THE SWORD AND THE SCALES

The United States and International Courts and Tribunals

The Sword and the Scales is the first in-depth and comprehensive study of attitudes and behaviors of the United States toward major international courts and tribunals, including the International Courts of Justice, World Trade Organization, and North American Free Trade Agreement dispute settlement systems; the Inter-American Court of Human Rights; and all international criminal courts. Thirteen chapters by American legal scholars map and analyze current and past patterns of promotion or opposition, use or neglect, of international judicial bodies by various branches of the U.S. government, suggesting a complex and deeply ambivalent relationship.

The United States has been, and continues to be, not only a promoter of the various international courts and tribunals but also an active participant in the judicial system. It appears before some of the international judicial bodies frequently and supports more, both politically and financially. At the same time, it is less engaged than it could be, particularly given its strong rule of law foundations and its historical tradition of commitment to international law and its institutions.

Cesare P. R. Romano is Professor of Law at Loyola Law School Los Angeles. In 1997, Professor Romano cofounded the Project on International Courts and Tribunals (PICT), becoming a world-renowned authority in the field of law and practice of international courts and tribunals. He has since directed PICT's American side. He is the author of numerous books and articles in the field of international courts and tribunals, including *The International Judges: An Introduction to the Men and Women Who Decide the World's Cases*. Before joining Loyola Law School, he taught and lectured at institutions throughout the United States and Europe.

The Sword and the Scales

THE UNITED STATES AND INTERNATIONAL COURTS AND TRIBUNALS

Edited by

CESARE P. R. ROMANO

Loyola Law School Los Angeles

CAMBRIDGE UNIVERSITY PRESS
Cambridge, New York, Melbourne, Madrid, Cape Town, Singapore,
São Paulo, Delhi, Dubai, Tokyo

Cambridge University Press
32 Avenue of the Americas, New York, NY 10013-2473, USA

www.cambridge.org
Information on this title: www.cambridge.org/9780521728713

© Cambridge University Press 2009

This publication is in copyright. Subject to statutory exception
and to the provisions of relevant collective licensing agreements,
no reproduction of any part may take place without the written
permission of Cambridge University Press.

First published 2009

Printed in the United States of America

A catalog record for this publication is available from the British Library.

Library of Congress Cataloging in Publication data

The sword and the scales : the United States and international courts and tribunals /
edited by Cesare P. R. Romano.
    p. cm.
Includes bibliographical references and index.
ISBN 978-0-521-40746-5 (hardback) – ISBN 978-0-521-72871-3 (pbk.)
1. International and municipal law – United States.   2. International law – United
States.   3. International courts.   4. United States. – Foreign relations.   I. Romano, Cesare
(Cesare P. R.)   II. Title.
KF4581.S86   2009
341.5′5 – dc22   2009001169

ISBN 978-0-521-40746-5 Hardback
ISBN 978-0-521-72871-3 Paperback

Cambridge University Press has no responsibility for the persistence or
accuracy of URLs for external or third-party Internet Web sites referred to in
this publication and does not guarantee that any content on such Web sites is,
or will remain, accurate or appropriate.

*To my children, Emma and Leo Guerrini Romano,
a new generation of Americans*

The law is not mere theory, but living force. And hence it is that Justice which, in one hand holds the scales, in which she weights the right, carries in the other the sword with which she executes it. The sword without the scales is brute force; the scales without the sword is the impotence of law.*

---

* Rudolph Von Jhering (German jurist, 1818–1892), *The Struggle for Law* (John Jay Lalor, trans., 1876) 1–2.

Contents

Preface		*page* xiii
Acknowledgments		xxv
Abbreviations		xxvii
Contributors		xxxi
1	**International Courts and Tribunals and the Rule of Law** *John B. Bellinger III*	1
	A. Dispute Resolution Tribunals	2
	B. International Criminal Tribunals	6
	C. The International Criminal Court	8
	D. Iraq High Tribunal	10
	E. Conclusion	10
2	**American Public Opinion on International Courts and Tribunals** *Steven Kull and Clay Ramsay*	12
	A. Past Public Opinion on International Courts and Tribunals (1942–2005)	13
	B. Attitudes of the American Public toward International Adjudication during the Second Term of the Bush Administration (2006)	20
	1. International Adjudication and the Case for U.S. Exceptionalism	20
	2. Detainee Treatment at Guantanamo Bay	24
	3. Charging Individuals and the ICC	25
	4. Torture	27
	C. Conclusion	28

3	Arbitration and Avoidance of War: The Nineteenth-Century American Vision *Mary Ellen O'Connell*	30
	A. International Arbitration and America: 1776–1872	31
	B. International Arbitration and America: 1872–1918	37
	C. Conclusion	44
4	The United States and the International Court of Justice: Coping with Antinomies *Sean D. Murphy*	46
	A. Antinomies in the U.S. Relationship with the ICJ	48
	1. American Realism versus Institutionalism	49
	2. American Exceptionalism versus Sovereign Equality	53
	3. Autonomous National Law versus National Law Embedded in International Law	55
	B. Techniques for Mediating the Antinomies	57
	1. Only States, Not Persons	61
	2. Circumscribed Jurisdiction	61
	3. State Influence on Selection of Judges	69
	4. No Direct Enforcement of Judgments in National Law	71
	5. Discursive and Political Constraints	72
	C. A Look at U.S. Cases before the ICJ	74
	1. The Overall Track Record	74
	2. Recent Cases	79
	D. Conclusion	97
5	The U.S. Supreme Court and the International Court of Justice: What Does "Respectful Consideration" Mean? *Melissa A. Waters*	112
	A. *From Breard to Medellin*: Aborted Dialogues between the ICJ and the Supreme Court	114
	B. Conceptualizing Treaty Dialogue with the ICJ: A Horizontal or Vertical Relationship?	117
	C. "Respectful Consideration" in Treaty Dialogue: In *Sanchez-Llamas*, Conceptualizing the Relationship Is Everything	121
	1. The Conservative Conception: Horizontal Dialogue with the ICJ	122
	2. The Liberal Conception: Vertical Dialogue with the ICJ	125
	D. Conclusion	128

6	**U.S. Attitudes toward International Criminal Courts and Tribunals**	131
	John P. Cerone	

    A. Early U.S. Attitudes toward International Justice and the Possibility of International Criminal Courts (from the Nineteenth Century to 1945)   133
        1. The Hague Peace Conferences (1899–1907)   133
        2. The Treaty of Versailles (1919)   133
        3. The League of Nations (1919–1945)   136
    B. U.S. Policy toward International Criminal Courts since World War II   137
        1. Nuremberg and Tokyo   137
        2. Early United Nations Efforts to Create an International Criminal Court   140
        3. The International Criminal Tribunals for the Former Yugoslavia and Rwanda   143
        4. The International Criminal Court   147
        5. Internationalized, Hybrid, and Related Criminal Tribunals   167
    C. Conclusion   180
        1. Commitment to Accountability   180
        2. Strong Preference for Domestic Resolution; Other Courts as Last Resort   180
        3. Security Council Control   181
        4. Other and Underlying Factors   181
        5. Historical Analysis of Policy Formulation   182
        6. The Limits of Pragmatism   182
        7. Postscript   183

7	**The United States and the Inter-American Court of Human Rights**	185
	Elizabeth A. H. Abi-Mershed	

    A. The Creation of the Inter-American Human Court of Human Rights: Accepted but Not Embraced   187
    B. Prospects for U.S. Acceptance of the Court's Contentious Jurisdiction   189
    C. Instances of Engagement between the United States and the Inter-American Court   191
    D. Concerns Cited as Holding Back U.S. Ratification of the American Convention and Acceptance of the Court's Contentious Jurisdiction   200
    E. The Mechanisms through Which the United States Engages with the Inter-American Court and Commission   202

F. The Nature of Current U.S. Support for the Regional
   Human Rights System 203
G. The Role of U.S. Jurists on and before the Court 204
H. The Role of the Inter-American Court in Protecting the
   Rights of U.S. Citizens 205
I. The Work of the Inter-American Court and Commission
   Influences International Human Rights Law; That, in
   Turn, Has an Effect on U.S. Law and Policy 206
J. Conclusion 208

8 **From Paradox to Subsidiarity: The United States
and Human Rights Treaty Bodies** 210
Tara J. Melish

A. Legal Context: The Human Rights Framework Applicable
   to the United States 223
B. Supervisory Treaty Body System and the Scope of U.S.
   Engagement 233
   1. Periodic Reporting Process 235
   2. Individual and Collective Complaint Procedures and
      Precautionary Measures 241
   3. Other Promotional Mechanisms 248
C. Interest Management: The Push-Pull of Domestic and
   Foreign Policy Agendas 249
   1. Foreign Policy Interests: Net Push Toward Greater
      Treaty Body Engagement 250
   2. Domestic Policy Interests: From Pull to Push – The
      Evolution of Domestic Social Struggles 256
D. Mediating Techniques for Promoting U.S. Engagement:
   Asserting Clear Lines and Recurring (Selectively) to
   Subsidiarity Doctrine 272
   1. Carving Out "No-Go" Zones: The Substantive
      Parameters of Treaty Body Competence 276
   2. Preferring "Political" to "Judicial" Controls in Human
      Rights Supervision and Interpretation 279
   3. Retaining Full Remedial and Policy-Making Discretion . 282
E. Honoring Subsidiarity Doctrine in Full: From
   International Defense to Domestic Challenge 285
   1. A National Office on Human Rights Implementation
      and Inter-Agency Coordination Body 290
   2. United States Commission on Human Rights 292
F. Conclusion: Institutionalizing Subsidiarity 295

9	**The U.S. and International Claims and Compensation Bodies**	297
	John R. Crook	
	A. The Iran–United States Claims Tribunal	298
	B. U.S. Role in the Creation and Operation of Holocaust Victims Compensation Mechanisms	306
	1. The Swiss Bank Claims Institutions	307
	2. Forced and Slave Labor Claims	311
	3. Other Holocaust-Related Programs	313
	4. Insurance Claims	313
	C. The UN Compensation Commission	314
	D. Conclusion	319
10	**Does the United States Support International Tribunals? The Case of the Multilateral Trade System**	322
	Jeffrey L. Dunoff	
	A. The Turn to Liberal Trade Policies	323
	B. The Birth of the International Trade System: From the International Trade Organization to the General Agreement on Tariffs and Trade	327
	1. The Original U.S. Draft	328
	2. The Drafting Process and Creation of the GATT	330
	C. The GATT Experience	333
	1. The Early Years	334
	2. The 1960s: The Fall of GATT Dispute Settlement and the Rise of Anti-Legalism	336
	3. The 1970s: Reconstruction and Revival	338
	4. 1980–1994: Aggressive Unilateralism and the Birth of the WTO	341
	D. The Uruguay Round Dispute Settlement Understanding	345
	1. Outline of the DSU	345
	2. U.S. Implementation and Debate over the DSU	346
	E. U.S. Experience under WTO Dispute Settlement	348
	F. Conclusion	354
11	**The United States and Dispute Settlement under the North American Free Trade Agreement: Ambivalence, Frustration, and Occasional Defiance**	356
	David A. Gantz	
	A. An Overview of Dispute Resolution under NAFTA	362
	B. Investment Disputes under Chapter 11	364
	C. Review of Unfair Trade Disputes under Chapter 19	375

	D. Government-to-Government Disputes under Chapter 20	385
	E. Conclusion	393

12 Dispute Settlement under NAFTA Chapter 11: A Response to the Critics in the United States   395
Susan L. Karamanian

    A. Investor-State Arbitration under NAFTA Chapter 11   396
        1. The Process   396
        2. The Claims   399
    B. The Criticism of NAFTA Chapter 11   404
        1. Intrusions into U.S. Sovereignty   404
        2. Due Process Concerns   406
    C. A Reality Check   408
        1. Exaggerations   408
        2. Moderate Concerns   412
    D. Conclusion   417

13 The United States and International Courts: Getting the Cost-Benefit Analysis Right   419
Cesare P. R. Romano

    A. Toward a Balanced Instrumental Approach   423
        1. International Courts Are More than "Dispute Settlers" and "Problem Solvers," and, Surprise!, They Do What They Are Supposed to Do   423
        2. International Courts Are Like Halloween Haunted Houses: They Spook Only the Naïve or Those Who Want to Be Spooked   428
        3. You Cannot Have International Courts That Are Always on Your Side   431
        4. International Courts, and the Services They Render, Are Global Public Goods   433
        5. Easy-Riding Will Cost You   436
        6. If You Do Not Understand Your Instruments, You Risk Blunting Them Unnecessarily   439
        7. The United States Needs International Courts, and International Courts Need the United States   442

Index   445

Preface

Among the phenomena that have characterized international relations since 1945, two are particularly noteworthy. The first is the rise of the United States to the status of "superpower." The second is the growth of international organizations and international law to cover areas of human activity hitherto left to individual states to manage and regulate. Both phenomena have experienced a sudden acceleration and qualitative transformation since 1990. The collapse of the Soviet Union has removed the only plausible rival of the United States, turning it into the sole superpower: the only nation in the world that has strategic interests to defend in every corner of the globe. At the same time, the increasing density and specialization of international legal regimes, which have been dubbed the *legalization* of world politics,[1] have given way in some areas to a further and separate stage of development. This stage can be called the *judicialization* of international relations.[2] Indeed, since the early 1990s, there has been a remarkable increase in the number of international judicial bodies, at both the regional and global levels. Nowadays, there are about eighteen permanent international courts and tribunals currently active in fields ranging from general questions of international law to specialized

---

[1] In 2000, *International Organization* – the leading international relations journal – devoted a special issue to the topic of legalization of international relations. Judith Goldstein et al., *Introduction: Legalization and World Politics*, 54 Int'l Org. 385 (2000). In particular, see Kenneth W. Abbott et al., *The Concept of Legalization*, 54 Int'l Org. 401 (2000).

[2] The proliferation of international courts and tribunals and the general increase in international adjudication have been hailed as some of the most significant changes in international law (and, correspondingly, international relations) of our time. *See generally* Laurence R. Helfer and Anne-Marie Slaughter, *Why States Create International Tribunals: A Response to Professors Posner and Yoo*, 93 Cal. L. Rev. 899, 910 (2005) ("Within the past decade the world has witnessed an explosion of international adjudication"); Chester Brown, *The Proliferation of International Courts and Tribunals: Finding Your Way through the Maze*, 3 Melb. J. Int'l L. 453, 454 (2002) ("The establishment of new fora for third party dispute settlement is undoubtedly one of the more striking international legal developments in recent years").

international law areas, such as human rights, trade, law of the sea, and criminal law.[3] These international bodies generate a considerable and steady flow of judgments, advisory opinions, orders, and warrants.[4] Aside from these international judicial bodies, there are at least another dozen that are dormant, or active at minimal levels, and about seventy other international institutions that exercise judicial or quasi-judicial functions.[5]

Not only there is correlation between the rise of America and the multiplication of international courts, but, to a large degree, there is also causation. The United States has been instrumental in or, at a minimum, has encouraged the creation of most of these international judicial bodies. The United States has a tradition of commitment to adjudication of international disputes that dates back more than two hundred years, the intellectual roots of which draw deep into the philosophical and religious movements that shaped the early days of the American republic. Of all nations, only the United Kingdom could possibly boast a similar pedigree. During the twentieth century, the United States showed dedication to the resolution of economic disputes through specialized tribunals and favored the creation of strong international institutions to regulate trade and settle disputes arising out of it. Reluctance from its allies – including the United Kingdom – notwithstanding, and after some initial hesitation, the White House insisted on having the Nazi leadership and the Japanese military tried instead of summarily executed.[6] Forty years later, it led the effort to create international courts for crimes committed in the former Yugoslavia, Rwanda, Sierra Leone, and Cambodia, to name a few. For more than a century, American nationals have been on the bench of many of these courts and tribunals in their personal capacity, and their contribution to the international jurisprudence has been on par with that of their country's great legal tradition.

---

[3] The first systematic classification of international courts and tribunals was published in Cesare P. R. Romano, *The Proliferation of International Judicial Bodies: The Pieces of the Puzzle*, 31 N.Y.U. J. Int'l L. Pol. 709, 739–48 (1999). It was reprinted in José E. Alvarez, *International Organizations as Law-Makers* (Oxford, 2005), at 404–7. The "synoptic chart" included in that article has been updated since. The most recent version (November 3, 2004) can be found at http://www.pict-pcti.org/publications/synoptic_chart.html.

[4] Karen Alter counts twenty-six international courts that have issued sixty-nine percent of their more than 15,000 decisions, opinions, and rulings since 1990. *See generally* Karen J. Alter, *Agents or Trustees? International Courts in Their Political Context*, 1 Eur. J. Int'l Relations 33 (2007).

[5] Synoptic chart, *supra* n. 3.

[6] For a chronicle of the role of the United States in the creation of the Nuremberg and Tokyo tribunals, *see* The United Nations War Crimes Commission, *History of the United Nations War Crimes Commission and the Development of the Laws of War* (1948), in particular pp. 454–61. It should be noted that the United States opposed the creation of international criminal tribunals after World War I. See *infra* Cerone, Chapter 6 of this volume, § A.2.

Despite – or perhaps because of – this record, observers, learned and casual, are puzzled by the ambivalent, and in some cases adverse, attitude that the United States has toward international courts and tribunals. More important, in recent years, the attitude of the United States toward international judicial institutions has become a point of contention with several countries, particularly, but not only, Europeans. The policy of the United States under the administration of President George W. Bush with regard to the International Criminal Court (ICC) is the most notorious, and probably extreme, case.

As this book aims to prove, the U.S. attitude toward international judicial institutions is much more complex than that. Indeed, the United States is more engaged with international courts and tribunals than some tend or want to see. The United States has been, and continues to be, not only a promoter of the various international courts and tribunals but also an active participant in the judicial system, appearing before some of the international judicial bodies frequently, and supporting more, both politically and financially. At the same time, it is also true that the United States is less engaged than it perhaps might be, particularly given its strong rule of law foundations.

A ROADMAP FOR THE READER

In recent years, the U.S. drift toward unilateralism has induced several international scholars to reassess U.S. attitudes and behaviors toward international law and institutions. Variably focusing on theories of American "exceptionalism" and "unilateralism" or, more generally, the American "tradition," they largely deal with how the preponderance of American power affects U.S. practice regarding international law – in some cases, more specifically the United Nations – and often concerning the use of force in particular.[7] Similarly, following the proliferation of international judicial bodies during the 1990s, there has been a remarkable scholarly production of works on international courts. These works tend to focus on certain structural issues (such as jurisdiction) or

---

[7] E.g., Stewart Patrick, "Multilateralism and Its Discontents: The Causes and Consequences of U.S. Ambivalence," *Multilateralism and U.S. Foreign Policy; Ambivalent Engagement* (Stewart Patrick and Shepard Forman eds., Lynne Rienner, 2002); John Murphy, *The United States and the Rule of Law in International Affairs* (Cambridge, 2004); *Unilateralism and U.S. Foreign Policy* (David M. Malone and Yuen Foong Khong eds., Lynne Rienner, 2003) 19; *American Exceptionalism and Human Rights* (Michael Ignatieff, ed., Princeton, 2005); Harold Hongju Koh, *On American Exceptionalism*, 55 Stan. L. Rev. 1497 (2003); Deborah L. Madsen, *American Exceptionalism* (Edinburgh,1998); Robert Kagan, *Of Paradise and Power: America and Europe in the New World Order* (Knopf 2003); David Skidmore, *Understanding the Unilateralist Turn in U.S. Foreign Policy*, 1 Foreign Policy Anal. 207 (2005); *U.S. Hegemony and International Organizations – The United States and Multilateral Institutions* (Rosemary Foot, S. Neil MacFarlane, and Michael Mastanduno eds., Oxford, 2003).

on certain courts (such as the International Criminal Court) but rarely have a holistic approach, touching on multiple international courts and a range of issues.[8]

Even though certain articles and books address U.S. practice vis-à-vis international tribunals – usually the rejection of the International Criminal Court and at times the problematic relationship with the International Court of Justice – this is the first comprehensive look at U.S. attitudes toward a very large range of judicial and, in the case of human rights bodies, quasi-judicial international institutions and procedures. Moreover, this book not only occupies an empty thematic niche; it also aims to provide further analysis for those scholars of international law and relations who are considering how current knowledge and theories need to be readjusted in the light of the rise of international judicial institutions.

Although this book provides empirical evidence about the factors that influence U.S. relations with a broad range of international courts, it is not exhaustive. Thus, although we addressed the question of relations with the International Court of Justice (ICJ) we mostly focused on the post-*Nicaragua* case phase (1986). We felt that the question of attitudes and behaviors toward the predecessor of the ICJ, the Permanent Court of International Justice, the main judicial body of the League of Nations, active between 1922 and 1939, is not crucial enough to warrant a chapter of its own.[9] The same applies to the case of the first permanent international court ever, the Central American Court of Justice, which operated between 1908 and 1918. Although the Court's jurisdiction was limited to Costa Rica, El Salvador, Guatemala, Honduras, and Nicaragua, the United States played a role in both its creation and its demise.[10]

---

[8] Among the notably few, see, José Alvarez, *International Organizations as Law-Makers* (Oxford, 2005).

[9] On the United States and the PCIJ, *see*, e.g., Denna Frank Fleming, *The United States and the World Court 1920–1966* (Russell & Russell, 1968); Michla Pomerance, *The United States and the World Court as a "Supreme Court of the Nations": Dreams, Illusions and Disillusions* (Nijhoff, 1996).

[10] The Central American peace conference that established the Court was held in Washington, D.C., in September 1907. Writing in 1908, James Brown Scott noted that "the two great Republics lying to the north [i.e., the United States and Mexico] have not only lent their friendly aid in the negotiation of the treaties and convention [creating the CACJ], but are prepared by peaceful and proper means to guarantee their execution." James Brown Scott, *The Central American Peace Conference of 1907*, 2 Am. J. Int'l L. 129, 143 (1908). On the issue of the Court's demise, see Jean Allain, *A Century of International Adjudication* (T.M.C. Asser, 2000), 89–91. *Cf.* Humphrey M. Hill, "Central American Court of Justice,", in *Max Planck Encyclopedia of Public International Law* (Rudolf Bernhardt ed., vol. 1 Oxford, 1992) 551, 553–54 (attributing termination of the Court not to the United States but rather to the fact that the treaty creating the Court had a term of ten years, which was yet to expire).

We touch only tangentially, in the final chapter, on the International Tribunal for the Law of the Sea (ITLOS). Currently, and as long as the United States does not ratify the United Nations Convention on the Law of the Sea, there is not much of a relationship to speak of. The ITLOS is one of the dispute settlement bodies provided for by the dispute settlement machinery of the United Nations Convention on the Law of the Sea.[11] The United States is one of the few developed countries not to have ratified that treaty. The fact that the dispute settlement machinery under the convention provides for compulsory adjudication of certain disputes is one of the reasons why ratification is stalled,[12] even though, during negotiations of the Convention, it was the United States that insisted on a compulsory and binding dispute settlement procedure.[13]

Equally omitted is the issue of the U.S. attitude toward the Court of Conciliation and Arbitration of the Conference/Organization on Security and Cooperation in Europe (CSCE/OSCE), an international organization to which the United States is party. It is a very minor body in the pantheon of international courts. The failure of the OSCE Court to attract even just one case since it was established in 1995 might be explained by many factors, one of which might be the opposition of the United States and the United Kingdom to its creation.[14]

---

[11] United Nations Convention on the Law of the Sea, art. 287, Dec. 10, 198, 1833 U.N.T.S. 397. *See generally* Andronico Adede, *The System for Settlement of Disputes under the United Nations Convention on the Law of the Sea: A Drafting History and a Commentary* (Nijhoff, 1987); *see also* Robin Churchill and Vaughan Lowe, *The Law of the Sea* (3rd ed. Juris, 1999).

[12] José E. Alvarez, *Judicialization and Its Discontents*, Am. Soc. Int'l L. (Jan. 31, 2008), at http://www.asil.org/ilpost/president/preso80131.html.

[13] United States, Draft Articles for a Chapter on the Settlement of Disputes, U.N. Doc. A/AC.138/97 (1973); Article 1 of the United States Proposal, 22, 28 GAOR Supp. No. 21, U.N. Doc. A/9021 (1973). *See also* the explanatory memorandum by the U.S. delegation, accompanying the United States Proposal, and distributed to members of the Working Group, quoted in Adede, *The System for Settlement of Disputes*, *supra* n. 11, at 15–16; Louis B. Sohn, *Settlement of Disputes Arising Out of the Law of the Sea Convention*, 12 San Diego L. Rev. 495, 496 (1975). *U.S. Presents Proposals at Preparatory Session for the Law of the Sea Conference*, 69 Dep't St. Bull. 394, 414 (1973) (statement by Ambassador Stevenson); *U.S. Defines Position on 200-Mile Economic Zone at Conference on the Law of the Sea*, 71 Dep't State Bull 232, 235 (1974) (statement by Ambassador Stevenson).

[14] For details of the negotiation process leading to the creation of the OSCE Court, *see* Michael Lucas and Oliver Mietzsch, "Peaceful Dispute Settlement and the CSCE," in *The CSCE in the 1990s: Constructing European Security and Cooperation* (Michael Lucas ed., Nomos, 1993) 96–97. *See also* Gerard Tanja, "Peaceful Settlement of Disputes within the Framework of the OSCE: A Legal Novelty in a Political-Diplomatic Environment," in *The Challenges of Change: The Helsinki Summit of the CSCE and Its Aftermath* (Arie Bloed ed., Nijhoff 1994) 70, 80–81.

Lastly, we did not address the question of attitudes of the United States toward courts of regional organizations to which the United States could not be a party (e.g., the European Court of Justice or the African Court of Human and Peoples' Rights). Other than generic statements encouraging regional integration and rule of law, there is little indication that the United States has any particular opinion, in favor of or against, any of these bodies. It does not support them in any meaningful way, nor does it oppose them.

Of course this book does not provide the only possible perspective. Being a study of attitudes and behaviors of the United States toward international courts *as observed from the United States*, it is largely a self-portrait. All authors in this book are Americans, writing from American schools, the U.S. government, or institutions based in the United States. Non-American views have been incorporated to the extent that all authors, at various stages of this project, have benefited from foreign commentary and criticism.

Finally, this book was written during the term of the second administration of President George W. Bush but was published when America had voted into power President Barack H. Obama, whose fundamental campaign message was the need to abandon the policies of the previous administration. Although the White House plays an important role in charting the course of U.S. foreign relations, and therefore on attitudes and behaviors toward international courts, as many of the chapters in this book should make clear, there are several other decision-making centers within the U.S. government that affect outcomes in our chosen field of investigation. Moreover, long-lasting factors such as American culture and history, the U.S. constitutional structure, and the unique post–Cold War position of the United States in the international community, rather than the view of this or that administration, probably have greater explanatory power over trends and fundamental attitudes of the United States toward international courts and tribunals.

THE BOOK, IN SHORT

The book begins with a chapter by John Bellinger, who, at the time this book was written, was the legal adviser to the U.S. Secretary of State. His piece is an accurate and carefully thought-out description of the attitude and behavior of the U.S. government under the George W. Bush presidency, although it probably suggests deep-seated attitudes common to several administrations during the last quarter of the twentieth century. He describes the U.S. approach as cautious and pragmatic. "[W]e evaluate the contributions that proposed international courts and tribunals may make on a case-by-case basis, just as we consider the advantages and disadvantages of addressing particular matters through international judicial mechanisms rather than diplomatic or other means."[15]

The American people seem to be less circumspect. In the second chapter, Steven Kull and Clay Ramsay describe the results of a nationwide survey – the first ever of this kind – of 1,023 Americans carried out in April 2006 by the Program on International Policy Attitudes at the University of Maryland. Remarkably, this was the most comprehensive examination ever conducted of the American public's attitudes toward international courts. The poll offered a wide range of arguments for and against U.S. participation in international tribunals; of types of cases that could be adjudicated; and of instances where the United States has been, or could be, ruled against in an international institution. Overall, the findings showed large majority support for participation in and compliance with international courts, tribunals, and other bodies, regardless of political orientations. Kull and Ramsay also show that this support is continuous with past majority attitudes held by Americans from the 1940s through the 1990s. The rise of the United States as the sole superpower and the war on terrorism have brought little change to these underlying attitudes. The particular political dynamics of the United States, its constitutional structure, and polity might explain why public support does not translate into pressure on the government to narrow the gap between what the people seemingly want and what the government does in practice.

All in all, American attitudes and behaviors toward international courts are highly contextual, changing between courts or dispute settlement procedures and between issues. Hence, to capture diversity and complexity, the book continues with a court-by-court analysis, addressing single facets of this multidimensional phenomenon.

Sean Murphy describes three essential antinomies in U.S. foreign relations, which might help explain the ambiguity of the U.S. position toward international adjudicative bodies. He uses the International Court of Justice as an example to illustrate the effects of these three antinomies, but his core analysis can probably be applied *mutatis mutandis* to any other international judicial body. One such antinomy is the fact that the United States operates on the basis of conflicting principles with respect to whether states should be treated as sovereign equals. A second is that the United States operates on the basis of conflicting principles with respect to whether international law should be "embedded" in U.S. law, including the manner in which international courts relate to U.S. law. Third, and finally, there is the eternal struggle between the "realist" and the "institutionalist" strains of international relations theory.

---

[15] *See*, John Bellinger, Chapter 1 of this volume.

Mary Ellen O'Connell supports and historicizes Murphy's insight on the antinomy between the realist and the intuitionalist approach by showing that its roots draw deep into the early days of the republic. Indeed, throughout the nineteenth century, both American pacifists and pragmatists advocated for the use of international arbitration as an alternative to war. Quakers, Mennonites, and then a broad array of Protestant denominations articulated idealistic reasons to support international adjudication of disputes. Early American leaders pragmatically realized that a small, new nation had little chance of winning wars against great powers. O'Connell's piece is not only of historical interest. She shows how the two positions resonated throughout much of U.S. history and how they still cast a long shadow on current debates about what the attitude and behavior of the United States should be.

Being a democracy, the United States is based on the principle of the division of powers. Thus, attitudes toward international courts vary among actors within the U.S. government. The president; Congress; the Supreme Court; the Departments of State, Defense, and Justice; the U.S. Trade Representative; as well as the governments of the fifty states, inter alia, all have particular and sometimes discordant perspectives on the issue. Although many of the chapters in this volume describe the attitudes of various executive and legislative branch actors, Melissa Waters focuses on the attitudes of the U.S. judiciary toward international tribunals. She does so through an in-depth analysis of the Supreme Court's decision in *Sanchez-Llamas v. Oregon*. Her analysis shows that even though all nine justices adopted identical language to describe the proper relationship between U.S. courts and international tribunals – one of "respectful consideration" of ICJ's rulings – there is considerable disagreement within the bench as to the precise contours of that relationship. Conservative justices view judicial dialogue with the ICJ as, at most, a horizontal relationship of coequal courts, whereas the liberal wing of the Court seems to envision a much more vertical relationship, in which the ICJ's rulings are entitled to a higher degree of deference in light of its special expertise in matters of treaty interpretation.

The next four chapters address the human rights and humanitarian law areas and reparations. John Cerone confirms the "instrumental" and "unidirectional" attitude of the United States in the case of international criminal tribunals. The United States supports international criminal courts only when the U.S. government has (or is perceived by U.S. officials to have) a significant degree of control over the court or when the possibility of prosecution of U.S. nationals is either expressly precluded or otherwise remote. He suggests that there is strong evidence that these factors are a constant of U.S. foreign policy, independent of who occupies the White House. If the United States is assured its nationals will not be prosecuted (or, at least, not without its consent), then it will engage in a balancing of interests to determine its level of support or opposition. In this case, variables, such as the particular circumstances involved or prevailing ideological leanings at the White House and Congress, will determine the outcome. To the extent that an administration's ideological strain in favor of accountability (typical of idealists and institutionalists) is stronger than its ideological strain opposed to the creation of international authority (the hallmark of realism), the prospect of U.S. support for a given international criminal court increases.

Moving on to the Inter-American Court of Human Rights and the panoply of quasi-adjudicatory United Nations human rights expert committees, the disconnect between the generally positive behavior of the United States and the underlying attitude emerges again. On one hand, the United States files reports; provides reams of information; appears before the committees and the Inter-American Commission and Court with large, high-level delegations; and tries to engage in substantive discussions. The behavior, in this regard, is superior to other member states, including several industrialized democracies. However, Elizabeth Abi-Mershed (in the case of the Inter-American system for the protection of human rights) and Tara Melish (in the case of United Nations human rights bodies) illustrate how this positive behavior, in reality, belies a problematic attitude that suggests the United States conceives these bodies mostly as a one-way road – that is, as tools to influence the conduct of other nations, rather than instruments to affect internal change, to provide a check on domestic institutions, or to promote self-reflection on human rights within the United States. This attitude can be explained as a manifestation of "exceptionalism," of the difficulty the United States has in accepting that it is just a state among a community of equals. Yet, the effect is to hamstring its capacity to seize and maintain the moral high ground in the international arena, a necessity if America wants to lead the world by persuasion and not coercion.

John Crook provides three examples of highly selective and carefully targeted instrumental use of international adjudicative processes to further specific and significant U.S. foreign policy goals: the Iran–United States Claims Tribunal, the mechanisms created to address the Holocaust claims, and the United Nations Compensation Commission. They are all unidirectional processes, purely so in the case of the latter two, and largely de facto so in the case of the Iran–U.S. Claims Tribunal, considering that the great majority of cases have been brought by U.S. nationals against Iran. These are also examples of the United States' legal creativity and the can-do attitude that is a general trait of the American culture. The shaping of legal tools and procedures to form new institutions to meet new needs is at the same time an expression of ingenuity and of a deep respect for the law and its rule.

The next three chapters consider the international trade and investment areas. In contrast to the foregoing, the economic arena is usually regarded as the domain in which the United States has the most favorable attitude. It is often pointed out that the United States has long been dedicated to the resolution of disputes through specialized tribunals; for example, that it favored, even in the teeth of European resistance, the judicialization of the General Agreement on Tariffs and Trade into the World Trade Organization (WTO) dispute settlement system; and that it is a leading advocate of, and pioneer in, arbitration to resolve disputes between investors and states.

However, Jeff Dunoff argues that the U.S. government's support for judicialized dispute settlement in international trade is based less on an abstract commitment to the rule of law in international relations than on pragmatic, short-term, and highly contextual calculations that this mechanism serves U.S. interests better than alternative arrangements. David Gantz, discussing dispute settlement under the North American Free Trade Agreement (NAFTA), argues that although the various arbitral procedures have worked reasonably well in resolving the types of disputes for which they were designed, this has occurred without generating much enthusiasm for any of them. Indeed, quite to the contrary, it has at times even generated opposition from the Congress, some government officials, civil society, and U.S. courts. Both Dunoff and Gantz harbor doubts about the long-term commitment of the United States to third-party adjudication in the trade arena, particularly at a time when the entry of China into the WTO and the expansion of free-trade agreements between the United States and several nations of the Americas might alter the delicate strategic balance on which support has, to date, been justified.

Gantz and Susan Karamanian show that, in the case of the NAFTA, many of the U.S. stakeholders (private and governmental) tend to be suspicious of third-party dispute resolution because of the loss of sovereign control compared to the utilization of national courts or diplomatic negotiations. Critics of NAFTA, who can be found across the whole range of the U.S. political spectrum, allege that the arbitral tribunals' review of domestic laws and judicial decisions undermines national sovereignty, impeding the ability of the nation to govern as it sees fit, and raises constitutional concerns. Further, the procedures used in the arbitration proceedings have come under attack, as they allegedly do not allow for an open, transparent, and consistent consideration of issues of public importance.

Lastly, in the final chapter, I abuse my position as editor of this book to be more overtly normative than the preceding chapters. My argument is that the current prevailing attitude is exceedingly contextual, and is the result of a fundamental misunderstanding of what international courts are for and about, what they can and cannot do. Improper conceptualization of international courts distorts the cost-benefit analysis underlying decisions by U.S. authorities of whether to support and engage them. The final chapter provides a few corrective analytical lenses to currently prevailing narrow instrumental views to show that the United States has more to gain, and less to lose, from more constructive engagement with international courts than superficial discussions might suggest. Of course, I need to stress that my reasoning might not be something that other contributors to this volume would necessarily endorse.

BEHIND THIS BOOK

This book is the culmination of a three-year research project undertaken by the Center on International Cooperation (CIC), New York University, and the Project on International Courts and Tribunals (PICT), and supported by a generous grant from the JEHT Foundation.

The Center on International Cooperation was established in 1996 to conduct a program of policy research and development on the management and financing of multilateral commitments.[16] For ten years (1997–2007), CIC was the American home of the Project on International Courts and Tribunals.[17] PICT's mission is to address the legal and institutional issues arising from the multiplication of international courts and tribunals and other dispute settlement bodies, as well as from the increased willingness of members of the international community to have recourse to such bodies. PICT couples academic research with concrete action aimed at facilitating the work of international courts and tribunals.

In 2004, building on CIC's work on multilateralism and U.S. foreign policy and on PICT's experience with the activities of the principal international judicial bodies, a project was launched to seek to help move the United States toward a more constructive role in international justice issues. The

---

[16] Over the years, CIC has refocused its efforts to enhance international responses to conflicts, humanitarian crises, and global security threats, through four main strands of activity: independent research; direct policy support to the UN and other multilaterals; direct engagement with Washington, D.C., as a critical player in the revitalization of multilateral institutions, in partnership with the Brookings Institution, USIP, and other DC-based institutions; and engagement with the global South, especially the rising and regional powers. For more information on CIC, see http://www.cic.nyu.edu.

[17] The Project on International Courts and Tribunals (PICT) was jointly established in February 1997 by the Center on International Cooperation (CIC), at New York University, and the Foundation for International Environmental Law and Development (FIELD), at the School of Oriental and African Studies, University of London. In 2002, the London "home" of PICT moved to University College London with the establishment at the Faculty of Laws of the Centre for International Courts and Tribunals. In 2007, PICT was reconfigured as a shared research agenda carried out by a network of institutions and individuals, namely Ruth Mackenzie at the Centre for International Courts and Tribunals, University College London; Thordis Ingadottir at Reykjavik University; Yuval Shany at Hebrew University; and Cesare Romano at Loyola Law School Los Angeles. For more information on PICT, see http://www.pict-pcti.org.

project, called "United States Attitudes and Behaviors towards International Courts and Tribunals," aimed to map and analyze current and past patterns of promotion or opposition, use or neglect, of international courts and tribunals, as well as international dispute settlement mechanisms, by various branches of the U.S. government.

Two meetings were the foci of the project. A preparatory meeting, held at The Hague in June 2005, and hosted by the T.M.C. Asser Instituut, advanced the research phase of the project. Papers were solicited from American legal scholars, and initial presentations were commented upon by European scholars. A second meeting, in the form of a public colloquium, was held in May 2006 in Washington, D.C., at The George Washington University School of Law. It brought together people from the various decision-making centers in the nation's capital and leading thinkers in the fields of international law and international relations.

This book collects some of the revised (sometimes extensively) papers presented at either or both the first and second meetings of this project.

Acknowledgments

This book is the result of a large collective effort, which involved, at various stages and in various capacities, numerous individuals and institutions. First of all, the project could not have taken place without the generosity of the JEHT Foundation, and in particular the encouragement and support of Garth Mentjes, Senior Program Manager, and his assistant Leila Saad.

The Center on International Cooperation, at New York University, was the place where the project was incubated and launched. A heartfelt thank you to all CIC's staff, but first and foremost to Shepard Forman, for encouraging me to take on this challenge, and to Bruce Jones for believing in this project and continuing to support it even when I left New York. Loyola Law School Los Angeles deserves a special mention as it became, during the summer of 2006, my new home and promptly welcomed me in its community of scholars. I am beholden to the deans and my colleagues for facilitating my research and allowing me to find the time to bring this long-overdue project to completion.

I would like to thank the institutions and the persons who hosted the two workshops that laid the foundations of this book: at T.M.C. Asser Instituut, Frans Nelissen, and Philip van Tongeren, and at The George Washington University School of Law, Professors Susan Karamanian and Sean Murphy. My gratitude goes to all those who participated in those meetings and provided useful feedback to the authors and crucial insight. At The Hague meeting: Peter Van den Bossche; Pablo Zapatero; Gerhard Hafner; Olivier Ribbelink; Avril McDonald; Norbert Wühler. At the Washington, D.C., meeting: Alice H. Henkin; Andrew Moravcsik; Andrew Solomon; Charlotte Ku; David Crane; David Skidmore; Denise Manning; Eric Biel; Gabor Rona; Harry Kruglik; James Bacchus; John Stompor; Jorg Philipp Terhechte; Karen Alter; Kim Holmes; Lee Caplan; Mark Moller; Peter Rutledge; Stephen J. Weber; Stephen Schwebel; Todd Buchwald; Uche Onwuamaegbu; Col. William Lietzau. A special thank you goes to Madeline Morris who attended both meetings. In addition to comments from several contributors to this volume,

I personally benefited from, and I am grateful for, the comments on the parts of the book I penned from friends, namely Yuval Shany, Karen Alter, and Larry Helfer, scholars whose influence on my own thinking cannot be overestimated.

Of course, I am forever indebted to the authors who attended all meetings, contributed chapters to this book, and had the patience to wait for me to sort out my personal and academic life: John Bellinger; Steven Kull; Clay Ramsay; Mary Ellen O'Connell; Sean Murphy; Melissa Waters; John Cerone; Elizabeth Abi-Mershed; Tara Melish; John Crook; Jeff Dunoff; David Gantz; and Susan Karamanian. And, of course, a big thank you to the research assistants who helped me throughout this project: Lindsey Raub and Adaobi Ukabam at New York University, and Melissa Keaney, Casey Johnson, and Jenna Gilbert at Loyola Law School.

My editor at Cambridge University Press, John Berger, deserves a special award for the superhuman patience he displayed as deadlines for submission of the manuscript came and went. John, I owe you another book!

Finally, this book has been a work in progress, with ups and downs, for about four years of my life. During that time, I moved between three different schools (New York University, Duke Law School, and Loyola Law School Los Angeles) and four houses. I owe my family a lot of time and attention, and a big apology for the bouts of saturnine moods caused by the making of this book that they had to endure.

Cesare P. R. Romano
Santa Monica, CA
November 4, 2008

Abbreviations

AB	Appellate Body (WTO)
ABA	American Bar Association
AD/CVD	antidumping/countervailing duty
AEI	American Enterprise Institute
AFL-CIO	American Federation of Labor and Congress of Industrial Organizations
AFR	Additional Facility Rules (ICSID)
APS	American Peace Society
ASPA	American Servicemembers' Protection Act
ATIF	Americans Talk Issues Foundation
ATS	Americans Talk Security
AU	African Union
BIT	Bilateral Investment Treaty
BRA	Boston Redevelopment Authority
BSE	Bovine Spongiform Encephalopathy
CAFC	U.S. Court of Appeals for the Federal Circuit
CAFTA	Central American Free Trade Agreement
CAP	Common Agricultural Policy
CAT	Convention Against Torture and Other Cruel, Inhuman or Degrading Treatment or Punishment
CBS	Columbia Broadcasting System
CCFR	Chicago Council on Foreign Relations
CCJ	Caribbean Court of Justice
CEDAW	Convention on the Elimination of All Forms of Discrimination Against Women
CFTA	U.S.–Canada Free Trade Agreement
CIT	U.S. Court of International Trade
CRC	Convention on the Rights of the Child
CRS	*Congressional Research Service*

CRT	Claims Resolution Tribunal
CSCE/OSCE	Conference/Organization on Security and Cooperation in Europe
DSU	Dispute Settlement Understanding
EC	European Communities
EC/EU	European Communities/European Union
ECC	Extraordinary Challenge Committee
ECCC	Extraordinary Chambers in the Courts of Cambodia
ECHR	European Court of Human Rights
ECJ	European Court of Justice
EU	European Union
FCN	Friendship, Commerce and Navigation
FHWA	U.S. Federal Highway Administration
FSC	Foreign Sales Corporation
FTA	Free Trade Agreement
GATT	General Agreement on Tariffs and Trade
GMO	genetically modified organism
HVIRA	Holocaust Victim Insurance Relief Act
IACHR	Inter-American Court of Human Rights
IAWG	Interagency Working Group on Human Rights
ICAO	International Civil Aviation Organization
ICC	International Criminal Court
ICCPR	International Covenant on Civil and Political Rights
ICEP	Independent Committee of Eminent Persons
ICERD	International Convention on the Elimination of All Forms of Racial Discrimination
ICESCR	International Covenant on Economic, Social and Cultural Rights
ICHEIC	International Commission for Holocaust Era Insurance Claims
ICJ	International Court of Justice
ICSID	International Centre for the Settlement of Investment Disputes
ICTR	International Criminal Tribunal for Rwanda
ICTY	International Criminal Tribunal for the Former Yugoslavia
IHT	Iraqi High Tribunal
IJC	International Joint Commission
ILC	International Law Commission
ILO	International Labour Organization
IMT	International Military Tribunal
ITC	U.S. International Trade Commission

ITLOS	International Tribunal for the Law of the Sea
ITO	International Trade Organization
JNOV	judgment notwithstanding the verdict
MTBE	methyl tert-butyl ether
NAAEC	North American Agreement on Environmental Cooperation
NAALC	North American Agreement on Labor Cooperation
NAFTA	North American Free Trade Agreement
NATO	North Atlantic Treaty Organization
NGO	nongovernmental organization
OAS	Organization of American States
OHADA	Organization for the Harmonization of Business Law in Africa
OLA	UN Office of Legal Affairs
OTP	Office of the Prosecutor
PCC	Policy Coordination Committee (PCC) on Democracy, Human Rights, and International Operations
PCIJ	Permanent Court of International Justice
PICT	Project on International Courts and Tribunals
PIPA	Program on International Policy Attitudes
RPF	Rwandan Patriotic Front
RTA	Reciprocal Trade Agreements Act
RUDs	Reservations, Understandings, and Declarations
SCSL	Special Court for Sierra Leone
STL	Special Tribunal for Lebanon
TPA	Trade Promotion Authority Act
TRIPs	Agreement on Trade Related Aspects of Intellectual Property Rights
UN	United Nations
UNCC	United Nations Compensation Commission
UNCITRAL	United Nations Commission on International Trade Law
UNSCR	United Nations Security Council Resolution
USTR	United States Trade Representative
USUN	U.S. Mission to the United Nations
WPP	Woman's Peace Party
WTO	World Trade Organization

Contributors

Elizabeth A. H. Abi-Mershed, Assistant Executive Secretary, Inter-American Commission on Human Rights

John B. Bellinger III, Partner, Arnold & Porter LLP, Washington, DC; Legal Adviser to the U.S. Secretary of State, 2005–2009

John P. Cerone, Professor of Law and Director of the Center for International Law and Policy, New England School of Law

John R. Crook, retired U.S. State Department lawyer, arbitrator on the Eritrea-Ethiopia Claims Commission and under NAFTA, and professorial lecturer at The George Washington University Law School

Jeffrey L. Dunoff, Charles Klein Professor of Law and Government and Director, Institute for International Law and Public Policy, Temple University Beasley School of Law

David A. Gantz, Samuel M. Fegtly Professor of Law and Director, International Trade and Business Law Program, University of Arizona, James E. Rogers College of Law; and Associate Director, National Law Center for Inter-American Free Trade

Susan L. Karamanian, Associate Dean for International and Comparative Legal Studies, The George Washington University Law School

Steven Kull, Director, Program on International Policy Attitudes, University of Maryland

Tara J. Melish, Associate Professor of Law and Director of the Buffalo Human Rights Center, University at Buffalo School of Law (SUNY)

Sean D. Murphy, Patricia Roberts Harris Research Professor of Law, The George Washington University

Mary Ellen O'Connell, Robert and Marion Short Chair in Law and Research Professor of International Dispute Resolution–Kroc Institute, University of Notre Dame

Clay Ramsay, Research Director, Program on International Policy Attitudes, University of Maryland

Cesare P. R. Romano, Professor of Law, Loyola Law School Los Angeles; and Co-Director, Project on International Courts and Tribunals (PICT)

Melissa A. Waters, Professor of Law, Washington University School of Law

1

International Courts and Tribunals and the Rule of Law

JOHN B. BELLINGER III*

It should be uncontroversial that the United States is among the world's leaders in supporting the development of international courts and tribunals. For example, in the economic arena, the United States has long been dedicated to the resolution of disputes through specialized tribunals, and we have continued that commitment through our cooperation with dispute settlement panels under the World Trade Organization. We have also been a leading advocate of ad hoc tribunals to resolve disputes between investors and states pursuant to bilateral and multilateral investment agreements.

This chapter, however, focuses on two other categories of international courts and tribunals: (1) tribunals for the resolution of state-to-state disputes over the rights and obligations of states under international law, such as the International Court of Justice (ICJ), and (2) criminal tribunals through which the international community seeks to hold individuals accountable for war crimes and other atrocities, including the International Criminal Tribunals for the former Yugoslavia (ICTY) and Rwanda (ICTR), the Special Court for Sierra Leone, and the International Criminal Court (ICC).[1]

Contrary to what is sometimes suggested, the United States believes that such state-to-state and criminal tribunals make valuable contributions and has therefore supported them in both word and deed. International courts and tribunals can assist states in resolving disputes that they have been unable to settle through ordinary diplomacy. They can provide an alternative to the

---

* The author was the Legal Adviser for the Department of State from April 2005–January 2009. He is currently a partner in the Washington, D.C.-based law firm of Arnold & Porter. This chapter contains the remarks made by the author on May 11, 2006, at The George Washington University School of Law.

[1] For a subsequent and more detailed statement by the author on the U.S. Government's views on international criminal tribunals, see "U.S. Perspectives on International Criminal Justice," Remarks by John B. Bellinger, III, at the Fletcher School of Law and Diplomacy, November 14, 2008. Available at http://2001-2009.state.gov/s/l/rls/111859.htm.

resolution of disputes or the adjudication of criminal liability through domestic courts that may be ill equipped or ill suited to address particular matters. They can also foster uniformity in the interpretation and application of international agreements.

Of course, the United States has sometimes had concerns about aspects of the work of particular tribunals. Our concerns about the ICC are well known. We also have some concerns about the operations of the ICJ as well as the efficiencies of the ICTY and the ICTR.

Our general approach to international courts and tribunals is pragmatic. In our view, such courts and tribunals should not be seen as an end in themselves but rather as potential tools to advance shared international interests in developing and promoting the rule of law, ensuring justice and accountability, and solving legal disputes. Consistent with this approach, we evaluate the contributions that proposed international courts and tribunals may make on a case-by-case basis, just as we consider the advantages and disadvantages of addressing particular matters through international judicial mechanisms rather than diplomatic or other means.

Because this approach requires close attention to context, I consider some examples of state-to-state and criminal courts and tribunals in turn and offer some thoughts on the types of contributions each may make and how we might best ensure that they fulfill their promise.

A. DISPUTE RESOLUTION TRIBUNALS

Tribunals for the resolution of traditional state-to-state disputes have historically played a useful role in providing a neutral, depoliticized forum to resolve disputes between states that are difficult to settle through regular diplomatic means. Sometimes this is because they involve contested facts and complicated legal issues, which can best be evaluated and resolved through a judicial process. In other cases, a large number of claims between states, often involving treatment of each others' nationals, may prove too complicated or time-consuming for states to resolve diplomatically, and an international tribunal may prove helpful in easing this burden. In still other cases, states may find it politically difficult to compromise on matters in dispute but can use a third-party decision-making mechanism to overcome the diplomatic impasse.

The most prominent Court in this category, the ICJ, celebrated its sixtieth anniversary in April 2006, and the Office of the Legal Adviser and the U.S. Embassy participated in events in The Hague to commemorate this important milestone. The United States has long supported the ICJ and has appeared before it in a significant number of cases. We have worked hard to maintain a seat for a judge from the United States and were extremely pleased in

November 2005 when Judge Thomas Buergenthal was reelected to the Court. One of my first trips abroad as legal adviser was to visit The Hague, and I very much enjoyed the opportunity to meet and exchange views with the members of the Court.

The United States has affirmatively looked to the ICJ in the past as a neutral forum to facilitate the resolution of disputes. In the wake of the seizure of the U.S. Embassy in Tehran, we looked to the Court to help enforce our rights under the Vienna Conventions on Diplomatic and Consular Relations. In the early 1980s, we agreed to submit to the ICJ a dispute with Canada over the maritime boundary in the Gulf of Maine. Later in the 1980s, we agreed with Italy to submit the ELSI case (concerning Elettronica Sicula) to the Court, inviting it to resolve a dispute arising under the U.S.-Italy Friendship Commerce and Navigation Treaty.

Our more recent experience before the Court has been in more politically charged cases that were not submitted by agreement. In the Oil Platforms case, Iran sought to use a friendship, commerce, and navigation treaty to challenge U.S. efforts to protect neutral shipping in the Persian Gulf from Iranian attacks. In the Lockerbie case, Libya sought to use an aviation terrorism convention to challenge the authority of the United Nations (UN) Security Council to impose sanctions for Libya's failure to cooperate in efforts to bring to justice those responsible for the bombing of Pan Am Flight 103. In a series of cases against NATO members, Serbia invoked the Genocide Convention in connection with NATO's actions to end atrocities in Kosovo. In the Breard, LaGrand, and Avena cases, implementation of the death penalty by the United States was challenged under the Vienna Convention on Consular Relations; even if those latter cases are not viewed as "political," they unquestionably invited the Court into a complex area beyond its expertise – namely, the domestic criminal justice system. Requests for advisory opinions from the Court on issues related to the Israeli-Palestinian conflict and the legality of nuclear weapons invited the Court into highly charged, fluid political disputes.

The use of the Court for such political matters carries risks. In the long run, the willingness of states to refer disputes to the Court depends on their confidence in its objectivity and impartiality and their sense that the court is an appropriate forum for resolution of the dispute in question. When the Court addresses sensitive political issues, there is a risk that its decisions may be viewed as reflecting its desired political outcomes rather than its dispassionate analysis of the facts and the law. Similarly, if the Court is asked to address issues that require expertise it does not have and cannot acquire, there is a substantial risk of decisions that simply do not make sense.

Of course, the Court does not control the types of cases that states choose to put before it. In this regard, states themselves must consider carefully the impact of the increasing referral of political matters on the Court's long-term institutional role.

As one example in this regard, the United States opposed the decision of the UN General Assembly in 2003 to seek an advisory opinion from the Court on matters related to the Israeli security barrier. We were concerned that the Court's involvement in these issues risked interfering with the agreed framework for direct negotiations between the Israelis and Palestinians to resolve the issues between them and risked politicizing the Court. We were also concerned that the Court's advisory opinion procedures were ill suited to accommodate a matter as factually complex as the one referred by the General Assembly, particularly without the full participation of the interested parties.

We believe that these concerns were largely borne out in the advisory opinion rendered by the Court. In practice, the opinion has made little meaningful contribution to efforts to resolve issues between the Israelis and Palestinians. Also, the Court's opinion is open to criticism on its treatment of both factual and legal issues, in some cases due more to process than to any fault on the part of the Court. For example, the fact that the General Assembly had already declared itself on many of the issues risks creating the impression that the Court was being used to advance a particular set of political claims.

Also of concern are efforts in some quarters to suggest that aspects of the Court's advisory opinion, such as that relating to the extraterritorial application of the International Covenant on Civil and Political Rights, have binding force on member states in contexts that go beyond those addressed in the advisory opinion. This of course is not the case. Under the ICJ statute, states are bound only by the decisions – not by the Court's reasoning underlying those decisions – in contentious cases to which they are parties, and advisory opinions have no binding force at all but rather serve to provide guidance on legal questions to the UN organ or specialized agency requesting them.

For this range of reasons, we hope that the General Assembly's decision to seek an advisory opinion in this case does not reflect an increased desire to use the Court's jurisdiction in similar cases in the future, because doing so would risk damaging the Court's credibility.

Although the Court does not control the matters referred to it, there are steps it can and should take to avoid assuming a role that calls into question its objectivity and nonpolitical character. In the Israeli security barrier case, for example, the Court could have declined to render an advisory opinion on the ground that the General Assembly's request was essentially that the Court adjudicate a contentious case without the consent of the affected parties rather than a bona fide request for an advisory opinion.

The Court's handling of the Oil Platforms case in 2003 is another example in which, in the view of the U.S. Government, the Court should have taken steps to avoid suggestions that it sought to play a political role. The Court dismissed that case on the merits of Iran's claim against the United States because Iran failed to meet its affirmative burden of showing that U.S. actions against Iran's platforms had affected commerce protected under the U.S.-Iran Treaty of Amity. Yet despite this conclusion, the Court went on to express views on, and indeed purported to decide, contentious issues concerning the law on the use of force that were unnecessary to its ultimate judgment.

The Court's treatment of these issues suggested a desire on its part to influence political decisions on matters wholly unrelated to the case before it – specifically, on questions then being considered related to the use of force in Iraq. One member of the Court, in a separate opinion, defended the Court's decision to address the use of force issues, indicating that in light of the contemporary debate about the law relating to the use of military force, when "supplied" with a case allowing it to do so, the Court should take every opportunity to participate in that debate.[2]

This simply is not a wise approach for the Court. States cannot have confidence in the objectivity of a tribunal if they fear its decisions will be motivated by the judges' agendas rather than by an objective and judicious analysis of the relevant facts and law. Judges must realize that whether they are "supplied" by states with like cases in the future depends on their ability to excel in a more traditional judicial role and that stepping outside that role may harm not only their own reputation but also the reputation of international tribunals in general.

Having stated this concern, I want to emphasize that an effective International Court of Justice serves our interests in advancing the rule of law and encouraging the peaceful resolution of disputes between states. This does not mean that we think the Court will be the best forum to resolve every dispute that may arise between states. In this regard, it is well known that the United States withdrew from the compulsory jurisdiction of the Court in 1985. This is consistent with our preference for assessing the suitability of particular disputes for resolution before the Court on a case-by-case basis. Moreover, we are not alone in taking this approach; indeed, only sixty-five states have accepted the Court's compulsory jurisdiction, and many of those have done so subject to reservations. We have also recently withdrawn from the Additional Protocol to the Vienna Convention on Consular Relations, which provides for ICJ jurisdiction over disputes under that convention. We did so because the Court's recent decisions in cases under the Vienna Convention provided for remedies that went well beyond those contemplated by the United States when it

---

[2] Case Concerning Oil Platforms (*Iran v. United States of America*), Judgment of 6 November 2003, Separate Opinion of Judge Simma, para. 6.

became party to that convention and, in our view, inappropriately interfered in our domestic criminal proceedings. In our view, disputes over the particular means of compliance with obligations under the Vienna Convention are more appropriately a matter for states to resolve through diplomatic means.

We will continue, however, to support the Court's role as a neutral, depoliticized forum for resolving disputes among states in appropriate cases. President George W. Bush's recent determination that the United States will comply with the Avena decision despite our continuing disagreement with both the Court's outcome and its reasoning demonstrates the depth of our respect for the Court's role and its judgments.[3] As it enters its next sixty years, we look forward to working with the Court, including its new president, Judge Roslyn Higgins, and with others in the international community to foster its effectiveness.

B. INTERNATIONAL CRIMINAL TRIBUNALS

I next turn to the role of international criminal tribunals. Consistent with our overall approach on rule of law issues, we favor solutions that will best establish and empower local institutions to ensure criminal justice and that will, in turn, inspire local ownership of the results. For this reason, we believe that, whenever possible, domestic solutions for criminal justice are preferable to international solutions. Helping states develop strong judicial institutions is a central part of our strategy for promoting the rule of law.

At the same time, the United States has often supported the use of international or hybrid courts to investigate and prosecute crimes that would be difficult to address through domestic courts. In some cases, this is because domestic courts lack the capacity or resources to address particular crimes. In other cases, the involvement of international actors may help increase domestic actors' confidence in the objectivity and legitimacy of criminal processes, especially when domestic societies may be deeply divided along political, ethnic, or other lines.

For example, in the cases of Rwanda and the former Yugoslavia, we supported the UN Security Council's creation of international criminal tribunals as a means to ensure accountability for the terrible crimes committed

---

[3] The U.S. Supreme Court subsequently ruled in March 2008 that the President lacked the authority to order state courts to comply with the ICJ's Avena decision. Mexico then submitted to the ICJ a request for an interpretation of the ICJ's Avena judgment, arguing that the United States disagreed with the Avena decision, and the U.S. Government responded by stating that the United States fully accepted the decision of the Court and was endeavoring to comply with it. The author appeared before the ICJ to argue the case on behalf of the U.S. Government. On January 19, 2009, the ICJ ruled that it did not have jurisdiction to hear Mexico's request for interpretation.

during the conflicts and to aid the process of postconflict reconciliation. These tribunals are wholly international in character: they are subsidiary organs of the Security Council, are made up of judges elected by the UN, and have jurisdiction over crimes arising under international law. The UN Security Council resolutions creating the tribunals require all states to cooperate fully with them, and the United States has done so since their inception. We provide about one-quarter of the total cost of each tribunal – in 2005 we contributed $35.5 million to the ICTR and $43.7 million to the ICTY; by the end of 2006, our total contributions to the two tribunals since their inception exceeded half a billion dollars. We do far more to show our support than just writing checks, however. The United States also cooperates with requests for information and access to witnesses from both the prosecution and defense to help ensure full and fair trials. Our political support has been strong as well. The United States has consistently pressured states to cooperate with the tribunals and to help the tribunals secure custody of indictees, including, in the case of Serbia, by withholding financial assistance. Finally, in June 2005, within months of being sworn in, Secretary Condoleezza Rice, made a point of meeting with the presidents and chief prosecutors of the ICTY and ICTR to confer with them on the progress and challenges of the tribunals and to express her support for their work.

Although we have strongly supported the ICTY and the ICTR, we have expressed concerns about their cost – which, together, amounts to more than $2 billion to date – and the efficiency of their operations. As a result, we have urged the ICTY and the ICTR to ensure that they adhere to their Security-Council-endorsed completion strategies to complete trials of first instance in 2008 and appeals in 2010. We recognize that this is a daunting endeavor that must be balanced with protecting the rights of the accused, but timely and effective trials are an important component of justice.

The international community followed a somewhat different model in creating the Special Court for Sierra Leone than it did for ICTY and ICTR. Instead of being created by a Security Council resolution, the Special Court was established pursuant to an agreement between the UN and the government of Sierra Leone. The Special Court has its seat in Sierra Leone and includes judges appointed by both the government of Sierra Leone and the UN secretary general, and its statute provides for the prosecution of crimes under both Sierra Leonean and international law. These elements provide a greater degree of local involvement than in the cases of ICTY and ICTR. This hybrid model, combining local and international features, may be a promising model for future cases.

As with ICTY and ICTR, the United States has provided extensive financial, technical, and political support to the Special Court for Sierra Leone. Most recently, and perhaps most important, the United States made substantial efforts at the highest levels of our government to press for the transfer of former Liberian president Charles Taylor to the Special Court. This included efforts to persuade the government of Nigeria, where Taylor had previously been granted exile, to facilitate his transfer, as well as our leading role in securing passage of a UN Security Council resolution allowing UN peacekeepers in Liberia to apprehend Taylor should he be found and transfer him to the Special Court.[4] Arrangements have largely been concluded to transfer him to The Hague, where the Special Court would hold his trial in facilities leased from the ICC, with legal proceedings exclusively under the jurisdiction of the Special Court. The major obstacle to his transfer is the identification of a country in which to imprison him should he be found guilty. Consultations are taking place in that regard, and we hope that a country, perhaps one that has not done much otherwise to support the Special Court, will soon show its commitment to international justice and agree to enforce any sentence that may be handed down.

Another matter currently unfolding is the effort by the United States and others to assist Lebanon to bring to justice those responsible for the assassination of former Lebanese Prime Minister Rafiq Hariri. The UN Security Council has passed a resolution requesting that the UN secretary general negotiate an agreement with the government of Lebanon for the establishment of a tribunal of an international character to address these matters.[5] The United States, France, and the United Kingdom have taken a leading role in the Council to help Lebanon see justice done in a volatile environment in the region. The Hariri assassination case demonstrates that there is no off-the-shelf solution to the complex issues raised by international criminal justice and that a pragmatic approach – along with considerable effort, both in public and behind the scenes – may be required to adapt existing models to the needs of a particular situation.

C. THE INTERNATIONAL CRIMINAL COURT

The United States does not support every example of international criminal tribunals. Our concerns about the ICC are well known. Although we share common goals with many ICC supporters, we disagree with the ICC's method for achieving accountability. From the U.S. perspective, the ICC lacks an adequate system of checks and balances, and the Rome Statute gives the ICC prosecutor the ability to initiate cases without appropriate oversight by

---

[4] UN Security Council Resolution 1638 (2005).
[5] UN Security Council Resolution 1664 (2006).

the UN Security Council. This creates a risk of politicized prosecutions and infringes on the Security Council's primary role under the UN Charter for the maintenance of international peace and security. In this connection, we object as a matter of principle to the ICC's claim of jurisdiction over persons from states that have not become parties to the Rome Statute.

The United States has nonetheless demonstrated that our differences over the ICC will not prevent us from finding ways to work with its supporters to bring to justice perpetrators of genocide, war crimes, and crimes against humanity. For example, we accepted adoption of the UN Security Council resolution referring the situation in Darfur to the ICC because we felt it was important for the international community to speak with one voice on accountability there.[6] Further, we have expressed our willingness for the Special Court for Sierra Leone to hold the trial of Charles Taylor in the ICC facilities in The Hague to minimize the risk that his trial could pose to security and stability in West Africa.

As we have said many times, we respect the decisions of states that have become parties to the Rome Statute; we ask in return that other states respect our decision not to do so and not to subject U.S. persons to the ICC's jurisdiction. We share with parties to the Rome Statute a commitment to preventing genocide, war crimes, and crimes against humanity and to ensuring accountability when they occur. We believe that divisiveness over the ICC distracts from our ability to pursue these common goals, and we hope that supporters of the Rome Statute will join us in constructive efforts to advance our shared values. EU Foreign Policy Chief Javier Solana said it well when he stated last year that there needs to be a "modus vivendi" between the United States and supporters of the ICC.

The contentious debate over the ICC has obscured the enormous and indispensable contributions that the United States has made in matters of international criminal justice. Our experience has been that establishing a tribunal, whether by Security Council resolution, treaty, or domestic statute, is only a first step. A state's real commitment lies in its efforts to ensure that wrongdoers are apprehended, that tribunals have adequate resources, and that full and fair trials are actually conducted. By these measures, the United States is certainly among the world's leaders in promoting international criminal justice.[7]

---

[6] Bush Administration officials subsequently stated that the United States would be prepared to offer assistance to the prosecutor, if it received an appropriate request. See "US Floats Possibility of Assistance to Hague Court," Washington Post, June 7, 2007, available at http://www.amicc.org/docs/4-26-08%20Wall%20Street%20Journal.pdf.

[7] The Bush Administration took a more pragmatic and nuanced approach toward the ICC in its second term. For a subsequent and more detailed statement by the author on the U.S.

D. IRAQ HIGH TRIBUNAL

The foregoing discussion also explains why the United States has been so disappointed at the lack of international support for the Iraq High Tribunal. The Iraqis determined that a domestic Iraqi trial mechanism was the best way to achieve justice and reconciliation in their country, and from the beginning, they sought international support for their effort. The United States responded swiftly to Iraqi requests, establishing the Regime Crimes Liaison Office and allocating $128 million to support the Iraqi-led process. However, with valued exceptions – including the British and Australian governments and several nongovernmental organizations (NGOs) such as the International Bar Association and the International Legal Assistance Consortium – these U.S. efforts have mostly stood alone. We have heard several reasons why governments and NGOs are reluctant to help, but none is compelling enough to justify a complete failure to assist the tribunal. From the U.S. perspective, it is difficult to reconcile the international community's de facto boycott of the tribunal with the insistent calls for justice and accountability that existed prior to the Iraq intervention.

E. CONCLUSION

The U.S. position on the Iraqi High Tribunal illustrates a more general theme that I address in closing. Like the rest of the world, we value appropriate international tribunals because they serve grander ambitions – resolving disputes and promoting international criminal justice. There is also a broad agreement, I believe, that international courts and tribunals are one tool among many to achieve these important ends. Maximizing their potential requires us to identify both the situations in which international courts and tribunals can play a role and the type of tribunal appropriate to each situation. It also requires courts and tribunals to be sensitive to the role they play in relations among states and to tailor their approaches to best meet the needs of states and of the international system. The United States has been and will continue

---

Government's views toward the ICC, see "The United States and the International Criminal Court: Where We've Been and Where We're Going," Remarks by John B. Bellinger, III, at the DePaul University College of Law, April 25, 2008. Available at http://2001-2009.state.gov/s/l/rls/104053.htm. For press coverage of the change in approach, see, e.g., "US Takes More Pragmatic View of World Court," Reuters, May 7, 2008, available at http://www.amicc.org/docs/5-7-2008_Reuters.pdf; "US Warms to Hague Tribunal," Wall Street Journal, June 14, 2006, available at http://www.amicc.org/docs/6-14-06%20Wall%20Street%20Journal.pdf; "US Accepts International Criminal Court," Wall Street Journal, April 26, 2008, available at http://www.amicc.org/docs/4-26-08%20Wall%20Street%20Journal.pdf.

to be a strong advocate for accountability and a strong supporter of efforts to bring peace and the rule of law to countries whose populations have suffered grave atrocities. In pursuit of accountability, we will endeavor to preserve an appropriate role for sovereign states in ensuring justice; craft responses to local conditions and needs; and keep the door open to a variety of accountability options in order to incorporate lessons learned, address new developments, and adapt to new challenges.

2

American Public Opinion on International Courts and Tribunals

STEVEN KULL AND CLAY RAMSAY[*]

Although the United States has historically played a seminal role in establishing international courts, tribunals, and a multitude of other quasi-judicial and implementation control bodies, it is also true that the U.S. government's support for, and participation in, these bodies has ebbed – perhaps reaching a low point at the beginning of the twenty-first century. Other chapters in this book address the attitudes of the U.S. government toward the various international courts and tribunals. A rarely explored question is whether the U.S. government's stance reflects a simultaneous decline in support among the American public. In particular, one could ask:

- Do Americans support having international bodies adjudicate compliance with treaties? Are they willing to subject the United States to their judgments?
- How do Americans react to the report of the United Nations (UN) Human Rights Commission (February 2006)[1] that found that the Guantanamo detention camps are inconsistent with international standards? Do they think the United States is obligated to change its practices according to the UN's findings and recommendations?
- Do Americans think the United States should participate in the International Criminal Court (ICC), even if, as the Bush administration has argued, it might be used against U.S. soldiers?

---

[*] Steven Kull and Clay Ramsay are the director and research director, respectively, of the Program on International Policy Attitudes, University of Maryland. We would like to acknowledge the valuable assistance of Evan Lewis (research associate, PIPA), and also of Stephen Weber, Mary Speck, and Stefan Subias (Knowledge Networks).

[1] United Nations Economic and Social Council, Commission on Human Rights, "Situation of Detainees at Guantanamo Bay," February 15, 2006. The full report can be accessed at http://www.globalsecurity.org/security/library/report/2006/guantanamo-detainees-report_un_060216.htm, or through the Official Documents System of the United Nations (URL subject to change).

- Do Americans think an international court should have the right to investigate possible cases of torture? Or is this a purely domestic matter? Whom do they view as responsible for torture: those who carried out the torture or those who gave the orders?

This chapter first briefly reviews the history of public opinion on international tribunals as measured by polls taken since the 1940s. It then focuses on a nationwide survey of 1,023 Americans, conducted by the Program on International Policy Attitudes (PIPA) at the University of Maryland and fielded by Knowledge Networks from April 18 to 24, 2006. This is the most comprehensive examination ever conducted of American public attitudes toward international tribunals.[2]

A. PAST PUBLIC OPINION ON INTERNATIONAL COURTS AND TRIBUNALS (1942–2005)

Past public opinion data on views of international courts and tribunals are extremely sparse and episodic, but show a clear pattern nonetheless. The American public has long had an open and positive attitude toward the United States participating in such institutions and accepting their decisions, although awareness of them has been low. The public seriously considers counterarguments to U.S. participation in international courts when they arise in poll questions, but it has a settled predisposition favoring international institutions for the settlement of disputes under the rule of law.

In 1942, seven in ten Americans (69 percent) said they would approve of having "a world court to try to settle international disputes when this war is over."[3] Of those who approved, virtually all (68 percent of the whole sample)

---

[2] The questionnaire and original report for the poll are available online in PIPA's Web publication, worldpublicopinion.org. Knowledge Networks, a polling, social science, and market research firm in Menlo Park, California, with a stratified random sample of its large-scale nationwide research panel, fielded the poll. This panel itself has been randomly recruited from the national population of households having telephones; households without Internet access are subsequently provided with free Web access and an Internet appliance. Thus the panel is not limited to those who already have home Internet access. The distribution of the sample in the Web-enabled panel closely tracks the distribution of U.S. Census counts for the U.S. population on age, race, Hispanic ethnicity, geographical region, employment status, income, education, and so on. Upon survey completion, the data were weighted by gender, age, education, and ethnicity. Fielding was conducted from April 18 to April 24, 2006, with a sample size of 1,023 American adults. The margin of error was ±3.1 percent for full-sampled questions and ±3.6 percent for three-quarter-sampled questions. More information about the methodology can be found at http://www.knowledgenetworks.com/ganp.

[3] American Institute of Public Opinion (Gallup), August 1942. Our thanks to the Roper Center for Public Opinion Research, University of Connecticut, for making available online through its IPOLL database all historical poll findings cited in this section.

said they would like to see the United States become a member of such a court. However, in the war years, only about a quarter (27%–28%) of Americans were aware of the "World Court" (as the questions phrased it – presumably the Permanent Court of International Justice) and believed their country was "a member" (again, as phrased).[4] After the formation of the International Court of Justice, 37 percent perceived of the United States as a participant by March 1946.[5]

In the 1960s, midway through the Vietnam War, a plurality or a majority of Americans expressed support for the idea of "submit[ting] the case of what to do about Vietnam" to an international body and "agree[ing] to accept the decision, whatever it happens to be." When Gallup asked this in January 1966, saying the "case" could be submitted to "the United Nations or the World Court," 49 percent thought accepting third-party adjudication was a good idea, whereas 36 percent thought it a bad idea.[6] In September 1966, Gallup asked the question again, simplifying it by naming only the United Nations as the decision maker: 52 percent then supported settlement by a third party, with 32 percent opposed.[7]

In the late 1980s, as ever larger cracks appeared in the structures of the Cold War, poll questions about international adjudication started to appear more frequently. One question put forth by the polling organization Americans Talk Security (ATS) provided a forceful counterargument that engendered a narrow plurality against international courts.[8] When offered two statements, 42 percent preferred: "The U.S. should abide by all World Court decisions, even when they go against us, because this sets an example for all nations to follow." Forty-seven percent preferred: "We should not feel bound to abide by all World Court decisions, because many nations that sit on the Court are hostile to the United States." Although this result is partly due to the fear of judges acting irresponsibly on the basis of the political inclinations of their home country, it may also be partly due to objectionable framing of the "pro" argument. Much research on how Americans view the United States' role in the world demonstrates that Americans resist high-toned arguments suggesting that the United States should be "an example for all nations to follow."

More important, other questions asked at the time demonstrated Americans' strong support for international adjudication. In March 1989, Roper

---

[4] Office of Public Opinion Research, November 1943, March 1945.
[5] National Opinion Research Center (NORC), March 1946.
[6] Gallup, January 1966.
[7] Gallup, September 1966.
[8] ATS, August 1988.

found clear majority support for accepting the International Court of Justice's decisions.[9] Respondents were asked:

> As you may know, there is an organization called the World Court that tries to settle international disputes peacefully among countries that accept its jurisdiction. If the World Court finds that actions by the United States government have violated international law, should the U.S. accept the Court's decisions or should it feel free to ignore the Court's decisions if it disagrees with them?

Fifty-eight percent said the United States should accept the Court's decisions; only 15 percent said the United States should ignore them, and 26 percent declined to answer.

In 1988, a very large majority favored the idea of establishing an international court to try individuals, foreshadowing the idea of the ICC. When asked "Would you favor or oppose creating an international court within the U.N. to deal with hijackers and terrorists?" 82 percent were in favor and only 15 percent opposed.[10] Although the poll question presented a cost-free picture of such a court, it nonetheless shows that most Americans were comfortable with the idea of expanding the UN system in this direction.

With the end of the Cold War in the early 1990s, there was renewed interest and a sense of possibility about international judicial institutions. In this environment, the questions just discussed were asked once again. In the ATS question that had previously revealed plurality resistance to abiding by World Court decisions, a bare majority (51 percent, up from 42 percent) now preferred the argument that the "U.S. should abide by all World Court decisions, even when they go against us," whereas only 40 percent (down from 47 percent) preferred the argument that "many nations that sit on the Court are hostile to the United States," and so the United States should not feel constrained by its decisions.[11] Similarly, Roper found those who thought that the United States should accept the Court's decision, should it find U.S. actions contrary to international law, rose to 65 percent, up from 58 percent in 1989.[12]

In 1992, a slight majority favored the argument that the United States ratify various UN human rights treaties, even when presented the strong counterargument that this "might require changes in U.S. law and practices and ... other countries would then have the right to question human rights conditions in the United States." Only 21 percent agreed with these arguments against

[9] Roper Organization, March 1989.
[10] ATS, May 1988.
[11] ATS, August 1988.
[12] Americans Talk Issues Foundation, December 1991.

ratification, whereas 51 percent thought "the United States should ratify these treaties because it would show we support worldwide standards of human rights and because it would increase the pressure on other countries to abide by them."[13]

In March 1993, the Americans Talk Issues Foundation (ATIF) conducted an experiment in which respondents were asked about the idea of amending the UN Charter to create a powerful international criminal court (much more powerful than the actual one that was created in 1998).[14] Those who supported such a court were then asked whether the idea of a U.S. president appearing in the dock someday would make them rethink their support. ATIF posed the following scenario:

> Some people think that the U.N. Charter should be changed so that top leaders, such as heads of state in different countries, could be arrested by the U.N. for certain serious crimes and then tried by an international criminal court, and if judged guilty would be punished. I am going to read you some things that leaders have done and ask if you approve or disapprove changing the U.N. charter to permit the U.N., upon due process of law, to bring leaders accused of these things to stand trial by an international criminal court.

Large majorities approved of this hypothetical and very muscular court, which would try leaders accused of:

- Making war on an ethnic group in that leader's country: 87 percent approved of a trial by an international criminal court.
- Invading and occupying a neighboring country: 86 percent approved of such a trial.
- Doing serious damage to the global environment: 86 percent approved of such a trial.
- Preventing a democratic election from taking place: 68 percent approved of such a trial.
- Acquiring nuclear weapons: 67 percent approved of such a trial.

Those who had approved of an international court trying one or more of the cases set forth here were then warned, "It is conceivable that a President of the United States or leaders of U.S. corporations might someday be arrested by the UN under this charter revision," and were then asked to reconsider their support. Support dropped, but a majority (52%–74% of the full sample) still favored the hypothetical court.

---

[13] Roper Organization, March 1992.
[14] ATIF, March 1993.

In 1998, the Rome Statute to create the ICC was opened for signature, and the debate over whether to ratify the Statute within U.S. policy circles intensified. The public remained receptive to creating the actual institution, just as it had been to the idea of one. Eighty-four percent favored the "trial of suspected terrorists in an International Criminal Court."[15] When PIPA and the Chicago Council on Foreign Relations (CCFR) presented the key arguments of American opponents of the ICC in polls, two-thirds of Americans still wanted to support the new court. The question ran as follows:

> A permanent International Criminal Court has been proposed by the UN (United Nations) to try individuals suspected of war crimes, genocide, and crimes against humanity. Some say the U.S. (United States) should not support the proposed Court because trumped up charges may be brought against Americans, for example, U.S. soldiers who use force in the course of a peacekeeping operation. Others say that the U.S. should support such a court because the world needs a better way to prosecute war criminals, many of whom go unpunished today. Do you think the U.S. should or should not support a permanent international criminal court?

Sixty-six percent thought the United States should support the ICC; just 29 percent thought it should not.[16]

Support for the United States' accepting compulsory ICJ jurisdiction was at modest majority levels at the end of the 1990s. The idea of compulsory jurisdiction was explained in the following way in a 1999 PIPA question[17]:

> The World Court is part of the United Nations. It makes rulings on disputes between countries based on treaties the countries have signed. Some countries have made commitments to accept the decisions of the World Court. Other countries decide in advance for each case whether to accept the court's decisions. Do you think the U.S. (United States) should or should not make the commitment to accept the decisions of the World Court?

Fifty-three percent thought the United States should make this commitment, and 38 percent thought it should not – very similar to the levels of support found in other questions regarding the ICJ at the close of the Cold War.

The September 11, 2001, attacks engendered a strong reaction among the American people that some think included a rejection of international and multilateral mechanisms. Poll questions asked at the time, however, do not show such a rejection. On the day after 9/11, NBC/*Wall Street Journal* asked about "several possible responses by the United States," including "build[ing]

---

[15] CCFR, November 1998.
[16] PIPA, October 1999.
[17] PIPA, October 1999.

a case against the people who are specifically responsible and seek[ing] justice in the World Court."[18] Three-quarters (75 percent) favored the United States doing this (62 percent strongly), with 22 percent opposed.

This openness to the use of international courts in terrorism cases extended even to jurisdiction over Osama bin Laden personally. A number of questions at the same time posed the scenario of capturing bin Laden and putting him on trial, with different kinds of courts described to respondents. In five questions that set forth differing options and conditions, those preferring that bin Laden be tried in an international court ranged from 37 to 52 percent.[19] The question that offered the fullest arguments on both sides posed the problem this way[20]:

> If Osama Bin Laden were captured, we would need to decide whether he would be tried in a federal court in New York or in an International Criminal Tribunal. Some say it would be better to have bin Laden tried in an International Criminal Tribunal because it would be more likely that the world would view the trial as impartial and less likely to lead to further terrorist attacks against the US. Others say it would be better to have bin Laden tried in New York because the crime took place in America and we can be more confident that justice will be done. Do you think it would be better to have bin Laden tried in an International Criminal Tribunal or in New York?

A slim plurality preferred to try bin Laden in an international court (49 percent) as opposed to a federal court in New York (44 percent).

In the same months, the U.S. government was introducing its new policy of special military tribunals for suspected terrorists. In November 2001, only four in ten (40 percent) thought these tribunals "should be entirely American proceedings."[21] A clear majority of 55 percent thought "these tribunals should have some international involvement or representation."

In the years immediately following, there was little or no sign that the run-up to, and the experience of, the Iraq War had affected Americans' positive opinions regarding international tribunals. From 1998 to 2004, the CCFR asked the public and an elite sample of four hundred foreign policy opinion leaders three times whether they would favor or oppose the "trial of international terrorists in an International Criminal Court." Among the public, four out of five favored such trials with no variation over the years (82%–84%). Among the elite sample, there was also significant support but with more fluctuation:

---

[18] PIPA, October 1999.
[19] PIPA, November 2001; Gallup/CNN/USA Today, November and December 2001; CBS/New York Times, December 2001.
[20] PIPA, November 2001.
[21] Newsweek, November 2001.

89 percent in 1998, down to 74 percent in 2002, and back up to 84 percent in 2004.[22]

CCFR's June 2002 poll asked a series of questions about whether specific international institutions need to be strengthened "to deal with shared problems" or whether "this would only create bigger, unwieldy bureaucracies."[23] A 56 percent majority thought the World Court needed to be strengthened, whereas 29 percent thought not. In December 2003, Saddam Hussein was captured, and there was discussion as to whether he should be tried by an international court. Offered a choice by Gallup and CBS of an Iraqi court, a U.S. military court, and an international court, a 48 to 50 percent plurality chose an international court.[24] In 2004, 57 percent thought the United States should accept compulsory jurisdiction for the decisions of the ICJ – slightly higher than the 53 percent who thought so in 1999.[25] Likewise, 69 percent thought the United States should accept adverse decisions by the World Trade Organization (WTO) dispute settlement system (up from 64 percent in 2002).[26]

In 2004, the Chicago Council also surveyed a sample of foreign policy opinion leaders, asking them some of the same questions the CCFR had asked the public.[27] The public's views were aligned with those of the leaders where international tribunals were concerned. Thus, 83 percent of the leaders favored compliance with unfavorable WTO rulings, as did 69 percent of the public. Seventy percent of the leaders favored participation in the ICC, as did 76 percent of the public.

However, the leaders mistakenly saw the public as holding views opposite to theirs. The elite sample was asked to estimate how the public would reply to the questions just discussed, and most leaders misperceived public opinion on international tribunals. Only 30 percent of leaders thought that a majority of the public supported ICC participation, and only 26 percent of leaders thought that a majority of the public favored compliance with unfavorable WTO rulings.

Overall, the existing public opinion record shows large majorities supporting the principle of international adjudication and modest majorities agreeing to accept adverse decisions. There has been strikingly little fluctuation in these

---

[22] CCFR, November 1998, June 2002, and June 2004.
[23] CCFR, June 2002.
[24] CNN/USA Today/Gallup, December 2003; CBS, December 2003.
[25] CCFR, June 2004; PIPA, October 1999.
[26] CCFR, June 2004 and June 2002.
[27] CCFR, June 2004. Elite responses are discussed throughout the report, "Global Views 2004: American Public Opinion and Foreign Policy," at http://thechicagocouncil.org/UserFiles/File/Global_Views_2004_US.pdf.

basic attitudes across the decades and little evidence of trends – with the possible exception of a warming to international adjudication as the Cold War ended. Still, the sporadic rhythm of earlier public opinion research, as well as the lack of comprehensiveness of the questions asked, naturally leaves doubts.

B. ATTITUDES OF THE AMERICAN PUBLIC TOWARD INTERNATIONAL ADJUDICATION DURING THE SECOND TERM OF THE BUSH ADMINISTRATION (2006)

Given the sweep of U.S. government actions from 2001 to 2008, which stressed unilateral action rather than the use of multilateral institutions, it is only natural to believe that these actions must have had some backing from the majority of the American public – presumably attitudes that result from the exigencies of the war on terrorism.

The survey designed and conducted by PIPA in April 2006[28] sought to test this hypothesis, especially by offering a wide range of arguments for and against U.S. participation in international tribunals, a range of the types of cases that could be adjudicated, and numerous instances in which the United States has been, or could be, ruled against in an international institution. The following sections discuss, first, how Americans respond to international adjudication when they are faced with counterarguments based on American exceptionalism. Second, American reactions to the Guantanamo Bay detainee camp and the strictures of the UN Human Rights Commission regarding it are addressed. Third, public attitudes toward the ICC and the larger question of charging individuals for war crimes and crimes against humanity are scrutinized. Finally, the issue of torture and the justifications sometimes proposed for it, as were presented in the poll, and respondents' reactions are assessed.

1. *International Adjudication and the Case for U.S. Exceptionalism*

The poll found that a very large majority favors having an international body, such as a court, judge compliance with treaties to which the United States is party. A large majority rejected the idea that the United States should receive exceptional treatment in the adjudication of treaty compliance. Arguments against international adjudication, however, held some sway, which suggests that Americans acknowledge there are some costs and risks associated with it.

When asked, "As a general rule, when the U.S. enters into international agreements, do you think there should or should not be an independent international body, such as a court, to judge whether the parties are complying

---

[28] See note 1 for methodological information.

with the agreement?" 76 percent said there should be such a body when the United States enters into international agreements, whereas 21 percent said that there should not be. This majority included two-thirds of Republicans (66 percent) and nearly all Democrats (88 percent).

Support was also quite strong when respondents were asked about the possibility of adjudicating a wide range of disputes. In every case, a majority expressed support, and in all but one case, a large majority did so. The highest support was for adjudication of disputes over whether states are abiding by treaties governing human rights (79 percent) or disputes over borders (74 percent). There were also strong majorities supporting the use of international bodies to adjudicate disputes over whether countries are enforcing environmental laws (69 percent), which countries have the right to fish in certain waters (66 percent), whether countries are enforcing labor laws (64 percent), and what rights nations give foreigners who are arrested and charged with a crime (64 percent). Curiously, the one type of dispute that fell below 64 percent support was about "when a country can give preferential trade treatment to another country." A bare majority of 51 percent supported adjudication in this instance, and 44 percent opposed it.

Republican support for international adjudication was not as robust as Democratic support but still constituted a substantial majority in every case except one. In cases involving preferential trade treatment, 57 percent of Republicans opposed such adjudication, whereas 62 percent of Democrats favored it.

Respondents also showed strong support for international agreements per se. For the three cases presented, support was overwhelming. Seventy-nine percent approved of "the international law that prohibits a nation from using military force against another nation except in self defense or to defend an ally" (71 percent of Republicans, 91 percent of Democrats). Eighty-six percent approved of the United States being part of "treaties that establish standards for protecting the human rights of their citizens" (87 percent of Republicans, 92 percent of Democrats). Eighty-two percent approved of the United States signing treaties that prohibit the use of torture (81 percent of Republicans, 90 percent of Democrats).

To dig deeper into respondents' views and find out how reliable they were, respondents were presented with a series of four arguments in support of, and four in opposition to, international adjudication and asked how convincing they found each one to be.

All four of the arguments in favor of international adjudication received overwhelming support. Eighty-five percent found convincing (41 percent very convincing) the argument that "[i]t is much easier for the U.S. to pursue its interests if the world is a place where countries are resolving disputes peacefully in accordance with international law." An equally large number (84 percent) found convincing (35 percent very convincing) the argument that "[w]e cannot simply let countries decide if they are in compliance with an agreement... [o]therwise they will find excuses for not really complying.... We need an objective party to judge whether they are complying." For these arguments, Republicans and Democrats who found them convincing were both in the 81- to 91-percent range.

Even the argument recognizing that the United States may "lose a case from time to time" generated 78 percent concurrence with the view that it is nonetheless "better for the U.S. to generally use international courts to resolve its disputes with other countries than to allow some disputes to escalate to destructive levels." Thirty-three percent found this view very convincing. The argument that did least well (69 percent convincing, 22 percent very convincing) proposed that the positive experience with the rule of law at home should be applied to the international sphere: "Because we use courts to resolve our disputes, the U.S. is a much better place to live than countries where the rule of law is weak. Since this works for us at home, we should generally try to resolve our international disputes in the same way." For these arguments, Republicans and Democrats who found them convincing were both in the 66- to 89-percent range.

None of the arguments against international adjudication did as well as the arguments in favor, but three out of four were nonetheless considered convincing by a majority. This suggests that most Americans acknowledge that there are costs and risks associated with international adjudication. However, when asked to weigh these costs and risks against the benefits, most come down in favor of international adjudication.

The most convincing argument against accepting international adjudication was that "judges from other countries cannot be trusted to be impartial ... because there are so many people in the world who are looking for opportunities to try to undermine the U.S." Sixty-five percent found the argument convincing, including not only 75 percent of Republicans but also 55 percent of Democrats. Polls around the world suggesting that U.S. foreign policy was unpopular at the time of the study may have enhanced this concern.

Somewhat less successful was an argument based on sovereignty concerns: "Submitting to international courts would violate the United States' sovereign right to protect its citizens and its interests." Although 58 percent said this was convincing, it did not have bipartisan appeal: 73 percent of Republicans found it convincing but only 47 percent of Democrats (51 percent found it unconvincing).

The weakest argument against adjudication started from a hard-core realist view stating that "[b]ecause the United States is the most powerful country in the world, it has the means to get its way in international disputes," and therefore, "[i]t has nothing to gain from submitting to the jurisdiction of international courts, where its arguments are put on the same footing as those of weaker countries." Only 48 percent found this convincing, whereas 51 percent found it unconvincing.

It proved much more acceptable to make an argument for exceptionalism based on responsibility, rather than on power alone:

> The United States uses its power in the world to do the right thing. Sometimes that means the U.S. must make the hard decisions that are not popular, but necessary for peace. Being subject to international courts would tie America's hands and undermine its ability to make the tough but necessary decisions.

Sixty-two percent found this argument convincing (23 percent very convincing), whereas 36 percent found it unconvincing (12 percent very unconvincing). Republicans overwhelmingly found that argument convincing (78 percent), and so did a modest majority of Democrats (54 percent); however, 46 percent of Democrats found it unconvincing.

After evaluating arguments for and against international adjudication, all respondents were asked (half of them for the second time) whether "[a]s a general rule, when the United States enters into international agreements, do you think there should or should not be an independent international body, such as a court, to judge whether the parties are complying with the agreement?"

Although majorities gave the arguments against adjudication careful consideration, most felt that the benefits of international adjudication still outweighed the costs. Seventy-one percent said that when the United States enters into an international agreement, an independent body should judge compliance – down 5 points from when they were asked the same question before evaluating the arguments. Twenty-five percent said no. Republicans were most affected by the arguments: 54 percent said no after pondering the arguments, down from 66 percent before hearing the arguments. Democrats and independents, however, were virtually unaffected (down 1.5 points each).

Overall, it appears that Americans found some arguments against international adjudication persuasive, primarily on the basis of themes that the United States should be viewed as exceptional. However, although these arguments may have given respondents pause, in the end Americans came down firmly in favor of international adjudication. This was true on the basis of the general question as well as the eight specific types of disputes presented (all of which were presented after respondents had evaluated the pro and con arguments).

Equally significant, seven out of ten rejected making a special exception for the United States in international treaties on human rights. Only 25 percent thought that as a general rule, "U.S. compliance with the treaty" should never be "subject to the judgment of an international body." Sixty-nine percent thought the United States should not claim a special exception." This included 63 percent of Republicans and 78 percent of Democrats.

2. Detainee Treatment at Guantanamo Bay

Perhaps the most apparent recent test of Americans' willingness to be subject to international third-party scrutiny was related to the February 2006 UN Commission on Human Rights evaluation of U.S. treatment of detainees held in Guantanamo Bay. Two in three Americans said the United States should change the way it treats detainees at Guantanamo Bay, as recommended by the UN Commission on Human Rights. An overwhelming majority wanted the United States to be part of treaties that limit what signatories can do when detaining individuals.

Respondents were told that "the U.S. participates in the UN Commission on Human Rights" and that the Commission's report "determined that the U.S. has held certain individuals for interrogation for several years without charging them with a crime, contrary to international conventions." They were then asked whether the United States should follow the Commission's recommendation to change these practices. Sixty-three percent said the United States "should change this practice," whereas 30 percent said the United States should not do so. Republicans were divided evenly, with 49 percent saying the United States should comply and 47 percent saying it should not; Democrats, however, were not evenly divided, with 76 percent in favor of compliance and 20 percent opposing compliance.

This support for following UN Human Rights Commission recommendations was consistent with the even larger support for the general principle that the United States participate in treaties on the treatment of detainees in the context of armed conflict, generally called the Geneva Conventions. An overwhelming 85 percent thought the United States should be part of treaties "that limit what the U.S. can do to detainees and what other countries can do when they detain Americans." This majority was bipartisan, with 85 percent of Republicans and 89 percent of Democrats approving.

These majorities were consistent with the findings of PIPA's 2004 study on torture and detention (conducted shortly after the Abu Ghraib scandal was revealed). In that study, PIPA tested the Bush administration's position that combatants who are terrorists, not conventional soldiers, do not come under the protection of "the laws governing the treatment of detainees." Respondents heard the argument that "because such people do not wear uniforms, do not fight in a conventional military fashion, and are not part of a nation that has signed these treaties, when dealing with them, the U.S.

should not be required to give them the rights provided by the treaties." Only 37 percent agreed with this position. On the contrary, 60 percent thought that "legally, the U.S. is required to treat all detainees in a way that is consistent with the treaties and, furthermore, not giving detainees the rights of the treaties would be immoral, set a bad example, hurt America's image and ultimately weaken the rule of law."

In 2004, respondents also were asked about specific legal requirements for the treatment of detainees in international treaties to which the United States is party – specifically, respecting a detainee's "right to a hearing in which the government makes its case for why the detainee should be held and the detainee can challenge the government's right to hold him or her." Eighty-one percent favored this requirement; 17 percent were opposed.

When Americans were presented some of these issues outside of the framework of treaty constraints, they gave more equivocal responses. When the Pew Research Center for the People and the Press asked in March 2006 whether they favored or opposed "the U.S. government's policy of holding suspected terrorists at Guantanamo Bay without formal charges or trials," responses were evenly divided – 44 percent in favor, 43 percent opposed.[29] Respondents were given no information about treaty requirements. Moreover, the presentation of this action as "the U.S. government's policy" surely lent it legitimacy and may have led some to believe that it was consistent with U.S. treaty commitments.

3. Charging Individuals and the ICC

The poll found majority support for giving international bodies the power to judge individuals charged with extreme violations of human rights when a national government is not performing this function. A large majority favored U.S. participation in the ICC even after hearing U.S. government objections. Where extreme violations of human rights are concerned, three out of five Americans favored giving international bodies the power to judge individuals when national governments fail to do so. This was true even when this view was challenged by a strong counterargument based on national sovereignty.

Respondents were first reminded that "[i]n most cases, the actions of individuals are simply governed by the laws of the country they live in." Then they were asked to choose between two positions. The position favoring international jurisdiction went as follows:

> In some cases there are individual actions that are of such significance, such as acts of torture or genocide, that there should be international laws governing these actions that are applied by an international court or tribunal if a nation does not enforce them.

[29] Q25e, http://people-press.org/reports/questionnaires/273.pdf.

The other position argued that granting such jurisdiction would violate the principle of national sovereignty:

> Only individual nations should make laws governing the acts of individuals, because having such international laws and giving international courts and tribunals the power to apply them would violate the sovereignty of nations.

Faced with these two arguments, 60 percent chose the first, supporting an international jurisdiction of last resort for grave human rights violations. Thirty-six percent chose the second, regarding national sovereignty as the more important principle. Partisan differences were slight. Among Republicans, 60 percent supported international jurisdiction as did 68 percent of Democrats. Among independents, only 44 percent were in support.

This response is consistent with attitudes over the years toward U.S. participation in the ICC. Seventy-four percent of one half-sample said the United States should "participate in the International Criminal Court that can try individuals for war crimes, genocide or crimes against humanity if their own country won't try them"; 21 percent were opposed to participation. Republicans and Democrats were both within the 77- to 80-percent support range, whereas independents were lower at 56 percent (26 percent were opposed and 18 percent gave no answer). This result was basically unchanged from a survey by the CCFR that asked the same question in 2002 and 2004.

When another half-sample presented the U.S. government argument against ICC participation, a large majority still favored it, although support was a bit lower. Respondents were presented a longer question that included the U.S. government's arguments regarding the ICC (also discussed earlier in the review of past polling):

> A permanent International Criminal Court has been established by the United Nations to try individuals suspected of war crimes, genocide, and crimes against humanity. Some say the U.S. should not support the Court because trumped-up charges may be brought against Americans, for example, U.S. soldiers who use force in the course of a peacekeeping operation. Others say that the U.S. should support the court because the world needs a better way to prosecute war criminals, many of whom go unpunished today. Do you think the U.S. should or should not support the permanent International Criminal Court?

In this context, support was 68 percent, with 29 percent opposed – again, virtually the same as when this question was asked in 2002 by CCFR. The counterargument clearly raised concerns among Republicans: only 45 percent favored participation in this question, with 52 percent opposed. Democrats, however, showed higher support than in the short question, with 85 percent favoring participation.

4. Torture

Respondents overwhelmingly endorsed U.S. participation in treaties prohibiting torture, and a large majority favored giving an international court the right to investigate when governments fail to take action against individuals who may have engaged in torture. A very large majority said that individuals who gave orders to torture should be held liable, as well as those who carried out the orders. Eighty-two percent (81 percent of Republicans, 90 percent of Democrats) approved of "the United States [having] signed a number of treaties that prohibit the use of torture."

Furthermore, a large majority favored giving an international court the right to investigate when governments do not take action against individuals who may have engaged in torture. Respondents were asked, "Do you think that states should or should not agree that if someone is tortured and no one is charged for it, that an international court should have the right to investigate to determine if someone should be charged?" Seventy percent said an international court should have this right; 26 percent disagreed. A clear majority of Republicans (57 percent) supported this type of jurisdiction, with 40 percent opposed. Among Democrats, 86 percent were in support.

Naturally, trying individuals for engaging in torture means holding them responsible even if they have been given orders to do so. This conundrum was posed to respondents, who were asked, "When acts of torture have been committed, who do you think should be held responsible – only persons who committed the acts of torture; only the person who gave the orders to use torture; both; or neither?" An overwhelming majority (77 percent) said that both those who committed torture and those who gave the orders should be held responsible. Only 12 percent said responsibility should lie only with those who gave the orders, and just 4 percent said responsibility should lie only with those who committed the acts. Republican and Democrat responses were essentially the same, with 75 percent of Republicans, 84 percent of Democrats, and 66 percent of Independents saying "both." "[T]he person who gave the orders" came in a distant second for each group of voters.

These majority positions are similar to those found in 2004, shortly after the eruption of the Abu Ghraib scandal.[30] At that time, PIPA found large majorities

---

[30] PIPA/Knowledge Networks Poll: "Americans on Detention, Torture and the War on Terrorism," PIPA (Washington D.C.), July 22, 2004. The full report and questionnaire can be accessed at http://www.worldpublicopinion.org/pipa/articles/btjusticehuman_rightsra/111.php?lb=brusc&pnt=111&nid=&id=.

supporting the principle of holding individuals responsible for their actions in regard to torture and abuse. When asked whether "government officials who engage in, or order others to engage in, torture or cruel and humiliating treatment as a way to get information should be tried and punished," 71 percent said they should be tried and punished and just 24 percent said they should not be tried and punished.

Consistent with this view of personal responsibility, in 2004, a large majority said that soldiers should have the right to disobey an order to engage in torture or abuse. Asked whether a soldier "ordered to take an action against a detainee that the soldier believes is in violation of international law should or should not have the right to refuse to follow the order," a remarkable 77 percent said that the soldier should have the right to disobey such orders, with only 19 percent saying a soldier should not have that right. It is important to note that the question did not specify that the action be in violation of international law – only that the soldier believed that it was. Thus, the public seems ready to give soldiers latitude in making such judgments.

C. CONCLUSION

Although it is somewhat surprising that, in the dramatic setting of the post–September 11 world, there should be such majority support for accepting the jurisdiction of international tribunals over U.S. policies, from a long-term perspective of U.S. involvement with the international system, such support is to be expected. Among the American people, majority support for international tribunals has coexisted with majority support for the United Nations and the overall framework of international law. The public's lack of information about the system's detail and its occasional frustrations with how the system performs in practice have been often mistakenly regarded as signs of weak support for the system's existence. This long-standing assumption, however, is disconfirmed by the available data.

A large majority of Americans see the United Nations as playing not simply a desirable but a necessary role in the world and would prefer to see the United States more fully assume the benefits and costs of a style of decision making that integrates the UN into the process.[31] Americans have long held these views about the larger context of international policy, which does not

---

[31] For example, Gallup (February 2005) found 64 percent saying, "The United Nations plays a necessary role in the world." Three out of five have consistently agreed with the statement, "When dealing with international problems, the U.S. should be more willing to make decisions within the United Nations, even if this means the United States will sometimes have to go along with a policy that is not its first choice" (CCFR June 2004, 66 percent; CCFR July 2006, 60 percent; PIPA October 2006, 61 percent).

directly include the additional normative value of the law. Consequently, it need not surprise us that, where international legal institutions are concerned, Americans, past and present, hold attitudes similar to those they hold toward the UN and see the benefits of participation and compliance as outweighing the costs in a normative order that maintains the legitimacy of law.

3

Arbitration and Avoidance of War: The Nineteenth-Century American Vision

MARY ELLEN O'CONNELL*

"[T]he American people...hate war and wish their country to do its share toward promoting peace with justice in the world."

Elihu Root, 1934[1]

What we need is "a moral substitute for war."

Jane Addams, 1904[2]

From the time of America's founding, its citizens embraced alternatives to the use of war for the settlement of international disputes. Early American political leaders understood the promise that these alternatives offered to a small, new nation.[3] At the same time, a significant portion of the American population came to this country committed to religious ideals of pacifism and nonviolence. Quakers, Mennonites, and then a broad array of Protestant denominations provided popular support to politicians willing to resolve disputes using peaceful methods. By the early nineteenth century, Christian pacifists were particularly promoting arbitration as an alternative to war. Later in the century, political parties included arbitration in their party platforms. For almost a hundred years, strong pacifist and pragmatist commitments resulted in popular support for international arbitration. Pacifist and pragmatist programs reached the pinnacle of their influence on U.S. foreign policy between

---

* Robert and Marion Short Chair in Law, Notre Dame University. With thanks for research assistance to Caoilte Joy, JD (2005), Gretchen Drenski, JD (2006), and Benjamin Hill, JD (2006).
[1] Philip C. Jessup, II, *Elihu Root* (1938) 444.
[2] John C. Farrell, *Beloved Lady: A History of Jane Addams' Ideas on Reform and Peace* (1967) 144.
[3] America's founders were well aware that international law, too, offered advantages to a people seeking to establish their sovereignty vis-à-vis other nations. *See* Mark Weston Janis, *The American Tradition of International Law, Great Expectations, 1789–1914* (2004): 53–54; Arthur Nussbaum, *A Concise History of the Law of Nations* (rev'd ed. 1954): 161.

1899 and 1918. In that period, Jane Addams, the Chicago-based social worker whose pacifism was grounded in her Christian faith, achieved international fame in pressing for alternatives to war. Elihu Root, the pragmatic secretary of war and secretary of state, worked tirelessly in the same period promoting the use of arbitration and international courts as alternatives to war. Both were winners of the Nobel Peace Prize.[4]

After World War I, however, with the continuing rise of American military and economic power, pragmatist arguments against war grew less persuasive to Americans. Religious-based pacifism also waned as the United States confronted fascism and communism – ideologies that American Christians increasingly believed had to be opposed by military force. By the end of the war, American enthusiasm for international arbitration had declined, and by the end of the twentieth century, it had virtually disappeared, replaced to some extent by enthusiasm for other institutions devoted to peaceful settlement, such as the United Nations and the International Court of Justice.

A. INTERNATIONAL ARBITRATION AND AMERICA: 1776–1872

The Founding Fathers would have been aware of arbitration, mediation, and negotiation as alternatives to war. All three methods have deep roots in the history of human communal living.[5] With the rise of international law in the seventeenth century, arbitration became a regular feature in the emerging literature. The Dutchman Hugo Grotius, who is considered the father of international law, promoted arbitration in his widely read treatise, *The Law of War and Peace*, first published in 1625. Grotius cites the Greek historian Thucydides for the point that "[i]t is not lawful to proceed against one who offers arbitration just as against a wrongdoer."[6] In addition to the literature, various treaties from this period mention arbitration. The famous Peace of Westphalia of 1648 required the parties to resolve disputes by "amicable settlement or legal discussion."[7]

---

[4] Root in 1912 and Addams in 1931.
[5] Mary Ellen O'Connell, *International Dispute Settlement* (2003) xxi.
[6] Hugo Grotius, I *De Jure Belli ac pacis Libri Tres* (Francis W. Kelsey trans., 1964): 562, 560–61. See also, VIII J. H. W. Verzijl, *International Law in Historical Perspective: Inter-State Disputes and Their Settlement* (1976): 52, and Grewe for the view that arbitration had only three great periods: classical Greece, the High and Late Middle Ages, and the nineteenth and early twentieth centuries. Grewe also finds nothing linking these periods. The evolution of arbitration was apparently episodic, not continuous. Wilhelm Grewe, *The Epochs of International Law* (Michael Byers trans. & ed., 2000): 104.
[7] The Articles of the Treaty of Peace, signed and sealed at Münster, in Westphalia, October 24, 1648, art. 73, I *Parry's Consolidated Treaty Series* (1969) 319; Treaty of Peace between the Empires and Sweden, concluded and signed at Osnabrück, October 24, 1648, *id.* at 148 (1969).

Emerich de Vattel, an influential eighteenth-century Swiss international law scholar and diplomat, also advocated the use of arbitration. His treatise on international law describes a number of seventeenth-century arbitrations as examples for states of his day to follow.[8] Vattel was apparently particularly influential in the young United States. Benjamin Franklin received three copies of Vattel's *Law of Nations* in 1775 and wrote to the sender: "the circumstances of a rising state make it necessary frequently to consult the law of nations."[9] It is not surprising, therefore, that the United States and Britain included a commitment to arbitrate in the Jay Treaty of 1794 that settled outstanding issues left from the War of Independence.[10] President George Washington endorsed the Jay Treaty primarily because the commitment to arbitrate was likely to "prevent war and to bring about the peaceful settlement of misunderstandings and quarrels."[11] Starting with the St. Croix River Arbitration of 1798, in which arbitrators determined much of the boundary between present-day Canada and the United States, 536 arbitral awards were made pursuant to the Jay Treaty between 1794 and 1804.[12]

Following this auspicious start, America's pacifist religious communities and the peace movement they inspired continued to promote peaceful settlement.[13] Early leaders of the peace movement began advocating arbitration as a substitute for war.[14] David Low Dodge, founder of the New York Peace Society, marshaled economic, political, and humanitarian rationales alongside religious objections in arguing that war was both wrong and unlawful. One of Dodge's supporters, a New York Presbyterian minister named Samuel Whelpley (1766–1817), took Dodge's pacifism one step further and argued that if countries disarmed and refused to fight, they could seek any needed protection in international arbitration, which would interpret and apply the law of nations.[15]

See also Nussbaum, *op. cit.*, at 116–17. The reference to "legal discussion" indicates arbitration, because negotiation and mediation are typically not restricted to legal discussion.

[8] Emmerich de Vattel, *The Law of Nations or the Principles of Natural Law, Applied to the Conduct and to the Affairs of Nations and of Sovereigns* (Charles G. Fenwick trans. of 1758 ed., 1916): 189–92. *See also* Christine Gray and Benedict Kingsbury, "Developments in Dispute Settlement: Inter-State Arbitration since 1945," *Brit. Ybk. Int'l L.* 97 (1992): 63.

[9] Nussbaum, *op. cit.*, at 161.

[10] The Jay Treaty arbitrations are considered the first law-based arbitrations (in contrast to diplomatic arbitration.) A. M. Stuyt, *Survey of International Arbitrations 1794–1938* (1939): vii.

[11] Merle Curti, *Peace or War: The American Struggle 1636–1936* (1936): 24.

[12] Janis, *op. cit.*, at 105, citing Nussbaum, *op. cit.*, at 128–9; Grewe, *op. cit.*, at 366. Claims commissions to settle property disputes between the United States and Britain were also established, but without as much success.

[13] Janis, *op. cit.*, at 98.

[14] *Id.*

[15] *Id.*, at 98, *citing* P. Brock, *Pacifism in the United States from the Colonial Era to the First World War* (1968): 450–66.

Such commitments to peace were widespread in early America, and despite the glorification of the War of Independence, U.S. leaders supported the peace movement both ideologically and institutionally. "No other government permitted so many men of conscience to avoid military service. No other country erected so many constraints against a peacetime standing army. No other people defined their collective identity so firmly with the work of redeeming the world for peace."[16] The peace movement created strong opposition to the War of 1812, drawing support from merchants, academics, clergy, and others.[17] The victory in 1815 dissipated much of the antiwar criticism, but the peace movement, which would last another hundred years, had been firmly established.[18]

After 1815, the peace movement took a new form: the private, voluntary society. The New York Peace Society was one of several regional religious groups that formed to emphasize the conflict between war and the New Testament. William Ladd, a retired New England sea captain and devout Christian, helped found a national pacifist organization, the American Peace Society (APS), in 1828 through grassroots campaigning in the Northeast and Midwest.[19] The APS combined Christianity and a belief in the peaceful resolution of international disputes, promoting negotiation, arbitration, and the formation of a Congress of Christian Nations.[20] Ladd's famous *Essay on a Congress of Nations* called for a two-tiered system of international justice: a congress of ambassadors from "civilized" nations who would create international law and an international court to arbitrate cases.[21]

The peace movement grew in strength throughout the 1830s and 1840s but divided over the question of the abolition of slavery. The APS was weakened particularly over this controversy. Whereas abolitionists such as William Lloyd Garrison were forging intellectual links between pacifism and abolitionism, it was becoming increasingly clear that the pro-slavery faction would fight to retain states rights with regard to slavery and other issues. Following violent outbreaks in the 1830s, the APS fractured between those supporting a defensive war and those adhering to strict pacifism.[22] The 1850s brought even deeper divisions over slavery, and further outbreaks of violence from abolitionist John Brown's attack at Harper's Ferry to Preston Brooks's beating of pacifist and

---

[16] Charles DeBenedetti, *The Peace Reform in American History* (1980): 17.
[17] *Id.* at 28.
[18] *Id.* at 30.
[19] Merle Eugene Curti, *The American Peace Crusade: 1815–1860* (1929): 43; Janis, *op. cit.*, at 103–10.
[20] DeBenedetti, *op. cit.*, at 38.
[21] Curti, *The American Peace Crusade: 1815–1860*, *op. cit.*, at 58.
[22] *Id.* at 42.

ardent abolitionist Charles Sumner on the floor of the U.S. Senate. Pure pacifists now began to reconsider their positions. Abelina Grimke Weld called for reformers to "choose between two evils," arguing that "all that we can do is to take the least, and baptize liberty in blood, if it must be so." By 1860, even Garrison had come out in full support of the Union. However, more than 1,500 conscientious objectors including Quakers, Mennonites, and members of other small religious sects refused to fight in the Civil War. [23]

Even while the American peace movement faced challenges at home, Elihu Burritt, the American philanthropist, linguist, and social activist, facilitated transatlantic organization and supported an international movement. Burritt, "the learned blacksmith," came to be known as "the symbol of the international peace movement of the mid-19th century."[24] Burritt helped organize several international peace congresses between 1848 and 1851, constituting the "greatest single accomplishment of the early movement."[25] The APS also pressed for arbitration of international disputes, as a practical measure to achieve international peace.[26] Other American internationalists such as Francis Lieber and David Dudley Field promoted international law, including international arbitration and interstate communication. Then in 1872, the United States and Britain participated in the Alabama Claims arbitration. The United States won the case, which was immediately held up as a triumph of peaceful settlement. The case rallied the peace movement to start lobbying for permanent machinery for the peaceful settlement of disputes, giving rise to the second phase of American enthusiasm for arbitration.[27]

Given the impact of the Alabama Claims arbitration on the subsequent twenty-five years of U.S. foreign policy with respect to the peaceful settlement of disputes, it is worth examining the case in some detail. It is an extraordinary episode.

The facts of the case began when the Confederate secretary of the navy sent James Bulloch to England to commission ships to augment the small Confederate Navy.[28] By then, Queen Victoria had already issued a Proclamation of Neutrality recognizing both the federal government and the Confederacy as belligerents.[29] Parliament passed the Foreign Enlistment Act, which

[23] DeBenedetti, *op. cit.*, at 58.
[24] Janis, *op. cit.*, at 110, *citing* P. Tolis, *Elihu Burritt: Crusader for Brotherhood* (1968): 1.
[25] Curti, *The American Peace Crusade: 1815–1860, op. cit.*, at 188.
[26] *Id.* at 189.
[27] *See* Martti Koskenniemi, *The Gentle Civilizer of Nations* (2001): 40; David Caron, "War and International Adjudication: Reflections on the 1899 Peace Conference," 94 A.J.I.L. (2000): 4; Janis, *op. cit.*, at 134–35.
[28] Eric C. Bruggink, "The Alabama Claims," 57 Ala. L. Rev. (1996): 339, 340.
[29] The United States only recognized the Confederacy as a rebel group within the United States.

prohibited British enlistment, and made it a misdemeanor to "fit out" armed ships for either side. However, in the early years of the American Civil War, segments of British society were pro-Confederacy, and Mr. Bulloch, under the guise of a private citizen, was able to commission the building of merchantmen ships in Britain. The three most notorious of those ships came to be called the *Alabama*,[30] the *Florida*,[31] and the *Shenandoah*.

Charles Francis Adams,[32] the U.S. ambassador to England during this time, heard about the *Alabama* being built. He complained to the British government numerous times. The British were unresponsive at first but were eventually embarrassed into action. Nevertheless, on July 28, 1862, the *Alabama* set sail with Bulloch on board.[33] Under the name *Enrica*, the *Alabama* appeared to be heading for a sea trial with civilian passengers on board. Once out to sea, the ship met a tugboat, the passengers disembarked, and it was fitted out for war. The *Alabama* then took on a mostly British crew, and on August 20, 1862, Captain Raphael Semmes, an American, joined the crew as the *Alabama*'s captain. The British still took no serious action. The United States said it would demand satisfaction.

Captain Semmes was instructed by the Confederate secretary of the navy to "do Northern commerce the greatest injury in the shortest time." The *Alabama* captured or destroyed at least 64 vessels, and in total, the Confederate ships captured three hundred Union ships. The attacks on northern vessels induced northern merchants to sail under the British flag to avoid capture. During the *Alabama*'s two-year life, the U.S. Navy had several opportunities to capture her but was not successful until June 1864 when the *Alabama* met the U.S.S. *Kearsarge* in the English Channel.[34] The *Kearsarge* sank the *Alabama*. Captain Semmes and most of the crew were picked up by a passing English steam-yacht.

While the *Alabama* was harassing Union ships and after its sinking, the press in the North demanded that the U.S. government take action, knowing that the *Alabama* and other Confederate cruisers had been outfitted by Great Britain. They wanted the United States to seek reparations. Despite the public outcry, Secretary of State William Seward did no more than write to British officials stating that the United States held the British responsible. The British did not accept liability, and President Lincoln did not pursue the matter.

---

[30] Originally known as No. 290 in the shipyard, and then the *Enrica* while in England.
[31] Originally known as the *Oreto* while being built in England.
[32] Son of President John Q. Adams. J. Gillis Wetter, 1 *The International Arbitration Process: Public and private* (1979) 57.
[33] There is some disagreement as to whether the British were too late to stop the *Alabama* from sailing because of accident, laziness, or deliberate delay. Wetter, *op. cit.*, at 41.
[34] Bruggink, *op. cit.*, at 341–42.

The dispute, however, was not forgotten, and in the following years, it continued to affect U.S.-British relations.[35] Letters were exchanged between U.S. Secretary of State Hamilton Fish and British Foreign Secretary the Earl of Clarendon stating their respective positions.[36] On May 8, 1871, after three years of negotiations, the United States and Great Britain signed the Treaty of Washington, which moved toward a final resolution of the dispute.[37] It established an arbitral tribunal with five arbitrators appointed by the U.S. president, the British queen, and the heads of state of Brazil, Switzerland, and Italy.

The tribunal met in Geneva on June 27, 1872, and reached its decision on September 14, 1872.[38] The arbitrators found by unanimous decision that Great Britain was liable for the actions of the *Alabama*.[39] They found by four votes to one that Britain was responsible for the *Florida*'s actions, and by three votes to two that it was responsible for the *Shenandoah*'s actions.[40] Great Britain was not liable for the actions of twelve other Confederate ships.[41] Finally, by a four to one vote, the arbitrators awarded the United States $15.5 million in gold for the direct damage claims.[42] Less than a year after the decision, on September 9, 1873, Great Britain paid the full amount to the U.S. Treasury.[43]

The *Alabama Claims* arbitration became famous and influential, energizing the peace movement in its advocacy of the peaceful settlement of disputes. Here was arguably the most powerful nation in the world, Britain, agreeing to arbitrate with a much weaker power. The Alabama Claims have been regarded as the high-water mark of international arbitration.[44] "While the idea of a permanent or at least a pre-existing dispute settlement mechanism is fairly old, it received a special thrust after the success of the Alabama Claims

---

[35] *Id.* at 35.
[36] *Id.* at 28, 35.
[37] V. V. Veeder, "Investor-State Disputes and the Development of International Law, Arbitral Lessons from the Private Correspondence of Queen Victoria and Lenin," 98 *Am. Soc'y Int'l L. Proc.* (2004): 33, 34.
[38] *Id.*, at 34. The award in the Alabama Claims Arbitration of September 14, 1872, can be found in Wetter, *op. cit.*, at 48.
[39] Wetter, *op. cit.*, at 50–51.
[40] *Id.* at 51.
[41] *Id.* at 52–54.
[42] *Id.* at 54.
[43] *Id.* at 170. Sir Edward Thornton called on Secretary of State Fish at the State Department and produced a certificate of deposit for $15.5 million and a receipt. Fish signed the receipt and gave it back to Thornton. That receipt is framed and still hangs as "both a grim reminder to British Governments of the penalties of carelessness in enforcing the rules of neutrality, and a priceless memento of the victories of peace." *Id.* at 170–71. (The author saw the receipt in the law library of the British Foreign and Commonwealth Office in the summer of 1982.)
[44] Stephen Schwebel, "The Reality of International Adjudication and Arbitration," 12 *Williamette J. Int'l L & Disp. Resol.* (2004): 359, 364.

arbitration of 1872."[45] "This arbitration is considered significant because of the international collegiate nature of the tribunal, the success of this mechanism in averting armed conflict, and the substantial sum of the final award."[46] After the Alabama Claims, support for arbitration became a "movement of impressive proportions," and the number of bilateral arbitration treaties increased.[47]

B. INTERNATIONAL ARBITRATION AND AMERICA: 1872–1918

From the 1870s through World War I, the peace movement was active, pressing for the further development of arbitration and international law. On June 17, 1874, the U.S. House of Representatives unanimously passed a motion requesting that the president try to insert arbitration clauses in all future treaties. In 1884, the Republican Party adopted peace and arbitration as a part of its presidential campaign platforms, as did all major parties soon after President Grover Cleveland was elected. Finally, in 1889, the first Universal Peace Congress since 1851 was convened. It was a symbol of the renewed interest in pacifism.[48] Arbitration clauses were included in fifty-nine treaties between 1823 and 1898.[49] Hundreds of arbitral awards were made.[50]

In addition, the peace movement devoted great energy toward the adoption of a general arbitration treaty with Britain.

> By the turn of the century, British and U.S. international law enthusiasts were exerting increasing influence upon their governments. In 1890, a resolution calling for the negotiation of general arbitral agreements was passed by the U.S. House and Senate, and in 1893, the British House of Commons unanimously resolved to cooperate with the United States in negotiating a general arbitration treaty. However, when the two governments finally drafted and signed such an agreement in 1897, the treaty failed to gain consent to ratification by three votes in the U.S. Senate.[51]

---

[45] V. S. Mani, "Development of Effective Mechanism(s) for Settlement of Disputes Arising in Relation to Space Commercialization," 5 *Sing. J. Int'l & Comp. L.* (2001): 191, 193.

[46] Henry T. King and James D. Graham, "Origins of Modern International Arbitration," 51 *Marquette Disp. Resol. J.* (1996): 42, 48; Howard N. Meyer, *The World Court in Action* (2002): 1–2.

[47] David P. Fidler, "War, Law, and Liberal Thought: The Use of Force in the Reagan Years," 11 *Ariz. J. Int'l & Comp. L.* (1994): 45, 62. Apparently the number of all treaties regardless of type increased in this period, but arbitration continued as a popular treaty topic following the Alabama Claims.

[48] DeBenedetti, *op. cit.*, at 64.

[49] Grewe, *op. cit.*, at 521.

[50] Grewe mentions counts of 177, 330, and 537 for the nineteenth century – varying apparently by differing classification criteria. "The boundary between arbitration and conciliation is frequently ambiguous, and this can make the classification of some cases controversial. However, there is no doubt that there were hundreds of arbitral awards...." *Id.* at 519.

[51] Janis, *op. cit.*, at 145.

President William McKinley had supported the general treaty, but it failed to win sufficient support, apparently because too many senators wanted to retain the right to approve every agreement to arbitrate. They did not wish to give up that control through agreeing to a general treaty.[52] Still, the movement pushed on. Starting in 1895, meetings were held at Mohonk, New York, where the arbitration idea was further developed into a plan for a world court. Participants envisioned that such a court would play the same role for nations that the U.S. Supreme Court played for individual states.

In the midst of all of this momentum, President McKinley's declaration of war on Spain in 1898 came as a terrible blow to the peace movement. The American public had for some time been incensed about Spain's treatment of its colonial subjects, especially in Cuba, just twenty some miles from Florida. When a U.S. Navy vessel, the *Maine*, was sunk in the Port of Havana, immediate suspicion turned on Spain. In negotiations, Spain granted concessions to the United States and offered to arbitrate remaining disputes, but McKinley rejected the offer. The United States went to war, easily defeating the Spanish and becoming a colonial power by acquiring Cuba, Puerto Rico, and the Philippines.

The American people were divided about the Spanish-American War. Some celebrated America's defeat of a former great power. Others were outraged – both by McKinley's failure even to attempt peaceful settlement and by the acquisition of colonies in disregard of America's anticolonial heritage. The war led to a movement opposed to imperialism and the formation of the Anti-Imperialist League. It also reenergized the peace movement.

Peace movement members generally held the view that the Spanish-American War might have begun in error, based on a mistaken belief that Spanish agents had sunk the *Maine*.[53] Mechanisms of peaceful settlement could have clarified the true cause of the *Maine* disaster, possibly avoiding the war, as well as the bloody insurgency in the Philippines and the ignominy of colonialism.[54] In the wake of the war, the peace movement began to resurge, marked by an increase in peace societies and support of prominent Americans who favored peace.[55] Despite these developments, the Senate affirmed the Paris Peace Treaty with Spain, and the Philippines were designated a territory of the United States. In reaction, the Anti-Imperialist League expanded and gained nationwide support, although not enough to defeat McKinley in the next presidential election in 1900. McKinley's reelection in 1900 dealt another

---

[52] Meyer, *op. cit.*, at 4–5.
[53] Caron, *op. cit.*, at 7.
[54] *Id.*
[55] David S. Patterson, "An Interpretation of the American Peace Movement, 1898–1914," *Peace Movements in America*.

blow to the peace movement. He won despite his failure to use arbitration, the waging of an imperial war, the costly insurgency in the Philippines, and the increasing reports of atrocities committed by U.S. troops against the Philippine population.[56]

Just when things seemed particularly grim from the peace movement's perspective, the Russian tsar, in a surprise move, invited nations to come together for a disarmament conference.[57] Leaders of the American peace movement seized on the occasion to lobby the tsar to add peaceful settlement to the conference agenda. The city of The Hague in the Netherlands was chosen as a neutral site, and in 1899 the First Hague Peace Conference was held. The tsar was interested in pursuing ways to avoid war not only to gain the benefits of peace but also in the interest of Russian security. The tsar realized Russia was not keeping pace with other world powers in acquiring the new technologies of war. In other words, Russia sought alternatives to the future wars it feared it could not win.[58] Delegates from twenty-six countries drafted four conventions, including one that set out rules and procedures for good offices, mediation, inquiry, and arbitration.

The British delegation formally proposed at the conference the institution of an international court for the settlement of disputes, known as "the American Plan" after the Mohonk proposal. Delegates failed to agree, however, on the formation of a permanent court, or even a permanent arbitral body. Eventually, they agreed on something they called the Permanent Court of Arbitration, consisting of a list of available arbitrators, a set of arbitration rules, and a small secretariat in The Hague.[59] No state was to be bound to have resort to it.

Despite the modest results for peaceful settlement, the U.S. delegation had been inspired in 1899 by the proposals for a court of compulsory jurisdiction. The United States encouraged more international conferences aimed at developing the machinery of peaceful settlement. In addition, the dramatic resolution of the Dogger Bank dispute added to the international enthusiasm for peaceful settlement. In 1906, Britain and Russia used a commission of inquiry to resolve the dispute that arose when Russian navy vessels on their way to fight Japan in a foggy night opened fire and sank a number of British fishing trawlers in the area of the Dogger Bank, off the English coast. The inquiry

---

[56] DeBenedetti, *op. cit.*, at 76.
[57] Meyer, *op. cit.*, at 11–12.
[58] Leila Nadya Sadat, "The Establishment of the International Criminal Court: From The Hague to Rome and Back Again," 8 J. Int'l L. & Prac., fn. 1 (1999) 97, citing, William I. Hull, *The Two Hague Conferences and Their Contributions to International Law* (1908): 3.
[59] See the Web site of the Permanent Court of Arbitration, at http://www.pca-cpa.org. See also P. Hamilton et al., *The Permanent Court of Arbitration: International Arbitration and Dispute Settlement, Summaries of Awards, Settlement Agreements and Reports* (1999).

demonstrated that the episode had been an accident and thus averted war between two great powers and, like the Alabama Claims, provided a dramatic example of the potential for peaceful settlement.[60] Another peace conference was duly called for 1907 where ten conventions were negotiated, including new rules for inquiry. The arbitration rules were modified and improved.

The United States and others tried diligently again in 1907 to get a permanent international court. They failed, again, largely owing to German opposition. The delegates in 1907 did agree nonetheless to the first multilateral treaty outlawing the use of force for a particular class of disputes: the Convention of 1907 Respecting the Limitation of the Employment of Force for the Recovery of Contract Debts.[61] The delegates also agreed to form a permanent prize court, although that court was never established.[62]

U.S. Secretary of State Elihu Root left The Hague ever more committed to the idea of judicial settlement of disputes. He promoted the idea in Central America, where governments succeeded in establishing the Central American Court of Justice in 1908.[63] The Central American Court was the first permanent court for the settlement of disputes between sovereign states.[64] It existed for ten years and might have gone on longer if the United States had taken a greater interest in promoting its survival.

In addition to the Central American Court, Root oversaw the establishment of the International Joint Commission (IJC) with Canada. The IJC was founded as a permanent institution for the regulation of joint resources and the resolution of boundary-related disputes. It continues to this day.

The United States also promoted the commitment to binding dispute resolution through bilateral agreements with South American and European states. Root was inspired by the large interest in binding arbitration and turned in the next year (February 10, 1908–January 23, 1909) to negotiating twenty-four bilateral arbitration agreements, creating binding commitments to arbitrate certain classes of disputes. The U.S. Senate demanded the right to give its advice and consent before any dispute could actually go to arbitration. It did

---

[60] *See* Richard Ned LeBow, "Accidents and Crises: The Dogger Bank Affair," 31 *Naval War Col. Rev.* (1978) 1.

[61] Hague Convention Respecting the Limitation of the Employment of Force for the Recovery of Contract Debts, October 18, 1907, 36 Stat. 2241.

[62] Hans-Jürgen Schlochauer, "Permanent Court of International Justice," 1 *Encyclopedia of Public International Law* (Rudolf Bernhardt ed., 1981) 163–164 [hereinafter EPIL]. A prize court would adjudicate claims to property arising in war such as the legality of seizing and selling enemy ships.

[63] Philip C. Jessup, 2 *Elihu Root* (1937) 50; *see also* Nobel Peace Prize, "Elihu Root," www.nobel.se/peace/laureates/1912/root-bio.html (last visited Nov. 24, 2008).

[64] Humphrey M. Hill, "The Central American Court of Justice," *EPIL, op. cit.*, at 41–44.

not want standing or automatic obligations, even though such approval clauses were criticized as undermining the promotion of peace. Nonetheless, Root's treaties were seen by Germany and Russia as powerful enough for those two countries to refuse to enter into them.[65]

Root's motivation in pursuing peaceful settlement of disputes was apparently not so much owing to religious belief – he was a Christian though no pacifist – but rather from his earlier career as a lawyer.[66] Root was comfortable with courts. He understood the mechanism and had a strong sense that courts provided the most practical and rational method for settling any dispute. Keeping the United States out of trouble was Root's ambition. He thought a robust rule of law and standing dispute settlement arrangements would help. His modesty and lack of personal ambition made it possible for powerful individuals such as Presidents McKinley, Theodore Roosevelt, and William Howard Taft to trust him. People believed he had the best interest of the country in mind in his search for peace, not his own career.

All in all, Root's favoring peaceful settlement by way of standing international adjudicative bodies was born out of pragmatic considerations.[67] This reflected the major philosophical movement of his day – pragmatism – which was related to the realist school that emerged in law around the same time.[68] Root did not believe all problems could be solved by courts. For example, he blamed the Germans for World War I. During the 1907 Peace Conference in The Hague, he concluded the Germans were not amenable to persuasion. They had to be fought, and Root advocated that the United States enter the war against the Germans on the side of the British.[69] Still, until his death he continued to believe in courts as the best approach to resolve most international disputes. In 1920, ten distinguished international jurists, including Root, drafted the Statute of the Permanent Court of International Justice, the first global court for the peaceful settlement of international disputes. He then worked for another eighteen years to persuade the U.S. Senate to give its consent to the Statute of the Permanent Court. It never did.

---

[65] *Id.* at 56–59.
[66] Adapted from Mary Ellen O'Connell, "Elihu Root and Crisis Prevention," 95 *Am. Soc'y Int'l L. Proc.* (2001): 115.
[67] *See*, e.g., Elihu Root, "The Sanction of International Law," 2 *A.J.I.L.* (1908): 451, 456.
[68] *See* Edward A. Purcell, "On the Complexity of 'Ideas in America': Origins and Achievements of the Classical Age of Pragmatism" (Review Essay on Louis Menand, *The Metaphysical Club: A Story of Ideas in America*. New York: Farrar, Straus & Giroux, 2001), 27 *Law & Soc. Inquiry* (2002): 967, 985–86.
[69] O'Connell, "Elihu Root and Crisis Prevention," *op. cit.*

The peace movement and Jane Addams, its most prominent leader in 1914 when the Great War began, took a view very different from Root's about the war. The outbreak of hostilities changed the landscape of the peace movement because it exposed the weaknesses and limitations of the practical peace reforms that dominated the discussions. These deficiencies and "the urgency of the war combined to force forward a new – indeed, the modern – peace movement."[70] Social progressives pushed for mediation, which was the basis of the platform of the Woman's Peace Party (WPP) formed by Carrie Chapman Catt and Jane Addams in 1915. The American Fellowship of Reconciliation was formed by Christian activists who condemned war in any form.[71]

Jane Addams worked tirelessly in both opposing U.S. entry into the war and in an effort to end the conflict. In addition to the WPP, she formed several other new peace organizations when the old-line groups held back.[72] She had worked for peace and theorized about peace throughout her long career in social work in Chicago. She was well educated, widely traveled, spoke several languages, and worked among immigrants from all over the world at Hull House, a center for education and social support. Addams formed alliances with like-minded people, especially women, throughout the United States and Europe. She believed women had a special role to play in war prevention:

> As women we are the custodians of the life of the ages and we will no longer consent to its reckless destruction. We are particularly charged with the future of childhood, the care of the helpless and the unfortunate, and we will no longer endure without protest that added burden of maimed and invalid men and poverty-stricken women and orphans which war places on us.... [W]e will no longer endure that hoary evil which in an hour destroys, or tolerate that denial of the sovereignty of reason and justice by which war and all that makes for war today render impotent the idealism of the race.[73]

Although Addams was a progressive and had ties to pragmatism (John Dewey, prominent scholar of pragmatism, was a close friend of hers), her commitment to peace was rooted in her Christianity, like America's traditional pacifists.[74] Addams worked for social reform but believed that for social reform to succeed, peace was necessary. She sought to shift people away from viewing war as glamorous toward viewing the work of creating healthy societies as

---

[70] DeBenedetti, *op. cit.*, at 91.
[71] *Id.* at 95.
[72] Farrell, *op. cit.*, at 140–41, 150–53.
[73] *Id.* at 140, quoting Jane Addams, 1915.
[74] *Id.* at 141.

heroic. With her great gifts for organization and publicity, she promoted arbitration, mediation, and international institutions aimed at preventing war.[75] She helped to organize an international congress of women in The Hague in 1915 to promote an end to the war in Europe. Addams and a delegation of women visited capitals throughout Europe to persuade the warring parties to accept mediation by neutral countries. The United States, the leading neutral country at the start of the war, was by 1915, however, already moving inexorably toward joining the allies and would not play a role in mediating peace.[76]

President Wilson's shift toward "active preparedness" in the fall of 1915 created a backlash of liberal criticism, evidenced by the creation of the American Union Against Militarism in 1916. However, Wilson was able to re-align himself with pacifists and progressives during his 1916 campaign, a coalition that helped him to win re-election. Wilson's calls for a "peace between equals" were immensely popular with pacifist progressives, but were soon forgotten after he cut off relations with Germany, and Congress declared war on April 2, 1917.[77]

The declaration of war split progressive reformers and peace activists. Reformers saw the war as an opportunity to pursue alternative agendas such as women's suffrage, workers' rights, and social welfare. Some among the internationalists hoped U.S. participation in the war would lead to an enduring world order for peace. However, Wilson's proposal for the League of Nations did not draw the overwhelming support of all internationalists (most notably, the philanthropist and industrialist Andrew Carnegie) because the issue became the focus of an increasingly bitter partisan political battle.[78]

Liberal internationalists were counterbalanced by the other emerging half of the peace movement: liberal pacifists. Whereas liberal internationalists viewed the path to peace through the cooperation of civilized nations, liberal pacifists "saw peace as a transnational process that subsisted in individual and group cooperation in the outworking of common values and institutions."[79] This split in the peace movement should not be overstated, however. Both groups came from the liberal Christian tradition, both saw peace as a process, and both were dominated by well-educated young men and women who "had been radicalized by their confrontation with war as was no other generation in American history before Vietnam."[80]

---

[75] *Id.* at 148–50.
[76] *Id.* at 159–69.
[77] DeBenedetti, *op. cit.*, at 98.
[78] Patterson, *op. cit.*, at 34.
[79] DeBenedetti, *op. cit.*, at 106.
[80] *Id.*

With America's entry into World War I, the country began its steady climb toward the status of a superpower. The practical and moral arguments for peaceful settlement by way of third-party adjudication, or even pure diplomacy, were heard in a very different context after the war. Adherents of pacifism did not disappear, but their moral arguments had to compete with moral arguments for the defeat of fascism and communism. The postwar pragmatic arguments counseled freedom to maneuver without becoming entangled by international institutions. The Covenant of the League of Nations mandated arbitration or adjudication to settle disputes and required the League Council to enforce arbitral awards or decisions against recalcitrant parties.[81] Soon after, the Permanent Court of International Justice was formed. The United States, however, joined neither the League nor the Court.

C. CONCLUSION

The inclusion of mandatory arbitration or adjudication in the League Covenant was the realization of a vision formulated in early America and nurtured for well over a century. Yet it also marked the end of popular enthusiasm for arbitration. Pragmatists like Root and pacifists like Addams turned their attention to the Permanent Court of International Justice and the League of Nations. The successors to these two leaders continue to this day in supporting international courts, such as the International Court of Justice and the International Criminal Court, as well as the United Nations. Contemporary support for these institutions cannot be compared with the pro-arbitration enthusiasm of the nineteenth and early twentieth centuries. Yet Americans are still deeply religious, and many U.S. leaders are still realists or pragmatists. These are the characteristics that resulted in American advocacy of arbitration for so long. Indeed, although at the start of the twenty-first century the United States may lack charismatic champions for alternatives to war like Addams and Root, as the next chapter shows, Americans have never lost their interest in such alternatives. Nor have American's leaders ever wholly rejected them. The United States, for example, has been a party to more International Court of Justice cases than any other state. It helped create the International Criminal Court and the World Trade Organization Dispute Settlement Understanding.

Some may nevertheless conclude that, because interest in arbitration declined in the United States as economic and military power grew, there is unlikely to be a higher level of commitment by U.S. leaders to courts

---

[81] Covenant of the League of Nations (1919), art. 12, 13, 13 A.J.I.L. 128, 134 (Supp. 1935).

and tribunals so long as the United States remains a superpower. Consider, however, that Britain was uniquely powerful when it agreed to the Alabama Claims, when it began advocating for a world court, and when it joined the Permanent Court of International Justice. An experience such as the Iraq War may at any time reawaken in America's leaders a new moral and pragmatic commitment to alternatives to war.

4

The United States and the International Court of Justice: Coping with Antinomies

SEAN D. MURPHY*

Since 1946, the United States has had an uneasy relationship with the International Court of Justice (ICJ, the World Court, or the Court). On one hand, the United States embraces the rule of law within its own society and, in principle, within the international system of states. The United States has been and remains an active participant in cases before the Court, appearing before it several times, more than any other state, even in recent years. On the other hand, the United States has never been willing to submit itself to the plenary authority of the Court and has typically reacted negatively to decisions by the Court that are adverse to U.S. interests. As is well known, in response to decisions that were reached by the Court, the United States refused to participate in the proceedings on the merits of the case brought by Nicaragua in 1984, withdrew from the Court's compulsory jurisdiction in 1986, and recently terminated its acceptance of the Court's jurisdiction over disputes arising under the Vienna Convention on Consular Relations.

This chapter addresses certain salient aspects of the U.S. relationship with the ICJ. Following this introduction, Part A briefly sets forth three antinomies (i.e., equally rational but conflicting principles) in U.S. foreign relations that have had important ramifications for the U.S. relationship with the Court from the outset. First, the United States operates on the basis of conflicting principles with respect to the relevance of international law and institutions for U.S. foreign policy. These conflicting principles have been referred to broadly in international relations theory as "realism" and "institutionalism." Although

---

* Patricia Roberts Harris Research Professor of Law, The George Washington University. My thanks for the opportunity to present this chapter at the T.M.C. Asser Institute in The Hague (May 2005), at The George Washington University Law School (May 2006), and at Georgetown Law School (February 2007). Further thanks to Kelly Dunn, JD (2008), Brooke Marcus, JD (2006), and José Arvelo-Vélez, JD (2006) for outstanding research assistance. As a matter of full disclosure, the author served as counsel for the United States in several of the cases discussed in this chapter.

discussion of the intricacies of such theories is beyond the scope of this chapter, realism at its core emphasizes the use of coercive state power in resolving interstate disputes. The realist has little faith in international institutions generally, insisting that they (including institutions for international dispute resolution) do not exert any independent influence on state behavior. The institutionalist asserts that the logic of realism does not adequately explain cooperation among states and thus places greater weight on the role that independent, judicial decision making has on interstate relations. The institutionalist sees long-term value in international courts as a means of efficiently and effectively coordinating state behavior. Both approaches represent powerful and deep-seated instincts in the American attitude toward international law and institutions, although, of the two, realism has tended to dominate.

Second, the United States operates on the basis of conflicting principles with respect to whether states should be treated as equal sovereigns or as units characterized by inescapable power differentials. Although the United States has historically articulated a desire for cooperation with other states as coequal sovereigns – and indeed has been in the vanguard in many respects in the promotion and development of international law and institutions built around the concept of sovereign equality – the United States has innate historical and cultural characteristics that push it toward an attitude of "exceptionalism" in its foreign policy, claiming itself entitled, formally and informally, to be treated differently from other states. Although similar in nature to the first antinomy stated earlier, this antinomy reflects certain factors quite unique to the United States, including its present role as the preeminent superpower, as an economic powerhouse, and as a country in certain respects uniquely insulated from vicissitudes of international relations. With respect to the U.S. relationship with the ICJ, this antinomy pulls the United States toward the Court as an institution before which all states are equal under law, but pushes it away when the Court fails to accommodate the special role of the United States on matters such as the maintenance of international peace and security.

Third, the United States operates on the basis of conflicting principles with respect to whether international law should be "embedded" in U.S. law, including the manner in which international courts relate to U.S. law. On one hand, the United States at its founding saw adherence to international obligations as an important means to establish the international legitimacy and security of a nascent republic and so adopted constitutional and judicial principles that promoted the idea of international law as being a part of national law and as superior to the law of the several states. On the other hand, the United States has developed democratic and constitutional traditions that make it difficult to adhere to and to implement internally international law. With respect to its democratic tradition, the United States has always accepted the importance and significance of a judiciary for the resolution of disputes but has also viewed unelected judges as potential agents for usurping popular governance, a concern that is aggravated when the judges in question are non-American and issuing their decisions from afar. Further, U.S. constitutional law creates significant obstacles to adherence to international law and institutions by dividing power between the president and the legislature and by maintaining a federal system that accords extensive rights to the several states.

Part B suggests that the ICJ was initially designed, in part, to accommodate such antinomies (which also exist with respect to other states, to varying degrees) by providing the means for mediating between these conflicting principles. For example, the formal manner for selecting judges and the types of jurisdiction granted to the Court are a means to satisfy and cultivate those principles that favor the existence and participation in a global court while at the same time acknowledging certain limitations on the Court in an effort not to aggravate conflicting principles. These techniques for mediating antinomies are discussed in the context of the history of the U.S. relationship with the Court from its inception to modern times.

Part C then briefly highlights the unfolding of these antinomies in some of the recent cases of the United States before the Court, with particular attention to the *Oil Platforms* case, the Israeli *Wall* advisory opinion, and the *Breard/LaGrand/Avena* cases. Although the United States fully participated in these cases and did not denounce the Court's decisions as without basis in law, the cases have brought the Court into square conflict with U.S. visions of realism, exceptionalism, and constitutional autonomy.

Among other things, Part D suggests that certain formal and informal means for mediating these antinomies may have been forgotten in the past twenty years, leading to a point at which the Court readily finds fault in the United States and the United States holds the Court in very low regard. In particular, whereas the Court's concern with its reputation and legitimacy in the first thirty years of its existence served as an important informal constraint in its relationship with the United States, over the past twenty years, that same concern has led to repeated clashes. The chapter concludes that these antinomies are unlikely to be resolved through the further development of formal or informal mediating techniques. In the near term, American policy makers will seek to avoid any involvement in matters before the Court, whereas the Court will embrace opportunities to speak to the legality of U.S. actions.

A. ANTINOMIES IN THE U.S. RELATIONSHIP WITH THE ICJ

An "antinomy" is a contradiction in principles that seem equally necessary and reasonable. In U.S. foreign relations, three core antinomies simultaneously pull the country toward and push it away from the idea of a meaningful international court. First, there is the conflict between "realism" and "institutionalism" in the way America thinks about securing its interests. Second, there is the conflict between the U.S. vision of itself as a unique entity that should not be subject to the same constraints of international law and institutions to which other states should be exposed and the U.S. vision of engaging with coequal sovereigns through uniform rules on trade, human rights, and other important issues. Third, there is the conflict between, in the first instance, U.S. democratic traditions that promote the autonomy of the U.S. legal system and local governance over local issues and, in the second instance, the U.S. willingness to embed its national law in international law. These antinomies – which are presented as broad concepts although they in practice have overlapping features – have had and will continue to have significant repercussions for the relationship with the ICJ.

1. American Realism versus Institutionalism

One antinomy of significance arises from the well-known divide within U.S. society, broadly stated, between realism and institutionalism lines of thinking.[1] The social contract theory advanced by Thomas Hobbes,[2] John Locke,[3] and Jean-Jacques Rousseau[4] to justify the origin of the state focused on the state as a creation by free individuals whose interests – security, freedom, order, justice, and welfare – the state must recognize and serve. As far as relations among states, Hobbes saw an environment of anarchy in which states fear each other, such that a state must use its military and economic power to pursue strategies and policies that advance that state's interests, which invariably conflict with the interests of other states. Although bargains may be struck between states that serve their mutual interests, such bargains are not and should not be driven by abstract ethical, moral, or legalistic considerations and once struck are often temporary or imposed coercively by one of the parties. Thus, international "law" (or rules or norms) and international "institutions" (or "regimes") may exist, but they do not exert independent influence on states. To the extent that

---

[1] There is, of course, an extraordinarily rich array of theories on international law and politics that cannot be done justice within this chapter. A sampling of these theories appears in *Foundations of International Law and Politics* (Oona A. Hathaway and Harold Hongju Koh eds., Foundation Press, 2005). For present purposes, very simplified models are used.
[2] Thomas Hobbes, *Leviathan* (Macmillan 1962) [1641].
[3] John Locke, *Second Treatise of Government* (Thomas P. Peardon ed., Prentice-Hall, 1952) [1698].
[4] Jean-Jacques Rousseau, *On the Social Contract: Discourse on the Origin of Inequality; Discourse on Political Economy* (Donald A. Cress trans. & ed., Hackett, 1987) [1762].

states are seen as abiding by such law, it is simply because political or economic factors encourage them to do so, not because of a fidelity to a "legal" system. Rather, states strive relentlessly to increase their relative power position vis-à-vis rival states regardless of international law or institutions. Frequently referred to as "realism" in international relations theory, this line of thinking appears to be deeply entrenched in U.S. policymaking; legions of American policymakers are fully versed in the seminal "realist" writings of Hans Morgenthau, Thomas Schelling, and Kenneth Waltz.[5]

The flip side of realism is institutionalism, which also has a place in U.S. policy making. Institutionalists assert that the contemporary nature of interstate relations is demonstrably not Hobbesian; rather, there is an extraordinary amount of cooperation among states that realism theory fails to explain. States pursue their national interests, but those interests include a desire for international law and institutions, such as impartial interstate dispute settlement, because cooperation often yields far greater benefits than noncooperation.[6] Among other things, institutionalists seek to develop a web of norms that will compel just, moral, and equitable behavior among states; to end warfare through the use of collective security, disarmament, and even criminal punishment; to use human rights as a normative tool for restraining government abuses of its people; and to make the world safe for democracy. The intellectual origins of institutionalism lie in the writings of Immanuel Kant, who called on states to establish a league of peace to prevent war.[7] At key points in American history, this line of thinking dominated U.S. foreign policy; typically, reference is made to Woodrow Wilson's Fourteen Points after World War I, to U.S. support for the myriad multilateral institutions that arose after World War II, and to the emphasis on human rights in the foreign policies of certain presidents, such as Jimmy Carter. At any given time, U.S. foreign policy may have elements of both realism and institutionalism. The George

---

[5] Hans J. Morgenthau, *Politics among Nations: The Struggle for Power and Peace* (2d ed., A.A. Knopf, 1955); Thomas C. Schelling, *The Strategy of Conflict* (Harvard, 1960); Kenneth Waltz, *Theory of International Politics* (McGraw Hill, 1979).

[6] See, e.g., Robert O. Keohane, *After Hegemony: Cooperation and Discord in the World Political Economy* (Princeton, 1984). Institutionalists are not interested in international courts simply out of a desire for international institutions. Although historically there have been "idealists" who favor international courts due to a belief that world government helps lead to world peace (and thus are necessarily a good thing), institutionalists favor institutions if they serve a useful purpose. Hence, although institutionalists as a general matter are more favorably inclined toward seeing the potential for international courts, much turns on whether any given court is operating in an effective and efficient way. Hence, even an institutionalist may resist U.S. involvement in the Court if the costs of that involvement are perceived, in the long term, as outweighing the benefits.

[7] Immanuel Kant, *Perpetual Peace: A Philosophical Essay* (M. Campbell Smith, trans., A. Robert Caponigri ed., Liberal Arts Press, 1948) [1795].

W. Bush administration was realist in its tendency to resist empowerment of international organizations but had elements of institutionalism in its neoconservative emphasis on the promotion of democracy.

This broad conflict in the U.S. attitude to foreign relations has affected its relationship with the Court. On one hand, institutionalism in the United States favors the existence of an effective and useful global court, whether or not the United States wins all its cases before it. For some, the very idea of a global court with an impartial panel of judges is strongly compelling; Thomas Franck has referred to such a vision as "messianic" – a belief that the rule of law institutions that have worked so well internally for the United States must be replicated on the international level.[8] On the other hand, realism in the United States wants to maintain the ability of the country to protect its national interests through resort to unilateral power and to that end has opposed a global court with plenary jurisdiction over international disputes involving it. For Franck, this is a "chauvinist" vision, one that views the rule of law known within the United States as unique to American history, culture, and values, such that replication of the rule of law internationally is not only implausible but also threatens national values and institutions.[9] Whereas the institutionalist strand led to the acceptance of the Court's compulsory jurisdiction in 1946 (discussed further in Part B), the realist strand virtually eviscerated that acceptance by attaching reservations to the acceptance. The presence, and even swinging back and forth, of these lines of thinking has fostered a constant tension between Washington, D.C., and The Hague, especially in recent years. Arguably the United States has pursued an impossible position of both embracing the idea of the Court and yet distancing itself from the inevitable effects of that idea.

This antinomy is not unique to the United States; other states have similar lines of thinking in their foreign policy. Indeed, the structural aspects built into the ICJ that are discussed in Part B – aspects that seek to mediate between the desire of states for an impartial, permanent judicial forum and the desire of states to control their exposure to ICJ decision making – may be seen as an effort to mediate between institutionalism and realism among all states. A further tension that arises, however, lies in the differences among states in how they strike a balance between these lines of thinking in their relationship to the Court. On one end of the spectrum – where realism dominates – lie

---

[8] Thomas Franck, "Messianism and Chauvinism in America's Commitment to Peace through Law," in *The International Court of Justice at a Crossroads*, 3, 6 (Lori F. Damrosch ed., Transnational, 1987); *see also* Mark Weston Janis, *The American Tradition of International Law: Great Expectations, 1789–1914* (Oxford, 2004) (finding that "to a surprising extent, the international courts of today were the work of nineteenth-century American Utopians by and large untrained in the law").

[9] Franck, *supra* note 8, at 6.

China and Russia, where the institutionalism line of thinking has never taken hold. Those states see no national interest in being exposed to the jurisdiction of the Court and have succeeded in never appearing before it in a contentious case. In effect, China and Russia have no relationship with the Court other than the presence of a judge of their nationality on the Court. A little further along the spectrum is the United States, the relationship of which with the Court is dominated by realism but with a patina of institutionalism.

Much further along the spectrum – moving into where institutionalism dominates – are the Europeans. For Europeans, the carnage of two world wars left them no choice but to opt for an institutionalist approach to foreign relations – a forsaking of national sovereignty and national prerogatives in favor of supranational institutions (the European Union, with its European Court of Justice, and the Council of Europe, with its European Court of Human Rights) that would generate and interpret law that would bind European states. As such, their attitude toward the ICJ leans toward the institutionalist end of the spectrum. Of the twenty-seven members of the European Union, for example, fifteen have accepted the Court's compulsory jurisdiction.[10] Finally, also largely on the institutionalism side of the spectrum are many of the developing states, such as Argentina, Democratic Republic of the Congo, Djibouti, or Nicaragua, all of which currently have cases pending at the Court. For them, the balance is also oriented toward the institutionalism approach because in most instances those states cannot rely on military or economic power to advance their national interests. By contrast, to the extent that embracing the Court provides a means to resolve intractable disputes among developing states, and a possible means to restrict the power of Western developed states, the World Court provides developing states with leverage that they would not otherwise have on their own. So although many developing nations have declined to expose themselves to the uncertainty of the Court's compulsory jurisdiction, they strongly favor the Court's existence, are quite interested in using it when possible to resolve disputes with neighbors, and are willing to use it on occasion against more powerful states, such as Djibouti's current case against France.

Differences in attitudes among these groups create tension. Realism-oriented states wish to downplay the authority and significance of the Court, wish to see it adopt a narrow approach to its jurisdiction, and are quick to challenge its integrity and impartiality whenever the opportunity arises.

---

[10] Austria, Belgium, Bulgaria, Denmark, Finland, Greece, Hungary, Luxembourg, Netherlands, Poland, Portugal, Slovakia, Spain, Sweden, and United Kingdom have adhered to the Court's compulsory jurisdiction. Cyprus, Czech Republic, Estonia, France, Germany, Ireland, Italy, Latvia, Lithuania, Malta, Romania, and Slovenia have not.

Conversely, institutionalism-oriented states tend to do the opposite, thus leading to serious divergences among states regarding the proper functioning, aim, and use of the Court.

2. American Exceptionalism versus Sovereign Equality

A second antinomy of significance arises from the conflict between accepting an international system fundamentally predicated on the equality of all states and, at the same time, insisting (formally and informally) on special prerogatives for major powers, most particularly the United States itself.[11] Although there are links with the "realism" line of thinking discussed earlier, exceptionalism is a somewhat different concept, in that whether a realism or institutionalism outlook is taken, the United States is often captivated by a belief that it simply should not be treated just like every other state.

The belief in the sovereign equality of all states is a fundamental principle of U.S. engagement in the international system. The international legal system, which the United States has done much to promote, is constructed around the concept of "the state," and the concept of all states having the same fundamental rights and obligations as an incident of their statehood. As asserted in the General Assembly's famous Declaration on Principles of International Law,

> All States enjoy sovereign equality. They have equal rights and duties and are equal members of the international community, notwithstanding differences of an economic, social, political or other nature. In particular, sovereign equality includes the following elements:
>
> 1. States are juridically equal;
> 2. Each State enjoys the rights inherent in full sovereignty;
> 3. Each State has a duty to respect the personality of other States;
> 4. The territorial integrity and political independence of the State are inviolable;
> 5. Each State has the right freely to choose and develop its political, social, economic and cultural systems.[12]

For this reason, the United States accepts that, in the plenary bodies of international organizations and at international negotiations of new treaties, tiny

---

[11] For a detailed discussion of how international law generally mediates between the principle of sovereign equality and a principle favoring prerogatives of great powers, see Gerry Simpson, *Great Powers and Outlaw States* (Cambridge, 2004).
[12] Declaration on Principles of International Law Concerning Friendly Relations and Co-operation among States in Accordance with the Charter of the United Nations, G.A. Res. 2625 (XXV), annex (Oct. 24, 1970).

states in terms of territory or population (such as Nauru) are entitled to the same formal status as behemoths (such as China).

At the same time, the conflicting vision of American exceptionalism pushes back against such notions of equality. Thus, in constructing the United Nations (UN) Security Council, the United States should be a permanent member with special rights and privileges that protect it from Security Council action. When establishing the World Bank or International Monetary Fund, a weighted voting system should be created that protects U.S. influence in the development of international economic policy. More recently, when creating international criminal tribunals, those that are focused on a particular country (e.g., Lebanon, Sierra Leone, Rwanda, or the former Yugoslavia) are acceptable, but the International Criminal Court is not, unless the United States has an ability to preclude prosecution of its nationals. In other words, this antinomy notes the conflict between a vision of international law and institutions in which all states participate as equal sovereigns and a vision of exceptionalism by which the United States habitually reaches for policies and structures that it alone controls or that apply generally to states but not to itself.

Such a tendency toward exceptionalism arises from a confluence of factors. Perhaps the most important is America's history over the past century as a country untouched by sustained armed conflict on its soil, protected by vast oceans from any serious threat of invasion (the sense of shock from and aggressive response to the isolated attacks of September 11 demonstrate this deeply felt sense of U.S. security). This history tends both to undermine arguments for why the United States must adhere to global norms and instruments and to foster an instinct to avoid "entangling" alliances that might draw it into the conflicts of other states. There are many other factors, including the demise of the Soviet empire, which eliminated the one dominant threat to the United States; the U.S. emergence as the sole global superpower, capable of projecting considerable power through unilateral action rather than relying on cooperation with other states; the increasingly conservative U.S. political environment vis-à-vis other developed states (including the existence of a concentrated and active conservative minority that, as Andrew Moravcsik has pointed out, has taken advantage of the fragmented nature of U.S. political institutions to resist implementation of international norms[13]); an indifference to the norms and institutions of other states caused by a belief that American norms and institutions, over time, have proven superior to anything found abroad (i.e., the United States leads others – it does not follow them); a distinctive "rights culture" that emphasizes negative protections against government interference

---

[13] *See* Andrew Moravcsik, "The Paradox of U.S. Human Rights Policy," in *American Exceptionalism and Human Rights* 147 (Michael Ignatieff, ed., Princeton, 2005).

in private liberties and does not emphasize, unlike other Western states and emerging democracies, activist provision by government of socioeconomic and welfare rights (i.e., entitlements to food, health care, etc.); and important although relatively recent demographic and cultural shifts that pull the United States away from even its traditional allies (i.e., the continuing and increasing role of Christian faith in the United States compared with the secularization of Europe; the gradual "Islamicization" of Europe caused by immigration, such that if Turkey joins the European Union, there will be more Muslims than Protestants in Europe).[14]

This presence of exceptionalism in U.S. relations with the World Court has two important effects. First, exceptionalists are inherently unhappy with any international institution that can issue pronouncements regarding the legality of U.S. conduct. For exceptionalists, an international court may be a good thing for keeping other states in line, but the United States almost always does the right thing, and, when it does not, any repercussions should flow from national legal and political institutions, not from abroad. Second, even when the ICJ is not passing on the legality of U.S. conduct, the exceptionalist is skeptical about the Court because it at times reaches conclusions that differ from those of the U.S. government, and therefore (for the exceptionalist) the Court is simply wrong.

3. Autonomous National Law versus National Law Embedded in International Law

A third antinomy arises from the conflict between favoring a national legal system that is embedded in international law, as a means of ensuring U.S. adherence to and implementation of its international obligations and disfavoring such incorporation to the extent that it transgresses national democratic and constitutional traditions that promote diffusion of power and governance of persons by their freely elected officials.

The United States at its founding saw adherence to international obligations as an important means to establish the international legitimacy and security of a nascent republic and so adopted constitutional and judicial principles that international law was a part of national law and superior to the law of the several states. The U.S. Constitution provides for treaties to be part of the "supreme law of the land"[15] and for the supremacy of federal law over state law.[16] Further, the Supreme Court has been favorably disposed toward the incorporation of

---

[14] Niall Ferguson, *The Widening Atlantic*, The Atlantic (Jan./Feb. 2005), at 40.
[15] U.S. Const., art. VI, § 2.
[16] *Id.*

customary international law into U.S. law[17] and to its interpretation whenever possible so as to avoid conflicts with international law.[18]

At the same time, strong currents in the American constitutional and democratic tradition seek to keep international law at a distance, such as through the doctrine of non-self-executing treaties and the trumping of customary international law by later-in-time statutes or "controlling executive acts."[19] Further, from the beginning of its history, America has been proud of the manner in which it has divided power among the three branches of its federal government and between the federal government and the several states. Such division of power was designed to promote a democratic but well-functioning government and to preclude concentration of power in a single organ. Although this constitutional tradition is a marvel, there can be little doubt that it has impeded the integration of the United States into the international legal system. Dividing power between the president and the Senate may have helped prevent the emergence of an American monarch in foreign policy, but it has also prevented presidents from embracing broad-ranging jurisdiction of a global court from the early twentieth century forward. Restraining the federal government from being able to regulate on certain matters of individual rights prevents a governmental denial of civil liberties, but places the United States in a difficult position internationally on matters such as regulating the freedom of speech of the tobacco industry or on matters of race. Dividing power between the federal government and the several states allows for greater local governance and numerous "laboratories" for developing laws, but it also makes it extraordinarily difficult for the United State to adhere to international norms that require greater national uniformity.

---

[17] See Ware v. Hylton, 3 Dall. 199, 281, 1 L.Ed. 568 (1796) (Wilson, J.) ("When the United States declared their independence, they were bound to receive the law of nations, in its modern state of purity and refinement."); The Nereide, 9 Cranch 388, 423, 3 L.Ed. 769 (1815) (Marshall, C.J.) ("[T]he Court is bound by the law of nations which is a part of the law of the land."); The Paquete Habana, 175 U.S. 677, 700 (1900) ("International law is part of our law, and must be ascertained and administered by the courts of justice of appropriate jurisdiction, as often as questions of right depending upon it are duly presented for their determination."); Banco Nacional de Cuba v. Sabbatino, 376 U.S. 398, 423 (1964) ("[I]t is, of course, true that United States courts apply international law as a part of our own in appropriate circumstances."); Texas Industries, Inc. v. Radcliff Materials, Inc., 451 U.S. 630, 641 (1981) (recognizing that "international disputes implicating ... our relations with foreign nations" are one of the "narrow areas" in which "federal common law" continues to exist); Sosa v. Alvarez-Machain, 542 U.S. 692, 729 (2004) ("For two centuries we have affirmed that the domestic law of the United States recognizes the law of nations.").

[18] See Murray v. The Charming Betsy, 2 Cranch 64, 118, 2 L.Ed. 208 (1804) ("[A]n act of Congress ought never to be construed to violate the law of nations, if any other possible construction remains."); Weinberger v. Rossi, 456 U.S. 25, 32 (1982) (the same); F. Hoffman-La Roche Ltd. v. Empagran, 542 U.S. 155, 164–65 (2004) (the same).

[19] The Paquete Habana, 175 U.S. at 700.

Consequently, there is an enduring schizophrenia in the U.S. constitutional and democratic tradition regarding the manner in which it incorporates international law, and this conflict is aggravated when the issue of courts is added to the picture. The United States has always accepted the importance and significance of a judiciary for the resolution of disputes; the importance and legacy of the Supreme Court from the early American republic to the present are ingrained in every American schoolchild. Yet the American democratic tradition strongly favors rule by the people principally through their popularly elected officials, such that there is an enduring suspicion of judges (local, let alone foreign) whose decisions do not hew closely to the laws enacted by the people. By and large, Americans do not favor their judges undertaking teleological interpretations of law; to the extent that laws need to be adapted, they look to the legislatures to do it. U.S. judges have been activist at times, both for conservative and liberal causes, but the practice does not sit well with the American democratic tradition and repeatedly evokes controversy. This conflict between a belief in an independent judiciary and distrust of activist judges explains in part the country's ambivalence to the ICJ (as well as efforts in some quarters to prevent judges from applying in U.S. courts norms generated outside the United States, whether formed by customary international law, within treaty regimes, or otherwise).

As discussed in Part C, this antinomy recently has presented the U.S. government with difficult issues regarding the relationship of ICJ decisions to the conduct of the law enforcement officials and courts of the several U.S. states.[20] Among other things, it has led to the acknowledgment that final judgments of the Court are binding as a matter of international law but to assertions by the Executive Branch that such judgments have no direct effect within the national legal system.

B. TECHNIQUES FOR MEDIATING THE ANTINOMIES

The World Court uses certain methods or mechanisms, formal or informal, to mediate the antinomies discussed in the previous section. Such techniques do not attempt to eliminate either of the conflicting principles captured by those antinomies; rather, the techniques take for granted the antinomies and seek to find a path between the conflicts presented. In essence, mediating

---

[20] See Andreas L. Paulus, *From Neglect to Defiance? The United States and International Adjudication*, 15 Eur. J. Int'l L. 783 (2004) ("The democratic tradition of the US, in which the government cannot rely on a majority in the legislature, sometimes stands in the way of the acceptance of rulings by 'unelected' international judges. Fifty state systems differ in their respect for international rulings.").

techniques[21] seek to play to tendencies of institutionalism, of sovereign equality, and of incorporation of international law into national law, while accepting that competing tendencies toward realism, exceptionalism, and autonomous national law circumscribe the role the Court may play. The discussion of such techniques here is combined with brief highlights of the history of the U.S. relationship with the ICJ.

As is well known, the predecessor to the ICJ, the Permanent Court of International Justice (PCIJ), was created in the aftermath of World War I. Caught up in the rising tide of institutionalism of the late nineteenth and early twentieth centuries and believing that reliance solely on international arbitration for the resolution of interstate disputes was not good enough, the United States became actively engaged in the negotiations that led to the establishment of the PCIJ.[22] Although arbitration had a role to play, American international lawyers and policy makers – such as Elihu Root – argued that it tended toward "an essentially political process of negotiation and compromise on the basis of expedience rather than the judicial procedure of impartial adjudication

---

[21] For discussions of such techniques, see W. Michael Reisman, *Systems of Control in International Adjudication and Arbitration* (Duke, 1992); Laurence R. Helfer and Anne-Marie Slaughter, *Toward a Theory of Effective Supranational Adjudication*, 107 Yale L.J. 273 (1997); Robert Adieh, *Between Dialogue and Decree: International Review of National Courts*, 79 N.Y.U. L. Rev. 2029 (2004); Laurence R. Helfer and Anne-Marie Slaughter, *Why States Create International Tribunals: A Response to Professors Posner and Yoo*, 93 Cal. L. Rev. 899 (2005).

[22] U.S. interest in international arbitration dates from early in its history (*see* Janis, *supra* note 8, at 97–116), but that interest for more than one hundred years was principally focused on disputes with its "mother country," the United Kingdom. The Treaty of Amity, Commerce and Navigation, Nov. 19, 1794, U.S.-U.K., 8 Stat. 116, T.S. No. 105 (commonly referred to as the "Jay Treaty" after U.S. Secretary of State John Jay), established three boards of arbitration to resolve disputes between the United Kingdom and its former colony. The Treaty of Washington, May 8, 1871, U.S.-U.K., 17 Stat. 863, T.S. No. 133, established four arbitrations for addressing Britain's conduct during the U.S. Civil War, including Britain's responsibility for allowing the construction of the Confederate raider *Alabama*. *See* Tom Bingham, *The Alabama Claims Arbitration*, 54 Int'l & Comp. L.Q. 1 (2005). Other U.S.-U.K. arbitrations addressed fur seals, the Venezuela-British Guiana boundary, and Alaska. In the years leading up to World War I, the United States entered into a few treaties providing for international arbitration, principally with Latin American states, but broader efforts foundered in the U.S. Senate.

The other principal U.S. interstate arbitration before World War II concerned Mexico. In September 1923, the United States and Mexico signed a convention in Washington, D.C. (which took effect in March 1924), creating a General Claims Commission. The purpose of the commission was to settle claims arising after July 4, 1868, "against one government by nationals of the other for losses or damages suffered by such nationals or their properties" and "for losses or damages originating from acts of officials or others acting for either government and resulting in injustice." Composed of three members (one each from the United States, Mexico, and a third country), the commission met from 1924 to 1937 in Washington, D.C., and Mexico City. Final settlement was reached in 1941.

of rights and duties in strict accordance with the rules of law."[23] The latter process was an option that states should have, because judicial decisions, being grounded more firmly in a rigorous application of law by persons not selected by the disputants, could serve as a means for definitively and convincingly resolving certain kinds of disputes. The United States had pressed without success for the creation of such a court at the 1907 Hague Peace Conference; then, after the carnage of world war, other states were willing to go along.

As is also well known, however, the U.S. Senate never consented to ratification of the Covenant of the League of Nations nor of the separate protocol embodying the Statute of the PCIJ. Although the PCIJ had its supporters in the United States, strong voices of realism and exceptionalism, particularly in the U.S. Senate, argued that submission to the jurisdiction of a world court would harm national interests and diminish or jeopardize national sovereignty. When put to a vote in 1935, adherence to the protocol secured fifty-two votes in favor and thirty-six against, thus falling seven votes short of a two-thirds majority.[24] Throughout the life of the PCIJ from 1922 to 1945 – during which time the court issued twenty-seven advisory opinions and thirty-two judgments[25] – the United States never participated in any litigation before the Court, although an American judge always served on it.[26] The substantive and procedural decisions of the PCIJ remain of interest today, because the Statute of the ICJ is essentially the same as that of its predecessor. Indeed, although states decided in the aftermath of World War II to create a new international court, they also decided to maintain continuity in its concept and function.[27]

Unlike the experience with the League of Nations, the United States joined the United Nations in 1945 and therefore ipso facto became a party to the ICJ statute.[28] Institutionalists emphasized that the success of a new system of international organizations to maintain peace and security, one built on the rule of law, necessarily entailed the creation of an international court. The U.S. delegation to the San Francisco conference reported to President Franklin D. Roosevelt that "[a]s the United States becomes a party to a Charter which places justice and international law among its foundation stones, it would

---

[23] *See* Francis Anthony Boyle, *Foundations of World Order* (Duke, 1999): 37; *see also* Michael Dunne, *The United States and the World Court, 1920–1935* (Pinter, 1988) at 17–46.
[24] 79 Cong. Rec. 1147 (1935). For an account, see Denna Frank Fleming, *The United States and the World Court: 1920–1966* at 117–137 (rev. ed. Russell & Russell, 1968).
[25] *See* Shabtai Rosenne, *The World Court and How It Works* at 16 (5th ed., Martinus Nijhoff, 1995).
[26] The PCIJ judges of U.S. nationality were John Bassett Moore (1922–28), Charles Evan Hughes (1928–30), Frank B. Kellogg (1930–35), and Manley O. Hudson (1936–42).
[27] *See* Amry Vandenbosch and Willard N. Hogan, *The United Nations: Background, Organization, Functions, Activities* (McGraw-Hill, 1952): 190.
[28] *See* UN Charter art. 93.

naturally accept and use an international court to apply international law and to administer international justice."[29] Testifying prior to the Senate's consent to ratification, the head of the U.S. delegation in San Francisco, Edward Stettinius, asserted that the Court will "have a most important part to play in the further development and strengthening of international law, just as the courts of England and America have helped to form the common law."[30] The State Department Legal Adviser (and later first American judge on the new Court) testified that the United States historically stood for

> the settlement of international cases by the judicial process; that we did try as far back as 1907 to establish a court; that such a court was established in 1922 and has been functioning ever since, and that while we did not go into that court, there was strong sentiment in this country, as you well know, for our becoming a party. Here we have provision for a Court, in the creation of which we have played an important part. Speaking for myself and for those who have been associated with me in this work, I think that we cannot too strongly urge... that we have here provided for the creation of an International Court of Justice that will be worthy of the name, and one that will make a great contribution to the maintenance of international peace and security. The Court is not as spectacular as some of the other organizations provided for in the Charter, but we think that it will serve an extremely important purpose, and that an International Organization without such a Court would be lacking in a very important essential.[31]

The UN Charter and the Court, of course, had their realist and exceptionalist detractors; some argued, among other things, that adherence to the Charter would "make slaves of our free citizens"[32] and that the ICJ would unconstitutionally usurp the jurisdiction of the Supreme Court "over all foreign disputes of this Nation."[33] Notwithstanding such views, the Senate in 1945 gave consent to ratification of the Charter, by a vote of eighty-nine to two.[34]

Even so, the United States did not embrace an international court that held wide-ranging and unconstrained authority. Structural aspects built into the Court sought to mediate between the desire of all states (including the United

---

[29] The Charter of the United Nations: Hearings before the Senate Committee on Foreign Relations, 79th Cong., 121 (1945) [hereinafter 1945 Senate Hearing] (report to the President on the Results of the San Francisco Conference, dated June 26, 1945).

[30] Id. at 219 (statement of Edward R. Stettinius, Jr., personal representative of the U.S. President to the San Francisco Conference).

[31] Id. at 344 (statement of Green H. Hackworth, U.S. Department of State Legal Adviser).

[32] Id. at 353 (statement of Mrs. Agnes Waters, legislative representative of the National Blue Star Mothers of America).

[33] Id. at 381 (statement of David Darrin, United Nations of Earth Association).

[34] 91 Cong. Rec. 8190 (1945).

States) for an impartial, permanent judicial forum and the desire of states to control their exposure to ICJ decision making (and, when exposed, to have their concerns be fairly heard and understood).

1. *Only States, Not Persons*

At the time of the creation of the ICJ, the idea that individuals might themselves pursue claims before an international tribunal was largely unknown. Consequently, the Statute of the Court provides that only states may appear before it in contentious cases, thus precluding voices that are not vested in the overall system of state sovereignty. This is an important design feature that provides states with a much greater comfort level regarding their exposure to the jurisdiction of the Court. Although today several states have accepted international courts that allow individuals to sue their own governments – such as the European Court of Human Rights – many others (including the United States) have been unwilling to do so. Were the International Court to have such jurisdiction, it would be a serious obstacle for U.S. participation, for it would invariably result in the Court passing upon matters that traditionally have been handled solely within the national legal system.

2. *Circumscribed Jurisdiction*

The dominant structural aspect controlling a state's exposure to the ICJ is that states cannot be sued absent their consent. Although there was considerable support at the San Francisco conference in favor of making the Court's jurisdiction compulsory, the United States and the Soviet Union were adamantly opposed. Faced with a deal breaker, the other nations backed down.[35] Consequently, under the Court's statute, consent to jurisdiction does not exist merely by virtue of a state being a party to the statute; separate express consent must exist. This requirement of state consent is why most of the 192 UN member states have never appeared before the Court in a contentious case and why the Court is regarded as an important but not dominant player in the field of international dispute resolution.

Although consent is needed, the statute is structured to make giving such consent as easy as possible. First, states can accept the Court's jurisdiction on an ad hoc basis for the adjudication of an existing dispute.[36] For example, the United States and Canada in 1981 jointly agreed to bring to the Court a

---

[35] See Ruth B. Russell, *A History of the United Nations Charter* at 884–90 (Brookings, 1958).
[36] Statute of the International Court of Justice, art. 36(1), 59 Stat. 1055, 3 Bemis 1153 [hereinafter ICJ Statute].

dispute over their maritime boundary.[37] That case, however, was the last time the United States agreed to bring a dispute to the Court on an ad hoc basis. Instead, bilateral disputes that might have been addressed by the Court under its ad hoc jurisdiction have been dealt with through bilateral negotiation[38] or through bilateral arbitration.[39] The United States has also promoted ad hoc arbitration directly between injured nationals and foreign states by coercing foreign states into accepting such jurisdiction.[40]

Second, states can adhere to a bilateral or multilateral treaty that expressly provides for ICJ jurisdiction when cases arise relating to the interpretation or application of the treaty.[41] (Treaties predating the existence of the ICJ that provide for jurisdiction of the PCIJ are also regarded under the statute as triggering ICJ jurisdiction.[42]) This form of jurisdiction is inherently limited, for the jurisdiction only arises from matters within the scope of the treaty. The narrower the scope of the treaty, the narrower the scope of the Court's jurisdiction. The breadth of the treaty may be addressed by including within it only a limited set of positive rights or obligations; it may also be addressed by clauses within the treaty that carve out issues, such as matters relating to national security.

Moreover, when ratifying a treaty providing for the World Court's jurisdiction over disputes, a state may be entitled to file a reservation to the provision on dispute resolution. For example, the Genocide Convention[43] sets forth various obligations of states with respect to preventing and punishing genocide, and it further provides that disputes arising under the convention between parties shall be submitted to the ICJ at the request of one of the parties.[44] However, when the United States ratified the Genocide Convention in 1988, it stated that before any dispute could be submitted to the Court under Article IX,

---

[37] See *Delimitation of the Maritime Boundary of the Gulf of Maine Area*, 1984 ICJ 246 (Oct. 12).
[38] See, e.g., Treaty with Mexico on Delimitation of Continental Shelf, June 9, 2000, U.S.-Mex., S. Treaty Doc. No. 106–39 (2000).
[39] See, e.g., *Heathrow Airport User Charges Arbitration*, 102 I.L.R. 215 (1992) (involving dispute between the United States and the United Kingdom over airport user charges at Heathrow Airport).
[40] See, e.g., *Compañía del Desarrollo de Santa Elena S.A. v. Costa Rica*, ICSID Case No. ARB/96/1, Final Award (Feb. 17, 2000), reprinted in 15 *ICSID Rev. – Foreign Investment L. J.* at 169 (2000). Costa Rica agreed to submit this and other disputes with U.S. investors to arbitration after being threatened by the United States with a loss of international financing and a suspension of U.S. aid to Costa Rica pursuant to the 1994 Helms Amendment. See 22 U.S.C. §2370a (2000).
[41] ICJ Statute, art. 36(1).
[42] *Id.*, art. 37.
[43] Convention on the Prevention and Punishment of the Crime of Genocide, Dec. 9, 1948, 78 U.N.T.S. 277.
[44] *Id.*, art. IX.

"the specific consent of the United States is required in each case."[45] Consequently, when Yugoslavia in 1999 sought to sue the United States under the Genocide Convention (for acts associated with the intervention in Kosovo), the ICJ found that – in light of the American reservation – there was no jurisdiction and therefore dismissed the case.[46]

The United States is a party to many treaties that confer jurisdiction on the Court, enabling it to sue and be sued thereunder.[47] In the wake of the *Nicaragua* decision (discussed later in the chapter), there has been repeated discussion within the U.S. government of withdrawing from dispute resolution provisions under such treaties, but the technical and political difficulties of doing so have so far left most of those provisions intact.

The last case brought to the Court by the United States under this form of jurisdiction was by an application filed in 1987 in the *ELSI* case.[48] In that case, the United States invoked a compromissory clause contained in a 1948 bilateral Treaty of Friendship, Commerce, and Navigation that provided for Court jurisdiction over disputes arising under that treaty.[49] The U.S. claim alleged expropriation of and interference with property of an American company's subsidiary in Sicily. The Court ultimately concluded that no harm had occurred from the alleged acts.

Since the *ELSI* case, the only other dispute pursued by the United States that might have led to the filing of an independent[50] claim before the ICJ appears to have been the "hushkits" dispute between the United States and Europe. On March 14, 2000, the United States initiated a dispute resolution proceeding by filing an application and memorial before the International Civil Aviation Organization (ICAO) Council in its capacity as a judicial body.[51] The dispute concerned a European Union (EU) regulation adopted in 1999

---

[45] *See* 28 ILM 782 (1989).
[46] See *Legality of Use of Force (Yugo. v. U.S.)*, 1999 ICJ 916 (June 2).
[47] *See* Table 4.1.
[48] *See Elettronica Sicula S.p.A. (ELSI) (U.S. v. Italy)*, 1989 ICJ 15 (judgment of July 20). Although the United States technically "sued" Italy at the ICJ, in fact the states agreed diplomatically in advance that the dispute would be brought before the ICJ, although Italy maintained its right to raise issues of jurisdiction and admissibility of the matter. As noted later, the two states also agreed to request that the Court form a chamber of five judges specified by the parties, which the Court did.
[49] Treaty of Friendship, Commerce, and Navigation, Feb. 2, 1948, U.S.-Italy, art. XXVI, 63 Stat. 2255, 79 U.N.T.S. 171.
[50] The United States did file a counterclaim based on a bilateral treaty of amity in the case brought by Iran for destruction of Iranian oil platforms in the Gulf. *See Oil Platforms (Iran. v. U.S.)*, 2003 ICJ 161 (Nov. 6), para. 9; *see* Pieter Bekker, Case Report: Oil Platforms (*Iran v. United States*), 98 Am. J. Int'l L. 550 (2004). The Court rejected that counterclaim.
[51] Such a dispute is brought under Article 84 of the Convention on International Civil Aviation, Dec. 7, 1944, 61 Stat. 1180, 15 U.N.T.S. 295 [hereinafter Chicago Convention], and Article 2 of the ICAO Rules for the Settlement of Differences, ICAO Doc. 7782/2 (2d ed. 1975).

relating to aircraft noise – one that imposed design-based restrictions on aircraft registered in, or operating into, Europe. In November 2000, the Council rejected certain preliminary objections raised by the EU.[52] In the aftermath of the ICAO Council decision, neither the United States nor EU member states exercised its right to appeal the Council's decision to the ICJ, in accordance with the procedure set forth in the Chicago Convention.[53] Rather, the EU member states filed their counter-memorial in December 2000 and the parties thereafter settled the matter.[54]

Since the 1980s, the United States has consistently declined to accept or incorporate into treaties compromissory clauses calling for adjudication of disputes by the ICJ. If the United States adheres to major multilateral treaties (such as the Genocide Convention) that contain such a clause, then the government typically files a reservation to that clause. If the United States adheres to major multilateral treaties that allow parties to opt for ICJ jurisdiction, then it declines to do so. Thus, should the United States ratify the 1982 UN Convention on the Law of the Sea, it has already announced that it will opt for compulsory arbitral dispute resolution, not resolution by the ICJ.[55] U.S. bilateral investment treaties now invariably call for investor-state arbitration before the International Centre for the Settlement of Investment Disputes (ICSID) or another forum,[56] a striking contrast to the earlier generation of treaties of

---

[52] *See* Decision of the ICAO Council on the Preliminary Objections in the Matter "United States and 15 European States (2000)" (Nov. 16, 2000) (on file with author).

[53] *See* Chicago Convention, *supra* note 49, art. 84 ("Any contracting State may, subject to Article 85, appeal from the decision of the Council to an ad hoc tribunal . . . or to the Permanent Court of International Justice.") Article 85 clarifies the ambiguity of Article 84 by noting that an ad hoc arbitral tribunal is relied upon where a party to a dispute has not accepted the Statute of the Permanent Court of International Justice and the parties to the dispute cannot agree on the choice of the arbitral tribunal. Although the Convention is not clear on whether a party to a dispute under Article 84 has the right to appeal an ICAO Council decision on jurisdiction, the International Court of Justice has decided that such appeal is possible. Appeal Relating to the Jurisdiction of the ICAO Council (India v. Pak.), 1972 ICJ 46, 60 (Aug. 18).

[54] *See* U.S. Dep't of State Press Release on U.S. Withdrawal of Complaint at ICAO (June 13, 2002), *at* http://www.state.gov/r/pa/prs/ps/2002/11096.htm. This dispute was only the second in ICAO's history that was addressed by the ICAO Council in its judicial capacity, the first being the dispute between India and Pakistan almost thirty years ago, which was appealed to the Court. *See* Appeal Relating to the Jurisdiction of the ICAO Council (India v. Pak.), *supra* note 51.

[55] *See* U.S. Secretary of State Letter of Submittal to the President, *in United Nations Convention on the Law of the Sea, with Annexes, and the Agreement Relating to the Implementation of Part XI of the United Nations Convention on the Law of the Sea, with Annex*, S. Treaty Doc. 103–39, V at IX-X (1994); *see also* Testimony of U.S. Dep't of State Legal Adviser William H. Taft, IV before the Senate Foreign Relations Committee (Oct. 21, 2003), at http://www.state.gov/g/oes/rls/rm/2003/25573.htm.

[56] *See*, e.g., Treaty Concerning the Encouragement and Reciprocal Protection of Investment, Oct. 25, 2004, U.S.-Uruguay, §B, at http://www.ustr.gov/Trade_Agreements/Bilateral/

Friendship, Commerce, and Navigation, which provided for ICJ jurisdiction over state-to-state disputes. Investment disputes arising under the North American Free Trade Agreement (NAFTA) are also sent to investor-state arbitration before ICSID[57] or an ad hoc panel operating under the UN Commission on International Trade Law (UNCITRAL) rules.[58] U.S. trade disputes – under agreements completed in the past fifteen years – are placed before World Trade Organization (WTO) panels,[59] panels operating under NAFTA Chapter 19[60] or 20,[61] or panels operating under bilateral trade agreements,[62] they are not submitted to the ICJ.

Third, under what is known as the "optional clause," the states that are parties to the ICJ Statute may by means of a unilateral declaration undertake that "they recognize as compulsory *ipso facto* and without special agreement, in relation to any other state accepting the same obligation, the jurisdiction of the Court in all legal disputes" involving issues of law or fact governed by rules of international law.[63] In 1946, the United States accepted the Court's compulsory jurisdiction, hoping that doing so would encourage other states to follow suit.[64] At the same time, it placed in its declaration certain reservations, including the so-called Connally reservation (or "amendment"), which

---

Section_Index.html. The current "model" bilateral investment treaty of the United States – on which the U.S.-Uruguay agreement was based – provides for disputes to be submitted to arbitration under ICSID or under the UN Commission on International Trade Law (UNICTRAL) rules or to another arbitral forum agreed on by the parties. *See* Treaty between the Government of the United States of America and the Government of Concerning the Encouragement and Reciprocal Protection of Investment, art. 24 (Nov. 2004), at http://www.state.gov/documents/organization/38710.pdf.

[57] *See, e.g., Waste Mgmt., Inc. v. Mexico*, Award, para. 98 (NAFTA Ch. 11 Arb. Trib. Apr. 30, 2004), reprinted in 43 ILM 967 (2004).

[58] *See, e.g., GAMI Investments, Inc. v. Mexico*, Final Award (NAFTA Ch. 11 Arb. Trib. Nov. 15, 2004).

[59] *See, e.g.*, Canada – Measures Affecting the Importation of Milk and the Exportation of Dairy Products, WTO Doc. WT/DS103/AB/RW2, WT/DS113/AB/RW2 (Dec. 12, 2002); Japan – Measures Affecting the Importation of Apples, WTO Doc. WT/DS245/AB/R (Nov. 26, 2003); Canada – Measures Relating to Exports of Wheat and Treatment of Imported Grain, WTO Doc. WT/DS276/R (Apr. 6, 2004); Canada – Measures Relating to Exports of Wheat and Treatment of Imported Grain, WTO Doc. WT/DS276/AB/R (Aug. 30, 2004).

[60] *See, e.g.*, Corrosion-Resistant Carbon Steel Flat Products from Canada, Full Sunset Review (NAFTA Ch. 19 Panel Oct. 19, 2004).

[61] *See, e.g.*, Cross-border Trucking Services (NAFTA Ch. 20 Arb. Trib. Feb. 6, 2001).

[62] *See, e.g.*, Free Trade Agreement, June 15, 2004, U.S.-Morocco, Ch. 20, at http://www.ustr.gov/Trade_Agreements/Bilateral/Section_Index.html.

[63] *See* ICJ Statute, art. 36(2); *see also* M. Fitzmaurice, *The Optional Clause System and the Law of Treaties: Issues of Interpretation in Recent Jurisprudence of the International Court of Justice*, 20 Austl. Y.I.L. 127 (1999); J.G. Merrills, *The Optional Clause Revisited*, 64 Brit. Y.B. Int'l L. 197 (1993).

[64] *See* U.S. Declaration Accepting the Compulsory Jurisdiction of the International Court of Justice (Aug. 26, 1946). At the time the U.S. declaration was submitted, Herschel V. Johnson, acting U.S. representative to the United Nations, asserted,

excluded from the jurisdiction of the Court "disputes with regard to matters which are essentially within the domestic jurisdiction of the United States of America *as determined by the United States of America*" (emphasis added). The purpose of this "self-judging" clause was to ensure that the U.S. government and not the Court's judges would decide, as a practical matter, whether a dispute is "domestic" in character and consequently outside the Court's jurisdiction. Because such a reservation in essence forecloses the ability of the Court to decide whether it has jurisdiction in a case,[65] many scholars and some ICJ judges have expressed doubts as to whether such a reservation is permissible,[66] but to date the Court has not definitively addressed the issue.

Early in the life of the Court, the Connally reservation proved to be a double-edged sword. Because the Court operates on a principle of reciprocity in application of its compulsory jurisdiction,[67] the reservation had the effect of entitling any state that the United States wished to sue to use the optional clause to invoke the reservation against the United States. When the United States sued Bulgaria in 1957 for an attack on an El Al aircraft flying over Bulgarian territory (resulting, among other things, in the death of six American nationals), Bulgaria responded that the matter was "essentially within" Bulgaria's "domestic jurisdiction," and thus outside the jurisdiction of the Court. The United States at first objected that such a response was in bad faith, but ultimately concluded that allowing the Court to decide whether Bulgaria's decision was in bad faith would defeat the entire point of the reservation and so withdrew its case.[68]

> One of the most elemental functions of the United Nations in the preservation of world peace is the development of procedures of pacific settlement. In these procedures, the role and functions of law is [sic] clear. We feel that international law is already sufficiently developed to serve as a guide and basis in international relations. We feel further that the best way of assuring its further development, and the only way of enabling it to fulfill its function, is by referring to a responsible international tribunal all disputes properly justiciable by such a tribunal.
>
> *See* 15 State Dep't Bull. 452 (Sept. 1, 1946). For Senate consideration, see Compulsory Jurisdiction, International Court of Justice: Hearings before a Subcommittee of the Senate Committee on Foreign Relations on S. Res. 196, 79th Cong., 2d Sess. (1946); see also S. Rep. No. 1835, 79th Cong., 2d Sess. (1946) (report of the Senate Foreign Relations Committee).

[65] *See* ICJ Statute, art. 36(6).
[66] *See Interhandel Case (Switz. v. U.S.)*, 1959 ICJ 6, 95 (Mar. 21) (separate opinion of Judge Lauterpacht); *Military and Paramilitary Activities in and against Nicaragua (Nicar. v. U.S.)*, 1984 ICJ 392, 601–02 (Nov. 26) (dissenting opinion of Judge Schwebel); *Fisheries Jurisdiction (Spain v. Can.)*, 1998 ICJ 432, 575 (Dec. 4) (dissenting opinion of Judge Vereshchetin).
[67] *See* ICJ Statute, art. 36(2) (allowing states to file declarations accepting compulsory jurisdiction "in relation to any other state accepting the same obligation").
[68] *See* Leo Gross, *Bulgaria Invokes the Connally Amendment*, 56 Am. J. Int'l L. 357 (1962).

Although in theory the Connally reservation could be invoked at will, the United States declined to do so in the case brought by Nicaragua in 1984, no doubt because it simply was not credible to declare that American attacks allegedly occurring in Nicaraguan territory were matters "essentially within the domestic jurisdiction of the United States." When the Court rejected other jurisdictional objections raised by the United States in the *Nicaragua* case,[69] in October 1985 the U.S. government announced that it was terminating its declaration accepting compulsory jurisdiction, in accordance with the terms of the U.S. declaration.[70] The termination became effective in 1986 and remains so today.

The reasons stated for terminating the declaration fell broadly into four areas.[71] First, the United States was clearly upset at the Court for finding that jurisdiction existed over Nicaragua's case, which resulted in the judges wading into the highly charged politics of President Reagan's Latin American policy. For the U.S. government, the Court's decision that Nicaragua had accepted the Court's compulsory jurisdiction, that El Salvador could not intervene at the jurisdiction stage, and that Nicaragua's claims were justiciable simply could not be correct as a matter of law. Second, the United States asserted that the benefits anticipated from accepting the Court's compulsory jurisdiction had not materialized. Originally, the United States accepted the Court's compulsory jurisdiction in the hope that other states would follow, but most states, including China and the Soviet Union, had not done so. Further, most of the cases that had advanced to the merits were not based on the Court's compulsory jurisdiction, and therefore such jurisdiction had not become a principal part of the Court's overall jurisprudence. The United States itself had tried seven times to sue a state before the ICJ on the basis of compulsory jurisdiction but had never been successful in doing so.[72] Third, the United States emphasized the costs of adherence to the Court's compulsory

---

[69] *See Military and Paramilitary Activities in and against Nicaragua (Nicar. v. U.S.)*, 1984 ICJ 392 (Nov. 26).

[70] *See* United States: Department of State Letter and Statement concerning Termination of Acceptance of ICJ Compulsory Jurisdiction, 24 ILM 1742 (1985). A year earlier, in an effort to forestall the *Nicaragua* case, the United States attempted to modify its declaration so as to exclude "disputes with any Central American state." 84 Dep't of State Bull. 89 (June 1984). The United States also declined to participate in the ensuing merits phase of the *Nicaragua* case, which led to a judgment against the United States on several counts. *See Military and Paramilitary Activities in and against Nicaragua (Nicar. v. U.S.)*, 1986 ICJ 14 (June 27). Thereafter, the United States ignored the Court's judgment and, as noted later, vetoed measures of implementation sought by Nicaragua at the Security Council.

[71] *See* Testimony of Abraham D. Sofaer, U.S. Dep't of State Legal Adviser, to the Senate Foreign Relations Committee (Dec. 4, 1985), reprinted in 86 Dep't of State Bull. 67 (Jan. 1986) [hereinafter Sofaer Testimony].

[72] *See infra* note 107.

jurisdiction, noting that three states had sued the United States on the basis of such jurisdiction.[73] Indeed, other states could undertake "hit-and-run" tactics, by waiting until they wished to sue the United States before filing a declaration accepting the Court's compulsory jurisdiction and then, after filing the case, withdrawing that declaration to avoid being sued. Finally, the United States attacked the credibility and impartiality of the judges of the Court, noting that most came from states that had not accepted the Court's compulsory jurisdiction. Moreover, because the judges must be elected by the General Assembly, and because the majority of states in the Assembly did not, and still do not, share the U.S. view on important international questions (including the special position of the permanent members of the Security Council in maintaining international peace and security), "[o]ne reasonably may expect at least some of the judges to be sensitive to the impact of their decisions on their standing with the U.N. majority."[74] Be that as it may, arguably the withdrawal of the acceptance of the Court's compulsory jurisdiction was, from the start, of little practical import, given the nature, scope, and effect of the Connally reservation.

Although the termination of this acceptance of the Court's compulsory jurisdiction may be unfortunate, the United States is in good company. The only permanent member of the Security Council that currently accepts the Court's compulsory jurisdiction is the United Kingdom; China, France, and Russia do not. Further, the United Kingdom's acceptance is conditioned by several significant reservations that make it quite difficult to sue it before the Court. Moreover, the vast majority of states have not accepted the Court's compulsory jurisdiction. Of 192 member states of the United Nations, only 65 have accepted the Court's compulsory jurisdiction as of December 2007,[75] and many of those acceptances contain significant conditions and reservations.[76]

---

[73] *Rights of Nationals of the United States in Morocco (Fr. v. U.S.)*, 1952 ICJ 176 (Aug. 27); *Interhandel (Switz. v. U.S.)*, 1959 ICJ 6 (Mar. 21); *Military and Paramilitary Activities in and against Nicaragua (Nicar. v. U.S.)*, 1986 ICJ 14 (June 27).

[74] Sofaer Testimony, *supra* note 70, at 69. Thomas Franck responded to the charge of bias against the United States by noting that (1) of the 115 judgments and advisory opinions issued between 1948 and 1985, the U.S. judge voted with the majority 82 times, and dissented in whole or in part only 15 times; (2) an examination of the dissents reveals that the U.S. judge disagreed with the majority "in circumstances that often fail to confirm the contention of bias"; and (3) "[i]n none of these cases could the majority be said to have taken a position that was contrary in any way to the U.S. national interest." *See* Thomas M. Franck, *Judging the World Court* 37 (Priority Press, 1986).

[75] *See* Table 4.1.

[76] *See, e.g.*, John R. Crook, *The International Court of Justice and Human Rights*, 1 Nw. U. J. Int'l Hum. Rts. 2 19 (2004).

TABLE 4.1. *List of states accepting the compulsory jurisdiction of the International Court of Justice*

Name of state	Year declaration was filed (Amended)	Name of state	Year declaration was filed (Amended)
Australia	2002	Liechtenstein	1950
Austria	1971	Luxembourg	1930
Barbados	1980	Madagascar	1992
Belgium	1958	Malawi	1966
Botswana	1970	Malta	1966 (1983)
Bulgaria	1992	Mauritius	1968
Cambodia	1957	Mexico	1947
Cameroon	1994	Netherlands	1956
Canada	1994	New Zealand	1977
Costa Rica	1973	Nicaragua	1929
Côte d'Ivoire	2001	Nigeria	1998
Cyprus	2002	Norway	1996
Democratic Republic of the Congo	1989	Pakistan	1960
		Panama	1921
Denmark	1956	Paraguay	1996
Djibouti	2005	Peru	2003
Dominica	2006	Philippines	1972
Dominican Republic	1924	Poland	1996
Egypt	1957	Portugal	1955 (2005)
Estonia	1991	Senegal	1985
Finland	1958	Slovakia	2004
Gambia	1966	Somalia	1963
Georgia	1995	Spain	1990
Greece	1994	Sudan	1958
Guinea	1998	Suriname	1987
Guinea-Bissau	1989	Swaziland	1969
Haiti	1921	Sweden	1957
Honduras	1986	Switzerland	1948
Hungary	1992	Togo	1979
India	1974	Uganda	1963
Japan	1958 (2007)	United Kingdom	1969 (2004)
Kenya	1965	Uruguay	1921
Lesotho	2000		
Liberia	1952		

3. *State Influence on Selection of Judges*

Once exposed to ICJ decision making, other structural aspects help assure states that their concerns will be fairly heard and understood. One such structural aspect is the manner in which judges are elected to the Court. On one hand, the de jure procedure entails a concurrent election of judges by the two principal organs of the United Nations (the General Assembly and the Security Council)[77] on the basis of the independence, character, and expertise of persons and not on their nationality.[78] Although judges are precluded from participating in cases in which they were previously involved (which, sometimes, can have the effect of preventing judges from sitting in some cases involving their own states),[79] there is no absolute bar to a judge sitting in a case involving a state of the judge's nationality.[80] The judges serve for nine-year terms and cannot be recalled or dismissed by the government of their nationalities during their tenure.

On the other hand, the procedure for selection of judges is not blind to nationality. No two judges on the Court may be of the same nationality.[81] The judges are to be selected so that the principal legal systems of the world are represented,[82] and as an informal matter, the seats of the judges on the Court are allocated according to regional quotas.[83] In contentious cases, if a party has no judge of its nationality sitting on the Court, it may appoint an ad hoc judge to sit in the case.[84] Further, although the permanent members of the Security Council do not have a "veto" with respect to the election of ICJ judges (a simple majority of eight votes is required),[85] the five permanent members are in a position to influence strongly the process. It should be no surprise that they have always had one of their nationals on the Court's bench.[86]

Having a judge of the state's nationality (or the state's region), of course, does not guarantee a decision in the state's favor. Cases are decided by majority of the whole bench. No "veto" power is accorded to judges from particular states. Moreover, some (but not all) studies indicate that historically judges have not automatically sided with their state of nationality.[87]

---

[77] ICJ Statute, arts. 4(1) and 8.
[78] *Id.*, art. 2.
[79] *Id.*, art. 17(2).
[80] *Id.*, art. 31(1).
[81] *Id.*, art. 3(1).
[82] *Id.*, art. 9.
[83] I *The Charter of the United Nations: A Commentary* 1162 (Bruno Simma ed. 2d ed., Oxford, 2002).
[84] ICJ Statute, art. 31(2) & (3).
[85] *Id.*, art. 10; *see* I *The Charter of the United Nations: A Commentary*, *supra* note 83, at 482. Normally voting by the Security Council requires a majority of nine.
[86] A judge from each of the permanent members has been on the Court since its inception, with the exception of a gap between 1967 and 1985 when there was no Chinese judge. *I The Charter of the United Nations: A Commentary*, *supra* note 83, at 1161. The ICJ judges of U.S. nationality to date have been Green Hackworth (1946–61), Philip Jessup (1961–70), Hardy Cross Dilliard (1970–79), Richard Baxter (1979–80), Stephen Schwebel (1981–2000), and Thomas Buergenthal (2000–present).
[87] *See* Edith Brown Weiss, Judicial Independence and Impartiality: A Preliminary Inquiry, in *Crossroads*, *supra* note 8, 123 at 134 (finding that "the record does not reveal significant

Even so, the Statute provides a means for two contending states to move the center of gravity of the Court closer to their value systems. Article 26 of the Statute allows the Court to establish a chamber (i.e., a small subgroup of the whole bench) of judges to decide a case. The Court typically is inclined to do so if both parties request it and identify the judges they wish appointed to such a chamber. Moreover, unlike under the Statute of the PCIJ, the chamber does not need to represent "the principal legal systems of the world"[88]; it can consist of judges from just certain regions. Thus, in the *Gulf of Maine* case, Canada and the United States informed the Court that they wished a chamber formed consisting of five judges identified by the parties.[89] In the *ELSI* case, Italy and the United States informed the Court that they, too, wished to have a chamber consisting of five specific judges.[90] In both cases, the states were clearly interested in having greater control over the legal and political attitudes being brought to the judicial table, and in both cases the Court played along. Despite this nod toward party control, the judgments of the chambers are technically[91] and, in practice, regarded as judgments of the Court as a whole.

In addition to jurisdiction over contentious cases between two states, the Court also has jurisdiction to issue advisory opinions on legal questions. The advisory jurisdiction may be invoked only by UN organs and by some of the specialized agencies of the UN, and the opinions, by definition, are nonbinding. Nevertheless, advisory opinions have juridical authority; they can serve to legitimate certain conduct of states and organizations and invariably have significance for a legal system in which judicial precedents are scarce. In practice, advisory opinions are relied on and cited as legal authority as frequently as are judgments rendered in contentious cases.

4. No Direct Enforcement of Judgments in National Law

International tribunals differ markedly in the manner in which their decisions are "embedded" in the national systems of the states that are subject to the

---

alignments, either on regional, political, or economic basis. There is a high degree of consensus among the judges on most decisions."); *see also* Dinah Shelton, *Legal Norms to Promote the Independence and Accountability of International Tribunals*, 2 Law & Prac. Int'l Cts. & Tribunals 27, 32 (2003); *but see* Eric A. Posner & Miguel de Figueiredo, *Is the International Court of Justice Biased?* (unpublished draft dated Dec. 2004); Eric Posner, *The Decline of the International Court of Justice* (unpublished draft dated Dec. 2004; finding that ICJ judges do not apply the law impartially but favor the interests of their home states or like-minded states).

[88] *See* PCIJ Statute, art. 9. For background, see Stephen M. Schwebel, *Ad Hoc Chambers of the International Court of Justice*, 81 Am. J. Int'l L. 831 (1987).

[89] *See* Delimitation of the Maritime Boundary of the Gulf of Maine Area, 1982 ICJ 3 (order of Jan. 20); *see also* Davis Robinson, David Colson, and Bruce Rashkow, *Some Perspectives on Adjudicating before the World Court: The Gulf of Maine Case*, 79 Am. J. Int'l L. 578 (1985).

[90] *See* Elettronica Sicula S.p.A. (ELSI) (U.S. v. Italy), 1987 ICJ 3 (order of Mar. 2).

[91] ICJ Statute, art. 27.

tribunal's jurisdiction.[92] Agreements creating international tribunals can make decisions directly enforceable in a national legal system, without any need for governments to take post hoc implementing action (e.g., through statutes or executive orders). This, too, is a technique for mediating between conflicting visions of what the tribunal should be.

In the spirit of institutionalism, ICJ judgments in contentious cases are binding on the parties, final, and without appeal.[93] Further, by the UN Charter, each UN member "undertakes to comply with the decision of the International Court of Justice in any case to which it is a party."[94] Yet when drafting the UN Charter and the ICJ Statute, states elected not to include any provisions addressing the legal effect of ICJ judgments within national legal systems, such as whether they provide a basis for private rights of action in national courts. Seen from the U.S. point of view, this is consistent with autonomous democratic and constitutional traditions. Moreover, as a concession to exceptionalism, the UN Charter provides that a party that prevailed before the Court may submit noncompliance with the ruling to the scrutiny of the UN Security Council, "which may, if it deems necessary, make recommendations or decide upon measures to be taken to give effect to the judgment."[95] Of all the cases decided on the merits in the Court's history, in only one did an applicant – Nicaragua – request that the Security Council take action to enforce the judgment. Needless to say, the United States vetoed a resolution to that effect.[96] An effort by private individuals to sue the U.S. government in U.S. courts, based, among other things, on the ground that U.S. actions violated the Court's decision, was dismissed because there is no private right of action to enforce an International Court decision in U.S. courts.[97]

5. *Discursive and Political Constraints*

In addition to formal or quasi-formal techniques, there are also certain political constraints that operate to mediate the antinomies.[98] The Court knows that

---

[92] *See,* e.g., Robert O. Keohane et al., *Legalized Dispute Resolution: Interstate and Transnational*, 54 Int'l Org. 457, 458 (2000).

[93] *See* ICJ Statute, arts. 59–60.

[94] UN Charter, art. 94(1).

[95] *Id.*, art. 94(2).

[96] *See* 25 ILM 1337, 1352–65 (1986); *see also* Constanze Schulte, *Compliance with Decisions of the International Court of Justice* 199–205 (Oxford, 2004); Colter Paulson, *Compliance with Final Judgments of the International Court of Justice since 1987*, 98 Amer. J. Int'l L. 434 (2004).

[97] *See Comm. of U.S. Citizens Living in Nicaragua v. Reagan*, 859 F.2d 929 (D.C. Cir. 1988).

[98] For a discussion regarding how a tribunal operates within a "strategic space" that is bounded not only by formal constraints but also by informal constraints that are both "discursive" and "political" in nature, *see* Richard H. Steinberg, *Judicial Lawmaking at the WTO: Discursive, Constitutional, and Political Constraints*, 98 Am. J. Int'l L. 247 (2004).

its legitimacy and credibility as an institution rest not only on the objective correctness of its legal reasoning but also on the acceptance of that legal reasoning by international lawyers, and more broadly by the global community of states.

Arguably "judicial law-making that consistently results in the loss of dispute settlement cases by a powerful member (as both a complainant and a respondent) would not be sustainable politically, for it would constitute a shift in property rights that would likely engender a political reaction."[99] As U.S. Supreme Court Justice Felix Frankfurter once wrote with respect to the U.S. Supreme Court,

> the Court's authority – possessed of neither the purse nor the sword – ultimately rests on sustained public confidence in its moral sanction. Such feeling must be nourished by the Court's complete detachment, in fact and in appearance, from political entanglements and by abstention from injecting itself into the clash of political forces in political settlements.[100]

The International Court is unlikely to issue a decision that, although perhaps regarded by its judges as soundly based in law, is regarded by international lawyers generally as misguided or by the global community at large as politically unacceptable. Were it to do so, its viability could be severely impaired. Instead, it strives to issue decisions that are likely to be well received within the international legal community and by its primary constituents: states. By doing so, it helps encourage states to submit cases, which in turn justifies its own significance and importance.

To a certain extent, this mediating technique has operated in the context of "admissibility" doctrines. Even if the Court finds that it has jurisdiction over a case, sometimes it has refused to pass upon the merits of the case. In doing so, the Court spares itself coming into conflict with aspects of the antimonies discussed earlier. For example, in certain cases, it has relied on the rule of customary international law known as the "local remedies rule" as a means of respecting decision making by states within their national systems. Under the rule, before a state may espouse a claim on behalf of its national, it must be shown that the latter has exhausted all available legal remedies in the courts and before the administrative agencies of the state against which the claim is brought. In 1959, the United States successfully avoided suit before the ICJ by invoking this rule[101]; in doing so, the Court in effect accepted that resolution of a dispute, at least in the first instance, should be left to U.S. courts. In another case in which the United States was the claimant, it successfully proved to

---

[99] Id. at 268–69.
[100] Baker v. Carr, 369 U.S. 186, 267 (1962) (dissenting opinion of Justice Frankfurter).
[101] See Interhandel Case (Switz. v. U.S.), 1959 ICJ 6 (Mar. 21).

the Court that the rule was satisfied.[102] In theory, the rule aims to permit states to remedy wrongs at the national level before they become a dispute on the international plane, where they might disrupt unnecessarily international relations. In practice, however, it also provides the Court with an opportunity to decline to pass upon a dispute that could place it in direct conflict with the tendency of some states toward strong constitutional autonomy. Similarly, the Court at times has seized on doctrines of standing[103] and mootness[104] to avoid passing upon highly charged disputes.

Even if a case reaches the merits phase, it is possible to detect judicial reasoning that reflects sensitivity to the political limits of the Court's authority. In the *Nuclear Weapons* advisory opinion, the Court engaged in a systematic analysis of why treaties and customary rules of international law did not prohibit the possession or use of nuclear weapons and then why certain principles of international humanitarian law did prohibit such use. The Court, however, could not quite bring itself to declare nuclear weapons unlawful in all circumstances. No doubt several of the judges were sensitive to the fact that nuclear weapons were unlikely to be eliminated because of a decision by the Court and that the most powerful states in the world rejected the idea that the possession and use of such weapons were in all circumstances unlawful. Further, the judges were likely conscious that a decision to that effect was not firmly grounded in international law; there were certainly no treaties that expressly stated as much, and the application of principles of international humanitarian law was plausible but not obvious. Consequently, the final conclusion reached was that the use of nuclear weapons as a general matter was unlawful, but that, in certain extreme circumstances involving the very survival of a state, such use might be lawful. Although this conclusion is problematic as a matter of legal analysis, it was a politically shrewd move by the Court, giving to the antinuclear movement strong language against the legality of nuclear weapons while allowing powerful states a basis for maintaining the status quo.

C. A LOOK AT U.S. CASES BEFORE THE ICJ

1. *The Overall Track Record*

Out of a total 111 contentious cases filed before the Court from 1946 to 2007, the United States was involved in twenty-one.[105] No other state has appeared before the Court so frequently. Moreover, other major powers such as China and Russia have never appeared before the Court in a contentious case.

---

[102] *See Elettronica Sicula S.p.A. (ELSI) (U.S. v. Italy)*, 1989 ICJ 15 (judgment of July 20).
[103] *South West Africa (Ethiopia v. S. Afr.; Liberia v. S. Afr.)*, 1966 ICJ 6 (July 18).
[104] *Nuclear Tests (Austr. v. Fr.; New Zealand v. Fr.)*, 1974 ICJ 253 (Dec. 20).
[105] *See* Table 4.2.

TABLE 4.2. *Contentious cases involving the United States at the International Court of Justice (ICJ)*

Applicant	Respondent	Name of case	Citation to case	U.S. overall prevailed?
Mexico	United States	Avena and Other Mexican Nationals	2004 ICJ 12 (Mar. 31) (merits judgment) Feb. 5, 2003 (provisional measures) (reprinted in 42 I.L.M. 309)	No (lost on provisional measures and on the merits)
Yugoslavia	United States	Legality of Use of Force	1999 ICJ 916 (June 2) (provisional measures)	Yes (dismissed for lack of jurisdiction)
Germany	United States	LaGrand	2001 ICJ 466 (June 27) (merits judgment) 1999 ICJ 9 (March 3) (provisional measures)	No (lost on both interim measures and on the merits)
Paraguay	United States	Vienna Convention on Consular Relations	1998 ICJ 426 (removal) (November 10) 1998 ICJ 266 (April 9) (provisional measures)	No (lost on provisional measures)
Iran	United States	Oil Platforms	2003 ICJ 161 (Nov. 6) 1996 ICJ 803 (Dec. 12) (preliminary objections)	No (regarding jurisdictional) Yes (regarding merits)
Libya	United States	Questions of Interpretation and Application of the 1971 Montreal Convention arising from the Aerial Incident at Lockerbie	2003 ICJ 152 (Sept. 10) (discontinuance) 1998 ICJ 115 (Feb. 27) (preliminary objections) 1992 ICJ 114 (Apr. 14) (provisional measures)	Discontinued due to settlement
Iran	United States	Aerial Incident of 3 July 1988	1996 ICJ 9 (Feb. 22) (removal)	Discontinued due to settlement

(continued)

TABLE 4.2 (continued)

Applicant	Respondent	Name of case	Citation to case	U.S. overall prevailed?
United States	Italy	Elettronica Sicula S.p.A. (ELSI)	1989 ICJ 15 (July 20)	No (lost on merits)
Nicaragua	United States	Military and Paramilitary Activities in and against Nicaragua	1991 ICJ 47 (Sept. 26) (removal) 1986 ICJ 14 (June 27) 1984 ICJ 392 (Nov. 26) (jurisdictional)	Discontinued
Canada	United States	Delimitation of the Maritime Boundary in the Gulf of Maine Area	1984 ICJ 246 (Oct. 12)	Not applicable although U.S. position largely sustained
United States	Iran	United States Diplomatic and Consular Staff in Tehran	1980 ICJ 3 (May 24) 1979 ICJ 7 (Dec. 15) (provisional measures)	Yes (won on provisional measures and on the merits)
United States	Bulgaria	Aerial Incident of 27 July 1955	1960 ICJ 146 (May 30) (removal)	Discontinued
United States	USSR	Aerial Incident of 7 November 1954	1959 ICJ 276 (Oct. 7) (removal)	Dismissed by the Court
Switzerland	United States	Interhandel	1959 ICJ 6 (Mar. 21) 1957 ICJ 105 (Oct. 24) (Interim protection)	Dismissed by the Court
United States	USSR	Aerial Incident of 4 September 1954	1958 ICJ 158 (Dec. 9) (removal)	Dismissed by the Court
United States	Czechoslovakia	Aerial Incident of 10 March 1953	1956 ICJ 6 (Mar. 14)	Dismissed by the Court
United States	USSR	Aerial Incident of 7 October 1952	1956 I.C.J 9 (Mar. 14) (removal)	Dismissed by the Court
United States	Hungary	Treatment in Hungary of Aircraft and Crew of the United States of America	1954 ICJ 99 (July 12) (removal)	Dismissed by the Court

Applicant	Respondent	Name of case	Citation to case	U.S. overall prevailed?
United States	USSR	*Treatment in Hungary of Aircraft and Crew of the United States of America*	1954 ICJ 103 (July 12) (removal)	Dismissed by the Court
Italy	France, United Kingdom, United States	*Monetary Gold Removed from Rome in 1943*	1954 ICJ 19 (June 15)	Dismissed by the Court
France	United States	*Rights of Nationals of the United States of America in Morocco*	1952 ICJ 176	Yes on some issues

In ten of the twenty-one cases, the United States was the applicant (or jointly agreed to the submission of the case to the Court), and the United States

- secured a boundary decision regarded by many as favorable to the U.S. position,[106]
- won one on the merits,[107]
- lost one on the merits,[108] and
- had to withdraw or accept removal of seven cases against Soviet bloc states because of lack of jurisdiction.[109]

---

[106] See *Delimitation of the Maritime Boundary of the Gulf of Maine Area*, 1984 ICJ 246 (judgment of Oct. 12).

[107] *United States Diplomatic and Consular Staff in Tehran (U.S. v. Iran)*, 1980 ICJ 3 (judgment of May 24). Although this judgment was in the United States' favor, the Court concluded its decision by chastising the United States for its failed effort to rescue the hostages in April 1980 (involving the death of eight U.S. soldiers), which the United States undertook from a belief that "the situation in Iran posed mounting dangers to the safety of the hostages." *Id.*, para. 32. The Court informed the United States that the operation was "of a kind calculated to undermine respect for the judicial process in international relations." *Id.*, para. 93.

[108] See *Elettronica Sicula S.p.A. (ELSI) (U.S. v. Italy)*, 1989 ICJ 15 (judgment of July 20).

[109] *Aerial Incident of 27 July 1955 (U.S. v. Bulgaria)*, 1960 ICJ 146 (order of May 30); *Aerial Incident of 7 November 1954 (U.S. v. U.S.S.R.)*, 1959 ICJ 276 (order of Oct. 7); *Aerial Incident of 4 September 1954 (U.S. v. U.S.S.R.)*, 1958 ICJ 158 (order of Dec. 9); *Aerial Incident of 10 March 1953 (U.S. v. Czech.)*, 1956 ICJ 6 (order of Mar. 14); *Aerial Incident of 7 October 1952 (U.S. v. U.S.S.R.)*, 1956 ICJ 9 (order of Mar. 14); *Treatment in Hungary of Aircraft and Crew of the United States of America (U.S. v. Hungary)*, 1954 ICJ 99 (order of July 12); *Treatment in Hungary of Aircraft and Crew of the United States of America (U.S. v. U.S.S.R.)*, 1954 ICJ 103 (order of July 12).

In eleven cases, the United States was the respondent, and

- two were settled or withdrawn before a decision on the merits by the Court,[110]
- three were dismissed by the Court on jurisdictional or admissibility grounds,[111]
- one was won on the merits,[112]
- one was partially won and partially lost on the merits,[113] and
- four were lost on the merits.[114]

Of the cases lost on the merits, none was taken to a damages phase, so a monetary judgment against the United States has not arisen.

As for whether it is possible to detect any trends looking at these cases chronologically, there might be said to be four periods:

High hopes (1950–59)	Several efforts by the United States to invoke the jurisdiction of the Court, without success; at the same time, success in avoiding the Court's jurisdiction
Benign neglect (1960–79)	Lengthy period viewing the Court as either a failure or as inconsequential
Reengagement and rejection (1980–87)	Return to the Court to handle both a territorial dispute and a major political crisis; bitter rejection of the Court after losing a politically charged Cold War case
Playing defense (1988–present)	Declining to bring any cases; aggressively defending against cases brought by others; resisting the Court without breaking from it; a turn to other fora (WTO, NAFTA, ICSID, United Nations Convention on the Law of the Sea arbitration)

---

[110] See *Aerial Incident of 3 July 1988 (Iran v. U.S.)*, 1996 ICJ 9 (Feb. 22) (ordering discontinuance of the case following a settlement); *Questions of Interpretation and Application Arising from the Aerial Incident at Lockerbie (Libya v. U.S.)*, 2003 ICJ 152 (Order of Sept. 10) (ordering discontinuance of the case).

[111] See *Legality of Use of Force (Yugo. v U.S.)*, 1999 ICJ 916 (June 2); *Interhandel (Switz. v. U.S.)*, 1959 ICJ 6 (Mar. 21); *Monetary Gold (Italy v. U.S., Fr., U.K.)*, 1954 ICJ 19 (June 15).

[112] *Oil Platforms (Iran v. U.S.)* (ICJ Nov. 6, 2003), 42 ILM 1334 (2003). At the same time, the Court in the *Platforms* case, as discussed later, engaged in an extensive analysis on why the U.S. use of force could not be justified as a matter of international law.

[113] *Rights of Nationals of the United States in Morocco (Fr. v. U.S.)*, 1952 ICJ 176 (Aug. 27).

[114] *Military and Paramilitary Activities in and against Nicaragua (Nicar. v. U.S.)*, 1986 ICJ 14 (June 27); *Vienna Convention on Consular Relations (Para. v. U.S.)*, Provisional Measures, 1998 ICJ 11 (Order of Apr. 9), *reprinted in* 37 ILM 810 (1998) (this case reached only the provisional measures stage, when the United States lost); *LaGrand Case (Ger. v. U.S.)*, 2001 ICJ 466 (June 27), reprinted in 40 ILM (2001): 1069; *Avena and Other Mexican Nationals (Mex. v. U.S.)*, 2004 ICJ 12 (Mar. 31) (merits judgment). In most of these cases, the United States prevailed on certain arguments before the Court that at least narrowed the scope of the Court's findings.

In addition to the Court's contentious jurisdiction, from 1946 to 2007, the ICJ issued twenty-four advisory opinions. The United States was involved in twenty-two of those advisory opinions either in the form of written or oral pleadings.[115] Again, no other state has participated in advisory proceedings so frequently. It is more difficult to see any discernible trends in this practice, although it appears that the United States was more enthusiastic about using the Court's advisory opinion jurisdiction early in the life of the Court, when it had greater influence in the General Assembly. In more recent years (e.g., the *Nuclear Weapons* advisory opinion, the Israeli *Wall* advisory opinion), the United States has opposed the asking of certain questions to the Court and, once asked, has argued that the Court should decline to answer the question.

2. Recent Cases

I. *Oil Platforms* Case

The realism/institutionalism antinomy is evident in the recent *Oil Platforms* case. The institutionalism strain in U.S. thinking resulted in the acceptance of a compromissory clause in the 1955 U.S.-Iran Treaty of Amity, providing for ICJ jurisdiction over disputes arising under that treaty.[116] At the same time, the realism strain sought to avoid application of international law and international dispute resolution to core national interests, thus resulting in the inclusion of a clause stating that the Treaty of Amity "shall not preclude the application of measures ... necessary to protect ... essential security interests."[117] Iran, a state weaker than the United States in terms of military and economic power, used the Court to challenge the deployment of U.S. power in the Persian Gulf, specifically U.S. attacks against Iranian oil installations in 1987–88. After the filing of Iran's 1992 application initiating the case, American realism might have led the United States simply to ignore it – to decline to participate in proceedings in which it had no comparative advantage vis-à-vis Iran and in which it was politically vulnerable to adverse findings. Yet the early 1990s was a period of resurgent institutionalism in the United States. Institutionalist landmarks of this period, which would not have been possible without proactive U.S. engagement, were the extraordinary multilateralism of the UN-authorized action against Iraq, the operation in Somalia, and the creation of new tribunals such as the UN Compensation Commission, as well as the war crimes tribunals for the former Yugoslavia and Rwanda.

---

[115] *See* Table 4.3.
[116] See Treaty of Amity, Economic Relations and Consular Rights, U.S.-Iran, Aug. 15, 1955, art. XX(1)(2), 8 U.S.T. 899, 284 U.N.T.S. 93.
[117] *Id.*, art. XX(1)(d).

TABLE 4.3 *Advisory opinions at the International Court of Justice showing U.S. participation*

Name of opinion	Year decided	U.S. written pleading	Oral pleading
Legal Consequences of the Construction of a Wall in the Occupied Palestinian Territory	2004	Jan. 30, 2004	
Difference Relating to Immunity from Legal Process of a Special Rapporteur of the Commission on Human Rights	1999	Oct. 7, 1998	
Legality of the Threat or Use of Nuclear Weapons	1996	June 20, 1995	Oct. 30–Nov. 15, 1995
Legality of the Use by a State of Nuclear Weapons in Armed Conflict	1996	June 10, 1994	Oct. 30–Nov. 15, 1995
Applicability of Article VI, Section 22, of the Convention on the Privileges and Immunities of the United Nations	1989	July 31. 1989 ICJ Pleadings p. 208	
Applicability of the Obligation to Arbitrate under Section 21 of the United Nations Headquarters Agreement of 26 June 1947 (1988)	1988	Mar. 25, 1988 ICJ pleadings p. 187	
Application for Review of the Judgement No. 333 of the United Nations Administrative Tribunal	1987	Mar. 5, 1985 ICJ pleadings p. 230	
Application for Review of Judgment No. 273 of the United Nations Administrative Tribunal	1982	ICJ pleadings p. 160	
Interpretation of the Agreement of 25 March 1951 between the World Health Organization and Egypt	1980	Aug. 27, 1980 ICJ pleadings p. 182	Oct. 21–23, Dec. 20 1980 ICJ pleadings p. 230
Legal Consequences for State of the Continued Presence of South Africa in Namibia (South West Africa) notwithstanding Security Council Resolution 276	1971	ICJ pleadings p. 843	
Certain Expenses of the United Nations	1962	February 1962 ICJ pleadings p. 180	May 21, 1962 ICJ pleadings p. 282
Constitution of the Maritime Safety Committee of the Inter-Governmental Maritime Consultative Organization	1960	ICJ pleadings p. 114	Apr. 26–May 4 1960 and June 8, 1960 ICJ pleadings p. 262

Name of opinion	Year decided	U.S. written pleading	Oral pleading
Admissibility of Hearings of Petitioners by the Committee on South West Africa	1956	ICJ pleadings p. 26	
Judgments of the Administrative Tribunal of the International Labour Organization upon Complaints Made against United Nations Educational, Scientific and Cultural Organization	1956	ICJ pleadings p. 184	
Voting Procedure on Questions relating to Reports and Petitions concerning the Territory of South West Africa	1955	Feb. 25, 1955 ICJ pleadings p. 69	
Effect of Awards of Compensation Made by the United Nations Administrative Tribunal	1954	ICJ pleadings p. 131	June 10–14, 1954 and July 13, 1954 ICJ pleadings p. 280
Reservations to the Convention on the Prevention and Punishment of the Crime of Genocide	1951	ICJ pleadings p. 23	
International Status of South West Africa	1950	ICJ pleadings p. 85	
Competence of the General Assembly for the Admission of a State to the United Nations	1950	ICJ pleadings p. 110	
Interpretation of Peace Treaties with Bulgaria, Hungary, and Romania	1950	Nov. 7, 1949 ICJ pleadings p. 131	Feb. 28, Mar. 1, and Mar. 30, 1950 ICJ pleadings p. 242
Reparations for Injuries Suffered in the Service of the United Nations	1949	Feb. 14, 1914 ICJ pleadings p. 19	
Conditions of Admission of a State to Membership in the United Nations (Article 4 of the Charter)	1948	Jan. 29, 1948 ICJ pleadings p. 19	

Thus, consistent with the spirit of that remarkable age, the United States elected to participate in the proceedings and ultimately pursued a strategy with realism and institutionalism prongs. The realism prong emphasized that states had not given the Court plenary jurisdiction over disputes; that the Court's jurisdiction only extended so far as states had consented; and that, in this case, the United States had not consented to review of its military operations through the vehicle of a largely commercial treaty. The United States succeeded on most of these points, successfully winnowing Iran's claims down to a single treaty provision concerning freedom of commerce between the two states[118] and convincing the bench that such commerce was not disrupted by the attacks on the oil platforms.[119]

At the same time, the United States had an institutionalist prong to its case. Arguing that the actions it took were necessary to protect "essential security interests" (and thus outside the scope of the treaty), the United States in essence sought to convince the Court that the attacks on Iranian oil platforms were legitimate self-defense. This prong held out hope that the Court would serve as an impartial arbiter of complicated facts and would acknowledge the rights of even a powerful state to defend itself, without an eye to the U.S. invasion of Iraq unfolding at the same time as oral hearings in the case. On this prong, the United States failed. Even though the Court found that the United States had not violated the Treaty of Amity by interrupting bilateral commerce with Iran, it had engaged in an extensive analysis of why the attacks on the oil platforms violated international law on the use of force, an analysis regarded as dicta thereafter by a U.S. Department of State legal adviser.[120]

In the *Oil Platforms* judgment, the Court neglected to resort to one of the mediating techniques available to address the realism/institutionalism antimony. The Court's willingness to address the legality of the use of force by the United States even though the Court had no jurisdiction over the case is a "pushing back" against the realist approach of denying the Court plenary jurisdiction. Although such action, or reaction, by the Court may be understandable, there may be collateral consequences.

First, the judgment exposes the Court to arguments that it was not acting as an impartial decision maker but was set on lecturing the United States at a time when use of military force in Iraq in 2003 was being harshly criticized.[121] Further, the fact that the "essential security interests" clause failed to insulate the United States from the Court casts into doubt the efficacy of such provisions in myriad existing treaties providing for ICJ jurisdiction and will encourage the U.S. government to periodically consider whether and how it might withdraw from or modify such treaties to avoid litigation.[122] Certainly, the cost-to-benefit

---

[118] *Id.*, art. X(1); *see Oil Platforms (Iran. v. U.S.)*, 1996 ICJ 803 (judgment on preliminary objections).

[119] *See Oil Platforms (Iran. v. U.S.)*, 2003 ICJ 161 (Nov. 6), paras. 98–99.

[120] *See* William H. Taft IV, *Self-Defense and the* Oil Platforms *Decision*, 29 Yale J. Int'l L. 295 (2004). The article identifies the author as Legal Adviser, U.S. Department of State, and contains no disclaimer that the views are personal.

[121] *See*, e.g., David H. Small, *The Oil Platforms Case: Jurisdiction through the – Closed – Eye of the Needle*, 3 L. & Prac. Int'l Courts & Tribunals 113 (2004) (critique by Organisation for Economic Co-operation and Development director of legal affairs, in his personal capacity).

[122] As noted in the next section, the United States terminated its acceptance of the Court's jurisdiction in March 2005 over matters arising under the Vienna Convention on Consular Relations.

analysis of this particular Treaty of Amity strongly suggests that it should be terminated: the United States has engaged in little economic activity and no consular activity with Iran for twenty-five years,[123] yet it is exposed at any time to suit by Iran under the treaty's compromissory clause. Moreover, many in the U.S. government will perceive the Court's willingness to lecture the United States as confirmation that compromissory clauses providing for the Court's jurisdiction should not be included in new treaties. Finally, the ultimate effect of the decision is probably to foreclose any possibility of U.S. adherence to the Court's compulsory jurisdiction. If there is no way to carve out national security interests without inviting the judges to engage in an extended discussion of the underlying matter, even in situations in which the United States ultimately succeeds in avoiding the Court's jurisdiction, then many will conclude that the United States has no business at the Peace Palace.

II. *Israeli Wall* Advisory Opinion

The United States' tendency toward exceptionalism may be seen in its attitude toward the recent advisory opinion on the legality of the barrier by Israel in the occupied West Bank of the Jordan River. On December 8, 2003, the General Assembly adopted a resolution asking the ICJ for an advisory opinion on "the legal consequences arising from the construction of the wall being built by Israel, the occupying Power, in the Occupied Palestinian Territory, including in and around East Jerusalem."[124] The resolution received ninety votes in favor, seventy-four abstentions, and eight opposed (including the United States). In opposing the resolution, the U.S. representative stated:

> The international community has long recognized that resolution of the [Israeli-Palestinian] conflict must be through negotiated settlement, as called for in Security Council resolutions 242 (1967) and 338 (1973). That was spelled out clearly to the parties in the terms of reference of the Madrid Peace Conference of 1991. Involving the International Court of Justice in this conflict is inconsistent with that approach and could actually delay a two-State solution and negatively impact road map implementation. Furthermore, referral of this issue to the International Court of Justice risks politicizing the Court. It will not advance the Court's ability to contribute to global security, nor will it advance the prospects of peace.[125]

---

[123] There do remain U.S. diplomatic and consular properties in Iran, although they are principally protected under other treaties. Arguably the United States benefited from the Treaty of Amity when private U.S. claims were being adjudicated before the Iran-U.S. Claims Tribunal, because the tribunal's decisions on occasion referred to certain standards set forth in the treaty. All U.S. private claims before the tribunal, however, have now been resolved.

[124] GA Res. ES-10/14 (Dec. 12, 2003).

[125] U.N. Doc. A/ES-10/PV.23, at 19 (Dec. 8, 2003).

The United States instead favored pursuing the "Quartet's road map" – a plan that the United States, the European Union, the Russian Federation, and the UN secretary-general developed in 2003 to further the process (initiated at the 1991 Madrid Conference) for peacefully resolving the Israeli-Palestinian conflict.[126] Thus, the United States was committed to an approach to the Israeli-Palestinian conflict entailing diplomacy by a restricted group of powers, not by the international community at large. The United States opposed submitting this matter to the World Court because doing so could intrude on the unique ability of the major powers to influence and shape the peace process.

Of course, in its written pleadings to the Court, the United States did not advance legal arguments predicated on exceptionalism, for there was no legal basis for doing so. Instead, it sought to take advantage of some of the mediating techniques referred to earlier. It argued that the Court should decline to answer the question of grounds of judicial propriety because the question was not an abstract inquiry, but, in essence, a bilateral dispute in disguise.[127] The United States hoped to convince the judges that they would be stepping over the bounds of the structural constraints on the Court's jurisdiction if they were to pass upon a dispute when the relevant parties to that dispute had not consented to jurisdiction. Implicit in this argument was a further argument that it was improper to decide a bilateral dispute between two parties when one of the parties had not yet even been recognized by the UN as a sovereign state (a decision in part controlled by the Security Council) and, therefore, could not appear before the Court. Further, the United States stressed that it was not for the Court to address an issue that was more properly addressed through political negotiations.[128]

Ultimately, the Court determined that answering the question would not impede the Middle East peace process. That conclusion was no doubt shared by a majority of states represented in the General Assembly, as was the Court's conclusion on the merits that Israel was violating international law by constructing the barrier. Yet from the perspective of American exceptionalism, the majority of states can very well be wrong about whether it is a good idea

---

[126] See Letter Dated 7 May 2003 from the Secretary-General Addressed to the President of the Security Council, annex, U.N.Doc. S/2003/529 (May 7, 2003) (containing "A Performance-Based Road Map to a Permanent Two-State Solution to the Israeli-Palestinian Conflict").

[127] Written Statement of the United States of America, paras. 3.3–3.10 (filed Jan. 30, 2004), Legal Consequences of the Construction of a Wall in the Occupied Palestinian Territory, Advisory Opinion. 2004 ICJ 136 (July 9). The United States made no oral submissions to the Court.

[128] Written Statement of the United States of America, para. 4.6 ("Any expression of legal views by the Court on the permanent status issues can be expected to make the necessary political accommodations between the parties on these issues far more difficult or even impossible.")

to involve the Court in this issue, and also misguided more generally in their opposition to Israeli policies. The Court's attitude in the advisory opinion may well reflect the dominant views of policy makers in other countries, but for the exceptionalist, that does not mean the Court is right.

III. Breard/LaGrand/Avena Cases

The recent cases concerning the treatment of aliens on death row in the United States highlights the antinomy created by the American democratic and constitutional tradition. The crux of the *Breard/LaGrand/Avena* line of cases is that aliens arrested by law enforcement officials often have not been advised of their right to have their consulate notified of their arrest, something states party to the Vienna Convention on Consular Relations (Vienna Convention) have agreed to do.[129] Some aliens, thereafter, have been convicted of serious crimes and sentenced to death. Paraguay, Germany, and Mexico each brought a case against the United States before the ICJ by invoking the Optional Protocol Concerning Compulsory Settlement of Disputes to the Vienna Convention on Consular Relations.[130] In each instance, the applicant asked the Court to indicate provisional measures of protection – namely, that the individuals would not be executed prior to a decision by the Court on the merits. Germany and Mexico also asked the Court for decisions on the merits regarding whether the United States had violated its obligations under the Vienna Convention and what consequences should flow from those violations. The United States has fully participated (when permitted) in all aspects of these cases before the Court, presenting extensive written and oral pleadings.

The U.S. reaction to the *Breard/LaGrand/Avena* line of cases may be considered in terms of both the Court's provisional orders and the decisions on the merits. In all three cases, the Court issued an order on provisional measures that the United States "take all measures at its disposal to ensure" (*Breard, LaGrand*) or "all measures necessary to ensure" (*Avena*) that the relevant aliens not be executed pending a final decision by the Court.[131] Prior to the Court's final judgment in the *LaGrand* case, the U.S. government argued both to the ICJ and to U.S. courts that such an order on provisional measures

---

[129] Apr. 24, 1963, art. 36, 21 U.S.T. 77, 101, 596 U.N.T.S. 261, 292.

[130] Apr. 24, 1963, 21 U.S.T. 325, 596 U.N.T.S. 487.

[131] Vienna Convention on Consular Relations (Para. v. U.S.), Provisional Measures, 1998 ICJ 11 (Order of Apr. 9), *reprinted in* 37 ILM 810, 819 (1998); Vienna Convention on Consular Relations (F.R.G. v. U.S.), Provisional Measures, 1999 ICJ 9 (Order of Mar. 3), *reprinted in* 38 ILM 308, 310 (1999); *Avena and Other Mexican Nationals (Mex. v. U.S.)*, Provisional Measures (Feb. 5, 2003), *reprinted in* 42 ILM 309, para. 59 (2003); *see* William Aceves, Case Report, 97 Am. J. Int'l L. 923 (2003).

was not legally binding and further that it had no direct effect in the U.S. legal system. Such a position has realism overtones, but the dominant feature appears to have been a concern to preserve the constitutional autonomy of the several states and a political concern with intruding on the democratic decision by those states to use the death penalty in their penal processes. Weighing that concern against the reality that the American constitutional system does incorporate international law, the U.S. government looked for credible legal arguments for why the Court's order was not binding and not a part of U.S. law. Thus, after the first provisional measures order was issued on April 9, 1998, in the *Breard* case, the U.S. Department of Justice filed a brief before the U.S. Supreme Court stating,

> The better reasoned position is that such an order is not binding. Article 41(1) of the ICJ statute provides that the ICJ shall have "the power to indicate any provisional measures which ought to be taken to preserve the respective rights of either power." Article 41(2) further states that, "[p]ending the final decision [of the ICJ], notice of the measures suggested shall forthwith be given to the parties and the Security Council." The use of precatory language ("indicate," "ought to be taken," "suggested") instead of stronger language (e.g.: the ICJ may "order" provisional measures that "shall" be taken) strongly supports a conclusion that ICJ provisional measures are not binding on the parties. The distinction in Article 41(2) between the "final decision" ultimately foreseen and the "measures suggested" in the interim also suggests that the "measures suggested" are not binding.
>
> Petitioners have relied on the United Nations Charter to argue that provisional measures are binding, but the language of the Charter does not support that conclusion. Article 94(1) provides that "[e]ach member... undertakes to comply with the decision of the [ICJ] in any case to which it is a party." "The decision," in the context of Article 94(1) of the Charter, evidently refers to the final decision of the International Court. Article 94(2) of the Charter elaborates that "[i]f any party to a case fails to perform the obligations incumbent upon it by a judgment rendered by the [ICJ], the other party may have recourse to the Security Council." Significantly, the Security Council has never acted to enforce provisional measures indicated by the ICJ. See Restatement [Third on the Foreign Relations Law of the United States], at 368 (discussing Security Council's response to ICJ's order indicating provisional measures in dispute between United Kingdom and Iran).
>
> Moreover, the ICJ itself has never concluded that provisional measures are binding on the parties to a dispute. That court has indicated provisional measures in seven other cases of which we are aware; in most of those cases,

the order indicating provisional measures was not regarded as binding by the respondent.[132]

In addition to these representations to the U.S. Supreme Court, the U.S. secretary of state sent a letter to the governor of Virginia requesting that he stay the execution of Breard because the "execution of Mr. Breard in the face of the Court's April 9 action could be seen as a denial by the United States of the significance of international law and the Court's processes in its international relations and thereby limit our ability to ensure that Americans are protected when living or traveling abroad."[133] Here, again, may be seen a balancing act, in which the State Department sought to uphold U.S. adherence to international law and institutions while respecting the constitutional autonomy of Virginia.

The Supreme Court denied the petitions for certiorari that had been filed in the case.[134] It did not focus on the binding nature of the ICJ's provisional measures order. Rather, it said that it was "clear that Breard procedurally defaulted his claim, if any, under the Vienna Convention by failing to raise that claim in the state courts."[135] Further, the Court stated,

> [W]hile we should give respectful consideration to the interpretation of an international treaty rendered by an international court with jurisdiction to interpret such, it has been recognized in international law that, absent a clear and express statement to the contrary, the procedural rules of the forum State govern the implementation of the treaty in that State.... This proposition is embodied in the Vienna Convention itself, which provides that the rights expressed in the Convention "shall be exercised in conformity with the laws and regulations of the receiving State," provided that "said laws and regulations must enable full effect to be given to the purposes for which the rights accorded under this Article are intended." Article 36(2), 21 U.S. T., at 101....
>
> Second, although treaties are recognized by our Constitution as the supreme law of the land, that status is no less true of provisions of the Constitution itself, to which rules of procedural default apply. We have held "that an Act of Congress ... is on a full parity with a treaty, and that when a statute which is subsequent in time is inconsistent with a treaty, the statute to the extent of conflict renders the treaty null." *Reid v. Covert*, 354 U.S. 1, 18 (1957) (plurality opinion).... The Vienna Convention – which arguably confers on

---

[132] Brief for the United States as *Amicus Curiae* at 46–51, *Breard v. Greene*, 523 U.S. 371 (1998) (Nos. 97–1390, 97–8214) (footnote omitted).
[133] Letter from Madeleine K. Albright, U.S. secretary of state, to James S. Gilmore III, governor of Virginia (Apr. 13, 1998), partially reprinted in 92 Am. J. Int'l L. 671–72 (1998).
[134] *Breard v. Greene*, 523 U.S. 371 (1998).
[135] *Id.* at 373.

an individual the right to consular assistance following arrest – has continuously been in effect since 1969. But in 1996, before Breard filed his habeas petition raising claims under the Vienna Convention, Congress enacted the Antiterrorism and Effective Death Penalty Act (AEDPA), which provides that a habeas petitioner alleging that he is held in violation of "treaties of the United States" will, as a general rule, not be afforded an evidentiary hearing if he "has failed to develop the factual basis of [the] claim in State court proceedings." 28 U.S.C. § 2254(a), (e)(2) [(2000]).[136]

After the Supreme Court denied the petitions for certiorari, the governor of Virginia decided not to stay the execution, and Breard was executed.

The World Court's order on provisional measures in the *LaGrand* case was issued on March 3, 1999, at 7 P.M. (Hague time) without having heard the views of the U.S. government.[137] In the late afternoon of March 3, the U.S. government transmitted the order to the governor of Arizona. Just before the scheduled execution, Germany filed a case before the U.S. Supreme Court against the United States and Arizona seeking a temporary restraining order or preliminary injunction to enforce the order of the ICJ. The U.S. solicitor general filed a letter opposing any stay, asserting that the "Vienna Convention does not furnish a basis for this Court to grant a stay of execution," and that "an order of the International Court of Justice indicating provisional measures is not binding and does not furnish a basis for judicial relief." In declining to exercise its original jurisdiction (with two justices dissenting), the Supreme Court explained in part,

> [A] foreign government's ability here to assert a claim against a State [i.e., Arizona] is without evident support in the Vienna Convention and in probable contravention of the Eleventh Amendment [to the U.S. Constitution] principles. This action was filed within only two hours of a scheduled execution that was ordered on January 15, 1999, based upon a sentence imposed by Arizona in 1984, about which the Federal Republic of Germany learned in 1992. Given the tardiness of the pleas and the jurisdictional barriers they implicate, we decline to exercise our original jurisdiction.[138]

In dissent, Justices Breyer and Stevens said that they favored a stay of the execution to give more time to brief fully "the jurisdictional and international

---

[136] *Id.*

[137] The ICJ's order was, for the first time, based wholly on the views of one party, without providing the opportunity to receive the views of the other party (here the United States) in writing or by oral hearing. The Court characterized its order as based on Article 75(1) of the Rules of the Court, which permits the Court to examine *proprio motu* (by its own motion) whether provisional measures should be ordered, although in fact there had been a request by Germany for such measures.

[138] *Germany v. United States*, 526 U.S. 111, 112 (1999).

legal issues involved."[139] The governor of Arizona decided not to stay. Walter LaGrand was executed on March 4, 1999.[140]

Although the executions in *Breard* and *LaGrand* in the face of the ICJ's order on the surface may suggest a complete U.S. disregard for the views of the Court, the United States took seriously the issue of whether it was bound by such orders and reached an entirely plausible conclusion that it was not. Yet the animating feature of the American position was the problem presented by federal-state relations. Criminal justice in the United States is a matter almost entirely left to the several states; persons committing crimes in this country are typically tried under state laws and often in state courts. Further, whether to adopt the death penalty is a matter left to each state; some have elected to include the death penalty as a possible sanction, whereas others have abolished or never had it. Those laws are adopted by the peoples of the states, through enactments by elected state legislators. The decision to convict a violent criminal and to impose the death penalty is a matter decided by the local community in the form of an indictment by a grand jury and a conviction and sentencing by a jury of the offender's peers. For the federal government to intrude on that process by declaring that an execution must be stayed because of the decision of a court consisting almost entirely of foreigners residing an ocean away would have been an extraordinary and deeply unpopular undertaking by any administration, Democratic or Republican.

Despite the executions in *Breard* and *LaGrand*, the U.S. government embarked on an aggressive campaign to educate and train state law enforcement officers regarding obligations arising under the Vienna Convention, to the point of printing cards that officers were to carry with them and read out when arresting an alien.[141] Moreover, after the Court held, in its judgment on the merits of the *LaGrand* case,[142] that provisional measures orders were binding and then the further provisional measures order was issued in the *Avena* case,[143] the United States did not publicly reject the *Avena* measures. Rather, it sought to implement them, albeit with extraordinary difficulty, principally

---

[139] *Id.* at 112–13.

[140] *See World Court's Effort to Stay Execution Fails*, Wash. Post, Mar. 4, 1999, at A16.

[141] *See* U.S. Dep't of State, Consular Notification and Access, at http://travel.state.gov/law/consular/consular_636.html; *see also* LaGrand (Ger. v. U.S.), 2001 ICJ 466, at para. 121, 123–24 (June 27), reprinted in 40 ILM 1069 (2001); Verbatim Record (Jan. 21, 2003), *Avena and Other Mexican Nationals (Mex. v. U.S.)*, Provisional Measures, ICJ Doc. CR 2003/2, paras. 3.13–3.22.

[142] *LaGrand Case (Ger. v. U.S.)*, Judgment, 2001 ICJ 466 (June 27), reprinted in 40 ILM 1069 (2001); *see* William J. Aceves, Case Report, 96 Am. J. Int'l L. 210 (2002).

[143] *Avena* (Provisional Measures), *supra* note 131, at para. 59.

by encouraging the commutation of death sentences of the relevant convicts by governors or parole boards.[144]

One of the central problems for the federal government in these cases concerned the "procedural default rule," a rule designed to help limit federal court review of state court decisions. In brief, under the procedural default rule, state law procedural rulings that are both sufficiently independent from federal law and adequate to sustain the judgment against the defendant ("procedural defaults") often preclude consideration of the merits of federal legal claims. Thus, if a defendant fails to file in state court proceedings a timely motion for a new trial or sentencing proceeding because he was not informed of his right to request consular notification, that procedural failure may bar filing such a motion not only thereafter before that state's courts but also before federal courts.

Turning to the judgments on the merits in *LaGrand* and *Avena*,[145] the Court found that the United States had violated its obligations under the Vienna Convention by not informing the aliens of their right of consular notification, by not notifying their consulates of their detentions, and by effectively depriving the consulates of the ability to communicate with and have access to the aliens. In both cases, the Court also found that the failure to provide judicial review of the aliens' convictions and sentences in light of the lack of notification constituted a further violation of the Vienna Convention. As for what the United States must do prospectively, in *LaGrand* the Court stated that, "should nationals of the Federal Republic of Germany nonetheless be sentenced to severe penalties," without their right to consular notification having been respected, the United States, "by means of its own choosing, shall allow the review and reconsideration of the conviction and sentence by taking account of the violation of the rights set forth" in the Vienna Convention.[146] The Court reached a similar finding on "review and reconsideration" with respect to the some fifty Mexican nationals at issue in the *Avena* case.[147] As to how such "review and reconsideration" should occur, the International Court found in both *LaGrand* and *Avena* that a procedural default rule cannot justify precluding review of a petitioner's claim.[148] Further, the Court found in both

---

[144] *See* Counter-Memorial of the United States, paras. 5.6–5.9 (Nov. 3, 2003), *Avena and Other Mexican Nationals (Mex. v. U.S.)*, Judgment (Mar. 31, 2004).

[145] *Avena and Other Mexican Nationals (Mex. v. U.S.)*, Judgment, 2004 ICJ 12 (Mar. 31), reprinted in 43 ILM 581 (2004); *see* Dinah L. Shelton, *Case Report*, 98 Am. J. Int'l L. 559 (2004).

[146] *LaGrand* (Judgment), *supra* note 142, para. 128(7).

[147] *Avena* (Judgment), *supra* note 145, para. 153(9).

[148] *LaGrand* (Judgment), *supra* note 142, paras. 90–91; *Avena* (Judgment), *supra* note 145, paras. 110–13, 153.

cases that Article 36 of the Vienna Convention creates "individual rights," which arguably means rights enforceable in U.S. courts.[149] Apparently with an eye to the U.S. approach of relying on governors and parole boards to commute death sentences in light of the Vienna Convention violations, the Court in *Avena* also stated that the process must entail "a procedure which guarantees that full weight is given to the violations of the rights set forth in the Vienna Convention" and "should occur within the overall judicial proceedings relating to the individual defendant concerned."[150] The Court specifically noted that "the clemency process, as currently practised within the United States criminal justice system, does not appear to meet the requirements."[151]

The initial fallout from the decisions on the merits in *LaGrand* and *Avena* is a story of the federal government encouraging the various states to take into account the decisions of the ICJ, without actually telling the states that they must do so as a matter of federal law. Not surprisingly, different courts went in different directions. In *Madej v. Schomig*, a federal district court found that the *LaGrand* judgment on the merits foreclosed strict reliance by U.S. courts on the procedural default rule for violations of the Vienna Convention.[152] In *Torres v. Oklahoma*, a concurring state court judge found that the state court was bound by the Vienna Convention Optional Protocol to abide by the International Court's *Avena* decision.[153] At the same time, a state court in *Cauthern v. Tennessee* concluded that, notwithstanding the International Court's judgments, the Vienna Convention does not create an individual right that is privately enforceable in the United States nor that violations of the Vienna Convention may be raised as part of a petition for postconviction relief.[154] Similarly, in *Medellín v. Dretke*, the Fifth Circuit found that the Supreme Court's order denying certiorari in the *Breard* case supported application of the procedural default rule regardless of what the International Court said in its *LaGrand* and *Avena* judgments, and further

---

[149] What the Court actually said was "Article 36, paragraph 1, creates individual rights, which, by virtue of Article I of the Optional Protocol, may be invoked in this Court by the national State of the detained person." *LaGrand* (Judgment), *supra* note 142, para. 77.

[150] *Avena* (Judgment), *supra* note 145, paras. 139–40.

[151] *Id.*, para. 143.

[152] *Madej v. Schomig*, 223 F.Supp.2d 968 (N.D. Ill. 2002).

[153] *Torres v. Oklahoma*, No. PCD-04-442, slip. op. at 2–5, 8–12 (Okla. Crim. App. May 13, 2004) (Chapel, J., concurring) (footnotes omitted), reprinted in 43 ILM 1227 (2004).

[154] *Cauthern v. Tennessee*, 145 S.W.3d 571 (Tenn. Crim. App. 2004); *see also United States v. Minjares-Alvarez*, 264 F.3d 980 (10th Cir. 2001); State v. Issa, 93 Ohio St. 3d 49 (2001) (according little value to the *LaGrand* judgment); *see generally* Christopher J. Le Mon, *Post-Avena Application of the Vienna Convention on Consular Relations by United States Courts*, 18 Leiden J. Int'l L. 215 (2005).

that the Vienna Convention did not create an individual right that is privately enforceable.[155]

In December 2004, the Supreme Court granted a writ of certiorari in the *Medellín* case. The U.S. government filed in February 2005 an amicus brief urging the Court to affirm the Court of Appeals. Playing strongly to the vision of democratic and constitutional autonomy, the government argued that Article 36 of the Vienna Convention does not provide a basis for private judicial enforcement in U.S. courts. The government supported this position through an analysis of the language and structure of the Convention (read in context), its ratification history, and state practice, as well as the long-standing position of the Executive Branch.[156] Although the International Court's position might imply a right of private judicial enforcement in U.S. courts, the government asserted, "While the ICJ's understanding of the Convention's requirements is entitled to respectful consideration, it is ultimately the responsibility of this [U.S. Supreme] Court to interpret the meaning of a federal treaty."[157] The government also argued that the Convention does not preclude application by U.S. courts of the procedural default rule. The government stated that the International Court was simply wrong when it found otherwise:

> [T]he ICJ in *LaGrand* concluded that applying procedural default to bar consideration of a challenge to a defendant's conviction and sentence violates [Vienna Convention] Article 36(2)'s requirement that laws of the forum state "must enable full effect to be given to the purposes for which the rights accorded under this Article are intended." But a general "full effect" clause cannot be understood to override application of rules that are as deeply embedded in the criminal justice system as rules of procedural default.... [W]hile the ICJ's interpretation of Article 36(2) is entitled to respectful consideration, it does not provide a basis for the [U.S. Supreme] Court to overrule its controlling decision in Breard.[158]

As for whether the International Court's decision in the *Avena* judgment could itself be privately enforced in U.S. courts, the government argued that it could not. The arguments were as follows: (1) although the United States adhered to the Optional Protocol to the Vienna Convention, that protocol operates only to grant jurisdiction to the ICJ over Vienna Convention disputes – it does not commit the United States to comply with the ICJ's judgment, nor does it make

---

[155] *Medellín v. Dretke*, 371 F.3d 270 (5th Cir. 2004). For a similar result before the Fifth Circuit in a different case, see *Plata v. Dretke*, 2004 WL 1814089 (5th Cir. Aug. 16, 2004).

[156] *See* Brief for the United States as Amicus Curiae Supporting Respondent, Medellín v. Dretke, No. 04-5928, at 18–30 (U.S.) (filed February 28, 2005).

[157] *Id.*, at 30.

[158] *Id.* at 31, 33.

the judgment privately enforceable in a criminal proceeding by an individual; (2) rather, U.S. compliance with ICJ judgments is addressed in the UN Charter, which creates an international duty upon the United States to comply with the judgment[159] but does not make the ICJ judgment privately enforceable in court; (3) the mechanism for taking noncompliance before the UN Security Council confirms that ICJ judgments were not meant to be privately enforceable; (4) the U.S. ratification history confirms this interpretation, as does the one U.S. court decision that has addressed the matter; (5) the ICJ Statute states that ICJ judgments have no binding effect except between the parties in the case, thus negating the possibility of private judicial enforcement; and (6) the ICJ itself stated that the U.S. obligation was to provide, *by means of its own choosing*, review and reconsideration, which means that the U.S. political branches are entitled to pursue the matter by a choice of their means.[160]

Despite this strong statement in favor of autonomy, the government accepted that it had an international obligation to abide by the ICJ's judgment and, further, decided that it had to do something about that obligation vis-à-vis the several states. Accordingly, President Bush on February 28, 2005, issued a memorandum to the Attorney General stating,

> The United States is a party to the Vienna Convention on Consular Relations (the "Convention") and the Convention's Optional Protocol Concerning the Compulsory Settlement of Disputes (Optional Protocol), which gives the International Court of Justice (ICJ) jurisdiction to decide disputes concerning the "interpretation and application" of the Convention.
>
> I have determined, pursuant to the authority vested in me as President by the Constitution and the laws of the United States of America, that the United States will discharge its international obligations under the decision of the International Court of Justice in the Case Concerning Avena and Other Mexican Nationals (*Mexico v. United States of America*) (*Avena*), 2004 ICJ 128 (Mar. 31), by having State courts give effect to the decision in accordance with general principles of comity in cases filed by the 51 Mexican nationals addressed in that decision.[161]

Thus, although the U.S. government argued against the direct incorporation into domestic law of international obligations emanating from the Vienna Convention or from the judgments of the International Court, the government proceeded to demand compliance by the states with the *Avena* judgment on the

---

[159] The U.S. government interpreted the "judgment" of the International Court to apply only to the dispositif, not to the Court's legal reasoning. *Id.*, at 38–39, n. 12.

[160] *Id.*, at 33–38.

[161] *See* Brief for the United States as Amicus Curiae, *supra* note 156, at attachment (memorandum from President George W. Bush for the Attorney General dated February 28, 2005).

basis of the president's "constitutional foreign affairs authority and his authority under Article 94 of the U.N. Charter."[162] In November 2006, the Texas Court of Criminal Appeals rejected the U.S. government's approach, stating that

> we hold that the President's memorandum ordering us to give effect to the ICJ *Avena* decision cannot be sustained under the express or implied constitutional powers of the President relied on by *Medellín* and the United States or under any power granted to the President by an act of Congress cited by *Medellín* and the United States. As such, the President has violated the separation of powers doctrine by intruding into the domain of the judiciary, and therefore, *Medellín* cannot show that the President's memorandum preempts [Texas procedural law].[163]

Finally, in *Medellín v. Texas*, the Supreme Court concluded that although the international treaties relating to consular relations and the International Court's jurisdiction may establish an *international* commitment upon the United States, neither the treaties at issue nor the International Court's decision established binding *internal* U.S. law in the absence of implementing legislation. Moreover, the Supreme Court found that the president lacks the power on his own to enforce international treaties or decisions of the International Court of Justice as against Texas.[164]

Overall, the U.S. government's approach can be seen within the context of the third antimony. The government's approach maintained the overall democratic and constitutional autonomy of the United States while simultaneously seeking to achieve compliance *as a matter of comity* with the ICJ's judgment. At the same time, the United States moved to ensure that it would never again be placed in such a position. On March 7, 2005, the government informed the UN secretary-general that it terminated its adherence to the Optional Protocol, thereby foreclosing future cases against the United States before the International Court based on the basis of that protocol.[165]

When one steps back from the intricacies of these cases, the overall thrust of both the Supreme Court's and ICJ's decisions may reflect an unfortunate movement away from the normal approaches for mediating the autonomous national law/embedded national law antinomy. In the context of both *Breard*

---

[162] *See id.*, at 42. The United States cited to various cases in support of the president's foreign affairs power: *United States v. Curtiss-Wright Exp. Corp.*, 299 U.S. 304 (1936); *Amer. Ins. Assoc. v. Garamendi*, 539 U.S. 396 (2003); *Dames & Moore v. Regan*, 453 U.S. 654 (1981); *United States v. Pink*, 315 U.S. 203 (1942); *United States v. Belmont*, 301 U.S. 324 (1937).

[163] *Ex Parte José Ernesto Medellín*, 223 S.W.3d 315, 348 (Tex. Crim. App. 2006).

[164] 128 S. Ct. 1346 (2008).

[165] Journal of the United Nations: Programme of Meetings and Agenda, No. 2005/48, at 13 (Mar. 12, 2005) (reporting receipt of the withdrawal on Mar. 7); *see* Charles Lane, *U.S. Quits Pact Used in Capital Cases*, Wash. Post, Mar. 10, 2005, at A1.

and *LaGrand*, the U.S. Supreme Court showed little sensitivity in trying to find a way forward for the United States in a manner consistent with its international obligations. The long-standing approach of the Supreme Court under the *Charming Betsy* doctrine[166] to interpret U.S. law, whenever possible and however possible, to avoid clashes with international law seems quite absent through the course of these proceedings. The issue of the death penalty is politically charged in the United States, and the issue of federalism is complicated, but the Supreme Court has found ways to uphold international commitments, even in recent years and even in situations in which federalism concerns are squarely at stake.[167]

As for the International Court, normally international dispute fora have accepted that they have the power to determine that a state has acted unlawfully and, as a consequence, to order reparations. Such fora, however, have generally avoided ordering of specific performance by a state, preferring not to interfere in internal national processes. Although ordering that specific acts be taken internally is by no means unprecedented,[168] international fora, by and large, accept that the autonomy of states must be respected – that there is only so far an international court or tribunal may go before its authority will be rejected. In the *Breard/LaGrand/Avena* line of cases, the ICJ showed considerable sensitivity to considerations of autonomy when it ordered that the United States, "by means of its own choosing . . . allow the review and reconsideration" of convictions and sentences. Yet despite this, the Court was remarkably willing to assume an authority to oversee the detailed circumstances of criminal law cases unfolding before U.S. state and federal courts, concerning crimes committed in the United States against U.S. nationals, and to order the United States to undertake further review of the cases through its judicial system. Were the Court's judgments firmly anchored in language of the Vienna Convention setting forth what type of remedy should flow from a violation, then the resistance of the United States to the Court's judgments would be much less defensible. As it is, however, it is understandable that the United States was a bit surprised to find that, by joining the Vienna Convention's Optional Protocol, it inadvertently laid the basis for the ICJ to upend U.S. state court proceedings.

---

[166] *See supra* note 17.

[167] *See, e.g., Garamendi, supra* note 162.

[168] *See, e.g., Arrest Warrant of 11 April 2000* (D.R.C. v. Belg.), 2002 ICJ 33 (ordering Belgium to cancel an arrest warrant issued by a Belgian judicial official because the warrant violated the international immunity of the Congo minister of foreign affairs). However, it may be noted that, in the *Arrest Warrant* case, the issuing of the arrest warrant itself was the unlawful act, whereas in *Breard/LaGrand/Avena* cases the conviction and death sentence were not themselves the unlawful acts.

For Europeans, the concept of a supranational court reaching decisions that directly affect the lives of individuals is nothing new; the European Court on Human Rights has existed for almost fifty years and has handed down hundreds of cases that reach deeply into the national legal systems of EU member states. Likewise, the European Court of Justice reaches directly into national legal systems in various ways. Regional human rights courts in the Americas and now in Africa have a less strong pedigree, but nevertheless, for states adhering to their jurisdiction, the concept of such supranational adjudication as having effects on internal decision making is understood. For Americans, however, there is no such tradition of allowing intrusion into the U.S. legal system (for example, the United States has never accepted the jurisdiction of the Inter-American Court of Human Rights).

One often sees reference to U.S. willingness to adhere to compulsory dispute settlement before the WTO, and explanations for doing so tend to focus on trade law being a more "technical" area or that the United States is in a relatively weaker position vis-à-vis other states (China, the EU, Japan) on trade matters than on other matters. Those issues are important, but it should also be noted that the outcome of WTO decision making does not directly intrude into the U.S. legal system. There is no mechanism by which a WTO panel decision has a legally binding effect on an internal U.S. entity, such as a state court. Rather, the result of a U.S. loss at the WTO is that the U.S. government has a choice to make: conform its law or practice or face WTO-authorized retaliation.[169]

The result in the *Breard/LaGrand/Avena* line of cases is different. There is no mechanism by which the United States can simply accept that Mexico will also not conduct full-fledged judicial review of the effects of violations of the Vienna Convention (were such an option available, the United States would likely accept it). Instead, the only avenue for redress is that directed by the ICJ, which purports to have a dispositive effect on the decision making of substate entities. In this sense, adherence to the jurisdiction of the International Court – in terms of its effects on U.S. democratic decision making and constitutional autonomy – is considerably different from adherence to WTO decision making.

D. CONCLUSION

The formal means for mediating antimonies have been largely unchanged since the inception of the Court: the Court has jurisdiction over many disputes,

---

[169] Similarly, in the context of NAFTA Chapter 11 dispute resolution, the United States has a choice: conform its law or practice (invariably, the law or practice of one of the several states with respect to a foreign investor) or pay damages.

but that jurisdiction is circumscribed (as recognized in Yugoslavia's *Legality of Use of Force* cases), the judges reflect the global community but also the major powers, and so on. Yet the Court may have entered a phase in which it is more likely to resist the constraints on its power contained within those formal means and less likely to attempt to reconcile antinomies. Although only states may appear before the Court, the Court now finds that a nonstate entity (Palestine) may do so if a dispute is submitted in the guise of an advisory opinion. Although its jurisdiction is circumscribed, the Court is comfortable engaging in an extended review of the legality of the use of military force by the United States based on a treaty that the Court has found was not violated. The Vienna Convention on Consular Relations and other relevant treaties contain no provisions regarding the effect of violations of the Convention on national court proceedings, but the Court sees no difficulty in determining that U.S. courts must engage in further judicial review of criminal convictions and sentences, trumping local procedural rules. One gets the impression that the Court – fifty years after its creation – is tired of some of the formal constraints that applied earlier in its life and, looking around at the robustness of dispute resolution in other international fora, is ready to expand the reach of its power.

Moreover, it may be that some of the informal means for mediating antinomies have been lost in the past twenty years. Whereas the Court's concern with its reputation and legitimacy in the first thirty years of its existence served as an important political constraint in the Court's relationship with all states, including the United States, over the past twenty years that same concern has led to several clashes with the United States foremost but also the United Kingdom and France. Having stood up to the United States in the *Nicaragua* case, the Court became a hero to the states of the developing world and ushered in a period of increased activity on its docket. Of the cases filed before the ICJ since its inception, approximately 40 percent were filed since the early 1990s.[170] Thus, whereas from 1947 to 1989 the Court received on its docket approximately two cases per year, after 1990 the Court received on average more than three cases per year. The U.S. withdrawal from the Court's compulsory jurisdiction has far from crippled the Court; arguably, it has enhanced the Court's stature as a place of authority in interstate relations unbeholden to the major powers. For the Court, the lesson may be not to tread lightly with respect to the United States but, rather, to tread heavily unless doing so would be viewed generally as bias.

In its foreign policies, contemporary America appears to be going a different route from much of the world, even its former close allies in Europe. The

---

[170] *See* Douglass Cassel, *Is There a New World Court?*, 1 Nw. U. J. Int'l Hum. Rts. 1 ¶ 18 (2004).

consequence is that the judges of the ICJ now reflect predominantly the views of states with which the United States often disagrees. Perhaps this reflects success in the prescription for the Court made by Richard Falk in his 1986 book *Reviving the World Court*.[171] Falk argued for the Court to turn away from what he viewed as Anglo-American and West European ways of thinking and move more toward reflecting the viewpoints associated with non-Western legal traditions (including, at that time, Marxist outlooks on law). Arguably, this is now what has happened, which has strengthened the Court's position among most states of the world but seriously alienated the United States.

The antinomies identified in Part A are unlikely to be resolved through the further development of formal or informal techniques for mediation. Although the United States is not happy with the decisions being rendered by the Court, there is no support in the global community for altering the formal mechanisms by which the Court operates. If the United States saw concrete benefits in being more closely associated with the Court, it might look for ways to improve relationships, but for the world's premier superpower, the benefits appear slim and the costs quite high. Consequently, the United States may take steps to remove itself further from the reach of the ICJ's jurisdiction by terminating some or all of the outstanding treaties that provide for the Court's jurisdiction. In the near term, U.S. policy makers will seek to avoid any involvement in matters before the ICJ, and the Court may well welcome opportunities to speak to the legality of U.S. actions.

The United States is a party to the bilateral and multilateral treaties contained in Table 4.4, which all address the issue of ICJ jurisdiction over disputes arising under the treaties. Nevertheless, the United States is not necessarily exposed to ICJ jurisdiction for all of the treaties listed herein. For some multilateral treaties, the United States filed a reservation when ratifying the treaty that rejects such jurisdiction (e.g., the Torture Convention, the Genocide Convention). Other multilateral treaties allow parties to file a declaration opting into ICJ jurisdiction, but the United States has filed no such declaration. Still other multilateral or bilateral treaties provide that parties may mutually agree to bring a dispute to the ICJ, but neither party can be compelled to do so. Consequently, in the third column, the table explains the nature of the ICJ's jurisdiction over treaty disputes involving the United States. (The table does not include treaties predating 1945, such as the Convention on International Civil Aviation, that provide for jurisdiction over disputes by the Permanent Court of Justice even though, per ICJ Statute Article 36, such treaties are also regarded as providing for ICJ jurisdiction.)

---

[171] Richard Falk, *Reviving the World Court* (Univ. of Virginia, 1986).

TABLE 4.4. *List of multilateral or bilateral treaties to which the United States is a party and that provide for International Court of Justice (ICJ) jurisdiction*[172]

Treaty name	Date U.S. ratified	Nature of ICJ jurisdiction
United Nations Convention against Corruption (multilateral)	Oct. 30, 2006	After failed negotiations and six months after efforts to initiate arbitration have failed, a party may refer a dispute to the ICJ. *See* art. LXVI (2).
		U.S. has reserved to ICJ jurisdiction under art LXVI.[173]
United Nations Convention against Transnational Organized Crime (multilateral)	Nov. 3, 2005	After failed negotiations and six months after efforts to initiate arbitration have failed, a party may refer a dispute to the ICJ. *See* art. XXXV (2).
		U.S. has reserved to ICJ jurisdiction under art. XXXV.[174]
Protocol against the smuggling of migrants by land, sea and air, supplementing the United Nations Convention against Transnational Organized Crime (multilateral)	Nov. 3, 2005	After failed negotiations and six months after efforts to initiate arbitration have failed, a party may refer a dispute to the ICJ. *See* art. XX (2).
		U.S. has reserved to ICJ jurisdiction under art. XX.[175]
Protocol to prevent, suppress, and punish trafficking in persons, especially women and children, supplementing the United Nations Convention against Transnational Organized Crime (multilateral)	Nov. 3, 2005	After failed negotiations and six months after efforts to initiate arbitration have failed, a party may refer a dispute to the ICJ. *See* art. XV (2).
		U.S. has reserved to ICJ jurisdiction under art. XV.[176]

(continued)

---

[172] This table is principally based on information from the UN treaty database, from U.S. Dep't of State, Treaties in Force (issued annually), and from information found at the ICJ Web site, http://www.ICJ-cij.org/ICJwww/ibasicdocuments/ibasictext/ibasictreatiesandotherdocs.htm (visited Dec. 15, 2007).
[173] *See* S. Exec. Rep. No. 109-18 (2006).
[174] *See* S. Exec. Rep. No. 109-4 (2005).
[175] *See id.*
[176] *See id.*

TABLE 4.4 *(continued)*

Treaty name	Date U.S. ratified	Nature of ICJ jurisdiction
International Convention for the Suppression of the Financing of Terrorism (multilateral)	June 26, 2002	After failed negotiations and six months after efforts to initiate arbitration have failed, a party may refer a dispute to the ICJ. *See* art. XXIV (1), (2).
		U.S. has reserved to ICJ jurisdiction under art. XXIV.[177]
International Convention for the Suppression of Terrorist Bombings (multilateral)	June 26, 2002	After failed negotiations and six months after efforts to initiate arbitration have failed, a party may refer a dispute to the ICJ. *See* art. XX (1).
		U.S. has reserved to ICJ jurisdiction under art. XX.[178]
Convention on the Prohibition of the Development, Production, Stockpiling, and Use of Chemical Weapons and on Their Destruction (multilateral)	Apr. 25, 1997	ICJ has jurisdiction over disputes if submitted "by mutual consent" of the parties. *See* art. XIV (2).[179]
Convention on the Marking of Plastic Explosives for the Purpose of Detection (multilateral)	Apr. 9, 1997	Six months after efforts to initiate arbitration, a party may refer a dispute to the ICJ unless the other party has reserved. *See* art. XI (1), (2).
		U.S. has not reserved to ICJ jurisdiction under art. XI (1).[180]
Convention for the Suppression of Unlawful Acts against the Safety of Maritime Navigation (multilateral)	Dec. 6, 1994	After failed negotiations and six months after efforts to initiate arbitration have failed, a party may submit the dispute to the ICJ unless the other party has reserved. *See* art. XVI (1), (2).
		U.S. has not reserved to ICJ jurisdiction under art. XVI.[181]

[177] *See* S. Exec. Rep. No. 107-2 (2001).
[178] *See* S. Exec. Rep. No. 107-2 (2001).
[179] *See* S. Exec. Rep. No. 104-33 (1996).
[180] *See* S. Exec. Rep. No. 103-15 (1993).
[181] *See* S. Exec. Rep. No. 101-18 (1989).

Treaty name	Date U.S. ratified	Nature of ICJ jurisdiction
Convention against Torture and Other Cruel, Inhuman, or Degrading Treatment or Punishment (multilateral)	Oct. 21, 1994	After failed negotiations and six months after efforts to initiate arbitration have failed, a party may submit the dispute to the ICJ unless the other party has reserved. *See* art. XXX (1), (2).
		U.S. has reserved to ICJ jurisdiction under art. XXX.[182]
International Convention of the Elimination of All Forms of Racial Discrimination (multilateral)	Oct. 21, 1994	If a dispute cannot be resolved by other means, a party may submit the dispute to the ICJ. *See* art. XXII.
		U.S. has reserved to ICJ jurisdiction under art. XXII to require consent on a case-by-case basis.[183]
United Nations Framework Convention on Climate Change (multilateral)	Oct. 15, 1992	ICJ jurisdiction exists if the parties by declaration have accepted such jurisdiction in relation to any party accepting the same obligation. *See* art. XIV (2).
		U.S. has not filed such a declaration.[184]
United Nations Convention against Illicit Traffic in Narcotic Drugs and Psychotropic Substances (multilateral)	Feb. 20, 1990	After all other efforts have failed, a party may refer a dispute to the ICJ unless the other party has reserved. *See* art. XXXII (1), (2), (4).
		U.S. has not reserved to ICJ jurisdiction under art. XXXII.[185]
Convention on the Prevention and Punishment of the Crime of Genocide (multilateral)	Nov. 25, 1988	ICJ has jurisdiction "at the request of any of the parties to the dispute." *See* art. IX. U.S. has reserved to ICJ jurisdiction under art. IX, requiring its consent on a case-by-case basis.[186]

(continued)

[182] *See* S. Exec. Rep. No. 101-30 (1990).
[183] *See* S. Exec. Rep. No. 103-29 (1994).
[184] *See* S. Exec. Rep. No. 102-55 (1993).
[185] *See* S. Exec. Rep. No. 101-15 (1989).
[186] *See* S. Exec. Rep. No. 98-50 (1984).

TABLE 4.4 *(continued)*

Treaty name	Date U.S. ratified	Nature of ICJ jurisdiction
Vienna Convention for the Protection of the Ozone Layer (multilateral)	Aug. 27, 1986	ICJ jurisdiction exists if the parties by declaration have accepted such jurisdiction in relation to any party accepting the same obligation. See art. XI (3), (4). U.S. has not filed such a declaration.[187]
International Convention against the Taking of Hostages (multilateral)	Dec. 7, 1984	Six months after efforts to initiate arbitration have failed, a party may submit the dispute to the ICJ unless the other party has reserved. See art. XVI (1), (2). U.S. has not reserved to ICJ jurisdiction under art. XVI.[188]
Convention on the Conservation of Antarctic Marine Living Resources (multilateral)	Feb. 18, 1982	ICJ only has jurisdiction "with the consent in each case of all Parties to the dispute," see art. XXV (2)[189].
Convention on Psychotropic Substances (multilateral)	Apr. 16, 1980	After other efforts have failed, a party may submit the dispute to the ICJ. See art. XXXI (1), (2). U.S. has not reserved to ICJ jurisdiction under art. XXXI.[190]
Convention on the Prevention and Punishment of Crimes against Internationally Protected Persons, including Diplomatic Agents (multilateral)	Oct. 26, 1976	After failed negotiations and six months after efforts to initiate arbitration have failed, a party may submit the dispute to the ICJ unless the other party has reserved. See art. XIII (1), (2). U.S. has not reserved to ICJ jurisdiction under art. XIII.[191]
Convention on the Political Rights of Women (multilateral)	Apr. 8, 1976	If a dispute cannot be resolved by negotiation or other means, the dispute shall be submitted to the ICJ. See art. IX. U.S. has not reserved to the ICJ jurisdiction under art. IX.[192]

[187] See S. Exec. Rep. No. 99-13 (1986).
[188] See S. Exec. Rep. No. 97-17 (1981).
[189] See S. Exec. Rep. No. 97-38 (1981).
[190] See S. Exec. Rep. No. 96-29 (1980).
[191] See S. Exec. Rep. No. 94-10 (1975).
[192] See S. Exec. Rep. No. 94-20 (1975).

Treaty name	Date U.S. ratified	Nature of ICJ jurisdiction
Patent Cooperation Treaty (multilateral)	Nov. 26, 1975	Any dispute not settled by other means may be brought before the ICJ. *See* art. LIX. U.S. has not reserved to ICJ jurisdiction under art. LIX.[193]
Convention for the Suppression of Unlawful Acts against the Safety of Civil Aviation (multilateral)	Jan. 26, 1973	After failed negotiations and six months after efforts to initiate arbitration have failed, a party may submit the dispute to the ICJ unless the other party has reserved. *See* art. XIV (1), (2). U.S. has not reserved to ICJ jurisdiction under art. XIV.[194]
Optional Protocol to the Vienna Convention on Diplomatic Relations Concerning the Compulsory Settlement of Disputes (multilateral)	Nov. 13, 1972	ICJ has jurisdiction over disputes unless the parties agree to arbitration. *See* art. I, II. U.S. has not reserved to ICJ jurisdiction under art. I.[195]
Universal Copyright Convention, signed at Geneva on September 6, 1952, as revised (multilateral)	Sept. 18, 1972	Provides that a dispute not settled by negotiation or other means shall be brought to the ICJ. *See* art. XV. U.S. has not reserved to ICJ jurisdiction under art. XV.[196]
Convention on the Suppression of the Unlawful Seizure of Aircraft (multilateral)	Oct. 14, 1971	After failed negotiations and six months after efforts to initiate arbitration have failed, a party may submit the dispute to the ICJ unless the other party has reserved. *See* art. XII (1), (2). U.S. has not reserved to ICJ jurisdiction under art. XII.[197]
International health regulations (multilateral)	Jan. 1, 1971	If a dispute cannot be resolved by other specified means, a party may submit the dispute to the ICJ *See* art. CVI (3). U.S. has not reserved to ICJ jurisdiction under art. CVI(3).[198]

(continued)

[193] *See* S. Exec. Rep. No. 93-2 (1973).
[194] *See* Treaties in Force 382-83 (2006).
[195] *See* Treaties in Force 412 (2006).
[196] *See* S. Exec. Rep. No. 92-32 (1972).
[197] *See* S. Exec. Rep. No. 92-8 (1971).
[198] *See* S. Exec. Rep. No. 91-18 (1970).

TABLE 4.4 *(continued)*

Treaty name	Date U.S. ratified	Nature of ICJ jurisdiction
Convention Placing the International Poplar Commission within the framework of Food and Agriculture Organization (multilateral)	Aug. 13, 1970	Disputes not settled by committee recommendation or other means shall be submitted to the ICJ. *See* art. XV. U.S. has not reserved to ICJ jurisdiction under art. XV.[199]
Convention for the Protection of Industrial Property signed at Paris on March 20, 1883 as revised (multilateral)	May 25, 1970	A dispute not settled by negotiation may be brought to the ICJ by a party unless the other party has declared itself not bound by this provision. *See* art. XXVIII (1), (2). U.S. has not reserved to ICJ jurisdiction under art. XXVIII.[200]
Convention on Privileges and Immunities of the United Nations (multilateral)	Apr. 29, 1970	Unless the parties agree to another method of settlement, disputes shall be referred to the ICJ. *See* art. VIII, sec. 30. U.S. has not reserved to ICJ jurisdiction under art. VIII.[201]
Consular Convention (bilateral with Belgium)	Nov. 6, 1969	After failed negotiations, a party may submit a dispute to the ICJ provided that the dispute does not concern a discretionary matter and local remedies have been exhausted. *See* art. XLVI.
Protocol relating to the Status of Refugees (multilateral)	Nov. 1, 1968	If a dispute cannot be resolved by other means, a party may submit the dispute to the ICJ. *See* art. IV. U.S. has not reserved to ICJ jurisdiction under art. IV.[202]
Supplementary Convention on the Abolition of Slavery, the Slave Trade, and Institutions and Practices Similar to Slavery (multilateral)	Dec. 6, 1967	If negotiations do not settle a dispute, the dispute shall be referred to the ICJ. *See* art. X. U.S. has not reserved to ICJ jurisdiction under art. X.[203]

[199] *See* Treaties in Force 499 (2006).
[200] *See* S. Exec. Rep. No. 91-13 (1970).
[201] *See* S. Exec. Rep. No. 91-10 (1969).
[202] *See* S. Exec. Rep. No. 90-14 (1968).
[203] *See* S. Exec. Rep. No. 90-17 (1967).

Treaty name	Date U.S. ratified	Nature of ICJ jurisdiction
Single Convention on Narcotic Drugs (multilateral)	May 25, 1967	If a dispute cannot be resolved by other means, a party may submit the dispute to the ICJ. *See* art. XLVIII (1), (2). U.S. has not reserved to ICJ jurisdiction under art. XLVIII.[204]
Agreement for Facilitating the International Circulation of Visual and Auditory Materials of an Educational, Scientific and Cultural Character (multilateral)	Oct. 14, 1966	When both parties to a dispute are members of the ICJ Statute, then a dispute may be submitted to the Court, unless the parties otherwise agree. *See* art. IX (1). U.S. has not reserved to ICJ jurisdiction under art. IX.[205]
Treaty of Amity and Economic Relations (bilateral with Togo)	Sept. 23, 1966	If a dispute cannot be resolved by other means, a party may submit the dispute to the ICJ. *See* art. XIV (2).
Convention on the Settlement of Investment Disputes between States and Nationals of Other States (multilateral)	May 11, 1966	If a dispute cannot be resolved by other means, a party may submit the dispute to the ICJ. *See* art. LXIV. U.S. has not reserved to ICJ jurisdiction under art. LXIV.[206]
Consular Convention (bilateral with Republic of Korea)	Oct. 16 1963	After failed negotiations, a party may submit a dispute to the ICJ provided that the dispute does not concern a discretionary matter and local remedies have been exhausted. *See* art. XVI.
Treaty of Friendship, Establishment, and Navigation (bilateral with Luxembourg)	Sept. 18, 1962	If a dispute cannot be resolved by other means, a party may submit the dispute to the ICJ. *See* art. XVII (2).
Amended Constitution of the International Rice Commission (multilateral)	Nov. 23, 1961	If a dispute cannot be resolved by other means, a party may submit the dispute to the ICJ. *See* art. XI. U.S. has not reserved to ICJ jurisdiction under art. XI.[207]

(continued)

---

[204] *See* S. Exec. Rep. No. 90-11 (1967).
[205] *See* S. Exec. Rep. No. 86-4 (1960).
[206] *See* S. Exec. Rep. No. 89-2 (1966).
[207] *See* Treaties in Force 244 (1963).

TABLE 4.4 *(continued)*

Treaty name	Date U.S. ratified	Nature of ICJ jurisdiction
Amended Agreement for the Establishment of the Indo-Pacific Fisheries Commission (multilateral)	Nov. 23, 1961	If a dispute cannot be resolved by other means, a party may submit the dispute to the ICJ. *See* art. XIII.
		U.S. has not reserved to ICJ jurisdiction under art. XIII.[208]
Treaty of Amity and Economic Relations (bilateral with Vietnam)	Aug. 28, 1961	If a dispute cannot be resolved by other means, a party may submit the dispute to the ICJ. *See* art. XIV(2).
Treaty of Friendship, Establishment, and Navigation (bilateral with Belgium)	Aug. 28, 1961	If a dispute cannot be resolved by other means, a party may submit the dispute to the ICJ. *See* art. XIX (2).
International Convention for the Prevention of Pollution of the Sea by Oil (multilateral)	May 4, 1961	If negotiations or arbitration do not settle a dispute, the dispute shall be referred to the ICJ. *See* art. XIII.
		U.S. has not reserved to ICJ jurisdiction under art. XIII.[209]
Convention on Offences and Certain Other Acts Committed on Board Aircraft (multilateral)	Sept. 5, 1960	After failed negotiations and six months after efforts to initiate arbitration have failed, a party may submit the dispute to the ICJ unless the other party has reserved. *See* art. XXIV (1), (2).
		U.S. has not reserved to ICJ jurisdiction under art. XXIV.[210]
Antarctic Treaty (multilateral)	Aug. 18, 1960	Any dispute not resolved by other means, may, with the consent in each case of all parties to the dispute, be sent to the ICJ. *See* art. XI (1), (2).[211]
Convention of Establishment (bilateral with France)	June 27, 1960	Disputes not settled by committee recommendation or other means shall be submitted to the ICJ. *See* art. XV.

[208] *See* Treaties in Force 264 (1963).
[209] *See* S. Exec. Rep. No. 87-4 (1961).
[210] *See* S. Exec. Rep. No. 91-4 (1969).
[211] *See* S. Exec. Rep. No. 86-10 (1960).

Treaty name	Date U.S. ratified	Nature of ICJ jurisdiction
Treaty of Friendship and Commerce (bilateral with Pakistan)	June 27, 1960	Disputes not settled by other means shall be submitted to the ICJ. See art. XXIII.
Treaty of Friendship, Commerce, and Navigation (bilateral with Republic of Korea)	July 10, 1957	Disputes not settled by other means shall be submitted to the ICJ. See art. XXIV.
Treaty of Friendship, Commerce, and Navigation (bilateral with the Netherlands)	July 9, 1956	Any dispute not resolved by other means shall be submitted to the ICJ. See art. XXV (2).
Treaty of Amity, Economic Relations, and Consular Rights (bilateral with Iran)	July 9, 1956	Any dispute not resolved by other means shall be submitted to the ICJ. See art. XXI (2).
Protocol Amending Slavery Convention signed at Geneva on September 25, 1926 (multilateral)	Mar. 7, 1956	Replaces PCIJ jurisdiction that exists under the 1926 Slavery Convention with ICJ jurisdiction. See art. III, annex. The 1926 Slavery Convention grants the PCIJ jurisdiction if a dispute cannot be settled by negotiation and the disputing parties are parties to the PCIJ Protocol. See art. VIII. U.S. has not reserved to ICJ jurisdiction under this protocol.[212]
Treaty of Friendship, Commerce, and Navigation (bilateral with the Federal Republic of Germany)	July 21, 1955	Any dispute not resolved by other means shall be submitted to arbitration or, upon agreement of the parties, to the ICJ. See art. XXVII (2).
Protocol for Limiting and Regulating the Cultivation of the Poppy Plant, and the Production of, International and Wholesale Trade in, and Use of Opium (multilateral)	Feb. 18, 1955	Unless the parties agree to another method of settlement, any dispute shall be referred to the ICJ. See art. XV(2). U.S. has not reserved to ICJ jurisdiction under art. XV.[213]

(continued)

[212] See S. Exec. Rep. No. 84-1 (1956).
[213] See S. Exec. Rep. No. 83-7 (1954).

TABLE 4.4 (continued)

Treaty name	Date U.S. ratified	Nature of ICJ jurisdiction
Universal Copyright Convention (multilateral)	Dec. 6, 1954	If a dispute cannot be resolved by negotiation or other means, the dispute shall be submitted to the ICJ. *See* art. XV. U.S. has not reserved to ICJ jurisdiction under art. XV.[214]
Economic Aids Agreement (bilateral with Spain)	Sept. 26, 1953	ICJ jurisdiction exists only by mutual agreement. *See* art. IX (1).
Treaty of friendship, Commerce, and Navigation (bilateral with Japan)	July 17, 1953	Any dispute not resolved by other means shall be submitted to the ICJ. *See* art. XXIV (2).
Treaty of friendship, Commerce, and Navigation (bilateral with Denmark)	July 17, 1953	Any dispute not resolved by other means shall be submitted to the ICJ. *See* art. XXIV (2).
Treaty of Amity and Economic Relations (bilateral with Ethiopia)	July 17, 1953	Disputes not settled by other means shall, at the request of a party, be submitted to the ICJ. *See* art. XVII.
Treaty of Friendship, Commerce, and Navigation (bilateral with Israel)	July 17, 1953	Any dispute not resolved by other means shall be submitted to the ICJ. *See* art. XXIV (2).
Treaty of Friendship, Commerce, and Navigation (bilateral with Greece)	July 17, 1953	Disputes not settled by other means shall be submitted to the ICJ. *See* art. XXVI (2).
Treaty of Friendship, Commerce, and Navigation (bilateral with Italy)	July 17, 1953	Any dispute not resolved by other means shall be submitted to the ICJ. *See* art. XXVI.
Agreement for Economic Assistance (bilateral with Israel)	May 9, 1952	Parties may submit claims to the ICJ by agreement and subject to each parties' recognition of the compulsory jurisdiction of the ICJ. *See* art. VIII.
Treaty of Peace with Japan (multilateral)	Feb. 14, 1952	Disputes not settled by a special claims tribunal shall be referred to the ICJ at the request of a party. *See* art. XXII. U.S. has not reserved to ICJ jurisdiction under art. XXII.[215]

[214] *See* S. Exec. Rep. No. 83-5 (1954).
[215] *See* S. Exec. Rep. No. 82-2 (1952).

Treaty name	Date U.S. ratified	Nature of ICJ jurisdiction
Convention on Road Traffic (multilateral)	Aug. 30, 1950	Disputes not settled by other means may be submitted to the ICJ. *See* art. XXXIII. U.S. has not reserved to ICJ jurisdiction under art. XXXIII.[216]
Treaty of Friendship, Commerce, and Navigation (bilateral with Ireland)	June 26, 1950	Any dispute not resolved by other means shall be submitted to the ICJ. *See* art. XXIII.
Economic Cooperation Agreement (bilateral with Portugal)	Sept. 28, 1948	Parties agree to submit any claims to the ICJ subject to the conditions of a party's acceptance of ICJ compulsory jurisdiction. *See* art. IX (1).
Economic Cooperation Agreement (bilateral with United Kingdom)	July 6, 1948	Parties agree to submit any claims to the ICJ subject to the conditions of a party's acceptance of ICJ compulsory jurisdiction. *See* art. IX (1).
Economic Cooperation Agreement (bilateral with Turkey)	July 4, 1948	Parties agree to submit any claims to the ICJ subject to the conditions of a party's acceptance of ICJ compulsory jurisdiction. *See* art. IX (1).
Economic Cooperation Agreement (bilateral with Sweden)	July 3, 1948	Parties agree to submit any claims to the ICJ subject to the conditions of a party's acceptance of ICJ compulsory jurisdiction. *See* art. IX (1).
Economic Cooperation Agreement (bilateral with Luxembourg)	July 3, 1948	Parties agree to submit any claims to the ICJ subject to the conditions of a party's acceptance of ICJ compulsory jurisdiction. *See* art. X (1).
Economic Cooperation Agreement (bilateral with Nationalist China)	July 3, 1948	Parties agree to submit any claims to the ICJ subject to the conditions of a party's acceptance of ICJ compulsory jurisdiction. *See* art. X (1).

(continued)

---

[216] *See* Treaties in Force 375 (2006).

TABLE 4.4 (continued)

Treaty name	Date U.S. ratified	Nature of ICJ jurisdiction
Economic Cooperation Agreement (bilateral with Iceland)	July 3, 1948	Parties agree to submit any claims to the ICJ subject to the conditions of a party's acceptance of ICJ compulsory jurisdiction. See art. X (1).
Economic Cooperation Agreement (bilateral with Norway)	July 3, 1948	Parties agree to submit any claims to the ICJ subject to the conditions of a party's acceptance of ICJ compulsory jurisdiction. See art. X (1).
Economic Cooperation Agreement (bilateral with Belgium)	July 2, 1948	Parties agree to submit any claims to the ICJ subject to the conditions of a party's acceptance of ICJ compulsory jurisdiction. See art. X (1).
Economic Cooperation Agreement (bilateral with Greece)	July 2, 1948	Parties agree to submit any claims to the ICJ subject to the conditions of a party's acceptance of ICJ compulsory jurisdiction. See art. X (1).
Economic Cooperation Agreement (bilateral with Netherlands)	July 2, 1948	Parties agree to submit any claims to the ICJ subject to the conditions of a party's acceptance of ICJ compulsory jurisdiction. See art. X (1).
Economic Cooperation Agreement (bilateral with Austria)	July 2, 1948	Parties agree to submit any claims to the ICJ subject to the conditions of a party's acceptance of ICJ compulsory jurisdiction. See art. IX (1).
Economic Cooperation Agreement (bilateral with Denmark)	June 29, 1948	Parties agree to submit any claims to the ICJ subject to the conditions of a party's acceptance of ICJ compulsory jurisdiction. See art. X (1).
Economic Cooperation Agreement (bilateral with France)	June 28, 1948	Parties agree to submit any claims to the ICJ subject to the conditions of a party's acceptance of ICJ compulsory jurisdiction. See art. X (1).

Treaty name	Date U.S. ratified	Nature of ICJ jurisdiction
Economic Cooperation Agreement (bilateral with Italy)	June 28, 1948	Parties agree to submit any claims to the ICJ subject to the conditions of a party's acceptance of ICJ compulsory jurisdiction. See art. X (1).
Treaty of Friendship, Commerce, and Navigation (bilateral with China)	May 28, 1948	Any dispute not resolved by other means shall be submitted to the ICJ. See art. XXVIII.
Protocol Amending the Convention for Limiting the Manufacture and Regulating the Distribution of Narcotic Drugs (multilateral)	Aug. 12, 1947	Any dispute not resolved by other means shall be submitted to the ICJ. See art. XXV. U.S. has not reserved to ICJ jurisdiction under art. XXV.[217]

[217] See S. Exec. Rep. No. 72-2 (1932).

5

The U.S. Supreme Court and the International Court of Justice: What Does "Respectful Consideration" Mean?

MELISSA A. WATERS*

For those interested in the attitudes of U.S. courts toward international tribunals, the 2005–6 Supreme Court term was slated to be a watershed moment. The nascent dialogue between the U.S. Supreme Court and the International Court of Justice (ICJ) over consular notification – begun eight years earlier[1] – was expected to reach its apex in *Sanchez-Llamas v. Oregon*.[2] In a series of decisions, the ICJ had held that the United States had violated its obligation, under Article 36 of the Vienna Convention on Consular Relations, to notify foreign nationals detained by the police of their right to contact their countries' consulates.[3] Moreover, the ICJ had ruled that the application of procedural default rules to consular notification claims violated Article 36 because it failed to give "full effect" to the purposes underlying the treaty. As a remedy for the treaty violation, the ICJ prescribed "review and reconsideration" of criminal proceedings involving consular notification claims that had been held by U.S. courts to be procedurally defaulted. Supreme Court watchers widely expected the Court in *Sanchez-Llamas* to decide what judicial deference, if any, was

---

* Professor of Law, Washington University Law School.
[1] *See* Vienna Convention on Consular Relations (Para. v. U.S.), 1998 I.C.J. 248 (Apr. 9); *Breard v. Greene*, 523 U.S. 371 (1998) (per curiam).
[2] 126 S.Ct. 2669 (2006). *Sanchez-Llamas* involved two consolidated appeals, *Sanchez-Llamas v. Oregon* and *Bustillo v. Johnson*. Sanchez-Llamas appealed from an Oregon Supreme Court ruling that suppression of incriminatory statements was not a required remedy for violation of his consular notification claim. *See id.* Bustillo appealed from a Virginia Supreme Court ruling that he had procedurally defaulted his treaty claim for violation of his consular notification rights. *See id.* In this chapter, I address only Bustillo's procedural default claims. For further discussion of the case, including the issues raised by Sanchez-Llamas, see Symposium, *Domestic Enforcement of Public International Law After* Sanchez-Llamas v. Oregon, 11 Lewis & Clark L. Rev. 1 (2007); Curtis A. Bradley, *International Decisions* — Sanchez-Llamas v. Oregon, 100 Am. J. Int'l L.882 (2006).
[3] *See LaGrand* Case (F.R.G. v. U.S.), 2001 I.C.J. 466, 479 (June 27); *Avena and Other Mexican Nationals* (Mex. v. U.S.), 2004 I.C.J. 12 (Mar. 31). *See*, in this book, Chapter 4 by Sean Murphy.

due the ICJ's interpretation of the Vienna Convention. More broadly, at stake was the extent to which the Supreme Court would choose to participate in dialogue on matters of treaty interpretation – and precisely what that dialogic relationship would look like – both with the ICJ and with the rapidly proliferating numbers of other international tribunals.[4]

At best, however, the Supreme Court's ruling in *Sanchez-Llamas* revealed a decided difference of opinion among the justices regarding the proper dialogic relationship between international tribunals and U.S. courts. All nine justices adopted identical language to describe that relationship: they agreed that the ruling of an international tribunal was entitled to "respectful consideration."[5] However, a close reading of the case reveals considerable disagreement among the justices as to the exact meaning of the term. Chief Justice Roberts, writing for a five-member majority,[6] seemed to view "respectful consideration" to mean little more than the sort of consideration that U.S. courts have long given to the courts of our treaty partners in treaty interpretation. Thus, the conservative members of the Court viewed judicial dialogue with the ICJ as, at most, a horizontal relationship of coequal courts. Under this view, the ICJ's interpretation of the Vienna Convention might have some persuasive value but otherwise was entitled to no special degree of deference.

Justice Breyer, writing for a three-member dissent,[7] seemed to envision a much more vertical relationship with the ICJ. In his conception, U.S. courts should recognize the ICJ as an international tribunal with special expertise in matters of treaty interpretation, the opinions of which are accordingly entitled to a greater degree of deference. The dissent argued that the Court should strive to avoid an interpretation of U.S. treaty obligations that would conflict with the ICJ's own interpretation. Indeed, it suggested that the Court should adopt a "modified reading" of its own precedent to avoid conflict with an ICJ treaty interpretation.

This chapter first provides some background on the history of the dialogue between the Supreme Court and the ICJ regarding consular notification, tracing the dialogue from the ICJ's ruling in *Paraguay v. United States* through the Supreme Court's decision in *Medellin v. Dretke*. It then explores the

---

[4] See Jenny S. Martinez, *Towards an International Judicial System*, 56 Stan. L. Rev. 429, 430 (2003): "[T]here are now more than fifty international courts, tribunals, and quasi-judicial bodies, most of which have been established in the past twenty years."
[5] See *Sanchez-Llamas*, 126 S.Ct. at 2683; *id.* at 2700 (Breyer, J., dissenting).
[6] Justices Scalia, Kennedy, Thomas, and Alito joined his opinion. See *id.* at 2673–74.
[7] Justice Breyer was joined in the dissent by Justices Stevens and Souter. See *id.* at 2674. Justice Ginsburg filed an opinion concurring in the judgment and joined the dissent's view that the Vienna Convention granted judicially enforceable rights. See *id.*

Sanchez-Llamas decision in detail, drawing lessons from the justices' opinions regarding the starkly different attitudes of the conservative and liberal wings of the Court toward dialogue with the ICJ.

A. FROM BREARD TO MEDELLIN: ABORTED DIALOGUES BETWEEN THE ICJ AND THE SUPREME COURT

In an important sense, dialogue between the Supreme Court and the ICJ regarding consular notification is part of the broader transnational dialogue taking place between the United States and anti–death penalty countries in the European Union and elsewhere regarding the validity of the death penalty.[8] In a series of cases beginning in 1998, several countries have brought complaints against the United States before the ICJ on behalf of their nationals currently awaiting execution in various states. At issue is the failure of local police authorities to comply with Article 36 of the Vienna Convention on Consular Relations, which requires authorities to notify foreign nationals, upon arrest or detention, of their right to contact their country's consulate.[9] In their complaints before the ICJ, these countries have argued that the failure of local police forces to notify detained foreign nationals of their consular notification rights violated U.S. treaty obligations and rendered void subsequent criminal proceedings against their nationals. The ICJ had jurisdiction over the complaints pursuant to the Vienna Convention's Optional Protocol Concerning Compulsory Settlement of Disputes (to which the United States was a party at the time of the various ICJ proceedings).[10]

---

[8] *See* Margaret E. McGuinness, Sanchez-Llamas, *American Human Rights Exceptionalism and the VCCR Norm Portal*, 11 Lewis & Clark L. Rev. 47, 54–58 (2007) (discussing the role of Article 36 litigation in U.S. death penalty cases). *See generally* Melissa A. Waters, *Mediating Norms and Identity: The Role of Transnational Judicial Dialogue in Creating and Enforcing International Law*, 93 Geo. L. J. 487 (2005) (discussing transnational dialogue regarding abolition of the death penalty).

[9] *See* Vienna Convention on Consular Relations, art. 36, Apr. 24, 1963, 21 U.S.T. 77, 596. U.N.T.S. 261: "[I]f he so requests, the competent authorities of the receiving State shall, without delay, inform the consular post of the sending State if, within its consular district, a national of that State is arrested or committed to prison or to custody pending trial or is detained in any other manner. Any communication addressed to the consular post by the person arrested, in prison, custody or detention shall be forwarded by the said authorities without delay. The said authorities shall inform the person concerned without delay of his rights under this subparagraph."

[10] The Optional Protocol grants the ICJ jurisdiction over "[d]isputes arising out of the interpretation or application of the Convention." *See* Vienna Convention on Consular Relations, Optional Protocol Concerning the Compulsory Settlement of Disputes art. 1, Apr. 24, 1963, 21 U.S.T. 325, T.I.A.S. No. 6820. The United States ratified the Optional Protocol in 1969 and withdrew from it in 2005. *See Sanchez-Llamas*, 126 S. Ct. at 2692 (Breyer, J., dissenting).

For the eight years prior to *Sanchez-Llamas*, the Supreme Court and the ICJ essentially engaged in a series of failed or aborted dialogues on consular notification. The first involved the execution in 1998 of Angel Breard, a Paraguayan national on Virginia's death row. Breard had not been notified upon arrest of his right to contact his consulate, but prosecutors argued that his Article 36 claim was procedurally defaulted under both Virginia law and federal habeas doctrine. Paraguay filed a complaint against the United States before the ICJ, alleging a violation of Article 36. Shortly before Breard's scheduled execution date, the ICJ issued a preliminary order stating that the United States "should take all measures at its disposal" to stay Breard's execution pending the ICJ's ruling on the merits of Paraguay's claim.[11] Breard and Paraguay then requested a stay of execution before the Supreme Court, asserting that "the Convention is the 'supreme law of the land' and thus trumps the procedural default doctrine."[12]

In *Breard v. Greene*, the Supreme Court refused to stay the execution. It acknowledged that the Court "should give respectful consideration to the interpretation of an international treaty rendered by an international court with jurisdiction to interpret [the treaty]."[13] It explained, however, that regardless of the outcome of the ICJ proceeding, Breard had procedurally defaulted his claim, and thus no remedy was available to him before the U.S. courts. The Court took the view that state procedural default rules were perfectly consistent with the Vienna Convention, which specified that rights under the treaty "shall be exercised in conformity with the laws and regulations of the receiving State."[14] "Laws," in the Court's view, included American procedural default rules. The State of Virginia executed Breard before the ICJ had an opportunity to rule on Paraguay's claim.

The ICJ's second aborted dialogue with the Supreme Court came three years later and involved Arizona's scheduled execution of a German national, Walter LaGrand. The ICJ again issued a preliminary order, requesting a stay of execution pending the outcome of ICJ proceedings between Germany and the United States.[15] Germany commenced litigation before the Supreme Court against the United States and Arizona, asking the Court to ensure enforcement of the ICJ order. The Supreme Court again refused to grant a stay of execution, emphasizing the Court's questionable subject matter jurisdiction and the lateness of the request (two hours before LaGrand's scheduled execution).[16]

---

[11] *Vienna Convention on Consular Relations (Para. v. U.S.)*, 1998 I.C.J. 248, 258 (Apr. 9).
[12] *Breard v. Greene*, 523 U.S. 371, 375 (1998) (per curiam).
[13] *Id.*
[14] *Id.* (quoting Vienna Convention on Consular Relations, *op. cit.*, art. 36(2)).
[15] See *LaGrand Case (F.R.G. v. U.S.)*, 2001 I.C.J. 466, 479 (June 27).
[16] See *Fed. Republic of Germany v. United States*, 526 U.S. 111 (1999).

Although Arizona executed LaGrand just hours after the Supreme Court's ruling, Germany continued to pursue its claim before the ICJ. In the *LaGrand* case, the ICJ issued a key ruling regarding the proper interpretation of the Vienna Convention with respect to procedural default rules.[17] It noted that application of a procedural default rule does not "in itself" violate Article 36.[18] Yet it took the position that when an individual had not been informed of his Article 36 rights, application of the procedural default rule violated the treaty because it failed to give "full effect" to the purposes for which the rights granted under Article 36 were intended.[19]

The third aborted dialogue between the ICJ and the Supreme Court involved an ICJ proceeding brought by Mexico on behalf of fifty-four Mexican nationals, many of whom were awaiting execution in various states. In its decision in *Avena*, the ICJ reiterated its interpretation of Article 36, stating that application of the procedural default rule to individuals who had not been informed of their Article 36 rights failed to give "full effect" to the treaty's purposes.[20] The ICJ emphasized that the appropriate remedy for such violations was "review and reconsideration" of the conviction and sentence. In its view, review and reconsideration was essential to remedy possible prejudice caused by the foreign national's inability to enlist his consulate's assistance in the initial criminal proceeding.[21]

In *Medellin v. Dretke*,[22] the Supreme Court was finally poised to engage in dialogue with the ICJ regarding the consular notification issue. In granting certiorari in the case, the Court agreed to decide whether U.S. courts were bound by the ICJ's ruling on procedural default or, in the alternative, whether "federal court[s] should give effect, as a matter of judicial comity and uniform treaty interpretation, to the ICJ's judgment."[23] Be that as it may, in *Medellin*, the nascent dialogue between the ICJ and the Supreme Court never took place. Before the Supreme Court could rule in the case, the Bush administration intervened. It issued a memorandum declaring that "the United States will

---

[17] It also issued a second key ruling in the case, holding that Article 36 creates individual rights that may be invoked by a State Party to the treaty on behalf of its detained national. See *LaGrand*, 2001 I.C.J. at 494.

[18] *Id.* at 497: "The problem arises when the procedural default rule does not allow the detained individual to challenge a conviction and sentence by claiming . . . that the competent national authorities failed to comply with their obligation to provide the requisite consular information 'without delay,' thus preventing the person from seeking and obtaining consular assistance from the sending State."

[19] See *id.*

[20] See *Avena and Other Mexican Nationals (Mex. v. U.S.)*, 2004 I.C.J. 12, 57 (Mar. 31).

[21] *Id.* at 65.

[22] 544 U.S. 660 (2005).

[23] *Id.* at 661–62.

discharge its inter-national obligations under the decision of the International Court of Justice [in *Avena*]... by having State courts give effect to the decision... in cases filed by the 51 Mexican nationals addressed in that decision."[24] Medellin filed a new habeas petition in state court, and the Supreme Court accordingly dismissed the writ of certiorari as improvidently granted.[25]

After eight years of litigation, and three failed forays into dialogue, the long-awaited Supreme Court decision addressing the deference due the ICJ's rulings finally came in *Sanchez-Llamas*. The case involved the consolidated appeals of Moises Sanchez-Llamas, a Mexican national tried and convicted in Oregon, and Mario Bustillo, a Honduran national tried and convicted in Virginia. Neither man had been informed by authorities of his consular notification rights at the time of arrest. Interestingly, unlike previous consular notification cases before the Supreme Court, neither appeal involved a capital offense. Sanchez-Llamas moved for suppression of certain incriminating statements that he had made during interrogation, asserting that they had been obtained in violation of Article 36. Bustillo, by contrast, had failed to raise his Article 36 claim until state habeas proceedings and thus had procedurally defaulted the claim under Virginia's procedural default rules. Although he was not one of the fifty-one individuals named in *Avena*, Bustillo argued that U.S. courts were bound to give deference to the ICJ's ruling with respect to procedural default of Article 36 claims.

The Supreme Court rejected both men's claims. It held that suppression is not a required remedy for Article 36 violations and that a state may treat a criminal defendant's Article 36 claim as procedurally defaulted when the defendant failed to raise the claim at trial.[26] The ICJ's previous rulings were applicable only to Bustillo's claim for procedural default: accordingly, this chapter limits its discussion to the procedural default issue and does not address the Court's holding with respect to suppression as a remedy for Article 36 violations.

B. CONCEPTUALIZING TREATY DIALOGUE WITH THE ICJ: A HORIZONTAL OR VERTICAL RELATIONSHIP?

With respect to dialogue with the ICJ, virtually the only point on which the conservative and liberal wings of the Court seem to agree is the proper language

---

[24] *See* Memorandum from President George W. Bush to the Attorney General re: Compliance with the Decision of the International Court of Justice in *Avena* (Feb. 28, 2005), available at http://www.whitehouse.gov/news/releases/2005/02/20050228-18.html.

[25] It noted that the new Texas proceeding "may provide Medellín with the very reconsideration of his Vienna Convention claim that he now seeks in the present proceeding." *Id.*

[26] *See Sanchez-Llamas*, 126 S. Ct. at 2675–76.

with which to describe that dialogue. In *Sanchez-Llamas*, both the majority and dissent agreed that U.S. courts should give "respectful consideration" to ICJ treaty interpretations.[27] However, their widely divergent conceptions of "respectful consideration" suggest that the justices view the dialogic relationship with the ICJ through starkly different lenses. The central point of disagreement is just how much deference, if any, is entailed in giving "respectful consideration" to ICJ rulings.

As an initial matter, all of the justices seem to agree that "respectful consideration" of international tribunals' treaty interpretations is useful because it promotes the important goal of uniformity in treaty interpretation. In *Sanchez-Llamas*, only the dissenting justices emphasized the key role of the ICJ itself in promoting uniformity.[28] This view certainly is consistent, however, with the Court's precedent on the importance of uniformity in treaty interpretation more generally. The Court has held, for example, that the judgments of other signatories' courts interpreting a given treaty are entitled to "considerable weight."[29] Accordingly, it has carefully considered foreign case law in interpreting a wide variety of treaties.[30]

Justice Scalia has gone even further in emphasizing the importance of uniformity. In his dissent in *Olympic Airways v. Husain*,[31] he chastised the majority for adopting an interpretation of the Warsaw Convention that conflicted with the prior rulings of intermediate appellate courts in two other countries. He noted that "it is reasonable to impute to the parties an intent that their respective courts strive to interpret the treaty consistently."[32] He further argued that "even if we disagree, we surely owe the conclusions reached by appellate courts of other signatories the courtesy of respectful consideration."[33]

For Justice Scalia in *Olympic Airways*, "respectful consideration" of *foreign* court judgments seemed to entail a considerable degree of deference to the courts of other signatory states in interpreting treaties.[34] Indeed, Justice Scalia arguably suggested a kind of rebuttable presumption in favor of the validity

---

[27] See id. at 2683; id. at 2685: "*LaGrand* and *Avena* are ... entitled only to the 'respectful consideration' due an interpretation of an international agreement by an international court; id. at 2700 (Breyer, J., dissenting) (noting that "the ICJ's decisions on this issue ... warrant our 'respectful consideration.'").

[28] See id. at 2700 (Breyer, J., dissenting).

[29] *Air France v. Saks*, 470 U.S. 392, 404 (1985).

[30] See, e.g., *El Al Israel Airlines, Ltd. v. Tsui Yuan Tseng*, 525 U.S. 155, 173–74 (1999); *Eastern Airlines, Inc. v. Floyd*, 499 U.S. 530, 550–51 (1991) (interpreting the Warsaw Convention).

[31] 124 S.Ct. 2065 (2004).

[32] Id. at 1232 (Scalia, J., dissenting).

[33] Id. at 1234 (Scalia, J., dissenting).

[34] See generally Melissa A. Waters, *Justice Scalia on the Use of Foreign Law in Constitutional Interpretation: Unidirectional Monologue or Co-Constitutive Dialogue?*, 12 Tulsa J. Comp. & Int'l L. 149 (2004).

of foreign court judgments in matters of treaty interpretation. He asserted, "Were we confronting the issue in the first instance, perhaps the Court could persuade me to its view, but courts in two other countries have already rejected this view, and their reasoning is no less compelling than the Court's."[35] Thus, Justice Scalia's opinion suggested, U.S. courts should defer to the prior ruling of a sister signatory court, so long as it offers a reasonable interpretation of the treaty – even if there are other, equally reasonable alternative interpretations. In other words, given the interest in uniformity, a foreign court's interpretation should receive deference unless the U.S. court can offer, in Justice Scalia's words, "a convincing explanation for its decision to depart from the foreign court's prior judgment."[36]

At issue in *Sanchez-Llamas* was the question whether "respectful consideration" of *international* court rulings entailed the same degree of consideration that is ordinarily extended to rulings by foreign signatory courts or whether it required some higher degree of deference. For the majority, the answer was clear: the ICJ's interpretation was entitled to no more consideration than would be enjoyed by foreign courts. The majority emphasized the essentially political nature of the ICJ, pointing out that its "principal purpose is to arbitrate particular disputes between national governments."[37] Thus, the ICJ's *Avena* ruling certainly had no binding force in this case: the majority noted that, as an arbitral tribunal, the ICJ's judgments have no binding force except between the parties in the case before it and do not constitute binding precedent "even as to the ICJ itself."[38] More important, the majority emphasized the primacy of the Supreme Court as the final arbiter on the meaning of treaties within the U.S. legal system – a role conferred upon the Court by the U.S. Constitution itself.[39]

---

[35] *Id.* at 1231 (Scalia, J., dissenting).
[36] *Id.* (Scalia, J., dissenting).
[37] *Sanchez-Llamas*, 126 S.Ct. at 2684.
[38] *Id.* The majority also contended that the ICJ's ruling should not be read as binding precedent, given the Bush administration's position in Vienna Convention litigation. *Id.*, noting that the president "has not taken the view that the ICJ's interpretation of Article 36 is binding on our courts." Moreover, it pointed out that subsequent to the ICJ's ruling in *Avena*, the United States had withdrawn from the Optional Protocol giving the ICJ jurisdiction in future Article 36 cases. It concluded, "Whatever the effect of *Avena and LaGrand* before this withdrawal, it is doubtful that our courts should give decisive weight to the interpretation of a tribunal whose jurisdiction in this area is no longer recognized by the United States." *Id.* The dissent, for its part, assumed without deciding that the ICJ's interpretation did not bind the Court in this particular case. *Id.* at 2700 (Breyer, J., dissenting).
[39] The majority commented, "[i]f treaties are to be given effect as federal law under our legal system, determining their meaning as a matter of federal law 'is emphatically the province and duty of the judicial department,' headed by the 'one supreme Court' established by the Constitution. It is against this background that the United States ratified, and the Senate gave its advice and consent to, the various agreements that govern referral of Vienna Convention disputes to the ICJ." *Id.* at 2685 (citations omitted).

Thus, the *Avena* ruling was "entitled *only* to the 'respectful consideration' due an interpretation of an international agreement by an international court."[40]

The conservative members of the Court who made up the majority in *Sanchez-Llamas* thus view treaty dialogue between the Court and the ICJ as involving, at most, a horizontal relationship of coequal tribunals. Through the conservative lens, "respectful consideration" of the *Avena* ruling does not seem to entail any higher degree of deference than the "considerable weight" ordinarily given to treaty interpretations by foreign signatory courts. Instead, in the conservatives' view, the Court's consideration of the ICJ's treaty interpretation is limited to whatever value it might have as persuasive authority – just as a treaty interpretation from any foreign signatory court would be. Indeed, as this chapter explores in Part C, the *Sanchez-Llamas* majority arguably went even further: it accorded to the ICJ ruling a level of "consideration" well below the sort of presumption of validity that Justice Scalia, in *Olympic Airways*, suggested would be appropriate to ascribe to interpretations by foreign signatory courts.

The liberal wing of the Court, by contrast, seems to envision treaty dialogue with the ICJ as involving a much more vertical relationship between the two tribunals. In its view, "respectful consideration" takes on a very different meaning in the context of dialogue with international courts: it entails at least some degree of U.S. court deference to treaty interpretations by international courts. The dissent in *Sanchez-Llamas* made two arguments with respect to the ICJ's ruling in *Avena*. First, it asserted that the goal of uniformity in treaty interpretation counseled strongly in favor of a greater degree of deference to the ICJ ruling.[41] The dissent suggested that the ICJ's interpretation of the Vienna Convention was owed deference because, at a minimum, the ICJ served as a reasonably accurate predictor of the views of foreign courts. After all, as the dissent pointed out, "the ICJ's position as an international court specifically charged with the duty to interpret numerous international treaties (including the Convention) provides a natural point of reference for national courts seeking ... uniformity."[42] In the dissent's view, foreign courts were likely to defer to ICJ interpretations of the Convention; thus, to promote the goal of uniformity, the Court should accord considerable deference to the *Avena* ruling.[43]

Second, and more important, the dissent suggested that the Court should give deference to ICJ rulings in recognition of the ICJ's special status as an international court. It explained, "'[R]espectful consideration' also reflects

---

[40] *Id.*
[41] *Id.* at 2700 (Breyer, J., dissenting).
[42] *Id.* (Breyer, J., dissenting).
[43] *See id.* (Breyer, J., dissenting).

an understanding of the ICJ's expertise in matters of treaty interpretation, a branch of international law. The ICJ's opinions 'are persuasive evidence' of what '[international] law is.'"[44] The dissent pointed out that the Supreme Court had "repeatedly looked to the ICJ for guidance in interpreting treaties and in other matters of international law."[45] Because the ICJ had a much more authoritative voice in such matters than ordinary foreign courts, the dissent suggested, its rulings were entitled to an accordingly greater degree of deference.[46]

Thus, far from the horizontal relationship of coequal courts envisioned by the Court's conservative wing, the dissenting Justices in *Sanchez-Llamas* posited a significantly more vertical dialogic relationship with international tribunals. In the dissent's conception of a vertical relationship, "respectful consideration" requires that U.S. courts look to international courts for "guidance" as to treaty interpretation and other matters within their special expertise.

C. "RESPECTFUL CONSIDERATION" IN TREATY DIALOGUE: IN *SANCHEZ-LLAMAS*, CONCEPTUALIZING THE RELATIONSHIP IS EVERYTHING

Although they use the same language – "respectful consideration" – to describe dialogue between U.S. courts and international tribunals, the conservative and liberal wings of the Court offer very different conceptions of the proper dialogic relationship between the courts. Not surprisingly, these differing conceptions resulted in starkly different approaches to dialogue with the ICJ in *Sanchez-Llamas*. The Court had previously held, in *Breard v. Greene*, that the application of procedural default rules did not violate Article 36 of the Vienna Convention. The petitioner in *Sanchez-Llamas* argued that the Court should reconsider this holding in light of the ICJ's contrary ruling in *Avena*. Through the "horizontal relationship" lens of the majority, the *Avena* ruling itself received short shrift. The majority engaged in dialogue with the ICJ, but it used that dialogue to instruct the international tribunal as to the importance of procedural default rules in the American legal system. The dissent's conceptualization of a "vertical relationship" with the ICJ, in contrast, resulted in a dialogue based on a strong degree of deference to the international tribunal. Indeed, in a move that calls to mind the *Charming Betsy*[47] canon of

---

[44] *Id.* at 2700–01 (Breyer, J., dissenting).
[45] *Id.* at 2701 (Breyer, J., dissenting).
[46] *See id.*
[47] *See Murray v. Schooner Charming Betsy*, 6 U.S. (2 Cranch) 64 (1804). Courts routinely apply the *Charming Betsy* canon to construe ambiguous federal statutes in such a manner that they would not violate either international treaties or customary international law. *See, e.g., TWA v. Franklin Mint Corp.*, 466 U.S. 243, 252 (1984).

statutory construction, the dissent suggested that the Court should strive to interpret its own precedent in a way that would *avoid* conflicts with ICJ treaty interpretations. Thus, *Sanchez-Llamas* reveals the profound significance of the conceptualization question on the character of the dialogue that the Court will conduct with international tribunals.

1. *The Conservative Conception: Horizontal Dialogue with the ICJ*

Relying on its conception of horizontal dialogue with international tribunals, the majority in *Sanchez-Llamas* took the position that there was simply no need to reconsider the Court's holding in *Breard*.[48] In its view, "even according [respectful] consideration" to the ICJ's *Avena* ruling, there was nothing in that ruling that counseled – much less required – a reexamination of *Breard*.[49] Consistent with its position that the ICJ's treaty interpretation was due no special deference, the majority considered *Avena* for its persuasive value only – and found that it had none.

In essence, the majority took the view that the ICJ's interpretation of the Vienna Convention was simply erroneous. It asserted that, under international law, "the procedural rules of domestic law generally govern the [domestic] implementation of an international treaty."[50] Moreover, it argued that the ICJ's interpretation was inconsistent with "the plain import of Article 36," which "makes clear that the rights it provides 'shall be exercised in conformity with the laws and regulations of the receiving State.'"[51] It concluded, "In the United States, this means that the rule of procedural default – which applies even to claimed violations of our Constitution, applies also to Vienna Convention claims."[52] Thus in the hands of the majority, the ICJ's key treaty interpretation in *Avena* – that the application of American procedural default rules failed to give "full effect" to Article 36 rights – received little "consideration" at all. Instead, giving no special deference to the ICJ ruling, the majority found that it had no persuasive value and discarded it.

One of the most interesting aspects of *Sanchez-Llamas* is the majority's use of dialogue to "educate" the international tribunal. It chided the ICJ for

---

[48] *Sanchez-Llamas*, 126 S.Ct. at 2672 ("Although the ICJ's interpretation deserves 'respectful consideration,' we conclude that it does not compel us to reconsider our understanding of the Convention in *Breard*.").

[49] *Id.* at 2673.

[50] *Id.* at 2685.

[51] *Id.*

[52] *Id.* The majority further contended that Bustillo had "point[ed] to nothing in the drafting history of Article 36 or in the contemporary practice of other signatories that undermines this conclusion."

its failure to understand the American criminal justice system, asserting that the *Avena* ruling was "inconsistent with the basic framework of an adversary system."[53] It explained:

> [The ICJ's] reasoning overlooks the importance of procedural default rules in an adversary system.... Procedural default rules are designed to encourage parties to raise their claims promptly and to vindicate "the law's important interest in the finality of judgments." The consequence of failing to raise a claim for adjudication at the proper time is generally forfeiture of that claim. As a result, rules such as procedural default routinely deny "legal significance" – in the Avena... sense – to otherwise viable legal claims.[54]

Indeed, the majority suggested that the ICJ's interpretation of the Convention may have stemmed from a bias in favor of the inquisitorial systems with which the ICJ was no doubt more familiar. It observed,

> Procedural default rules generally take on greater importance in an adversary system such as ours than in the sort of magistrate-directed, inquisitorial legal system characteristic of many of the other countries that are signatories to the Vienna Convention.... In an inquisitorial system, the failure to raise a legal error can in part be attributed to the magistrate, and thus to the state itself. In our system, however, the responsibility for failing to raise an issue generally rests with the parties themselves.[55]

The majority opinion in *Sanchez-Llamas* thus can be read as an attempt to use dialogue with the ICJ as a means to educate the international court. By emphasizing the significance of the procedural default rule as part of the "basic framework" of the adversarial system, the majority called on the ICJ to take into account the special requirements of adversarial systems in interpreting the Vienna Convention. Moreover, this use of dialogue to educate the ICJ further reinforced the majority's conceptualization of the courts' dialogic relationship as a horizontal one between two coequal tribunals.

To be sure, this conservative brand of "horizontal dialogue" with the ICJ was not exactly the kind of dialogue that most transnationalist legal scholars and human rights advocates were hoping for. It is nevertheless an important kind of dialogue in its own right. As I have argued elsewhere, dialogue with foreign and international courts need not entail automatic deference to those courts' views.[56] To be sure, transnational judicial dialogue can play an important educative role for U.S. judges: in some contexts, U.S. courts may find foreign

---

[53] *Id.* at 2673.
[54] *Id.*
[55] *Id.* at 2686.
[56] *See* Waters, Mediating Norms, *op. cit.*, at 556–57.

or international judicial decisions to be particularly instructive. However, judicial education is a two-way street, and in other contexts, it is entirely appropriate for U.S. courts to use transnational judicial dialogue as a way to educate foreign or international courts on important aspects of the American legal system.

The key advantage of the conservatives' "horizontal dialogue" conception, then, is that it ensures that communication between U.S. and foreign courts is not merely a unidirectional monologue in which U.S. judges serve as passive recipients of international legal norms. Instead, in the conservative conception of horizontal dialogue among coequal tribunals, U.S. judges can contribute to a co-constitutive dialogue in which key American legal norms influence international courts' work.[57]

The conservative justices' horizontal dialogue conception suffers from a significant weakness, however. It does little to promote the goal of uniformity in treaty interpretation, the importance of which both conservative and liberal justices alike have repeatedly emphasized. By giving so little deference to the ICJ's treaty interpretation in *Avena*, for example, the Court hampered the ability of the ICJ to serve as a "natural point of reference"[58] for domestic courts seeking to interpret the Vienna Convention consistently with the courts of other treaty partners.

Of course, the extent to which the ICJ really does serve as a "natural point of reference" for foreign courts is an empirical question well beyond the scope of this chapter. It certainly seems to be a logical assumption, however; and indeed, at least one foreign court has already adopted the ICJ's interpretation of the Vienna Convention in *Avena*. In a consular notification case very similar on its facts to *Sanchez-Llamas*, the German Constitutional Court recently held that German procedural default rules must give way to accommodate claims for violations of Article 36.[59] The court considered and rejected the Supreme Court's "respectful consideration" approach in *Sanchez-Llamas*, instead emphasizing that judicial deference to the ICJ's rulings would promote the goal of uniformity in treaty interpretation.[60] In light of this goal, the German Constitutional Court held that courts in Germany have a constitutional obligation to conform their decisions to those of the ICJ and other

---

[57] *See id.*
[58] *Id.* at 2700 (Breyer, J., dissenting).
[59] *See* Bundesverfassungsgericht (BVerfG – Federal Constitutional Court), 2 BvR 2115/01 (Sept. 19, 2006), available at http://www.bundesverfassungsgericht.de/entscheidungen/ rk20060919_2bvr211501.html. *See generally* Jana Gogolin, Avena *and* Sanchez-Llamas *Come to Germany – The German Constitutional Court Upholds Rights under the Vienna Convention on Consular Relations*, 8 German L.J. 261 (2007).
[60] *See id.* at para. 61.

international tribunals, so long as that obligation can be discharged consistently with other provisions in the German constitution.[61]

Thus, the German Constitutional Court adopted a vertical dialogue approach that went well beyond even the dissent's approach in *Sanchez-Llamas*. To the extent that other foreign courts follow the German court's lead, the *Sanchez-Llamas* majority's horizontal dialogue conception may well result in the Supreme Court finding itself increasingly out of step with foreign signatory courts in treaty interpretation.

2. The Liberal Conception: Vertical Dialogue with the ICJ

In stark contrast to the majority's approach, the dissent in *Sanchez-Llamas* offered a conception of dialogue with the ICJ that was significantly more vertical in orientation (although it certainly did not go as far as the German Constitutional Court has done). The most striking aspect of the dissent's approach is its nuanced analysis of the interaction between the ICJ's ruling in *Avena* and the Supreme Court's prior precedent in *Breard*. In essence, the dissent argued that, whenever possible, the Court should interpret both an ICJ ruling and the Court's own precedent in a way that enables it to avoid a conflict between the two courts.

The dissent began by chastising the majority for *creating* an unnecessary conflict with the ICJ, stating:

> Today's decision interprets an international treaty in a manner that conflicts not only with the treaty's language and history, but also with the ICJ's interpretation of the same treaty provision. In creating this last-mentioned conflict,... the Court's decision is unprecedented.[62]

The dissent suggested that the ICJ's opinions in *Avena* and other consular notification cases were open to different interpretations. It then accused the majority of adopting an extreme interpretation of the ICJ's opinions – one that permitted the Vienna Convention to trump *all* procedural default rules, and possibly other kinds of procedural rules as well. The dissent argued that the majority had thus unfairly painted the international tribunal as having "creat[ed] an extreme rule of law" that reflected a lack of understanding of

---

[61] *See id.* at para. 22. Specifically, the German court held that courts have an obligation to conform their decisions to rulings of international tribunals where "(a) the Federal Republic of Germany is a party to the relevant international treaty, (b) it accepts the jurisdiction of the relevant international court, and (c) no superior law, like the German constitution, is violated by the implementation of a given competent international court decision." Gogolin, *Avena* and *Sanchez-Llamas, op. cit.*, at 270.

[62] *Id.* at 2702.

the American adversarial system.[63] By construing the ICJ's opinions in this negative light, the majority had failed to accord the "respectful consideration" due to an international tribunal.[64]

The dissent argued, in essence, that "respectful consideration" required a more restrained reading of the ICJ's opinions.[65] It then offered its own alternative interpretation of the ICJ's ruling in *Avena*. It asserted that, "fairly read,"[66] *Avena* did not hold that the Vienna Convention "necessarily trumps all procedural default rules,"[67] as the majority claimed. Instead, the dissent argued that the ICJ had merely interpreted Article 36 as precluding the application of procedural default rules "when, but only when, it is the failure of the arresting authorities to inform the defendant of his Convention rights that prevented the defendant from bringing his claim sooner."[68]

Given this restrained interpretation, the ICJ's ruling in *Avena* seems perfectly consistent with the requirements of the adversarial system. After all, as the dissent pointed out, "procedural default rules themselves typically excuse defaults where a defendant shows 'cause and prejudice.'"[69] Thus in the dissent's view, Article 36 does not require procedural default rules to give way in a case where an arrested foreign national (or his lawyer) is aware of his consular notification rights and the foreign national "sleeps on his rights."[70] Instead, it requires procedural default rules to give way only in a fairly narrow set of circumstances: "where the State failed to inform the defendant of his consular access rights, *and* the defendant was not aware of those rights, *and* the State is unwilling to provide some other effective remedy, for example...an ineffective-assistance-of-counsel claim."[71] In the dissent's view, this narrow construction of Article 36 was a "perfectly reasonable interpretation"[72] of the ICJ's ruling in *Avena*. It added, "the Court's reluctance to give...*Avena* this perfectly reasonable interpretation reflects a failure to provide in practice the 'respectful consideration' that we all believe the law demands."[73]

---

[63] *See id.*: "The majority's argument...overlooks what the ICJ actually said, overstates what it actually meant, and is inconsistent with what it actually did."
[64] *See id.*
[65] *See id.*: "To show that kind of respect, we must read the opinions in light of the Convention's underlying language and purposes and ask whether, or to what extent, they require modification of a State's ordinary procedural rules."
[66] *Id.* at 2699.
[67] *Id.*
[68] *Id.* at 2703.
[69] *Id.*
[70] *Id.*
[71] *Id.*
[72] *Id.*
[73] *Id.*

Having thus construed the ICJ's ruling in *Avena* in a way that rendered the Vienna Convention's requirements consistent with American procedural rules, the dissent then turned to the Court's own precedent regarding the Vienna Convention. In *Breard v. Greene*[74] (decided prior to *Avena*), the Court had held that Article 36 did not trump federal procedural default doctrine. In *Sanchez-Llamas*, the dissent asserted that *Breard* could be read consistently with the ICJ's later ruling in *Avena*. First, it argued that federal and state procedural default rules are treated differently under the Supremacy Clause, and the only issue in *Sanchez-Llamas* was the application of Article 36 to *state* rules. As a result, "reading the Convention to require the *state* courts to set aside... procedural default rule[s]... would not call into question, let alone overrule," *Breard*'s holding with respect to *federal* rules.[75]

Second, and more important, the dissent suggested that *Breard* itself should be given a restrained interpretation that would avoid conflict with the ICJ's ruling. Again emphasizing its restrained interpretation of *Avena*, the dissent asserted that the ICJ had merely "interpret[ed] Article 36 to require state procedural default rules *sometimes* to give way to the Convention, namely, when those rules prevent effective remedy by barring assertion of a claim because of a delay caused by the Convention violation itself."[76] It argued that *Breard*'s holding should be read in a similar restrained manner – "i.e., as not saying that the Convention *never* trumps any procedural default rule."[77]

Finally, and most significantly, the dissent claimed that a modified reading of *Breard* was appropriate as a matter of *stare decisis*. It pointed out that the Court had revisited prior treaty interpretations in the past "when new international law has come to light."[78] It argued that the ICJ's post-*Breard* rulings in *LaGrand* and *Avena* amounted to a "'significant... subsequent development' of the law sufficient to lead to a reconsideration of past precedent."[79] Thus, in the dissent's view, even if some degree of *re*-interpretation of *Breard* was required to avoid a conflict with the ICJ rulings, such a move was perfectly justified in light of the international tribunal's post-*Breard* interpretations of the Convention.

Not surprisingly, the dissent's vertical conception of dialogue with international tribunals yielded an opinion in which "respectful consideration" entailed considerably more deference to the ICJ's ruling in *Avena* than was

---

74 523 U.S. 371 (1998).
75 *Sanchez-Llamas*, 126 S.Ct. at 2704.
76 *Id.* at 2704.
77 *Id.*
78 *Id.*
79 *Id.*

evident in the majority's opinion. More important, however, the dissent's vertical dialogue approach resulted in an opinion that went to great lengths to avoid creating a conflict between the Court's own jurisprudence on the Vienna Convention and the ICJ's treaty interpretation in *Avena*. The dissent would avoid the conflict by applying a sort of analogue to the *Charming Betsy* canon of statutory construction. It asserted that both the international court's ruling and the Court's own precedent were susceptible of more than one interpretation. Accordingly, the dissent argued, the Court should construe both *Avena* and *Breard* in a manner that would permit the Court to avoid creating a conflict between domestic criminal procedure doctrine and the United States' international law obligations.

The justices in the *Sanchez-Llamas* dissent thus approach dialogue with international tribunals very differently from the approach taken by the German Constitutional Court, discussed earlier in this chapter. Both emphasize the goal of uniformity in treaty interpretation and view the ICJ as a "natural reference point" and thus a key actor in promoting uniformity. For the German court, however, vertical dialogue requires that courts treat the ICJ's treaty interpretations as binding in most situations. For the *Sanchez-Llamas* dissent, by contrast, dialogue with the ICJ is slightly *less* vertical: "respectful consideration" does not require absolute deference to an ICJ treaty interpretation but *does* require that courts give the ICJ's ruling more deference than the "considerable weight" extended to rulings by foreign signatory courts. In the dissent's conception, "respectful consideration" requires the Supreme Court to engage in a nuanced dialogue with international tribunals. In that nuanced dialogue, the Court should seek accommodation between international tribunals' treaty interpretations and the Court's own precedent. In the dissent's view, a restrained interpretation of *both* courts' rulings interpreting a given treaty would enable the Supreme Court to avoid placing the United States in violation of its international law obligations, while still accommodating the needs (and asserting the primacy of) the American legal system.

D. CONCLUSION

Sanchez-Llamas reveals the very different roles that judicial dialogue with international tribunals can play in U.S. courts' interpretation of treaties. For the majority, the ICJ's ruling in *Avena* was simply erroneous and thus had no persuasive value in the Court's interpretation of the Vienna Convention. Nevertheless, the majority engaged the ICJ's ruling at some length, using dialogue not to inform its own decision making but instead to inform the ICJ itself: dialogue became a means to educate the international tribunal on what the majority viewed as the unique role of procedural default rules in the American adversarial system.

The dissent, by contrast, would use judicial dialogue with the ICJ to inform the Court's decision making. In its conception, dialogue becomes the starting point for a nuanced analysis of the interplay between an international court ruling and the Court's own precedent interpreting a given treaty. The goal of such judicial analysis is to avoid, wherever possible, decisions that will place the United States in violation of its treaty obligations.

Regardless of one's views with respect to their specific application in *Sanchez-Llamas*, both the majority's and the dissent's conceptions of dialogue have significant value. The majority's horizontal dialogue conception emphasizes the independent role of the Supreme Court as a transnational actor in its own right. The majority views the Court's relationship with international tribunals as one of coequal courts extending "respectful consideration" to one another out of a sense of international comity. Thus, the majority makes clear that the Court is perfectly capable of engaging in dialogue with international courts and, in that dialogue, playing a powerful gatekeeping role in scrutinizing international court rulings for their consonance with key American legal norms.

Yet the dissent's more vertical conception of dialogue seems superior in some significant respects. First, it does a better job of promoting the important goal of uniformity in treaty interpretation, preserving the ICJ's key role as a common point of reference for signatory courts. Second, by striving to adopt restrained interpretations of both international court rulings and the Court's own precedent, the dissent uses dialogue to ensure that the Court avoids needlessly placing the United States in violation of international law. In *Sanchez-Llamas*, the attempt to interpret *Avena* and *Breard* to avoid a conflict may have been at times a bit of a stretch. But, the analytical approach itself seems to be a sensible (if creative) extension of well-established principles of statutory construction that are perfectly familiar to the Court. Those principles hold that in engaging in interpretive work, where fairly possible, the Court should assume that the United States does not intend to violate its international law obligations. Adapting such an approach to interpret both international tribunals' and the Court's own decisions regarding treaty interpretations would enable the Court to show "respectful consideration" to international court decisions. At the same time, it would ensure that such consideration does not dissolve into blind deference.

The modest goal of this chapter has been to draw out and study the majority's and dissent's starkly divergent approaches to "respectful consideration" in *Sanchez-Llamas*, in an effort to better understand the differing conceptions on the current U.S. Supreme Court of judicial dialogue with international tribunals. Of course, the Court's opinion in *Sanchez-Llamas* leaves open key questions regarding the meaning of "respectful consideration" in contexts other than the Vienna Convention. For example, the Federal Circuit has grappled recently with the meaning of "respectful consideration" – and the application of *Sanchez-Llamas* – in the international trade context.[80] Here, and in a variety of other arenas, much conceptual and theoretical work remains to be done in developing a fully articulated conception of the proper dialogic relationship between U.S. courts and international tribunals.

[80] *See, e.g., Cummins v. United States*, 454 F.3d 1361 (Fed. Cir. 2006) (applying "respectful consideration" standard to ruling of World Customs Organization). *See generally* Patrick C. Reed, *Relationship of WTO Obligations to U.S. International Trade Law: Internationalist Vision Meets Domestic Reality*, 38 Geo. J. Int'l L. 209 (2006).

6

U.S. Attitudes toward International Criminal Courts and Tribunals

JOHN P. CERONE*

This chapter aims to provide a description of U.S. policy on the subject of international criminal courts and tribunals, both at present[1] and historically, and how that policy has been, and continues to be, developed. It is not intended to provide a critique of that policy. The merits of policy positions are examined only insofar as they shed light on the origins of or motivations underlying those positions.

As an initial matter, it is essential to formulate a definition of the term "international criminal court" as it is used in this study. The characterization of a court as "international" may be influenced by a range of factors. To comprehend the full range of U.S. policy positions, it is important to include not only those characteristics that jurists would consider relevant but also those that are relevant for policy makers, whether legally relevant or not (and whether reasonable or not). Thus, relevant criteria could include the following: whether the court is a creature of international law (i.e., whether the court has international legal personality, subjective or objective); whether its legal basis is an international legal instrument; the nature of the acts to be prosecuted

---

* John P. Cerone is Professor of Law and Director of the Center for International Law and Policy at the New England School of Law. He has served as a confidential legal advisor to several international criminal courts and was involved in the establishment of the Special Court for Sierra Leone and the Extraordinary Chambers in the Courts of Cambodia. Most recently, he was a Visiting Professional in Chambers at the International Criminal Court. The views expressed by the author are not attributable to any of his present or former employers. Much of the research presented herein was gathered through interviews with officials of the U.S. government, various other governments, the United Nations, each of the international criminal courts surveyed, and nongovernmental organizations working on international justice issues.

[1] This study was undertaken from 2005 to 2008, during the second term of the administration of U.S. President George W. Bush.

(including their gravity, the implication of political – moral or material – interests of the international community, or their connection to international law); the composition or manner of selection of the staff or officials of the court; the source of funding; the mandate; whether the court is related to or forms part of a national legal system; the source of the court's jurisdiction; the scope of its jurisdiction; whether the court is labeled "international"; whether its creation or functioning is linked to the United Nations or another international organization; whether the court's operations are beyond the control of states (or beyond the control of a small number of states, or of any single state); and the law to be applied by the court.

The quintessential example of an international criminal court is the International Criminal Court (ICC), established by the 1998 Rome Statute.[2] An inquiry including any of the foregoing considerations would lead to the conclusion that the ICC is an international criminal court. A less central case of an international criminal court would be the Special Court for Sierra Leone, which, although treaty-based, has a number of characteristics normally associated with a domestic court, including the inclusion of Sierra Leonean law within its subject matter jurisdiction and the inclusion of domestic personnel. Toward the periphery of this concept of an international criminal court would be an institution such as the Extraordinary Chambers in the Courts of Cambodia, which are a creature of domestic legislation, are located within the domestic judiciary, apply domestic law (which incorporates international norms), and are primarily staffed by Cambodian personnel. At the outer limit of this conception, or perhaps even beyond it, would be an institution such as the Iraqi High Tribunal, which is a national court without international legal personality, staffed by national personnel, prosecuting perpetrators under domestic law on ordinary bases of jurisdiction (territory and nationality) and without any connection to an international organization. The only factors giving this institution an international veneer are the nature of the acts prosecuted, the source of funding, and the possible appointment of foreign (or "international") officials or advisors.

Finally, it should be noted that there is no coherent U.S. policy on international criminal courts generally. This is in part because of the multifaceted nature of international criminal courts and more generally because the U.S. perspective is an amalgamation of diverse views reduced in some cases to written form, which is itself subject to varying interpretations.

---

[2] Rome Statute of the International Criminal Court, July 17, 1998, 37 ILM 999.

A. EARLY U.S. ATTITUDES TOWARD INTERNATIONAL JUSTICE AND THE POSSIBILITY OF INTERNATIONAL CRIMINAL COURTS (FROM THE NINETEENTH CENTURY TO 1945)

1. *The Hague Peace Conferences (1899–1907)*

The United States has been a strong supporter of the international regulation of armed conflict since at least the nineteenth-century codifications of international humanitarian law. Indeed, the Lieber Code, drafted at the request of the U.S. government for the regulation of the conduct of the armed forces during the U.S. Civil War, had a tremendous impact on the elaboration of the rules of humanitarian law set forth in the Hague Conventions of 1899 and 1907.

Although the United States has demonstrated consistent commitment to the promotion of international humanitarian law (subject to a recent weakening of support for international law generally), this is only tangentially related to the topic of the present study. The issue of whether international law should provide rules for the regulation of armed conflict is quite different from whether there should be an international mechanism with jurisdiction to prosecute individuals for violation of those rules. In addition, it must be noted that humanitarian law, or the *jus in bello,* is a body of law distinct from the *jus ad bellum* – the law that regulates the recourse to the use of armed force. Whereas the United States supports the development of generally applicable rules for the regulation of armed conflict, it is more reluctant to submit the question of the legitimacy of the use of force by the United States to legal regulation.

Although the Hague Peace Conferences did not deal with the issue of an international criminal court, they did consider the creation of an international court for resolving disputes between states. The report of the U.S. delegation makes clear that, although the U.S. government was deeply committed to the establishment of an international court, it was also, along with most of the participating powers, unwilling to submit to compulsory jurisdiction matters that implicated strong national interests.[3] Nonetheless, the United States welcomed the creation of the Permanent Court of Arbitration, with its purely consent-based jurisdiction, in part because of the role it would play in developing an international jurisprudence.[4]

2. *The Treaty of Versailles (1919)*

Article 227 of the Treaty of Versailles provided that Kaiser Wilhelm II (the former German emperor) was to be prosecuted by an international tribunal for

---

[3] Report of the U.S. delegation to the Hague Peace Conference, 1899.
[4] *Id.*

"a supreme offence against international morality and the sanctity of treaties."[5] The tribunal was to consist of judges from the victorious powers: the United States, Great Britain, France, Italy, and Japan.[6]

According to Telford Taylor, the United States was opposed to the idea of an international tribunal from the beginning. Accountability for war crimes did not rank high in President Woodrow Wilson's list of priorities. He was far more concerned with a "moderate peace, a viable democratic government for Germany, and, most of all, a League of Nations to secure future peace."[7] The U.S. delegation was instructed to express serious reservations, rejecting the tribunal and opposing the trial of the Kaiser, who, in the meantime, had found refuge in the neutral Netherlands.[8]

The U.S. representatives to the 1919 Paris Peace Conference indeed made strenuous legal objections to the proposed tribunal and prosecution of the Kaiser, while at the same time expressing the desire of the U.S. government that "those responsible for violations of the laws and customs of war should be punished for their crimes, moral and legal."[9] The American members of the Commission on Responsibility of Authors of the War, appointed by the Conference, noted that the "differences which have arisen between them and their colleagues lie in the means of accomplishing this common desire."[10] In particular, they objected to the creation of an international tribunal, prosecution for violations of the laws of humanity, the prosecution of a head of state, and the idea of "negative criminality" (i.e., prosecution for failure to prevent violations).[11]

Finding no way "to harmonize the[ir] differences without an abandonment of principles which were fundamental,"[12] the U.S. delegation strongly expressed its refusal to endorse the creation of the proposed international criminal court. According to its official "Memorandum of Reservations,"

> In view of their objections to the uncertain law to be applied, varying according to the conception of the members of the high court as to the laws and principles of humanity, and in view also of their objections to the extent of

---

[5] Treaty of Versailles, Article 227.
[6] Telford Taylor, *The Anatomy of the Nuremberg Trials: A Personal Memoir* 15 (Alfred A. Knopf, 1992).
[7] *Id.*
[8] *Id.*
[9] Memorandum of Reservations at 127.
[10] *Id.*
[11] *Id.* at 129.
[12] Commission on the Responsibility of the Authors of the War and on the Enforcement of Penalties, Report Presented to the Preliminary Peace Conference, March 29, 1919, Annex II: Memorandum of Reservations Presented by the Representatives of the United States to the Report of the Commission on Responsibilities, reprinted in 14 Am. J. Int'l L. 95 (1920).

the proposed jurisdiction of that tribunal, the American representatives were cnstrained to decline to be a party to its creation.... They therefore refrained from taking further part either in the discussion of the constitution or of the procedure of the tribunal.[13]

Indeed, with regard to the "unprecedented"[14] proposal to create an international tribunal, the U.S. representatives were

> unable to agree, and their views differ so fundamentally and so radically from those of the Commission that they found themselves obliged to oppose the views of their colleagues in the Commission and to dissent from the statement of those views as recorded in the report.[15]

They proposed instead that "acts affecting the persons or property of one of the Allied or Associated Governments should be tried by a military tribunal of that country."[16] As for acts affecting more than one country, they could be tried "by a tribunal either made up of the competent tribunals of the countries affected or of a commission thereof possessing their authority."[17] This tribunal "would be formed by the mere assemblage of the members, bringing with them the law to be applied, namely, the laws and customs of war, and the procedure, namely, the procedure of the national commissions or courts."[18]

Such a mechanism would address the concerns of the U.S. delegation regarding what they perceived as the ex post facto nature of an international tribunal. The U.S. representatives believed that

> the nations should use the machinery at hand, which had been tried and found competent, with a law and procedure framed and therefore known in advance, rather than to create an international tribunal with a criminal jurisdiction for which there is no precedent, precept, practice, or procedure.[19]

By creating a joint, multinational tribunal or commission, "existing national tribunals or national commissions which could legally be called into being would be utilized, and not only the law and the penalty would be already declared, but the procedure would be settled."[20] Only under these conditions

---

[13] *Id.*
[14] *Id.*
[15] *Id.* at 140.
[16] *Id.* at 146.
[17] *Id.*
[18] *Id.* at 142. This is essentially what is contemplated in Article 229 of the Versailles Treaty, the second paragraph of which provided, "Persons guilty of criminal acts against the nationals of more than one of the Allied and Associated Powers will be brought before military tribunals composed of members of the military tribunals of the Powers concerned."
[19] *Id.*
[20] *Id.* at 147.

and with these limitations might the United States participate in "a high tribunal, which they would have preferred to call, because of its composition, the Mixed or United Tribunal or Commission."[21]

Notwithstanding these objections, the United States grudgingly went along with the inclusion of Article 227 in the final draft of the Treaty of Versailles, but only after negotiating language that would reduce the prospects of it being implemented.[22]

3. *The League of Nations (1919–1945)*

Early in its existence, the Council of the League of Nations had before it a proposal to create an international criminal court. An Advisory Committee of Jurists, appointed by the Council in February 1920, recommended the creation of a High Court of International Justice, which would be competent to criminally prosecute individuals for violations of the "universal law of nations."[23] This proposal was eventually rejected by the League. According to the Third Committee of the League Assembly, it was "best to entrust criminal cases to the ordinary tribunals as is at present the custom in international procedure." While recognizing that "crimes of this kind" might "in future be brought within the scope of international penal law," consideration of the issue was, "at the moment, premature."[24]

According to UN Special Rapporteur Richard Alfaro, this rejection "reflected the views of those who had opposed the establishment of an international jurisdiction for the trial of the First World War criminals, for certain legal reasons, to wit: that there was no defined notion of international crimes; that there was no international penal law; that the principle *nulla poena sine lege* would be disregarded; that the different proposals were not clear; and that inasmuch as only States were subjects of international law, individuals could only be punished in accordance with their national law."[25] This of course closely parallels the position taken by the U.S. delegation to the Paris Commission on Responsibilities.

More than a decade later, under the auspices of the League of Nations, a treaty was elaborated that would have created an international criminal court

---

[21] *Id.*
[22] Taylor, *supra* n. 5, at 15.
[23] Report on the Question of International Criminal Jurisdiction by Richard J. Alfaro, Special Rapporteur, Yearbook of the International Law Commission, 1950, vol. II, A/CN.4/15, at para. 15.
[24] *Id.*, at para. 16.
[25] *Id.*, at para. 17.

to prosecute the crime of terrorism. This treaty failed to attract ratification and consequently never entered into force.[26]

Expressing contemporary views on the matter, Manley Hudson, U.S. jurist and former judge of the Permanent Court of International Justice, wrote in 1944,

> Instead of attempting to create an international penal law and international agencies to administer it, perhaps attention may more usefully be given to promoting the cooperation of national agencies in such matters as extradition, judicial assistance, jurisdiction to punish for crime, and coordinated surveillance by national police. Whatever course of development may be imminent with reference to political organization, the time is hardly ripe for the extension of international law to include judicial process for condemning and punishing acts either of States or of individuals.[27]

Hudson speculated that "[t]he local impact of anti-social acts inspires the desire of States to safeguard local condemnation and local punishment, and impingement on national prerogatives in this field will become possible only as the need for international action is clearly demonstrated."[28] Arguably, the horrors of World War II provided the necessary demonstration.

B. U.S. POLICY TOWARD INTERNATIONAL CRIMINAL COURTS SINCE WORLD WAR II

1. Nuremberg and Tokyo

The United States was strongly supportive of the establishment of the International Military Tribunals (IMTs) at Nuremberg and Tokyo after World War II. As one of the four victorious allies responsible for creating the Tribunals, the United States played a central role in shaping their design and operation.

However, as recalled by Telford Taylor, the United States was initially unsupportive of the Russian proposal to establish an international tribunal for the trial of "major war criminals."[29] Indeed, Roosevelt initially endorsed Churchill's counterproposal to summarily execute them.

---

[26] *Id.*, at para. 26. Manley O. Hudson, *International Tribunals: Past and Future* 186 (Carnegie Endowment for International Peace and The Brookings Institution 1944).
[27] *Id.*
[28] *Id.*
[29] Taylor, *supra* n. 5, at 34.

Taylor primarily credits Secretary of War Henry L. Stimson with the reversal of this position. In negotiations within the U.S. government, the War Department emerged as the dominant entity.[30] Taylor also noted that Stimson had the support of the military:

> Stimson's ascendancy also foreclosed American support for the British summary-execution plan. In his insistence that the Nazi leaders stand trial, the Secretary had the strong support of both the Army Chief of Staff, General George C. Marshall, and the army's principal lawyer, Judge Advocate General Myron C. Cramer.[31]

The U.S. government's preference for a "judicial" solution to the problem of war criminals was ultimately made clear in the Yalta Memorandum, which had been prepared to guide U.S. President Roosevelt when he attended the Yalta conference.

> We think that the just and effective solution lies in the use of the judicial method. Condemnation of these criminals after a trial, moreover, would command maximum public support in our own times and receive the respect of history. The use of the judicial method will, in addition, make available for all mankind to study in future years an authentic record of Nazi crimes and criminality.[32]

This same memorandum envisions the creation of an International Military Tribunal, to be established by Executive Agreement, and formed the groundwork of the later drafts submitted by the United States for an international agreement. The memorandum was initialed by Secretary Stimson, Secretary of State Edward R. Stettinius Jr., and Attorney General Francis Biddle.

Ultimately, support for the Tribunal came from the highest levels of the U.S. administration, including President Truman. Taylor notes that Truman, soon after taking office, made clear that he opposed summary execution and supported the establishment of a tribunal.[33]

The IMT at Nuremberg was established on the basis of the London Agreement, a treaty concluded among the four allies, and the IMT for the Far East (Tokyo) was created by a special proclamation of General MacArthur, acting as supreme commander of the Allied Forces. Both Tribunals were given jurisdiction to prosecute crimes against peace, war crimes, and crimes against

---

[30] *Id.*
[31] *Id.* at 35.
[32] Memorandum to President Roosevelt from the Secretaries of State and War and the Attorney General ("Yalta Memorandum"), January 22, 1945, at http://www.yale.edu/lawweb/avalon/imt/jackson/jack01.htm.
[33] *Id.* at 32.

humanity. Thus, the Tribunals were charged with prosecuting not only violations of the *jus in bello* but also violations of the *jus ad bellum*. Significantly for the purposes of this chapter, their jurisdiction was limited to prosecuting those fighting on behalf of enemy states. According to Article 6 of the London Charter, the Tribunal had the power to prosecute only those who were "acting in the interests of the European Axis countries." Thus, there was no possibility of prosecuting those fighting on behalf of the Allies.

Although U.S. support for the creation of the IMTs may appear inconsistent with the position taken by the U.S. delegation to the 1919 Paris Conference, it is worth noting the similarities between the IMTs and the U.S. counterproposal detailed in its 1919 Memorandum of Reservations. Echoing the U.S. vision of a joint, multinational military tribunal, the Nuremberg Tribunal pointed out,

> The Signatory Powers created this Tribunal, defined the law it was to administer, and made regulations for the proper conduct of the Trial. In doing so, they have done together what any one of them might have done singly; for it is not to be doubted that any nation has the right thus to set up special courts to administer law.[34]

Nonetheless, a key difference remained. The accused were clearly prosecuted on the basis of international law and not under the domestic law of the Signatory Powers. As noted by the Tribunal, the IMT Charter "is the expression of international law existing at the time of its creation."[35]

Some observers find U.S. support for the IMTs ultimately grounded in the confluence of internationalism and exceptionalism.[36] Although the Tribunals

---

[34] Judgment of the Nuremberg Tribunal, 1946. In addition, the Yalta Memorandum cites an Aide Memoire from the British Embassy indicating the UK government's willingness to cooperate in the establishment of "Mixed Military Tribunals to deal with cases which for one reason or another could not be tried in national courts." Its reference to "Mixed Military Tribunals" bears a strong similarity to the term preferred by the U.S. delegation to the 1919 Commission on Responsibilities – "Mixed or United Tribunal or Commission."

[35] *Id.* It should be noted, however, that the U.S. discomfort with the notion of the "laws of humanity," expressed repeatedly by the U.S. representatives to the 1919 Commission on Responsibilities, still existed in 1945. According to the Yalta Memorandum, Hitler's prewar atrocities were "neither 'war crimes' in the technical sense, nor offenses against international law." Nevertheless, this would not stand in the way of the "declared policy of the United Nations" that these crimes would be punished. In early drafts of the London Charter prepared by the United States, there was no reference to Crimes against Humanity. The analogous provision referred to "atrocities and offences" committed in violation of "any applicable provision of the *domestic law* of the country in which committed." Formulation of the Nürnberg Principles – Report by J. Spiropoulos, Special Rapporteur, *Yearbook of the International Law Commission*, 1950, vol. II, A/CN.4/22, at para. 2. Ultimately, this lingering discomfort was reflected in the conservative approach taken to the codification of Crimes against Humanity in the Nuremberg Charter. Crimes against Humanity could only be prosecuted if committed in conjunction with another crime within the jurisdiction of the Tribunal.

[36] Interview with former State Department official (name withheld), December 13, 2005.

were in some respects international, they were also viewed as mechanisms of the occupying powers and, in part, as arms of the U.S. military.[37] As international tribunals subject to a wide measure of U.S. control, their existence and operation were compatible with contemporary American tendencies toward internationalism while alleviating any concern about ceding power beyond U.S. reins. Although the United States did not have exclusive control of the Tribunals, the government was assured that U.S. nationals would not be prosecuted, because the personal jurisdiction of the Tribunals was limited to those who were acting in the interests of enemy states.

2. Early United Nations Efforts to Create an International Criminal Court

The establishment of an international criminal court was on the United Nations' (UN's) agenda from early on in its existence. In 1946, acting on the initiative of the U.S. delegation,[38] the UN General Assembly affirmed the principles of international law recognized in the Charter and judgment of the Nuremberg Tribunal, and mandated the Committee on the codification of international law to

> treat as a matter of primary importance plans for the formation, in the context of a general codification of offences against the peace and security of mankind, or of an International Criminal Code, of the principles recognized in the Charter of the Nuremberg Tribunal and in the judgment of the Tribunal.[39]

The following year saw the negotiation of the text of the Genocide Convention. An early draft prepared by the Secretariat included as appendices alternative proposals for a permanent and an ad hoc international criminal court to try and punish acts of genocide.[40] In its comments on the draft Convention, the United States proposed that the issue of establishing an international criminal court be considered separately.[41]

Although the United States supported the creation of ad hoc tribunals to prosecute genocide, it expressed concern that the attachment of a treaty creating a court to the draft Genocide Convention might jeopardize the successful

---

[37] The U.S. preference for a military tribunal was made clear in the Yalta Memorandum. It stated, "We would prefer a court of military personnel, as being less likely to give undue weight to technical contentions and legalistic arguments."

[38] *Formulation of the Nürnberg Principles* – Report by J. Spiropoulos, Special Rapporteur, *Yearbook of the International Law Commission*, 1950, vol. II, A/CN.4/22, at para. 29.

[39] G.A. Res. 1/95, 11 December 1946.

[40] Draft Convention on Genocide, Dc. A/362, 25 August 1947. The proposals for these courts drew heavily from the text of the 1937 Convention.

[41] Communications Received by the Secretary-General, Doc. A/401, 27 September 1947.

conclusion of the latter.[42] It also noted that the "problem of the institution of [an international penal] tribunal, competent to try international crimes generally, is of such a magnitude as to necessitate a separate project, having the most careful consideration, and inviting the largest number of States possible to become party thereto."[43] It suggested instead that the Genocide Convention expressly include an obligation to work toward the establishment of a permanent international criminal court, and that, pending the establishment of such an institution, States Parties should create ad hoc tribunals as needed. It also proposed that the International Law Commission (ILC), the successor entity of the Committee on the codification of international law, be mandated to explore the possibility of creating a permanent court.[44]

In subsequent debates in the Sixth Committee, the United States continued to voice strong support for retaining language in the Genocide Convention that would provide a foundation for the future development of an international criminal court.[45] The U.S. delegate noted that "[i]t was precisely because it had been felt that national courts might not be sufficiently effective in the punishment of genocide that States had realized the need for an international convention on the subject." He also pointed out that such a court's jurisdiction would be consent based.

Subsequently, the General Assembly, in the same resolution adopting the text of the Genocide Convention, invited the ILC to "study the desirability and possibility of establishing an international judicial organ for the trial of persons charged with genocide or other crimes over which jurisdiction will be conferred upon that organ by international conventions."[46] The Commission turned to this task the following year.

In 1950, the General Assembly designated a Committee consisting of seventeen UN Member States, including the United States, for the "purpose of

---

[42] Id.
[43] Id.
[44] Id. In its comments, the United States also objected to the inclusion of universal jurisdiction in the draft Convention. Among the reasons for its objection to this provision was "that it would apparently seek to establish a rule of law applicable to nationals of States which have not consented to it, namely, such States as may not ratify the convention." Id.
[45] Consideration of the draft Convention on Genocide, 98th Meeting of the Sixth Committee, November 10, 1948.
[46] G. A. Res. 3/260, 9 December 1948. The adoption of the Genocide Convention was strongly condemned by the president of the American Bar Association, who specifically objected to the possibility that "public officials as well as private citizens are to be made amenable to international tribunals for a variety of ill-defined and ambiguous acts of 'genocide' – to the extent that the causing of 'mental harm' to a member of a group or complicity in so doing is an act of genocide." F. Holman, *International Proposals Affecting So-Called Human Rights*, 14 Law & Contemp. Probs. 479 (1949). His views were subsequently endorsed in part by U.S. Senator John Bricker. J. Bricker, *Making Treaties and Other International Agreements*, 289 Annals Am. Acad. Pol. & Soc. Sci. 134 (1953).

preparing one or more preliminary draft conventions and proposals relating to the establishment and the statute of an international criminal court."[47] The U.S. delegate, George Morris, chaired the Committee, which met in Geneva in August 1951. When the Report of the Geneva Committee was considered by the Sixth Committee in the fall of 1952, Morris, then representing the United States on the Sixth Committee, seemed to voice modest support for the creation of an international criminal court, stating that the "United Nations was on the threshold of a potentially great idea."[48] However, a week later he clarified that the United States "neither favored nor opposed the establishment of an international criminal court."[49]

In the face of a wide range of views on the subject, including strong opposition from the United Kingdom,[50] Morris played a conciliatory role. For example, he pointed out that many of the delegates' objections to the creation of a court by a General Assembly resolution had been alleviated by a series of "agreements for the safeguarding of national interests."[51] In particular, he noted that the Geneva Committee had agreed that "no government should be bound to accept the court's jurisdiction for its own nationals; recognition of the court's jurisdiction could be the subject of a specific convention."[52] Thus, although the United States appeared to be amenable to the creation of an international criminal court, the court envisioned would have jurisdiction only over those individuals whose state of nationality had recognized the court's jurisdiction by treaty.

The UN continued its work on the draft statute for five more years, but differences among UN Member States, exacerbated by the nascent Cold War, led the UN to abandon its efforts on this project.[53] Among the more controversial aspects of the draft statute was the definition of the crime of aggression.[54]

---

[47] G.A. Res. 5/489, 12 December 1950.
[48] Consideration of the Report on the Committee on International Criminal Jurisdiction, 322nd Meeting of the Sixth Committee, 8 November 1952, at para. 18.
[49] Consideration of the Report on the Committee on International Criminal Jurisdiction, 328th Meeting of the Sixth Committee, 17 November 1952, at para. 29.
[50] Consideration of the Report on the Committee on International Criminal Jurisdiction, 321st Meeting of the Sixth Committee, 7 November 1952, at para. 26 and following.
[51] Consideration of the Report on the Committee on International Criminal Jurisdiction, 322nd Meeting of the Sixth Committee, 8 November 1952, at para. 17.
[52] Consideration of the Report on the Committee on International Criminal Jurisdiction, 322nd Meeting of the Sixth Committee, 8 November 1952, at para. 16.
[53] Ferencz, *An International Criminal Court: A Step toward World Peace*, vol. 2, 1980, pp. 36–38, Oceana.
[54] Report of the Sixth Committee, Doc. A/3770, 6 December 1957, at para. 5 and following. See also G.A. Res. 12/1186, 11 December 1957. The United States has traditionally resisted efforts to define aggression. For example the United States opposed the inclusion of a definition of aggression in the UN Charter. 5 Whiteman, *Digest of International Law* 740 (1965). This

It was not until 1981 that the UN General Assembly would request that the ILC return to the task of elaborating an international criminal code,[55] and the creation of an international criminal court would not find a place on the UN agenda until 1989. There is likely a link between this renewed interest in the UN and a change of attitude toward the matter in Washington, D.C. Indeed, in the United States, support for an international criminal court resurfaced in the late 1980s. In 1988, the U.S. Congress passed legislation urging the president to "begin discussions with foreign governments to investigate the feasibility and advisability of establishing an international criminal court to expedite cases regarding the prosecution of persons accused of having engaged in international drug trafficking or having committed international crimes."[56] However, this same piece of legislation was careful to preserve the possibility of an exemption for U.S. nationals. It stipulated, "Such discussions shall not include any commitment that such court shall have jurisdiction over the extradition of United States citizens."[57]

In 1989, Trinidad and Tobago placed the question of an ICC back on the agenda of the UN General Assembly, which requested the ILC to prepare a draft statute.[58]

3. The International Criminal Tribunals for the Former Yugoslavia and Rwanda

The United States was the driving force behind the establishment of the International Criminal Tribunals for the former Yugoslavia (ICTY) and Rwanda (ICTR), contributing the greatest share of political and financial muscle.

After the end of the Cold War, the United States became preeminent and gained a substantial degree of control, primarily through the Security Council, over UN mechanisms, providing an impetus to make greater use of them.[59] Thus, when faced with growing pressure to act in the face of widely publicized atrocities in the former Yugoslavia and Rwanda, the Clinton administration responded by promoting the creation of the ICTY and ICTR.[60]

---

controversy remains in the context of continuing negotiations over the definition for aggression as a crime within the subject matter jurisdiction of the International Criminal Court.

[55] G.A. Res. 36/106, 10 December 1981.
[56] PL 100-690, 102 Stat. 4267 (1988).
[57] Id.
[58] G.A. Res. 44/39, 4 December 1989.
[59] Interview with David Scheffer, former U.S. ambassador for War Crimes Issues, March 31, 2005; interview with former State Department official (name withheld), December 13, 2005; interview with former State Department official (name withheld), May 11, 2006.
[60] Id. But see D. Scheffer, Three Memories from the Year of Origin: 1993, 2 J. Int'l Crim. Justice, No. 2, 353 (2004).

Both Tribunals have jurisdiction to prosecute war crimes, genocide, and crimes against humanity. Unlike the IMTs, violations of the *jus ad bellum* are not within their subject matter jurisdiction. As ad hoc Tribunals, they have limited territorial and temporal scope. Although U.S. personnel are theoretically subject to prosecution by either Tribunal, the nature of the Tribunals' jurisdiction and the political framework within which the Tribunals operate make such an event unlikely, which reduced the likelihood of any U.S. opposition. Another factor bolstering U.S. support for the Tribunals is the ability of the United States to influence their operations. This influence, although limited, expresses itself through the staffing of the tribunals with a number of U.S. citizens, several of whom were former government employees, and through the "silent influence" of the United States – the mere fact that the staff of the Tribunals are aware that, without the support of the United States, the tribunals would not exist.[61]

It is also clear that, without the support of the United States, the ICTs would never have come into being. The initial declarations of a number of Member States expressed genuine skepticism at the idea of a Security Council–created international tribunal.[62] The establishment of the ICTY was a U.S. idea, and it was the United States that pushed it through the Security Council.[63]

Many observers credit then-U.S. Ambassador to the UN Madeleine Albright with the creation of the ICTY.[64] Her expressions of support rang of high ideals. Upon the establishment of the ICTY, she stated, "There is an echo in this chamber today. The Nuremberg principles have been reaffirmed. The lesson that we are all accountable to international law may finally have taken hold in our collective memory."[65]

U.S. President Clinton also expressed strong support for the ICTY and ICTR in a 1995 speech at the University of Connecticut:

> With our purpose and with our position comes the responsibility to help shine the light of justice on those who would deny to others their most basic human rights. We have an obligation to carry forward the lessons of Nuremberg. That

---

[61] Interview with ICTY official (name withheld), April 3, 2005.
[62] See Zacklin, *Bosnia and Beyond*, 34 Va. J. Int'l L. 277 (1994): "In my twenty years of experience in the United Nations, I have never encountered as much skepticism as has surrounded the establishment of this Tribunal. Even now, though the Tribunal has actually been established, member states and United Nations organs continue to question whether this Tribunal will work."
[63] Interview with UN official (name withheld), March 27, 2005.
[64] *Id.*
[65] Madeleine K. Albright, *UN Security Council Adopts Resolution 808 on War Crimes Tribunal*, 4 U.S. Dept. of St. Dispatch No. 12, Art. 5 (March 22, 1993).

is why we strongly support the United Nations War Crimes Tribunals for the former Yugoslavia and for Rwanda.[66]

Clinton reiterated his support in a 1997 address before the UN General Assembly and also endorsed the creation of a permanent international criminal court, saying,

> [W]e must maintain our strong support for the United Nations war crime tribunals and truth commissions. And before the century ends, we should establish a permanent international court to prosecute the most serious violations of humanitarian law.[67]

A number of official statements of support for the Tribunals have, of course, also been made by the former U.S. Ambassador at Large for War Crimes Issues Pierre Prosper, and his predecessor David Scheffer.[68]

The ad hoc Tribunals, and the ICTY in particular, enjoy broad support in the U.S. Congress. Congressional support has been important in putting pressure on the administration to act in support of the Tribunals.[69]

U.S. support for the Tribunals has taken a variety of forms. In addition to the financial support that the United States provides as the largest contributing Member State of the United Nations,[70] the U.S. government has also provided significant additional direct support, including through in-kind contributions. The United States had also provided a large number of gratis personnel, until the Fifth Committee of the General Assembly put a stop to it.[71]

Its political support has been manifested in its continued advocacy for the Tribunals in UN fora, as well as through the creation of the Rewards for Justice Program[72] and its continuing efforts to pressure states to cooperate with the Tribunals, including through conditionality. In addition, as noted earlier, the Tribunals employ a number of U.S. citizens, many in key and top-level

---

[66] William J. Clinton, *Remarks at the University of Connecticut in Storrs*, 31 Wkly. Comp. Pres. Docs. 1840, 1842 (Oct. 23, 1995).

[67] William J. Clinton, *Remarks to the 52d Session of the United Nations General Assembly in New York City*, 33 Wkly. Comp. Pres. Docs. 1386, 1389 (Sept. 29, 1997).

[68] See various statements of support on the Web site of the U.S. State Department Office of War Crimes Issues at http://www.state.gov/s/wci.

[69] Interview with Nina Bang-Jensen, executive director of the Coalition for International Justice, June 16, 2005; interview with Richard Dicker, Human Rights Watch, March 9, 2005.

[70] By the end of 2006, U.S. financial support totaled more than $500 million. Statement of John Bellinger, May 11, 2006.

[71] Interview with ICTY official (name withheld), April 3, 2005. Presumably, the Fifth Committee acted to ensure that the ICTY and ICTR could still be representative of the whole UN membership and that a handful of nations would not be overrepresented in the staff.

[72] Through this program, the U.S. government pays significant financial rewards in return for information leading to the apprehension of certain individuals indicted by the tribunals. *See*, e.g., Public Law 106-277 (October 2000).

positions.⁷³ As with many of these factors, this serves as an expression of U.S. support, as well as an influence in bolstering U.S. support.

Some advocates within the nongovernmental organization (NGO) community have perceived a cooling of U.S. support for the Tribunals in the era following the adoption of the Rome Statute creating the ICC, which they attribute to a cooling toward international justice generally.⁷⁴ Others, however, have perceived a shift of increasing support, which they attribute to the Bush administration's desire to demonstrate the value of ad hoc, Security-Council-controlled tribunals, and, in the case of the Rwanda Tribunal, the virtue of carrying out justice locally, in contrast to the ICC.⁷⁵ It seems more likely that both have occurred and that they have resulted in a dynamic equilibrium of sorts that still equates with a generally supportive attitude.

Be that as it may, U.S. support of the ad hoc international criminal tribunals has been largely consistent. Official criticism has generally been limited to concerns about efficiency and accountability of staff members (particularly with respect to the ICTR),⁷⁶ which may be linked to a latent suspicion of international bureaucracies.

A possible exception to this otherwise consistent support would be situations in which the operations of the Tribunals have directly conflicted with U.S. foreign policy objectives. For example, the review of the NATO bombing of Serbia in 1999, undertaken by the Office of the Prosecutor (OTP) of the ICTY,⁷⁷ infuriated opponents of the ICC within the U.S. government.⁷⁸ Similarly, U.S. government officials were upset by the indictment of Radovan Karadzic in the run-up to the Dayton Accords.⁷⁹ Some observers suggest that this attitude was also reflected in NATO's failure to arrest Karadzic and also Ratko Mladic – two of the ICTY's most wanted.⁸⁰ Similar allegations have been made concerning U.S. interference in the ICTR's efforts to prosecute members of the Rwandan Patriotic Front (RPF).⁸¹

---

73 The United States has always had a U.S.-nominated judge on the ICTY, two of whom have been ICTY president. In addition, U.S. nationals have occupied the largest number of senior positions in the Office of the Prosecutor and Registry.
74 Id.
75 Interview with John Stompor, Human Rights First, March 8, 2005.
76 See Opening Statement of Pierre-Richard Prosper before the Committee on International Relations of the U.S. House of Representatives, February 28, 2002.
77 See Final Report to the Prosecutor by the Committee Established to Review the NATO Bombing Campaign against the Federal Republic of Yugoslavia (2000).
78 Interview with former State Department official (name withheld), August 24, 2001.
79 Id.
80 Interview with ICTY official (name withheld), March 27, 2005.
81 In her 2007 book *Peace and Punishment*, former ICTY/R spokeswoman Florence Hartmann claims that the U.S. government pressured Carla del Ponte, former ICTR prosecutor, to drop

4. The International Criminal Court

By the mid-1990s, it became apparent that the ad hoc approach was unsustainable, a phenomenon that some have dubbed "tribunal fatigue."[82] From the U.S. perspective, this left two options: reverting to domestic systems or developing a permanent international criminal court.[83] At this time, the U.S. government appeared very supportive of the idea of establishing a permanent international criminal court.

In 1995, President Clinton expressed this support when he stated that "nations all around the world who value freedom and tolerance [should] establish a permanent international criminal court to prosecute, with the support of the United Nations Security Council, serious violations of humanitarian law."[84] On July 30, 1997, Congress expressed its support for the creation of an international criminal court in House Joint Resolution 89, reminding Clinton of his earlier expressions of support and calling on him "to continue to support and fully participate in negotiations at the United Nations to conclude an international agreement to establish an international criminal court."[85]

Nonetheless, there was a broad spectrum of views within the U.S. government, and each agency had its own concerns. Whereas the State Department as a whole was in favor of establishing an international criminal court, there was resistance from the intelligence community and the Joint Chiefs of Staff.[86] Through interagency dialogue, some of the rough edges were smoothed, and interagency consensus in favor of establishing an international criminal court was ultimately achieved.[87]

---

her investigations into alleged international crimes committed by members of the RPF. She asserts that the United States acted at the request of Rwandan president Paul Kagame, former leader of the RPF, as a quid pro quo for Rwanda's consent to an Article 98 Agreement with the United States. Hartmann also claims that del Ponte's refusal to halt the investigations is what led to the appointment of a new ICTR Prosecutor in September 2003. F. Hartmann, *Peace and Punishment*, Flammarion (2007). *See also* S. Aulich, *Behind Curtains of International Justice*, interview with Florence Hartmann, The European Courier, October 11, 2007 (http://europeancourier.org/47.htm – revisited the site on 4/2/2009).

[82] "Challenges Confronting International Justice Issues," address by David J. Scheffer at New England School of Law, Ambassador at Large for War Crimes Issues, January 14, 1998.
[83] Interview with David Scheffer, former U.S. Ambassador for War Crimes Issues, March 31, 2005.
[84] 31 Wkly. Comp. Pres. Docs. at 1843. At the same time, his reference to the "support of the Security Council" may indicate that he was envisioning a particular control mechanism for such a court.
[85] H.J. Res. 89, 105th Cong. (July 30, 1997).
[86] Interview with David Scheffer, former U.S. Ambassador for War Crimes Issues, March 31, 2005.
[87] *Id.*

I. The Rome Conference – June–July 1998

The U.S. delegation to the Rome Conference, led by then-U.S. Ambassador at Large for War Crimes Issues David Scheffer, was the largest of any government. A number of U.S. agencies, including the Departments of Justice, State, Defense, and Treasury; the Joint Chiefs of Staff; and the intelligence community, had all been involved in developing the U.S. position at Rome.[88]

The U.S. delegation arrived in Rome with a number of concerns that it sought to be addressed during the conference. Broadly, these fell into three categories: the crimes that would fall within the subject matter jurisdiction of the court, the way in which cases would be triggered, and the exposure of U.S. personnel.[89] In general, the delegation engaged in what it considered to be a constructive approach – to influence the Conference to accede to U.S. demands in the hope of establishing a court acceptable to the United States.[90]

To the NGO community, it was clear that the U.S. delegation wanted to limit the jurisdictional reach of the ICC.[91] The delegation wanted either Security Council control or a clear exemption for nationals of non-States Parties.[92] The United States pushed particularly hard on three issues: bases of jurisdiction, *proprio motu* investigations by the prosecutor, and peacekeeper exemptions.[93] It resorted to particularly strong-arm tactics. According to NGO reports, U.S. officials were calling capitals threatening to cut off aid, going after the smaller, weaker states, especially in Africa.[94] Even if these states did not have much political weight, they had numerical significance.

Although many of its concerns were addressed, a few key issues were not resolved to the satisfaction of the U.S. government. Thus, U.S. support cooled considerably following the adoption of the Rome Statute. Indeed, the United States was one of only a handful of states that voted against the adoption of the Rome Statute.

Shortly after the adoption of the Rome Statute, Scheffer testified before the Senate Foreign Relations Committee, setting forth the reasons why the delegation voted against adoption. The United States objected to the breadth of the court's jurisdiction, in particular, its jurisdiction over nationals of non-States Parties (absent a Security Council referral), the *proprio motu* power of

---

[88] Sen. Subcomm. on Intl. Operations of the Comm. on For. Rel., *Is a U.N. International Criminal Court in the U.S. National Interest?*, 105th Cong. 11 (July 23, 1998).
[89] Interview with David Scheffer, former U.S. Ambassador for War Crimes Issues, March 31, 2005.
[90] *Id.*
[91] Interview with diplomat (non-U.S.) involved in the Rome negotiations (name withheld), March 26, 2005.
[92] *Id.*
[93] *Id.*
[94] *Id.*

U.S. Attitudes toward International Criminal Courts and Tribunals 149

the prosecutor, the possibility of a definition for the crime of aggression that would not maintain the "vital linkage" with a prior decision by the Security Council, and the inclusion of a "no reservations" clause.[95]

One of the other witnesses testifying at the Senate hearings on the International Criminal Court was John Bolton, introduced at the hearing as "Former Assistant Secretary of State for International Organization Affairs; Senior Vice President, American Enterprise Institute."[96] At the time of the 1998 hearing, Bolton had served in a prior administration but was then employed by the conservative think tank, the American Enterprise Institute (AEI). Bolton's comments before the Senate committee demonstrate a very different attitude toward the idea of an international criminal court in general:

> Unfortunately, support for the ICC concept is based largely on emotional appeals to an abstract ideal of an international judicial system, unsupported by any meaningful evidence, and running contrary to sound principles of international crisis resolution. Moreover, for some, faith in the ICC rests largely on an unstated agenda of creating ever more comprehensive international structures to bind nation states in general and one nation state in particular. Regrettably, the Clinton administration's naive support for the ICC has left the U.S. in a worse position internationally than if we had simply declared our principled opposition in the first place.[97]

He concluded that the United States "should oppose any suggestion that we cooperate, help, fund or generally support the work of the prosecutor. We should isolate and ignore the ICC."[98] He described his policy proposal as the "Three Noes: no financial support, directly or indirectly; no collaboration; and no further negotiations with other governments to improve the statute."[99] This approach was "likely to maximize the chances that the ICC will wither and collapse, which should be our objective."[100]

As articulated in a July 2002 Congressional Research Service report, the United States, and in particular the U.S. Congress, would have three options: "to withhold all cooperation from the ICC and its member states in order to prevent the ICC from becoming effective, to continue contributing to the development of the ICC in order to improve it, or to adopt a pragmatic approach based solely on U.S. interests."[101]

---

[95] *Id.* at 12–15.
[96] *Id.* at 28.
[97] *Id.*
[98] *Is a U.N. International Criminal Court in the U.S. National Interest?*, 105th Cong. at 31.
[99] *Id.* at 32.
[100] *Id.*
[101] Jennifer Elsea, Congressional Research Service, *U.S. Policy Regarding the International Criminal Court* 3 (July 9, 2002).

II. The Decision to Sign the Rome Statute

The Rome Statute was open for signature until December 31, 2000. There was a split view within the U.S. government over whether to sign. The Department of Defense, and the Joint Chiefs of Staff in particular, did not want to sign; however, it should be noted that there was division even within the Pentagon.[102]

On December 31, 2000, the last day that it was open for signature, and during the final days of the Clinton administration, the U.S. signed the treaty. Upon signing, however, President Clinton made clear that the United States was not prepared to ratify the treaty in its present form, citing continuing concerns about "significant flaws" in the Statute. (This language was heavily negotiated to satisfy the Department of Defense.[103]) He remarked that, despite the U.S. signature, "I will not, and do not recommend that my successor, submit the treaty to the Senate for advice and consent until our fundamental concerns are satisfied."[104]

Nonetheless, it appeared that the United States might ultimately be prepared to ratify the treaty if it was successful in obtaining certain concessions from the other signatory states, and it signed to maintain its seat at the discussion table.[105] The general attitude of the U.S. government at this time appeared to be that the ICC in principle was a good thing but that it needed adjustments to be acceptable to the United States.[106]

III. The Bush Administration and Notification of Intent Not to Become a Party

Shortly after the Clinton administration signed the Rome Statute, George W. Bush was sworn in as the new U.S. president. Under his administration, the attitude of the U.S. government toward the ICC would shift from cautious support to outright opposition. Some observers believe that this shift was immediate and that the position immediately became one of intense hostility. Others perceived a more gradual shift.

Those who perceived an immediate shift to intense hostility point to the greater wariness about international law and institutions on the part of Bush, Vice President Dick Cheney, and a number of their appointees,

---

[102] Interview with former State Department official (name withheld).
[103] *Id.*
[104] William J. Clinton, *Statement on the Rome Treaty on the International Criminal Court*, 31 Wkly. Comp. Pres. Docs. 4 (Dec. 31, 2000).
[105] Interview with David Scheffer, former U.S. Ambassador for War Crimes Issues, March 31, 2005.
[106] *Id.*

including Secretary of Defense Donald Rumsfeld[107] and Under Secretary of State for Arms Control and International Security John Bolton.[108] Further, Bolton, whose anti-ICC position was clearly set forth in the Senate hearings described earlier, had an influence greater than his title would ordinarily imply because he was perceived to have helped Bush win the 2000 presidential election.[109]

This shift in the Executive must also be seen against the backdrop of prevailing skepticism on Capitol Hill. Most Democrats were at best tepid in their support for the ICC,[110] and key Republican legislators, such as Tom DeLay and Jesse Helms, shared the Bush administration's profound visceral hostility toward it.

Some observers also attribute increasing opposition to the ICC to the perception that it is "too European" or "too human rights-based."[111] Certainly, Europe has become the dominant political supporter of the ICC. However, there also seems to be a concern that the work of the ICC is more likely to be dominated by Continental European jurisprudence. The frequent references by the ICTY to jurisprudence of the European Court of Human Rights, for example, fuel this perception. Others have emphasized the central role of NGOs in the creation of the court, suggesting that NGOs "hijacked" the Rome Conference and continue to influence developments from a position beyond the interstate process. Still others cite the holding of the International Court of Justice in *Congo v. Belgium* that the customary law of head of state immunity, while barring prosecution in foreign courts, may not bar prosecution before international criminal courts.[112]

In any event, a number of events that occurred after the change in administration seemed to reinforce, if not augment,[113] the U.S. government's initial hostility toward the ICC. The most dramatic of these were the September 11, 2001, attacks on the Pentagon and World Trade Center. The War on Terror,

---

[107] The Defense Department under Rumsfeld was firmly opposed to the ICC. See Rumsfeld's comments issued by the U.S. Department of Defense, May 6, 2002.

[108] Bolton was subsequently appointed U.S. representative to the United Nations.

[109] Bolton was a key official in the Florida recount that secured Bush his election victory.

[110] Very few Democrat legislators have gone on record as supporting U.S. adherence to the ICC Statute. Even Chris Dodd, who was the chief opponent of the anti-ICC provisions of the American Servicemembers' Protection Act, described later, stated during the ASPA debates that he would not support U.S. ratification of the ICC Statute.

[111] Interview with Defense Department official (name withheld), March 29, 2005. Interview with State Department official (name withheld), March 31, 2005.

[112] Case Concerning the Arrest Warrant of 11 April 2000 (*Dem. Rep. Congo v. Belgium*), 2002 ICJ 3 (Feb. 14).

[113] Some observers have indicated that U.S. opposition could not be more intense than it was from the inception of the Bush administration. Interview with NGO official (name withheld), December 11, 2006.

launched in response to those attacks, led to a greater projection of U.S. armed force abroad. In this new context, the existence of the ICC, the subject matter jurisdiction of which potentially encompasses violations of the *jus ad bellum*, is seen as a possible restraint on that use of force. The 9/11 attacks also reinforced the U.S. notion of exceptionalism. The attacks seemed to confirm to the U.S. government that it was not similarly situated to other states.

The Rome Statute received its sixtieth ratification in April 2002. It thus became clear that the treaty would enter into force on July 1, 2002. The Bush administration had already indicated that it would not proceed with ratification. In a speech following the passage of the 2001 Commerce Budget Bill, Bush had this to say:

> Section 630 prohibits the use of appropriated funds for cooperation with, or assistance or other support to, the [ICC].... [This] clearly reflects that Congress agrees with my Administration that it is not in the interests of the United States to become a party to the ICC treaty.[114]

On May 6, 2002, the Bush administration, through John Bolton, widely regarded as the chief opponent to the ICC within the U.S. administration, sent a letter to the UN, as depository of the treaty, stating that "the United States does not intend to become a party to the [ICC] treaty. Accordingly, the United States has no legal obligations arising from its signature on December 31, 2000."[115] The purpose of this statement was presumably twofold: to make clear the U.S. opposition to ICC jurisdiction over U.S. nationals and to relieve the United States of any legal obligation it may have undertaken upon signing the treaty.[116]

On that same date, Marc Grossman, Under Secretary of State for Political Affairs, spoke at the Center for Strategic and International Studies about the United States and the ICC. In his speech, Grossman said that the U.S. decision to withdraw its signature from the treaty was not an easy one to make, and "after years of working to fix this flawed statute, and having our constructive proposals rebuffed, it [was] our only alternative."[117] He stated that the principles that the United States stands for – such as "states, not international institutions are primarily responsible for ensuring justice in the international system... [and] the best way to combat these serious offenses is to build domestic judicial

---

[114] George W. Bush, *Statement on Signing the Departments of Commerce, Justice, and State, the Judiciary, and Related Agencies Appropriations Act*, 2002, Wkly. Comp. Pres. Docs. 1723, 1724 (Nov. 28, 2001).

[115] Press Release, John R. Bolton, Under Sec'y of State for Arms Control and Int'l Sec., *International Criminal Court: Letter to UN Secretary General Kofi Annan* (May 6, 2002), at http://www.state.gov/r/pa/prs/ps/2002/9968.htm.

[116] Vienna Convention on the Law of Treaties, art. 18.

[117] Press Release, Marc Grossman, Under Sec'y for Political Affairs, *American Foreign Policy and the International Criminal Court* (May 6, 2002), at http://www.state.gov/p/9949.htm.

systems, strengthen political will and promote human freedom"[118] – are not consistent with the Rome Statute. Reflecting the U.S. concerns expressed at Rome, Grossman listed four critiques of the ICC, saying that it "undermines the role of the United Nations Security Council in maintaining international peace and security,"[119] "[it] creates a prosecutorial system that is an unchecked power,"[120] "[it] asserts jurisdiction over citizens of states that have not ratified the treaty . . . [which] threatens U.S. sovereignty,"[121] and "[it] is built on a flawed foundation . . . [and] these flaws leave it open for exploitation and politically motivated prosecutions."[122] He concluded by stating that "the United States respects the decision of those nations who have chosen to join the ICC; but they in turn must respect our decision not to join the ICC or place our citizens under the jurisdiction of the court."[123]

Pierre Prosper, in his capacity as Ambassador for War Crimes Issues, held a press briefing the same day to state that "[t]he President has made clear that – what he wanted to do today was to make our intentions clear and to not take aggressive action or wage war, if you will, against the ICC or the supporters of the ICC."[124] The remarks of Grossman and Prosper appeared to indicate that the United States, although not supporting the ICC, would refrain from interfering in the ICC's operations in relation to the States Parties to the Rome Statute. In sum, over the course of seventeen months, the U.S. attitude appeared to shift from cautious optimism to strict neutrality (nonsupportive, noninterference).

IV. Attempts to Exempt U.S. Nationals from ICC Prosecution

The desire to shield U.S. servicemembers from prosecution before non-U.S. courts is one of the oldest elements of U.S. policy toward the ICC. For decades, the United States has been careful to include jurisdictional exemptions for its forces in Status of Forces Agreements. However, efforts to shield nationals from possible ICC prosecution have been undertaken with unusual breadth and fervor.

By the time of the notification of intent not to become a party, the United States had begun to pursue aggressively a strategy for limiting the exposure of all U.S. citizens to the jurisdiction of the ICC. According to the

---

[118] *Id.*
[119] *Id.*
[120] *Id.*
[121] *Id.*
[122] *Id.*
[123] *Id.*
[124] Press Release, Pierre-Richard Prosper, U.S. Ambassador for War Crimes Issues, *Issues Update* (May 6, 2002), at http://fpc.state.gov/9965.htm.

State Department fact sheet on the ICC, the United States would "work together with other nations to avoid any disruptions that might be caused by the treaty. The treaty itself provides for this, specifically in Article 98. We intend to pursue Article 98 agreements worldwide."[125] By June 2005, the government, at times applying tremendous political and financial pressure, had persuaded one hundred states to sign Article 98 agreements, whereby those states would undertake not to surrender U.S. citizens to the ICC.

The United States also worked through the Security Council to obtain an exemption for peacekeepers from non–States Parties. After intense pressure tactics by the United States, including vetoing the renewal of a peacekeeping operation, the Security Council on July 12, 2002, adopted Resolution 1422, which requested that the ICC refrain from proceeding with investigation or prosecution of any case "involving current or former officials or personnel from a contributing State not a Party to the Rome Statute over acts or omissions relating to a United Nations established or authorized operation."[126] Resolution 1422, which was adopted under Chapter VII of the UN Charter, also "decide[d] that Member States shall take no action inconsistent with"[127] this request. This resolution was renewed by the Security Council the following July. However, in the wake of revelations about egregious detainee abuse by U.S. forces at Abu Ghraib, the United States was unable to secure a second renewal in 2004.

At the same time, the U.S. Congress was preparing legislation to support these efforts. In August 2002, Bush signed into law the American Servicemembers' Protection Act (ASPA).[128] This legislation, dubbed the "Hague Invasion Act" by human rights NGOs, contains provisions restricting U.S. cooperation with the ICC,[129] making U.S. support of peacekeeping missions largely contingent on achieving ICC exemption for all U.S. personnel,[130] cutting off military assistance to states that refuse to sign Article 98 agreements,[131] and granting

---

[125] Fact Sheet, Bureau of Political-Military Affairs, *The International Criminal Court* (Aug. 2, 2002), at http://www.state.gov/t/pm/rls/fs/2002/23426.htm.

[126] S.C. Res. 1422 ¶ 1, U.N. Doc. S/RES/1422 (July 12, 2002).

[127] *Id.* at 3.

[128] According to some observers, proponents of the ASPA had introduced it in the hope of preventing the ICC from coming into existence. Indeed, the ASPA would likely have been passed in the fall of 2001, before the ICC Statute attracted sufficient ratifications to enter into force, had it not been for a temporary change in Senate leadership that saw the Democrats gain control just long enough to drop the bill from that session's legislative agenda. Thus, the ASPA could not be passed until August of the following year, by which time the ICC Statute had entered into force.

[129] 22 U.S.C.A. § 7423 (West 2002).

[130] *Id.* at § 7424.

[131] *Id.* at § 7426.

the president permission to use "all means necessary and appropriate"[132] to free U.S. citizens and allies from ICC-ordered detention or imprisonment. The legislation, however, contains waivers that enable the president to avoid application of these measures where necessary.[133] The scope of such considerable measures was increased in December 2004 with the enactment of the so-called Nethercutt Amendment, as part of the U.S. Foreign Appropriations Bill. This legislation permits the termination of other forms of economic aid (not limited to military assistance). In introducing the legislation, Senator Jesse Helms stated,

> [The purpose of the ASPA is] to protect [Americans] from a U.N. Kangaroo Court where the United States has no veto. . . . Let me state for the record, to be absolutely certain there is no mistake made about it, (1) this amendment will prohibit U.S. cooperation with the court, including use of taxpayer funding or sharing of classified information; (2) it will restrict a U.S. role in peacekeeping missions unless the United Nations specifically exempts U.S. troops from prosecution by this international court; (3) it blocks U.S. aid to allies unless they too sign accords to shield U.S. troops on their soil from being turned over to the court; and (4) it authorizes the President to take any necessary action to rescue U.S. soldiers, any service man or woman, improperly handed over to that Court.[134]

Helms also expressed doubts as to the impartiality of the ICC, stating that "these crimes and these cases would be tried before judges who could be from North Korea, Cuba or other unfriendly places."[135]

The U.S. administration has relied on this legislation to cut off aid to a number of U.S. allies,[136] at times to the detriment of other U.S. foreign policy objectives. For example, the United States terminated military assistance to Trinidad and Tobago, which inhibits them from preventing illegal narcotics from getting into the United States.[137]

---

[132] *Id.* at § 7427.
[133] In addition, pursuant to a Senate amendment, Section 2015 of the law expressly permits the United States to render assistance to international efforts to bring to justice foreign nationals accused of genocide, war crimes, or crimes against humanity.
[134] Congressional Record – Senate, at s10042, October 2, 2001.
[135] 140 Cong. Rec. S96, 101 (Jan. 26, 1994).
[136] Washington had cut off military aid to Mexico, Costa Rica, Venezuela, Ecuador, Peru, Bolivia, Paraguay, Uruguay, Brazil, Barbados, St. Vincent and The Grenadines, Trinidad and Tobago, Croatia, Serbia, Montenegro, Malta, Mali, Niger, Kenya, Tanzania, Lesotho, South Africa, and Namibia. Jess Bravin, "U.S. Warms to Hague Tribunal – New Stance Reflects Desire to Use Court to Prosecute Darfur Crimes," *Wall Street Journal*, p. A4, June 14, 2006.
[137] Interview with Richard Dicker, Human Rights Watch, March 9, 2005. See also, statements of military officials, infra.

V. Increasing Expressions of Hostility toward the ICC

By this time, the U.S. attitude toward the ICC had become one of outright opposition. In early 2005, ICC supporters within the NGO community described the U.S. attitude toward the ICC as "intensely hostile."[138] One NGO official noted that he was "baffled by the degree to which the U.S. government has been willing to slap around long-term allies like Jordan and the Baltic states for their being Parties to the Rome Statute."[139]

Indeed, the rhetoric of U.S. government officials shifted increasingly toward the position outlined by Bolton in 1998. Bolton's views had been aired in a 1999 speech drafted for consideration by then-President Clinton and for the purposes of analyzing possible foreign policy options. Bolton, then still a senior vice president for the AEI, wrote for Clinton's use:

> I plan to say nothing more about the ICC during the remainder of my administration, I, however, instructed the secretary of state to raise our objections to the ICC on every appropriate occasion, as part of our larger campaign to assert American interests against stifling, illegitimate, and unacceptable international agreements. The plain fact is that additional "fixes" over time to the ICC will not alter its multiple inherent defects, and we will not advocate any such efforts. We will leave the ICC to the obscurity it so richly deserves.[140]

Although this policy was rejected by Clinton, it seems to have been given some life under the Bush administration. During his term, Bush made a number of statements that demonstrated his administration's opposition to the ICC. To troops preparing to deploy for Afghanistan, he proclaimed,

> As we prepare our military for action, we will protect our military from international courts ... with agendas of their own.... You might have heard about a treaty that would place American troops under the jurisdiction of something called the [ICC]. The United States cooperates with many other nations to keep the peace, but we will not submit American troops to prosecutors and judges whose jurisdiction we do not accept.[141]

In his campaign for reelection against Senator John Kerry, he reminded the public that he had "made a decision not to join the International Criminal

---

[138] Id.
[139] Id.
[140] John Bolton, *Speech Two: Reject and Oppose the International Criminal Court* 36, http://www.cfr.org/content/publications/attachments/International_Criminal_Court.pdf (1999).
[141] George W. Bush, *Remarks to the 10th Mountain Division at Fort Drum, New York*, Wkly. Comp. Pres. Docs. 1189, 1231 (July 19, 2002).

Court in The Hague, which is where our troops could be brought to – brought in front of a judge, an unaccounted judge. I don't think we ought to join that."[142]

As noted earlier, Members of Congress have also expressed deep opposition to the ICC. In June 2005, then-House Majority Leader Tom DeLay remarked,

> The ICC is a threat not only to the sovereignty of the United States and the constitutional rights of American citizens; it is an overreaching distortion of the United Nations Charter and its mission. The ICC would, in effect, disregard not only Federal and State laws, but also the Uniform Code of Military Justice, thereby establishing a rogue court in which foreign judges can indict, try, and convict American troops for broadly defined and openly interpreted crimes, all without any of the fundamental legal rights guaranteed by the United States Constitution.... The United Nations' mission is to protect and promote human rights around the globe, to exhort with clarity and courage the principles of justice and liberty to those who would seek to oppress them. The ICC, on the contrary, could be an instrument of undemocratic score-settling, a shadowy kangaroo court in which despots and their diplomats can humiliate and even imprison the men and women who have the courage to do the work the U.N. refuses to do.[143]

VI. Abu Ghraib

As noted earlier, a consistent theme in the U.S. attitude toward the ICC under both the Clinton and Bush administrations has been the desire to limit the exposure of U.S. personnel to prosecution by the ICC. However, this central concern seemed to have broadened under the Bush administration. Whereas the Clinton administration focused on the possibility of prosecution of U.S. troops, the Bush administration seemed to be concerned about prosecutions of leadership as well.[144] Arguably, the decision to invade Iraq in the face of a large international opposition and lacking explicit UN endorsement may have played a role in this shift.

---

[142] George W. Bush, *Presidential Debate in St. Louis, Missouri*, Wkly. Comp. Pres. Docs. 2289, 2293 (Oct. 15, 2004). *See also* Bravin, *supra* note 136 (quoting Bush during a 2004 presidential debate as stating that the ICC is a "body based in the Hague where unaccountable judges and prosecutors can pull our troops or diplomats up for trial"). The fact that Bush mentioned the ICC twice during the presidential debates indicates that his campaign regarded this as a winning issue.

[143] Congressional Record, at H4634, June 16, 2005.

[144] Interview with former State Department official (name withheld); interview with State Department official (name withheld), November 3, 2005.

From the perspective of the U.S. government, the calls for criminal prosecution of senior U.S. officials for the Abu Ghraib crimes highlighted the problems with the ICC system of complementarity. There was serious concern within the U.S. government that if the ICC had jurisdiction in this case, it could conclude that there has been an unwillingness on the part of the United States to prosecute senior officials under a theory of complicity or superior responsibility.[145] Admittedly, there are segments of the international community, both governmental and nongovernmental, that would reach such a conclusion, whether pursuant to political motivations or otherwise. Because the United States had little confidence in the ICC's ability to insulate itself from these perspectives and even feared that ICC officials may share them, its hostility toward the ICC increased.

Yet after Abu Ghraib, it became increasingly difficult for the United States to publicly cite fear of politically motivated prosecutions as an objection to the ICC. It was forced to strengthen and emphasize its more principled objections.

VII. Strengthening Preference for Resolution at the National Level

U.S. hostility toward the ICC combined with other perennial national concerns, including shielding U.S. personnel from prosecution by foreign courts and fear of interference with national policy objectives, to create a new policy line – that an international criminal court is not a good thing, even in principle, and that prosecution of atrocities should be returned to the domestic sphere, or as close as possible to that sphere.

As stated by Prosper before the Senate Committee on the Judiciary,

> [T]he international practice should be to support sovereign states seeking justice domestically when it is feasible and would be credible....[146] International tribunals are not and should not be the courts of first redress, but of last resort. When domestic justice is not possible for egregious war crimes due to a failed state or a dysfunctional judicial system, the international community may through the Security Council or by consent step in on an ad hoc basis as in Rwanda and Yugoslavia.[147]

He summarized the Bush administration's policy as "encourage[ing] states to pursue credible justice rather than abdicating the responsibility. Because justice and the administration of justice are a cornerstone of any democracy,

---

[145] *Id.*

[146] Press Release, Pierre-Richard Prosper, U.S. Ambassador for War Crimes Issues, *War Crimes in the 21st Century* [¶ 31] (Oct. 26, 2004), at http://www.state.gov/s/wci/rm/38309.htm.

[147] Press Release, Pierre-Richard Prosper, U.S. Ambassador for War Crimes Issues, *Address at the Peace Palace in the Hague* [¶ 8] (Dec. 19, 2001), at http://www.state.gov/s/wci/rm/8053.htm.

pursuing accountability for war crimes while respecting the rule of law by a sovereign state must be encouraged at all times."[148]

Where there is no possibility for credible justice at the national level, Prosper indicated a U.S. preference for regional solutions. This policy line was manifested in U.S. proposals to find a regional solution to the situation in Darfur.

VIII. The Darfur Referral

In September 2004, then-U.S. Secretary of State Colin Powell announced the view of the U.S. government that the killings in Sudan's Darfur region constitute genocide.[149] The United States led international condemnation of the atrocities and called on the United Nations to initiate a full investigation.[150]

The following week, in Resolution 1654, the UN Security Council requested the secretary-general to "rapidly establish an international commission of inquiry in order immediately to investigate reports of violations of international humanitarian law and human rights law in Darfur by all parties, to determine also whether or not acts of genocide have occurred, and to identify the perpetrators of such violations with a view to ensuring that those responsible are held accountable."[151] Shortly thereafter, the International Commission of Inquiry on Darfur was established and began working.

In its January 2005 report to the secretary-general, the Commission "strongly recommend[ed] that the Security Council immediately refer the situation of Darfur to the International Criminal Court, pursuant to article 13(b) of the ICC Statute."[152]

On March 31, 2005, after months of intense negotiations, the UN Security Council by its Resolution 1593 referred the situation in Darfur to the ICC.[153] In the negotiations leading up to the adoption of that resolution, the United

---

[148] Press Release, Pierre-Richard Prosper, U.S. Ambassador for War Crimes Issues, *The Campaign against Terrorism: Military Commissions and the Pursuit of Justice* [¶ 22] (Dec. 4, 2001), at http://www.state.gov/s/wci/rm/8584.htm.

[149] The U.S. House of Representatives had two months earlier similarly declared that genocide was occurring in Darfur.

[150] Secretary Colin L. Powell, Testimony before the Senate Foreign Relations Committee Washington, D.C., September 9, 2004.

[151] Report of the International Commission of Inquiry on Darfur to the United Nations Secretary-General. Pursuant to Security Council Resolution 1564 of 18 September 2004. Geneva, January 25, 2005, p. 2.

[152] Report of the International Commission of Inquiry on Darfur to the United Nations Secretary-General, January 25, 2005. Because Sudan is not a party to the Rome Statute and would not otherwise consent to ICC jurisdiction over Darfur, a Security Council resolution was required to bring the situation within the Court's competence.

[153] S.C. Res. 1593 ¶ 1, U.N. Doc. S/RES/1593 (March 31, 2005).

States demonstrated strong resistance to the referral, leading some observers to conclude that U.S. opposition to the ICC had become overtly hostile to the point of compromising the ability of the UN to respond to the atrocities being committed.[154]

However, the official position of the United States was simply that the ICC was not a suitable forum. The United States had instead proposed a "Sudan Tribunal" that would be "created and mandated by a U.N. Security Council resolution and administered by the U.N. in conjunction with the African Union (AU)." The proposed tribunal, U.S. officials said, "would allow the AU to continue its leadership role . . . [and] would contribute to the development of the African Union's overall judicial capacity on the continent."[155] This approach fit in with the U.S. policy of delivering justice closer to the victim community and would avoid what U.S. officials described as the "colonial" approach of Europeans judging Africans.[156]

This proposal took a variety of forms.[157] Under one version, it was proposed that the "Sudan Tribunal" would eventually be folded into the emerging, but not yet established, African Court of Human and Peoples' Rights. The United States was prepared to fully fund this Tribunal.[158]

These proposals were seen by other members of the Security Council as an attempt by the United States to marginalize the ICC, belying an intention to prevent the ICC from becoming a credible institution.[159] This perception was reinforced when Prosper, explaining the U.S. position, bluntly stated, "We don't want to be party to legitimizing the ICC."[160]

It is difficult to ascertain the true design of the United States, because there seemed to be no single, uniform intention. In all probability, the amalgamation of views included those who wanted to undermine the ICC, those who were convinced of the need to bolster the African Union and to conduct

---

[154] Interview with diplomat (non-U.S.) involved in the negotiations (name withheld), March 26, 2005; interview with John Stompor, Human Rights First, March 8, 2005; *U.S. Thwarts Justice for Darfur*, Human Rights Watch, March 24, 2005.

[155] Press Release, Judy Alta, Washington File United Nations Correspondent, *African Union Tribunal Proposed for War Crimes in Darfur* [5–6] (Feb. 2005), at http://usinfo.state.gov/af/Archive/2005/Feb/10-767752.html.

[156] Interview with State Department official, March 31, 2005.

[157] *U.S. Proposes New Regional Court to Hear Charges Involving Darfur, Others Urge ICC*, 99 Am. J. Int'l L. 501 (2005); U.S. Department of State Daily Press Briefing, February 1, 2005.

[158] Remarks of Secretary of State Condoleezza Rice before the Senate Foreign Relations Committee, February 16, 2005.

[159] Interview with diplomat (non-U.S.) involved in the negotiations (name withheld), March 26, 2005.

[160] Human Rights Watch, *Human Rights News, U.S. Fiddles over ICC while Darfur Burns* [¶ 6], http://hrw.org/english/docs/2005/01/31/usint10091.htm (Jan. 31, 2005).

prosecutions on the regional level, and those who simply wanted to see the African Court of Human and Peoples' Rights get off the ground.

Ultimately, the United States failed to garner support for its proposed Sudan Tribunal, and it allowed the referral to go through by abstaining. However, the United States achieved a substantial concession in exchange for agreeing to abstain. Security Council Resolution 1593 provided far more than a mere exemption from ICC jurisdiction of nationals of states not parties to the treaty establishing the Court. In paragraph 6 of that resolution, the Council decided that

> nationals, current or former officials or personnel from a contributing State outside Sudan which is not a party to the Rome Statute of the International Criminal Court shall be subject to the exclusive jurisdiction of that contributing State for all alleged acts or omissions arising out of or related to operations in Sudan... unless such exclusive jurisdiction has been expressly waived by that contributing State.[161]

In other words, rather than simply referring the case to the ICC, while exempting from its jurisdiction peacekeepers from states not parties to the ICC treaty, the Security Council at the behest of the United States government decided that *only* those states would have jurisdiction. In doing so, the Council not only purported to limit the jurisdiction of the ICC but also to circumscribe the jurisdiction of all Member States of the United Nations. Although the reservation of "exclusive jurisdiction" is commonly found in bilateral arrangements between troop-contributing states and host states, the effect of such a provision is to deprive the host state of jurisdiction without affecting the jurisdiction of other states. Resolution 1593 purports to multilateralize this obligation instantly.[162] This remarkable use of Security Council power to legislate for the entire international community effectively limits the rights of all countries to exercise jurisdiction over international crimes even when their national was the victim, absent an express waiver by the contributing state.

This provision was likely included to stave off attempts to bring cases in foreign domestic courts under a theory of universal jurisdiction. Thus, the breadth of this provision resonates beyond U.S. opposition to the ICC and indicates broader concerns about exposure of U.S. personnel to prosecutions anywhere in the world.

However, in the months following this diplomatic defeat in the Security Council, the U.S. view of the Darfur referral seemed to shift slightly. Indeed,

---

[161] S.C. Res. 1593, *supra* note 152, ¶ 6.
[162] *Id.*

U.S. government officials at times seemed to express satisfaction with the referral. For example, addressing an international conference in September 2005, State Department Legal Adviser John Bellinger stated,

> Even on issues such as those involving the ICC, where the United States has voiced political concerns, we have undertaken to work with the international community through the Security Council to a satisfactory resolution. Thus, Secretary Rice worked hard last spring to find an acceptable formula for a Security Council resolution to address the issue of accountability in Sudan. While the United States continues to maintain fundamental objections to the ICC, we did not veto UNSCR 1593, which referred the situation in Darfur to the ICC, because we recognized the need for the international community to work together to end the atrocities in Sudan and speak with one voice-to bring to account the perpetrators of those crimes.[163]

Although such statements may have initially been attempts to save face following diplomatic defeat, they may also have fed back into the U.S. attitude, perhaps contributing to yet another shift toward a more moderate stance regarding the ICC.[164] Indeed, by late 2008, the language had shifted from non-opposition to acceptance. In November 2008, Bellinger remarked,

> We've re-emphasized as a core principle of our policy our respect for the decisions of other states to join the ICC, and have acknowledged that the court can have a valuable role to play in certain cases. On this point, Darfur is exhibit A. In 2005, in one of the first major policy decisions of Secretary Rice's tenure at the State Department, the United States accepted the decision of the UN Security Council to refer the Darfur situation to the ICC. We have said that we want to see the ICC's Darfur work succeed and indicated our willingness to consider an appropriate request for assistance from the ICC in connection with the Darfur matter, consistent with applicable U.S. law.[165]

---

[163] Press Release, John B. Bellinger, III, U.S. Dept. of State Legal Adviser, *United Nations Security Council Resolutions and the Application of International Humanitarian Law, Human Rights and Refugee Law* [¶10] (Sept. 9, 2005), at http://www.usmission.ch/Press2005/0909BellingerIHLSanRemo-2.htm.

[164] See also the Statement of the U.S. Representative during the 53rd Plenary Meeting of the General Assembly, A/60/PV.53, November 23, 2005: "While our concerns about the Court have not changed, we would like to move beyond divisiveness on the issue.... While we have preferred a different mechanism [for Darfur], we believed that it was important for the international community to speak with one voice and to act decisively. Consequently, we accepted referral of the Darfur situation by the Security Council to the Court. Those events demonstrate that there can be common ground when both sides are willing to work constructively."

[165] John B. Bellinger, III, U.S. Dept. of State Legal Adviser, "U.S. Perspectives on International Criminal Justice," Remarks at the Fletcher School of Law and Diplomacy, November 14, 2008.

In November 2005, U.S. Assistant Secretary of State Jendayi Frazer indicated a willingness on the part of the United States to assist the ICC in Darfur prosecutions. On November 1, she told the House International Relations Committee "that if the ICC requires assistance, the United States stands ready to assist... we don't want to see impunity for any of these actors... we stand ready to assist."[166]

By the spring of 2006, the U.S. government began to make other noises questioning the wisdom of its earlier approach to the ICC. With regard to aid cut-offs required by the ASPA, U.S. Secretary of State Condoleezza Rice acknowledged in March 2006 that the U.S. government may be "shooting ourselves in the foot," expressly acknowledging that the ASPA requirements interfered with other U.S. foreign policy objectives:

> We do have certain statutory requirements concerning the ICC. I think you're probably aware of, as I testified yesterday, that we're looking at the issues concerning those situations in which we may have, in a sense, sort of the same as shooting ourselves in the foot, which is, I guess, what we mean. By having to put off aid to countries with which we have important counterterrorism or counterdrug or in some cases, in some of our allies, it's even been cooperation in places like Afghanistan and Iraq. And so I think we just have to look at it. And we're certainly reviewing it and we'll consult with Congress about it. But I think it's important from time that we take a look to make sure that we're not having a negative effect on the relationships that are really important to us from the point of view of getting our security environment – improving the security environment.[167]

In a recent interview, State Department Legal Advisor John Bellinger gave further support to the view that the ICC is no longer regarded as a "rogue court," acknowledging that "it has a role to play in the overall system of international justice."[168]

IX. The Call to Move the Taylor Prosecution to The Hague

On March 29, 2006, former Liberian president Charles Taylor was arrested and surrendered to the Special Court for Sierra Leone. Shortly after his arrest, amid concerns for regional stability prompted by his impending prosecution, the United States called for his trial to be moved to The Hague. Pursuant to

---

[166] H.R. Subcomm. on Africa, Global Human Rights, and Intl. Operations of the Comm. On Intl. Relations, *Sudan: Losing Ground on Peace?*, 109th Cong. 16, 29 (Nov. 1, 2005).

[167] Press Release, Condoleezza Rice, Sec. of State, *Trip Briefing* (March 10, 2006), at http://www.state.gov/secretary/rm/2006/63001.htm.

[168] Bravin, *supra* note 136.

this proposal, Taylor would still be prosecuted by the Special Court, but the trial would take place using the facilities of the ICC in The Hague. Taylor was transferred to the ICC Detention Centre in The Hague on June 20, 2006. The U.S. government was heavily involved in facilitating the transfer.[169]

The announcement of this proposal by the U.S. government stands in sharp contrast to its zealous attempts to prevent the Darfur referral, as well as its general pattern of attempts over the past few years to remove any reference to the ICC in, for instance, resolutions and other official documents of intergovernmental organizations. Previously, the U.S. objective of preventing official acts that could be perceived to legitimize the ICC in any way seemed to prevail above most other competing interests. It now appeared that the importance of this objective may have begun to diminish.

The transfer of the Taylor proceedings to The Hague also provided a vehicle for improving relations between the U.S. government and the ICC. U.S. officials held numerous discussions with ICC officials to facilitate the transfer.[170] These discussions required the establishment of new contacts and served to strengthen existing relationships among officials, broadening the prospects for other forms of cooperation between the two entities.

X. The Moderation of the U.S. Position

The Darfur referral and the transfer of the Taylor case signaled a new phase in the U.S. relationship with the ICC. Moreover, subsequent statements and actions by the U.S. Executive demonstrated increasing recognition of the value of the ICC.

In June 2006, U.S. Assistant Secretary of State for African Affairs Jendayi Frazer publicly acknowledged the constructive role of the ICC.[171] Speaking at a press conference in Uganda about the situation there, she noted that "the ICC indictment [of rebel Leader Joseph Kony] is extremely important and it is part of the process of accountability, and ending impunity."[172] She also cited the case of Charles Taylor as evidence that "you can achieve peace and accountability." Later that year, the U.S. ambassador to Uganda explained that the United States does not perceive the ICC arrest warrants as obstacles to peace talks. "[I]nstead," he remarked, "it is the reason why we have peace talks today."[173]

---

[169] Interview with State Department official (name withheld), July 21, 2006.
[170] Interview with State Department official (name withheld), July 21, 2006.
[171] Presidential waiver, October 2, 2006.
[172] Transcript of June 20, 2006 press conference, Entebbe, Uganda.
[173] "ICC-phobic U.S. offers court rare praise for Uganda rebel charges," Agence France Presse quoting Ambassador Steven Browning, November 16, 2006.

The Bush administration also subsequently waived many of the ASPA and Nethercutt funding restrictions imposed on countries that failed to become parties to bilateral nonsurrender agreements.[174]

In one of the clearest indications of this change of attitude, the Bush administration in the summer of 2008 indicated its support of the ICC prosecution of Sudanese President Omer Al-Bashir.[175] The United States also refused to endorse a Security Council resolution that indicated possible support for a request that the prosecution of Al-Bashir be deferred.[176] In the fall of 2008, Bellinger noted,

> [I]n recent months, we have opposed efforts by some countries to invoke Article 16 of the ICC Statute to defer the investigation and prosecution of Sudanese President Al Bashir. The irony of the United States' support for the court in opposing an Article 16 deferral is often noted by the press; what I hope will get equal attention is the still-greater irony that some strong supporters of the court seem so willing to consider interfering with the Court's prosecution of an individual responsible for genocide.[177]

An increasing openness toward the International Criminal Court was also to be found in Congress. In September 2006, Congress approved legislation eliminating some of the aid restrictions imposed by the ASPA on states parties to the ICC Statute. Individual members of Congress have also recently made statements in support of the ICC.[178]

Moderation of the U.S. position was facilitated by a number of factors, including the transfer of the Taylor case and the need to retrospectively characterize the Darfur referral as a positive development. Another major factor

---

[174] A number of countries have refused to become parties to these agreements. The U.S. military has been influential in securing waivers for these states. *See* Statements of General Brantz J. Craddock before the Senate Armed Services Committee, March 14, 2006 and September 19, 2006, and House Armed Services Committee, March 7, 2005 and March 16, 2006. It encouraged the granting of waivers by pointing out that China has begun providing military assistance to these countries.

[175] "Sudan President Defiant in Darfur," BBC News, July 23, 2008.

[176] "Security Council Decides to Extend Mandate of African Union-United Nations Hybrid Operation in Darfur by 14 Votes in Favour, 1 Abstention," UN News Press Release, July 31, 2008.

[177] John B. Bellinger, III, U.S. Dept. of State Legal Adviser, "U.S. Perspectives on International Criminal Justice," Remarks at the Fletcher School of Law and Diplomacy, November 14, 2008.

[178] *See* "A Shift in the Debate on International Court; Some U.S. Officials Seem to Ease Disfavor," *Washington Post*, November 7, 2006 (quoting Senator Patrick Leahy as stating, "The ICC has refuted its critics, who confidently and wrongly predicted that it would be politicized and manipulated by our enemies to prosecute U.S. soldiers"); "Rescue Darfur Now," *Washington Post* Op-Ed by Senator John McCain and former Senator Bob Dole (calling on the U.S. government to "publicly remind Khartoum that the International Criminal Court has jurisdiction to prosecute war crimes in Darfur").

has been the fact that all of the ICC cases to date dovetail with U.S. foreign policy interests. All of the situations before the Court – the Central African Republic, Uganda, the Congo, and Darfur – are situations where the United States supports external scrutiny. Further, three of the situations – the Central African Republic, the Congo, and Uganda – were brought to the ICC by the governments of those states. As such, the prosecutor is not intervening in a situation in which the government would prefer to handle the matter domestically.[179] The fourth situation, Darfur, was undertaken at the behest of the Security Council, which, from the U.S. perspective, has been the preferred mode of ICC operation.

This change of attitude also coincided with personnel changes within the U.S. government. The neoconservatives lost influence. Rumsfeld resigned. Delay left Congress. Helms died. Bolton failed to win the Congressional support necessary to retain his appointment as U.S. representative to the United Nations. The waning of their influence, and of their ideological objection to the very idea of an international criminal court, allowed room for pragmatists to assume a greater role.

In sum, since 1998, the United States has shifted through each of the options identified by the Congressional Research Service noted earlier – from constructive engagement, to firm opposition, to pragmatic exploitation.

In the early 1990s, the United States was a supporter of the idea of a permanent international criminal court. After the Rome Conference, at which the United States was not completely successful in having its concerns addressed, U.S. support waned. Nonetheless, it remained engaged in the preparations for the establishment of the Court and ultimately signed the Rome Statute to enable continued participation.

U.S. support lessened upon the election of George W. Bush, who brought with him an administration that was generally anti-internationalist. This sentiment was augmented following the attacks of September 11, 2001. By the spring of 2002, opposition was clear, although it maintained an official position of neutrality, as expressed by U.S. officials upon the withdrawal from the Rome Statute. This opposition became increasingly visible, manifesting itself in the passage of legislation and the adoption of diplomatic strategies that appeared to constitute frontal attacks against the ICC.

Recent developments, including the Darfur referral, the transfer of the Taylor trial to The Hague, and the waiver of ASPA restrictions, indicate a

---

[179] Indeed, the prosecutor has been criticized for being overly cautious in his approach. The Pre-Trial Chambers have resorted to holding hearings to pressure the prosecutor to act. *See,* e.g., Decision Inviting Observations in Application of Rule 103 of the Rules of Procedure and Evidence, ICC-02/05–10, 24.07.2006.

lessening propensity for ideologically rooted or visceral responses[180] and a recognition of the value of the ICC in the attainment of other foreign policy objectives. This has led the State Department legal adviser to characterize the present U.S. attitude as "pragmatic."[181]

5. Internationalized, Hybrid, and Related Criminal Tribunals

In general, the United States has adopted more favorable positions with respect to so-called hybrid or internationalized tribunals. There is little or no possibility of prosecution of U.S. personnel in these fora, and each has a closer connection to the legal system of the country in which the atrocities occurred.

I. Sierra Leone

The Special Court for Sierra Leone (SCSL) is considered to be a hybrid court because of its synthesis of international and domestic elements. Unlike the ICTY and ICTR, which were established by the United Nations Security Council as UN subsidiary bodies, the legal basis for the SCSL is a treaty between the UN and Sierra Leone.[182] Thus, the SCSL is not a UN organ, and the Sierra Leonean government was deeply involved in its creation. Its Management Committee, drawn from a Group of Interested States, carries out the oversight.[183] The substantive criminal law to be applied by the Court, codified in the Statute of the SCSL, was derived from both international law and domestic law.[184] Finally, the personnel of the Court are also mixed, employing both international and national staff.

As with the ICTR and ICTY, the United States was the prime mover behind the creation of the Special Court for Sierra Leone.[185] It was also strongly

---

[180] Although the U.S. administration has continued its anti-ICC rhetoric to some degree, this may simply serve as a smokescreen to create the appearance that U.S. opposition remains firm.

[181] Statement of John Bellinger, U.S. Department of State Legal Adviser, 29th Roundtable on Current Problems of International Humanitarian Law, September 8, 2006. See also Bellinger, in this book, Chapter 1. See also "The United States and International Law," remarks of John Bellinger at The Hague, June 6, 2007: the Darfur referral, the offer of assistance to the OTP in Darfur, and the transfer of the Taylor proceedings "reflect our desire to find practical ways to work with ICC supporters to advance our shared goals of promoting international criminal justice."

[182] Agreement between the United Nations and the Government of Sierra Leone on the Establishment of a Special Court for Sierra Leone preamble (Jan. 16, 2002), at http://www.sc-sl.org/scsl-agreement.html.

[183] Id. at art. 7.

[184] Id. at art. 1.

[185] Interview with diplomat (non-U.S.) involved in the negotiations (name withheld), March 26, 2005; interview with former SCSL official (name withheld), March 7, 2005. One NGO official

supported by the United Kingdom, though the United States and the United Kingdom divided over certain details, such as the scope of the Court's temporal jurisdiction.[186]

In the SCSL, the Bush administration saw an opportunity to build an international justice mechanism that would conform more closely to the model espoused by the United States as preferable to the ICC.[187] The SCSL was created in cooperation with the Sierra Leonean authorities, it does not have the authority to bind other states or otherwise require their cooperation, it is funded primarily by voluntary contributions, and peacekeepers are exempt from its jurisdiction, subject to a Security Council override. Some claim that hostility within the UN's Office of Legal Affairs toward the establishment of the SCSL was a response to what it perceived as an attempt by the United States to undermine the ICC.[188]

Whether this motivation to showcase the SCSL as an ICC alternative was present from the beginning or whether it evolved along with negotiations on the design of the Court is unclear. In any event, the United States was strongly supportive from its inception. Indeed, some assert that it was the U.S. government that initially approached the Sierra Leonean government, inviting it to request the United Nations to establish the SCSL.

Although not unanimous, the U.S. Congress was extraordinarily and uncharacteristically supportive of the SCSL.[189] This support likely emerged from the confluence of three factors: it provided an opportunity to make the U.S. Congress seem pro-accountability, as well as an opportunity to criticize the UN, by, for example, citing the failure of the United Nations Mission in Sierra Leone; the sensationalism of the amputee issue appealed to the camera-chasing members of Congress; and those harboring anti-Clinton sentiment saw this as an opportunity to publicize the failure of the Lomé Accords.[190]

---

viewed the United States as only one of several significant promoters of the Court, including Canada, the Netherlands, and, of course, Sierra Leone. Interview with Alison Smith, No Peace without Justice, March 24, 2005.

[186] Interview with diplomat (non-U.S.) involved in the negotiations (name withheld), March 26, 2005.

[187] Interview with David Scheffer, March 31, 2005. The decision to create the Court had already been taken under the Clinton administration. *Id.* Nonetheless, continued U.S. support under the Bush administration was critical to the ultimate establishment of the Court in 2002.

[188] Interview with diplomat (non-U.S.) involved in the negotiations (name withheld), March 26, 2005; interview with former SCSL official (name withheld), March 7, 2005.

[189] Interview with former SCSL official (name withheld), March 7, 2005; interview with Nina Bang-Jensen, Coalition for International Justice, June 16, 2005.

[190] Interview with former SCSL official (name withheld), March 7, 2005.

The Department of Defense, which had been a recent source of opposition to international criminal courts, did not express opposition to the creation of the SCSL and at times seemed affirmatively supportive.[191] Their support was largely due to the fact that David Crane, who had been employed at the Pentagon, was appointed as prosecutor.

Again, U.S. support has taken a variety of forms. As noted earlier, the United States was the driving force behind the creation of the SCSL. Ambassador Richard Holbrooke as well as Scheffer and Prosper all helped to push the court along.[192] In addition, the United States has been the largest financial contributor to the operations of the Court.[193]

The United States was highly influential in the design of the Court. A number of states, including the United States, made it clear from the beginning that the SCSL would not have Chapter VII authority, despite the desire of the Sierra Leonean government for a Security Council resolution to that effect.[194] Thus, unlike the ICTY and ICTR, the Special Court was not given authority to compel cooperation from states. Possibly as a result of tribunal fatigue, the United States also wanted the SCSL to be outside of the UN structure and to be funded through voluntary contributions.[195]

The continuing political support of the United States was evident when the SCSL ran into financial difficulty in 2004. The U.S. Mission to the United Nations (U.S.UN) asked the secretary-general to intervene on the funding issue. The secretary-general would have to go to the Security Council to ask for authorization to go to the General Assembly to get authorization to make a subvention grant.[196] The United States prompted the secretary-general to seek this authorization from the Security Council and then pushed it through.[197] It then followed up by ensuring proper language was used in the General Assembly resolutions authorizing the subvention grant.[198] The SCSL then received a subvention grant for 2005, enabling it to continue operations.

---

[191] Interview with former SCSL official (name withheld), March 7, 2005; interview with former SCSL official (name withheld), April 15, 2006.

[192] Interview with diplomat (non-U.S.) involved in the negotiations (name withheld), March 26, 2005; interview with former SCSL official (name withheld), March 7, 2005; interview with David Scheffer, March 31, 2005.

[193] Fact Sheet, Office of the Press Secretary, *Fact Sheet: United States and G8 Renew Strong Commitment to Africa* (July 8, 2005), at http://www.whitehouse.gov/news/releases/2005/07/20050708-3.html.

[194] Interview with diplomat (non-U.S.) involved in the negotiations (name withheld), March 26, 2005.

[195] Interview with former SCSL official (name withheld), March 7, 2005; interview with diplomat (non-U.S.) involved in the negotiations (name withheld), March 26, 2005.

[196] *Id.*

[197] *Id.*

[198] *Id.*

Senior U.S.UN officials have also intervened with the office of the UN Controller.[199] The Office of the Controller was dragging its heels in dispersing funds to the SCSL. Some have speculated that this was because the SCSL was created as an institution outside of the UN framework or perhaps for reasons similar to those evoking hostility from the UN Office of Legal Affairs (OLA).[200] In any event, U.S.UN intervened to secure cooperation from the Controller's office.

Another major factor bolstering U.S. support, and with respect to which the United States played a central role, is the limited personal jurisdiction of the SCSL.

I.A. THE PEACEKEEPER EXEMPTION. The scope of personal jurisdiction of the SCSL was a matter of concern for a number of UN Member State delegations.[201] These delegations initially sought to limit the personal jurisdiction of the Court to Sierra Leonean nationals.[202] Indeed, this was stipulated in the original draft statute of the Court.[203] However, the finally agreed-on text did not include a nationality limitation. Instead, the Court's personal jurisdiction is limited to

> persons who bear the greatest responsibility for serious violations of international humanitarian law and Sierra Leonean law committed in the territory of Sierra Leone since 30 November 1996, including those leaders who, in committing such crimes, have threatened the establishment of and implementation of the peace process in Sierra Leone.[204]

In the course of the negotiations, the nationality limitation was dropped in exchange for an exemption for peacekeepers.[205] Article 1 of the SCSL Statute excludes peacekeepers from the personal jurisdiction of the Court unless their sending state is unwilling or unable to prosecute. Even if it is established that the sending state is unwilling or unable to prosecute, the Security Council must still approve the prosecution before it can proceed.[206] Thus, not only does

---

[199] Interview with diplomat (non-U.S.) involved in the negotiations (name withheld), March 26, 2005.
[200] Interview with former SCSL official (name withheld), March 7, 2005.
[201] Interview with diplomat (non-U.S.) involved in the negotiations (name withheld), March 26, 2005.
[202] Id.
[203] Id.
[204] *Statute of the Special Court for Sierra Leone* art. 1 (Jan. 16, 2002), at http://www.sc-sl.org/scsl-statute.html.
[205] Interview with diplomat (non-U.S.) involved in the negotiations (name withheld), March 26, 2005.
[206] *Statute of the Special Court for Sierra Leone*, art. 1 (Jan. 16, 2002), at http://www.sc-sl.org/scsl-statute.html.

this establish a precedent for a peacekeeper exemption but it also enables the United States, as a veto-wielding permanent member of the Security Council, to prevent the prosecution of peacekeepers sent by its allies, for example, from Nigeria, without Security Council approval. This is essentially the kind of exemption that the United States sought at the Rome Conference.

I.B. THE APPOINTMENT OF AN AMERICAN PROSECUTOR. Another major factor in U.S. support for the SCSL was the appointment of David Crane as prosecutor. The United States lobbied intensely to get him appointed. OLA was supporting another candidate – Ken Flemming.[207] The UN secretary-general was undecided between Crane and Flemming and expressed a desire to see other candidates. Several high administration officials and even members of Congress applied pressure to UN Secretary-General Kofi Annan to get Crane appointed.[208] This of course exacerbated the existing tensions with OLA.

Some observers would infer that the key issue for the United States is control of who could be indicted.[209] In the case of the SCSL, the appointment of an American who was previously employed at the Pentagon reassured the United States, and the Department of Defense in particular. Further, it may be that the appointment of a former member of the U.S. military, who brought with him a team of former military servicemembers, gave the SCSL more of a Nuremberg feel, further facilitating support for it.

Prosper's office supported Crane for a number of reasons. They wanted someone with management experience; Crane had been a senior executive at the Pentagon. They also liked the fact that he was a former judge advocate (having retired from the army in 1996), again mirroring the IMT model. His Africa background was another factor. Crane was also a former teacher of Prosper's then-deputy.[210]

Some have speculated, however, that the State Department as a whole was not as keen on the selection of Crane as prosecutor.[211] When Crane was initially deployed to Sierra Leone, he and several of his handpicked senior staff had top-secret clearance, thus providing them access to all of the cables

---

[207] Interview with former SCSL official (name withheld), March 7, 2005; interview with NGO official involved in the negotiations, March 24, 2005.

[208] Interview with former SCSL official (name withheld), March 7, 2005.

[209] Interview with diplomat (non-U.S.) involved in the negotiations (name withheld), March 26, 2005; interview with John Stompor, Human Rights First, March 8, 2005; interview with ICTY official (name withheld), March 27, 2005; interview with former State Department official (name withheld), December 13, 2005.

[210] Interview with former SCSL official (name withheld), April 15, 2006.

[211] Interview with diplomat (non-U.S.) involved in the negotiations (name withheld), March 26, 2005; interview with former SCSL official (name withheld), March 7, 2005.

between Washington and Freetown.[212] This access was lost when he and his team started carrying out investigations in neighboring Liberia. Some have suggested that this loss of clearance was an expression of disapproval by the State Department.

Crane's relationship with the State Department and, as a result the relationship between the SCSL and the U.S. government worsened considerably upon the unsealing of the Taylor indictment.[213]

I.C. THE UNSEALING OF THE TAYLOR INDICTMENT. On June 4, 2003, the SCSL unsealed the indictment of Charles Taylor, then president of Liberia. On that date, Taylor was participating in a peace conference in Ghana. Although it was apparent to most observers that Crane was planning to indict Taylor, and given the SCSL's numbering of indictments it was clear that there had been a sealed indictment, the State Department apparently found major fault with Crane's timing.

The timing of the unsealing of the indictment was not coincidental. Indeed, the prosecutor's strategy was to demonstrate the power of the rule of law by stripping Taylor of his political power in front of his peers.[214] Crane gave twenty-four-hour notice to concerned parties, including the U.S. government, of his intent to unseal the indictment. State Department officials tried unsuccessfully to persuade him to refrain from doing so.[215]

Key State Department officials and members of the National Security Council were infuriated by Crane's decision.[216] For months after the indictment was unsealed, the State Department cut off all communication with the OTP of the SCSL.[217] During this period, the U.S. ambassador in Freetown refused access to all personnel.[218]

Nonetheless, many observers credit the unsealing of the indictment with the hastening of Taylor's departure from Monrovia.[219] With the consent of the U.S. government, Taylor was subsequently granted refuge in Nigeria. After Taylor's arrival in Calabar, Nigeria, the U.S. Executive appeared reluctant

---

[212] Interview with former SCSL official (name withheld), March 7, 2005.
[213] Interview with former SCSL official (name withheld), March 7, 2005; interview with former SCSL official (name withheld), April 15, 2006.
[214] Interview with former SCSL official (name withheld), April 15, 2006.
[215] *Id.*
[216] *Id.* Interview with former SCSL official (name withheld), April 15, 2006.
[217] *Id.*
[218] *Id.*
[219] Interview with John Stompor, Human Rights First, March 8, 2005; "Charles Taylor, Indicted," *Washington Post*, June 5, 2003, at A32; Ward, *Might v. Right: Charles Taylor and the Sierra Leone Special Court*, 11 Hum. Rts. Br. 8, 8 (2003); Remarks of Alex Vines, Human Rights Watch, before House International Relations Committee, October 3, 2003.

to push Nigeria, a key ally, into surrendering Taylor to the SCSL. The U.S. Congress was divided as to how to handle Taylor.[220] In early 2004, the U.S. government seemed to be equivocating on this issue.[221] By late 2004, however, the new U.S. ambassador had reopened dialogue, and began appealing to the Nigerian government (at least publicly) to surrender Taylor to the court.[222]

By the spring of 2005, the political winds had shifted. There seemed to be a growing recognition within the U.S. government that the best solution to the Taylor problem was prosecution before the Special Court. In an overwhelming show of support for the SCSL, the U.S. Congress, on May 10, 2005, adopted Congressional Resolution 127, urging Nigeria to "expeditiously transfer" Taylor to the Special Court.[223] The resolution, which passed the House by a vote of 421 to 1 and was unanimously endorsed by the Senate, also noted that "the Special Court for Sierra Leone has contributed to developing the rule of law in Sierra Leone and is deserving of support"[224] and included statements by Crane on the threat posed to Liberia's stability by Taylor's continuing evasion of justice. The United States also played a leading role in getting the Security Council to pass a resolution allowing UN peacekeepers in Liberia to arrest Taylor.[225]

Following the exertion of pressure on Nigeria and Liberia by both the Executive and Congress, Taylor was finally surrendered to the Court on March 29, 2006. Members of Congress had earlier made clear to the newly elected president of Liberia that U.S. aid was dependent on Liberian cooperation with the transfer of Taylor to the Court.[226] On March 22, during a visit to the United States, Liberian president Ellen Johnson-Sirleaf called for Taylor's swift surrender to face trial.[227]

On March 28, Taylor disappeared from his home in Calabar, Nigeria. At the time of Taylor's disappearance, Nigerian President Obasanjo was en route to Washington, D.C. Members of Congress publicly urged Bush to refuse to meet with Obasanjo unless Taylor was brought to justice.[228] Upon arrival,

---

[220] Interview with former SCSL official (name withheld), March 7, 2005.
[221] Interview with John Stompor, Human Rights First, March 8, 2005.
[222] Remarks of Pierre-Richard Prosper before the Africa Subcommittee of the House International Relations Committee, June 24, 2004.
[223] H.R. Con. Res. 127, 109th Cong. [¶ 14] (May 4, 2005); see also "Bring Charles Taylor Justice," *New York Times* Op-Ed by Congressman Ed Royce, May 5, 2005.
[224] *Id.* at [¶ 10].
[225] UNSC Resolution 1638, deciding "that the mandate of the United Nations Mission in Liberia (UNMIL) shall include the following additional element: to apprehend and detain former President Charles Taylor in the event of a return to Liberia and to transfer him or facilitate his transfer to Sierra Leone for prosecution before the Special Court for Sierra Leone."
[226] Interview with former SCSL official (name withheld), March 7, 2005.
[227] "Nigeria Pressed by UN Court to Arrest Liberia's Ex-leader," *New York Times*, March 27, 2006.
[228] Statement of U.S. Senator Barack Obama on Charles Taylor, March 28, 2006.

Obasanjo was informed by senior State Department officials that unless Taylor was turned over to the Special Court, Bush would not meet with him.[229] Within hours, Taylor was apprehended and turned over to the Special Court.

As noted earlier, the U.S. government, citing concern for West African regional stability, called for Taylor's trial to be conducted in The Hague, using the facilities of the ICC.[230] Taylor would still be tried by the SCSL, but in an ICC courtroom. Taylor was transferred to the ICC Detention Centre in The Hague on June 20, 2006. The U.S. government was heavily involved in the transfer negotiations.[231]

I.D. INCREASING INTERNATIONALIZATION OF THE SCSL. In many ways, the Special Court has evolved into an increasingly international court. The nature of its jurisdiction, its personnel, and even its subject matter jurisdiction have all gradually moved to the international end of the spectrum. The Court itself has held that it is an international court and as such may prosecute even sitting heads of state.[232] The deputy prosecutor, initially envisioned by the treaty establishing the Court to be a Sierra Leonean, was an international/foreigner whose appointment was facilitated by an amendment to the treaty. Defendants have been tried only for violations of international law; no charges have been brought on the basis of the provisions of Sierra Leonean law included in the Statute (for a variety of reasons, including the Lomé Amnesty). Now its most prominent trial, that of Charles Taylor, may be moved to The Netherlands. It appears that the hybrid nature of the Court is increasingly a formal matter. This transformation does not seem to have elicited opposition from the U.S. government, raising questions as to the strength of its desire for a more domestic-oriented tribunal.

II. Cambodia

The Extraordinary Chambers in the Courts of Cambodia (ECCC) differ significantly from the Special Court for Sierra Leone in that they form part of Cambodia's domestic judiciary. They were created on the basis of domestic legislation, and their subject matter jurisdiction is circumscribed by this same

---

[229] Interview with NGO official (name withheld), April 3, 2006; interview with SCSL official (name withheld), April 4, 2006.

[230] "President Discusses Democracy in Iraq with Freedom House," Office of the Press Secretary, March 29, 2006; see also SC Res. 1688 (2006).

[231] Interview with SCSL official (name withheld), April 4, 2006; interview with State Department official July 21, 2006.

[232] *Prosecutor v. Taylor*, Decision of the Appeals Chamber on Immunity from Jurisdiction, SCSL-03-01-I-059, May 31, 2004.

domestic law. Although Cambodia has entered into a treaty with the UN with regard to the work of the ECCC, this treaty regulates UN involvement and imposes certain obligations on Cambodia and the UN with respect to the court's operations. It does not serve as the constitutive instrument of the ECCC.

The Chambers are staffed by both Cambodian and foreign[233] staff and officials. However, unlike the SCSL, the Cambodian officials constitute the majority. To ensure that decisions are not made through a purely Cambodian majority, decisions of the Chambers require a super-majority, including at least one foreign judge.

Initially, the United States supported the creation of an accountability mechanism for the Khmer Rouge atrocities. It had consistently funded documentation efforts and was heavily involved in the initial negotiations to establish the ECCC. Indeed, Scheffer has been credited with the idea of requiring a super-majority for judicial decisions, thus facilitating resolution of what had been a highly contentious issue during the negotiations.[234] In 2001, Prosper stated that the United States had been "encouraging both the Royal Government of Cambodia and the United Nations to be flexible in their approaches and to expeditiously finalize an agreement to ensure credible justice is achieved in the establishment of the Extraordinary Chambers."[235]

In addition, as with the other hybrids, U.S. support was facilitated by the employment of restrictive language in circumscribing the scope of the Chambers' jurisdiction. The Chambers have jurisdiction to prosecute only "Suspects," who are defined essentially as those members of the Khmer Rouge who committed international crimes from 1975–1979.[236]

Nonetheless, U.S. political support for the ECCC has been lukewarm. This is attributable in part to conflicting views within Congress and opposition to the Chambers on the part of a number of human rights NGOs. Congressional ambivalence results from the fact that different Cambodian diaspora groups,

---

[233] The Cambodian legislation establishing the ECCC refers to "foreign," as opposed to "international," judges and prosecutors. See, e.g., articles 9, 11, 16, and 18, Law on the Establishment of the Extraordinary Chambers, as amended on October 27, 2004 (NS/RKM/1004/006). Use of the term "foreign" underscores the fact that the Extraordinary Chambers are closer to the domestic end of the hybrid spectrum. It may also be used to affirm that the foreign officials are not hierarchically superior to the Cambodian officials, and possibly as a reminder that the former are operating within a foreign, rather than international, system.

[234] Interview with NGO official involved in the negotiations (name withheld), June 16, 2005. U.S. Senator John Kerry was also involved in the negotiations. Id.

[235] Press Release, Pierre-Richard Prosper, U.S. Ambassador for War Crimes Issues, Address at the Peace Palace in the Hague [¶ 20] (Dec. 19, 2001), at http://www.state.gov/s/wci/rm/8053.htm.

[236] Law on the Establishment of the Extraordinary Chambers, with inclusion of amendments as promulgated on 27 October 2004 (NS/RKM/1004/006), art. 2.

as constituencies of several members of Congress, have different views on the Chambers.[237] Although all of these groups want to see an accountability process, they are divided as to whether the Extraordinary Chambers can provide credible justice. Human rights NGOs have similar concerns as to whether the Chambers will be able to act independently in light of the Cambodian government's track record.[238]

During the first year of the Chambers' operation, the United States did not provide any funding. This was in part attributable to the fact that, until recently, U.S. legislation specifically precluded[239] the U.S. government from providing financial assistance to the central government of Cambodia and, in particular, "to any tribunal established by the Government of Cambodia" unless the Secretary of State "determine[d] and reporte[d] to the Committee on Appropriations that: (1) Cambodia's judiciary is competent, independent, free from widespread corruption, and its decisions are free from interference by the executive branch; and (2) the proposed tribunal is capable of delivering justice, that meets internationally recognized standards, for crimes against humanity and genocide in an impartial and credible manner."[240] This provision appeared in Appropriations legislation for several years.[241]

---

[237] Interview with Nina Bang-Jensen, Coalition for International Justice, June 16, 2005.
[238] See, e.g., "Kingdom of Cambodia: Amnesty International's Position and Concerns Regarding the Proposed "Khmer Rouge" Tribunal," April 25, 2003; "Cambodia: Opposition MP Jailed after Sham Trial," Human Rights Watch Report, August 9, 2005; Extraordinary Chambers of the Courts of Cambodia, Letter from Human Rights Watch to the Secretariat of the Rules and Procedure Committee, November 17, 2006.
[239] However, certain statutory exceptions were made, none of which are relevant to the present analysis.
[240] Foreign Operations Appropriations Act, 2005. This provision was introduced by a member of Congress whose staffer had spent significant time in Cambodia and had reported a very poor human rights record. Several officials have indicated that it is highly unlikely that the secretary of state could have made such a determination, particularly with respect to the first requirement.
[241] According to the Congressional Research Service, "Restrictions on U.S. assistance largely reflect congressional disapproval of Prime Minister Hun Sen's seizure of power in 1997 and concerns about ongoing political violence. Since 1998, foreign operations appropriations legislation has barred U.S. assistance to the central government of Cambodia and to the Khmer Rouge tribunal and instructed U.S. representatives to international financial institutions to oppose loans to Cambodia, except those that meet basic human needs. U.S. assistance may be provided only to Cambodian and foreign NGOs and to local governments. Statutory exceptions allow for U.S. assistance to the central government of Cambodia for reproductive, maternal, and child health care, preventing and treating HIV/AIDS and other infectious diseases, basic education, combating human trafficking, rule-of-law programs, cultural and historic preservation (Angkor Wat), counter-narcotics, and developing international adoptions procedures. For most of these activities, however, U.S.AID collaborates with the central government of Cambodia but continues to provide funding only through NGOs." Congressional Research Service, "Cambodia: Background and U.S. Relations," July 8, 2005.

In the Committee Report accompanying the 2005 Appropriations Act, the Committee noted,

> The Committee again restricts assistance to the Cambodian Government, with few exceptions, and notes that the budget request does not contain funding for a United States contribution to the Khmer Rouge tribunal. The Committee directs that no funds be made available for a contribution to the tribunal unless the Secretary of State reports to the Committee that the tribunal is capable of delivering justice that meets internationally recognized standards of justice for crimes against humanity and genocide in an impartial and credible manner.[242]

This tribunal-specific provision, however, was removed in the 2006 Appropriations Act, perhaps signaling a moderation of the U.S. position. Nonetheless, the blanket prohibition on aid to the central government still posed an obstacle to direct assistance to the Tribunal.[243]

Most observers agree that, if it were not for this legislative obstacle, the United States would have been likely to support the Extraordinary Chambers financially for at least two reasons.[244] First, as special chambers within the domestic Cambodian legal system, they conform more closely to the model that the Bush administration put forth as the ideal. Second, the United States had already provided a significant amount of financial support to the nongovernmental Documentation Center for Cambodia, knowing that the records of this organization would play a crucial role in any prosecutions that occur before the Extraordinary Chambers.

Throughout the ECCC's first year of operation, the United States maintained a wait-and-see approach to the issue of whether to provide any form of direct support to the ECCC. Corruption allegations,[245] as well as a perceived lack of progress at early plenary sessions of the ECCC,[246] posed new impediments to U.S. support.

---

[242] Senate Report 109-96, Department of State, Foreign Operations, and Related Programs Appropriations Bill, 2006, pg. 39.
[243] However, there may be some room to maneuver around this funding prohibition in the 2006 Appropriations Act. The act contains an exception making funds available for "activities to support democracy, the rule of law, and human rights"; Section 554(b), 2006 Foreign Operations Appropriations Act. The State Department must, however, consult with the Committee prior to "the obligation of assistance for the central Government of Cambodia." Section 520; see also Committee Report accompanying the 2006 Appropriations Act.
[244] Interview with Nina Bang-Jensen, Coalition for International Justice, June 16, 2005; interview with NGO official (name withheld), April 6, 2006.
[245] OSJI Press Release, "Corruption Allegations at Khmer Rouge Court Must Be Investigated Thoroughly," February 14, 2007.
[246] Interview with intergovernmental organization official (name withheld), February 7, 2007.

However, in early 2008, Cambodian officials reported that the United States expressed the possibility of directly supporting the ECCC. According to the Cambodian Foreign Ministry, U.S. diplomats had offered the possibility of financial support if the Cambodian government acceded to a U.S. request for an advisory role at the ECCC.[247] Although this request was initially resisted by Phnom Penh, a compromise was eventually reached whereby a U.S. national would be deployed to the ECCC under the auspices of the UN. As a result, the United States announced in summer 2008 that it would begin to provide funding.[248]

III. Other Courts with an International Dimension

The United States has been largely supportive of other courts with an international dimension, including the internationalized Kosovo and East Timorese court systems and the Bosnian War Crimes Chamber. The United States has provided political, financial, and other material support for these mechanisms.

For example, the United States provided personnel to assist in the work of each of these institutions. U.S. prosecutors and judges served in the internationalized courts of East Timor, Kosovo, and Bosnia. The United States also provided direct financial support to each of these institutions.

The United States has also been credited with the creation of the Bosnian War Crimes Chambers.[249] According to a number of sources, the Chambers would not have come into existence without the exertion of U.S. political pressure, as well as the initial financial contribution of the United States, which opened the door to funding by other states.[250]

U.S. support was again facilitated by the fact that each of these mechanisms is closer to the national end of the hybrid spectrum, bringing them within the U.S. preference for resolution at the national level. They each sat essentially as domestic courts staffed in part by foreign nationals and applying in part international law. The creation of each also dovetailed with other U.S. foreign policy objectives in the relevant regions. However, in some instances that support has been interrupted by the emergence of competing foreign policy considerations. This was seen most dramatically in relation to U.S. support for the Special Panels for Serious Crimes in East Timor. Although the United

---

[247] "U.S. Seeks Role in Cambodian KRouge Trials: Official," *AFP*, January 17, 2008.
[248] "US Plans to Pledge Funds for KRouge Court," AFP, August 25, 2008. By early 2009, the United States had dispersed $1.5 million in funding for the ECCC. State Department Daily Press Briefing, February 18, 2009.
[249] Interview with international official of the Bosnian War Crimes Chamber (name withheld), November 3, 2005.
[250] Interview with international official of the Bosnian War Crimes Chamber (name withheld), November 3, 2005.

States continued to support the Panels in their prosecution of East Timorese perpetrators, it was not supportive of East Timor's efforts to prosecute Indonesian officials. Indonesia is viewed by the United States as a key ally in the War on Terror, as well as having strategic value because of its location.

The most recent quasi-international criminal court to be supported by the United States is the Special Tribunal for Lebanon (STL), which was established to prosecute certain "terrorist attacks" occurring in Lebanon since October 2004.[251] Similar to the hybrid mechanisms described earlier, the STL is composed of a mix of international and Lebanese officials.

The jurisdiction of the Tribunal is narrowly circumscribed. The STL's jurisdiction encompasses only the assassination of former Lebanese prime minister Rafiq Hariri and other related attacks between October 1, 2004, and December 12, 2005. The Tribunal can take jurisdiction over subsequent related attacks only with the consent of the Security Council. Thus, any member of the Security Council may veto jurisdiction over acts committed after December 2005. Further, the STL's subject matter jurisdiction is limited to crimes under Lebanese law.[252] A participant in the negotiations has indicated that these jurisdictional limitations were included at the behest of the United States to ensure that the Tribunal could not take jurisdiction over the conduct of Israeli forces during the 2006 conflict between Israel and Hezbollah/Lebanon.[253]

An institution at the farthest end of the hybrid spectrum (i.e., the least international in nature) would be the Iraqi High Tribunal (IHT) which has been robustly supported by the United States. Not only has the United States provided extensive political and financial support but the institution itself was essentially a U.S. creation. Having a central role in the creation of the court, the United States was able to ensure that U.S. personnel would not be subject to its jurisdiction. Indeed, the initial Statute for the Tribunal expressly limited its jurisdiction to Iraqi nationals.

It must be borne in mind that the IHT was created during a time in which the United States was still an occupying force in Iraq and thus in possession of broad power over the creation of Iraqi institutions. This was also during the peak of U.S. hostility toward the ICC. Thus, the United States rejected a role for the ICC or even the creation of a hybrid along the lines of the Sierra Leone model. Instead, it saw the creation of the IHT as an opportunity to show that even trials of former heads of state and other senior officials could be conducted at the national level.

---

[251] UN SC Resolution 1757 (2007).
[252] Id. at Annex.
[253] Interview with U.N. official involved in the negotiation over the Tribunal's jurisdiction (name withheld), March 22, 2007.

In general, as hostility toward international institutions has increased, the United States has shown increasing support for hybrid institutions. However, as with other international criminal justice mechanisms, U.S. support for the hybrids has been strongly influenced by competing foreign policy objectives, as well as the possibility of prosecution of U.S. nationals, especially U.S. agents.

C. CONCLUSION

Essentially, the official position of the U.S. government may be summarized as follows:

1. The United States is in principle committed to justice and accountability for all.
2. It is best to prosecute crimes, including all international crimes, at the national level. Prosecution by any other court (including domestic courts of other countries)[254] should be the absolute last resort.
3. The Security Council should have the final word on prosecution by any other court.

1. *Commitment to Accountability*

The United States is in principle committed to accountability. Notwithstanding changes of administration, a strong ideological strain in favor of accountability permeates all branches of the U.S. government and public.

This does not mean, however, that the United States seeks accountability at any cost. Even in cases in which the U.S. attitude toward international criminal courts is at its most favorable, these institutions are not viewed as ends in themselves. The U.S. approach is pragmatic – each institution is assessed in terms of its ability to advance U.S. interests, which include, but are not limited to, promoting accountability and the rule of law on the international level.

When accountability efforts at the domestic level fail, the United States resorts to a balancing of interests. When international accountability efforts conflict with strong national interests, those interests will prevail.

2. *Strong Preference for Domestic Resolution; Other Courts as Last Resort*

Despite its support for the ad hoc tribunals, there was a belief in the Bush administration that the ICTY in particular had not been successful in making

---

[254] There are of course strong parallels with the U.S. position on the exercise of universal jurisdiction.

changes for the affected people or the affected region. The United States insists that it is far better to have courts trying people locally, contributing to the sense of ownership by the affected communities.

The U.S. government has also pointed to the ICC as even further removed from the affected communities, emphasizing the fact that the first four situations before the Court are all in Africa. The United States emphasized that African crimes should be prosecuted in Africa, distinguishing this from the "colonial" approach of the ICC in which Africans are "prosecuted by their former colonial masters in The Hague."

3. Security Council Control

The United States is strongly interested in maintaining the primacy of the Security Council in matters of peace and security. The United States regards the existence of the ICC as a threat to this primacy. Most observers assert that this position is a direct consequence of the status of the United States as a permanent member of the Council. Indeed, some would argue that the degree of U.S. support for a tribunal directly corresponds to its degree of control over the mechanism.

4. Other and Underlying Factors

The U.S. attitude seems to be influenced by a range of factors, including such variables as ideological leanings of those in power and the strength of certain personalities (proponents or opponents). The impact of such variables tends to be moderated over time. Sentiments that appeared to underlie the Bush administration's hostility toward international criminal courts include the following:

1. belief in the superiority of the U.S. justice system, and U.S. governance generally;
2. belief that the United States, in light of its global preeminence, activities, and responsibilities, is not similarly situated to other states and that therefore its agents should not be subject to the same constraints and legal liabilities as those of other states;
3. suspicion of international/multilateral institutions (perceived to have a greater tendency toward inefficiency, bias, and corruption);
4. perception of international criminal courts as being unrealistic, "too European," or "too human rights–based"; and
5. fear of accountability mechanisms outside of any U.S. control, coupled with fear that "everyone is out to get us."

The relationship between the principles on which the United States publicly grounds its policy and the other identified factors is complex. The extent to which there are ideological objections and visceral responses by those in power corresponds to an increasing likelihood of a top-down approach to policy making. As these objections and responses become moderated over time, the normal interagency process of policy formulation regains the space necessary to perform its function.

5. Historical Analysis of Policy Formulation

The historical survey in this chapter reveals certain consistent themes underlying U.S. attitudes toward international criminal courts. One consistent element would appear to be the (un)likelihood of prosecution of U.S. nationals. The United States has tended to support international criminal courts when the U.S. government has (or is perceived by U.S. officials to have) a significant degree of control over the court or when the possibility of prosecution of U.S. nationals is either expressly precluded or otherwise remote. This was certainly the case for the post–World War II military tribunals, as well as the Security Council ad hoc tribunals. U.S. support for the hybrid tribunals was similarly facilitated by the inclusion of jurisdictional limitations and other assurances of nonprosecution of U.S. nationals.

If the United States is assured that U.S. nationals will not be prosecuted (or, at least, not without its consent), it will engage in a balancing of interests to determine its level of support or opposition. Ideological leanings will of course color this balancing of interests and at times define some of those interests. To the extent an administration's ideological strain in favor of criminal accountability is stronger than its ideological strain opposed to the creation of international authority, the prospect of U.S. support of a given international criminal court seems to increase.

6. The Limits of Pragmatism

This balancing of interests approach corresponds with Bellinger's description of the U.S. approach as "pragmatic." In a May 2006 statement to the colloquium of authors of this book, Bellinger stated,

> In our view, such courts and tribunals should not be seen as an end in themselves but rather as potential tools to advance shared international interests in developing and promoting the rule of law, ensuring justice and accountability, and solving legal disputes. Consistent with this approach, we evaluate the contributions that proposed international courts and tribunals may make

on a case-by-case basis, just as we consider the advantages and disadvantages of particular matters through international judicial mechanisms rather than diplomatic or other means.[255]

Although Bellinger does not spell out the possible disadvantages in much detail, the practice of the United States indicates that not all such considerations relate to the high-minded ideals cited in the preceding sentence. Of course, the United States considers these high-minded ideals in its calculation of interests but not to the exclusion of lower minded considerations.

For some critics, a pragmatic approach that permits consideration of purely national self-interests, and perhaps even the interests of individual government officials, is inappropriate when it comes to judicial settlement of disputes. For them, the idea of the selective use of courts creates an internal tension – that selective judicial enforcement is inconsistent with the very idea of a court. This tension is exacerbated considerably in the value-laden criminal realm, with its punitive dimension, and *a fortiori* when it comes to prosecution of individuals for such morally heinous crimes as those that typically spring to mind in the present context.

This is perhaps the greatest challenge to the U.S. position. The idea of a court comes with a lot of ideological baggage, some of which resounds in other value-laden areas of international law. Indeed, international law as a whole has been permeated by the development of human rights law, as well as older notions of equality before the law and other principles of natural justice. Although this baggage may not be essential to a court's technical operation, it still serves an important purpose. Courts find their credibility and legitimacy in that baggage. Selectivity of use diminishes a court's legitimacy. A pragmatic approach that overlooks this factor may ultimately prove impractical.

7. Postscript

As this book goes to press, Barack Obama has just begun his term as the 44th President of the United States. There is a strong expectation that his policy positions regarding international institutions will be significantly

---

[255] "International Court and Tribunals and the Rule of Law," Statement by John Bellinger, legal advisor, at George Washington School of Law, Washington, D.C., May 11, 2006. This instrumental use of international courts is clearly visible in the creation of the STL. The jurisdiction of the Tribunal is essentially limited to a single crime. Although it may be appropriate for politics to play a role in shaping a court's subject matter jurisdiction, even in relation to conduct that has already been committed, it may lead to a manipulation of jurisdiction to single out particular perpetrators for prosecution. It could also lead to a de-contextualization of, and thus misapprehension of, conduct.

different from those of his immediate predecessor.[256] The rhetoric of the Obama administration so far seems to support this expectation. Newly appointed U.S. Ambassador to the UN Susan Rice stated during her first appearance in the Security Council that the ICC "looks to become an important and credible instrument for trying to hold accountable the senior leadership responsible for atrocities committed in the Congo, Uganda, and Darfur." She also confirmed that "we support the ICC investigation and prosecution of war crimes in Sudan, and we see no reason for an Article 16 deferral."[257]

Although it is too soon to tell whether U.S. policy toward international criminal courts will change significantly under President Obama, the positive tone adopted by his administration seems to augur in favor of a continuation of the trend toward constructive engagement already in evidence during the latter years of the Bush administration.

---

[256] "Under Obama, US Drops Hostility to ICC: Experts," AFP, March 22, 2009. Although this expectation may or may not be warranted, civil society groups are availing themselves of this perceived window of opportunity to encourage a policy shift toward a more favorable disposition vis-à-vis the ICC. See, e.g., ICC Task Force Report, American Society of International Law, 2009.

[257] Statement by Ambassador Susan Rice in the Security Council, USUS Press Release # 020(09), January 29, 2009. Ambassador Rice reiterated U.S. support for the ICC's work in Darfur on March 4, 2009, following the issuance of an ICC arrest warrant for Sudanese President Omer Al-Bashir. Statement by Ambassador Susan Rice on the ICC's arrest warrant for Sudanese President Bashir, USUS Press Release # 039(09), March 4, 2009.

7

The United States and the Inter-American Court of Human Rights

ELIZABETH A. H. ABI-MERSHED[*]

[T]he last half century has witnessed the internationalization of human rights and the humanization of international law.[1]

The recognition of the individual as the holder of rights and that respect for such rights may require specific responses from the state has brought about fundamental changes in international law over the last half-century. Regional human rights systems have played a vital role in this development of international law and have gained steadily increasing legitimacy. All the member states of the Organization of American States (OAS), the Council of Europe, and the African Union are subject to regional human rights supervision.

The OAS is the world's oldest regional organization,[2] and the primary multilateral forum for the United States and its hemispheric neighbors. The essential purpose of the OAS is to strengthen peace and security in the Americas, and the inter-American human rights system is an essential tool in the pursuit of this regional objective.[3] Ratification of the OAS Charter creates a minimum

---

[*] Assistant Executive Secretary, Inter-American Commission on Human Rights. The opinions presented in this chapter are those of the author and do not necessarily reflect those of the Organization of American States or the Inter-American Commission on Human Rights.
[1] Thomas Buergenthal (former president of the Inter-American Court of Human Rights), *The Normative and Institutional Evolution of International Human Rights*, 19 Hum. Rts. Qtrly 703 (1997) 722.
[2] It dates back to the First International Conference of American States, held in Washington, D.C., from October 1889 to April 1890.
[3] The Inter-American Commission provides comprehensive information about its work online at http://www.cidh.org. The site includes the instruments of the system, as well as all published reports and a search mechanism. The Inter-American Court provides information at http://www.corteidh.or.cr.

set of human rights obligations for a member state.[4] States may opt to expand those obligations by ratifying any or all of a series of regional human rights treaties.[5]

The system provides two organs to supervise member-state compliance with regional human rights obligations: the Inter-American Commission on Human Rights ("Commission") and the Inter-American Court of Human Rights ("Court"). The Commission carries out a diverse range of quasi-judicial and quasi-political supervisory functions. The Court has three specific roles: (1) it exercises contentious jurisdiction with respect to those states that have ratified the American Convention on Human Rights ("American Convention") and accepted that form of jurisdiction, (2) it has the competence to issue provisional measures with respect to those same states, and (3) it may issue advisory opinions at the request of any member state, the Commission, or other relevant organs of the OAS.

This chapter reviews attitudes of the United States toward the Inter-American Court and attempts to reflect the ambiguity of a perspective that recognizes the Court's utility for certain purposes but has declined to consider further engagement with it. Although the chapter focuses on the Inter-American Court, it includes some references to the more engaged and complex relationship the United States maintains with the Inter-American Commission.

The OAS and its human rights mechanisms play a necessary role in the resolution of some of our most serious hemispheric challenges. These institutions are important not only for some member states but also provide a forum and opportunities for all, including the United States, to advance the protection of basic rights in the Americas.[6]

---

[4] Charter of the Organization of American States, art. 1, Apr. 30, 1948, 2 U.S.T. 2394, reprinted in IACHR, Basic Documents Pertaining to Human Rights in the Inter-American System (hereinafter "Basic Documents"), OEA/Ser.L/V/I.4 rev. 12, 31 Jan. 2007, at 115.

[5] These treaties include the American Convention on Human Rights (hereinafter "American Convention"), Additional Protocol to the American Convention in the Area of Economic, Social and Cultural Rights "Protocol of San Salvador," Protocol to Abolish the Death Penalty, Inter-American Convention to Prevent and Punish Torture, Inter-American Convention on Forced Disappearance of Persons, Inter-American Convention on the Prevention, Punishment and Eradication of Violence against Women "Convention of Belém do Pará," Inter-American Convention on the Elimination of All Forms of Discrimination against Persons with Disabilities, all reprinted in Basic Documents, *supra*.

[6] In a speech given at the OAS in 2001, President George W. Bush indicated that the organization has an "important role" to play in dealing with issues of hemispheric concern. "In lands where liberty is threatened by corruption, drugs and human rights abuses, the OAS is helping to combat these destructive forces. Along borders where tensions run high, the OAS helps build confidence and avoid crises. And in lands where freedom's hold is fragile, the OAS is there to strengthen it." Quoted in *Fact Sheet on the Organization of American States*, U.S. Mission to the Organization of American States, Nov. 5, 2004, at http://www.state.gov/p/wha/rls/fs/37856.htm.

A. THE CREATION OF THE INTER-AMERICAN HUMAN COURT OF HUMAN RIGHTS: ACCEPTED BUT NOT EMBRACED

The idea of an inter-American court to monitor compliance with human rights obligations dates back to the origins of the regional human rights system itself.[7] The regional system developed in stages, beginning with the adoption by the OAS member states of the American Declaration of the Rights and Duties of Man in 1948.[8] The member states began looking forward at that time to the possible creation of a judicial organ of supervision. The Inter-American Commission was created by resolution of the Fifth Meeting of Consultation of Ministers of Foreign Affairs in 1959 to serve as a quasi-judicial and quasi-political mechanism of supervision.[9] The notion of a judicial treaty-based organ of supervision was finally given concrete form with the adoption in 1969 of the American Convention, the treaty that established the Inter-American Court of Human Rights.[10] The Court was established in operational terms shortly after the entry into force of the Convention in 1978.[11]

Even before the American Convention on Human Rights had been drafted, the United States had clearly articulated a position with respect to its own possible participation in such a regime:

> The United States . . . has since its birth as a nation strongly defended human rights. The promotion of respect for human rights in the inter-American system is therefore supported by the United States. While the United States, because of its Federal Government, does not find it possible to enter into multilateral conventions with respect to human rights or with respect to an Inter-American Court of Human Rights, it, of course, raises no objection to other states entering into conventions on these subjects should they find it possible to do so. Accordingly, while the United States has voted in favor of

---

[7] *See generally* IACHR, Basic Documents, *supra*, 11–12, recounting the creation and initial history of the Court.

[8] American Declaration of the Rights and Duties of Man, adopted by the Ninth International Conference of American States, Bogotá, Colombia, 1948, reprinted in Basic Documents, *supra*, at 15.

[9] Fifth Meeting of Consultation of Ministers of Foreign Affairs, Santiago, Chile, Aug. 12–18, 1959, Final Act. Doc. OEA/Ser.C/II.5, 4–5.

[10] Organization of American States, American Convention on Human Rights, arts. 52–69, Nov. 22, 1969, O.A.S.T.S. No. 36, 1144 U.N.T.S. 123.

[11] The Statute of the Court was approved by the OAS General Assembly in La Paz, Bolivia, in 1979, Resolution AG/RES. 448, reprinted in IACHR, Basic Documents, *supra*. The Court held its first meeting on June 29 and 30, 1979, at OAS headquarters in Washington D.C., and the Court was officially installed at its headquarters in San José, Costa Rica, on September 3, 1979. See OAS, Inter-American Court of Human Rights, Proceedings of the Installation, San José Costa Rica, Sept. 1979.

Resolution VIII, Human Rights [creating the Inter-American Commission on Human Rights and calling for a convention to be drafted], it reserves its position with respect to its participation in the instruments or organisms that may evolve.[12]

The United States did not oppose the creation of the Inter-American Court. In fact, it even facilitated its establishment by participating very actively in the drafting of the American Convention, including those articles concerning the proposed Inter-American Court of Human Rights.[13] In terms of the mechanics of the U.S. government's participation, an Interdepartmental Committee on Foreign Policy Relating to Human Rights, an interagency group that advised the State Department on human rights policy issues, reviewed draft versions of the proposed Convention in 1968 and 1969.[14] The U.S. government submitted detailed written comments and proposed amendments to the draft in 1969, submitted supplementary observations during the drafting conference, and participated actively in the drafting sessions.[15]

The U.S. position paper prepared for the drafting conference indicated generally that it would seek "a convention (a) suitable for the Inter-American system, (b) within range of ratification by all, or nearly all, the members of the OAS, and (c) preferably one which the U.S. can also consider favorably – if not now, at least at some future time."[16] With respect to the proposed Inter-American Court, the position was to support the creation of such a tribunal as long as acceptance of compulsory jurisdiction was optional.[17]

Broadly speaking, insofar as the Court's jurisdiction over contentious cases was defined as optional, requiring an express act of acceptance by a State Party

---

[12] Marjorie M. Whiteman, 5 Digest of International Law, Dept. of State Pub. 7873, vol. 5, Ch. XIII, Rights and Duties of States, sec. 16, "Human Rights," 235 (1965).

[13] *See generally*, Conferencia Especializada Interamericana sobre Derechos Humanos, San José, Costa Rica, 7–22 de noviembre de 1969, Actas y Documentos, OEA/Ser.K/XVI/1.2.

[14] *See Report of the United States Delegation to the Inter-American Conference on Protection of Human Rights*, San José, Costa Rica, Nov. 9–22, 1969. This report is available in the archives of the Columbus Memorial Library of the OAS; pertinent parts are reprinted in Thomas Buergenthal and Robert Norris, 3 *Human Rights: The Inter-American System* (1982) part 2, ch. III.

    The U.S. Delegation comprised five members. The head of the delegation was the then-U.S. member of the International Law Commission, and the alternate was a member of the U.S. Mission to the OAS. The delegation also included two members from the State Department and one from the Department of Justice.

[15] *Id.*

[16] U.S. Position Paper for the Inter-American Human Rights Conference, San José, Costa Rica, Nov. 7–22, 1969, prepared by Walter J. Landry, on file at the IACHR, at ii.

[17] *Id.* at iv (specifying: "The U.S. should oppose revision which would make acceptance of Court jurisdiction automatic on ratification of the Convention").

to the Convention, the creation of the Inter-American Court enjoyed broad support from all the member states that participated in the drafting, including the United States.[18]

B. PROSPECTS FOR U.S. ACCEPTANCE OF THE COURT'S CONTENTIOUS JURISDICTION

A review of developments over the years indicates that although the United States is probably not any closer to ratifying the American Convention or accepting the contentious jurisdiction of the Inter-American Court of Human Rights, there have been and continue to be instances of engagement with the system that have an impact on both the system and the conduct of the U.S. government.

Engagement with the system has to some extent reflected the measure in which various U.S. administrations have incorporated human rights as a foreign policy priority and have sought to exercise influence in the consolidation of democracy and human rights in the Americas.

Thus, as part of its emphasis on the protection of human rights as a foreign policy goal, the Carter administration actively sought to strengthen the regional machinery for protecting human rights and its relevance in the hemisphere. It was active on human rights issues within the context of the OAS generally, and President Carter signed the American Convention on Human Rights and submitted it to the Senate for its advice and consent.[19] It may be noted that, consistent with a long-standing U.S. practice, although the Carter administration endorsed ratification, it did so pursuant to a declaration to the effect that the substantive rights recognized in the Convention would not be considered self-executing.[20]

---

[18] It may be noted that it was proposed at one point during the drafting sessions that the seat of the Commission, Court and their respective secretariats be located in Virginia, near the home of the drafter of that state's Declaration of Rights. The Brazilian delegation that presented the proposal, which did not find any support, indicated that if the United States had not ratified the Convention within one year after its entry into force, the OAS Council could select another seat. *Id.* 51–52.

[19] The United States signed the American Convention on June 1, 1977. See IACHR, Basic Documents, *supra*, signatures and current status of ratifications, at 51. *See generally*, David Forsythe, *The United States and the Organization of American States*, 13 Hum. Rts. Qtrly 66, at 85–88, reviewing actions of the Carter administration in support of the inter-American human rights system. *See also* Tom Farer, *The Rise of the Inter-American Human Rights Regime: No Longer a Unicorn, Not Yet an Ox*, 19 Hum. Rts Qtrly 511 (1997) at 521 (noting President Carter's role in urging other regional states to ratify the American Convention).

[20] *See* Message from the President of the United States Transmitting Four Treaties Pertaining to Human Rights, S. Exec. Doc. F, 95th Cong., 2d Sess. 1 (1978). The United States has

Efforts toward ratification in subsequent years have been few and far between. In June 1993, in his address before the World Conference on Human Rights, Secretary of State Warren Christopher indicated that the Clinton administration was taking up the ratification of pending human rights treaties, looking first to the International Convention on the Elimination of All Forms of Racism. It would then turn to the Convention on the Elimination of All Forms of Discrimination Against Women, the American Convention, and the International Covenant on Economic, Social and Cultural Rights.[21] While the World Conference was underway, a member of the House of Representatives presented remarks in the House encouraging the Clinton administration to retake the question of ratification of the American Convention and three other human rights treaties.[22] This initiative was perhaps spurred in part by free trade negotiations then underway between the United States and a number of countries of the Americas and the need to ensure adherence to minimum labor and human rights standards throughout the region.[23] The following month, a congressional seminar was organized to examine the contents of the treaties and their significance.[24]

A working group of the American Bar Association (ABA) issued a report recommending ratification of the American Convention that garnered some support from the State Department and the National Security Council.[25] It should be noted that the ABA to date maintains a policy favoring support for ratification of the American Convention.[26] Shortly thereafter, however, the majority in the Senate shifted, and the initiative lost momentum. It has been reported that, at least twice since 1994, the State Department considered recommending possible ratification but took no action due in some measure

---

held the position that the provisions of the American Convention should not be understood as self-executing since the time of the drafting of the American Convention. See Lawrence LeBlanc, *The OAS and the Promotion and Protection of Human Rights*, at 21 (1977). It should be noted that the submission to the Senate included a series of proposed reservations.

[21] "Democracy and Human Rights: Where America Stands – Secretary of State Warren Christopher Addresses World Conference – Transcript," U.S. Department of State Dispatch, June 21, 1993.

[22] Hon. John J. La Falce, "United States Should Ratify Human Rights Treaties," Extension of remarks – June 16, 1993, at http://thomas.loc.gov/cgi-bin/query/z?r103:E16Jn3–125.

[23] See Opening Statement of Andrew Reding, Congressional Seminar, "International Human Rights Treaties: Time to Ratify," sponsored by Rep. John J. LaFalce (NY) and Sen. Paul Wellstone (MN), July 21, 1993.

[24] Congressional Seminar, "International Human Rights Treaties: Time to Ratify," sponsored by Rep. John J. LaFalce (NY) and Sen. Paul Wellstone (MN), July 21, 1993.

[25] Remarks of Professor Douglass Cassel, delivered during the conference "The United States and the Inter-American Human Rights System," sponsored by Columbia Law School Human Rights Institute, CEJIL and ASIL, New York, April 7, 2008.

[26] "International Law Section Policy – Human Rights – American Convention," at http://www.abanet.org/intlaw/leadership/policy.html.

to expected opposition from the then-chair of the Senate Foreign Relations Committee.[27]

Although there has not been strong governmental interest in ratification of the American Convention in recent years, the question merits a couple of comments. First, given that the United States ratified the International Covenant on Civil and Political Rights,[28] the provisions of which are very similar to those of the American Convention, ratification of the latter would not impose on the United States more extensive, or markedly distinct, obligations than those contained in the former. Second, to the extent that facts on the ground may prompt or require deeper engagement on human rights issues in the hemisphere, U.S. ratification of the American Convention would substantially increase its authority in this area.

There are no signals suggesting that U.S. administrations to date have given serious consideration to accepting the obligatory jurisdiction of the Inter-American Court. The arguments that militate in favor of ratification of the Convention apply in general terms with respect to acceptance of the Court's contentious jurisdiction. The American Convention is the centerpiece of the regional human rights system. Its norms, coupled with the monitoring actions of the Commission and Court, form an integrated system of protection. The system produces advances in the protection of basic rights precisely because the norms and the monitoring mechanisms work together. Nonetheless, ratification of the Convention does not require submission to the jurisdiction of the Court; several countries currently hold that status.[29]

C. INSTANCES OF ENGAGEMENT BETWEEN THE UNITED STATES AND THE INTER-AMERICAN COURT

Given that the United States has not yet ratified the American Convention, nor, *a fortiori*, accepted the contentious jurisdiction of the Inter-American Court, the instances in which there has been engagement between it and the Court relate primarily to the exercise of advisory jurisdiction.[30]

---

[27] Douglass Cassel, *The Inter-American Court of Human Rights: Promise and Peril*, in Commentaries, Center for International Human Rights: Northwestern Law, at http://www.law.northwestern.edu7depts/clinic/ihr.

[28] 999 U.N.T.S. 171, 6 ILM 368 (adopted Dec. 19, 1966; ratified by U.S. June 8, 1992).

[29] Dominica, Grenada, and Jamaica are party to the Convention but have not accepted the contentious jurisdiction of the Court.

[30] Article 64 of the American Convention establishes the Court's competence to issue advisory opinions:

1. The member states of the Organization may consult the Court regarding the interpretation of this Convention or of other treaties concerning the protection of human rights in the

Since the Court was established in 1979, it has issued nineteen advisory opinions. Many of these have had a substantial impact on the evolution of human rights law in the region. As Dinah Shelton has written, the Inter-American Court has the capacity to "shape the interpretation and application of the Convention, Declaration and other human rights instruments"; "[a]dvisory opinions in particular are well-suited to the enunciation of general legal principles which may contribute to the development of human rights law in the Western hemisphere."[31] Those developments feed into the larger process of the evolution of international human rights law, which in turn does have some eventual impact on the conduct of the United States.[32]

Over the years, by way of advisory opinions, the Court has elaborated on some fundamental questions in the region, including impermissible limitations on journalistic expression,[33] the non-derogability of habeas corpus and fundamental due process guarantees in states of emergency,[34] the status of the American Declaration as a source of legal obligation for member states,[35] the legal consequences of the failure of a party to the Vienna Convention on Consular Relations to provide notification to a detained foreigner of his or

> American states. Within their spheres of competence, the organs listed in Chapter X of the Charter of the Organization of American States, as amended by the Protocol of Buenos Aires, may in like manner consult the Court.
> 2. The Court, at the request of a member state of the Organization, may provide that state with opinions regarding the compatibility of any of its domestic laws with the aforesaid international instruments.

[31] Dinah Shelton, *Improving Human Rights Protections: Recommendations for Enhancing the Effectiveness of the Inter-American Commission and Inter-American Court of Human Rights*, in 3 Am. Univ. J. Int'l Law Pol. 334 (1988).

[32] The Inter-American Court's advisory opinions on habeas corpus and judicial guarantees in states of emergency, for example, have been influential throughout the region. See I/A Court H.R., *Habeas Corpus in emergency situations* (arts. 27(2), 25(1) and 7(6) American Convention on Human Rights). Advisory Opinion OC-8/87 of January 30, 1987, Ser. A No. 8; *Judicial guarantees in States of Emergency* (arts. 27(2), 25 and 8 American Convention on Human Rights). Advisory Opinion OC-9/87 of October 6, 1987, Ser. A No. 9. Recently they have been cited by *amici curiae* in litigation concerning the right of detainees held at Guantanamo Bay to file for habeas corpus relief. See Brief *Amicus Curiae* of the American Bar Association in support of petitioners, *Boumediene v. Bush*, on writs of cert., Aug. 24, 2007; Brief of *Amici Curiae* Amnesty International et al., *Boumediene v. Bush*, op. cit.

[33] I/A Court H.R., *Compulsory membership in an association prescribed by law for the practice of journalism* (Arts. 13 and 29 American Convention on Human Rights). Advisory Opinion OC-5/85 of November 13, 1985. Series A No. 5.

[34] I/A Court H.R., Advisory Opinion OC-8/87, *op. cit*; Advisory Opinion OC-9/87, *op. cit*.

[35] I/A Court H.R., *Interpretation of the American Declaration of the Rights and Duties of Man within the framework of Article 64 of the American Convention on Human Rights*. Advisory Opinion OC-10/89 of July 14, 1989, Ser. A No. 10.

her right to contact a consular official,[36] and the due process rights of migrant workers.[37]

As in the case of the International Court of Justice, advisory opinions of the IACHR are not binding but rather set forth authoritative interpretations.[38] As with the ICJ, certain organs and agencies of the OAS, such as the Commission, are authorized to request opinions. In addition, member states may also present such requests. The scope of the Inter-American Court's advisory jurisdiction is quite broad, given that it may address questions concerning not only the American Convention but also other human rights treaties applicable in the region. At the request of a state, the Court may also examine the compatibility of domestic legislation with an applicable treaty.[39]

Any time a request for an advisory opinion is made, the Court notifies all the OAS member states. As in the case of the International Court of Justice (ICJ), member states may choose to present written observations, as well as to participate in the public hearing held to inform the Court's formulation of each such opinion. The Court also receives written and oral submissions from representatives of civil society.

Whereas the United States has been involved in twenty-two of the twenty-four advisory proceedings brought before the World Court, in the form of written or oral pleadings,[40] it has participated in only three of the nineteen processes before the Inter-American Court.[41]

The most significant of these for evaluating the present attitude of the United States toward the Court is the Advisory Opinion on *The Right to Information on Consular Assistance in the Framework of the Guarantees of the Due Process of*

---

[36] I/A Court H.R., *The Right to Information on Consular Assistance in the Framework of the Guarantees of the Due Process of Law*. Advisory Opinion OC-16/99 of October 1, 1999, Ser. A No. 16.

[37] I/A Court H.R., *Juridical Condition and Rights of Undocumented Migrants*. Advisory Opinion OC-18/03 of September 17, 2003, Ser. A No. 18.

[38] On advisory opinions of the ICJ, *see* Sean D. Murphy, "The United States and the International Court of Justice: Coping with Antinomies," in the present volume, at section C.1.

[39] For example, in 1984, Costa Rica requested that the Court provide an advisory opinion on draft legislation. I/A Court H.R., Proposed Amendments of the Naturalization Provisions of the Constitution of Costa Rica. Advisory Opinion OC-4/84 of January 19, 1984, Ser. A No. 4.

[40] *See* Sean D. Murphy, *supra*, at section D.

[41] I/A Court H.R., The Effect of Reservations on the Entry into Force of the American Convention on Human Rights (Arts. 74 and 75). Advisory Opinion OC-2/82 of September 24, 1982, Ser. A No. 2; Interpretation of the American Declaration of the Rights and Duties of Man within the Framework of Article 64 of the American Convention on Human Rights. Advisory Opinion OC-10/89 of July 14, 1989, Ser. A No. 10; The Right to Information on Consular Assistance. In the *Framework of the Guarantees of the Due Process of Law*. Advisory Opinion OC-16/99 of October 1, 1999, Ser. A No. 16.

Law.[42] The request was filed by Mexico in December 1997 and was connected to a series of cases filed by Paraguay, Germany, and Mexico against the United States over violations by the latter of the Vienna Convention on Consular Relations ("Vienna Convention").[43]

The request consisted of a number of sub-questions, the objective of which was to analyze the legal consequences that would attach if a state failed to notify a detained foreigner of his or her right under the Vienna Convention to contact a consular official. Mexico framed the questions in the context of criminal prosecution involving the possible application of the death penalty, also under scrutiny by the ICJ. The request provoked the broadest participation by member states and representatives of civil society in the history of the Court's advisory opinion practice.[44]

Considering the potential repercussions for the pending matters before the ICJ, the United States fully participated in proceedings, submitting a written memorial, presenting arguments during the public hearing, and filing final written observations. The presentations were extensive and reflected a substantial investment of time and effort. At the public hearing, the United States was represented by a team of highly experienced attorneys – three from the State Department and one from the Department of Justice.

In pertinent part, the United States argued that the Court should not exercise its advisory jurisdiction over the question because it considered that the matter amounted to a disguised contentious case against the United States, the Vienna Convention is not a human rights treaty, and the Vienna Convention is a treaty of universal application that finds its proper mechanism for resolution of disputes in the ICJ, where, indeed, it was being discussed. On the substance of the questions presented, the United States essentially posited that consular notification was not a human right or a prerequisite for the observance of due process, that failure to notify a detainee of this right in no way implicated equal protection guarantees, and that there was no legal basis to conclude

---

[42] I/A Court H.R., Advisory Opinion OC-16/99, *op cit*. For an overview of the opinion, *see generally* William J. Aceves, *International Decision: The Right to Information on Consular Assistance in the Framework of the Guarantees of the Due Process of Law*, 94 A.J.I.L. 555 (2000).

[43] On the *Breard/LaGrand/Avena* series of cases, see Sean D. Murphy, *supra*, at section C.2.III.

[44] The public hearing before the Inter-American Court in 1998 included the presentation of positions by representatives of the governments of Mexico, Costa Rica, El Salvador, Guatemala, Honduras, Paraguay, the Dominican Republic, and the United States. The Inter-American Commission participated, as it customarily does in all proceedings before the Court. There were presentations as well by representatives of Amnesty International, the *Comisión Mexicana para la Defensa y Promoción de Derechos Humanos* (CMDPDH) Human Rights Watch/Americas, the Center for Justice and International Law (CEJIL), the International Human Rights Law Institute of De Paul University College of Law, Death Penalty Focus of California, Minnesota Advocates for Human Rights, and several U.S. attorneys involved in aspects of death penalty litigation.

that failure to notify would invalidate criminal proceedings against a foreign defendant.

In its advisory opinion of October 1, 1999, the Court affirmed in strong terms that the right to information on consular assistance is an individual right giving rise to corresponding obligations on the part of the receiving state, that it falls within the corpus of human rights protections, that it enables due process rights to have practical effect in concrete cases, and that the failure to notify is prejudicial to the right to due process. The Court concluded that application of the death penalty is subject to the strictest scrutiny, and its imposition subsequent to a violation of due process would constitute a violation of the right to life.[45]

The Inter-American Court's opinion was the first at the international level to affirm that a state's failure to provide consular notification implicates fundamental rights of the detained defendant, particularly in death penalty cases, thereby giving rise to responsibility to subject any sentence imposed to judicial review. It was the first in a series of findings at the international level. The Inter-American Court dealt with the advisory opinion following aborted proceedings before the ICJ in the *Breard Case*[46] and while proceedings on the *LaGrand Case* were pending.[47] The Inter-American Court's opinion was cited in the *Avena* proceedings before the ICJ[48] and has been cited in proceedings within the United States.

This line of developments provoked changes in the conduct of the U.S. government. On one hand, it prompted the United States to begin taking consular notification more seriously than it had in the past. For example, in January 1998, following the presentation of its written observations on the request, and just prior to the public hearing before the Inter-American Court, the State Department published a handbook on consular notification designed to inform law enforcement officials of their responsibilities in the case of detained foreign nationals.[49] Although the United States continued to maintain that failure

---

[45] I/A Court H.R., Advisory Opinion 16, *op cit.*
[46] *Vienna Convention on Consular Relations (Para. v. U.S.)*, Provisional Measures, 1998 ICJ 11 (Order of April 9), reprinted in 37 ILM 810, 819 (1998).
[47] *Vienna Convention on Consular Relations (F.R.G. v. U.S.)*, Provisional Measures, 1999 ICJ 9 (Order of March 3), reprinted in 38 ILM 308, 310 (1999).
[48] See ICJ, Verbatim Record, Year 2003, CR 2003/25, Public sitting Dec. 15, 2003, case concerning *Avena and Other Mexican Nationals (Mexico v. United States of America)*.
[49] The handbook is titled *Consular Notification and Access: Instruction for Federal, State and Local Law Enforcement and Other Officials Regarding Foreign Nationals in the United States and the Rights of Consular Officials to Assist Them* and is available online. During the public hearing before the Inter-American Court on Advisory Opinion 16, the United States presented a copy of the handbook as a means of illustrating that, notwithstanding its legal arguments, the government was taking measures to respond to prior omissions of law enforcement agents.

to notify did not give rise to any state responsibility, it acknowledged that some of its officials had not been aware of the notification requirements and changed its conduct in terms of making a better effort to comply with the terms of the treaty.

In February 2005, following the *Avena* decision, the White House issued a memorandum to the attorney general indicating that, pursuant to U.S. status as a party to the Vienna Convention, and the Optional Protocol giving the ICJ jurisdiction to resolve disputes arising thereunder, the United States would discharge its obligations under the *Avena* decision by "having State courts give effect to the decision in accordance with general principles of comity in cases filed by the 51 Mexican nationals addressed in that decision."[50]

On the other hand, just weeks later, President Bush decided to withdraw acceptance of jurisdiction of the ICJ with respect to that protocol. It should be noted that during the hostage crisis in Teheran in 1979, the United States relied on this same protocol and jurisdictional clause to initiate a case against Iran before the ICJ. U.S. courts have yet to affirm that the Vienna Convention generates rights that are susceptible to enforcement by the judiciary.

U.S. participation in these advisory proceedings reflected a strong sense of self-interest. The United States approached the proceedings not to address abstract legal questions but rather to defend its position in ongoing litigation at home and before the ICJ.[51] With respect to the other two instances in which it participated in advisory proceedings, the submissions also reflected an interest in defending a U.S. position from the perceived risk of an adverse interpretation.

Previously, the United States had filed both written and oral observations in the proceedings on the advisory opinion on the *Interpretation of the American Declaration of the Rights and Duties of Man within the Framework of Article 64*

---

[50] See Sean D. Murphy, *supra*, at section D.

[51] At the same time, it may be noted that the United States did not participate in the proceedings on Advisory Opinion 18, "Juridical Condition and Rights of the Undocumented Migrants," Advisory Opinion OC-18 of September 17, 2003, Ser. A No. 18, which was presented by the government of Mexico in May 2002, just two months after the U.S. Supreme Court issued its opinion in *Hoffman Plastic Compounds v. NLRB* (535 U.S. 137 (2002)). In *Hoffman Plastics*, the Supreme Court had decided that an award of back pay by the NLRB to an unfairly fired undocumented worker was precluded by federal immigration policy. In its request to the Inter-American Court, Mexico asked that the Court examine a series of questions concerning the labor rights of migrant workers and the principles of equality, nondiscrimination and equal protection of and before the law, and the extent to which international obligations could be subordinated to the pursuit of domestic policy objectives. The *Hoffman Plastics* case was cited by a number of the *amici curiae* who intervened in the proceedings. Although the request and response did not directly raise the *Hoffman Plastics* case, it was seen by many as closely related.

of the American Convention on Human Rights.[52] This opinion was issued in response to a request filed by the government of Colombia for an interpretation as to whether Article 64 of the American Convention authorizes the Inter-American Court to render advisory opinions concerning the interpretation of the American Declaration. It will be recalled that Article 64 authorizes the Court to issue advisory opinions relative to the American Convention "or other treaties" concerning the protection of human rights in the region.

In response to the Court's invitation to submit observations, the U.S. government presented a memorial and participated in the public hearing held at the Court's headquarters.[53] The U.S. position, as summarized by the Court in its opinion, was that the latter should not issue an opinion because the Declaration "is not and never has been a treaty" so that the question did not fall within the terms of Article 64.[54] The United States went on to indicate that, if the Court did address the normative status of the Declaration, its view was that the text was drafted as a set of aspirational principles and not as a legal instrument aiming to create binding obligations. The U.S. delegation indicated that the Declaration lacked the "precision necessary to resolve complex legal questions."[55] It considered that, in terms of normative value, the Declaration served as a statement of "basic moral principles and broad political commitments and as a basis to review the general human rights performance of member states, [but] not as a binding set of obligations."[56] Finally, it commented that those who would convert it into a binding instrument had good intentions but that "good intentions do not make law" and that legal obligations could not be imposed through a process of "reinterpretation" or "inference."[57]

The United States had correctly anticipated that the Inter-American Court was likely to use the request presented to issue a finding as to the legal nature of the American Declaration, a question of particular interest for member states of the OAS that had not yet ratified the American Convention, like the United States. In deciding that the request presented was admissible, the Court determined that the issuance of an opinion primarily required an

---

[52] I/A Court H.R., *Interpretation of the American Declaration of the Rights and Duties of Man within the Framework of Article 64 of the American Convention on Human Rights.* Advisory Opinion OC-10/89 of July 14, 1989, Ser. A No. 10.
[53] The U.S. government was represented at that hearing by its ambassador to Costa Rica, an attorney-adviser in the Office of the Legal Adviser of the Department of State, and a senior political adviser from the Mission to the OAS.
[54] I/A Court H.R., OC-10/89, *op cit*, para. 17.
[55] *Id.*, para. 12.
[56] *Id.*
[57] *Id.*

interpretation of the scope of Article 64 of the American Convention and thus fell within the scope of its advisory jurisdiction.[58]

In dealing with the substance of the request, the Court determined that, in fact, the American Declaration is not a treaty in accordance with the definition under international law, because it was not drafted on that basis.[59] At the same time, the Court took into account that the Declaration was drafted as an initial system of protection; that the American Convention itself expressly provides that its terms may not be interpreted to exclude or limit the effects of the American Declaration; that human rights provisions must be interpreted in light of the evolution of that body of law within international law; and that the Charter of the OAS sets forth general human rights obligations that, through agreement and practice, are understood to include those set forth in the American Declaration.[60] Accordingly, the Court determined that the American Declaration does constitute a source of legal obligation for states that have ratified the OAS Charter.[61]

Previously, in 1982, the United States had presented a written memorial during the proceedings on the advisory opinion concerning the *Effect of Reservations on the Entry into Force of the American Convention on Human Rights* (arts. 74 and 75).[62] The Inter-American Commission requested the Court to issue an advisory opinion as to whether the Convention would enter into force for a state presenting a reservation on the date of ratification of the treaty or upon the expiration of the term of twelve months for states to raise objections set forth under the Vienna Convention on the Law of Treaties.[63] The basic position outlined by the United States in its memorial was that reservations constitute modifications in the treaty regime and that the principle of reciprocity requires that the other parties have the chance to accept or reject those changes before the ratifying state acquires rights under the treaty.[64]

In its opinion, the Court gave particular weight to the special character of human rights treaties as multilateral instruments "enabling States to make binding unilateral commitments not to violate the human rights of individuals

---

[58] *Id.* para. 24.
[59] *Id.* paras. 32–33.
[60] *Id.* paras. 34–42.
[61] *Id.* paras. 43 and 45.
[62] I/A Court H.R., *The Effect of Reservations on the Entry into Force of the American Convention on Human Rights* (arts. 74 and 75). Advisory Opinion OC-2/82 of September 24, 1982, Ser. A No. 2.
[63] Vienna Convention on the Law of Treaties, art. 20(5), 1155 U.N.T.S. 331, 8 ILM 679, entered into force Jan. 27, 1980.
[64] I/A Court H.R., Advisory Opinion OC-2/82, Series B: Pleadings, Oral Arguments and Documents, No. 2, pp. 24–36.

within their jurisdiction."[65] The Court determined that a treaty that attributes such importance to the "protection of the individual that it makes the right of individual petition mandatory as of the moment of ratification" cannot be deemed to have intended to provide for a delay in entry into force of up to a year, and that the American Convention entered into force, with or without reservations, at the time of the deposit of ratification.[66]

The purpose of the foregoing review is not to suggest that advisory opinions are similar to decisions in contentious cases; they are not. Rather, the purpose is to demonstrate a level of engagement, with the idea that the will and capacity to engage with the organs of the system suggest the possibility for further developments.

Although the United States is not subject to the Court's jurisdiction, it does pay attention to the Court's decisions in individual cases concerning other countries, and references to those decisions show up periodically in the formulation of U.S. foreign policy. To mention one clear example, judgments of the Inter-American Court have been cited in the State Department's Country Reports on Human Rights for many years as indicators of the human rights situation in various countries of the region.[67] To take an example, looking at the report for 2004,[68] the section on Peru includes references to the *Berenson Mejía Case*[69] decided by the Inter-American Court in December of that year, as well as the cases of *Maria Teresa de la Cruz Flores*[70] and *García Asto and Ramírez Rojas*[71] then pending before the Inter-American Court. The section on Suriname refers to the *Case of Moiwana Village*,[72] then pending a decision by the Court. The section on Venezuela refers to cases of disappearance then pending before the Court,[73] and the section on Paraguay refers to judgments

---

[65] I/A Court H.R., Advisory Opinion OC-2/82, Ser. A No. 2, para. 33.

[66] *Id.*, paras. 33–34.

[67] *See generally* "Human Rights as a Component of Foreign Policy," comments of Robert P. Jackson, U.S. Dept. of State, in *Human Rights in the International System, Enforcing Global Governance*, a conference report (Woodrow Wilson International Center for Scholars 2004), at 27, 39 (referring to the importance of these reports and human rights concerns generally in the formulation of foreign policy).

[68] Country Reports on Human Rights Practices for 2004, report submitted to the Committee on International Relations, U.S. House of Representatives, and the Committee on Foreign Relations, U.S. Senate, by the Department of State, at http://www.state.gov/g/drl/rls/hrrpt/2004/41771.htm.

[69] I/A Court H.R., *Lori Berenson Mejía Case*. Judgment of November 25, 2004, Ser. C No. 119.

[70] I/A Court H.R., *De la Cruz Flores Case*. Judgment of November 18, 2004, Ser. C No. 115.

[71] I/A Court H.R., *García Asto and Ramírez Rojas Case*. Judgment of November 25, 2005, Ser. C No. 137.

[72] I/A Court H.R., *Case of Moiwana Village*. Judgment of June 15, 2005, Ser. C No. 124.

[73] I/A Court H.R., *Blanco Romero et al. Case*. Judgment of November 29, 2005, Ser. C No. 138.

issued in the cases of *Panchito López*[74] and *Canese*.[75] In a related sense, the section on Guatemala refers to the killing in 2004 of a witness in the *Bámaca Case*[76] previously decided by the Court.

D. CONCERNS CITED AS HOLDING BACK U.S. RATIFíCATION OF THE AMERICAN CONVENTION AND ACCEPTANCE OF THE COURT'S CONTENTIOUS JURISDICTION

There are three interrelated issues that are cited with some regularity as raising concerns with respect to possible ratification of the American Convention, a necessary precondition to possible acceptance of the contentious jurisdiction of the Court. These issues are abortion, the death penalty, and federalism.

The language of Article 4 of the American Convention refers to the right to life and the requirement that it be protected by law, "and, in general, from the moment of conception." The drafting history of the Convention expressly indicates that the words "in general" were included in this formulation to permit the continuity of the diversity of practices that existed even at that time with respect to abortion.[77] The Commission has interpreted this to signify that the Convention neither requires nor prohibits that abortion be available.

Article 4 also refers to the conditions under which a state party may apply the death penalty without breaching its obligations under the Convention. Although the Convention is not abolitionist, it is based on the premise that capital punishment may only be applied for the most serious crimes and in accordance with the principles of due process. Article 4 expressly provides that the death penalty may not be extended to any crime to which it does not already apply at the time of ratification. The application of the death penalty has been raised as a ratification issue with respect to the limitations established in Article 4, as well as with respect to the fact that, except in very limited classes of cases, the death penalty in the United States is a matter of state law and jurisdiction, not federal law. The issue brings up questions of federalism

---

[74] I/A Court H.R., "*Instituto de Reeducación del Menor*" ("*Panchito López*") *Case*. Judgment of September 2, 2004, Ser. C No. 112.

[75] I/A Court H.R., *Ricardo Canese Case*. Judgment of August 31, 2004, Ser. C No. 111.

[76] I/A Court H.R., *Bámaca Velásquez Case*. Judgment of November 25, 2000, Ser. C No. 70. See also Order of the Inter-American Court of November 20, 2003, Provisional Measures in the Bámaca Velásquez Case (recounting the background to the issuance of the protective measures, and the status of implementation to that point).

[77] *See, inter alia*, IACHR, Inter-American Yearbook on Human Rights 1968 (1973), pp. 97, 321; OAS, *Conferencia Especializada Interamericana sobre Derechos Humanos, San José, Costa Rica, 7–22 de noviembre de 1969, Actas y Documentos*, pp. 57, 121, 160.

and the tension that sometimes arises among international, national, and local standards.[78]

The implementation of international human rights law tends to raise special challenges in federal systems, such as that of the United States. Interestingly, and not by chance, because the Americas include federations such as Canada, Brazil, Argentina, Mexico, and the United States, the American Convention contains a special provision concerning federal systems. Article 28(1) provides that, in the case of federal states, the national government "shall implement all the provisions of the Convention over whose subject matter it exercises legislative and judicial jurisdiction." Article 28(2) indicates,

> With respect to provisions over whose subject matter the constituent units of the federal state have jurisdiction, the national government shall immediately take suitable measures, in accordance with its constitution and its laws, to the end that the competent authorities of the constituent units may adopt appropriate provisions for the fulfillment of this Convention.

As Thomas Buergenthal has explained, "Article 28 is an anachronism which harks back to the days of the League of Nations. Few modern international human rights instruments contain comparable clauses."[79] In fact, the International Covenant on Civil and Political Rights takes a different approach in indicating that it applies in federal systems without limitation or exception.[80] It is noteworthy that this Article was included in the American Convention pursuant to insistence by the United States delegation.[81]

In its report on the conference held to draft the American Convention in 1969, the U.S. delegation placed great emphasis on the treaty's treatment of federalism. The report noted that the Convention sets a "new standard for the protection of human rights, . . . [and] does so in a unique way in that it does not weaken the authority which constituent units of a federal state have over such matters."[82] More specifically, the report indicated,

> [f]or the United States, the most important article is Article 28 (Federal Clause) which provides that a national government is bound by the provisions of the Convention over whose subject matter it exercises jurisdiction. A national government is not obliged, however, to exercise its authority with

---

[78] On this question generally, see Richard J. Wilson, *The United States Position on the Death Penalty in the Inter-American Human Rights System*, 42 Santa Clara L. Rev. 1159 (2002).

[79] Thomas Buergenthal, *"The Inter-American System for the Protection of Human Rights,"* Anuario Jurídico Interamericano 1981 at 85–87 (OAS 1982), reprinted in Thomas Buergenthal and Dinah Shelton, *Protecting Human Rights in the Americas* 465 (4th ed. 1995).

[80] *See id.*

[81] *Id.*

[82] Report, *supra*, introduction at iii.

respect to provisions over whose subject matter the constituent units of the federal state (i.e., the individual states of the U.S.) have jurisdiction.[83]

Federal systems give rise to special challenges insofar as the language of Article 28 creates ambiguity with respect to certain questions of state responsibility, particularly in the case of systems in which treaties are not self-executing.[84] Yet the Inter-American Commission and Court have looked to basic principles of interpretation under international law and the Vienna Convention on the Law of Treaties to affirm that international obligations must be understood to apply throughout national territory and that limitations of national law cannot be invoked to evade compliance with such obligations.[85]

The U.S. position toward the American Convention presents something of a contradiction in this sense. On one hand, the U.S. delegation insisted on including a federal clause in the American Convention, notwithstanding which the Senate never advanced in the process of advice and consent. On the other hand, years later the United States ratified the Covenant on Civil and Political Rights, which expressly provides that federal states are responsible for the implementation of all obligations undertaken throughout their jurisdictions without exception or limitation.

E. THE MECHANISMS THROUGH WHICH THE UNITED STATES ENGAGES WITH THE INTER-AMERICAN COURT AND COMMISSION

The interface between the Inter-American Court and Commission and any member state is the Ministry of Foreign Affairs, or, for the United States, the State Department. This governmental agency is then responsible for coordinating interagency or interentity consultation and information gathering as part of the state's participation in the regional human rights system. In the case of the United States, the State Department, through the Office of the Legal Adviser and the U.S. Mission to the OAS, plays the predominant role in communications with the Commission or Court. The Department of Justice often plays a role in the formulation of legal positions as well.

The role of the State Department in formulating policy is reflected in examples of U.S. participation in proceedings before the system as described

---

[83] *Id.* at 13.
[84] *See generally* Buergenthal, *The Inter-American System, supra*, at 466 (identifying some of the problems that arise from the formulation of Article 28).
[85] *See generally* IACHR, Resolution 1/90, Cases 9768, 9780, and 9828, Mexico, May 17, 1990, para. 96.v; Report 102/05, Case 12.080, Friendly Settlement, Sergio Schiavini and María Teresa Schnack, Argentina, October 27, 2005, para. 26.

earlier. It may also be noted that, insofar as the U.S. government provides financial support for the operations of the Commission, Congress has a role in authorizing the expenditure of those funds, and the U.S. Mission to the OAS plays an important role in facilitating that funding.

F. THE NATURE OF CURRENT U.S. SUPPORT FOR THE REGIONAL HUMAN RIGHTS SYSTEM

Historically, the United States has been more closely involved with the Inter-American Commission than the Inter-American Court. Whereas the United States has provided substantial additional financial contributions to the Commission (beyond the normal quota allocation), it has not done so for the Court. The United States also provides important political support for the work of the Commission, but it addresses the work of the Court in a much more limited way. Nonetheless, political and financial support for the Commission have an impact on the strength of the system as a whole, including the Court, because it is the Commission that submits cases to the Court.

In a speech representative of U.S. support, the Ambassador to the OAS referred to the Commission as the "crown jewel" of the inter-American system, and indicated that the government "is proud to be its largest financial supporter." He went on to indicate that

> [t]he Commission provides a valuable fact-finding role that no Court can duplicate. While it does review cases presented before it like other tribunals, it also makes site visits to countries in the hemisphere where abuses of human rights have been reported. It makes country reports. The Commission often requests governments to take precautionary measures pending more detailed reviews of matters. Democratic governments pay attention to the concerns of the Commission and usually make good faith efforts to address them.[86]

The support for the Commission may be contrasted to very scarce references by the United States to the work of the Court. To give one example, in a fact sheet on the OAS published on the State Department's Web site, there is a section on human rights titled "Human Rights: The Inter-American Commission." The section refers to the autonomy and independence of the Commission as crucial attributes, and reviews several of its competences as well as some specific achievements. The only reference to the Court is found in the general

---

[86] "The United States and the Future of the Organization of American States," Remarks of Amb. John F. Maisto, U.S. Permanent Representative to the OAS, to the Midwest Association of Latin American Studies, Webster University, St. Louis, MO, Nov. 12, 2004, at http://www.state.gov/p/wha/rls/rm/38197.htm.

statement that the Commission and Court "give the OAS an active and, at times, forceful role in promoting and protecting human rights."[87]

At the same time, it must be taken into account that financial and political support for the Commission necessarily have a role in strengthening the system in general terms and have an impact over the longer term on the work of the Court. More specifically, the Commission participates in the litigation of all contentious cases before the Court and has been the primary proponent of requests for advisory opinions over the Court's history. Actions that strengthen the Commission's capacity with respect to the case system, or even with respect to activities such as on-site visits and thematic activities, can and usually do eventually have some impact on its work before the Court, albeit indirectly.

G. THE ROLE OF U.S. JURISTS ON AND BEFORE THE COURT

Although all member states may nominate and elect members of the Inter-American Commission, only states parties to the American Convention may nominate and elect judges to the Inter-American Court of Human Rights. Consequently, whereas the Commission has included a number of U.S. nationals as members over the years, only one U.S citizen has served on the Inter-American Court, having been nominated by another member state.[88]

Costa Rica nominated Thomas Buergenthal during the first elections for the Court, and he served from 1979 to 1991. Now a member of the ICJ, this distinguished jurist played a crucial role in establishing some of the jurisprudential bases of the regional human rights system. He was a member of the Court through the issuance of its first eleven advisory opinions, which, as mentioned earlier, dealt with such fundamental issues as the legal status of the American Declaration, limitations on journalistic expression, and the non-derogability of habeas corpus and basic judicial guarantees in states of emergency. In terms of his work on contentious cases, among others, he participated in the formulation of the decision on the first such case, the seminal *Velásquez Rodríguez* judgment.[89] That decision established principles on state responsibility and due diligence that continue to serve as benchmarks in international law.

Given that the regional human rights system includes substantive and procedural elements drawn from its constituent national legal systems, including

---

[87] Fact sheet, *op cit*.
[88] *See generally* Douglass Cassel, A *United States View of the Inter-American Court of Human Rights*, in The Modern World of Human Rights: Essays in Honour of Thomas Buergenthal 214 (Inter-American Institute of Human Rights 1996) (arguing that, as a nonparty, the United States is losing an important opportunity to nominate U.S. judges and thus include their perspective in the formulation of the Court's jurisprudence).
[89] I/A Court H.R., *Velásquez Rodríguez Case*. Judgment of July 29, 1988. Ser. C No. 4.

civil law, common law, and Dutch-Roman law, it is desirable that the composition of the supervisory bodies reflects, at some level, that diversity of legal experience. However, given that the United States, Canada, and several Caribbean member states have yet to ratify the Convention, the common law perspective has more limited influence in the formulation of regional jurisprudence. Moreover, given that there is a highly dynamic interplay in the region between national legal systems and international law and institutions, it is desirable that jurists be able to contribute to these institutions on the basis of their experience and perspective from the national level.

In this regard, it may also be noted that a substantial number of lawyers from the United States have participated in proceedings on both advisory and contentious cases before the Inter-American Court. For example, as referred to earlier, law professors and attorneys from the United States participated in the proceedings on *The Right to Information on Consular Assistance* Advisory Opinion. U.S. lawyers have also represented victims and their families in a number of contentious cases before the Court. U.S. nationals also serve on the respective legal staffs of the Inter-American Court and Commission.

H. THE ROLE OF THE INTER-AMERICAN COURT IN PROTECTING THE RIGHTS OF U.S. CITIZENS

It is noteworthy that, although the United States is not subject to the obligatory jurisdiction of the Court, the Court has been called on to issue decisions affecting the rights of U.S. citizens vis-à-vis other countries. For example, in the *Blake Case*, the Court dealt with a denial of justice by the State of Guatemala for the disappearance and murder of Nicholas Chapman Blake, a U.S. citizen who had been working as a journalist in Guatemala.[90]

More recently, the Court decided the case of U.S. citizen Lori Berenson, imprisoned on terrorism charges in Peru.[91] The Court dealt with the case of Efraín Bámaca, a Guatemalan citizen and the husband of U.S. attorney Jennifer Harbury, after he was detained, tortured, and disappeared at the hands of the Guatemalan military.[92] In addition to determining that Mr. Bamaca's rights had been violated, the Court found the State of Guatemala responsible for having denied his wife and family justice.[93]

---

[90] I/A Court H.R., *Blake Case*. Judgment of January 24, 1998. Ser. C No. 36.
[91] I/A Court H.R., *Case of Lori Berenson-Mejía v. Perú*. Judgment of November 25, 2004. Ser. C No. 119.
[92] I/A Court H.R., *Bámaca Velásquez Case*. Judgment of November 25, 2000. Ser. C No. 70.
[93] *Id.* paras. 195–96.

I. THE WORK OF THE INTER-AMERICAN COURT AND COMMISSION INFLUENCES INTERNATIONAL HUMAN RIGHTS LAW; THAT, IN TURN, HAS AN EFFECT ON U.S. LAW AND POLICY

The inter-American human rights system has grown from being an incipient effort to establish basic standards to exercising a tremendous capacity to effectuate positive change in human rights law and policy throughout the Americas. Member states have changed constitutions, laws, policies, and practices based on decisions of the Commission and the Court. In a growing number of instances, national courts are citing jurisprudence of the Inter-American Commission and Court as a necessary element informing the interpretation and application of national law. The inter-American human rights system is accorded substantial and growing legitimacy and relevance as a regional actor.

In the direct sense, the jurisprudence of U.S. courts to date indicates that neither the American Declaration nor the American Convention is considered to create individual rights that would be enforceable before national courts.[94] In essence, in the instances in which either or both instruments have been invoked, the judicial response has been that the former was not drafted as a treaty and the latter has not been ratified by the United States. U.S. courts indicate that, although the OAS Charter establishes the Inter-American Commission, its determinations are nonbinding recommendations, aimed at the executive and legislature and not the judiciary.[95]

Although developments concerning the right to consular notification in the context of the death penalty have produced the unintended consequence of U.S. withdrawal from the Optional Protocol to the Vienna Convention on Consular Relations, thereby prompting some to question the utility of the efforts made to invoke international mechanisms, it must be recalled that, concurrent with those developments, we have seen the U.S. Supreme Court follow another line of jurisprudence to reverse its earlier holdings and declare the execution of juvenile offenders unconstitutional. *Roper v. Simmons* drew on developments in international law in recognizing the overwhelming weight of international opinion against the juvenile death penalty. One of those developments, it should be noted, is the work of the Inter-American

---

[94] *See*, for example, *Garza v. Lappin*, 253 F.3d 918 (7th Cir. 2001) (No. 01-2441) (denying petition for stay of execution). Garza had filed for a stay of execution based the findings of the Inter-American Commission in Report 52/01 (Case 12.243, Juan Raul Garza, U.S., April 4, 2001) that admission during sentencing of evidence of unadjudicated prior crimes committed in Mexico was incompatible with provisions of American Declaration. The Seventh Circuit found that the regional norms did not create an enforceable right of action for Garza.

[95] For one example of this fairly consistent approach, *see Thompson v. State of Tennessee*, 134 S.W. 3d 168; 2004 Tenn. LEXIS 370, May 12, 2004.

Commission in the cases of *Domingues*[96] and *Beazley*[97] against the United States, finding the execution of juveniles incompatible with the terms of the American Declaration of the Rights and Duties of Man.[98] Whereas the Commission's reports are not expressly cited in the *Roper* decision, they were placed before the Supreme Court in briefs of *amici curiae*.[99]

In this sense, the work of the Commission and Court is increasingly part of the lexicon of human rights law and practice, including in the United States. Although it would exceed the scope of this chapter to review the work of the Commission in monitoring the human rights situation in the United States, it is important to note that the former began dealing with U.S. petitions in the 1980s. It was at that time that the Commission began analyzing the imposition of the death penalty in the United States under the norms of international law, an issue with which it remains deeply engaged. It was in the early 1980s that the Commission carried out its first visits to U.S. immigration detention centers, another issue with which it continues to work. The Commission's work with respect to the United States has expanded over the years to incorporate a broad range of human rights questions.[100]

Although U.S. courts have not attributed direct legal effect to regional norms within the national legal system, they have cited such norms in explaining the content of international human rights law.[101] The work of the Court and Commission has been admitted as evidence and served as context in diverse judicial proceedings in federal and state courts.[102] It must always be taken into account that the relationship between national and international law is dynamic and that the perspectives of those whose work influences or is

---

[96] IACHR, Report No. 62/02, Merits, Case 12.285, Michael Domingues, United States, October 22, 2002.

[97] IACHR, Report No. 101/03, Merits, Case 12.412, Napoleon Beazley, United States, December 29, 2003.

[98] IACHR, Report No. 101/03, Case 12.412, Napoleon Beazley, United States, December 29, 2003; Report 62/02, Case 12.285, Michael Domingues, United States, October 22, 2002.

[99] Brief of *Amicus Curiae* Former U.S. Diplomats, 2003 U.S. Briefs 633, July 19, 2004; Brief of *Amici Curiae* Nobel Peace Prize recipients, 2003 U.S. Briefs 633, July 19, 2004.

[100] *See generally*, Tara Melish, "From Paradox to Subsidiarity: The United States and Human Rights Treaty Bodies," in the present volume, at section B, recounting many of the cases brought before the Commission against the United States.

[101] *See, e.g., Filartiga v. Pena-Irala*, 630 F.2d 876 (1980) (citing the American Convention in support of the finding that torture is universally condemned as a matter of international law); *Forti v. Suarez-Mason*, 672 F. Supp. 1531, at 1542 (1987).

[102] *See, e.g., Doe v. Saravia*, 2004 U.S. Dist. LEXIS 27452, November 16, 2004 (granting admission into evidence of the Commission report on the case of Monsignor Romero, Report 37/00, Case 11.481, El Salvador, April 13, 2000); *Ordinola v. Hackman*, 478 F.3d 588 (4th Cir. 2007) (citing as context Inter-American Court decision on the Case of Barrios Altos, Ser. C No. 75 (2001), in decision on extradition of an alleged perpetrator to Peru under bilateral extradition treaty).

influenced by that relationship are hardly monolithic.[103] Although the U.S. legal system does not embrace international norms as such, the work of the Inter-American Court and Commission is becoming increasingly present in U.S. litigation, and perhaps more important, in the training provided in U.S. law schools.

J. CONCLUSION

Given that the United States has not ratified the American Convention and it has yet to seriously consider accepting the contentious jurisdiction of the Inter-American Court, a chapter on the U.S. relationship with the Inter-American Court may appear abstract. However, even though the United States does not accept determinations of the Inter-American Court and Commission as having binding authority, these organs contribute to the evolution of regional standards in human rights law and practice that eventually have an impact on regional law, policy, and politics, in which the United States has a very direct and tangible interest, and even on the U.S. legal system itself. As Douglass Cassel has reflected, "international human rights law must be understood and evaluated as part of a broader set of interrelated rights-protecting processes."[104] The fact that there are inconsistencies and weaknesses in recognition and implementation does not negate that developments in international law can reshape the discourse of national law and policy, and "facilitate international and transnational processes that reinforce, stimulate, and monitor these domestic dialogues."[105]

The work of the Inter-American Court has steadily gained legitimacy, as has that of the system as a whole. That legitimacy has, over time, encouraged additional member states to accept the contentious jurisdiction of the Court.[106] As the system continues to generate increased legitimacy, it also generates improved levels of compliance with decisions of the Court and Commission. This in turn generates greater engagement with other processes within the system, such as the friendly settlement procedure, precautionary measures,

---

[103] *Compare*, e.g., the approach to the American Declaration in *Celestine v. Butler*, 823 F.2d 74, at 79 (5th Cir. 1987) (No. 87–4536) (rejecting argument based on American Declaration and OAS Charter not on jurisdictional grounds but for lack of substantive content) *with Chen v. Ashcroft*, 85 Fed. Appx. 700, at 705, 2004 U.S. App. LEXIS 421 (10th Cir. 2004) (No. 03–2078) (indicating that neither American Declaration nor other international instruments cited create any binding obligation for the United States).
[104] Douglass Cassel, *International Human Rights Law in Practice: Does International Human Rights Law Make a Difference?*, 2 Chi. J. Int'l L. 121 (2001) 122.
[105] *Id.*
[106] Of the thirty-five member states, as of 2008, twenty-one are subject to the contentious jurisdiction of the Inter-American Court.

country reports, or thematic initiatives. The experience of the inter-American system indicates that legitimacy must be constructed; it is not a given. The growing legitimacy and relevance of the system in the region should continue to open new possibilities for engagement with the member states, including the United States.

To the extent that the United States articulates a strong interest in effecting positive change in support of democracy and human rights in the region, ratification of the American Convention and acceptance of the Court's contentious jurisdiction would strengthen its authority and capacity. The inter-American system places a unique emphasis on the relationship between democracy and human rights. The OAS Charter refers to representative democracy as a necessary condition for peace and security, and the Commission and Court have defined that, in a democratic society, human rights, the guarantees that apply to such rights, and the rule of law form a triad in which each element defines itself, and complements and depends on the others for meaning and content. The inter-American system offers strong and specialized tools to uphold values that are central to U.S. domestic and foreign policy. It becomes complicated for the United States to support or insist on member state compliance with obligations under a treaty to which it is not party and gives rise to perceived contradictions in U.S. policy.

8

From Paradox to Subsidiarity: The United States and Human Rights Treaty Bodies*

TARA J. MELISH**

In the battle for democracy and human rights, words matter, but what we do matters much more.[1]

It is frequently said that the United States has a paradoxical human rights policy.[2] On the one hand, the United States embraces human rights principles as a founding national ideology[3] and has supported the enhancement of human rights and democracy as a core premise of its foreign policy since the end of World War II, when it played a leading role in birthing the international human rights regime.[4] Indeed, the promotion of human rights and democracy abroad is a central motivating tenet of U.S. foreign policy,

---

* The original version of this chapter was published in the *Yale Journal of International Law* (YJIL), volume 34, pp. 389–462 (2009). It has been adapted and substantively modified for inclusion in this book by permission of YJIL.
** Visiting Professor, University of Notre Dame School of Law, Spring 2009. Associate Professor of Law, University at Buffalo School of Law, SUNY. JD, Yale Law School; BA, Brown University. I extend my gratitude to Robert K. Harris, Steven R. Hill, and Mark P. Lagon of the U.S. Department of State for their helpful conversations on issues discussed in this chapter, as well as to Sean Murphy, Susan Benesch, Rick Wilson, and Cesare Romano for their valuable comments on an earlier draft. All views expressed herein are those of the author alone.
[1] Warren Christopher, "Democracy and Human Rights: Where America Stands," transcript of U.S. Secretary of State's address to 1993 World Conference on Human Rights, June 21, 1993, in U.S. State Dep't Dispatch No. 25, June 23, 1993 [hereinafter Christopher].
[2] *See, e.g.*, Andrew Moravcsik, "The Paradox of U.S. Human Rights Policy," in Michael Ignatieff, ed., *American Exceptionalism and Human Rights* (Princeton: Princeton University Press, 2005), 147–97.
[3] *See, e.g.*, U.S. Dep't of State, *Fundamentals of U.S. Foreign Policy* (1988), 24 ("The cause of human rights forms the core of American foreign policy [as] it is central to America's conception of itself."); Christopher, *op. cit.* ("America's identity as a nation derives from our dedication to the proposition 'that all Men are created equal and endowed by their Creator with certain unalienable rights.'").
[4] *See* Mary Ann Glendon, *A World Made New: Eleanor Roosevelt and the Universal Declaration of Human Rights* (New York: Random House, 2001).

manifested in the nation's extensive foreign assistance commitments, political and financial support of international human rights bodies, linking of bilateral aid to human rights improvements, and annual reporting on the human rights situation of 194 nations of the world.[5] National public opinion polls, moreover, suggest that roughly eighty percent of Americans believe that human rights inhere in every human being, whether the government formally recognizes those rights or not.[6] Equal numbers express not only their support for U.S. ratification of human rights treaties but also their belief that international supervision over those treaty commitments, by a court or other independent body, is necessary.[7]

Yet despite strong external and internal human rights commitments, the United States has appeared to flinch, even recoil, when it comes to direct domestic application of human rights treaty norms, especially as those norms are interpreted by international supervisory bodies. Whether through the executive, the legislature, or the courts, the nation has insisted that human rights treaties are non-self-executing domestically and has remained ambivalent toward international adjudicatory fora that may judge it on its own human rights treaty commitments. The United States has renounced international bodies that have issued judgments against it on human rights matters, declined to affirmatively accept the contentious jurisdiction of human rights bodies, and even fought the creation of new international bodies with adjudicatory

---

[5] The U.S. Department of State, under congressional mandate, has been reporting annually on human rights conditions in countries around the world since 1976. Since 2002, these *Country Reports on Human Rights Practices* have been supplemented by an annual report to Congress on the specific actions taken by the U.S. government to encourage respect for human rights around the world, in compliance with section 665 of the Foreign Relations Authorization Act, Fiscal Year 2003, Pub. L. No. 107-228, 116 Stat. 1350 (codified as amended at 22 U.S.C. §§ 2151n, 2304 (2000 & Supp. VII 2007)). *See*, e.g., U.S. State Department, *Supporting Human Rights and Democracy: The U.S. Record 2006* (2006). Of course, U.S. foreign policy has also served over the years to consolidate the power of many dictators and repressive governments responsible for systematic human rights abuse.

[6] *See* The Opportunity Agenda, "Human Rights in the United States: Findings from a National Survey," Public Opinion Research on Human Rights in the U.S. (by Belden Russonello & Stewart), Aug. 2007, at 12 (finding that 80 percent of Americans support this proposition, whereas only 18 percent endorse view that "rights are given to an individual by his or her government").

[7] *See*, e.g., Steven Kull et al., "Americans on International Courts and Their Jurisdiction over the US," The WorldPublicOpinion.org/Knowledge Networks Poll, May 11, 2006, at 3. The poll finds that 79 percent of Americans believe that there should be an independent international body, such as a court, to judge whether the United States and other states parties are abiding by the international human rights treaties they ratify. Indeed, of all subject matters commonly governed by treaty (i.e., border disputes, fishing rights, environment, human rights, trade, labor, investments, and protection of aliens), human rights treaties received the highest percentage of support for the proposition that independent international tribunal supervision over compliance was necessary. *Id.*

competence over its citizens. It is this apparent paradox of U.S. human rights policy – outwardly prodigious, inwardly niggardly – and its underlying set of "antinomies"[8] that a growing literature has sought to document and explain, often through the lens of U.S. exceptionalism.[9]

This chapter offers a new narrative based in interest-group management. It does so by taking a closer look at the U.S. human rights paradox from the perspective of U.S. engagement with the international human rights treaty bodies that exercise formal supervisory jurisdiction over it.[10] This engagement, once negligible, has expanded quite significantly over the last decade, a byproduct of the United States' careful navigation through a diverse set of political pressures. It is thus useful to view the distinct ways and degrees in which this engagement manifests itself, especially with respect to the varied competences that treaty bodies exercise along the supervisory spectrum. Doing so allows us to take a closer look at the actual reasons why the United States may shrink from full engagement with certain international processes, while accepting others fully. Such a frame can, in turn, reveal important insights for predicting what the United States can and will do in the future, why, and under what preconditions or constraining guidelines. Importantly, it also allows us to begin to imagine a set of institutional arrangements and coordinating mechanisms that can help to address the underlying concerns, particularly as they relate to recurrently raised federalism, separation of powers, and countermajoritarian objections.

My central claim is that a closer, more searching look at the nature and scope of U.S. treaty-body engagement policy – especially at the plurality of disaggregated policy interests that determine its evolving and often asymmetric contours – reveals that the U.S. human rights paradox may not in fact be so paradoxical. To the contrary, given U.S. engagement policy's modern doctrinal anchoring in one of international human rights law's most foundational principles – the principle of subsidiarity[11] – it may be precisely the foundation

---

[8] Sean D. Murphy, "The United States and the International Court of Justice: Coping with Antinomies," Chapter 4 in this volume (defining antinomies as "equally rational but conflicting principles" and discussing three that underlie U.S. foreign policy: realism vs. institutionalism, exceptionalism vs. sovereign equality, and autonomous national law vs. internationally embedded domestic law).

[9] See, in particular, contributions in Michael Ignatieff, ed. *American Exceptionalism and Human Rights*, op. cit.; Moravcsik, "The Paradox of U.S. Human Rights Policy," op. cit. (presented as conference paper in proceedings giving rise to this book project).

[10] Human rights treaty bodies refer to the committees or commissions of independent experts set up under key human rights treaties to supervise, through quasi-adjudicatory and promotional powers, state-party compliance with treaty undertakings.

[11] The principle of subsidiarity, discussed further in this chapter, governs the appropriate relationship among international, national, and subnational levels of supervision in the shared project of ensuring human rights protection for all individuals. Foundational to international human

necessary to build a strong and sustainable domestic human rights policy over the long term. Achieving this, however, will require a fundamental shift in thinking and strategy among many domestic advocates. That shift is one that draws from the insights of an interest mediation perspective to transform the current U.S. engagement emphasis on the negative dimension of the subsidiarity principle from a shield into a sword. That is, the tools of the subsidiarity principle must not be permitted to be used only defensively by U.S. actors to shield domestic legislative and judicial processes from international intervention. They must also be used offensively to routinize, within the bounds of U.S. federalism, an internal process of domestic self-reflection and localized democratic deliberation on how we, in our own local communities, wish to protect internationally recognized human rights to best ensure the dignity of the human person.

The challenge for domestic human rights advocates, I argue, is not to reject the negative dimensions of subsidiarity (as is the tendency today), dimensions that are core to U.S. interest-management techniques, but rather to firmly embrace them, while likewise finding new ways of working flexibly and effectively within the subsidiarity paradigm to institutionalize a framework for respecting the positive half. In this way, advocates may ensure that U.S. engagement policy is directed not only outward, toward an international audience, but, just as critically, inward to our own domestic constituencies at home. It is this vital shift in U.S. human rights policy – from partial subsidiarity (paradox) to genuine subsidiarity – that is the focus of this chapter.

Yet a doctrinally anchored, interest-mediation perspective on U.S. human rights policy does not only help to chart a path toward the future. It also helps to explain the present and past. It offers, in this regard, a fuller, more empirically plausible and realistic account of U.S. human rights policy than can parallel accounts sounding in "U.S. exceptionalism," whether of a "rights cultural" or "structural" variety.[12] Indeed, a closer look at the actual ways in which the United States engages with human rights treaty bodies – and, specifically, at the varying mediating techniques[13] it employs to ensure its engagement comports

---

rights law, it has been broadly defined as "the principle that each social and political group should help smaller or more local ones accomplish their respective ends without, however, arrogating those tasks to itself." Paolo G. Carozza, *Subsidiarity as a Structural Principle of International Human Rights Law*, 97 Am. J. Int'l L. 38, 38 n.1 (2003) (providing a "simplified working definition").

[12] See Moravcsik, *op. cit.* (discussing "rights cultural" and "structural" narratives of U.S. exceptionalism, and defending the latter).

[13] The term "mediating techniques" is used here in relation to the tactics, methods, and postures employed by the U.S. government in modulating its human rights engagement policy to take into account the countervailing pressures faced from a diversity of interest groups, at both domestic and foreign policy levels, each urging greater or lesser levels of U.S. engagement.

with evolving U.S. domestic and foreign policy interests – suggests that academic prognostications that the United States will resist further engagement with human rights bodies may be short-sighted. Whereas prominent observers of the "U.S. human rights paradox" have suggested that we should not be optimistic about further U.S. engagement in the international human rights regime, given certain structural conditions that set the United States apart from other nations,[14] I argue that this view may be overly static in its portrayal of the predicted behavior of relevant social actors, even under unreservedly correct, "thicker" explanations of U.S. ambivalence to human rights law.[15] Specifically, while correctly focusing on domestic special interest politics and the unique ability of veto players in the United States' highly decentralized and fragmented political structure to block treaty ratification notwithstanding supportive domestic majorities (especially under Republican Senate majorities), such a view fails to take account of the diverse and dynamic ways that civil society advocates – of both liberal and conservative persuasions – take advantage of changing positions and new strategic openings for advancing their substantive policy preferences.

In particular, by focusing too narrowly on conservative politics, veto players, and formal treaty ratification procedures, the view fails to take account

---

This usage differs slightly from the term's primary use in the scholarly literature to describe the justiciability doctrines and other judicial restraint techniques used by courts and tribunals, at both national and international levels, to accommodate separation of powers, federalism, subsidiarity, and sovereignty concerns. *See*, e.g., Alexander Bickel, *The Least Dangerous Branch* 112 (Bobbs-Merrill 1962) (discussing domestic judiciary's "passive virtues" and quoting Justice Brandeis's assertion that the "mediating techniques of not doing" were the most important thing the U.S. Supreme Court did); Murphy, *op. cit.* (discussing and citing other scholarly discussions of "mediating techniques" used by international tribunals to promote engagement by States).

[14] *See* Moravcsik, "The Paradox of U.S. Human Rights Policy," *op. cit.* Professor Moravcsik identifies four such structural conditions (external power, democratic stability, conservative minorities, and fragmented political institutions), concluding that "[t]he United States is exceptional primarily because it occupies an extreme position in [these] four structural dimensions of human rights politics, from which we would expect extreme behavior on the part of any government." *Id.* at 150–51.

[15] *See id.* Professor Moravcsik argues convincingly that a "thicker," "pluralist" explanation that focuses on the instrumentality of partisan politics and conservative policy agendas in explaining U.S. human rights behavior is more plausible empirically than "thinner" accounts that attribute U.S. ambivalence to a unique American "rights culture," one predisposing Americans to oppose human rights treaty commitments. He nonetheless reads his analysis as suggesting a "sobering conclusion": "U.S. ambivalence toward international human rights commitments is not a short-term contingent aspect of specific American policies, but it is woven into the deep structural reality of American political life." *Id.* at 197. Consequently, "The institutional odds against any fundamental change in Madison's republic are high. To reverse current trends would require an epochal constitutional rupture – an Ackermanian 'constitutional moment'. . . . Short of that, this particular brand of American ambivalence toward the domestic application of international human rights norms is unlikely to change anytime soon." *Id.*

of the equally relevant strategies and campaigns of liberal politics, including their regular employ of the many "deblocking" opportunities presented by the fragmented U.S. political structure. Likewise, it insufficiently addresses the ways the U.S. government acts in a mediating role between these countervailing persuasions, including those operating at the foreign policy level: bowing more or less to one or the other, yet always within the bounds of a principled, rule-bound policy position. Under this light, any prediction that the United States will not further engage with human rights treaty bodies may be missing critical domestic movements and changing visions of political agency that suggest the contrary.

This is particularly true as advocates and interest groups adapt their strategies to the hard reality of U.S. ratification of an increasing number of human rights treaties and persistent engagement with international supervisory procedures. The fundamental domestic debate has in many ways thus changed. It is no longer *whether* the United States will ratify, but rather *how* domestic advocates will use U.S. ratification and international engagement to achieve their distinct domestic policy agendas at home and what measures or methodologies the U.S. government will adopt to mediate these countervailing pressures.

To address these important issues, this chapter proceeds in six parts. Following this introduction and a brief explanation of the subsidiarity principle, Part A provides an overview of the legal framework that structures current U.S. human rights treaty body engagements at the national and international levels. Part B supplements this review by examining the specific ways the United States[16] in fact engages with the three principal competences exercised by the UN, OAS, and ILO supervisory treaty body systems: periodic reporting, quasi-adjudication, and promotional activities. It concludes that U.S. engagement with these competences is in fact far more robust than popular notions of the "U.S. human rights paradox" would suggest.

Part C seeks then to explain this discrepancy. It suggests that U.S. engagement policy is best viewed not as a static or structural given, but rather as a complex mediation among a variety of pressures exerted on policy makers by powerful actors at both the foreign and domestic policy levels. Disaggregating those pressures, the analysis emphasizes the role of four distinct groups that contribute to the pragmatic calculus undertaken in shaping U.S. human rights policy. These include "realists" and "institutionalists" at the foreign policy level and groups I call "insulationists" and "incorporationists" at the

---

[16] Throughout this chapter, "United States" is used to refer to the state agents who express the policy position of the nation before international treaty bodies. Although frequently represented by the U.S. State Department, the position asserted represents that of the "State" and is informed by many complex processes.

domestic policy level, each seeking alternately greater or lesser substantive and procedural engagement with human rights bodies, in accordance with their group-specific policy interests. While scholars in the various camps of international relations theory tend to explain U.S. engagement policy with primary emphasis on *one* of these four groups,[17] it is the complex interaction and competing interests of *each* of them, I argue, that determine the precise coordinates at which U.S. policy can most accurately be mapped.

To explain how this complex management process is effectuated, Part D identifies the principal mediating techniques employed by the United States in its current treaty body engagements, each designed to accommodate distinct sets of competing interest-group pressures. While each of these mediating techniques is solidly anchored in foundational international law doctrines of sovereignty and subsidiarity, each nonetheless draws on only the negative dimensions of those doctrines. Corresponding to doctrines of non-interference and deference to domestic political processes, this selective posture allows the United States to effectively manage competing interest group pressures, pursuing an engagement policy that at once permits active U.S. engagement with international procedures, appeases the most vocal critiques of such engagement (at both domestic and foreign-policy levels), and allows the United States to remain in formal compliance with the external procedural obligations it has assumed under international law through treaty ratification.

What it does not do, as currently pursued, is facilitate *internal* domestic reflection on the nation's treaty-based human rights commitments. Indeed, responsive to the dominant pressures exerted at present on U.S. policy makers from both within and without government, these mediating techniques draw on only half of subsidiarity's blueprint. This partial and selective embrace of the tools envisioned by international human rights law's subsidiarity principle has conduced to a signal, yet predictable, outcome: U.S. engagement policy has to date been pursued principally, if not wholly, as a foreign policy objective, not as a domestic policy one. That is, contrary to the primary purposes of international human rights law, the United States engages with international human rights bodies not with an eye toward better protecting human rights within its own jurisdictional boundaries but rather with a view toward influencing the policies of *other* sovereign states and the international community generally. Part E

---

[17] These camps include those dedicated to realism, institutionalism, liberalism, and constructivism. For a general descriptive overview, see Oona A. Hathaway, *Do Human Rights Treaties Make a Difference?*, 111 Yale L.J. 1935 (2002). Though neither liberalism nor constructivism refers in name to "insulationists" or "incorporationists," the emphasis of liberalism on domestic political structures and processes focuses it on the veto-player politics of the former, just as constructivism's privileging of the role of non-state actors and their persuasive discourses focuses it on the tactics and strategies of the latter.

discusses this conflict, the structural opportunities for addressing it, and the importance of giving the principle of subsidiarity its full and intended meaning in international human rights law. The piece continues by looking at where U.S. policy can be expected to lead in coming years, as U.S. policy makers continue to chart a middle course through difficult and shifting pressures. This middle course is one that does not reject but rather solidly embraces supervisory human rights treaty body processes, albeit under a vision of their jurisdiction as strictly subsidiary to domestic decision-making processes. The challenge for domestic advocates, I argue, is to ensure that this subsidiarity principle is embraced in its full dimensionality, not only in its negative facets. An outline of how this might be institutionally pursued and structured in the United States is discussed in Part E.

* * *

Before turning to these important issues, a brief reflection on the subsidiarity principle in international human rights law is warranted.[18] First off, this principle should not be confused with the narrower, more rigid rule of the same name that has developed since 1993 in the European Union to govern the constitutional relationship between the Union and its member states.[19] Often equated with U.S. federalism,[20] which draws from but does not replicate subsidiarity's

---

[18] For the fullest account of this principle, see Carozza, *op. cit.*

[19] This principle is reflected in Articles 1, 2, and 5 of the (Maastricht) Treaty on European Union, as updated by the Protocol of Amsterdam. Although the broad essence of subsidiarity is reflected in Article 1, which requires that "decisions [be] taken ... as close as possible to the citizen," it is the practical operationalization of the principle in article 5 that has been the focus of the EU subsidiarity "rule": "The Community shall act within the limits of the powers conferred upon it by this Treaty and of the objectives assigned to it therein. In areas which do not fall within its exclusive competence, the Community shall take action, in accordance with the principle of subsidiarity, only if and insofar as the objectives of the proposed action cannot be sufficiently achieved by the Member States and can therefore, by reason of the scale or effects of the proposed action, be better achieved by the Community. Any action by the Community shall not go beyond what is necessary to achieve the objectives of the Treaty."

[20] The similarities between EU subsidiarity and U.S. constitutional federalism have spawned a vast comparative literature. *See*, e.g., George A. Bermann, *Taking Subsidiarity Seriously: Federalism in the European Community and the United States*, 94 Colum. L. Rev. 332 (1994); W. Gary Vause, *The Subsidiarity Principle in European Union Law – American Federalism Compared*, 27 Case W. Res. J. Int'l L. 61 (1995); Gerald L. Neuman, *Subsidiarity, Harmonization, and Their Values: Convergence and Divergence in Europe and the United States*, 2 Colum J. Eur. L. 573 (1996); Cary Coglianese and Kalypso Nicolaidis, "Securing Subsidiarity: The Institutional Design of Federalism in the United States and Europe," in *The Federal Vision: Legitimacy and Levels of Governance in the United States and the European Union* (K. Nicolaidis & R. Howse, ed., New York: Oxford University Press, 2001).

Other literature has explored the nuances and complexities of the concept across subject matters and jurisdictions. *See*, e.g., Neil MacCormick, *Questioning Sovereignty: Law, State, and Nation in the European Commonwealth* 151–55 (New York: Oxford University Press, 2000)

premises, the rule is directed to dividing legislative competences[21] between vertically overlapping sovereignties, with the higher level preempting the lower in its carefully prescribed fields of authority.[22] The principle of subsidiarity that structurally underlies international human rights law is both broader and less rigid than its modern European namesake.[23] This is true even as it is fully consistent with, and complementary to, both the narrower EU subsidiarity rule and American constitutional federalism.

The primary differentiating feature between the two lies in their respective objects of protection. Unlike its narrower rule-based instantiation, the safeguarded object of which is the sovereignty interests of formal political units within a given constitutional structure, the principle of subsidiarity begins and ends with the human person – specifically, with the inherent dignity of the socially situated human being. Society and government are thus viewed as integrated into a protective layering of facilitative support, or *subsidium*, designed to ensure that such dignity finds genuine expression in meaningful, appropriate, context-specific ways. Such support does not aim to preempt "lower" competences but rather to assist and strengthen them such that they are capable of meeting needs directly where and when they arise, at the level closest

---

(distinguishing "market subsidiarity," "communal subsidiarity," "rational legislative subsidiarity," and "comprehensive subsidiarity"); Giandomenico Majone, "Regulatory Legitimacy in the United States and the European Union," in *The Federal Vision, op. cit.* at 252 (noting increased demand in the EU for local control in the nineties led to shift in subsidiarity's interpretation from "total" harmonization to "optional" and "minimum" harmonization, just as similar demands in the United States in the seventies and eighties led to a shift from "preemptive" to "cooperative federalism").

[21] For an argument that subsidiarity should likewise be incorporated into the judicial doctrine of the European Court of Justice, which has so far resisted Maastricht's governing principle, see Edward T. Swaine, *Subsidiarity and Self-Interest: Federalism at the European Court of Justice*, 41 Harv. Int'l L. J. 1 (2000); Florian Sander, *Subsidiarity Infringements before the European Court of Justice: Futile Interference with Politics or a Substantial Step Towards EU Federalism*, 12 Colum. J. Eur. L. 517 (2006).

[22] Lower political units, bound by the higher, are thus required to harmonize their laws to conform to the rules and directives of the higher authority, whenever higher action is expressly authorized or, given its scale or effects, sanctioned as "necessary" and proportional to achieve treaty objectives. *See* Maastricht Treaty, *op. cit.* art. 5.

[23] *See* Carozza, *op. cit.* at 52 (underscoring that "[i]t would truly impoverish our discourse and reduce our capacity for understanding to limit subsidiarity to a technical European rule that does not grow up out of that ground"). Carozza provides the long history to the concept, which dates back to classical Greece, tracing its intellectual history through medieval scholasticism; seventeenth-century secularist theory; the work of eighteenth- and nineteenth-century titans such as Montesquieu, Locke, Tocqueville, Lincoln, and Proudhon; and nineteenth-century Catholic social theory, until finally transposed from social philosophy into positive law by Germany in its post–World War II drive to undo the massive centralization of national socialism and to devolve power to the Länder. It was formally enshrined in the Maastricht Treaty in 1992 (and further proceduralized in the 1996 Protocol of Amsterdam), taking on a particularly European meaning that is nonetheless still quite contested.

to the affected individual. In this way, subsidiarity represents the constitutive scaffolding to what may usefully be visualized as a series of nested circles, with the individual human person sitting at the center, surrounded concentrically by progressively larger social groupings of family, civic solidarity associations, local government, nation-state, and, ultimately, intergovernmental bodies and transnational social networks.

To best ensure the dignity interests of their constituent members, each of these connective layers holds concurrent duties of both *non-interference* and *assistance* to their interior or smaller units. On the one hand, larger, more comprehensive organizations have a "negative" duty not to interfere in the freedom of inner groupings to meet their own human dignity needs in ways that accord with their own realities. "It requires that problems be solved where they occur, by those who understand them best, and by those who are most affected by them."[24] It thus mandates that a respectful degree of latitude and discretion be given to smaller communities to interpret and implement human rights in ways that authentically accord with local understandings, mores, and particularized conditions. This follows not only from the fact that local needs are best appreciated by local actors but also from the fact that we live in a plural world in which the value of human dignity can be instantiated in a diversity of ways, each of which may fully accord with the broad purposes to which human rights aim. It is the formalized tools of this *negative* aspect of subsidiarity that the United States tends to invoke exclusively, often in conjunction with appeals to U.S. federalism, in defending its domestic human rights record and insulating it from outside pressures or influences.

Yet just as the subsidiarity principle does not tolerate preemption of smaller social or political units, neither does it support wholesale devolution to them.[25] Accordingly, whenever interior bodies cannot accomplish the good to which human rights aim without assistance, exterior groupings have a "positive" responsibility to intervene – by, for example, "directing, watching, urging, restraining, as occasion requires and necessity demands"[26] – to assist them

---

[24] J. E. Linnan, *Subsidiarity, Collegiality, Catholic Diversity, and Their Relevance to Apostolic Visitations*, 49 The Jurist 399, 403 (1989), *cited in* Dinah Shelton, "Subsidiarity, Democracy and Human Rights," in *Broadening the Frontiers of Human Rights: Essays in Honour of Asbjorn Eide* 43 (Donna Gomien ed., Oslo: Scandinavian University Press, 1993). The passage continues: "Only when their efforts fail should the matter be placed before a higher authority." *Id.* at 43–44.

[25] *See, e.g.*, Robert K. Vischer, *Subsidiarity as a Principle of Governance: Beyond Devolution*, 35 Ind. L. Rev. 103 (2001) (arguing that the "compassionate conservatism" platform of the Republican Party purports to enact the lessons of Catholic teachings on subsidiarity but in so doing advocates wholesale devolution to local authorities, neglecting subsidiarity's core focus on assistance from higher authorities).

[26] Carozza, *op. cit.* at 41, quoting Pius XI's 1931 papal encyclical, *Quadragesimo Anno: Encyclical Letter on Reconstruction of Social Order*.

in fulfilling the objectives of the common good. This requires that comprehensive monitoring mechanisms be set up – separately, at local, national, and international levels – that can track progress and setbacks at lower levels, providing support, an external check, and facilitative assistance whenever locally unremedied abuses or systemic problems are perceived. International human rights law, accordingly, envisions a constitutive framework of monitoring, supervision, and facilitation that allows this subsidiary relationship to play itself out flexibly within a broad variety of institutional structures and mediating procedures.[27] This is true not only at the international level but also, just as importantly, at the national and subnational levels.

In short, the subsidiarity principle in human rights law is directed at ensuring that the heavy lifting of human rights interpretation and implementation occurs at the domestic level, as close as possible to affected individuals. International treaty bodies correspondingly see their role as inherently supplemental, designed not to usurp or preempt but to facilitate, assist, and strengthen indigenous and localized implementation efforts. The principle of subsidiarity thus provides an important middle way through the polarizing tensions and cross-talk that currently dominate U.S. discourse on domestic human rights incorporation, particularly in its unhelpful setting of sovereignty and federalism in opposition to internationalism and human rights.[28] These dueling

---

[27] Modern international human rights treaty bodies, for example, exercise this subsidiary responsibility through each of their recognized competences. Thus, periodic reporting processes are designed precisely to stimulate and regularize *domestic* monitoring, enforcement, and self-appraisal processes, with the broad participation of all members of society. *See, e.g.,* Comm. on Economic, Social and Cultural Rights, General Comment 1, *Reporting by States Parties* (Third session, 1989), U.N. Doc. E/1989/22, annex III at 87 (1989) (identifying objectives of periodic reporting). The issuance of general comments aims to offer advice and guidance, drawn from the comparative experience of other states, for state consideration in implementing, modifying, and enforcing their own policies. Special rapporteurs work to identify best practices and common pitfalls across jurisdictions, stimulating and promoting issue-specific dialogue among a multiplicity of actors working on a common problem. Further, individual complaint processes, activated only when domestic remedies have proved ineffective in addressing a concrete human rights abuse, aim at ensuring, through a variety of tools, that an appropriate remedial scheme is effected by local actors. In fact, to ensure that such interventions are proportional and offered only where necessary, a series of institutional restraint doctrines have been adopted to guide treaty body conduct, particularly where complaints procedures are at issue. These include, among others, the exhaustion of domestic remedies rule, the margin of appreciation doctrine, "reasonableness" and other appropriate interest-balancing and proportionality tests, the fourth instance formula, and friendly settlement and "good offices" conciliation, all of which are important tools of subsidiarity. They also include recognition of the permissibility of reservations, understandings, and declarations and, specifically, respect for the non-self-execution doctrine.

[28] This discourse, which extends over an enormous literature, is in many ways succinctly encapsulated in the popular-media exchange between Peter Spiro, Jack Goldsmith, and Curtis Bradley in *Foreign Affairs*, in which "sovereignty" and "internationalism" are antagonized. *See* Peter J. Spiro, *The New Sovereigntists: American Exceptionalism and Its False Prophets*, Foreign Affairs,

postures, through their tendency to minimize the important constitutional values and democratic insights offered by the opposing position, tend toward communicative deadlock and heel-digging.[29] Subsidiarity, by contrast, merges the core democratic insights of both positions.[30] It values the procedural facilitation of international bodies and national monitoring, while respecting the primacy of localized process in determining appropriate means toward common ends. That is, it sees as its objective the authentic instantiation of human rights values in locally relevant, contingent, and meaningful ways, by local actors – not as cookie-cutter transplants determined and imposed by international experts, as is frequently claimed by those who resist human rights treaty incorporation on sovereignty, federalism, or majoritarian grounds.[31]

Subsidiarity, in this way, rejects the notion that respect for universal human rights is synonymous with singular or absolutist outcomes or interpretations, which only an international body is competent to define.[32] To the contrary, it understands that, given the plurality of human communities, the broad

---

Nov./Dec. 2000, at 1 (describing sovereigntists as "insulationist" and "anti-international"); Curtis A. Bradley and Jack L. Goldsmith, *Letter to the Editor*, Foreign Affairs, Mar./Apr. 2001, at 188 (rejecting Spiro's "unalloyed internationalism" as ignoring importance of state consent); Peter J. Spiro, *"What Happened to the "New Sovereigntists?"* Foreign Affairs, foreignaffairs.org, July 28, 2004 (predicting that the United States will finally be forced to "bend to international norms" after Iraq War debacle). See also Curtis A. Bradley, *The Treaty Power and American Federalism*, 97 Mich. L. Rev. 390 (1998) (concluding that U.S. government must "make a choice": human rights treaties *or* American federalism).

[29] See generally Curtis A. Bradley and Jack L. Goldsmith, *Treaties, Human Rights, and Conditional Consent*, 149 U. Pa. L. Rev. 399, 468 (2000) (noting that "the exaggeration and impatience that characterize the opposition to RUDs [reservations, understandings, and declarations] threaten to make U.S. officials less inclined, not more inclined, to continue their involvement with international institutions").

[30] The constitutive relationship among democracy, subsidiarity, and human rights has been initially explored in Dinah Shelton, *op. cit.*

[31] See, e.g., Jack Goldsmith, *Should International Human Rights Law Trump U.S. Domestic Law?* 1 Chi. J. Int'l L. 327, 338–39 (2000). As Professor Carozza has underscored, "A subsidiarity-oriented understanding of human rights and international law does not care to ask whether 'state sovereignty' must either resist or give way to international harmonization and intervention but, instead, whether the good that human rights aim at realizing can be accomplished at the local level, and if not, what assistance is necessary from a more comprehensive association to enable a smaller unit to realize its role." Carozza, *op. cit.* at 66.

[32] This is equally true for quasi-adjudicatory treaty bodies, such as the UN treaty body committees, and for supranational "courts," such as the European Court of Human Rights and the Inter-American Court of Human Rights. Although court rulings and remedial orders are binding on the parties to the litigation, they tend to be drafted in sufficiently broad terms to permit significant latitude to states in determining the contours of appropriate implementation at the domestic level. The remedial orders of the Inter-American Court, for example, increasingly require the participation of victims in the determination of the specific concrete measures that will give effect to the broad principles laid down by the Court. See Tara J. Melish, "Inter-American Court of Human Rights: Beyond Progressivity," in Malcolm Langford, ed., *Social Rights Jurisprudence: Emerging Trends in Comparative and International Law* (New York: Cambridge University Press 2008).

purposes of human dignity that human rights norms encapsulate must be given concrete form in locally relevant ways and that these instantiations will take a wide diversity of forms across the culturally rich tapestry of human society. As such, international processes are designed first and foremost to require that processes are established *and routinized* at the domestic level to resolve human rights complaints locally and to ensure that these are operating effectively and reliably. International bodies will intervene only when domestic institutions prove ineffective in resolving human rights issues, and then with the primary objective of strengthening local processes through constantly innovating forms of facilitative assistance, or *subsidium*.

Whether human rights treaty law becomes a more permanent fixture in U.S. law and policy making in the coming years will depend in large measure on the extent to which this positive dimension of the subsidiarity principle is constructively embraced by U.S. policy makers and, most importantly, by domestic interest groups – actively employed to formalize and institutionalize *domestic supervisory and monitoring processes*, at local, state, and federal levels, as a national project (rather than an international one). Such internally reflective processes – supported by a national institutional framework – must aim to continually assess and reassess national and local progress and setbacks in human rights achievement, debate the normative content of those rights, listen to citizen views on where deficiencies arise and how potential solutions might be crafted, and chart locally and nationally relevant paths toward fuller domestic human rights achievement. The promotion of such internal deliberative processes around the normative meaning of rights is in fact precisely the object to which international human rights law is directed.[33]

It is important to underscore, in this respect, that the United States' historic ambivalence to human rights treaty body engagements does not relate to either human rights or international supervisory regimes per se; both are fully consistent with and complementary to U.S. democracy, federalism, and rights culture. Rather, U.S. ambivalence is responsive to a particular static and absolutist way of conceiving human rights and international supervision that has been propagated and popularized over the past half-century by partisan U.S. interest groups. Although this rights absolutism is key to the rhetoric and group-mobilization strategies of many domestic advocates (of both liberal and conservative persuasion), it fails to acknowledge two of the principal underlying tenets of international human rights treaty law and supervision: First, its subsidiary nature vis-à-vis domestic protection efforts and, second, its

---

[33] It has been observed, for example, that "from a Liberal perspective, *a* – if not *the* – primary function of public international law is... *to influence and improve the functioning of domestic institutions*" and that, accordingly, "human rights law is the core of international law." Anne-Marie Slaughter, *A Liberal Theory of International Law*, 94 ASIL Proc. 240, 246 (2000) (emphasis in original).

focus on domestic process and progressivity, not universalized or standardized, top-to-bottom policy prescriptions or outcomes. A renewed focus on these tenets would reveal that the U.S. human rights paradox, at least in its modern manifestation and as applied within the U.S. territorial jurisdiction, is not in fact so paradoxical. To the contrary, once given an institutional framework to express itself domestically, it may be precisely the foundation for ensuring a sustainable domestic U.S. human rights policy over the long term.[34]

A. LEGAL CONTEXT: THE HUMAN RIGHTS FRAMEWORK APPLICABLE TO THE UNITED STATES

It is frequently contended that the United States ratifies few international human rights treaties. Although this may be true in relative terms, it does not accurately reflect the scope of commitments the United States has in fact undertaken under international human rights law, particularly over the past two decades. Under growing pressure from domestic and international constituents and with strong bipartisan support, the United States has ratified an increasingly broad spectrum of human rights treaties, under Republican and Democratic administrations alike. Thus, under the administrations of George H. W. Bush, William J. Clinton, and George W. Bush, the United States has ratified the International Covenant on Civil and Political Rights (ICCPR),[35] the Convention Against Torture and Other Cruel, Inhuman or Degrading Treatment or Punishment (CAT),[36] the International Convention on the Elimination of All Forms of Racial Discrimination (CERD),[37] the Genocide Convention,[38] a series of ILO treaties on labor rights,[39] and the two Optional Protocols to the Convention on the Rights of the Child in the areas

---

[34] It may also provide important insights for a more sustainable U.S. policy toward other international tribunal engagements, such as with the International Court of Justice.

[35] International Covenant on Civil and Political Rights, Dec. 16, 1966, S. Exec. Doc. E, 95-2 (1978), 999 U.N.T.S. 171 [hereinafter ICCPR]. The ICCPR was ratified by the United States on June 8, 1992.

[36] Convention Against Torture and Other Cruel, Inhuman or Degrading Treatment or Punishment, Dec. 10, 1984, S. Treaty Doc. No. 100-20 (1988), 1465 U.N.T.S. 85 [hereinafter CAT]. The CAT was ratified by the United States on October 21, 1994.

[37] International Convention on the Elimination of All Forms of Racial Discrimination, Dec. 21, 1965, S. Exec. Doc. C, 95-2 (1978), 660 U.N.T.S. 195, 212 [hereinafter CERD]. The CERD was ratified by the United States on October 21, 1994.

[38] Convention on the Prevention and Punishment of the Crime of Genocide, Dec. 9, 1948, 102 Stat. 3045, 78 U.N.T.S. 277 [hereinafter Genocide Convention]. The Convention was ratified by the United States on November 25, 1988.

[39] See, e.g., Convention concerning the Abolition of Forced Labour, June 25, 1957, S. Treaty Doc. 88-11, 320 U.N.T.S. 291 (ratified by the United States on September 25, 1991); Convention Concerning the Prohibition and Immediate Action for the Elimination of the Worst Forms of Child Labour, June 17, 1999, 2133 U.N.T.S. 161 (ratified by the United States on December 2, 1999). As of 2008, the United States has ratified a total of fourteen ILO treaties.

of children in armed conflict and the sale of children, child prostitution, and child pornography.[40] The United States has also ratified human rights treaties relating to slavery,[41] refugees,[42] and the political rights of women,[43] among others,[44] and has ratified the OAS Charter, which subjects it to the promotional and quasi-adjudicatory jurisdiction of the Inter-American Commission on Human Rights with respect to the full scope of internationally recognized rights enshrined in the American Declaration on the Rights and Duties of Man.

Taken together, these treaties cover a vast spectrum of rights – of a civil, cultural, economic, political, and social nature – and extend horizontally under three distinct supranational supervisory systems, each with its own set of promotional and quasi-adjudicatory powers. In this sense, although critical attention is often focused on the U.S. failure to ratify certain internationally popular treaties, including the Convention on the Rights of the Child (CRC), the Convention on the Elimination of All Forms of Discrimination Against Women (CEDAW), the American Convention on Human Rights, and the International Covenant on Economic, Social and Cultural Rights (ICESCR), it must be recognized that the scope of international commitments implicated by these treaties has already, in large measure, been undertaken by the United States pursuant to the treaties that it has ratified.[45] This reality complicates

---

[40] Optional Protocol to the Convention on the Rights of the Child on the involvement of children in armed conflict, May 25, 2000, 2173 U.N.T.S. 222 (ratified by the United States on December 23, 2002); Optional Protocol to the Convention on the Rights of the Child on the sale of children, child prostitution and child pornography, G.A. Res. 54/263, Annex II, at 6, 54 U.N. GAOR, Supp. No. 49, U.N. Doc. A/54/49 (2000) (ratified by the United States on December 23, 2002).

[41] *See, e.g.*, Slavery, Servitude, Forced Labour and Similar Institutions and Practices Convention of 1926 (Slavery Convention of 1926), 60 L.N.T.S. 253; Protocol Amending the Slavery Convention, Dec. 7, 1953, 182 U.N.T.S. 51; Supplementary Convention on the Abolition of Slavery, the Slave Trade and Institutions and Practices Similar to Slavery, Sept. 7, 1956, 226 U.N.T.S. 3.

[42] Protocol Relating to the Status of Refugees, Oct. 4, 1967, 606 U.N.T.S. 267.

[43] Convention on the Political Rights of Women, July 7, 1954, 193 U.N.T.S. 135; Inter-American Convention on the Granting of Political Rights to Women, May 2, 1948, O.A.S. T.S. No. 3 (ratified by the United States on March 22, 1976).

[44] The United States has ratified all four Geneva Conventions. As it recognizes, it has also "entered into many bilateral treaties (including consular treaties and treaties of friendship, commerce, and navigation) that contain provisions guaranteeing various rights and protections to nationals of foreign countries on a reciprocal basis," some of which may be invoked directly in U.S. courts. *See* Office of the U.N. High Comm'r for Human Rights, "Core Document Forming Part of the Reports of States Parties: United States," ¶ 151, U.N. Doc. HRI/CORE/USA/2005, Jan. 16, 2006.

[45] There is indeed wide overlap in the rights protected in distinct human rights treaties. This is apparent in the substantial substantive overlap (both direct and indirect) in the rights enshrined in the ICCPR and ICESCR, as well as by the express inclusion of varying numbers of both sets of rights in virtually all other human rights treaties, including the European Convention,

the utility to partisan actors of wholesale opposition to currently nonratified treaties.[46] It also undermines claims that the United States fails to ratify human rights treaties out of a cultural commitment to "negative" or libertarian conceptions of rights or, relatedly, a cultural aversion to economic, social, and cultural rights, two frequently raised but factually uncompelling explanations.[47]

    American Convention, African Charter, CERD, CEDAW, and CRC. Although it is therefore undoubtedly correct that the oft-purported "cultural aversion to socioeconomic ('positive') rights in the strong sense of welfare entitlements or labor rights," is not a credible reason for U.S. ambivalence to human rights (*see* Moravcsik, "The Paradox of U.S. Human Rights Policy," *op. cit.* at 163), the proffered reasons for reaching that conclusion are misdirected. *Id.* (concluding that because "the international human rights system strictly separates civil and political rights from socioeconomic ones," the "United States could, therefore, at any time simply ignore socioeconomic documents, while ratifying and implementing civil and political ones").

[46] Indeed, CEDAW, CRC, and ICESCR subject matters are regularly taken up through ICCPR, CERD, CAT, and ILO convention supervisory procedures.

[47] U.S. law, at local, state, and federal levels, provides significant and far-reaching protections for economic and social rights, including the rights to housing, health, education, work, social security, unionization, and other basic labor guarantees. National opinion polls, moreover, reflect that the majority of Americans identify many of these guarantees not as mere "privileges" but as personally held, individual rights, secured as part of the American heritage and in fact constitutive of the rights enshrined in the U.S. Constitution. *See*, e.g., Cass R. Sunstein, *The Second Bill of Rights: FDR's Unfinished Revolution and Why We Need it More than Ever* (Basic Books 2004) (noting that the majority of Americans would be surprised to learn that the rights to social security and education were not constitutionally protected), 62–63 (noting, too, a 1991 survey of U.S. citizens in which strong majorities identified adequate housing, a reasonable amount of leisure time, adequate provision for retirement years, an adequate standard of living, and adequate medical care as "a right to which he is entitled as a citizen" and not as "a privilege that a person should have to earn.").

    A 2007 national survey similarly found that strong majorities of Americans not only believe but "*strongly* believe" that a core set of social rights are human rights. These include equal access to quality public education (82%), access to health care (72%), living in a clean environment (68%), fair pay for workers to meet the basic needs for food and housing (68%), freedom from extreme poverty (52%), and adequate housing (51%). Only slim minorities believe these are not human rights. The Opportunity Agenda, "Human Rights in the United States: Findings from a National Survey," *op. cit.* at 3–4.

    Although currently lacking a direct federal constitutional basis, such rights are guaranteed in many state constitutions and came close to federal constitutional incorporation in the late 1960s and early 1970s. *See*, e.g., Sunstein, *op. cit.* at 5; William E. Forbath, *Constitutional Welfare Rights: A History, Critique and Reconstruction*, 69 Fordham L. Rev. 1821, 1823 (2001); William E. Forbath, *Not So Simple Justice: Frank Michelman on Social Rights, 1969–Present*, 39 Tulsa L. Rev. 597, 612 (2004) (noting U.S. Supreme Court on verge of recognizing constitutional basis for array of economic and social rights, in line with domestic social views, when the slim Nixon victory in 1968 ushered in judicial appointments that stopped process).

    At the same time, traditional distinctions between "negative" and "positive" rights, particularly as reified in classic "sets" of rights, have never been tenable as a factual matter, all rights possessing both negative and positive dimensions in the sense of duties to act reasonably and duties not to act arbitrarily. *See*, e.g., Stephen Holmes and Cass R. Sunstein, *The Cost of Rights: Why Liberty Depends on Taxes* (W.W. Norton 1999); Tara J. Melish, *Rethinking the "Less as More" Thesis: Supranational Litigation of Economic, Social, and Cultural Rights in the Americas*, 39 NYU J. Int'l L. & Pol. 171 (2006).

These are pretexts for other interests at play.[48] Indeed, in its interactions with international treaty bodies the United States regularly addresses the "positive" dimensions of its human rights obligations as well as a wide spectrum of economic, social, and cultural rights,[49] as it does in its own domestic legislation.

In this regard, it is also useful to note that although the United States has been slow to ratify many treaties – primarily because of the blocking opportunities presented by the fragmentation of the U.S. political structure – virtually all core human rights treaties have, since the late 1970s, been signed by the U.S. executive, indicating at least a political commitment to the rights and obligations enshrined therein and a present, if revocable, intent to be bound in the future.[50] President Carter signed the ICESCR, ICCPR, CERD, and the American Convention in 1977 and CEDAW in 1980. President Reagan signed the Genocide Convention in 1986, and President Clinton signed the CRC and its two Optional Protocols in 1995 and 2000, respectively.

Likewise, the administration of George H. W. Bush presided over U.S. ratification of the ICCPR in 1992, having urged Senate consent in 1991, and President Clinton, who presided over U.S. ratification of the CERD and CAT in 1994 and ILO Convention 182 in 1999, strongly promoted U.S. ratification of the ICESCR, CEDAW, and CRC from the beginning of his administration in 1993.[51] The George W. Bush administration, moreover, not only presided

---

[48] This is not to say that those who perpetuate them as part of a cultural myth of America are using them as pretext but rather that their underlying motivations rest on political-ideological foundations of a more partisan nature. For discussion, see Part C.2 *infra*.

[49] This is particularly true in U.S. reporting under the ICCPR and CERD, in which the United States regularly addresses the positive measures it has taken to respect and ensure the rights to nondiscrimination, equal protection, due process, and judicial protection with respect to health, housing, education, and employment. See, e.g., U.S. State Department, "Periodic Report of the United States of America to the U.N. Committee on the Elimination of Racial Discrimination Concerning the International Convention on the Elimination of All Forms of Racial Discrimination, April 2007," at http://www.state.gov/g/drl/hr/race/cerd_report/ (visited Apr. 25, 2007) [hereinafter "U.S. CERD Report 2007"], ¶¶219–78 (addressing the right to work; the right to form and join trade unions; the right to housing; the right to public health, medical care, social security, and social services; the right to education and training; and the right to equal participation in cultural activities). The United States also addresses these dimensions of economic and social rights with respect to contentious cases lodged against it with the Inter-American Commission on Human Rights, which has jurisdiction over all of the rights in the American Declaration on the Rights and Duties of Man, including the rights to health, education, unionization, housing, and social security.

[50] Vienna Convention on the Law of Treaties art. 18, *opened for signature* May 23, 1969, 1155 U.N.T.S. 331, 8 I.L.M. 679 (1969) (stating that signature obliges certain conduct until a State's intention not to ratify is made clear). In 2002 the Bush administration "unsigned" a treaty to indicate its lack of both obligations thereunder and intent to ratify. See Edward Swaine, *Unsigning*, 55 Stan. L. Rev. 2061 (2003).

[51] See, e.g., Christopher, *op. cit.* at 1. There is wide recognition that Senate consent failed because of the Republican takeover of Congress in 1994.

over the ratification of the two Optional Protocols to the CRC in 2002 but, after an initial decision to step back from the negotiation process, reinitiated active engagement in the final stages of the substantive drafting of the newly adopted UN Convention on the Rights of Persons with Disabilities (CRPD).[52] It did so under active pressure from both domestic constituencies[53] and members of the U.S. House of Representatives.[54] CEDAW, for its part, has consistently garnered strong, even bipartisan, support in Congress, with Senate Democratic leaders committing in 2008 to bring it to a full Senate vote as soon as politically opportune. Although likely to face intense targeted opposition from antiabortion lobbies, which by continuing to politicize it in absolutist terms may succeed in blocking it still, CEDAW is expected to receive supermajority support.

This treaty-related behavior, from Republican and Democratic administrations alike, suggests two important conclusions. First, it suggests that, despite popular rhetoric to the contrary, the United States does not in principle perceive inherent contradictions between such regimes and U.S. domestic law, policy, or interests. If it did, such treaties would neither be signed by the President nor ratified by Senate supermajorities. Second, given the established track-record of speedy human rights treaty ratification with Democratic control of the Senate and Executive, it can be concluded that the nation's

---

[52] Convention on the Rights of Persons with Disabilities, G.A. Res. 61/106, art. 5, U.N. Doc. A/RES/61/106 (Dec. 6, 2006) [hereinafter CRPD]. The CRPD received eighty-four signatures on the opening day, more than any human rights treaty in history. Although the United States formally participated in all eight sessions of the UN Ad Hoc Committee charged with drafting the CRPD, it announced its intention not to ratify at the second session in June 2003. *See* Statement of Ralph F. Boyd, U.S. assistant attorney general for civil rights, to the UN General Assembly Ad Hoc Committee on a Comprehensive and Integral International Convention on the Protection and Promotion of the Rights and Dignity of Persons with Disabilities, June 18, 2003, USUN Press Release #89 (03), at http:www.usunnewyork.usmission.gov/03print_089.htm (visited Apr. 20, 2007) [hereinafter Boyd Statement]. The U.S. delegation thereafter ceased to make substantive proposals, reinitiating its active engagement in the drafting process only at the seventh session in January 2006.

[53] See discussion in Part C.2.III *infra*.

[54] *See* House Concurrent Resolution 134 (expressing the sense of Congress that the United States should support a UN convention on disability rights and thereby urging: "(1) the United States to play a *leading role* in the drafting of a United Nations convention and to work toward its adoption ... and (2) urg[ing] the President to instruct the Secretary of State to send to the UN Ad Hoc Committee meetings a U.S. delegation that includes individuals with disabilities who are recognized leaders in the U.S. disability rights movement.") (emphasis added). The resolution was unanimously adopted by the House International Relations Committee in 2004 but failed to be scheduled for a vote on the House floor by majority leader Tom Delay (R-TX). Members of the House committee, together with the Congressional Human Rights Caucus, met directly with members of the U.S. State Department to express their sense of urgency that the United States reinitiate a leadership role in the CRPD drafting process, given the United States' historic protagonism in advancing disability rights.

political branches reasonably anticipate being subject to human rights treaty regimes as an inevitable outcome of swings in the political process.[55] Within this context, any view that says the United States institutionally or "culturally" resists human rights commitments appears incomplete.

The better explanation, as advanced by Professor Moravcsik, rests in the distinct ways that conservative minority special interest groups exert their influence over veto players in the ratification process, particularly within the U.S. Senate.[56] Through rhetorical resort to stereotypes and "rights absolutism"[57] that portray international procedures as undemocratic, authoritarian, communistic, and hence "anti-American," these interest groups have historically succeeded in turning the rhetorical debate into one related to American rights culture and states' rights, rather than simply as a rough-and-tumble domestic wrestling match over the shape of distinct social policy outcomes, within the *methodological framework* of human rights commitments and supervisory monitoring procedures. This "thicker" explanation should not, however, lead to dire predictions that the status quo will persist[58] but rather to a more searching look at what special interest groups are doing and how their interests intersect or fail to intersect with the promotion of international human rights law.

Special interest groups traditionally at the forefront of the fight against U.S. adherence to international human rights treaties over the past two decades appear in fact to have begun to reassess their positions and modify their strategies, finding ways that recurrence to such treaties may in fact advance their domestic and international agendas. They have increasingly demanded greater U.S. participation in drafting the terms of international human rights

---

[55] Strong Democratic control of the Senate has historically been an important facilitating condition for the ratification of human rights treaties. Moravcsik calls it a "necessary condition" based on a review of a set of core treaties ratified from 1945 to 2000. *See* Moravcsik, *op. cit.*, at 184 ("[T]he Senate has never ratified an international human rights treaty (even with reservations) when Democrats held fewer than 55 seats."). It is important to recall, however, that ILO Convention 182 as well as the two CRC optional protocols were ratified under Republican Senate majorities in 1999 and 2002, respectively.

[56] *Id.* at 186–87 (noting that "[a]ll other things being equal, the greater the number of 'veto players,' as political scientists refer to those who can impede or block a particular government action, the more difficult it is for a national government to accept international obligations" and highlighting three characteristics of the U.S. political system that engender veto players: "super-majoritarian voting rules and the committee structure of the Senate, federalism, and the salient role of the judiciary in adjudicating questions of human rights").

[57] Rights absolutism can be defined as an unwillingness to recognize that human rights law permits reasonable restrictions on all individual rights and that states are granted a (variable, but generally quite wide) margin of discretion in determining their nature and scope in distinct contextual settings.

[58] Moravcsik, *op. cit.*, at 197 (predicting no change absent some unexpected "epochal constitutional rupture – an Ackermanian 'constitutional moment'").

agreements and even sought U.S. ratification of certain human rights treaties.[59] This activity, taken together with the renewed mobilization of groups traditionally in favor of human rights treaty compliance – particularly through the coordination of the U.S. Human Rights Network[60] – is leading to a distinctly new situation for U.S. engagement with international human rights supervisory bodies and will lead to growing opportunities and challenges for all parties involved.

Increased civil society engagement (from both sides of the political spectrum) is being met, moreover, by growing institutionalization of human rights coordination within the U.S. government, particularly from the U.S. State Department, which is increasingly broadening its oversight from an exclusive focus on the human rights situation in *other* countries to *domestic* human rights achievement. In this regard, it is useful to recall that it was not in fact until 1976 – the year the ICCPR and ICESCR entered into force – that the U.S. government began to systematically monitor human rights achievement at all, in any country. In that year, Congress amended the Foreign Assistance Act to require the Secretary of State to transmit to it "a full and complete report" every year concerning "respect for internationally recognized human rights in each country proposed as a recipient of U.S. assistance."[61] The next year, the first forebear to the current position of Assistant Secretary of State for Democracy, Human Rights, and Labor was appointed,[62] and an Interagency Working Group on Human Rights and Foreign Assistance was established.[63] Yet these focal points were mandated exclusively to report on the human rights situation

---

[59] See discussion *infra* Part C.2.
[60] Founded in 2003, the U.S. Human Rights Network is a loosely coordinated community of more than 250 human rights organizations and 1,000 individuals committed to ensuring that U.S. human rights treaty commitments have effect for domestic communities. See http://www.ushrnetwork.org/ (visited Apr. 20, 2007).
[61] This limited reporting requirement was authorized in the 1976 International Security Assistance and Arms Export Control Act, Pub. L. No. 94-329, 90 Stat. 729, which included an amendment to § 502B of the Foreign Assistance Act of 1961, Pub. L. No. 87-195, 75 Stat. 424 (codified as amended in scattered sections of 22 U.S.C.). The requirement was expanded in 1978's International Development and Food Assistance Act, Pub. L. 95-424, 92 Stat. 937, to include each member of the United Nations. The report was to be based on the internationally recognized human rights ideals detailed in the 1948 Universal Declaration of Human Rights, G.A. Res. 217A, U.N. GAOR, 3d Sess., at 71, U.N. Doc. A/810 (1948). In 1998, the mandate was extended to religious freedom. See International Religious Freedom Act, § 102(b)(1), 22 U.S.C. § 6412 (1994 & Supp. V 1999).
[62] It was at the time called coordinator (and then assistant secretary) for human rights and humanitarian affairs. The latter named bureau was renamed the Bureau for Democracy, Human Rights, and Labor under the Clinton administration.
[63] See Hauke Hartmann, *U.S. Human Rights Policy under Carter and Reagan, 1977-1981*, 23 Hum. Rts. Q. 402, 417 (2001).

of *other* countries, particularly those receiving U.S. foreign assistance.[64] They had no mandate to report on the human rights situation *within* the United States itself. It was not until two decades later – on the fiftieth anniversary of the Universal Declaration of Human Rights – that an interagency group was specifically mandated to coordinate executive agency response to domestic human rights concerns.[65]

Although that body, the Interagency Working Group on Human Rights Treaties (IAWG), functioned in that form for only two brief years, it represented a fundamental turning point for the orientation of U.S. human rights policy. Created by Executive Order 13107, issued by President Clinton on December 10, 1998, it was mandated to promote coordination among U.S. executive agencies in ensuring compliance with the human rights treaties the United States has ratified and supporting the work of international human rights mechanisms, including the UN, ILO, and OAS.[66] The order states that "[i]t shall be the policy and practice of the Government of the United States, being committed to the protection and promotion of human rights and fundamental freedoms, fully to respect and implement its obligations under the international human rights treaties to which it is a party, including the ICCPR, the CAT, and the CERD."[67] Critically, it further charges all executive departments and agencies to "maintain a current awareness of United States international human rights obligations" relevant to their functions and to ensure that such functions are performed "so as to respect and implement those obligations fully."[68] This duty includes "responding to inquiries, requests for information and complaints about violations of human rights obligations that fall within [each agency's] areas of responsibility."[69]

The IAWG, for its part, was given a series of concrete coordination and oversight functions. These included coordinating the preparation of both treaty compliance reports to the UN, OAS, and other international organizations and responses to contentious complaints lodged therewith, as well as overseeing a review of all proposed legislation to ensure its conformity with international human rights obligations. It was also mandated to ensure that plans for public outreach and education on human rights provisions in treaty-based and domestic law were broadly undertaken and to ensure that an annual review of U.S.

---

[64] *See* Foreign Assistance Act of 1961, Pub. L. No. 87-195, 75 Stat. 424 (codified as amended in scattered sections of 22 U.S.C.) § 502(B); *see also* Hartmann, *op. cit.*, at 417 (describing limited economic focus of Human Rights Bureau's Interagency Group).
[65] Exec. Order No. 13107, 63 Fed. Reg. 68,991 (1998), 38 ILM 493 (1999).
[66] *Id.* §1.
[67] *Id.* §1(a) (emphasis added).
[68] *Id.* §2.
[69] *Id.* §§2–3.

reservations, declarations, and understandings to human rights treaties takes place. Finally, and notably, the Working Group was charged with ensuring that all nontrivial complaints or allegations of inconsistency with or breach of international human rights obligations be reviewed to determine whether any modifications to U.S. practice or laws are in order.[70]

The change of administrations in January 2001 meant that the work of the IAWG was never fully institutionalized. On February 13, 2001, it was superseded – in form, if not function – by President George W. Bush's National Security Presidential Directive, which reorganized the National Security Council system.[71] Specifically, the Bush Directive transferred the duties of the Human Rights Treaties IAWG established under Executive Order 13107 to a newly established Policy Coordination Committee (PCC) on Democracy, Human Rights, and International Operations, to be directed by the Assistant to the President for National Security Affairs.[72] With the national security structure thrown into disarray by the September 11 attacks later that year, the PCC was not, however, formally constituted. It was not until 2003 that the staffs of the State Department and National Security Council, aware of a growing number of overdue periodic reports, began to work again on an ad hoc basis in preparing the relevant reports.[73]

Since then, U.S. responses to international human rights treaty bodies have been coordinated by the Office of the Legal Adviser of the U.S. State Department, with the assistance, when necessary, of legal consultants with expertise in the area and of other executive agencies and departments, particularly the National Security Council and the Departments of Justice, Homeland Security, the Interior, Defense, Health and Human Services, and Labor. This is true both for the preparation of U.S. periodic reports on domestic compliance with human rights treaties and of U.S. responses to individual complaints and precautionary measures.[74] Although this work is done on an ad hoc basis, without dedicated staff and resources, the framework for a more structured response is at least technically in place. This framework requires formal reconstitution and the infusion of resources and staff that ideally, at least with respect to periodic reporting functions, are functionally independent of the Office of

---

[70] *Id.* §4.
[71] National Security Presidential Directive, Feb. 13, 2001, at http://www.fas.org/irp/offdocs/nspd/nspd-1.htm (abolishing the system of Interagency Working Groups established under the Clinton administration).
[72] *See id.*
[73] Interview with Mark P. Lagon, Deputy Assistant Sec'y of State, Bureau of Int'l Affairs, U.S. Dep't of State, & Robert K. Harris, Assistant Legal Adviser, U.S. Dep't of State (Feb. 1, 2007) [hereinafter Lagon-Harris Interview].
[74] For their part, responses to ILO complaints and periodic reports are prepared principally by the U.S. Department of Labor.

the Legal Adviser – more like the current structure for preparing the State Department's country reports on the human rights situation in *other* nations.[75] It is important to note that whereas this latter mandate remains limited to non-U.S. jurisdictions, the 2006 report recognized for the first time that the U.S. government, too, has fallen short of international standards in some areas.[76]

This movement within the executive branch[77] is being matched by movements within the legislative and judicial branches. The judicial branch is increasingly, if slowly and cautiously – and in the face of certain powerful resistance[78] – referring to comparative human rights jurisprudence in resolving domestic disputes and interpreting domestic statutory and constitutional law.[79]

---

[75] The State Department has a sizable staff of attorneys working exclusively on preparing Annual Country Human Rights Reports, a permanent staff that is assisted by the staffs of U.S. embassies and consulates around the world. A similar mechanism could be set up through which a permanent staff of attorneys within the State Department or other federal agency or entity, preferably with an autonomous monitoring mandate, is assisted by the staffs of federal offices in the fifty states, together with the voluntary inputs of state officials.

[76] U.S. State Department, "2006 Country Reports on Human Rights Practices," at http://www.state.gov/g/drl/rls/hrrpt/2006/ (visited Apr. 20, 2007). *See also* Brian Knowlton, "U.S. Releases Report on Human Rights in 2006," *Int'l Herald Tribune*, Mar. 6, 2007.

[77] Although President Obama has taken no action yet on a proposed Executive Order to revitalize and strengthen the Clinton-era IAWG, he issued an Executive Order on March 11, 2009 establishing a more limited-mandate White House Council on Women and Girls that would function under a similar interagency structure. *See* Executive Order No. 13506, 74 Fed. Reg. 11,271 (Mar. 16, 2009).

[78] Justice Antonin Scalia has been the most vocal judicial opponent of referring to foreign law in domestic jurisprudence. *See, e.g., Atkins v. Virginia*, 536 U.S. 304, 347–48 (2002) (Scalia, J., dissenting). A minority of representatives within the U.S. House of Representatives has likewise resisted this trend, introducing two House resolutions in 2004 and 2005, respectively, that sought to legislatively preclude domestic courts from referring to "judgments, laws, or pronouncements of foreign institutions" in determining the meaning of U.S. laws. *See* H.R. Res. 568, 108th Cong. (2004); H.R. Res. 97, 109th Cong. (2005). Although voted out of committee, the two proposals, which garnered seventy-four and eighty-four House cosponsors, respectively, were never brought to a vote in the full House. A similar bill was introduced to the U.S. Senate in 2005 but did not make it out of committee. It is important to note that Supreme Court justices, including Justice Scalia, have indicated constitutional objections to such legislative initiatives on separation of powers grounds. *See* Tony Mauro, "Scalia Tells Congress to Stay Out of High Court Business," *Legal Times*, May 19, 2006.

[79] For recent Supreme Court examples, *see, e.g., Roper v. Simmons*, 543 U.S. 551 (2005); *Laurence v. Texas*, 539 U.S. 558 (2003); *Grutter v. Bollinger*, 539 U.S. 344 (2003); *Atkins v. Virginia*, 536 U.S. 304 (2002). Of course, the Court has long referred to international law in general, either as federal common law or in interpreting domestic statutes to not conflict with international treaty commitments. *See, e.g., Murray v. The Charming Betsy*, 2 Cranch 64 (1804); *The Paquete Habana*, 175 U.S. 677 (1900); *Banco Nacional de Cuba v. Sabbatino*, 376 U.S. 398 (1964). For reviews and discussion of this jurisprudence, both as a contemporary and historical matter, *see*, for example, Vicki Jackson, *Constitutional Comparisons: Convergence, Resistance, Engagement*, 119 Harv. L. Rev. 109 (2005); Steven G. Calabresi and Stephani Dotson Zimdahl, *The Supreme Court and Foreign Sources of Law: Two Hundred Years of Practice and the Juvenile Death Penalty Decision*, 47 Wm. & Mary L. Rev. 743 (2005); Sarah H. Cleveland, *Our International Constitution*, 31 Yale J. Int'l L. 1 (2006).

The Senate Judiciary Committee, for its part, created a new Sub-Committee on Human Rights and the Law in 2007, reauthorizing it in 2009.[80] Such Senate bodies, together with the bipartisan Congressional Human Rights Caucus, could play a critical role in coordinating with a new National Human Rights Commission, National Human Rights Office, and reconstituted IAWG or PCC,[81] particularly if the latter entities were given a specific legislative reporting mandate,[82] to ensure that all branches of government are adhering to their treaty-based human rights obligations. At a minimum, the playing field for domestic advocates in pushing their respective policy agendas has been materially altered in recent years, changing the opportunity structure for using human rights language to achieve distinct policy ends. Opponents and proponents have taken note, adjusting their strategies accordingly.

B. SUPERVISORY TREATY BODY SYSTEM AND THE SCOPE OF U.S. ENGAGEMENT

Although scarcely covered by the U.S. media establishment and hence not well known outside narrow advocacy circles,[83] the United States has remained actively engaged in the work of supranational human rights treaty bodies, consistent with its international treaty commitments. "Human rights treaty bodies" refer to the committees or commissions of independent experts[84] set up under key human rights treaties to supervise, through quasi-adjudicatory and promotional powers, state party compliance with treaty undertakings. There are currently eight United Nations (UN) human rights treaty bodies operating under the auspices of the UN Office of the High Commissioner on Human Rights, four of which exercise direct supervisory jurisdiction over the United States.[85] These include the Human Rights Committee, the Committee

---

[80] *See* David Johnston, "New Judiciary Subcommittee Is to Focus on Civil Liberties," *New York Times*, Dec. 14, 2006, A33.

[81] See Part E *infra* (proposing these new entities).

[82] Such a reporting mandate might be similar to the one given to the State Department under the Foreign Assistance Act. The benefit of a legislative mandate is that it cannot be abolished through executive order with periodic changes in the White House.

[83] For a discussion of the phenomenological biases of the media as a participant in the international legal process, see Monica Hakimi, *The Media as Participant in the International Legal Process*, 16 Duke J. Comp. & Int'l L. 24 (2006).

[84] Such experts are nominated and elected by the States parties to the treaty but serve in their personal capacities, generally for renewable four-year terms. Most treaties require them to be persons of high moral authority and recognized competence in the field of international human rights law; in practice, they have various skill sets and backgrounds.

[85] The United States is not subject to the jurisdiction of the other four: the UN Committee on Economic, Social and Cultural Rights, the UN Committee on the Elimination of All Forms of Discrimination Against Women, the UN Committee on the Rights of Persons with Disabilities, and the UN Committee on Migrant Workers and their Families.

Against Torture, the Committee on the Elimination of All Forms of Racial Discrimination, and the Committee on the Rights of the Child.[86] The United States is also subject to the supervisory jurisdiction of the Inter-American Commission on Human Rights, one of the two principal human rights organs of the Organization of American States (OAS),[87] as well as the International Labour Organization's (ILO) Committee of Experts and Committee on Freedom of Association.[88]

Although not courts in the sense of having competence to issue legally binding rulings on the matters and parties before them, these treaty bodies often exercise quasi-adjudicatory functions that closely approximate that role.[89] Most are empowered to receive petitions of alleged human rights violations from either individual or collective complainants,[90] review evidentiary or informational submissions, find facts, interpret legal rules, and issue nonbinding decisions or recommendations. Such recommendations are increasingly accompanied by follow-up and compliance reporting requirements, designed to ensure that appropriate measures are taken by states to give domestic legal effect to treaty body pronouncements. These quasi-judicial functions, exercised under jurisdictional rules and procedures highly similar to those of international judicial bodies,[91] are supplemented by functions of a more overtly

---

[86] Although the United States has not yet ratified the Convention on the Rights of the Child, it has ratified the two optional protocols thereto, each of which entails a periodic reporting obligation to the Committee on the Rights of the Child.

[87] The other is the Inter-American Court of Human Rights, the contentious jurisdiction of which the United States has not recognized. For more on the Court, see Elizabeth A. H. Abi-Mershed, "The United States and the Inter-American Court of Human Rights," Chapter 7 in this volume; *see also* Melish, "Inter-American Court of Human Rights," *op. cit.*

[88] The former has mandatory supervisory jurisdiction over the ILO's core labor standards, two of which the United States has ratified: No. 105 on the Abolition of Forced Labor and No. 182 on the Elimination of the Worst Forms of Child Labor. The latter exercises contentious jurisdiction over collective complaints involving freedom of association regardless of whether the member state has ratified ILO treaties; as of 2008, it has considered forty-nine complaints against the United States. See Steve Charnovitz, *The ILO Convention on Freedom of Association and Its Future in the United States*, 102 Am. J. Int'l L. 90, 92 (2008).

[89] *See* UN Human Rights Comm., General Comment 33, *The Obligations of States Parties under the Optional Protocol to the International Covenant on Civil and Political Rights*, ¶ 11, U.N. Doc. CCPR/C/GC/33 (Nov. 5, 2008) ("While the function of the Human Rights Committee in considering individual communications is not, as such, that of a judicial body, the views issued by the Committee under the Optional Protocol exhibit some important characteristics of a judicial decision. They are arrived at in a judicial spirit, including the impartiality and independence of Committee members, the considered interpretation of the language of the Covenant, and the determinative character of the decisions.").

[90] The UN and OAS mechanisms have individual standing rules, whereas the ILO has jurisdiction over collective complaints lodged by, and on behalf of, workers' or employers' organizations.

[91] Compare, for example, the jurisdictional rules for receiving contentious complaints of the Inter-American Commission on Human Rights (a quasi-judicial body) and the Inter-American

promotional nature, such as periodic reporting procedures and their accompanying committee conclusions and recommendations, the issuance of general comments or observations, onsite visits, and general reports on distinct human rights matters or issues.

U.S. engagement with these bodies extends over the full range of treaty body activities, including each of the three principal types of supervisory mechanisms: periodic reporting processes, individual and collective complaints procedures, and special mandate or promotional mechanisms. Because the scope of engagement with each of these mechanisms speaks so powerfully to the parameters of U.S. human rights policy, each merits slightly closer attention here.

1. *Periodic Reporting Process*

The quintessential function of human rights treaty bodies is a periodic reporting process.[92] Periodic reporting reflects the subsidiary nature of human rights law vis-à-vis domestic law and is designed to assist states in their central obligation under human rights treaty law: to ensure that protected rights have domestic legal effect through the adoption of "appropriate" or "necessary" measures, determined in context. States parties are thus required to submit reports on the appropriate measures they have adopted to give effect to the rights recognized in the treaty and on the progress and setbacks made in the enjoyment of those rights.[93]

> Court of Human Rights (a judicial body). Both bodies – like the UN committees and the European Court of Human Rights – require the exhaustion of domestic remedies, proof of concrete personal harm to identified individuals, imputation of conduct-based causal responsibility to the state for that harm, and similar *ratione temporis* and *ratione loci* requirements. The principal difference between the two is that the case-based conclusions of judicial bodies, like the Court, are formally binding on the parties to the dispute, whereas those of quasi-adjudicatory bodies, like the Commission and UN treaty bodies, are recommendary in nature. An expectation exists nonetheless that such recommendations will be given effect in the domestic jurisdiction, with treaty bodies increasingly requesting follow-up reports on the measures taken toward this end.
>
> [92] An exception is the Inter-American Commission on Human Rights, which, despite an explicit competence to supervise a periodic reporting process (*see* American Convention on Human Rights art. 42, Nov. 22, 1969, 1144 U.N.T.S. 123, O.A.S.T.S. No. 36, at 1 (1969)), has declined to formally pursue it over the years. A periodic reporting function has been set up under the Additional Protocol to the American Convention in the Area of Economic, Social and Cultural Rights and guidelines have recently been drawn up by the Inter-American Commission for the preparation of reports by States parties. See, e.g., OAS General Assembly Resolution 2074 (XXXV-O/05).
>
> [93] To do so, they are expected to undertake a thorough and comprehensive review of national legislation, administrative rules and procedures, and practices to assess conformity with treaty commitments, to determine whether new policy making is required by identifying areas of strength and weakness, and to continually monitor the actual situation with respect to each treaty-recognized right for progress and setbacks in levels of enjoyment and protection.

Each of the core UN human rights treaties envisions a mandatory periodic reporting process under the supervision of the relevant treaty body committee. An initial report must generally be provided within one year, followed by a periodic report every two to five years or as the Committee so requests.[94] The United States has undertaken periodic reporting requirements under the CERD, the CAT, the ICCPR, the two Optional Protocols to the CRC, and certain ILO conventions it has ratified. Although the United States – not unlike most other nations – has frequently been late in submitting its reports,[95] it has actively engaged with the supervisory treaty bodies in the periodic reporting process, particularly as nongovernmental organizations (NGOs) have become increasingly savvy in using international procedures and pressure points to ensure timely, substantive, and participatory reporting.

In this regard, the United States submitted its first report under the ICCPR to the Human Rights Committee in Geneva in 1994, defending it in 1995. This was followed by its first CAT report in 1999 and its first CERD report in 2000.[96] These reports were defended before the UN Committee on Torture and the UN Committee on the Elimination of Racial Discrimination, respectively, in 2000 and 2001. In 2005, the United States submitted its combined second and third CAT reports and its combined second and third ICCPR reports,[97] defending each in Geneva in 2005 and 2006, respectively. It presented its combined fourth, fifth, and sixth report to the CERD Committee in 2007, which it defended in 2008. It has regularly submitted reports as well – on a two-year periodic basis – to the ILO Committee of Experts.[98]

The supervisory procedures associated with periodic reporting tend formally to be characterized as a process of "constructive dialogue" between treaty bodies and states parties.[99] After a state party submits its written report,

---

[94] Most human rights treaties require periodic reports to be submitted every four to five years. CERD, by contrast, requires reports to be submitted every two years. This has led to serious backlogs in the Committee's ability to review states' periodic reports and the Committee's increasing request for states to prepare and submit combined reports on a four-year schedule.

[95] This delay owes to several mostly institutional factors. First, until early 1999 the United States lacked any dedicated body with explicit competence to prepare and supervise such reports, causing many deadlines to be missed. While a coordinating mechanism exists today, it continues to lack dedicated staff and resources, thus constraining its capacity to produce reports on time, especially given the significant institutional coordination and commitment needed for their production. It is for this reason that the institutional mechanisms proposed in Part E, *infra*, are so crucial.

[96] The United States missed its CERD report due dates in 1995, 1997, and 1999 and thus submitted its combined first, second, and third reports as a single document in 2000.

[97] These were submitted one and seven years late, respectively.

[98] *See* U.S. Dep't of Labor, Bureau of Int'l Labor Affairs, International Labor Organization (ILO), http://www.dol.gov/ilab/programs/oir/ILO.htm (recognizing requirement of regular submission of U.S. reports to ILO supervisory bodies).

[99] *See, e.g.*, Philip Alston, *U.S. Ratification of the Covenant on Economic, Social and Cultural Rights: The Need for an Entirely New Strategy*, 84 Am. J. Int'l L. 365, 370 (1990) (noting

the treaty body prepares a list of priority issues that the state party should be prepared to discuss at a scheduled hearing in Geneva.[100] On the basis of the state party's written report, its oral presentations, and any additional information made available to the committee, the supervising committee prepares a public report in which it identifies areas of progress and areas of concern with respect to the state's human rights achievement. It then draws conclusions and sets forth recommendations for how the state party might take further measures in areas where deficiencies or weaknesses were identified. Although technically a friendly process, treaty-based reporting has become increasingly adversarial over the years as treaty bodies have gained prominence and international authority.[101] As a result, their recommendations are often interpreted, at least by domestic and international advocacy groups and some international media sources, as a binding "legal decision" requiring immediate domestic execution by national authorities. This view is often reinforced by committee requests that the state party submit additional information if committee questions were not answered fully in oral proceedings, a request sometimes construed by advocates as a requirement to report on follow-up measures.

U.S. participation in this process is marked by five major characteristics, each determinative in appreciating the mediated nature of U.S. engagement policy. First, the United States prepares extensive and detailed reports to the committee. In contrast to many states, which often submit incomplete or insufficiently inclusive reports,[102] the United States closely hews to the committee-issued guidelines in preparing its consistently lengthy and comprehensive submissions.[103] These reports address each substantive rights-based

---

that periodic reporting function is "based on the assumption that a constructive dialogue between the Committee and the state party, in a non-adversarial, cooperative spirit, is the most productive means of prompting the government concerned to take the requisite action.").

[100] These questions are often based on the information provided to treaty bodies in civil-society-prepared "shadow reports," prepared to highlight and correct misstatements or generalizations in official state reports; fill in overlooked areas with accurate facts, details, and statistics; and generally present an alternative view for the expert UN committee to consider in assessing state progress and setbacks and in making recommendations for domestic improvements.

[101] This growing prominence and global authority have in many ways emboldened treaty bodies to be more confrontational with U.S. delegations. Cf. Murphy, op. cit. ("For the [ICJ], the lesson [of increasing global authority unbeholden to major powers] may be not to tread lightly with respect to the United States but, rather, to tread heavily unless doing so would be viewed generally as bias.").

[102] The UN Human Rights Committee, for example, has regularly lamented the lack of comprehensiveness in state party reports. See, e.g., General Comment No. 2, op. cit., ¶1. As a result, it has issued guidelines to assist states in preparing reports under the respective treaties. "Consolidated guidelines for States reports under the International Covenant on Civil and Political Rights: 26/02/2001," CCPR/C/66/GUI/Rev.2 (2001).

[103] The U.S. third periodic report to the UN Human Rights Committee, for example, was 120 single-spaced pages, covering U.S. achievements with respect to each of the twenty-seven

provision in the relevant treaty, how U.S. law protects the right, the types of claims that are regularly brought to U.S. courts to protect it, and the outcomes of major court decisions, particularly those of the U.S. Supreme Court. In this respect, the United States tends to be very good at reporting on formal legal protections emanating from the three branches of government, focusing on the outcomes of high-profile judicial decisions and the legislation or policy positions enacted to give formal effect to rights. It is less good at critically describing gaps in coverage and at documenting progress or setbacks in the statistical enjoyment of rights over the population and distinct subgroups within it, particularly at the state level.[104] It is here that the treaty bodies generally focus their questions and direct their recommendations, relying on NGO submissions to fill in the missing pieces and to ask further probing questions. In response, the United States, keen on improving its performance, is increasingly opening the reporting process to a greater degree of transparency among nongovernmental actors and greater substantive comprehension, explicitly seeking input and data for its reports from U.S. NGOs[105] and state attorney generals.

Second, the United States participates in Geneva-based meetings – and increasingly in contentious OAS proceedings[106] – with large, high-level interagency delegations. According to State Department officials, it does so to demonstrate the seriousness with which the United States takes the human rights supervisory process. It thereby seeks to set an example for other states, encouraging them to engage the process with a similar degree of seriousness and material commitment. It is important, in this regard, to highlight that the United States sends not only a high-level official spokesperson to present and defend its report but also a full delegation of high-level officials from each of the major executive agencies and departments to present and answer

---

substantive rights guaranteed in the ICCPR. See CCPR/C/USA/3 (Nov. 28, 2005). The United States' 2007 CERD Report is more than 170 pages and includes coverage with respect to each provision of the CERD, as well as separate annexes on examples of state-level civil rights programs, the U.S. legal position on the Western Shoshone case, and new domestic laws adopted since 2000, when the United States submitted its first CERD report. See U.S. CERD Report 2007, op. cit.

[104] In response to Committee requests for the United States to discuss state-level progress and setbacks, the U.S. has included an annex to its 2007 CERD Report in which it provides examples of civil rights programs in Illinois, New Mexico, Oregon, and South Carolina.

[105] The State Department and other executive departments and agencies have increasingly been meeting with civil society representatives, at the latter's request, before and after treaty body hearings in Geneva to take their views into account.

[106] Although this has not historically been the case, a change has occurred over the last five or six years in which larger interagency delegations are appearing at hearings before the Inter-American Commission on Human Rights.

committee questions in their respective areas of competence.[107] This level of engagement reflects the high standard requested of governments by the Geneva-based committees to ensure the effectiveness of the process.[108]

Third, the United States consistently affirms, particularly in its oral presentations to treaty bodies, that it recognizes that it is not perfect and has definite gaps to fill.[109] The central message of the treaty-mandated reports is thus that the United States "is trying in good faith to bring its domestic practices into compliance with international standards."[110] Within this context, it formally welcomes the views of the treaty body as part of a constructive dialogue aimed at assisting it in identifying areas of weakness in its own internal process, affirming that committee suggestions are appropriately taken into consideration.[111] According to U.S. representatives, what grates U.S. officials is not the process

---

[107] At its most recent appearances before the UN Human Rights Committee and Committee Against Torture, for example, the U.S. delegation comprised more than thirty government officials from at least six executive agencies or departments.

[108] See, e.g., Human Rights Committee, General Comment 2, "Reporting guidelines" (Thirteenth session, 1981), U.N. Doc. HRI\GEN\1\Rev.1 at 3 (1994), ¶4: "The Committee wishes to state that, if it is to be able to perform its functions under article 40 as effectively as possible and if the reporting State is to obtain the maximum benefit from the dialogue, it is desirable that the States representatives should have such status and experience (and preferably be in such number) as to respond to questions put, and the comments made, in the Committee over the whole range of matters covered by the Covenant."

Although the UN treaty bodies tended to acknowledge this effort in its initial reports, they have declined to do so in later reports as the relationship with the United States has grown more contentious on matters relating to the Iraq War and counterterrorism measures. Compare "Concluding Observations of the Human Rights Committee: United States of America, 03/10/95," CCPR/C/79/Add.50 (1995), ¶¶267–68 (expressing appreciation of high quality of report, "participation of high-level delegation which included a substantial number of experts in various fields relating to the protection of human rights in the country," and well-structured replies) with "Concluding Observations of the Human Rights Committee: United States of America," CCPR/C/USA/CO/3/Rev.1 (Dec. 18, 2006) (no mention of high-level delegation or quality of process).

[109] See, e.g., Remarks to the U.N. Committee Against Torture by Harold Hongju Koh, U.S. Assistant Secretary of State for Democracy, Human Rights and Labor, Geneva, Switzerland, May 10, 2000 ("Although we are proud of our record in eliminating torture, we acknowledge continuing areas of concern within the United States. Although our commitment is unambiguous, our record is not perfect."); Remarks to the UN Human Rights Committee by Robert Harris, Legal Adviser, U.S. Department of State, Geneva, Switzerland, July 17, 2006 (noting that the United States recognizes that it has gaps to fill in its human rights record under ICCPR); see also Briefing on the State Department's 2006 Country Reports on Human Rights Practices by Condoleezza Rice, U.S. Secretary of State, Washington, D.C., Mar. 6, 2007 ("We do not issue these reports because we think ourselves perfect, but rather because we know ourselves to be deeply imperfect, like all human beings and the endeavors that they make. Our democratic system of governance is accountable, but it is not infallible.").

[110] See, e.g., Harold Hongju Koh, A United States Human Rights Policy for the 21st Century, 46 St. Louis U. L.J. 293, 308 (2002).

[111] See, e.g., Harris Remarks, op. cit. (noting that the United States welcomes committee's views and that such views are appropriately taken into consideration by agencies of U.S. government).

itself – which, they affirm, is genuinely appreciated, particularly for the opportunity to orally defend U.S. policy positions on human rights internationally – but when committee members appear unopen to dialogue on debatable issues and insensitive to areas of simple disagreement, particularly as they relate to U.S. jurisdictional concerns on the substantive limits of treaty body competence.[112]

Fourth, and relatedly, members of official delegations and those who prepare reports tend to recognize the genuine utility of the reporting process for gaining a better understanding of the precise ways in which the United States is and is not in compliance with international standards.[113] That is, despite prominent unilateralist or realist strains within many departments and agencies of government, the process of engagement has revealed for many the real utility of periodic reporting for gaining a better understanding of the national reality and where the country stands vis-à-vis international human rights law. This realization militates in favor of greater U.S. engagement – both for purposes of pushing other states to engage to a similar degree and for promoting the involvement of an increasing number of federal, state, local, and nongovernmental actors in the reporting process. The U.S. government, for example, is increasingly meeting with civil society organizations to follow up on concerns articulated at treaty body sessions and to discuss the establishment of mechanisms for coordinating information on state and national human rights monitoring and achievement.[114]

Finally, although the United States manifests a high degree of openness and willingness to answer treaty body questions in virtually all areas of domestic human rights policy, there are certain policy issues that it declines to address other than "as a matter of courtesy." These predominate in two areas: one, the territorial scope of treaty body competence and, two, the intersection of human rights and humanitarian law.[115] The United States insists that UN and OAS

---

[112] Lagon-Harris Interview, *op. cit.*

[113] This appreciation, often acknowledged to be unexpected, has been consistently expressed in multiple fora by government officials responsible for preparing treaty reports. This is equally true in public meetings between U.S. departments and agencies, treaty bodies, and domestic advocacy groups and in private interviews or conversations in which this author has taken part. *See*, e.g., Interviews with Steven Hill, Robert Harris, and Mark Lagon, U.S. Department of State, Feb. 2007.

[114] U.S. State Department officials, as well as those from Justice, affirm that they are always open to meeting and working with domestic groups on human rights issues. Interagency meetings involving representatives of the Departments of State, Justice, Homeland Security, and Defense have been held on multiple occasions with the U.S. Human Rights Network and other civil society organizations to discuss the periodic reporting process and follow-up measures thereto.

[115] Statement of Mark P. Lagon, Deputy Assistant Secretary of State for International Organization Affairs, Media Roundtable with Senior Government Officials at presentation of U.S. periodic report under the ICCPR to UN Human Rights Committee, Geneva, July 17, 2006 ("There are

treaty bodies lack jurisdiction to consider U.S. human rights policy as it affects persons outside its territorial boundaries and as it intersects with the law of armed conflict, which, it asserts, prevails as *lex specialis* at points of intersection and hence falls outside treaty body jurisdiction.[116] The United States has, in this sense, adopted a highly technical and legalized posture with respect to the scope of treaty body competence, asserting its prerogative to decline to answer questions that exceed that competence as the United States defines it. Although this is an explicit mediating posture adopted by the United States to shield its foreign policy and national security interests within the context of active engagement with human rights treaty bodies,[117] it has nonetheless put the United States in an increasingly adversarial position vis-à-vis the treaty bodies.

2. Individual and Collective Complaint Procedures and Precautionary Measures

Just as the United States actively engages in mandatory periodic reporting processes under all relevant treaty regimes, it likewise engages in individual and collective communication procedures wherever they are mandatory. The United States has not, however, *optionally* acceded to any such procedure. Thus, it has not recognized the right of individuals to initiate individual communications or claims procedures under the ICCPR, CAT, or CERD, nor has it recognized the contentious competence of the Inter-American Court of

---

some issues that will come up in this defense that have to do with the war on terrorism and the United States conduct of it. It is our firm belief that those issues in large part lie beyond the scope of the treaty, those things that have to do with conduct outside of the territory of the United States or those that belong to the questions of law of war rather than human rights law. Nonetheless, the United States will answer those controversial questions as a courtesy to the committee, and importantly, as a matter of openness in the international community.").

[116] On the former point, see "Third Periodic Reports of States Parties due in 2003: United States of America," CCPR/C/USA/3 (2005), Annex 1 ("Territorial Application of the [ICCPR]"), 109–11. This posture predates but supports the U.S. "war on terror" policy of holding suspected terrorists and "enemy combatants" outside of U.S. territory, such as in Guantanamo Bay, Cuba, or on offshore vessels. Significantly, the extraterritoriality point is pressed as a matter of human rights *treaty law*, even while accepting the Supreme Court's decision in *Rasul v. Bush*, 542 U.S. 466 (2004), that the U.S. judiciary may exercise jurisdiction over extraterritorial abuses taking place in loci over which the U.S. exercises effective ("exclusive") authority and control. This constitutional exception to the extraterritoriality principle is effectively identical to that recognized in international human rights law generally. *See, e.g., Coard et al. v. United States*, Case 10.951, Report N° 109/99, Sept. 29, 1999, Inter-Am.Comm.H.R, para. 37 ("In principle, the inquiry turns not on the presumed victim's nationality or presence within a particular geographic area, but on whether, under the specific circumstances, the State observed the rights of a person *subject to its authority and control*.") (emphasis added).

[117] See discussion *infra* Part D.1.

Human Rights, the properly judicial (as opposed to quasi-judicial) organ of the regional human rights system.[118] These adjudicatory and quasi-adjudicatory procedures provide legal standing for individuals within a state party's jurisdiction to bring contentious claims alleging that the state is responsible, through its conduct, for violating the individual's treaty-protected rights. Although most human rights treaty bodies can issue only findings and recommendations, not legally binding rulings,[119] they nonetheless act in an adjudicatory capacity in considering the claims that come before them – finding facts, issuing legal conclusions and remedial recommendations, and initiating follow-up mechanisms to supervise compliance with their case-based recommendations.

There are, however, two *mandatory* mechanisms in international human rights law that allow individuals to bring human rights complaints against the United States, as well as one mechanism for collective complaints. The first is the case-based contentious jurisdiction of the Inter-American Commission on Human Rights (Commission). The second is the precautionary measure or early warning/urgent action procedure recognized respectively by the Commission and the UN human rights treaty bodies.[120] Finally, the United States is subject to a collective complaints procedure regarding compliance with ILO labor rights treaties, through which labor and employer organizations may bring complaints against the United States before the ILO Committee on Freedom of Association.[121] The United States recognizes and engages with each of these three sets of procedures, appearing and presenting arguments at all procedural stages of litigation.

With regard to individual complaints procedures, the most significant and extensively used of the two applicable to the United States is the quasi-adjudicatory petitions process of the Inter-American Commission on Human

---

[118] Each of these nonmandatory procedures requires the deposit of an independent instrument of jurisdictional recognition for operativity.

[119] The exception, of course, is the Inter-American Court of Human Rights, the findings of which are "final" and "binding" on all OAS Member States that have accepted its jurisdiction. See American Convention on Human Rights, *op. cit.*, arts. 67–68.

[120] The formal competence of treaty bodies to issue these measures is generally established in their respective rules of procedure. *See*, e.g., Rules of Procedure of the Inter-American Commission on Human Rights, art. 25, OEA/Ser.L/V/I.4 rev. 12 (2007) at 171 ("In serious and urgent cases, and whenever necessary according to the information available, the Commission may, on its own initiative or at the request of a party, request that the State concerned adopt precautionary measures to prevent irreparable harm to persons."). For information on the CERD's urgent action or early-warning procedure, see Office of the U.N. High Comm'r for Human Rights, Comm. on the Elimination of Racial Discrimination: Monitoring Racial Equality and Non-Discrimination, http://www2.ohchr.org/english/bodies/cerd (last visited Apr. 4, 2009).

[121] These will not be substantively addressed here. For an assessment, see Charnovitz, *op. cit.* The full range of cases and complaints against the United States can be accessed at International Labour Organization, International Labour Standards, http://www.ilo.org/ilolex/english/caseframeE.htm (follow "United States" hyperlink) (last visited Apr. 4, 2009).

Rights. Formally established in 1959, the Commission is mandated under the OAS Charter to "promote the observance and protection of human rights and to serve as a consultative organ of the [OAS] in these matters."[122] In this regard, the Commission has both quasi-adjudicative and promotional functions.

Persons within the jurisdictional boundaries of the United States at the time of an alleged violation can therefore bring human rights complaints through this supranational mechanism for violation, to their detriment, of any of the rights recognized in the American Declaration on the Rights and Duties of Man, including the rights to health, education, property, life, due process, judicial protection, and nondiscrimination.[123] To date, the majority of cases lodged against the United States have involved persons on death row claiming due process denials with respect to the rights to life and to judicial protection,[124] including through failure to provide consular notification to nonnationals. This U.S. case pattern owes primarily to limited public awareness in the United States about the regional human rights system and its adjudicatory competence over concrete instances of domestic human rights abuse.

Nevertheless, the Commission has considered a growing number of U.S. cases beyond the death penalty context, increasingly so in recent years. These have involved the rights of indigenous persons to ancestral territory,[125] voting

---

[122] Charter of the Organization of American States art. 106, Apr. 30, 1948, 2 U.S.T. 2394, 119 U.N.T.S. 3 (entered into force Dec. 13, 1951); *see also id.* arts. 3, 16, 51, 112, 150. The Commission has affirmed that, consistent with its Statute and Rules of Procedure, it has jurisdiction to consider individual petitions lodged against the United States, as with all thirty-five OAS member states, by virtue of the United States's 1951 ratification of the OAS Charter. *See, e.g., Sánchez v. United States*, Petition 65/99, Inter-Am. C.H.R., Report No. 104/05, OEA/Ser.L/V/II.124, doc. 5 ¶ 50 (2006) ("United States of America deposited its instrument of ratification of the OAS Charter on June 19, 1951 and has been subject to the Commission's jurisdiction since 1959, the year in which the Commission was created."); *see also Roach v. United States*, Case 9647, Report No. 3/87, OEA/Ser. L./V/II.71. doc. 9 rev. 1 (1987).

[123] American Declaration of the Rights and Duties of Man, OAS Res. XXX, International Conference of American States, 9th Conf., OAS Doc. OEA/Ser. L./V/II.23, doc. 21 rev. 6 (1948). Article 1 of the Commission's Statute defines the human rights the Commission is competent to apply as "[t]he rights set forth in the American Convention on Human Rights, in relation to the States Parties thereto" and "[t]he rights set forth in the American Declaration of the Rights and Duties of Man, in relation to the other member states." OEA/Ser.L/V/I.4 rev. 12 at 163 (2007).

[124] *See, e.g., Medina v. United States*, Case 12.421, Inter-Am. C.H.R., Report No. 91/05, OEA/Ser.L/V/II.124, doc 5 (2005); *Workman v. United States*, Case 12. 261, Inter-Am. C.H.R., Report No. 33/06, OEA/Ser.L/V/II.127, doc. 4 rev. 1 (2007) (admissible). A great number of these cases have dealt with failures to provide consular notification under the Vienna Convention on Consular Relations.

[125] *Dann v. United States*, Case 11.140, Inter-Am C.H.R., Report No. 75/02, OEA/Ser. L./V/II.117. doc. 7 rev. 1 (2002); *Cherokee Nation v. United States*, Case 11.071, Inter-Am. C.H.R., Report No. 6/97, OEA/Ser.L/V/II.a5, doc. 7 (1997).

rights in the nation's capital,[126] summary deportations,[127] abortion,[128] abuses committed during U.S. military action abroad where effective authority or control was maintained over the alleged victims,[129] capital punishment of minors,[130] and the rights of interdicted refugees and detainees held in Immigration and Naturalization Service detention facilities and at Guantanamo Bay.[131] They have likewise involved freedom from extraordinary rendition, the right not to be deported where HIV treatment is not available in the return country,[132] border controls,[133] the right to reparation for civil rights abuses,[134] welfare reform,[135] and the right to police enforcement of domestic violence restraining orders,[136] among others.

Although U.S. responsibility for rights violations is frequently found, the majority of cases lodged against the United States with the Commission are found inadmissible, either in pre-admissibility vetting procedures[137] or after admissibility hearings. This is principally because of jurisdictional defects in petitioners' arguments, including failure to properly exhaust domestic

---

[126] *Statehood Solidarity Committee v. United States*, Case 11.204, Inter-Am. C.H.R., Report No. 98/03, OEA/Ser. L/V/II.114, doc. 70 rev. 2 (2003).

[127] *See, e.g., Smith v. United States*, Case 8-03, Inter-Am. C.H.R., Report No. 56/06, OEA/Ser.L/VII.127, doc. 4 rev. 1 (2007); *Armendariz v. United States*, Case 526-03, Inter-Am. C.H.R., Report No. 57/06, OEA/Ser.L/V/II.127, doc. 4 rev. 1 (2007).

[128] *"Baby Boy" v. United States*, Case 2141, Inter-Am. C.H.R., Res. No. 23/81, OEA/Ser.L/V/II.54, doc. 9 rev. 4 (1981).

[129] *Coard v. United States*, Case 10.451, Inter-Am. C.H.R., Report No. 109/99, OEA/Ser.L/V/II.106, doc 6 rev. (1999) (U.S. attacks on Grenada); *Disabled Peoples' International v. United States*, Case 9213, Inter-Am. C.H.R. 198, OEA/Ser.L/V/II.71, doc. 9 rev. 1 (1987) (U.S. attacks on Grenada); *Hill v. United States*, Case 9213, Inter-Am., Report No. 3/96, OEA/Ser.L/V/II.91, doc. 7, at 201 (1996) (closing case after full reparation provided to alleged victims of U.S. attack on civilian hospital in Grenada); *Salas v. United States*, Case 10.573, Inter-Am. C.H.R., Report No. 31/93, OEA/Ser.L/V/I.85, doc. 9 rev. (1993) (U.S. invasion of Panama).

[130] *See, e.g., Patterson v. United States*, Case 12.439, Inter-Am. C.H.R., Report No. 25/05, OEA/Ser.L/V/II.124 doc. 5 (2005) (17 years old when committed crime); *Thomas v. United States*, Case 12.240, Inter-Am. C.H.R., Report No. 100/03, OEA/Ser.L/V/II.118 (2003) (17 years old when committed crime); *Roach v. United States*, Res. No. 3/87, OEA/Ser.L/V/II.71 doc. 9 rev. 1, ¶¶ 46–49 (1987).

[131] *Haitian Ctr. for Human Rights v. United States*, Case 10.675, Inter-Am. C.H.R., Report No. 51/96, OEA/Ser.L/V/II.95 doc. 7 rev. at 550 (1997); *Ferrer-Mazorra v. United States*, Case 9903, Inter-Am. C.H.R., Report No. 51/01, OEA/L/V/II.111 doc. 20 rev. at 1188 (2000).

[132] These two cases do not yet have formal admissibility reports.

[133] *Sánchez v. United States*, Petition 65/99, Inter-Am. C.H.R., Report No. 104/05, OEA/Ser.L/V/II.124 doc. 5 (2005) (found inadmissible).

[134] *Shibayama v. United States*, Petition 434-03, Inter-Am. C.H.R., Report No. 26/06, OEA/Ser.L/V/II.127 doc. 4 rev. 1 (2007).

[135] *Poor People's Economic Human Rights Campaign v. United States* (1999, dismissed without prejudice for failure to identify individual victims).

[136] *Gonzales v. United States*, Petition 1490-05, Inter-Am. C.H.R., Report No. 52/07 (2007).

[137] In this case, no public record of the filing is maintained.

remedies, lack of victim standing, failure to state a prima facie claim, or lack of *ratione temporis, ratione personae,* or *ratione loci* jurisdiction. These defects most frequently stem from petitioners' conflation of the case-based and promotional competences of the Commission and an effort to extract strong, absolutist human rights statements from it without framing the controversy as a concrete justiciable case.[138] In this respect, the U.S. position often rests on reminding the Commission of the limited nature of its jurisdiction and the importance of not exceeding it or acting as a court of fourth instance in any particular case.

Within this context, the United States participates reliably in individual petitions processes before the Commission, as it has since at least 1977, the year President Carter signed the American Convention on Human Rights.[139] As the cases have become more varied and complex, U.S. participation in hearings has likewise become more active, extensive, and substantive, with strong positive effects for the system as a whole. Although the United States has frequently argued that the Declaration, as a nontreaty, creates no binding obligations for it, its submissions nonetheless consistently address both the admissibility and merits of the underlying claim. The United States today substantively briefs and argues all questions posed by alleged victims and their representatives in each stage of case-based proceedings[140] at the Commission's Washington, D.C., headquarters, at times arriving with full interagency delegations of experts in the distinct fields under consideration.[141] It increasingly also invites local or state authorities in whose jurisdiction the alleged violation took place.

At the same time, while the United States hastens to emphasize that the final recommendations of the Commission are in fact just that – nonbinding

---

[138] *See* Melish, "Rethinking the 'Less as More' Thesis," *op. cit.,* 207–74 (discussing common jurisdictional errors in framing contentious claims); Tara J. Melish, "The Inter-American Commission on Human Rights: Defending Social Rights through Case-Based Petitions," in Malcolm Langford, ed., *Social Rights Jurisprudence: Emerging Trends in Comparative and International Law* (Cambridge University Press, 2008).

[139] Although earlier cases had been lodged against the United States, it was in 1977 that the first case to proceed to a merits decision was submitted. *See "Baby Boy" v. United States,* Case 2141, Inter-Am. C.H.R., Res. No. 23/81, OEA/Ser.L/V/II.54, doc. 9 rev. 1 ¶ 1 (1981). The United States extensively briefed this abortion-related case, using the regional instruments' *travaux préparatoires* to support its argument that regional norms protecting the right to life did not proscribe abortion absolutely, but rather allowed it to proceed under reasonable state regulation.

[140] This includes pre-admissibility, admissibility, merits, and follow-up/compliance stages. With respect to the latter, the United States attended its first follow-up meeting in March 2007 to discuss compliance with the IACHR's recommendations. *See Dann v. United States,* Case 11.140, Report No. 75/02, Inter-Am. C.H.P. OEA/Ser.L/V/II.117, doc. 1 rev. (2002).

[141] This is particularly true in cases dealing with national security issues.

recommendations – it likewise takes measures to consider the propriety of those recommendations and, to the extent that state agency behavior is implicated, to give state agents the opportunity to independently consider and give effect to the Commission's conclusions and recommendations. Similar to the practice of other federal nations, decisions of the regional body are procedurally transmitted to the responsible federal department or agency and/or state attorney generals for follow-up, within the bounds of their responsibilities, competence, and discretion.[142] In this sense, the U.S. State Department treats the Commission's recommendations in much the same way it treats ICJ decisions that affect state and local agents: it transmits the recommendations or decision to the competent authority, leaving it to them – in function of federalism considerations – to determine the appropriate response under the circumstances.[143] Speaking on the issue most recently in *Medellín*, the U.S. Supreme Court has appeared to endorse this approach.[144]

The United States responds in a similar way to requests for precautionary measures, whether by the Inter-American Commission or UN treaty bodies, such as the CERD.[145] Precautionary measures are urgent interim measures of protection designed to prevent the occurrence or continuance of alleged human rights abuses that threaten irreparable harm, particularly until the merits of the underlying claim is considered. They are issued based on a prima facie assessment, without prejudgment on the underlying merits, of written communications that suggest abuse may be occurring.[146] Although the United States regularly contests the competence of treaty bodies to issue

---

[142] Interview with Steven R. Hill, Att'y Adviser, Office of the Legal Adviser, U.S. Dep't of State, in Washington, D.C. (Feb. 8, 2007) [hereinafter Hill Interview].

[143] For a discussion of the U.S. response to ICJ provisional measures and merits decisions in the *Breard*, *LaGrand*, and *Avena* cases, see Murphy, *op. cit.* ("The initial fallout from the decisions on the merits in *LaGrand* and *Avena* is a story of the federal government encouraging the several states to take into account the decisions of the ICJ, without actually telling the states that they must do so as a matter of federal law.") (noting that "the United States sought to implement [provisional] measures... principally by encouraging the commutation of death sentences of the relevant convicts by governors or parole boards" and by "embark[ing] on an aggressive campaign to educate and train state law enforcement officers regarding U.S. obligations arising under the Vienna Convention, to the point of printing cards that officers were to carry with them and read out when arresting an alien").

[144] *Medellín v. Texas*, 128 S. Ct. 1346 (2008).

[145] The CERD Committee issued an "urgent action" request under its early-warning procedure to the United States in March 2006 with respect to the Western Shoshone Peoples of the Western Shoshone Nation, giving the United States four months to respond on the measures it has taken in response. The United States has responded both in writing directly to the Committee and in Annex II of its 2007 CERD Report, *op. cit.*, in which it provides background information on the case and U.S. responses to the underlying claim over the years.

[146] *See, e.g.*, Rules of Procedure of the Inter-American Commission on Human Rights, art. 25, *op. cit.* ("The granting of such measures and their adoption by the State shall not constitute a prejudgment on the merits of a case.").

such measures, the State Department nonetheless follows a policy of formally transmitting requests for precautionary measures as an informational notice to the appropriate attorney general or responsible federal agency.[147] It also engages in associated hearings on the propriety of interim measures and on follow-up thereto, reporting on the measures it has taken to ensure that precautionary measure requests are brought to the attention of the relevant body or bodies and, where compliance follows, on the steps taken by that body in response to the measures. Although far from the norm, federal and state agents have on occasion complied with precautionary measure requests issued by the Inter-American Commission.[148]

In sum, although the United States asserts that these contentious complaints procedures generate nothing more than recommendations for the United States to take under advisement – and participates in associated proceedings expressly on that basis – it nonetheless treats the process as a formal, adjudicatory one.[149] It actively engages in all stages of proceedings, employing the full set of procedural rights available to it to defend U.S. policy interests within the jurisdictional constraints of the Commission's competence. Where defects are identified, processes are at times initiated to consider whether further measures are necessary to address the underlying concern.[150] This is true of both individual complaints procedures under the jurisdiction of the Inter-American

---

[147] Hill Interview, *op. cit.* Such transmittals do not propose or encourage any particular action, but are sent to the relevant authority for that authority to respond to in its discretion.

[148] *See*, e.g., *Ramos v. United States*, Case 12.430, Inter-Am. C.H.R., Report No. 1/05, OEA/Ser.L/V/II.124, doc. 7 ¶ 89 (2005) (noting U.S. indication that federal district court judge in Texas had postponed setting an execution date in light of the petition before the Commission and request for precautionary measures) ("The Commission observes that this arrangement has given practical effect to the Commission's precautionary measures by preserving Mr. Moreno Ramos' life and physical integrity pending the Commission's consideration of his complaint, and the Commission commends the efforts taken within the Texas judicial system to preserve Mr. Moreno Ramos' right of effective access to the inter-American human rights system.").

[149] Notably, following submission of the *Baby Boy* case to the IACHR in 1977, four members of the U.S. House of Representatives sent a letter to the IACHR in 1979, "in a spirit of cooperation and with the intent of furthering the work of the Commission," requesting an opinion on "whether, if the United States loses, it would be subject to trade and diplomatic sanctions similar to those imposed upon Cuba by the O.A.S. following, and partially on account of, the human rights violations of the Castro regime?" It also requested suggestions on "how legislation might be shaped in order to eliminate any doubts as to U.S. compliance with IACHR standards in this regard." "*Baby Boy*" *v. United States*, Case 2141, Inter-Am. C.H.R., Res. No. 23/81, OEA/Ser.L/V/II.54, doc. 9 rev. 1 (1981), ¶19.

[150] In other instances, the United States will indicate that it is taking measures to address the issue even while asserting that the Commission lacks competence to consider it. *See*, e.g., *Medina v. United States*, Case 12.421, Inter-Am. C.H.R., Report No. 31/05, ¶ 43 (2005) (asserting Commission's lack of competence over Vienna Convention on Consular Relations, but submitting nevertheless that the United States takes its obligations thereunder "very seriously and has since 1998 undertaken an intensive, on-going and now permanently institutionalized effort to improve compliance by federal, state and local government officials ... includ[ing]

Commission and the collective complaints mechanism of the ILO, in which U.S. participation is equally extensive.[151]

3. Other Promotional Mechanisms

The United States also actively engages with UN, OAS, and ILO treaty bodies in other noncontentious ways aimed at facilitating more robust human rights promotion at the domestic level. This may include coordinating with civil society on treaty-based requirements to prepare national programs of action to give treaty commitments domestic effect[152] or issuing invitations to UN and OAS special rapporteurs and independent experts to come to the United States to undertake onsite visits or otherwise discuss issues under their special mandates. The United States has, for example, authorized and cooperated with the Inter-American Commission on Human Rights as it has undertaken onsite visits to Florida, Puerto Rico, New York, California, Kansas, Pennsylvania, Louisiana, and Texas to look into alleged abuses in the areas of state and federal detention facilities and with respect to migrant laborers and their families.[153] U.S. cooperation is also expected should the Commission take up pending proposals to investigate other alleged abuses in the United States, such as housing discrimination and inappropriate use of electroshock weapons by local police forces.

Similarly, the United States regularly accepts and facilitates country visits by UN special rapporteurs and independent experts who request invitations to visit the United States to engage in constructive dialogue with federal and state officials, NGOs, and civil society more broadly – most recently by the UN Special Rapporteurs on the subjects of protecting human rights while countering terrorism,[154] human rights of migrants,[155] and racial discrimination. Such

---

the publication of a 72-page brochure on Vienna Convention requirements as well as pocket reference cards for arresting officials and a training video").

[151] As of January 2008, the ILO Committee on Freedom of Association had decided forty-nine cases involving the United States, cases in which it frequently recognized the nation's reliable and engaged participation.

[152] ILO Convention 182, for example, requires ratifying states to develop a National Program of Action on ensuring child labor rights. The U.S. government initiated a process of review with civil society organizations but ultimately concluded that no additional measures were necessary.

[153] For a list of all IACHR on-site visits, see http://www.iachr.org/visitas.eng.htm.

[154] Press Release, OHCHR, Special Rapporteur on the Rights of Migrants to Visit United States, UN Doc. HR/07/04 (Apr. 27, 2007) (announcing a U.S. invitation for country visit in May 2007).

[155] See Eliane Engeler, "U.N. rights expert to probe U.S. treatment of illegal immigrants [sic]," *Associated Press*, Apr. 27, 2007 (reporting on U.S.-facilitated visit in May 2007, with scheduled stops in California, Arizona, Texas, Florida, Georgia, New York, and Washington, D.C.). The UN expert was, however, denied access to certain facilities in Texas by local authorities.

UN experts are mandated to develop a regular dialogue with relevant governmental and nongovernmental actors, exchange information, make recommendations, and identify and promote best practices on measures to respect and ensure fundamental human rights. Consistent with the U.S. approach to periodic reporting processes, U.S. officials have at times noted that special rapporteurs, through the noncontentious dialogue they engender with an array of domestic governmental and nongovernmental actors, represent one of the most promising ways of promoting change within the United States.[156]

C. INTEREST MANAGEMENT: THE PUSH-PULL OF DOMESTIC AND FOREIGN POLICY AGENDAS

As the preceding section's examination reveals, U.S. engagement with international human rights treaty bodies is quite robust. The question of interest, then, is how this level of engagement can be reconciled with popular notions that the United States actively resists the domestic application of human rights norms and thumbs its nose at human rights treaty body regimes? The answer, I argue, lies in interest management. Specifically, it resides at the intersection of domestic and foreign policy pressures, and the mediating postures the United States employs to steer a middle course through them. As with all international tribunals, engagement with human rights bodies involves important push-pull dynamics among a plurality of interest groups, with some urging greater engagement (the "push toward" factor) and others resisting engagement (the "pull away" factor). These push-pull vectors operate simultaneously at the foreign policy level and at the domestic policy level. The U.S. position has modulated within these countervailing tendencies, resting at momentary middle grounds within the four corners of the dynamic[157] as interest politics change and distinct strategic opportunities evolve.

What appears clear, however, is that the United States is moving decisively toward greater engagement with international human rights treaty bodies. This shift is due both to growing pressures to engage at the foreign policy level and to a gradual diffusion of interests in domestic constituencies opposed to engagement. The net effect of the two dynamics, both accelerating since the 1990s, is an ever more robust engagement policy, albeit one that operates within clearly parametered constraints that represent the continuing power of "pull back" interests.

---

[156] Hill Interview, *op. cit.*
[157] Viewed diagrammatically, this dynamic may be seen as operating over a plane with domestic and foreign policy interests along one axis and push-pull tendencies along another. The U.S. policy position locates itself within this four-cornered plane at convergence points along the various and shifting vectors.

Although the motivations for each shift are independent of each other, their effects are mutually reinforcing and equally constitutive of the parameters of U.S. human rights policy. To demonstrate the various levers in this interest-management process, the following two sections look, respectively, at the push-pull dynamic as it plays out, first, at the foreign policy level between "realist" and "institutionalist" persuasions in the foreign policy establishment and, second, at the domestic policy level between groups I call "insulationists" and "incorporationists."

Because these labels are so important to the analysis, it should be emphasized that the four corresponding groups are neither ideologically based nor exclusive in their membership. Rather, each bundles adherents to one of four distinct instrumental approaches to interest achievement, each directed to fostering a political environment most conducive to a given foreign or domestic policy agenda. Their memberships are thus variable and politically contingent, with adherents straddling or moving into or out of groupings depending on the precise issue at stake and shifting appreciations of policy opportunities.

1. *Foreign Policy Interests: Net Push Toward Greater Treaty Body Engagement*

A body of scholarship has arisen of late, looking more closely at the foreign policy dimension of U.S. human rights engagement and domestic policy making. In particular, whereas accounts of the U.S. human rights paradox often focus narrowly on domestic politics and the partisan cleavages that historically linked human rights with "anti-Americanism" and thus assured for forty years, through veto-player politics, that the United States would neither ratify newly adopted human rights treaties nor adopt broad-based "human rights" campaigns at home, this new literature turns attention back to the countervailing influence of diplomatic and foreign policy pressures on changing formal U.S. behavior on human rights questions within its own jurisdiction.[158]

This influence cannot be ignored. Just as it was determinative in influencing the federal response to the U.S. civil rights movement in the 1950s and 1960s, when the international human rights regime was first emerging,[159] so, too, is it determinative today, fifty years later, as that regime has matured into a set of legitimacy-bestowing international instruments and institutions. Two intellectual camps have been most determinative in this regard, both heavily

---

[158] See, e.g., Mary L. Dudziak, *Cold War Civil Rights: Race and the Image of American Democracy* (Princeton University Press, 2000); Carol Anderson, *Eyes off the Prize: The United Nations and the African American Struggle for Human Rights, 1944–1955* (Cambridge University Press, 2003).

[159] *See* Dudziak, *op. cit.*, chaps. 3–5.

represented in the U.S. foreign policy establishment. They include groups broadly referred to as "realists" and "institutionalists."[160]

Realists include those who, following either classical or neo-structural versions of international relations' realism theory, understand State behavior as influenced by one of two realpolitik determinants: the raw power of a more powerful State or an objective expectation of material benefit, such as trade benefits, economic assistance, or debt reduction.[161] Realists in the U.S. foreign policy establishment thus tend to reject the usefulness of international institutions or norms, seeing them as mere window-dressing for real power and interest. They seek instead to preserve the unconstrained prerogative of the United States, as a world superpower, to protect national interests and respond to foreign threats by all available means, including unilateral power whenever necessary.

Institutionalists, on the other hand, see greater instrumental utility in engaging actively with both international institutions and global norms – including human rights norms. While they, too, believe that States act exclusively in accordance with their instrumental interest,[162] they see these interests as being increasingly interwoven with participation in international cooperative, peace-building, and dispute-resolution institutions.[163] U.S. engagement with international institutions thus constitutes for institutionalists an important and instrumental foreign policy tool for promoting and defending U.S. interests abroad, while conferring key reputational benefits, ever more salient in global politics particularly in the international human rights field.[164]

While realists dominated U.S. human rights policy during the Cold War,[165] and remain highly influential in the foreign policy establishment today, institutionalists have gained increasing prominence over the last two decades with the dramatic proliferation of international institutions and rapid expansion of the international human rights architecture. Within this context, the push-pull dynamic over U.S. human rights policy as a foreign policy objective has shifted

---

[160] For a brief overview of "realist" and "institutionalist" positions, see Murphy, *op. cit.*

[161] For influential classical accounts of realism, see, for example, Hans Morgenthau, *Politics Among Nations: The Struggle for Power and Peace* (New York: Alfred A. Knopf, 1948); and Kenneth Waltz, *Theory of International Politics* (McGraw-Hill 1979). More recent "neo realist" scholarship has sought to refine these classical understandings by drawing upon concepts in game theory and law and economics. See Jack Goldsmith & Eric Posner, *The Limits of International Law* (Oxford University Press, 2005).

[162] Harold Hongju Koh, *Why Do Nations Obey International Law*, 106 Yale L.J. 2599, 2649 (1997) (referring to both as "instrumental interest theories").

[163] *See, e.g.*, Robert O. Keohane, *After Hegemony: Cooperation and Discord in the World Political Economy* (Princeton University Press, 1984).

[164] Andrew T. Guzman, *A Compliance-Based Theory of International Law*, 90 Cal. L. Rev. 1823 (2002) (suggesting a reputation-based model of state compliance with international law).

[165] *See generally* Hartmann, *op. cit.*

determinatively toward institutionalists, those favoring active U.S. engagement with supranational human rights treaty regimes. For this group, human rights engagement serves two primary strategic foreign policy goals: first, renewal of U.S. moral leadership in multilateral settings and, second, promotion of human rights and democratic reforms in *other* countries. Both are directed to furthering national security and global public order objectives, independent of any domestic policy implication.

First, institutionalists appreciate that the international standing of U.S. diplomats and their ability to lead in international processes of global dispute resolution are compromised by the nation's failure to ratify core human rights instruments and engage in their supervisory procedures. This failure, which has left the nation increasingly in the formal company of rogue or failed states,[166] renders it out of step with its democratic partners and subjects it to charges of hypocrisy by less democratic nations where the United States seeks human rights improvements or security safeguards.[167] On a real and practical level, this impairs the United States' ability to get its national security and other global security priorities accomplished within multilateral settings, at times making disagreement with the United States a "principled" human rights stand in itself for nations.[168] In this sense, ratification and engagement

---

[166] The United States stands alongside Somalia, a nation lacking a functional government, as the only two nations among 194 UN Member States that have not ratified the Convention on the Rights of the Child. The United States likewise stands among only eight nation-states not to have ratified the CEDAW.

[167] *See*, e.g., Harold Hongju Koh, "Why America Should Ratify the Women's Rights Treaty (CEDAW)," 34 *Case W. Res. J. Int'l L.* 263, 269 (2002) [hereinafter Koh, *CEDAW*] ("[F]rom my direct experience as America's chief human rights official, I can testify that our continuing failure to ratify CEDAW has reduced our global standing, damaged our diplomatic relations, and hindered our ability to lead in the international human rights community.... In particular, our European and Latin American allies regularly question and criticize our isolation from this treaty framework both in public diplomatic settings and private diplomatic meetings.") (reflecting testimony to Congress); Statement of Patricia Derian, Assistant Secretary, Bureau of Human Rights and Humanitarian Affairs, Department of State, in U.S. Congress, Nov. 1979 (affirming to Senate Foreign Relations Committee that "failure...to ratify [ICCPR, ICESCR, CERD, and CAT] has a significant negative impact on the conduct of [U.S.] human rights policy," undermining its "credibility and effectiveness") (cited in Moravcsik, *op. cit.*, at 194).

[168] The United States has found that it is increasingly on the losing side of votes at the UN. U.S. representatives have, accordingly, recognized that the mere fact that the United States takes a strong stand on an issue may cause a number of states to vote against it, even if they have no independent interest in doing so. A recent illustration occurred in a 2006 vote in a UN treaty drafting committee regarding the inclusion of a politicized reference to "foreign occupation" in the treaty's preamble. Little support had been expressed in the drafting committee for the phrase outside of one regional block. Nonetheless, upon U.S. insistence on a state-by-state roll-call vote on the issue (in a treaty otherwise agreed to by consensus), the United States could garner the support of only four other nations. An overwhelming 102 states voted affirmatively to

serve as a tool through which the United States can reseat itself within the "international community," reassert its moral leadership role, and hence better promote its national security agenda in multilateral settings, where most international work gets done. For institutionalists, this has been a particular priority following the widely internationally condemned unilateral actions taken by the United States following the September 11 terrorist attacks.

The second factor, most commonly articulated by the U.S. State Department, involves recognition that full compliance by the United States with international human rights treaty body procedures increases the visibility and legitimacy of the procedures themselves, ratcheting up expectation levels for their regular and concerted use, and thereby prodding other states to take the procedures more seriously. Indeed, U.S. executive agencies recognize that human rights treaty bodies – by providing an international spotlight for gross abuses, giving voice to individuals and civil society groups seeking greater human rights protections and transparency at home, and providing legitimacy to domestic human rights and democracy movements – have initiated important conversations and processes in countries around the world, particularly in transitional states.[169] They also recognize that while the U.S. failure to ratify specific treaties has not likely caused other states to forego ratification, it may embolden some to turn ratification into an empty political act, used as a rhetorical device to claim greater commitment to human rights than the United States without making corresponding changes in their policies and practices at home.[170]

In this sense, although the foreign policy establishment may remain skeptical, or at best agnostic, about the usefulness of engagement for the United States' *domestic* human rights record, it nonetheless fully recognizes and values the importance of treaty body engagement for promoting human rights

---

retain the text, with 8 states abstaining. The dearth of support the United States could muster in an official UN vote of this nature sent an unmistakable message. A similar message was conveyed in the November 2006 General Assembly elections of members of the International Law Commission, the first such election in which the U.S. nominee failed to be elected to the international body. See ILC, *2006 election of the International Law Commission*, at http://untreaty.un.org/ilc/2006election.htm (visited Apr. 25, 2007).

[169] See White House, "National Security Strategy of the United States of America," Mar. 16, 2006 (supporting human rights treaty bodies as an explicit part of the U.S. National Security Strategy), at http://www.whitehouse.gov/nsc/nss/2006/nss2006.pdf (visited Apr. 20, 2007). In December 2006, the U.S. State Department issued "Guiding Principles on Non-Governmental Organizations," a set of ten principles to guide U.S. human rights policy around the world, in recognition that NGOs "are essential to the development and success of free societies and that they play a vital role in ensuring accountable, democratic government." See http://www.state.gov/g/drl/rls/77771.htm (visited Apr. 20, 2007).

[170] With respect to the frequency of treaty ratification as an empty political act, see generally Oona Hathaway, *Do Human Rights Treaties Make a Difference?*, 111 Yale L. J. 1935 (2002).

and democracy in *less democratically stable states*.[171] By actively and constructively engaging with these procedures – through high-level government participation, comprehensive reporting, well-prepared and legally argued oral and written interventions, civil society participation, and a high degree of transparency – the United States thus seeks, through its example, to encourage other states to do the same. It is, in this sense, constitutive of the United States' already heavy human rights investments in its broader national security agenda,[172] a key strategy for promoting good practices in *other* states and hence contributing to global security as a whole.[173]

These two general "push" factors appear to be the dominant influences motivating U.S. engagement policy with international treaty bodies. They are, however, blunted at the margins by certain "pull away" or "realist" tendencies. These, led by foreign-policy-focused national security entities, such as the National Security Council and Department of Defense – with the legal buttress of the U.S. Justice Department[174] – tend to be little concerned by most of what human rights tribunals do and hence have less interest in determining U.S. engagements with them. They are more concerned with the implications of U.S. engagement with *other* international courts and tribunals discussed in this volume, such as the International Criminal Court (ICC) or the International Court of Justice (ICJ),[175] that more directly touch on state-to-state national security and international defense prerogatives. This follows from the fact that human rights tribunals do not tend to deal directly with interstate or transjurisdictional disputes that may involve threats to national security or other interests emanating from abroad[176] – for which realists seek to maintain

---

[171] It serves, in this sense, to help restore a balance between ratifying nations whose formal treaty commitments find analogues in domestic policy and practice and those that do not.

[172] The United States invests heavily and plays an active role in promoting human rights abroad. This takes shape through its annual country reports on the human rights situation of 194 countries around the world, its substantial bilateral and multilateral aid, support of international human rights treaty bodies, and substantial diplomatic efforts.

[173] In this respect, although some note that U.S. *ratification* has little effect on other states' decision to ratify or not, *see* Moravcsik, *op. cit.* (finding little empirical evidence to support common claim), the level and scope of U.S. *participation* in treaty body processes or lack thereof can be expected to have a notable effect on the scope of other states' participation, given the ratchet-up effect it has on community expectations.

[174] The U.S. Department of Justice under the George W. Bush administration has played a central role in crafting legal arguments to resist international engagement and provide justification for "war on terror" policies that often put the United States at loggerheads with the rest of the world. In so doing, it has increasingly been at policy odds with the U.S. Department of State. *Cf.* Neil Lewis, "Justice Dept. under Obama Is Preparing for Doctrinal Shift in Policies of Bush Years," *New York Times*, Feb. 2, 2009, at A14.

[175] See chapters 6 and 4, respectively.

[176] Optional interstate complaint mechanisms, though rarely used, are in fact established under most human rights treaties. Notably, the United States has recognized the competence of the

a supple and unconstrained response capability. Rather, they deal exclusively with U.S. conduct vis-à-vis persons subject to its *own* jurisdiction. As such, the geopolitical calculations of engagement tend to be distinct from, and less sensitive than, those related to most other international tribunals.

Realist tendencies nonetheless recognize that too full an engagement with human rights treaty bodies might function in practice to constrain U.S. warmaking or defense functions, especially as exercised abroad. Foreign policy realists thus pull back in areas where this might occur. That is, whereas institutionalists, for the reasons noted earlier, tend to prevail on the question of engagement once treaty ratification has been effected, their realist counterparts play an important role in policing the boundaries of human rights supervision, "pulling back" against the institutionalists' "push forward" wherever human rights supervision may conceivably circumscribe U.S. national security discretion and war-related undertakings.

The United States has mediated these push-pull concerns by adopting an engagement policy that participates fully in human rights treaty body mechanisms, *except* to the extent they purport to address extraterritorial concerns or matters that overlap with international humanitarian law or the law of armed conflict. That is, the United States has adopted a foreign policy position that supports active U.S. engagement with human rights treaty bodies in all but these two sensitive areas defined as beyond the jurisdictional competence of international human rights supervision. Although these positions put the United States in an increasingly adversarial posture vis-à-vis human rights treaty bodies, given extraterritorial abuses committed in response to the 9/11 terrorist attacks and the U.S. war against Iraq and Afghanistan,[177] they may be seen as a core mediating technique between U.S. institutionalist and realist positions with respect to achieving its varied foreign policy objectives.

UN Human Rights Committee to examine interstate complaints against it under the ICCPR. *See* 138 Cong. Rec. S4781–01 (daily ed., April 2, 1992).

[177] The U.S. "pull-back" posture has the express effect of opening a space to which contested practices may be removed without the threat of supervisory censure by human rights treaty bodies. This has created growing international alarm as the United States has increasingly moved "war on terror" abuses off-shore, including the holding of "enemy combatants" in Guantanamo Bay, third-party states, and off-shore vessels, and engaged in the practice of extraordinary rendition. *See*, e.g., Margaret L. Satterthwaite, *Rendered Meaningless: Extraordinary Rendition and the Rule of Law*, 75 Geo. Wash. L. Rev. 1333 (2007).

Prior to the U.S. presentation of its second and third periodic report to the UN Human Rights Committee in July 2006, a member of the UN Committee lamented privately to this author the fact that the United States had not submitted its report on time, the report being due *before* the 9/11 attacks in 2001. Had the report been submitted on time, the Committee would not have had to focus so narrowly on the high-profile abuses in Guantanamo, Abu Graib, and other extraterritorial loci, and could have addressed itself more fully to the more general human rights issues affecting the U.S. population as a whole.

2. Domestic Policy Interests: From Pull to Push – The Evolution of Domestic Social Struggles

The foreign policy considerations just described have dominated in determining current U.S. engagement modalities with human rights treaty bodies over the last decade. The prior question of *whether* the United States will in fact ratify a given treaty, and thus open itself to treaty body engagement, remains a decision in which domestic politics are distinctly paramount. The push-pull dynamic on U.S. decision makers at this level functions not between foreign policy institutionalists and realists but between domestic groups we may term "insulationists" and "incorporationists." The former seek to *insulate* domestic law from the influence of international human rights constructions, finding a domestic environment free from human rights methodologies and migrations more amenable to achieving their substantive political policy preferences. They oppose U.S. ratification of human rights treaties and vigorously object to the use of human rights norms by domestic courts. Incorporationists, by contrast, find the mediating influence of international human rights law on domestic politics *helpful* to their domestic policy agenda, which generally favors broader individual rights interpretations, with fewer permissible restrictions. They thus seek to *incorporate* international human rights norms and human rights methodologies into domestic law and decision-making processes, through treaty ratification, local monitoring and interpretation initiatives, treaty body engagement, grassroots mobilization, judicial oversight, and direct implementing legislation at local, state, and federal levels.

This push-pull dynamic has played out in virtually every domestic social struggle since the international human rights regime first emerged sixty years ago. Thus, the civil rights era demands of incorporationists in the fifties and sixties for the federal government to ensure respect for internationally protected human rights guarantees of racial equality were quickly countered by insulationists' initiatives to launch "states' rights" movements,[178] red-baiting campaigns against rights advocates (and internationalism generally), and the fateful Bricker Amendment, a concerted attempt to constitutionally insulate domestic law from all treaty-related modifications.[179] These insulation initiatives, intersecting with Cold War politics, led to a series of actions and political

---

[178] These movements, which included the founding of a "states' rights" political party, sought to insulate local segregationist and abusive policies from the illumination of federal constitutional, statutory, and treaty law.

[179] For an animating description of the process through which the proposed constitutional amendment (and a watered-down version of it) failed, *see* Anderson, *op. cit*. Had it passed it still of course would have required approval in three-quarters of U.S. states to take effect. U.S. Const., art. V.

compromises that ensured that human rights remained off the domestic policy-making agenda for the next quarter century. Since the 1970s, this dynamic has played out with similar intensity over "family values," abortion, parental rights, and personal lifestyle-choice debates, with incorporationists seeking broad human rights statements from international treaty bodies to incorporate into domestic advocacy and litigation strategies and insulationists seeking to foreclose all reference by domestic legislatures and courts to international decisions or comparative rights jurisprudence.[180]

In this politicized struggle over the control of legal rights meaning, domestic policy insulationists – fewer in number but better in organization, funding, and insider/beltway political contacts – have historically been dominant.[181] The reasons for this, at least from the perspective of treaty ratification, are reviewed by Professor Moravcsik in his discussion of the "U.S. human rights paradox."[182] They center on two factors: first, the extreme decentralization and fragmentation of U.S. political institutions, which make them uniquely amenable to veto-group politics, and, second, a strong conservative minority that has consistently utilized veto players, most notably in the U.S. Senate, to achieve its insulationist agenda. Indeed, employing a culturally resonant rhetoric sounding in constitutional democracy, this minority has historically been successful in rallying partisan affiliates and mobilizing veto players to block ratification of human rights treaties, either by bottlenecking them in the Senate Foreign Relations Committee or by foreclosing the ability to achieve super-majority advice and consent in the full Senate.

The powerful political and financial lobby of these interest groups and their unique control over veto players in the political process – particularly over Republican majorities in the Senate – explain the U.S. historic failure to ratify human rights treaties apace with similarly minded nations, those equally committed to domestic human rights guarantees.[183] It nonetheless fails as a reliable explanatory framework for predicting U.S. human rights engagements in the twenty-first century. Such an explanation would have to

---

[180] *See*, e.g., H.R. Res. 568, 108th Cong. (2004); H.R. Res. 97, 109th Cong. (2005) (seeking to preclude domestic courts from referring to "judgments, laws, or pronouncements of foreign institutions" in determining the meaning of U.S. laws).

[181] Liberal advocacy and community-based groups readily recognize that they have been insufficiently successful in organizationally linking their grassroots campaigns and local support with beltway politics, and hence have had a much less effective influence in Washington than their numbers should indicate.

[182] *See* Moravcsik, *op. cit.*

[183] It also helps to explain why the United States, after ratifying the ICCPR, CERD, and CAT in 1992 and 1994, did not ratify the CRC and CEDAW from 1994 to 2006, when Republicans held majorities in the Senate and "family values" groups were actively lobbying beltway veto players against ratification.

account for three closely related facts: one, U.S. ratification of an increasingly broad spectrum of human rights treaties in the 1990s that failed, over time, to generate or sustain strong issue-specific oppositional lobbies (including the ICCPR, CERD, CAT, and child-protective labor rights treaties); two, active U.S. engagement in the international supervisory regimes corresponding to these treaties, including in areas of substantive overlap with nonratified treaties, such as the CRC, CEDAW, and ICESCR; and, three, the altered opportunity structure both of the above factors create for domestic advocates – that is, those pushing for greater engagement, and those pulling away from it – as they perpetually recreate and evolve their strategies to better achieve distinct substantive policy preferences in changing political environments.

That is, a fully explanatory description of U.S. human rights politics must account not only for the structural *potential* for mobilized political lobbies to block treaty ratification.[184] It must account as well for the shifting *incentive structure* for them to do so over time and the relative *receptivity* of the population (and hence potential veto players) to traditional insulationist arguments. As these environmental factors change, so too does the importance of "extreme decentralization" as a structural condition favoring – rather than disfavoring – insulation. At the same time, insulationism, like incorporationism, has always been an instrumental strategy for its proponents, supported to create a domestic political environment most conducive to particular policy agendas. As soon as it ceases to bring comparative advantage, it will be discarded and replaced by a new set of strategies and supporting ideologies. This is precisely what we are beginning to see today.

The United States is thus faced in the twenty-first century with a new set of domestic pressures in its human rights engagement policy. It is no longer exclusively a *push-pull* dynamic between "liberal" and "conservative" interest groups, with the latter consistently prevailing – as they did from the 1950s to 1980s – through their unique ability to block ratification of human rights treaties, and hence, together with a particular brand of politically-resonant rights absolutism, preempt human rights conversations from deepening domestically. Rather, with U.S. ratification of core human rights treaties in the 1990s, it is increasingly becoming a *push-push* dynamic in the twenty-first century. That is, liberal interest groups, true to their incorporationist heritage, continue to push for greater U.S. engagement with human rights treaties and treaty bodies as a means of bringing domestic law, policies, and practice more fully into line with internationally recognized human rights norms, norms

---

[184] The mere existence of a vocal conservative minority and institutional amenability to veto politics as a treaty-blocking option does not, in itself, speak to the *utility* of insulationist strategies to the conservative political agenda.

they have spent decades constructing.[185] Conservative interest groups, for their part, faced with a growing incorporationist reality, have increasingly realized that insulationism alone may not be helpful to their agendas, particularly as they relate to lifestyle, personal choice, and "family values" issues. Many such groups are thus urging the United States not to *dis*engage with international human rights bodies but rather to *engage* more fully – albeit with a distinct agenda. That is, they do not seek the *domestication* of presently recognized international norms, as do liberals, but rather – in a strategic reversal of process – the *internationalization* of socially conservative rights constructions more amenable to their domestic policy agenda, which may then be subject to incorporation at some later date. Where opportunities emerge, traditional insulationists are increasingly using partisan political connections to press the U.S. diplomatic (and legislative) corps to undertake this agenda on their behalf.[186]

Because this transition is so important for understanding current U.S. human rights politics, it is useful to highlight the constitutive processes that led to it. The techniques the United States adopts to mediate between these dueling push-push pressures will be taken up more fully in Part D.

I. Diminishing U.S. Receptivity to Insulationism

Historically, insulationism has been employed by socially and politically conservative interest groups as a way to bypass the mobilizing influence of human rights law on those wishing to effect equality or dignity-based change in the U.S. social structure. Because such change is rhetorically consistent with the promise of the U.S. Constitution – indeed, with the country's national narrative[187] – it has been necessary to create an ideational structure that pits international human rights law against U.S. constitutional democracy, framing the former as undemocratic and even anti-American. This is possible through a rhetorical manipulation of international human rights law that equates it with absolutist, externally defined policy outcomes, intrinsically and automatically superior to domestic determinations. In fact, both sides of the political spectrum have tended to rely on *rights-absolutist* constructions to appeal to their respective constituencies, one side affirming that international treaty law

---

[185] Notably, they have often helped construct these norms in the mold of strong U.S. constitutional rights protections.
[186] *See*, for example, discussion in Part C.2.III *infra*.
[187] *See* Jack M. Balkin, "*Brown* as Icon," in Balkin ed., *What "Brown v. Board of Education" Should Have Said* 5 (NYU Press, 2001) (describing as the "Great Progressive Narrative" that "widely held and often repeated story of deep resonance in American culture, which sees America's basic ideals of liberty and equality as promises for the future to be achieved eventually through historical struggle").

requires the immediate modification of domestic law to conform strictly to international treaty body views and policy preferences, the other that international law constructions conflict with deliberative democracy at home.

It is in fact precisely this rights absolutism that is responsible for the contentiousness of human rights treaty law engagements in U.S. domestic politics and, specifically, the historic ability of veto politics to successfully block human rights treaty ratifications. That is, opponents have mobilized influential veto players by representing human rights law as a doctrine of foreign-determined meaning imposed on nonconsenting domestic populations. Nationalistic urgency is then tied to ratification-blocking campaigns by asserting that ratification will force the United States to adopt a set of externally defined policies that are morally or socially objectionable to a large segment of the population. Although this once took the form of imagining UN bodies as communist-inspired institutions that would force communities to desegregate their schools, eateries, pools, and public accommodations and lead to widespread miscegenation[188] – issues that could mobilize powerful domestic constituencies against ratification – it now asserts that adhesion to currently unratified human rights treaties, such as the CRC and CEDAW, will require immediate mandatory legalization of same-sex marriage, provision of abortion and contraception on demand, decriminalization of prostitution, the turning over of child rearing to the state, and other measures that could not currently be achieved through national-level democratic processes alone.[189]

It is this caricatured vision of human rights treaty law – one permitting of no national discretion in the crafting of "appropriate" policies – that gives rise and animating force to "national sovereignty," "states' rights," and other "rights-cultural" objections.[190] These objections, although plainly instrumental given

---

[188] *See*, for example, William Fleming, *Danger to America: The Draft Covenant on Human Rights*, 37 A.B.A. Journal 739, 794-99 (1951) (claiming that the Draft Covenant on Human Rights is the "perfect embodiment of... unmitigated socialism"); Frank E. Holman, *International Proposals Affecting So-Called Human Rights*, 14 Law & Contemp. Probs. 479, 483 (1949 (claiming that the Universal Declaration of Human Rights will force the United States to allow interracial marriages).

[189] The same strategy has been used with the Equal Rights Amendment to the U.S. Constitution, with opponents arguing in the 1970s that it would lead to women being drafted by the military and to public unisex bathrooms. Today it is warned that its passage would compel courts to approve same-sex marriage and deny Social Security benefits for housewives and widows. *See* Juliet Eilperin, "New Drive Afoot to Pass Equal Rights Amendment," *Washington Post*, Mar. 28, 2007, A1, A4 (citing arguments of Eagle Forum President Phyllis Schlafly and other conservative opponents); *see also* Phyllis Schlafly, *Time to Unsign CEDAW* (Feb. 14, 2007) at http://www.eagleforum.org/column/2007/feb07/07–02-14.html (visited Apr. 20, 2007).

[190] It also gives rise to academic critiques of human rights advocacy. *See*, e.g., David W. Kennedy, *The International Human Rights Movement: Part of the Problem?* 15 Harv. Hum. Rts. J. 99 (2001).

the subsidiary structure of human rights law, have high political traction in the U.S. popular mind-set and hence are effective mobilizing tools for capturing key veto players to block ratification when perceived as politically advantageous.

This blocking process reliably works, however, only to the extent a politically influential minority can be convinced, or can convince core constituencies, of two critical factors with respect to any given human rights treaty: one, that ratification will compel the immediate adoption of laws and policies determined by *external* (not domestic) decision makers; and, two, that such policies are socially or morally repugnant or otherwise contrary to group interests. Both propositions have become increasingly difficult to sustain over the past decade, as the U.S. ratification record reveals.

First, the idea that human rights treaty ratification will compel the United States blindly to adopt externally defined policies is today unsupportable. As a legal matter, the United States has removed all basis for doubt over the issue by adopting the consistent practice of attaching non-self-execution clauses to human rights treaties upon ratification.[191] Such clauses stipulate that any change to domestic law required by international treaty commitments must be implemented through the *ordinary legislative process*, in which federal, state, and local voices may all be heard, not through direct judicial constructions unmediated by "deliberative democracy."[192] This policy, directly responsive to rights-absolutist constructions that sustain "states' rights" and "national sovereignty" rhetoric, effectively removes the key mobilizing rationale behind policy-driven opposition to ratification initiatives.[193] At the same time, it has become increasingly clear, as a factual matter, that U.S. ratification of the ICCPR, CERD, CAT, ILO Convention 182, and the two CRC optional protocols – and submission to the jurisdiction of their supervisory treaty bodies – has not forced the United States to adopt extremist policies that were not fully vetted by domestic political processes. There is no reason to believe that this

---

[191] In providing its advice and consent to the ICCPR in 1992, for example, the Senate declared that "the provisions of Article 1 through 27 of the Covenant are not self-executing." 138 Cong. Rec. S4781, at S4784 (1992). The Senate stated that the declaration was meant "to clarify that the Covenant will not create a private cause of action in U.S. Courts." S. Rep. No. 102-23, at 15 (1992).

[192] In its decision in *Medellín v. Texas*, 128 S. Ct. 1346 (2008) the Supreme Court appeared to adopt a different, more expansive interpretation of non-self-execution that does not conform to the Senate's stated intent in attaching such clauses to human rights treaties. *Medellín*, 128 S. Ct. at n.2.

[193] This concern over direct judicial enforcement of human rights treaty law tends to be the principal objection of opponents of U.S. human rights incorporation. *See*, e.g., Jack Goldsmith, *Should International Human Rights Law Trump U.S. Domestic Law?* 1 Chi. J. Int'l L. 327 (2000).

will not likewise be true with U.S. ratification of additional treaties, such as the CRC, CEDAW, CRPD, and the ICESCR.

Second, given broad social, cultural, and attitudinal changes in the United States over the last two decades, domestic policy changes claimed to be required by human rights treaty ratification simply are not sufficiently unpalatable to U.S. interest groups in the twenty-first century to sustain veto politics for all but a small number of content-specific treaties. Such treaties are generally those associated with women and children's role in the family and their access to contraception, abortion, and "integral health services." These issues – like those on sexual orientation, marriage, prayer, and Israel – are those on which socially conservative minority groups continue to hold powerful domestic sway.[194] This narrowing environment in which veto politics can effectively function follows from the changing interest politics and shifting political alliances that social struggle and norm internalization have brought with time. Indeed, as the principal social struggles turned in the past half-century from race and Cold War divisions to "moral values" and "lifestyle choice" issues, old social alliances broke down and the treaty-opposition agenda narrowed, becoming more issue specific and less capable of mobilizing influential players across broad social sectors.[195] At the same time, many politically and financially influential domestic groups – such as the U.S. business and legal communities – that once reliably opposed incorporation have today become, for a diversity of self-interested and non-self-interested motivations, active proponents of U.S. ratification of human rights treaties.[196] The U.S. business community, for example, has taken energetic part in ILO treaty drafting processes (particularly where child labor protections are at issue), actively lobbying the Senate Foreign Relations Committee for speedy ratification and attaining it even under strong Senate Republican majorities.[197]

---

[194] Significantly, this sway was magnified in the eight years of the George W. Bush presidency, given the special access such groups had to the White House and formal positions of power.

[195] Interestingly, it has necessitated that many conservative groups, long opposed to internationalism, have had to extend their strategic embrace to like-minded allies beyond domestic borders.

[196] The American Bar Association was a powerful and highly influential opponent of human rights treaties in the late forties and fifties, see, e.g., Fleming, op. cit. (citing arguments of the ABA President); it today actively supports ratification of CEDAW, CRC, ICESCR, and the American Convention, albeit with a standard set of reservations, understandings and declarations (RUDs).

[197] This was true with both ILO Convention 182 and the two optional protocols to the CRC, each ratified under Republican Senate majorities with the support of the U.S. business community. See, e.g., "U.S. Business Community's Letter to the Senate Foreign Relations Committee: ILO Convention on the Worst Forms of Child Labor", Sept. 23, 1999, at http://www.uscib.org/index.asp?documentID=1352 (visited Apr. 20, 2007) (providing reasons U.S. business

Given the nature of the U.S. political structure, these shifting alliances have led to a predictable outcome. With broad national support for human rights treaty ratification generally, targeted pro-ratification lobbying by certain influential groups, and veto players mobilizable only with respect to limited "family value" subject matters, the United States proceeded to ratify the ICCPR, CERD, CAT, and a variety of labor and child rights treaties in the 1990s and early 2000s. It will not be long before additional treaties are ratified, particularly where coordinated civil society ratification campaigns intersect with Democratic control of the U.S. Senate, as will be the case in at least 2009 and 2010.

II. Creeping Incorporation, Despite Insulationist Obstruction

At the same time, it has become increasingly clear that strategies focused on insulation alone – most notably, ratification blocking and the inclusion of a standard package of reservations, understandings, declarations with treaty ratification[198] – are no longer reliable in insulating the U.S. domestic system from human rights methodologies and migrations. This has resulted from the many innovative and constantly adapting strategies undertaken by incorporationists over the years, designed to circumvent the blocking potential of traditional insulationist tactics. Whereas these traditional tactics have focused on *top-down* insulation, mobilizing federal veto players through rhetorical appeals to states' rights and federalism-based safeguards on localized experimentation, the new incorporationist strategies seek in fact to operationalize these appeals: they start at the grassroots and *incorporate upward*. In this regard, it is important to underscore that while "extreme decentralization" or "political fragmentation" has been identified as a structural factor of the U.S. political system that favors *top-down insulation*,[199] it is – just as critically – a structural factor of the U.S. political system that favors *filter-up incorporation*.[200] The

---

community, including U.S. Chamber of Commerce and Business Roundtable, supports U.S. ratification). The U.S. business community has also become a strong and influential supporter of universal health insurance in the United States. *See*, e.g., Jonathan Cohn, "What's the One Thing Big Business and the Left Have in Common?" *New York Times*, April 1, 2007.

[198] For the package of Reservations, Understandings, and Declarations (RUDs) under the CERD, ICCPR, and CAT, see 140 Cong. Rec. S7634–02 (daily ed., June 24, 1994), 138 Cong. Rec. S4781–01 (daily ed., April 2, 1992), and Cong. Rec. S17486–01 (daily ed., Oct. 27, 1990). Of course, not all RUDs are aimed at insulation; many are required by constitutional constraints and are fully consistent, in both letter and spirit, with international law.

[199] *See* Moravcsik, "The Paradox of U.S. Human Rights Policy," *op. cit.*, at 186–90, 197.

[200] In view of this in the judicial field, William Brennan famously called on state courts to continue to expand strong individual rights protections under state constitutions, given federal judicial

ability of the two in our Madisonian democracy to "resist and frustrate the measures of the other"[201] has been one of the defining characteristics of U.S. human rights politics from the late twentieth to early twenty-first centuries. This can be seen in a wide variety of modern incorporationist tactics.

First, with ratification of certain domestically popular human rights treaties impeded at the federal level by veto politics, incorporationists have gone straight to their local and state governments seeking direct localized incorporation, with growing success rates. With respect to CEDAW and the CRC, for example, governmental bodies in scores of U.S. states, territories, cities, and localities have adopted resolutions or instruments endorsing the conventions or adopting them on behalf of their jurisdictions.[202] These initiatives have at times been accompanied by innovative community-based supervision and other follow-up procedures to monitor local-level progress in achieving treaty-related commitments and to ensure implementation of locally relevant solutions to the problems identified. Initiatives in San Francisco,[203] Berkeley,[204]

"backsliding" in the 1970s. William J. Brennan, Jr., *State Constitutions and the Protection of Individual Rights*, 90 Harv. L. Rev. 489–504 (1977).

[201] "Federalist 46" (James Madison) (discussing U.S. federal structure); *cf.* Moravcsik, *op. cit.*, at 197 ("The institutional odds against any fundamental change [in U.S. human rights policy] in Madison's republic are high.")

[202] *See*, e.g., Chicago City Council, Resolution (Feb. 11, 2009) (resolving to "advance policies and practices [that] are in harmony with the principles of the Convention on the Rights of the Child in all city [sic] and organizations that address issues directly affecting the City's children."); Koh, CEDAW, *op. cit.*, at 274 and nn. 48–50 ("Far from CEDAW imposing unwanted obligations on local governments, local governments are in fact responding to the demands of their citizens, who have become impatient at the lack of federal action to implement these universal norms into American law.").

[203] For a copy of the San Francisco city ordinance, see San Francisco, Cal., Administrative Code, ch. 12K (2001), at http://www.sfgov.org/site/uploadedfiles/cosw/cedaw/pdf/appenda.pdf (visited Apr. 20, 2007). The San Francisco initiative represents an experiment in localized replication of UN periodic reporting, constructive dialogue, and expert recommendation processes. It specifically establishes a local CEDAW Task Force, composed of eleven elected representatives from both government and civil society, to work with the Human Rights Commission and city departments to identify discrimination against women and girls and to implement human rights principles at the city level. For related documents, *see* http://www.sfgov.org/site/dosw_page.asp?id=19725 (visited Apr. 20, 2007). *See generally* Stacy Laira Lozner, *Diffusion of Local Regulatory Innovations: The San Francisco CEDAW Ordinance and the New York City Human Rights Initiative*, 104 Colum. L. Rev. 768 (2004).

[204] On February 27, 2007, the Berkeley City Council adopted a resolution requiring the city manager to supervise a periodic reporting process on the city's progress in eliminating racial discrimination, in accordance with the CERD. *See* Resolution No. 63,596-N.S. Eliminating Racial Discrimination. The Office of the City Manager thereupon created a template and sent it to every city agency in Berkeley seeking information on racial discrimination. The first Berkeley City report, submitted on June 26, 2007, was likewise to be sent to the UN CERD Committee in anticipation of its February 2008 review of the United States as a whole, as well as the attorney general of California.

New York City,[205] Pennsylvania,[206] and Massachusetts[207] have been particularly noteworthy, although forms of localized human rights incorporation are apparent at the grassroots throughout the country.[208] City and state governments are, in response, increasingly taking a human-rights-based approach to community problem solving, including with respect to the few treaties that vocal conservative minorities continue to be able to block at the federal level.[209]

Second, even where federal ratification is attained, non-self-execution clauses have posed a prima facie, if often overstated, dilemma for domestic human rights advocates. These jurisdictional clauses bar domestic courts from entertaining private causes of action arising directly under treaty law, requiring instead that independent causes of action be identified under U.S. statutory,

---

[205] In New York City, a bill was introduced to the city council in late 2004 to turn CEDAW and CERD into statewide principles of governance, to be interpreted and applied by state and city human rights commissions with competence over local disputes, reported on by city government, and periodically reviewed by a city task force. See Bill, Int. 512-A "New York City Human Rights Government Operations Audit Law." The bill would require that city government departments and programs review their policies and programs to determine their effects on women and racial minorities and report on those impacts for review by a city task force. For information on the New York City Human Rights Initiative, http://www.nychri.org/frame.html (visited Apr. 20, 2007). The bill is up for reintroduction in 2009.

[206] In 2002, the Pennsylvania House of Representatives passed a resolution establishing a House committee to "study and investigate the integration of human rights standards in Pennsylvania's laws and policies." See House Resolution 473 (2002). In 2003, House Resolution No. 144 reestablished the select committee to continue its work. Public hearings were held throughout the state on the rights to health, housing, employment, transportation, and nutrition, and the House Select Committee's conclusions and recommendations were issued on November 30, 2004.

[207] In Massachusetts, House Bill No. 706 was proposed in 2005 to establish a special commission to review the integration of international human rights standards into the commonwealth's laws and policies. It would authorize the state legislature to investigate human rights abuses through a series of public hearings, drawing conclusions and making recommendations for changes in state and local policy.

[208] In Chicago, for example, a local city council adopted a right-to-housing bill that brought in significant federal dollars. "National truth commissions" or "community hearings" to expose locally identified deficiencies in U.S. policies and practices vis-à-vis core human rights instruments have also been undertaken locally around the country. See, e.g., Poor Peoples' Economic Human Rights Campaign, National Truth Commission: Shining a Light on Poverty in the USA, at http://www.economichumanrights.org/ntc_report1.shtml (visited Apr. 20, 2007). Efforts at local periodic reporting on human rights compliance are also being advanced in Portland, Oregon, and Milwaukee, Wisconsin.

[209] This is particularly true with respect to CEDAW and the CRC. The United States has also not ratified the ICESCR and American Convention. The reasons, however, do not appear to be veto politics but simply the lack of any organized domestic constituency pushing strongly for ratification of either. That is, although there is no vocal minority actively obstructing ratification, neither is there yet any strong domestic advocacy movement pushing for ratification.

constitutional, or common law. Incorporationists have responded by increasingly pressing domestic courts to apply human rights treaty law not directly, but rather indirectly – used as a nonbinding interpretive aid or source of persuasive authority in discerning meaning under independent private causes of action.[210] U.S. courts, with their long historical pedigree of reference to international law, foreign practice, and foreign court judgments, have often been willing to adopt this approach, particularly with respect to state and federal constitutional provisions that are direct analogues to treaty-based norms, such as due process and cruel and unusual treatment or punishment.[211] State courts, the principal protagonists in cooperative judicial federalism, may be especially amenable to such human rights migrations in interpreting state constitutional guarantees. This is particularly true where such guarantees have been directly influenced in their drafting by international human rights law[212] or where they include normative protection for rights – such as those to health, education, welfare, or human dignity – that have no direct federal constitutional parallels and thus for which comparative foreign law and human rights sources are particularly useful.[213] Although insulationist resistance to this judicial methodology remains sharp,[214] the movement toward greater U.S. judicial reliance on transjurisdictional human rights dialogues is unmistakable; it represents an area of growing U.S. human rights incorporation of ratified, and even unratified, treaty law.[215]

---

[210] In the U.S. Supreme Court's 2006 term, all nine justices endorsed the view that treaty interpretations by international tribunals were entitled to "respectful consideration" by U.S. courts. *Sanchez-Llamas v. Oregon*, 126 S.Ct. 2669, 2683 (2006); *id.* at 2700 (Breyer, J., dissenting).

[211] *See, e.g.*, Cleveland, *op. cit.*; Jackson, "Constitutional Comparisons," *op. cit.* at 109 ("references to foreign and international sources occur episodically in constitutional decisions throughout the [Supreme] Court's history"); Harold Hongju Koh, *International Law as Part of Our Law*, 98 Am. J. Int'l L. 43, 43–45 (2004); Gerald L. Neuman, *The Uses of International Law in Constitutional Interpretation*, 98 Am. J. Int'l L. 82, 83–84) (2004).

[212] *See, e.g.*, Vicki Jackson, *Constitutional Dialogue and Human Dignity: States and Transnational Constitutional Discourse*, 65 Mont. L. Rev. 15, 21–27 (2004) (describing influence of Universal Declaration of Human Rights on text of Montana Constitution).

[213] *See, e.g.*, Martha F. Davis, *The Spirit of Our Times: State Constitutions and International Human Rights*, 30 N.Y.U. Rev. L. & Soc. Change 359 (2006).

[214] This resistance was perhaps most powerfully manifested in two resolutions introduced to the U.S. House of Representatives in 2004 and 2005, respectively, although neither came to a full vote. Each expressed the sense of their cosponsors that "judicial determinations regarding the meaning of the laws of the United States should not be based on judgments, laws, or pronouncements of foreign institutions unless such foreign judgments, laws, or pronouncements inform an understanding of the original meaning of the laws of the United States." H.R. Res. 568, 108th Cong. (2004), at http://thomas.loc.gov/cgi-bin/query/D?c108:1:./temp/~mdbsmtQvNi:: (visited Apr. 20, 2007); H.R. Res. 97, 109th Cong. (2005), at http://thomas.loc.gov/cgi-bin/query/D?c109:2:./temp/~mdbsmtQvNi:: (visited Apr. 20, 2007).

[215] The methodology, given the noncontrolling nature of its inputs, allows domestic judges to draw not only on the growing set of international human rights treaty norms that the

Third, as with non-self-execution clauses, incorporationists have not been deterred by declarations or understandings attached to human rights treaties upon ratification that purport to affirm that U.S. laws are fully in compliance with treaty norms and hence require no modification. Rather, incorporationists have persistently used treaty body procedures – particularly periodic reporting and contentious complaints – to draw attention to perceived gaps and deficiencies in U.S. law, policies, and practices and to press government officials to respond to identified problems within a human rights framework. They have done so by working not only to attain strong issue-specific conclusions and recommendations from treaty bodies but, most important, to then ensure that those conclusions and recommendations are effectively addressed through increasingly institutionalized mechanisms and participatory processes at federal, state, and local levels. At the same time, "shadow report" procedures that accompany periodic reporting processes[216] are now regularly used by incorporationists as a teaching and awareness-raising tactic, employed as a means to train local communities in how to use human rights methodologies and understandings to address problems of local concern and to frame dialogues with governmental entities. The grassroots analyses produced from shadow reporting exercises are then used not only for formal reporting purposes in Geneva[217] but, most significantly, for pressing local, state, and federal officials for meaningful, socially relevant reforms in domestic communities.

Finally, the continued success of federal veto politics in blocking certain treaties, such as the CEDAW and CRC, that raise sensitive issues for socially conservative minorities has not stopped domestic advocates from using international treaty body supervision to engage those very same issues, albeit under

---

United States has ratified – including their case-specific interpretations by treaty bodies and foreign courts in factually-similar cases – but also norms that the United States has not ratified but that are widely seen as legitimate guiding principles for the conduct of nations, such as those in the Universal Declaration of Human Rights (UDHR) or CEDAW. *See generally* Jackson, "Constitutional Comparisons," *op. cit.* at 111 (noting several U.S. Supreme Court opinions between 1949 and 1970 referring to UDHR).

[216] "Shadow reports" are parallel reports to the official treaty body reports prepared by the U.S. government. They aim to highlight and correct misstatements or generalizations in official U.S. reports; fill in overlooked areas with accurate facts, details, and statistics; and generally present an alternative view for the expert UN committee to consider in assessing U.S. progress and setbacks in human rights enjoyment under the supervised treaty and in making recommendations for improvements.

[217] The U.S. Human Rights Network has played an important role in coordinating the large numbers of domestic advocates who travel to Geneva to participate in the supervisory process, both by consolidating issue-specific and local shadow reports into a single accessible U.S. NGO report and in coordinating advocates in making timely, effective statements to the UN committees and in presenting appropriate information that is easily accessible to Committee experts as they question U.S. representatives.

other treaties. Pressed by civil society advocates, the UN Human Rights Committee, Torture Committee, and Racial Discrimination Committee thus regularly question U.S. representatives – who provide detailed responses – on the measures taken to give legal effect to rights related to women's reproductive health and safety, gender violence, children's rights abuses, discrimination in housing, education, health care, indigenous land rights, and employment, as well as to the disparate impacts of a wide range of U.S. policies on grounds of race, ethnicity, age, sex, religion, and sexual-orientation.

There are in fact virtually no substantive issues arising under the CEDAW, CRPD, CRC, or ICESCR that cannot in some way be addressed under the ICCPR, CERD, and CAT supervisory procedures. The same is true of the contentious individual complaints procedure supervised by the Inter-American Commission on Human Rights, which allows complaints to be lodged against the United States with respect to the full spectrum of internationally recognized rights. Incorporationist strategies have thus altered in fundamental ways the incentive structure that has historically justified mobilizing veto players to block certain treaties. Today, that incentive structure has largely been reversed: given U.S. commitments under the ICCPR, CERD, CAT, ILO treaties, and the American Declaration, there is little functional reason to oppose – and growing functional reasons to support – U.S. ratification of the CEDAW, CRPD, CRC, ICESCR, and the American Convention.[218]

III. Responding to Incorporation's Advances: Reappropriating Rights

This just-described reality has fundamentally changed the political environment in which traditional opponents of treaty ratification pursue their own domestic policy agenda, complicating their efforts to cordon off the domestic legal system from international interpretations that might differ from their preferred views. Many appear to be realizing that old strategies focused on ratification blocking alone are insufficient and that failure to reassess their strategies may mean missing out on critical agenda-advancing opportunities. Such interest groups have thus appeared increasingly to focus critical energies on ensuring that new international agreements reflect their interests and agendas at the drafting stage.

---

[218] This is particularly true with respect to the American Convention nonratification of which insulates the United States from no new obligations but rather serves only to prevent the United States from nominating and electing U.S. nationals to serve as judges on the Inter-American Court of Human Rights. This follows from the close substantive parallels between the American Declaration and American Convention and the fact that the Court's jurisdiction is not mandatory upon ratification of the Convention; a separate opt-in instrument must be filed with the OAS. *See* American Convention, *op. cit.*, art. 62.

The most notable of these shifts involves the increasingly active participation of traditionally insulationist NGOs in international human rights fora. Many such groups now have a regular and active lobby at UN meetings and conferences, especially those related to women, children, health, and family structure. A strong, but single, example has been the drafting negotiations behind the new UN Convention on the Rights of Persons with Disabilities (CRPD), in which the U.S.-based "pro-life" movement maintained a highly visible presence and sustained political lobby over the four-and-a-half years of the treaty's negotiation. It did so with a core aim of reshaping the international meaning of rights-based terms related to reproduction, family, child rearing, and "life," using political affinities within the Bush administration to compel the U.S. government to pursue its policy agenda in the negotiation process.

In fact, although the United States announced at the start of the treaty-drafting process in 2003 that it did not intend to participate actively in the negotiating process,[219] under sustained pressure from socially conservative activist groups it changed course at the penultimate session in early 2006. The United States announced the reason for its reentry as a manifestation of its strong interest in shaping the terms of the new human rights treaty – principally out of its long-term interest in ensuring the strength and consistency of international law as a general matter, but also, specifically, to avoid the inclusion of any language that might be substantively objectionable to the United States.[220] The actual textual amendments proposed by the U.S. delegation, however, spoke more forthrightly to its immediate motivations. These included: strengthened language on the role of the family in dependent caregiving; the deletion of references to "health services," a term understood by antiabortion groups as an international code word for abortion services; and the insertion of "and worth" after each treaty reference to "inherent dignity," a proposal associated with the embrace of the human fetus within the protective scope of human rights law. It also included the addition of a new draft

---

[219] The United States provided oral testimony essentially declaring no need for an international instrument given the availability of national laws prohibiting discrimination on the basis of disability and declared its intention not to ratify the Convention. *See* Boyd Statement, *op. cit.* ("It is the position of the United States today that . . . the most constructive way to proceed is for each Member State, through action and leadership at home, to pursue within its borders the mission of ensuring that real change and real improvement is brought to their citizens with disabilities. Thus we hope to participate in order to share our experiences . . . but given our comprehensive domestic laws protecting those with disabilities, not with the expectation that we will become party to any resulting legal instrument.").

[220] This official change of policy was declared and explained by the U.S. delegation in public-information side meetings at the Seventh Session of the Ad Hoc Committee charged with negotiating the treaty text. This author served as UN representative of a U.S.-based disability organization in the treaty drafting process.

article – the first of its kind in international human rights law – guaranteeing a right not to be denied food or fluids when dependent on life support, a thinly disguised attempt to internationalize the Terri Schiavo case in human rights terms.[221] While the United States failed to achieve sufficient support for removal of "health services," it did succeed in getting substantial textual revisions to the health and family provisions, the addition of "and worth," as well as inclusion of the essence of its food and hydration provision.[222]

On the basis of these successes, the conservative NGO movement has intimated support for U.S. ratification of the CRPD. At a minimum, it has signaled that the time for wholesale rejection of international human rights law has passed. In speaking of the CRPD, a conservative commentator recently wrote in the *Weekly Standard*:

> Can anything good come out of the United Nations? Actually, yes... The positive impact [of conservative NGO participation in the CRPD drafting negotiations] teaches a valuable lesson. Many conservative organizations eschew obtaining NGO status with the United Nations because they loathe internationalism, disdain the U.N., and expect America not to be bound by these agreements.
>
> But such standoffishness is woefully shortsighted. Like it or not, many of the most important social and legal policies of the twenty-first century are going to be materially influenced by international protocols such as this one. These agreements are molded substantially behind the scenes by NGOs – most of which are currently leftist in their political outlooks and relativistic in their social orientation. This makes for a stacked deck. *If conservatives hope to influence the moral values of the future, they are going to have to hold their collective noses and get into the game.*[223]

We should increasingly expect to see this: a more active engagement by traditionally insulationist NGOs in the construction of normative meaning at the international level – accompanied by more vigorous pressure on

---

[221] This author monitored all UN Member State proposals as they were made. Although the U.S. drafting proposals had partisan undertones and derivations, the United States played a positive role overall in mediating diverse international interests within the negotiations. Its renewed participation in the drafting process in 2006 was welcomed by all governments and civil society actors.

[222] The much longer draft provision was, in a final compromise deal, significantly condensed and consolidated into a subprovision of the right-to-health article, which reads: "States Parties shall:... (f) Prevent discriminatory denial of health care or health services or food and fluids on the basis of disability."

[223] Wesley J. Smith, "A Worthwhile U.N. Initiative! A Welcome Defense of the Disabled from an Unlikely Organization," *Weekly Standard*, Jan. 29, 2007, Vol. 12, Issue 19.

sympathetic U.S. officials to engage human rights organs in pursuit of this norm-reappropriation agenda.[224]

Such a policy was in fact almost adopted twenty-five years ago by the U.S. antiabortion movement, which – given a legally and politically unamenable domestic environment – came close to converting to incorporationism. Indeed, whereas states' rights and other insulationist arguments prevailed in the 1950s and 1960s, when race and poverty were the dominant social struggles and human rights law clearly favored desegregation and racial equality initiatives, the political climate shifted in the 1970s, as the cultural wars transitioned toward Vietnam, women's rights, and lifestyle choices. Specifically, in the loosened political climate of the seventies, "rights cultural" or "states' rights" arguments no longer served the substantive policy agenda of opponents of abortion, contraception, and alternative family structures. These groups increasingly found themselves on the losing side of both *federal* and *state* legislation and high court decisions.

Consequently, in 1977, sensing a potential opportunity in the U.S. signature that year of the American Convention on Human Rights, the U.S. antiabortion movement turned to international human rights law. Catholics for Christian Political Action and Lawyers for Life filed a contentious complaint, *Baby Boy v. United States*, with the Inter-American Commission on Human Rights on behalf of an aborted fetus, alleging that domestic abortion law, at state and federal levels alike, violated international human rights law.[225] Specifically, they saw strategic potential in the American Convention's guarantee of the "right to life," a legal protection that, according to Article 4 of the treaty's text, begins "in general, *from the moment of conception*." Drawing on this favorable provision (sans the introductory qualifier), the U.S. antiabortion petitioners asserted that an absolute prohibition on abortion, permitting of no restrictions, was mandated by the United States' international law commitments and that

---

[224] As an example of U.S. officials carrying out conservative social movement agendas abroad, two conservative members of the U.S. House of Representatives went so far as to send a letter to the Special Rapporteur on the Rights of Women of the Inter-American Commission on Human Rights in early 2007, in anticipation of the Rapporteur's scheduled trip to Nicaragua to meet with women's groups and the government. In it, the Special Rapporteur was instructed not to discuss a legislative bill then before the Nicaraguan Congress that proposed adding life and health exceptions to the country's comprehensive abortion ban, threatening cuts to U.S. financial support of the Inter-American Commission if he did.

[225] Specifically, petitioners alleged that the United States was in violation of "Baby Boy's" right to life given its failure to respond appropriately to the Massachusetts Supreme Court's 1977 acquittal of a manslaughter conviction of the treating doctor and, by extension, the U.S. Supreme Court's 1973 decision in *Roe v. Wade* and *Doe v. Bolton*. See "Baby Boy" v. United States, Res. 23/81, Case 2141, Inter-Am. Comm. H.R. (Mar. 6, 1981),

the United States was legally bound to follow this international construction of rights-based meaning.

Had the U.S. antiabortion movement won this case, its activists would undoubtedly have demanded that U.S. law submit to the authoritative and final conclusions of international human rights treaty bodies. As it turns out, they lost. The Inter-American Commission, over two dissents, agreed with the U.S. government's position that the right to life does not mandate an absolute prohibition on abortion but rather allows for reasonable restrictions in line with domestic political choices.[226] By the time the 4–2 decision was issued in 1981, however, the political winds had again shifted in the United States and, with Ronald Reagan in the presidency, the domestic political climate had become distinctly amenable to the conservative "family values" policy agenda. Consequently, the mantle of "states' rights" and "national sovereignty" was again taken up to insulate local decision-making structures – *in which absolutist constructions of the right to life could still effectively be pursued* – from the influence of evolving human rights law and international constructions, which have consistently rejected rights absolutism.

These conservative advocates may today rue that they did not take a more dualist approach twenty-five years ago – pushing for conservative constructions at the international level, while insulating domestically until those constructions were more fully consolidated. This is the process that appears to be being pursued today.[227]

D. MEDIATING TECHNIQUES FOR PROMOTING U.S. ENGAGEMENT: ASSERTING CLEAR LINES AND RECURRING (SELECTIVELY) TO SUBSIDIARITY DOCTRINE

What do these instrumental realignments mean for the United States and its future engagement with human rights treaty bodies? The U.S. position is often presented, inaccurately and unhelpfully, as monolithically opposed to human rights treaty body engagement. In fact, it is most useful to view U.S. human rights policy in fluid and responsive terms: as a careful mediation between distinct political pressures – from realist and institutionalist tendencies at the foreign policy level, liberal and conservative and/or incorporationist

---

[226] Alongside Brazil, the U.S. government had expressly opposed an absolutist meaning of the right to life in the drafting of the American Convention in 1969, as well as in the American Declaration on the Rights and Duties of Man. *See id.*

[227] It can be seen in multiple international fora – both in norm-creating conferences and meetings of the United Nations, its specialized agencies, and regional organizations of States and in the increasing involvement of conservative U.S. organizations in policy debates on abortion in countries around the world.

and insulationist persuasions at the domestic policy level, and "political process" versus "legal process" preferences more generally. The United States, in its policy positions, mediates these pressures, bowing more or less to one or the other at distinct political conjunctures and with shifting electoral politics. Yet, importantly, as its engagement practice reveals, it does so always within the parameters of a clearly articulated and jurisdictionally focused set of legal principles that frame and anchor the U.S. policy position.

These principles, drawn from the lettered texts and doctrines of international law, serve as essential mediating tools in the articulation of U.S. human rights policy. Indeed, as presently invoked, they appear to be advanced with a distinct policy aim: to set bright-line rules with respect to the scope of treaty body competence in precisely those areas that make conservative critics, at both domestic and foreign policy levels, most politically exercised. The resulting U.S. posture at once accommodates those concerns, particularly as articulated through federalism, sovereignty, and national security objections – the priority concerns of domestic policy insulationists and foreign policy realists – while opening a viable political space in which active U.S. engagement with human rights treaty bodies may feasibly be pursued, both as an international project (as has been the case to present) and a national one (a challenge still pending).

Significantly, the United States justifies this policy response not through resort to any exceptionalist notion of its power or political culture but rather through formal, repeated, and insistent resort to two of international law's most foundational building blocks: the doctrine of *sovereignty* and the *principle of subsidiarity*. Both doctrines are not only applicable to and regularly recurred to by all nations of the world in their own engagement policies but are foundational to the very rule of law and effective protection of human rights in the global public community. As such, formal U.S. reliance on them as the basis for its treaty body engagement policy lays a sturdy foundation for constructively advancing U.S. human rights policy toward the future, especially as advocates seek to strengthen and build the domestic dimension of the subsidiarity relationship. Their strategic use as a mediating device in U.S. engagement policy nonetheless comes clearly into focus upon considering that the United States currently invokes them before treaty bodies exclusively in their negative components: as doctrines of *non-interference* and *deference* in domestic political processes. Largely absent from the discourse is a parallel focus on their more positive aspects of assistance and support in strengthening domestic processes of human rights enforcement.

The current U.S. policy posture with respect to international treaty body engagement has three framework parts: (1) a bright-line, doctrinal statement of the substantive and spatial boundaries of treaty body jurisdiction, with a view to preserving the flexibility of foreign policy responsiveness in times of war or threats to global public order; (2) a close attention to the technical-jurisdictional boundaries of "contentious" dispute mechanisms versus "promotional" ones, narrowing access to the former and preferring reliance on the latter; and (3) an aggressive insistence on the nonbinding nature of all international treaty body decisions and conclusions, aimed at underscoring the primacy of domestic political process.[228] These three positions are advanced in virtually all international treaty body engagements, frequently as a direct preface to legal briefs and oral arguments. The first draws heavily on the negative dimensions of sovereignty doctrine, the latter two on those of subsidiarity.

While domestic advocates often view these three positions as a manifestation of the United States' stubborn refusal to accede to the binding rules of international law, they are, in many respects, just the opposite: a mediating posture that *relies* on the formal rules of international law to *allow* the United States to engage with supervisory human rights bodies on the widest diversity of subject matters feasible at a given political conjuncture. This rule-based, jurisdictional approach serves a number of ends. On the one hand, it creates a rhetorical or juridical comfort zone in which both conservative minorities can be politically appeased and foreign policy objectives pursued *within* the formal letter of U.S. human rights treaty commitments; this allows the United States to attend to oppositional concerns while simultaneously confuting charges of exceptionalism. On the other hand, and most consequentially from the domestic standpoint, by changing the relevant vocabulary of resistance, it functions to diffuse and transcend the "rights cultural" rhetoric that has historically given rise to exceptionalist demands at home. Indeed, that rhetoric has served as the primary basis for mobilizing domestic resistance to human rights treaty ratification and engagement, used to caricature human rights law in absolutist terms as contrary to and in direct conflict with U.S. constitutionalism, democracy, and sovereignty.[229]

---

[228] Although the three are frequently in tension, each plays a necessary role in defining the level of U.S. engagement with international treaty bodies at any given time. Advocates seeking a shift in levels or degrees of U.S. engagement would do well to pay close attention to how their strategies affect the equilibria achieved by these mediating techniques with respect to the underlying competing pressures.

[229] Although rarer to find in the U.S. State Department, which consistently takes a more multilateralist and international law-based approach, this "rights cultural" rhetoric continues to be used by some attorneys in the U.S. Department of Justice as a rationale for why the United States should not ratify human rights treaties. For a recent published example, see Tracey R. Justesen and Troy R. Justesen, *An Analysis of the Development and Adoption of the United Nations Convention Recognizing the Rights of Individuals with Disabilities: Why the United States Refuses to Sign this UN Convention*, 14(2) Hum. Rts. Brief 36, 39–41 (2007). For a counterperspective, see Tara J. Melish, *The UN Disability Convention: Historic Process, Strong Prospects, and Why the U.S. Should Ratify*, 14(2) Hum. Rts. Brief 37, 46 (2007).

The jurisdictional aggressiveness of the U.S. human rights policy may thus most profitably be interpreted as a mediating strategy in itself, designed to transcend this rhetorical and absolutist view of human rights law, and to bring it back in line with the actual foundations of human rights law. Thus, U.S. practice is to insist before human rights treaty bodies that the United States *will not accept human rights law on absolutist terms*. Rather, the United States underscores, it will accept human rights law and treaty body engagements *only* under terms that allow it (1) to engage in legitimate self-defense if national security is threatened, (2) to be the primary and final interpreter of how international law commitments will be translated into domestic laws and policies, and (3) to ensure that those laws and policies are determined in the first instance by the political branches rather than the courts. These positions do not contradict but rather are fully consistent with international human rights law, which is based on the principle of subsidiarity and the sovereign decision-making authority of democratic states.[230] What sets U.S. human rights policy apart from other states, then, is not its insistence on these legal principles – which other states equally expect to be respected in their relationship with treaty bodies – but rather its forthrightness and hyperlegalized defense of them in international contexts.[231] This jurisdictional aggressiveness is often popularly misconstrued as a rejection of human rights law itself, rather than simply a rejection of absolutist constructions of that law. U.S. exceptionalism in this respect is often more a question of tone and political sensitivity than of content.

It is here, however, that the mediating nature of the U.S. position is clearest. Although the aggressiveness of U.S. insistence on the primacy of domestic law and the limits of treaty body jurisdiction operates, in many ways, as a liability, it is also a goal: a rhetorical tactic to appease domestic opponents of human rights engagements by making clear that, in actively engaging with

---

[230] "Sovereignty," in this sense, refers not to antiquated international law notions of a "sovereign's sovereignty" – the prerogative to do as the sovereign pleases within the domestic jurisdiction, insulated from international law – but rather to the modern democracy-based notion of "the people's sovereignty." W. Michael Reisman, *Sovereignty and Human Rights in Contemporary International Law*, 84 Am. J. Int'l L. 866, 869 (1990); *see also id.* at 872 ("International law is still concerned with the protection of sovereignty, but, in its modern sense, the object of protection is not the power base of the tyrant who rules directly by naked power or through the apparatus of a totalitarian political order, but *the continuing capacity of a population freely to express and effect choices about the identities and policies of its governors.*") (emphasis added) ("[T]he word 'sovereignty' can no longer be used to shield the actual suppression of popular sovereignty from external rebuke and remedy.").

[231] That is, the United States is not exceptional in accepting treaty commitments only to the point of political feasibility. It is exceptional only in its forthright and aggressive defense of that policy in international and domestic fora, a defensiveness attributable both to the nation's own hyperlegalized culture and, relatedly, to the fierceness of domestic politics on the underlying issues.

human rights treaty bodies, the United States has not surrendered any of its sovereignty, constitutional commitment to a federal form of government, or ability to engage in national defense. It demonstrates that the United States has staked out a firm legally based position from which it can safely and reliably defend democratic institutions against perceived over-reaching by international treaty bodies. With these assurances in place, opponents may be willing to relinquish their "rights cultural" arguments that human rights law conflicts with American constitutional democracy. It may thus open the door to a more sustainable human rights policy over the long term, especially at the domestic level.

1. Carving Out "No-Go" Zones: The Substantive Parameters of Treaty Body Competence

The first mediating strategy employed by the United States draws on sovereignty doctrine to assuage realist and institutionalist pressures at the *foreign policy level*.[232] As discussed, whereas institutionalists in the foreign policy establishment push for greater U.S. treaty body engagement, foreign policy realists pull away from it, seeing international human rights supervision as an unnecessary and unwelcome constraint on the United States' power and prerogative to respond by all means necessary to foreign threats, particularly in times of war and armed conflict. With an eye toward appeasing both interests, the United States has adopted a mediating policy focused on the parameters of its sovereign consent to treaty body jurisdiction. It supports a policy of "full" jurisdictional engagement with international human rights treaty bodies *within their* ratione materiae *and* ratione loci *competence*. The United States then defines these jurisdictional parameters, using positivist international law doctrines, as exclusive of alleged abuses arising, first, in situations of armed conflict, and, second, extraterritorially – both traditional areas of strong foreign policy sensitivities. It resorts to the full set of internationally accepted methods of treaty interpretation, consistent with the Vienna Convention on the Law of Treaties, to support this jurisdictional interpretation, including ordinary meaning, the *travaux préparatoires*, state practice, the context surrounding the treaty at its conclusion, and the views of eminent public jurists.[233]

---

[232] Professor Murphy refers to a similar tension as the antinomy of exceptionalism versus sovereign equality. Murphy, *op. cit.*

[233] *See*, e.g., "Third periodic reports of States parties due in 2003: United States of America," CCPR/C/USA/3 (2005), Annex 1 ("Territorial Application of the [ICCPR]"), pp. 109–11 (relying on ordinary meaning, *travaux préparatoires*, U.S. practice, context at conclusion, and views of eminent public jurists, identified expressly as proper means of interpretation under the Vienna Convention on the Law of Treaties). Although the U.S. interpretation is not always persuasive,

Although this posture has become the focal point of scholarly and advocacy critique of U.S. human rights policy since 2001 – given deliberate removals of rights-abusive conduct to extraterritorial loci and other recent "war on terror" abuses – it is useful to take a step back and view it in larger perspective, outside of abusive applications, for what it represents at its core: *a mediation tactic.* Faced with powerful pressures to disengage *entirely* with international supervisory bodies should competence be exercised over U.S. military interventions or "war on terror" subjects – as the United States has done with other international tribunals, such as the ICC[234] or ICJ[235] – the U.S. decision to remain actively engaged in human rights treaty procedures while carving out limited subject matter "no-go" zones may be viewed, more positively, as a compromise strategy to conserve U.S. human rights engagement in *all other areas of domestic human rights abuse.* This is an enormous field, and U.S. willingness to engage it should not be minimized.[236]

It is important to note, moreover, that the U.S. position in this regard is not new. It represents a long-term policy on the part of the U.S. government, regularly raised in international fora wherever U.S. conduct in situations of war, war-related recovery, or conflict abroad has been challenged.[237] Initially advanced in the 1950s as a pragmatic concern in the ICCPR drafting process

---

it is prima facie credible. More important, it is consistently and persistently advanced across international supervisory jurisdictions. This is true before the Committee Against Torture, the Human Rights Committee, the Inter-American Commission on Human Rights, and even special mandate procedures, such as UN Special Rapporteurs and Independent Experts.

[234] In May 2002, President George W. Bush renounced the United States' prior signature of the Rome Statute of the International Criminal Court, asserting in a letter to the UN Secretary-General that "the United States has no legal obligations arising from its signature on December 31, 2000."

[235] The United States withdrew from the ICJ's compulsory jurisdiction in 1986, following the Court's adverse decision against it in *Military and Paramilitary Activities in and Against Nicaragua (Nicar. v. U.S.)*, 1986 I.C.J. 14 (June 27). On March 7, 2005, following another merits loss, it terminated the Court's treaty-specific jurisdiction over it with respect to alleged breaches of the Vienna Convention on Consular Relations. *See* Journal of the United Nations: Programme of Meetings and Agenda, No. 2005/48, at 13 (Mar. 12, 2005) (reporting UN Secretary-General's receipt of U.S. withdrawal notice to Convention's Optional Protocol).

[236] It covers areas such as discrimination, political participation, due process, health, housing, prison conditions, education, labor rights, and access to justice. U.S. opening to international supervision with respect to these domestic areas represents an important advance. This, of course, is not to say that advocates should not continue to challenge the legitimacy of the "no-go" zones, particularly unjustifiable uses of them to commit human rights abuse. It is only to say that U.S. human rights policy should not be judged exclusively on the basis of no-go zones.

[237] From 1992 to 1999, for example, the United States made these arguments in litigation before the Inter-American Commission on Human Rights involving its responsibility for the incommunicado detention of 17 civilians during the 1983 U.S. invasion of Grenada. *See Coard et al. v. United States*, Case 10.951, Report N° 109/99, Sept. 29, 1999, Inter-Am.Comm.H.R (1999). Although the United States argued in the alternative that it had not violated the rights of the

with respect to the U.S.-led post–World War II recovery process in Europe and Japan,[238] it in many ways today reflects the United States' self-awareness as the world's sole remaining military superpower in a world in which international law constitutes "an effective but limited structure."[239] In consequence of that awareness, and consistent with realist pressures, the United States has persistently rejected jurisdictional recognition of treaty body authority in situations of extraterritorial and armed conflict. This posture enables it to maintain maximum flexibility to respond to threats to national security and global public order – including the leeway to engage in what has been termed "operational noncompliance"[240] – without having to justify its conduct before international expert bodies through resort to legitimate or permissible restrictions on rights, such as those required to protect the rights and security of others.[241]

Significantly, in rejecting treaty body supervision in these limited areas, the United States does not claim immunity from the binding rules of international human rights and humanitarian law, nor that human rights or humanitarian abuses do not occur within no-go zones. Rather, its argument is a narrow jurisdictional one: Treaty bodies, as a technical matter, *lack jurisdiction* over

---

alleged victims under either the American Declaration or the Geneva Conventions, its principal arguments centered on questions of admissibility – that is, that the Commission lacked jurisdiction over the law of armed conflict, which prevailed as *lex specialis*, and, secondarily, over the extraterritorial conduct of a State.

[238] The resulting language in art. 2 of the ICCPR ("within its territory *and* subject to its jurisdiction") remains at the center of the U.S. policy position on the extraterritorial scope of human rights treaty obligations. See "Third periodic reports of States parties due in 2003: United States of America," CCPR/C/USA/3 (2005), Annex 1, 109–11.

[239] W. Michael Reisman, *Unilateral Action and the Transformations of the World Constitutive Process: The Special Problem of Humanitarian Intervention*, 11 Eur. J. Int'l L. 3, 9–10 (2000).

[240] Jacob Katz Cogan, *Noncompliance and the International Rule of Law*, 31 Yale J. Int'l L. 189, 191 (2006) (defined as "noncompliance that keeps a partially effective system, such as international law, operational by reconciling formal legal prescriptions with changing community policies or by bridging the enforcement gap created by inadequate community mechanisms of control").

[241] Human rights law is in fact designed to allow for this sort of practical accommodation. It expressly allows for justified restrictions on the enjoyment of rights, both in the general interest and, specifically, in times of national emergency. Human rights bodies consistently, moreover – whether explicitly or implicitly – provide a higher margin of discretion to states in crafting such justified restrictions in national security situations. *See, e.g., Ireland v. United Kingdom*, Judgment of 18 Jan. 1978, Eur. Ct. H.R., Series A, no. 25, para. 214; Lawless judgments of 7 April and 1 July 1961, Eur. Ct. H.R., Series A, nos. 2 & 3. Philip Alston, UN Special Rapporteur on extrajudicial, summary or arbitrary executions, has accordingly urged the United States to adopt this human-rights-based approach: rather than argue that human rights law does not apply in situations of armed conflict and thereby resist supervision, the United States might more usefully argue that its actions represent "justified" conduct in times of war or armed conflict within the frame of human rights law. Press Release, Office of the High Comm'r for Human Rights, Special Rapporteur on Extrajudicial, Summary, or Arbitrary Executions, U.N. Doc. HR/07/51 (Mar. 28, 2007). The United States has decided that it prefers not to take this course, at least not at present or as an exclusive option.

the United States in such areas, given the United States' historically based and persistently expressed position on the scope of its treaty undertakings. Under this view, human rights complaints in this sensitive foreign policy and rights-balancing area are valid but best reserved to political mechanisms of control: media attention, political pressure, congressional oversight and investigation mechanisms, international censure, and diplomatic pressure. These controls are understood as best capable of advancing the shared community goal of global human rights protection – both in most effectively restoring fundamental rights protections as soon as any national or global threat diminishes[242] and by removing a structured disincentive to responsive unilateral action in situations of humanitarian crisis or other threats to global public order to which the international community cannot or will not respond.[243]

This is, however, the only area in which the United States should be expected to refuse supervision in its engagement policy. It is a bow to the power of foreign policy realists, enabling the United States to continue its otherwise substantively plenary engagement policy and thereby attend to other domestic and foreign policy pressures and agendas.

2. Preferring "Political" to "Judicial" Controls in Human Rights Supervision and Interpretation

The second set of mediating tactics operates to accommodate the tension not between realists and institutionalists but between engagement as a foreign policy objective and domestic-level resistance to that engagement by those who view it as a threat to constitutional democracy. Such domestic resistance, often rooted in simple partisan political preferences, generally manifests itself in two classic arguments. The first involves classic federalism concerns.[244] The second departs from the perceived "undemocratic" nature of treaty bodies, in the sense that their members are not elected by nor directly accountable to U.S. citizens and relatedly are called on to interpret treaties that reflect *global*

---

[242] For a supportive view of this approach in the United States' domestic jurisdiction in times of war, see William H. Rehnquist, *All the Laws but One: Civil Rights in Wartime* (Random House, 1998) (discussing suspension of habeas corpus and other civil rights protections in times of war in United States).

[243] It may, in this sense, be viewed as part of a global constitutive process that, although open to abuse under certain ideological postures, functions over the long term to build more enduring international institutions and community mechanisms of control.

[244] *See*, e.g., Curtis A. Bradley, *The Treaty Power and American Federalism*, 97 Mich. L. Rev. 390 (1998) (asserting that treaty power is inconsistent with principle that the national government's powers are limited and enumerated and that states have rights to legislate independently in certain spheres, concluding that government must therefore "make a choice": human rights treaties *or* American federalism).

majoritarian mores, not necessarily U.S. ones.[245] This counter-majoritarian critique, paralleling similar critiques at the domestic level with respect to the role of the U.S. judiciary in interpreting broadly worded constitutional rights, is amplified where international tribunals are concerned, particularly given rhetorical assertions that such courts will compel the United States to adopt foreign rights constructions that conflict with democratically determined domestic understandings. This follows not only from the fact that treaty-based human rights norms tend to be drafted at a high level of generality, open to widely diverse interpretations by different social and cultural mediators,[246] but also from common objections that international "experts" or "judges" have no necessary connection to the United States and are elected principally by foreign sovereigns that may have interests or agendas averse, or even hostile, to those of the United States.

Significantly, both of these "states' rights" and "democratic deficit" objections are voiced most vehemently in one area of particular insulationist concern: the possibility of direct *judicial* enforcement of human rights treaty law. Insulationists object to such enforcement both by U.S. federal courts[247] and by supranational human rights treaty bodies exercising adjudicatory or quasi-adjudicatory powers.

The United States answers these objections through the regular use of three specific procedural devices drawn from the negative dimension of the principle of subsidiarity. Each is designed to preserve the primacy of *political* control mechanisms (the preferred decision-making environment of insulationists) by limiting the jurisdictional competence of judicial or quasi-adjudicatory bodies over raw human rights complaints.

---

[245] *See, e.g.*, Roger P. Alford, *Misusing Sources to Interpret the Constitution*, 98 Am. J. Int'l L. 57, 59 (2004) (discussing his view of "international countermajoritarian difficulty"); Curtis A. Bradley, *International Delegations, the Structural Constitution, and Non-Self-Execution*, 55 Stan. L. Rev. 1557, 1558 (2002–03) ("By transferring legal authority from U.S. actors to international actors – actors that are physically and culturally more distant from, and not directly responsible to, the U.S. electorate – these delegations may entail a dilution of domestic political accountability."); *cf.* John O. McGinnis and Ilya Somin, *Should International Law Be Part of Our Law?* 59 Stan. L. Rev. 1175 (2007) (limiting critique to "raw international law," that is, that which has not been endorsed by the domestic political process).

[246] *See, e.g.*, Goldsmith, *op. cit.* at 338–39 ("In and among pluralistic democratic societies, there is a reasonable scope for disagreement about what broadly worded human rights norms require. When the human rights community demands that the United States make international human rights treaties a part of domestic law in a way that circumvents political control, it evinces an intolerance for a pluralism of values and conditions, and a disrespect for local democratic processes.").

[247] *Id.* at 332 ("Domestic incorporation of the ICCPR... would constitute a massive, largely standardless delegation to federal courts to rethink the content and scope of nearly every aspect of domestic human rights law.").

The first involves the regular attachment of non-self-execution declarations to human rights treaties upon ratification. Such declarations assert that treaty norms do not create private causes of action for direct enforcement by the domestic judiciary. Rather, to be judicially cognizable they must first be given locally relevant content in domestically enforceable implementing legislation. This tactic bows directly to institutionalists and indirectly to incorporationists, but, in a concession to insulationists, insists that any incorporation be done by domestic legislatures or other political processes, not courts.

The second subsidiarity-based mediating tactic extends the same principle upward, from the domestic judiciary to the international treaty body system. It takes advantage of the fact that international treaty law generally makes judicial or quasi-judicial complaints mechanisms *optional* for States parties. In an effort to mediate competing institutionalist and insulationist pressures, the United States thus affirmatively accepts the jurisdiction of human rights treaty bodies for purposes of active and regular engagement, but only with respect to *non-adjudicatory* functions. Where given a choice, the United States reliably declines to accept the contentious jurisdiction of treaty bodies, voluntarily submitting only to periodic reporting and other promotional functions that focus on "constructive dialogue" with international supervisory bodies, not rights "adjudication." U.S. compliance with treaty obligations can thereby be discussed and debated in general ways, without an international adjudication that a specific policy or practice has violated the rights of distinct individuals and hence requires a specific remedial response, independent of domestic appreciation of the matter.

Finally, a third set of subsidiarity-based procedural devices is used in the few instances in which the United States is in fact mandatorily subject to international adjudicatory or case-based claims processes as a requirement of membership in a given intergovernmental organization.[248] In such circumstances, the United States trains heavily on the subsidiarity-based jurisdictional rules that limit treaty body competence over contentious cases, such as the exhaustion of domestic remedies requirement, the "fourth instance formula," and strict *ratione materiae, personae, loci,* and *temporis* limitations. These procedural devices, recognized in all international adjudicatory fora, are designed to give effect to the principle that human rights treaty bodies should never arrogate to themselves functions that can more immediately and effectively be undertaken at more local levels. U.S. engagement practice is correspondingly characterized by an emphasis on the extensive opportunities the litigant is or was afforded to address the issue through domestic legal and political

---

[248] The OAS and ILO have such compulsory membership requirements.

processes and the ultra vires nature of international jurisdiction where domestic processes provide full due process of law and effective redress to the alleged victim.

3. Retaining Full Remedial and Policy-Making Discretion

The United States employs a fourth mediating technique likewise derived from subsidiarity's negative dimension. This technique draws not on procedural devices designed to limit the exercise of adjudicatory competence, as do the former three, but rather on a subsidiarity-based doctrine of substantive deference applicable once competence is in fact asserted. Premised on the understanding that local actors are in the best position to appreciate the complexity of circumstances on the ground and, correspondingly, to understand what measures may be most effective for internalizing human rights values in distinct contexts, that doctrine mandates that a certain *margin of discretion* be given to competent authorities in the determination of rights abuse and in the crafting of appropriate responsive measures to it.[249] This subsidiarity-based deference doctrine is given regular effect in treaty body practice: both through the standard of review used to assess state compliance with treaty undertakings and, more broadly, through the general recognition that treaty body conclusions are recommendatory in nature only, providing states ample leeway to tailor responses appropriately to local conditions and constraints.

This fourth subsidiarity-based mediation tactic is articulated in U.S. engagement practice through regular U.S. assertions that all treaty body conclusions and recommendations, although welcome and appropriately taken into broader political account, are *nonbinding* and have *no independent domestic legal force*. Such nonbindingness is asserted with equal degrees of force with respect to the final recommendations issued by treaty bodies under contentious individual complaints procedures and those derivative of constructive dialogue and periodic reporting. By doing so, the United States seeks to underscore its full retention of plenary discretion to adopt its policies the way it chooses, notwithstanding U.S. submission to and engagement with international supervisory procedures.

In making this assertion, the United States does not affirm anything that is new to international law: the nonbinding nature of human rights treaty body supervision is, as a matter of international human rights law, uncontroversial, as is the ability of states parties to adopt measures of their sovereign choosing

---

[249] For a discussion of this doctrine as it has developed in the European system, see Howard Charles Yourow, *The Margin of Appreciation Doctrine in the Dynamics of European Human Rights Jurisprudence* (Utrecht: Martinus Nijhoff, 1996).

in giving effect to treaty obligations.[250] Rather, the United States uses this policy to speak directly to domestic constituencies, underscoring to insulationists that U.S. engagement will not force it to adopt policies that have not been fully mediated through the democratic process. This important mediating tactic nevertheless puts increasing strain on U.S. relationships with international tribunals. It also invites charges of paradox and double standards from domestic and international quarters alike, who often read U.S. assertions of the nonbindingness of the views and recommendations of *treaty bodies* as an assertion of the nonbindingness of the *treaty commitments* themselves. The U.S. government labors to clarify this distinction at the international level, consistently affirming its full acceptance of all treaty obligations duly undertaken. Consistent with interest management, it works less hard to make the distinction clear at the domestic level.

* * *

In light of the foregoing analysis, one might expect the United States to adopt the following postures toward treaty body engagements over the coming years. Reflecting a careful management of the underlying interest-group pressures, each reflects the continuing application of the sovereignty and subsidiarity-based mediation techniques just discussed.

- The United States will continue to ratify internationally popular human rights treaties, accelerating the process where coordinated domestic lobbying campaigns converge with Democratic majorities in the Senate. Such treaty ratifications will likely consist of the CRPD and CEDAW, as first priorities; the American Convention on Human Rights and the CRC, as second priorities; and, finally, the ICESCR.[251]

- These treaties will continue to be accompanied by non-self-execution clauses and other declarations and understandings designed to protect

---

[250] *See, e.g.*, Certain Attributes of the Inter-American Commission on Human Rights, Advisory Opinion, Inter-Am. Ct. H.R., OC-13/93 (Ser. A) No. 13, ¶ 29 (1993) (authority of Commission to find violation does not confer "authority to rule as to how a legal norm is adopted in the internal order," which "is the function of the competent organs of the State"). There are, of course, limits to the measures that a state can adopt and still purport to be giving effect to treaty obligations. These limits are generally expressed in the idea of an appropriate "margin of appreciation" to be granted a state, given local actors' greater appreciation of the facts on the ground, or the "reasonableness" of government conduct in aiming to achieve a given end, taking account of conflicting duties, burdens, and resource constraints.

[251] The United States is unlikely to ratify the Migrant Workers Convention, a treaty that – unlike other core UN human rights conventions – has not received a high level of support from the international community.

the primacy of domestic political processes in the determination of the scope and contours of domestic human rights protections.

- The United States will continue to participate actively in periodic reporting processes at the UN level, as well as through other promotional mechanisms envisioned in UN, ILO, and OAS law. In so doing, it will take a leading international role in identifying ways to make the process more efficient and less cumbersome for government actors, especially as its reporting obligations continue to grow with the ratification of new treaties.

- The United States will continue to decline to accept the contentious jurisdiction of UN treaty bodies.

- All individual contentious complaints of human rights abuse against the United States will instead be processed by the Inter-American Commission on Human Rights, in which the United States will continue to actively and constructively engage. This follows largely from the United States' greater familiarity with the system's rules and actors and ability to influence its direction and growth.

- The United States will ratify the American Convention with a view to seating a U.S.-nominated judge on the Inter-American Court of Human Rights. This will be undertaken to better influence the direction of inter-American jurisprudence, increasingly important to the United States as more contentious U.S. cases are brought to the Inter-American Commission on Human Rights.

- The United States will not, however, accept the Court's jurisdiction over U.S. cases. This policy will continue for the foreseeable future, at least until the United States has a greater degree of confidence in the Court's self-imposed jurisdictional limits and, most decisively, has established a politically based institutional setup for determining the content of effective remedies at the domestic level.[252]

- The United States will continue to resist international supervisory jurisdiction over extraterritorial abuses and those committed in armed conflict, even as it takes measures to prevent such abuses or to respond to them once they occur.

Notably, U.S. human rights policy should be expected to embrace these engagement postures irrespective of party control of the White House. Indeed, whether the White House occupant is a liberal Democrat or a conservative Republican, she or he will face the same powerful set of competing

---

[252] As a political matter, the United States is also unlikely to accept the contentious jurisdiction of the Court while Canada has similarly declined to do so.

interest-group pressures at both the foreign and domestic policy levels, and will need to find a principled yet flexible way to balance and accommodate them in a single policy posture.[253] In this complex interest-management process, the mediating techniques derived from the principles of subsidiarity and sovereignty should be expected to continue to play a dominant role. This is both because of their firm doctrinal (and hence ideologically neutral) basis in international law and because of their inherent flexibility in responding to new sets of evolving pressures and demands.

It is not, then, stasis that should be expected in U.S. human rights engagement policy, but rather continually evolving and responsive interactions among a wide variety of domestic and international actors, each with vastly different, often conflicting interests. The three predictable constants will be an active attention to the foreign policy benefits of engagement, a continuing emphasis on the primacy of domestic-level democratic decision-making processes, and adherence to a core set of doctrinally anchored mediating techniques designed to effectively mediate the two.

E. HONORING SUBSIDIARITY DOCTRINE IN FULL: FROM INTERNATIONAL DEFENSE TO DOMESTIC CHALLENGE

This chapter has aimed thus far to disentangle some of the motivating pressures and interests that are constitutive of today's U.S. human rights policy. In so doing, it has endeavored to demonstrate that U.S. human rights policy is best viewed not as a static or fixed structural given but rather as a careful mediation among the varied interest groups that successfully exert power and sustained influence on U.S. policy makers. This vantage point serves a number of important ends. Most significantly, it serves as a civic reminder that U.S. policy making is neither structurally predetermined nor undertaken hegemonically in a political vacuum; it is determined by domestic actors with agency, creativity, and constantly adapting political strategies that interact with each other and their environment as part of a constitutive, contested, constantly evolving process.[254] In this respect, it is vital to underscore the deep irony that results in too heavy a focus by scholars and advocates on the fixedness of the "U.S. human rights paradox," whether attributed to U.S. rights culture, U.S.

---

[253] In an interview given aboard Air Force One, President Obama responded to a question about the release of Guantanamo detainees by asserting that "there is still going to be some balancing that has to be done and some competing interests that are going to have to be addressed." "Reassurance on the Economy, and Addressing Afghanistan," *New York Times*, Mar. 8, 2009, at A1.

[254] *See generally* William M. Reisman, *Necessary and Proper: Executive Competence to Interpret Treaties*, 15 Yale J. Int'l L. 316, 323–30 (1990) (noting that law is never static; it changes as parties continually shape behavior in accordance with law, in reliance on it, and in the context of multiple factors that shape and limit options).

global hegemony, or "the deep structural reality of American political life."[255] That irony lies in the fact that civil society, pressed with the constant assertion that the United States *does not* or *will not* engage domestically on human rights matters, may stop *seeking* engagement. In a political democracy, when any group ceases to persistently pursue constructive policy engagement, its interests cannot be expected to be represented in mediated political outcomes.

This political reality is, in fact, directly reflected in today's U.S. human rights engagement policy. That policy has been determined at the intersection of pressures from three primary interest groups: foreign policy institutionalists, foreign policy realists, and domestic policy insulationists. Notably absent in the equation are domestic policy incorporationists. Although these vital social protagonists have been vigorously active at the local level, working with grassroots communities and effecting local change through a variety of innovative initiatives aimed at local government, incorporationists are the first to underscore that they have been least effective in mobilizing their broad base of constituents to influence national policy makers and beltway politics, through, for example, coordinated lobbying and nationally directed political action campaigns. The unremarkable consequence is that incorporationist interests are not today meaningfully reflected in U.S. treaty body engagement policy. Rather, reflecting institutionalists' concerns for international diplomacy, that policy has been pursued principally, if not wholly, as a foreign policy objective. It is directed to demonstrating *to other nations* the United States' strong commitment to human rights, to international law, and to participation in international institutions, not to effecting domestic self-reflection, civic discussion, and constructive change within the internal legal order.

Indeed, the most notable aspect of U.S. treaty body engagement policy today is precisely its lack of any explicit goal of strengthening domestic human rights protection. To the contrary, the U.S. position has been that the nation already has strong domestic rights protections and that, beyond certain modifications determined to be necessary *before* ratification, it does not need to make additional internal changes in its laws and policies.[256] Accordingly, even as the United States recognizes before international bodies that it is not perfect, has gaps to fill, and that human rights fulfillment is evolutionary, there is currently no institutional mechanism in place to systematically gather and process information from domestic actors on how the United States could improve its human rights protections. Likewise, although the United States prepares reports for submission to treaty bodies with a high degree of comprehension and detail, complying strictly with the technical aspects of its

---

[255] Moravcsik, *op. cit.* at 197.
[256] *Core document, op. cit.*

reporting requirements, it lacks any formal institutional mechanism to receive systematically the inputs of civil society into that process, to circulate outputs, to debrief the nation on its findings, or to encourage national reflection on how identified deficiencies might be remedied.

From a democracy standpoint, it is here that the central puzzle of U.S. human rights policy is located: how can such overt lack of institutional attention to facilitating domestic deliberative human rights processes be reconciled with the United States' formal insistence, as part of its treaty body engagement policy, on the *secondary* role of international treaty bodies and the *primacy* of domestic processes in the interpretation and protection of international human rights treaty norms? The disconnect lies in the United States' selective and partial use of the tools of international human rights law's subsidiarity principle to mediate the conflicting pressures faced from dominant interest groups. That is, in its treaty body engagement policy, the United States carefully invokes only the *negative* half of subsidiarity's project: the "non-interference" principle, the notion that discretion should be left to more local units to determine the content of rights without intervention or assistance from "higher" ones. This exclusive fragment of subsidiarity doctrine corresponds directly to the political coordinates at which the policy agendas of U.S. institutionalists and U.S. insulationists intersect – the former favoring treaty body engagement, the latter resisting any domestic effects thereof.

The problem is that the structural integrity of human rights law cannot endure subsidiarity's expedient fracture into constituent halves; it is constituted irreversibly of *both* the non-interference principle *and* that of intervention or assistance, each of which serves as a structural check on the other in the service of human dignity. Indeed, just as subsidiarity's negative dimension guards against drift into centralized bureaucracy or authoritarianism, so, too, does its positive dimension stand as a bulwark against collapse into simple devolution or pure unchecked discretion. By invoking only subsidiarity's negative side and, then, only vis-à-vis the U.S. relationship with international treaty bodies – not within the U.S. body politic itself – the United States undermines first principles of international human rights law, reimagining it as a simple exercise in local devolution.

This partial recognition accounts for why supervisory treaty body concern is so often raised in relation to U.S. reliance on certain doctrinal tools emanating from subsidiarity's negative dimension (such as the non-self-execution doctrine), despite such tools' solid foundation in international human rights law and broad parallel use by other nations.[257] Indeed, that concern arises not in

---

[257] Australia, Canada, India, Kenya, Mexico, and the United Kingdom, among many others, for example, likewise recognize the non-self-execution doctrine.

relation to the tools themselves, which, in conjunction with subsidiarity-based monitoring mechanisms, are fully sanctioned by international law. Rather, it relates to their regular employ *in the absence of* effectively functioning domestic monitoring and supervisory mechanisms that reflect subsidiarity's affirmative dimension. Thus, for instance, although both the United States and Canada apply the non-self-execution doctrine in implementing human rights treaties, international concern tends to be expressed with respect to the former only. This is because Canada employs the doctrine not in isolation but in symmetry with an integrated system of national, provincial, and local human rights institutions.[258] These institutions are mandated to serve in a subsidiarity capacity – internalizing and domesticating human rights values in locally relevant, democratically sanctioned, and indigenized ways, as close as possible to the individual yet within a supportive national structure.

A fuller recognition of the comprehensive nature of subsidiarity thus illuminates the central U.S. human rights challenge for the future: *How to give substance to the affirmative aspects of subsidiarity in national human rights policy, while continuing to honor and respect the negative aspects*. Indeed, this appears to be the path most capable of effectively accommodating all domestic interest groups. This is true both at the foreign policy level and, most directly, at the domestic level in mediating the vital tensions between incorporationists and insulationists – the former seeking greater incorporation of human rights methodologies and monitoring arrangements into the domestic legal and political system, the latter wishing to protect the primacy of domestic legal process and the boundaries of state consent. A focus on subsidiarity principles serves both ends. It does so by allowing the contested struggle over the meaning of rights, and their application to concrete, real-world situations, to take place within domestic control mechanisms, yet aided by the methodological framework and general *subsidium* of monitoring and implementation mechanisms at the local, state, and federal levels.

The central challenge for the future, therefore, lies in figuring out how to implement creative tools and institutionalized mechanisms to advance such processes at the national and subnational levels – that is, to erect the constitutive scaffolding necessary to link the individual, family, civic solidarity associations, and local, state, and national governments in a common subsidiarity-based project that places human dignity at its center. Such tools should be designed to listen to local and national communities as they discuss

---

[258] For an excellent discussion, see Koren L. Bell, Note, *From Laggard to Leader: Canadian Lessons on a Role for U.S. States in Making and Implementing Human Rights Treaties*, 5 Yale Hum. Rts. & Dev. L.J. 255 (2002).

and debate the contours of their own rights, to solicit their solutions for how to respond to deficiencies, and then to parlay those notions into concrete legislative, advocacy, and executive proposals at local, state, and federal levels. This project will, moreover, require a rethinking of traditional incorporationist objections to classic subsidiarity tools like the non-self-execution doctrine, shifting perspective to embrace them as *democracy-enhancing* and *deliberation-forcing* tools – ones that do not block human rights incorporation but rather actively aid the process of internalizing human rights norms in locally relevant ways.

By doing so, advocates may succeed – through organized pressure, active engagement, and a constructive shift in human rights strategy to accommodate the genuine democracy-based interests of all groups – in compelling the United States to expand its treaty body engagement policy beyond its current status as an exclusively international project, into a genuinely domestic one. That project would be one self-consciously based in the principle of subsidiarity, designed to support and sustain the localized decision-making capacities of U.S. communities to continually self-reflect on where they are, where they want to go, and how to get themselves there, within the methodological frame of international human rights law. In this way, the international treaty body system can serve its true subsidiary purpose.

The question is, how do we structure this? International human rights law, in function of its basis in subsidiarity doctrine, tends to offer an institutional outline, even while recognizing the wide variety of institutional arrangements that states adopt to govern themselves.[259] At the national level, two general levels of institutional supervisory arrangements are called for: one for state *implementation*, the other for state *monitoring*. Both should be established in the United States as a matter of priority.[260]

The following two sections consider each of these national-level institutional arrangements as they might profitably be established in the United States. Each of these arrangements is nevertheless fully replicable at "lower" levels of political organization – by states, counties, cities, and towns. Indeed, such institutional layering of supervisory authority is core to subsidiarity's premise,

---

[259] *See*, e.g., CRPD, *op. cit.*, art. 33, (recognizing need of states parties to establish national implementation mechanisms "in accordance with their system of organization" and national monitoring mechanisms "in accordance with their legal and administrative systems").

[260] Drawing expressly on the proposals in this chapter, as well as the recommendations of a Blueprint Advisory Group, a formal proposal to establish both national mechanisms was submitted to the Obama administration in October 2008. *See* Catherine Powell, Am. Constitution Soc'y for Law & Politics, *Human Rights at Home: A Domestic Policy Blueprint for the New Administration* (2008), *available at* http://www.acslaw.org/files/C%20Powell%20Blueprint.pdf.

ensuring that decision making and monitoring occur as close as possible to the individual.

1. A National Office on Human Rights Implementation and Inter-Agency Coordination Body

The first national institutional arrangement required by an effective subsidiarity-based regime is an executive branch "focal point" on implementation.[261] Ideally in the form of a National Office on Human Rights Implementation, such a focal point would be dedicated to taking care that the nation's international human rights treaty undertakings are appropriately implemented in the domestic jurisdiction.[262] As the national face for human rights implementation efforts, the focal point should be based in the Executive Office of the President and led by a person of recognized competence and expertise in the field of human rights. That individual, through the National Office, would be responsible for overseeing national efforts on human rights matters.

Importantly, as an orchestrating body, its purpose would not be to take over the administrative functions of other agencies, nor to be responsible for implementing programs or policies, outside those on transparency, capacity-building, human rights training, and small grants programs for innovative local human rights initiatives. Rather, consistent with subsidiarity, it would be dedicated to taking care that the nation's human rights commitments were being appropriately implemented in the domestic jurisdiction, through each of the nation's many competent departments and agencies. To this end, it would be assisted at the federal level by a coordination mechanism composed of a senior-level representative from each of the major agencies and departments of government.[263] Each member would be personally responsible for overseeing, coordinating, and reporting on human rights mainstreaming efforts in her or his department, as well as responding to agency-related complaints of human rights abuse. The National Office on Human Rights would act as a back-stop on these efforts, providing coordination, a mechanism for the sharing of best

---

[261] There is an increasing emphasis in international law and development theory on ensuring government focal points. Such focal points generally take the shape of a dedicated office within government or other policy-coordinating body. *See, e.g.*, CRPD, *op. cit.*, art. 33(1) ("States Parties... shall designate one or more focal points within government for matters relating to the implementation of the present Convention....").

[262] The U.S. Constitution invests the President with the power and duty to "take Care that the Laws be faithfully executed." U.S. Const. Art. II, § 3. This undertaking includes enforcement of treaties, which form part of the "supreme Law of the Land." *Id.* Art. VI.

[263] *See* CRPD, *op. cit.*, art. 33(1) ("States Parties... shall give due consideration to the establishment or designation of a coordination mechanism within government to facilitate related action in different sectors and at different levels.").

practices, encouragement, and advice. To ensure this essential orchestrating role, the coordination mechanism should ideally be chaired by the head of the National Office on Human Rights.

While the United States lacks any executive branch focal point for domestic-level human rights treaty implementation, it has formally established a coordination mechanism. Envisioned by President Clinton's 1998 Executive Order 13107 and reorganized under President Bush's 2001 National Security Presidential Directive, that mechanism must be revitalized and given life through new infusions of personnel, resources, and specific human rights mainstreaming mandates, with appropriate corresponding tools of transparency and sanction where deficiencies are identified in agency or department conduct.

It is essential, however, that such a revitalized coordination mechanism be accompanied by a National Office on Human Rights Implementation. Without a centralized, permanent, and dedicated focal point to orchestrate the human rights mainstreaming work of agency and department heads, the coordination mechanism alone will not be maximally effective. This has been the experience of the current Policy Coordination Committee (PCC) on Democracy, Human Rights, and International Operations, which has not functioned other than in an ad hoc fashion. This experience owes in large part to the absence of a dedicated executive focal point that has human rights treaty implementation as its exclusive mandate and area of expertise. Rather, the PCC has been headed by the Assistant to the President for National Security Affairs, for whom domestic-level human rights treaty implementation may be neither a priority nor interest.

A National Office on Human Rights Implementation would thus work with a coordination mechanism to ensure that each of the critical functions expressed in Executive Order No. 13107 are carried out by the appropriate authority or authorities, including the following:

- responding to inquiries, requests for information, and complaints about violations of human rights obligations that fall within each authority's areas of responsibility;
- coordinating the preparation of treaty compliance reports to the UN, OAS, and other international organizations;
- coordinating responses to contentious complaints lodged with the same organizations;
- overseeing a review of all proposed legislation to ensure its conformity with international human rights obligations;
- ensuring that plans for public outreach and education on human rights provisions in treaty-based and domestic law are broadly undertaken;

- ensuring an annual review of U.S. reservations, declarations, and understandings to human rights treaties; and
- ensuring that all nontrivial complaints or allegations of inconsistency with or breach of international human rights obligations are reviewed to determine whether any modifications to U.S. practice or laws are in order.[264]

In addition to these competences, the National Office on Human Rights Implementation would likewise have the important mandate to report to Congress and to the nation annually on national human rights progress and to make recommendations on new legislation or policies that might periodically be required on the basis of information received. In this way, Congress would be regularly informed of human rights implementation measures taken throughout the nation and could supplement efforts where gaps in coverage were identified or new forms of spending were required.

The National Office would also, however, play an important facilitation role with respect to the human rights implementation initiatives undertaken by state and local authorities. It could collect information, share best practices, provide publicity, shine a national spotlight on abusive situations, and promote the scaling up of the nation's most successful local experiments with human rights implementation. The Office would act as a centralizing repository for information generated from a variety of programs, agencies, and private sector sources on national human rights achievement, problem areas, and setbacks and could be held to political account for failures to supervise or intervene where systemic or gross abuses were uncovered.

In short, the National Office on Human Rights Implementation would serve as the nation's focal point for ensuring that federal, state, local, and private entities were adequately supported and incentivized to implement effective and appropriate human rights policies for themselves, as close as possible to affected individuals. In this way, its mandate would be to help obviate the need for individuals to seek human rights protections and enforcement at international or even national levels. Rather, consistent with the positive dimensions of subsidiarity, it would function to ensure those protections were provided effectively at the immediate site of abuse.

2. *United States Commission on Human Rights*

Yet, an implementation mechanism alone is not enough to ensure an effective national system of subsidiarity-based protection for human rights. An executive

---

[264] Executive Order 13107, *op. cit.* §§2–4.

focal point must be accompanied by a fully institutionalized national-level *monitoring* framework to ensure that all individuals have the ability to participate in national-level scrutiny and public oversight of U.S. human rights implementation commitments.[265] Such a body, ideally in the form of a U.S. Commission on Human Rights, would serve as an independent check on implementation failures, providing a forum through which individuals could report abuses and seek political or quasi-judicial address at the domestic level, before needing to recur to international treaty bodies.

To be maximally effective it should be instituted and financed by government, but functionally independent of the political branches, consistent with the Paris Principles.[266] Most countries honor this function by creating a national human rights commission or ombudsperson's office, bodies that can be further replicated within subnational political units, as close to the individual as necessary.[267]

Many U.S. states and cities in fact have bodies called "human rights commissions" or "human relations commissions."[268] Few, however, interpret their mandate as extending beyond investigating complaints of discrimination.[269] A U.S. Commission on Human Rights would serve to encourage states and localities to broaden their own mandates to encompass the full field of rights recognized in the Universal Declaration of Human Rights and in the treaties ratified by the United States. A subsidiarity-based relationship would then be engaged in which the national body would serve to support the human rights protection and promotion activities of more local commissions, ensuring that protection efforts are provided throughout the nation's diverse communities at the level closest to the affected individual.

---

[265] *See, e.g.*, CRPD, *op. cit.*, art. 33.2 ("States Parties shall... maintain, strengthen, designate or establish within the State Party, a framework, including one or more independent mechanisms, as appropriate, to promote, protect and monitor implementation of the present Convention. When designating or establishing such a mechanism, States Parties shall take into account the principles relating to the status and functioning of national institutions for protection and promotion of human rights.").

[266] National Institutions for the Promotion and Protection of Human Rights ("The Paris Principles"), G.A. Res. 48/134, U.N. Doc. A/Res/48/134 (Mar. 4, 1994) [hereinafter Paris Principles].

[267] The International Coordinating Committee of National Human Rights Institutions counts more than 100 national human rights institutions worldwide. U.N. Doc. A/AC.265/2006/CRP.5 (2006), n. 4.

[268] There reportedly are only three states – Alabama, Arkansas, and Mississippi – that do not have any form of a state or local human rights or human relations commission. *See* Kenneth L. Saunders & Hyo Eun (April) Bang, "A Historical Perspective on U.S. Human Rights Commissions," *Harvard Univ. John F. Kennedy Sch. of Gov't Executive Session on Human Rights Commissions & Criminal Justice*, No. 3 (June 2007), at 11.

[269] The U.S. Commission on Civil Rights has a similarly limited mandate.

Within this subsidiarity orientation, the U.S. Human Rights Commission would have a broad promotional and protective mandate.[270] It would be able to issue relevant reports and guidelines on rights-respecting behavior by distinct social actors. These would include nonbinding guidelines or guiding principles on appropriate conduct in prisons, police stations, administrative agencies, and other fora in which human rights abuses frequently occur, as well as the power and responsibility to make regular (nonbinding) recommendations to all relevant stakeholders, including particularly Congress, executive agencies and departments, and the legislatures of the many states. Such recommendations would be offered in a constructive spirit of cooperation, indicating areas of concern and offering assistance in identifying the most effective measures of response in consultation with affected citizens and local or national authorities.

A national human rights commission would also engage in regular human rights education and training programs,[271] as well as receive complaints from individuals about alleged human rights violations, initiate investigations, offer mediation services, arrive at findings, and issue recommendations to the parties and/or to relevant local authorities.[272] It would be competent to hold nationwide thematic hearings on distinct human rights issues, especially where common themes emerged from state and local hearings, and engage in independent monitoring of national human rights conditions through a variety of means, including investigations, inquiries, and surveys. In this respect, it could gather statistics from local and state human rights commissions on the numbers and types of issues and complaints they were addressing, and ensure the broad availability of human rights documents and materials. It would thereby serve as an important conduit for receiving and processing the results of localized discussions, policies, and experiments around the nation, with a view to discussing and sharing them among a national audience.

A U.S. Commission on Human Rights would thus self-consciously be based in the principle of subsidiarity, ensuring that its interventions were aimed at supporting local decision making, participatory engagement, and community-centered implementation processes. Its work would be directed to supporting

---

[270] Paris Principles, *op. cit.*, Part A, ¶ 2 ("A national institution shall be given as broad a mandate as possible, which shall be clearly set forth in a constitutional or legislative text, specifying its composition and its sphere of competence.").

[271] The Paris Principles explicitly affirm that national human rights institutions "*shall*, inter alia, have the following responsibilities.... To assist in the formulation of programs for the teaching of, and research into, human rights and to take part in their execution in schools, universities and professional circles; [and] [t]o publicize human rights and efforts to combat all forms of discrimination ... by increasing public awareness, especially through information and education and by making use of all press organs." *Id.* ¶¶ 3, 3(f)-3(g) (emphasis added).

[272] *Cf. id.* Part D.

localism, states' rights, and the vital experimentation they foster, while serving in a capacity to illuminate problematic areas where national policy intervention may be necessary in function of subsidiarity's positive assistive aspect.

In this way, a U.S. Human Rights Commission would serve as an independent check to ensure that individuals throughout the United States had effective local mechanisms through which their rights could effectively be protected in meaningful and appropriate ways at the immediate site of abuse, without needing to resort to international human rights treaty bodies for additional assistance and support.

F. CONCLUSION: INSTITUTIONALIZING SUBSIDIARITY

In his statement before the 1993 World Conference on Human Rights, U.S. Secretary of State Warren Christopher affirmed that "[i]n the battle for democracy and human rights, words matter, but what we *do* matters much more."[273] This continues to be the slogan of the U.S. State Department in its engagement policy with international human rights treaty bodies. That is, the United States engages such bodies in a procedurally exacting, substantively responsive, and high-level way, with the aim of setting an example for other states in deepening their own sovereign engagements with human rights treaty body supervision.

Yet what the United States in fact does in its engagement policy constitutes only half of what it seeks to encourage other states to do. The United States does not wish to encourage other states to use treaty ratification primarily as a foreign policy tool, formally preparing and presenting reports, answering questions, and then leaving the process in Geneva, away from the critical reflection of domestic constituencies. Such a process would serve no useful domestic-level purpose, either in terms of strengthening democratic institutions or enhancing human dignity. To the contrary, the United States aims to use its influence to encourage the world's governments to bring those international processes and commitments *home*, to discuss them with civil society, to monitor their own internal human rights progress, and to work to correct areas of deficiency through local innovation, transparency, and corrective experimentation. That is, the United States aims to ensure that international supervision truly serves its intended *subsidiary* purpose: to accompany and impel forward domestic processes of human rights monitoring, supervision, and remediation at national, municipal/state, and local levels.

In this respect, if the United States genuinely wishes to set a positive, constructive example for other states, it must – as Secretary Christopher

---

[273] Christopher, *op. cit.*

underscored – not only talk the talk, but walk the walk, demonstrating through self-directed action its commitment to domestic human rights processes. This cannot include engagement with the mere formalisms of international treaty obligations, using them to shield domestic processes from the influence of treaty body engagement. Rather, it must include engagement with the substance and spirit of them. This means institutionalizing domestic processes for using treaty body engagement as the impetus for a regular conversation and self-analysis of how well we are in fact standing up to human rights commitments, as we understand them in our complex and diverse communities and in the concrete contexts in which we live. It means monitoring national-level statistics and collecting regular information from the states with respect to each recognized right, regularly listening to citizens about the ways in which they feel their rights are or are not being addressed, actively considering their proposals for effective solutions, and systematically analyzing complaints of abuse and what remedies are in place to address them. Within this process, the inputs of international actors and comparative national experience can be highly instructive, even as they are never determinative for the precise contours of U.S. policy. That is, human rights engagement is not only or even principally about having a conversation at the international level; it is about starting and sustaining a *domestic* conversation, one that begins at the smallest and most local of places and works its way up to town, state, and federal authorities, within a national facilitative structure.

A U.S. treaty body engagement policy structured in this way – with the focus on domestic processes and responsive accountability to local needs – would go a long way toward transforming U.S. human rights policy from a noted example of paradox for the rest of the world to a genuine model of how human rights law and international treaty body engagement can be used, in function of subsidiarity principles, to deepen democratic processes, strengthen civil society participation, and internalize human rights protections in locally relevant, factually responsive, and genuinely meaningful ways.

9

The U.S. and International Claims and Compensation Bodies

JOHN R. CROOK[*]

From its earliest days, the United States has often pursued its policy goals through vigorous engagement in international institutions created to resolve large numbers of claims on the basis of law.[1] The 1794 Jay Treaty between the fledgling United States and the United Kingdom is perhaps best remembered for creating the boundary commission that resolved the disputed St. Croix River Boundary, but it also created two other commissions to address large numbers of legal claims by British and U.S. citizens. The first, which addressed ship seizure claims, succeeded. The second, dealing with colonial-era American debts, failed, for reasons that students of modern dispute settlement processes will find instructive.[2]

---

[*] John R. Crook is an arbitrator on the Eritrea-Ethiopia Claims Commission and under North American Free Trade Agreement and teaches international arbitration at The George Washington Law School. During three decades as a State Department lawyer, he served as U.S. agent at the Iran–U.S. Claims Tribunal in The Hague and was deeply involved in creating the UN Compensation Commission in Geneva. He edits the *American Journal of International Law*'s section on contemporary U.S. practice in international law.

[1] David J. Bederman, "Historic Analogues of the UN Compensation Commission," in *The United Nations Compensation Commission: Thirteenth Sokol Colloquium* (Richard B. Lillich, ed., Irvington, N.Y., Transnational Publishers, 1995), 257; David J. Bederman, *The United Nations Compensation Commission and the Tradition of International Claims Settlement"* 27 N.Y.U.J. Int'l L. & Pol. (1994), 1; John R. Crook, "Mass Claims Processes: Lessons Learned over Twenty-Five Years," in *Redressing Injuries through Mass Claims Processes: Innovative Responses to Unique Challenges* (Int'l Bureau, Permanent Court of Arbitration, ed., Oxford, Oxford University Press, 2006), 41–42.

[2] The commission created to address unlawful vessels seizures by the Royal Navy and by French privateers outfitted in U.S. ports was successful, issuing 565 awards. The second commission, created to address colonial-era debts to British creditors, deadlocked and failed. See Crook, "Mass Claims Processes," *op. cit.*, 41–42; Manley O. Hudson, *International Tribunals* (Washington, D.C., Carnegie Endowment for International Peace and Brookings Institution, 1944), 3; Richard B. Lillich, *The Jay Treaty Commissions*, 38 St. John's L. Rev. (1963), 38; Jackson H. Ralston, *International Arbitration from Athens to Locarno* (Stanford, Stanford University Press, 1929), 191–93.

Throughout the latter decades of the nineteenth century and the early decades of the twentieth, the United States was a frequent participant in mixed claims commission with its American neighbors.[3] It also participated in claims commissions with Germany, Austria, and Hungary that addressed extensive claims stemming from World War I. Then, however, such claims commissions fell out of fashion. Their work often took years, and some commissions failed to complete their dockets.[4] With a few limited exceptions, international claims processes handling large numbers of claims did not figure in U.S. legal policy or practice for many years after World War II.

This chapter sketches three cases in which these processes were revived and effectively used between 1980 and 2000. It each case, the U.S. government and U.S. officials played central roles in creating new international legal institutions that helped to advance significant U.S. policy goals. The chapter's conclusion suggests that the lessons learned from these institutions can have enduring relevance and that such institutions could again form a useful element of U.S. legal policy.

A. THE IRAN–UNITED STATES CLAIMS TRIBUNAL

The Iran–United States Claims Tribunal was a direct result of the dramatic deterioration of the previously extensive political and economic relationships between the United States and Iran following the success of the Iranian revolution in January and February 1979. Before the revolution, "U.S. companies serviced and supplied the oil fields of Iran and purchased large quantities of oil. U.S. bank institutions held most of Iran's dollar deposits and were major lenders ... to Iran. U.S. suppliers of military equipment and services had very substantial contracts in process. U.S. companies were involved in numerous construction and manufacturing projects in Iran and operated major subsidiaries there. And U.S. firms were major sources of varying types of goods imported into Iran."[5]

Following waves of antigovernment protests throughout Iran, the Shah of Iran left the country on January 16, 1979. The Ayatollah Khomeini returned

---

[3] See, e.g., A. H. Feller, *The Mexican Claims Commissions, 1923–34* (New York, Macmillan, 1935); Bert L. Hunt, *Report of the Agent for the United States. American and Panamanian General Claims Arbitration under the Conventions between the United States and Panama of July 28, 1926, and December 17, 1932* (Washington, D.C., Government Printing Office, 1934).

[4] Crook, "Mass Claims Processes," *op. cit.*, 42.

[5] Robert Carswell and Richard J. Davis, "The Economic and Financial Pressures: Freeze and Sanctions," in *American Hostages in Iran: The Conduct of a Crisis* (Warren Christopher et al., eds., New Haven, Yale University Press, 1985), 173. (Carswell was deputy secretary of the Treasury during 1979–81; Davis was assistant secretary of the Treasury responsible for economic sanctions programs.)

to Iran on February 1, 1979, and established a government of his supporters on February 4.[6] In the following months, the United States initially sought to maintain a correct, even if cooler, relationship with the new regime. The two governments concluded agreements aimed at the orderly termination of extensive prior programs of military cooperation and other matters. However, there were clear warning signs that the relationship could not continue smoothly. Leftists seized the U.S. Embassy in Tehran on February 14, 1979, shortly after Ayatollah Khomeini's return. Revolutionary guards acting at the call of the new government cleared the embassy, but the size of the U.S. official presence was thereafter sharply reduced.

During this period, many large Iranian commercial entities were taken over by, or fell under the control or direction of, revolutionary groups or committees. Many of these entities acted to curtail or end previously extensive banking, investment, and economic relationships with Western, particularly U.S., firms. Often this was done with little regard for contractual obligations or the rights of foreign partners, and some Iranian parties attempted to draw on letters of credit provided by the Western party as security for its performance. Prior to November 1979, these events resulted in approximately forty cases in U.S. courts against Iranian government and its instrumentalities.[7] Some of this litigation was accompanied by efforts to attach Iranian assets in the United States and abroad.

Matters took a dramatic turn for the worse in October 1979, when President Carter decided that the ailing shah should be admitted to the United States for cancer treatment. On November 4, 1979, a large mob of revolutionary students swamped the defenses of the U.S. Embassy in Tehran, taking sixty-six U.S. personnel hostage there and at the Iranian Foreign Ministry.[8] The Iranian prime minister and foreign minister pledged to assist the embassy, but were powerless to do so and soon resigned. The revolutionary authorities subsequently approved the students' actions and called for their continuation; the

---

[6] This discussion of the Iran–U.S. Claims Tribunal rests in part on the author's recollections but also draws heavily on two works collecting reflections of senior U.S. officials involved in the hostage crisis. Christopher's collection, *op. cit.*, includes many useful accounts by U.S. participants. Andreas F. Lowenfeld et al., *Revolutionary Days: The Iran Hostage Crisis and The Hague Claims Tribunal: A Look Back* (Huntington, N.Y., Juris Publishing, 1999), records reflections of some of these same officials and other participants and observers at a 1996 conference at New York University Law School. There is an extensive bibliography on the Tribunal in *The Iran–United States Claims Tribunal and the Process of International Claims Resolution* (David R. Caron and John R. Crook, eds., Ardsley, N.Y., Transnational Publishers, 2000), 477. See also Peter G. Bourne, *Jimmy Carter* (New York, Scribner, 1997); Kathryn Koob, *Guest of the Revolution* (Nashville, Thomas Nelson Publishers, 1982); and Gary Sick, *All Fall Down: America's Tragic Encounter with Iran* (New York, Random House, 1985).

[7] Thomas Shack in Lowenfeld, *op. cit.*, 28.

[8] Thirteen black and female hostages were released in November 1979. Bourne, *op. cit.*, 455.

International Court of Justice later found that this made the Islamic Republic of Iran responsible for their actions under international law.[9]

Early on the morning of November 14, Iranian Foreign and Finance Minister Bani-Sadr announced that Iran would withdraw precipitously billions of dollars of Iranian deposits in U.S. banks.[10] A few hours later, the United States responded to the unraveling of events by invoking U.S. emergency legislation and freezing roughly $12 billion of Iranian official assets held in the New York Federal Reserve and in U.S. banks in the United States, and as dollar deposits in U.S. banks overseas. More than half was in the United States; the remainder was in U.S. banks' overseas branches.[11] Thereafter, almost all of the U.S. firms that had attempted to maintain vestiges of past relationships with Iranian partners withdrew any remaining expatriate personnel and gave up their contracts and investments as lost. There was a race to the courthouse by U.S. commercial entities that had suffered losses on their investments or contracts. At least four hundred suits were filed in U.S. courts, often accompanied by attempts to attach Iranian official assets.[12] A system of Treasury Department licenses was put in place, under which the Treasury would allow the filing of cases against Iranian parties, including prejudgment attachments, but would not allow entry of judgments.[13]

It is beyond the scope of this chapter to replicate the complex web of U.S. litigation and Treasury Department licenses affecting Iranian assets operating during 1979 and 1980. It is sufficient to recall that there were extensive claims by U.S. banks, businesses, and individuals against Iran pending in U.S. courts at the time. U.S. officials involved in resolving the hostage crisis took as a starting point that any eventual resolution had to provide some mechanism addressing these claims. Although Iran sought during the negotiations to have the claims and the related litigation terminated by Executive fiat, the U.S. side was not prepared to do so, both for constitutional reasons and to avoid the appearance of paying ransom for the hostages' return. Roberts B. Owen, the State Department Legal Adviser during this period and a major architect of the final settlement, recalls that the notion of canceling the private U.S. claims

---

[9] *United States Diplomatic and Consular Staff in Tehran (USA v. Iran)*, 1980 I.C.J. Rep. 3, 35. See James Crawford, *The International Law Commission's Articles on State Responsibility* (Cambridge, Cambridge University Press, 2002), 121–22.

[10] Carswell and Davis in Christopher, *op. cit.*, 176.

[11] *Id.* at 205.

[12] Thomas Shack, U.S. counsel for Iran during this period, knew of about 400 post-freeze cases. Lowenfeld, *op. cit.*, 30. See Michael F. Hertz, "The Hostage Crisis and Domestic Litigation: An Overview," *The Iran–United States Claims Tribunal 1981–1983: Seventh Sokol Colloquium* (Richard B. Lillich, ed., Ardsley-on-Hudson, N.Y., Transnational Publishers, 1984) 136.

[13] Carswell and Davis in Christopher, *op. cit.*, 185–86.

"was never seriously entertained at any point in the process."[14] The picture was further complicated because several major U.S. banks, in addition to holding large Iranian deposits, also had extended large loans to Iran. Any settlement had to include some mechanism for sorting out these relationships, including a means to resolve any disputed amounts or other disputes between U.S. and Iranian bankers.

Reflecting the turbulent political situation inside Iran, no reliable channel for serious negotiations was available until after the elected Iranian parliament (the Majlis) and a relatively stable government were finally in place in the late summer of 1980. Discussions opened with a pair of meetings in Germany between Deputy Secretary Christopher and an Iranian representative in September 1980.[15] On September 22, Iraq invaded Iran. This added pressure on Iran to find a settlement to lessen its diplomatic isolation, but also diverted Iranian policy makers and made it impossible for Christopher's interlocutor to travel.

During the months when there were no active negotiations, officials in the Department of State, operating under strict confidentiality, worked on concepts for settlement that included a possible claims tribunal. State Department Deputy Legal Adviser Mark Feldman and Counselor of International Law Gerald Rosberg were major actors in this work.[16] Speaking at New York University Law School in 1996, Feldman recalled the process:

> We knew all along that we had two broad options for claims settlement. One was a lump sum agreement and the other was some kind of dispute settlement procedure. There wasn't any clear preference for a long time. Lump sum meant we could get money done with ... [But,][c]ould you possibly get enough money to make the deal acceptable for the American community?
>
> The problems on arbitration were enormous, the complexity ... the magnitude, the diversity of the claims, the previous experience in international claims settlement, with tribunals in the post World War I period ... There were a lot of reasons to be concerned about it. I don't know how the decision was taken. All I know is, the message came over from Bob Carswell [Deputy Secretary of the Treasury during the crisis] sometime in the summer of 1980 that we in the State Department should be working up an arbitration agreement.[17]

---

[14] Owen in Lowenfeld, *op. cit.*, 60. See Christopher, "Introduction," in Christopher, *op. cit.*, 5; Owen, *Id.* at 303.
[15] Bourne, *op. cit.*, 468; Christopher in Christopher, *op. cit.*, 3; Owen, *Id.* at 297, 305–6; Mark B. Feldman "Drafting the Claims Settlement Agreement," in Lowenfeld, *op. cit.*, 92.
[16] *Id.* at 91.
[17] *Id.* at 94.

Feldman recorded that the State Department lawyers thereafter prepared a "very long arbitration agreement."[18]

The details of the final negotiating process are beyond the scope of this chapter.[19] The final intensive negotiations, with senior Algerian government officials playing a key intermediary role, did not begin until November 1980, following the defeat of President Carter in that year's elections. Participants recount that a major Iranian goal at the outset of the final negotiations was a U.S. undertaking to nullify private claims against Iran. As noted earlier, U.S. officials believed they could not do so, constitutionally or politically. Accordingly, the United States insisted on some substitute procedure to address U.S. claims.[20] Following intense negotiations with and through the Algerian intermediaries, on December 19, "Iran accepted the general principle of an arbitration process with a $1 billion security fund to be replenished when it fell to the $500,000 level."[21]

A few days later, in a late December meeting in Washington, the Algerian intermediaries insisted that the U.S. draft arbitration text was too long and complicated. Feldman and his colleagues undertook a hurried and drastic pruning job, reducing the document from twenty-five pages to three-and-a-half.[22] The drafters relied on the UNCITRAL arbitration rules (then relatively new and untested)[23] as a default mechanism to address numerous issues that could not be treated in detail.[24] With a few small but important last-minute modifications to meet Iranian requirements, the resulting text became the Claims Settlement Declaration, a relatively brief document that has served well as the constitution of the Iran–U.S. Claims Tribunal.[25]

The complex package of agreements to end the crisis came together at the last minute; the hostages were still holding on the runway in Tehran as Ronald Reagan took the oath of office to succeed Jimmy Carter.[26] However,

---

[18] *Id.* at 95.
[19] My favorite account of events leading to the final settlement is Roberts Owen's, in Christopher, *op. cit.*, 297.
[20] Feldman in Lowenfeld, *op. cit.*, 96.
[21] *Id.* at 97; Owen in Christopher, *op. cit.*, 309.
[22] *Id.* at 312.
[23] These rules, today widely used in international commercial and investment arbitration, were adopted by the UN Commission on International Trade Law in April 1976 and were later endorsed by the UN General Assembly (GA Res. 31/98, Dec. 15, 1976). The rules as originally adopted are reprinted in II *Yearbook of Commercial Arbitration* (1977) ii, 161, and 15 ILM (1976), 702.
[24] Feldman in Lowenfeld, *op. cit.*, 99–105.
[25] I have elsewhere described the Claims Settlement Declaration as "a notable illustration of the role that skillful legal analysis and craftsmanship can play in international affairs." David D. Caron and John R. Crook, "Tribunals as Institutions," in Caron and Crook, *op. cit.*, 7.
[26] Bourne, *op. cit.*, 473.

there was a serious question whether the new administration would honor the deal concluded by its predecessor, including the new claims settlement process. The Reagan campaign had harshly criticized efforts to end the crisis through negotiations.[27] Indeed, some commentators argued in early 1981 that the Algiers Accords had been the product of coercion and so were not legally binding on the United States.[28]

In the event, all three branches of the federal government lined up in support of the Algiers Accords, albeit sometimes without enthusiasm. Following a month-long review of the agreements, the incoming Reagan administration grudgingly concluded that they should be carried out. Secretary of State Al Haig's State Department issued a statement on February 18, 1981, confirming that the United States would implement the agreements:

> Our position up until now has been that the United States, of course, will honor its obligations under international law. Because of the complexity of the agreements and the extraordinary conditions under which they were negotiated, we have undertaken a review to determine precisely what our obligations are under them. . . .
>
> Having considered all the circumstances carefully, we have decided to approve implementation of the agreements in strict accordance with the terms of the agreements. . . .
>
> The conclusion of the agreements was a legal exercise of Presidential authority. . . . We did not find it necessary to reach a conclusion as to the legally binding character of these agreements under international law. . . .
>
> It should be well understood that the decision to faithfully implement the agreements does not represent a precedent for future actions by the U.S. Government in similar situations. The present Administration would not have negotiated with the Iran for release of the hostages. Future acts of state-sponsored terrorism against the United States will meet swift and sure punishment.[29]

---

[27] See Lloyd Cutler (President Carter's White House Counsel) in Lowenfeld, *op. cit.*, 43, and Owen, *Id.* at 59: "[M]any of President Carter's critics, including Ronald Reagan's advisers, took the position at the time that quite apart from the question of ransom, just the act of talking or negotiating with a terrorist government was totally unacceptable."

[28] For critical analysis of the argument that the Algiers Accords were coerced and therefore void and unenforceable under the principles of Article 52 of the Vienna Convention on the Law of Treaties, see Oscar Schachter, "International Law in the Hostage Crisis: Implications for Future Cases," in Christopher, *op. cit.*, 369–373.

[29] State Department Statement, Implementation of Hostage Agreement (Feb. 18, 1981), 81 *Dept. of State Bull.* (Mar. 1981), 17, and Lowenfeld, *op. cit.*, A-99-A-100. Roberts Owen attended a ceremony for the returned hostages where Secretary Haig emphasized his view that the United States should not have negotiated for their return. "How's that for a tasteful welcome home message?" asked Owen. *Id.* at 62.

Following its review, the Reagan administration issued the Executive Order required to suspend U.S. litigation of claims that the Claims Settlement Declaration required to be presented to the new international tribunal.[30]

The administration thereafter successfully defended the actions taken by it and the Carter administration to regulate U.S. litigation against Iran and to require U.S. claimants to pursue their claims in the new international process. In July 1981, the U.S. Supreme Court upheld these measures in *Dames & Moore v. Reagan*.[31] Justice Rehnquist's majority opinion strongly affirmed the Executive's power to settle the claims of U.S. nationals through a claims settlement agreement, although the Court's assessment of the prospects for the new claims tribunal was less than whole-hearted:

> Our conclusion is buttressed by the fact that the means chosen by the President to settle the claims of American nationals provided an alternative forum, the Claims Tribunal, which is capable of providing meaningful relief. The Solicitor General also suggests that the provision of the Claims Tribunal will actually enhance the opportunity for claimants to recover their claims.... Although being overly sanguine about the chances of United States claimants before the Claims Tribunal would require a degree of naiveté which should not be demanded even of judges, the Solicitor General's point cannot be discounted.[32]

The Court emphasized that the U.S. Congress also supported implementation of the Algiers Accords:

> Just as importantly, Congress has not disapproved of the action taken here. Although Congress has held hearings on the Iranian Agreement itself, Congress has not enacted legislation or even passed a resolution, indicating its displeasure with the Agreement. Quite the contrary, the relevant Senate Committee has stated that the establishment of the Tribunal is "of vital importance to the United States" S. Rep. No. 97-71, p. 5 (1981). We are thus clearly not confronted with a situation in which Congress has in some way resisted the exercise of Presidential authority.[33]

The Iran–United States Claims Tribunal got underway during 1981 as envisioned by the Algiers Accords and successfully completed most of its large commercial claims by 1990.[34] The Tribunal did not make corresponding progress with the approximately 2,800 small claims on its docket, which were

---

[30] Executive Order 12294, Suspension of Litigation against Iran (Feb. 24, 1981).
[31] *Dames & Moore v. Reagan*, 453 U.S. 654 (July 2, 1981).
[32] 453 U.S. 687.
[33] 453 U.S. 687–88. (Court's footnotes omitted.)
[34] There is a substantial literature on the Tribunal. In addition to Caron and Crook, *op. cit.*, 477, see David D. Caron et al., *The UNCITRAL Arbitration Rules* (Oxford, Oxford University Press, 2006), 995.

settled by a lump-sum settlement agreement between the two governments in 1990.[35] A few politically sensitive dual national claims also remained for several years after 1990.

The Tribunal lingers on today, twenty-eight years after its inauguration, in what one former U.S. agent has termed its "long twilight."[36] The generally slow pace of Tribunal activity in its latter years largely results from decisions made by the two governments and by the Tribunal in its early years to postpone until the end a number of huge and complex cases involving the parties' prerevolutionary military cooperation and sales relationships.[37] The briefing and collection of evidence in these cases have dragged on for years, although in recent years, some of them have become more active; the Tribunal held sixty days of hearings in Iran's claims involving military properties held by private U.S. entities for which the U.S. government has refused export licenses.

Throughout the Tribunal's long life, the U.S. 50 percent share of the Tribunal budget[38] has been included as part of the budget of the Department of State Legal Adviser's Office and has been faithfully paid (subject to a few delays caused by the vicissitudes of the U.S. budget process). The United States has promptly made appointments to fill vacancies resulting from the occasional resignations of U.S. arbitrators. Although the views of particular private claimants tended to reflect their relative success (or lack of it) in the Tribunal process, the U.S. commercial claimant community generally gave the process grudging approval.[39] Notwithstanding the continuing poor state of U.S.-Iranian bilateral relations, the United States continues to this day to participate actively in the process of arbitrating the small group of large intergovernmental claims remaining on the docket.

U.S. courts have likewise supported the process through the years. Because Tribunal awards in favor of U.S. claimants have been paid from the security account created by the Algiers Accords, there has been no need for U.S. claimants to go into U.S. courts to enforce their awards. Litigation has arisen only in rare cases, principally when Iran (which does not benefit from the security account) has sought to enforce awards in its favor. U.S. courts have held that the Tribunal's awards are enforceable in the United States under

---

[35] John R. Crook, "Mass Claims Processes," *op. cit.*, 45–46.
[36] Lucy F. Reed, "The Long Twilight: An Agent's View of the Closing Stages," Caron and Crook, *op. cit.*, 339.
[37] Ronald J. Bettauer, "The Task Remaining: The Government Cases," Caron and Crook, *op. cit.*, 355.
[38] As of May 2007, the Tribunal's annual budget is about 6 million euros.
[39] See Brice M. Clagett, "The Perspectives of the Claimant Community," Caron and Crook, *op. cit.*, 62. ("While the litigation did indeed proceed at a stately pace that was frustrating for the claimants, ultimately prejudice was largely avoided by realistic interest awards and eventual payment in full.... All in all, disposition of virtually all of the large private claims... within twelve years is not a disgraceful record.")

the New York Convention.[40] The U.S. Federal Circuit Court of Appeals has upheld the 1990 lump-sum settlement of the small claims against claims that the failure to secure full payment including interest constituted a taking.[41]

B. U.S. ROLE IN THE CREATION AND OPERATION OF HOLOCAUST VICTIMS COMPENSATION MECHANISMS

The processes leading to the creation in the 1990s of new mechanisms to compensate Holocaust victims tended to be more complex, and to involve a wider array of U.S. and other actors, than the other processes discussed in this chapter (i.e., the Iran–U.S. Claims Tribunal and the UN Compensation Commission). Ambassador Stuart E. Eizenstat, a senior official in the Commerce, State, and Treasury Departments during the Clinton administration, played a particularly important role as the administration's high-level representative in the negotiations leading to several of these processes.[42] Other U.S. officials or agencies also were involved, but the form and extent of their activities varied. U.S. instrumentalities involved in these issues included U.S. courts, members of Congress, Executive Branch officials, state banking and insurance regulators, and local government officials, all in varying ways and proportions.

For reasons combining morality with practical domestic and international politics, official U.S. entities at multiple levels supported efforts to provide compensation,[43] although there were differences regarding emphasis and modalities. Ambassador Eizenstat highlights the role of domestic political pressures in energizing U.S. action, including the central role of U.S. Jewish groups:

> Were domestic Jewish political pressures also a major reason for sustained, high-level U.S. engagement in the Holocaust negotiations? Yes.... There is nothing insidious about this. Jews are hardly the only group seeking to influence government officials. They are all part of a peculiarly American way of making foreign policy.[44]

---

[40] *Iran Aircraft Ind. v. AVCO Corp.*, 980 F.2d 141 (2d Cir. 1992); *Ministry of Defense v. Gould, Inc.*, 887 F.2d 1357 (9th Cir. 1989), cert. den. 110 S. Ct. 1319 (1990), noted 84 A.J.I.L. 556 (1991).
[41] *Abrahim-Youri v. United States*, 139 F.3d 1462 (Fed. Cir. 1997) (rejecting claim that government's lump-sum settlement of the small claims constituted a constitutional taking because it did not provide for 100 percent interest on settled claims).
[42] *Digest of United States Practice in International Law* 2000 (Sally J. Cummins and David P. Stewart, eds., Washington, D.C., International Law Institute, 2001) 445. Ambassador Eizenstat's memoir of these events provides a lively description of the issues and of the complex of litigation, government interventions, and negotiations required to resolve them. Stuart E. Eizenstat, *Imperfect Justice* (New York, Public Affairs, 2003).
[43] On the mix of morality and political forces propelling U.S. action, see *Id.* at 4–5.
[44] *Id.* at 6.

Herein lies a crucial distinction between these claims and the corresponding claims of persons who suffered grave injuries at the hands of the Japanese government and Japanese firms during World War II. Persons concerned about possible claims against Japan were less numerous and less able to mobilize U.S. public and Congressional support.[45] Moreover, these claims faced serious legal obstacles not present with the Holocaust claims. In 1951, Japan and the United States concluded a Treaty of Peace, which in Article 14(b) expressly waived all reparations claims of the Allied Powers and their nationals.[46] Although there were attempts to litigate claims against Japan in U.S. courts, these typically foundered on the waiver of claims in the Peace Treaty.[47] Because of the postwar division of Germany, there was no corresponding treaty of peace and waiver of reparations claims against Germany, so U.S. action addressing Holocaust claims was not constrained by past agreements. Finally, it must be said that Japan has been far less willing to acknowledge past abuses and to entertain claims.

The Holocaust claims mechanisms created in the 1990s were largely rooted in long-standing and acrimonious disputes among private actors. They usually matched Holocaust victims or their heirs against banks, insurers, and manufacturing companies accused by the claimants of having taken or withheld their property (rights to bank accounts or under insurance policies), of subjecting them to forced or slave labor, or of other wrongful conduct. Most of the institutions created to address these claims were based on agreements adhered to by the private disputing parties (including court-approved settlements), not on treaties or other international law instruments. Private entities provided significant amounts of the funds distributed (although governments also provided significant funding in some cases). Nevertheless, U.S. officials played active roles in negotiating several of these arrangements, the State Department concluded international agreements to support them, and the Justice Department took action in U.S. courts supporting the international claims settlement processes.

1. *The Swiss Bank Claims Institutions*

The best known of these institutions is the Claims Resolution Tribunal for Dormant Bank Accounts in Switzerland (hereinafter, "Claims Resolution

---

[45] Tellingly, there is no index entry for "Japan" in Eizenstat's book.
[46] Treaty of Peace, United States and Japan, Sept. 8, 1951, 3 U.S.T. 3168, 136 U.N.T.S. 45. See Sean D. Murphy, *United States Practice In International Law. Volume 1: 1999–2001* (Cambridge, Cambridge University Press, 2002), 153–57.
[47] See *Id.*; 2000 U.S. Digest, *op. cit.*, 505–42.

Tribunal" or "CRT"), an institution with a turbulent history.[48] The CRT process grew out of longstanding tension between major Swiss banks and Jewish groups and individuals. The claimants contended that the banks had concealed and wrongfully denied access to accounts opened in the 1930s and 1940s by clients who perished in the Holocaust and otherwise wrongfully profited from dealings with the Nazis. A 1995 meeting between Swiss bankers and high-level Jewish representatives to discuss the issue reportedly went badly, increasing ill will and mistrust.[49] In the United States, these tensions ultimately led in the mid-1990s to high-profile public criticism, threats of state and local regulatory action and class action litigation against the banks. Senator Alphonse D'Amato of New York and other political figures mounted aggressive public attacks on the banks.[50] Threats of sanctions by local financial officers and other officials became a powerful current in local politics in New York City and State and elsewhere. In 1998, the Department of State publicly opposed imposition of sanctions on the banks by local U.S. jurisdictions, but encouraged the Swiss government to consider means to resolve the disputes.[51]

Following heated Senate hearings chaired by Senator D'Amato in April 1996 and in the face of mounting public pressure on the banks, representatives of the banks and major Jewish organizations agreed in May 1996 to create the Independent Committee of Eminent Persons (ICEP), headed by Paul Volcker, to carry out an independent audit of wartime accounts. In response to class action lawsuits filed against the banks in the fall of 1996 and following several serious public relations missteps by the Swiss government and banks,[52] the ICEP and the Swiss Federal Banking Commission subsequently agreed on arrangements to create and monitor a Claims Resolution Tribunal (CRT-I) to determine such claims.[53] This process was launched in July and October 1997, when the Swiss Bankers Association published the names of 5,570 non-Swiss account holders with accounts dormant since 1945. The initial CRT-I process was largely designed and paid for by the banks, which retained control over key threshold determinations. A key step was the identification and publication by the banks of the names of potentially relevant account holders. This process

---

[48] On the initial stage of the Swiss bank claims process, *see* Thomas Buergenthal, *Arbitrating Entitlement to Dormant Bank Accounts*, 15 ICSID Rev. – For. Investment L. J. 301 (2000); Lucy Reed, "Arbitration Principles in Resolving Holocaust Bank Claims," in *Institutional and Procedural Aspects of Mass Claims Settlement Systems* (Int'l Bureau, Permanent Court of Arbitration, ed., The Hague, Kluwer Law International, 2000) 59.
[49] Eizenstat, *op. cit.*, 59.
[50] *Id.* at 61–69
[51] Murphy, *op. cit.*, 148.
[52] Eizenstat, *op. cit.*, 92–98.
[53] Ambassador Eizenstat or other U.S. officials do not appear to have played a direct role in the negotiations to create CRT-I.

of publication proceeded piecemeal, contributing to suspicions about the process by claimants and some observers. Lists of additional potentially relevant account holders were published several times as the CRT process evolved, including 21,000 names of account holders published in early 2001 and another 3,000 names published in January 2005.[54]

Recognizing that Holocaust survivors, victims, and their heirs could not be expected to present documents such as bank books, death certificates, or wills, the CRT-1 rules established a low evidentiary standard. In other respects, the process was cumbersome and expensive. It initially did not prioritize claimants by age or other indicia of need. It did not adopt the techniques for processing large numbers of similar claims together on the basis of common issues or characteristics being implemented during this same period by the UN Compensation Commission. It instead emphasized cumbersome claim-by-claim assessment, utilizing distinguished international arbitrators as decision makers on several types of issues, including some minor ones. The arbitrators' role may have helped to dampen claimants' suspicion and acrimony, but the process required substantial commitments of their (expensive) time. Overall, the CRT-1 process was neither efficient nor economical; a former staff member described it as "expensive, labour-intensive, cumbersome and complex."[55]

The agreements creating the CRT-I process did not end U.S. litigation against the Swiss banks. Class action lawsuits filed against them in 1996 and 1997 on behalf of approximately 18,000 claimants continued and were consolidated in the Eastern District of New York under Chief Judge Edward R. Korman.[56] This litigation included claims both that the banks had wrongly retained victims' assets and that they had laundered looted assets and transacted in the proceeds of slave labor. The litigation and attendant bad publicity in the United States became a running sore for some of the major banks, which were seeking at that time to enhance their stature as significant players in the U.S. and other international markets and were contemplating mergers requiring U.S. regulatory approval.[57] Ambassador Eizenstat made intense but unsuccessful efforts to mediate a settlement of the litigation over the spring and summer of 1998.[58] Thereafter, under pressure from Judge Korman and the

---

[54] William Glaberson, "Swiss Banks Publish Names from Holocaust," *New York Times*, Jan. 13, 2005, C18.

[55] Suzannah Linton, *Righting a Wrong or Prolonging the Agony? The Work of the Claims Resolution Tribunal for Dormant Accounts in Switzerland*, 12 Leiden J. Int'l L. 373, 388 (1999).

[56] In re Holocaust Victims Assets Litigation, No. CV 96–4849 (E.D.N.Y.).

[57] During the late 1990s, the Swiss Bank Corporation and the Union Bank of Switzerland were preparing the merger that produced UBS AG. Eizenstat, *op. cit.*, 125.

[58] *Id.* at 115–64.

threat of sanctions by New York State banking authorities, the parties agreed in 1999 to a large, complex, and wide-ranging settlement.[59] The settlement, finally approved in July 2000, resolved both claims that the banks had wrongfully pocketed victims' accounts and that they had wrongfully benefited from financial transactions with the Nazi regime.[60] The U.S. Department of Justice appeared at the fairness hearing on the proposed settlement and supported its adoption.

Pursuant to the settlement, the banks created a fund of $1.25 billion to be funded in installments over four years; $800 million of the fund was available to bank depositors and their heirs and the balance to other specified types of claims for property losses and other Holocaust-related injuries. Following the settlement, the CRT process was expanded, and a number of other institutions, including the International Organization for Migration in Geneva, were enlisted to assist in claims collection and resolution. As of early 2005, about $700 million reportedly had been paid from the $1.25 billion settlement, including $220 million to bank account owners or their heirs.[61] The process of distributing the settlement fund continues; in April 2005, the U.S. court approved the largest CRT award to date, a $21.8 million payment to the surviving members of two Viennese families that set up a trust account with an unnamed Swiss bank in 1938 to protect ownership of a large sugar refinery. Following the German annexation of Austria, the bank deliberately violated the terms of the trust account and assisted in the sale of enterprise to Nazi supporters.[62]

As discussed later, the U.S. Swiss bank litigation and the ensuing settlement were paralleled by similar U.S. litigation against European insurance companies and several major European firms alleged to have wrongfully benefited from the abuses of the Nazi era. These also gave rise to private agreements creating mass claims processes dealing with tens or hundreds of thousands of claims. Ambassador Eizenstat and other U.S. officials supported creation of these processes and sometimes played an active role in the negotiations leading to their creation. The United States entered into related international

---

[59] *Id.* at 166–86.
[60] *In re* Holocaust Victim Assets Litigation, 105 F. Supp. 2d 139 (E.D.N.Y. Aug. 9, 2000). See 2000 U.S. *Digest, op. cit.*, 445; Murphy, *op. cit.*, 148; *Introduction to the Claims Resolution Process*, http://www.crt-ii.org/introduction.phtm (visited May 4, 2007).
[61] Glaberson, *op. cit.*; Advertisement, "Holocaust-Era Swiss Bank Claims," *New York Times*, Jan. 19, 2005, A17.
[62] Claims Resolution Tribunal Award Maria Victoria Altmann *in re* Account of Osterreichische Zuckerindustrie AG Syndicate, Claim No. 215866/MC (Apr. 13, 2005), 44 ILM 1307 (2005). See William Glaberson, "For Betrayal by Bank and Nazis, $21 Million," *New York Times*, Apr. 14, 2005, A1; Ryan Pearson, "12 Heirs of Nazi Victims Win Swiss Bank Claim," *Washington Post*, Apr. 15, 2005, A5.

agreements with several governments, and the U.S. Department of Justice acted in U.S. courts to support the transfer of claims to the alternative claims processes.

2. Forced and Slave Labor Claims

Ambassador Eizenstat and other U.S. officials played a central role in bringing about a 2000 agreement among the German government, major German industrial concerns, and claimant groups to settle claims that the firms wrongfully benefited from forced and slave labor during World War II.[63]

In the early 1950s, the Federal Republic of Germany began large programs to provide financial support to the State of Israel and compensation to broad classes of individuals who suffered in concentration camps during the Nazi era. Under agreements concluded with Israel and with the Conference on Jewish Material Claims Against Germany and subsequent agreements with other countries, Germany paid more than $60 billion to more than 500,000 Holocaust survivors.[64] However, these programs did not address the full universe of injured persons. They initially were limited to German nationals or refugees, although in the 1960s, they were extended to nationals of some other countries pursuant to bilateral agreements between Germany and the other countries concerned.[65] Further, they did not address claims for forced or slave labor in industrial facilities or camps other than concentration camps.[66]

Following the example of the U.S. litigation against Swiss banks, in the late 1990s, major German firms such as Daimler-Chrysler, Bayer, BMW, Siemens, and Krupp and major German banks became the target of high-visibility litigation and adverse public comment in the United States.[67] Claimants contended that these firms or their corporate predecessors had used forced or slave labor during the Nazi era or were otherwise complicit in Nazi abuses. The U.S. litigation became an issue in U.S.-German relations and led to bilateral negotiations aimed at creating a mechanism to resolve the situation. In February 1999, a number of major German firms jointly pledged to create a fund constituted with contributions from major German corporations and banks to compensate surviving victims of slave and forced labor and other victims.

---

[63] Eizenstat, *op. cit.*, 205–78.
[64] *Id.* at 14–15.
[65] The United States and Germany concluded agreements in 1995 and 1999, providing for 37.5 million DM to be paid to the United States as compensation for distribution to U.S. national claimants who were victims of Nazi persecution. Murphy, *op. cit.*, 105–6.
[66] *Id.* at 136–37.
[67] Eizenstat, *op. cit.*, 229–78; Murphy, *op. cit.*, 137.

Victims' representatives did not immediately accept this initiative. Over the next seventeen months, intense negotiations addressed the definition of eligible claimants, the amounts to be contributed, and the allocation of the funds among eligible claimants and states. Ambassador Eizenstat played an active role seeking to facilitate these negotiations involving government representatives, German firms, claimants, and private lawyers. Agreement was reached on these matters in March 2000.[68] The German government and companies agreed to create a 10 billion DM fund – the Foundation, "Remembrance, Responsibility, and the Future" – to compensate persons who suffered a variety of injuries, including those forced to labor for German enterprises and others who suffered personal injury or property losses at the hands of German companies. (At that time, 10 billion DM equaled approximately $4.9 billion.) Persons forced to work as slave laborers while held in concentration camps, ghettoes, or in other places of confinement under comparable conditions are eligible to receive up to 15,000 DM each (at that time about $7,350). Other forced laborers who worked under less bitter conditions are eligible to receive lesser amounts. In exchange, victims' representatives agreed to voluntarily dismiss the U.S. lawsuits.

With these matters resolved, the German Bundestag adopted legislation creating the foundation and authorizing claims by victims for forced and slave labor and certain other claims, as well as claims by victims or their heirs for property loss or damage, including claims against German banks and insurance companies. Arrangements to implement the claims process were addressed in a joint statement signed in July 2000 on behalf of the German government and by representatives of German companies; the U.S., Israeli, and other governments; and victims' representatives and law firms. The same day, the United States and Germany signed an Executive agreement recording that "the President of the United States has concluded that it would be in the foreign policy interests of the United States for the Foundation to be the exclusive forum and remedy for the resolution of all asserted claims against German companies arising from their involvement in the National Socialist era and World War II" and committing the United States to "recommend dismissal on any valid legal ground" of such claims in U.S. courts.[69]

The United States thereafter filed a statement of interest in each of the approximately fifty-five cases filed in U.S. courts against German concerns

---

[68] *Id.* at 139.

[69] Agreement Concerning the Foundation "Remembrance, Responsibility, and the Future" (United States-Germany), July 17, 2000, 39 ILM (2000) 1298. See 2000 *U.S. Digest, op. cit.*, 448–50; International Organization for Migration, German Forced Labour Compensation Programme, *Slave or Forced Labourer under the Nazi Regime* and *Compensation for Property Loss* (undated pamphlets) (on file with author).

raising wartime claims. This document represented to the court that it would be in the foreign policy interests of the United States for the foundation process to be the exclusive remedy for resolution of covered claims.[70] In general, U.S. courts gave effect to the U.S. statement of interest and dismissed suits against German and other companies involving claims falling within the scope of the new claims processes. One federal district judge was not prepared to accept a voluntary dismissal unless the German Bundestag made changes to the program it had approved; the Second Circuit directed a writ of mandamus to the judge, instructing her to alter her opinion to eliminate the suggestion of directing foreign lawmakers.[71]

3. Other Holocaust-Related Programs

A corresponding process of public pressure and litigation in the United States contributed to France's decision to augment a previously created process to assess and provide compensation for certain claims for wartime abuses.[72] Austria also agreed with the United States to create a process to address claims by Jews and others injured during the Nazi period; the United States again agreed to file statements of interest in U.S. courts urging that the new processes should be the exclusive forum for addressing covered claims.[73]

4. Insurance Claims

Public pressure in the United States and other countries, including pressure by U.S. state insurance regulators, again stimulated negotiations leading to the creation in October 1998 of the International Commission for Holocaust Era Insurance Claims (ICHEIC), chaired by former Secretary of State Lawrence Eagleburger.[74] A senior State Department officer represented the United States

---

[70] Excerpts of the U.S. Statement of Interest are at 2000 U.S. Digest, op. cit., 450–60.
[71] In re Austrian and German Holocaust litigation, 250 F.3d 156 (2d Cir. 2001). See Murphy, op. cit., 144.
[72] Eizenstat, op. cit., 315–37; see Eric Freedman, "The French Commission for the Compensation of Victims of Spoliation: A Critique," Redressing Injuries, op. cit., 139. On U.S. litigation related to creation of the French program, see Michael J. Bayzler and Amber L. Fitzgerald, Trading with the Enemy: Holocaust Restitution, the United States Government, and American Industry, 28 Brook. J. Int'l L. 697–99 (2003).
[73] Agreement Concerning the Austrian Fund "Reconciliation, Peace and Cooperation" (Reconciliation Fund), U.S.-Austria, 40 ILM (2001). See Murphy, op. cit., 150; Hannah Lessig, Richard Rebernik, and Nicola Spitzy, "The Austrian General Settlement Fund: An Overview," Redressing Injuries, op. cit., 699–700; Ian Urbina, "Austria Offers Amends to Nazi-era Survivors," Int'l Herald Tribune, Oct. 17, 2003, 10; Nora Boustany, "For Holocaust Families, Restitution and Reconnection," Washington Post, Nov. 24, 2004, A1.
[74] Murphy, op. cit., 145–47.

in ICHEIC matters, and Ambassador Eizenstat was involved in finalizing the procedures to be used in handling claims against German companies.[75]

In the 1920s and 1930s, life insurance policies were an important savings and investment vehicle for many Europeans. ICHEIC was intended to address claims relating to insurance policies issued between 1920 and 1945 to persons who died under Nazi persecution. The ICHEIC completed its work in March 2007. According to its final statistical report, the ICHEIC claims process resulted in a total of 48,263 offers of settlement, with a value of more than $300 million.[76] The process, which took nine years, was criticized in its initial years for delays and high operating costs.[77]

As in the case of the German forced labor claims, the U.S. Executive Branch, through the Justice Department, acted to support the IHEIC process. The United States supported successful challenges to the constitutionality of U.S. state insurance laws aimed at providing redress to claimants through domestic procedures. In *American Insurance Association v. Garamendi*, the U.S. Supreme Court overturned California's Holocaust Victim Insurance Relief Act (HVIRA), which required, inter alia, insurance companies doing business in California to disclose publicly information concerning Holocaust-era policies. The Supreme Court found the HVIRA unconstitutional because it conflicted with federal policy favoring resolution of these claims through the internationally agreed process.[78]

C. THE UN COMPENSATION COMMISSION

The United Nations Compensation Commission (UNCC) in Geneva has been a highly successful, if not particularly well-known, international claims institution. The UNCC completed work on its caseload of more than 2.6 claims in July 2006; as of May 2007, it had paid out about $22 billion in compensation. The average success rate of all categories of completed claims is approximately 14.9 percent.[79] With claims processing completed, the UNCC now operates with a small secretariat to implement payments to claimants as additional funds become available.

The U.S. Department of State played a central role in the UNCC's creation and successful operation. Writing in 1994, the lawyer heading the

---

[75] Eizenstat, *op. cit.*, 266–68.
[76] See http://www.icheic.org/pdf/stats-19mar07.pdf (visited May 8, 2007).
[77] See "Too Late, Too Slow, Too Expensive," *The Economist*, Aug. 2, 2003, 12; *Line to Nowhere*, Id. at 61.
[78] *American Insurance Association v. Garamendi*, 539 U.S. 396 (2003).
[79] UNCC Web site, at http://www2.unog.ch/uncc (visited May 4, 2007). The UNCC Web site includes a thorough bibliography on the Commission.

State Department's claims office described the U.S. role in the following terms:

> It is hard to imagine a better recent example of the U.S. Government playing a fundamental role in the creation of a new international institution. The United States was the driving force behind the relevant provisions in the Security Council resolutions that established the Commission, developed drafts of and pressed for the adoption of all of the key decisions of the UNCC Governing Council during its early period, and worked assiduously behind the scenes to ensure that the Commission would become an effective body.[80]

The establishment of the UNCC, and the major role played by the United States in its creation, had much to do with the unique international situation at the time of Iraq's August 1990 invasion and occupation of Kuwait. The invasion came at a time when the international system was undergoing fundamental transformations. The Berlin Wall came down in 1989. The Union of Soviet Socialist Republics was beset by internal stresses and could not continue the military and political competition with the West that marked the Cold War. The Soviet leadership was prepared to contemplate new relationships with the West. Although it could not yet be said that the Cold War had ended, these circumstances created political space that allowed much greater cooperation between the United States and the Soviet Union. The transformation in the relationship between the superpowers was particularly evident in the Security Council. For a brief period in the early 1990s, to an extent not seen before and not likely to be seen again, the Council played the role of vigorous protector of international peace and security envisioned by Chapter VII of the United Nations Charter.

Following the August 1990 invasion, President George H. W. Bush, Secretary of State James Baker, and other senior U.S. officials quickly settled on a strategy incorporating recourse to the Security Council as an important element in forging a vigorous international response.[81] It is beyond the scope of this chapter to describe the course of diplomacy prior to the Gulf War, but several of the resolutions adopted by the Security Council during this period laid the foundations for the UNCC. In October 1990, the Council adopted Resolution 674, a mandatory Chapter VII resolution addressing human rights and other abuses by Iraq, including hostage taking, threatening diplomatic

---

[80] Ronald J. Bettauer, "Establishment of the United Nations Compensation Commission: The U.S. Government Perspective," in Lillich, *The United Nations Compensation Commission*, op. cit., 29. I was counselor for legal affairs in the U.S. Mission in Geneva 1990–95 and was involved in much of the behind-the-scenes work that Bettauer cites.

[81] See James A. Baker, III, *The Politics of Diplomacy: Revolution, War & Peace, 1989–1992* (1995), 275–328.

establishments in Kuwait, abuse of Kuwaiti civilians, and theft and destruction of Kuwaiti property.[82] Paragraph 8 of Resolution 674 "[r]eminds Iraq that under international law it is liable for any loss, damage or injury arising in regard to Kuwait and third States, and their nationals and corporations, as a result of the invasion and illegal occupation of Kuwait by Iraq."

The materials I reviewed do not trace the precise parentage of paragraph 8; Secretary Baker's memoirs do not discuss the resolution. Nevertheless, the Security Council's resolutions during this period were all heavily influenced by the United States; as State Department lawyer Ron Bettauer makes clear, "[t]he United States was the driving force behind the relevant provisions of the Security Council resolutions" establishing the UNCC.[83] It therefore seems highly probable that the thinking behind paragraph 8 was largely, if not exclusively, "made in the U.S.A."

Following the successful conclusion of military operations against Iraq in Operation Desert Storm in March 1991, the Security Council turned to defining the terms for ending the conflict and restoring international peace and security. The primary vehicle for doing so was the wide-ranging Security Council Resolution 687,[84] sometimes described as "the mother of all Security Council resolutions."[85] In paragraph 16, the Security Council

> reaffirms that Iraq . . . is liable under international law for any direct loss, damage, including environmental damage and the depletion of natural resources, or injury to foreign Governments, nationals or corporations, as a result of Iraq's unlawful invasion and occupation of Kuwait.

In paragraph 18, the Council decided "to create a fund to pay compensation for claims that fall within paragraph 16 and to establish a Commission that will administer the fund." Paragraph 19 directed the UN secretary-general to develop recommendations to the Security Council regarding creation and operation of the fund and commission. The secretary-general's recommendations were adopted and the compensation fund created by Security Council Resolution 692.[86]

The United States played a central role in drafting both Resolutions 687 and 692. Moreover, as Bettauer notes, it likewise was a major actor in the work

---

[82] S/RES/674 (1990), Oct. 29, 1990.
[83] Ronald J. Bettauer in Lillich, *The United Nations Compensation Commission, op. cit.*, 29, 31–32.
[84] S/RES/687 (1991), Apr. 3, 1991, 30 ILM (1991) 846.
[85] Prior to the opening of allied military operations in Operation Desert Storm in January 1991, Saddam Hussein famously promised that the ensuing conflict would be "the mother of all battles."
[86] S/RES/692 (1991), May 20, 1991.

of the UNCC's Governing Council both during its organizational stages and in later years. I can affirm from personal experience that the key decisions adopted by the UNCC Governing Council during its early years establishing the framework for the UNCC claims process were based on proposals and texts initiated by the U.S. delegation.

The United States also played a vital role in assuring funding for the UNCC during its initial years. The Security Council resolutions envisioned that the claims process would be funded with a portion of the proceeds of Iraqi oil exports, but Iraq declined for several years to export oil on the terms set by Security Council Resolution 706 (1991) and subsequent resolutions. This left the UNCC without a source of funds for salaries and operating costs, let alone for paying approved awards of compensation. To address this situation, the U.S. State Department, with the concurrence of the Department of the Treasury (the holder of blocked Iraqi assets), was instrumental in developing and obtaining approval of Security Council Resolution 778 in October 1992.[87] Under this Chapter VII resolution, states holding Iraqi oil or the proceeds of Iraqi oil sales paid for after sanctions were imposed in August 1990 were required to transfer those funds or the proceeds of the oil to a UN escrow account. Thirty percent of the transferred funds were then allocated to the UNCC. No state was required to transfer more than $200 million or 50 percent of the total transferred. This mechanism provided the funds that kept the UNCC going during its early years.[88] The United States, which held the largest amount of frozen Iraqi assets held by any country, took domestic action to implement Resolution 778[89] and provided 50 percent of all funds eventually generated through this process.[90]

The vigorous U.S. support for creation and operation of the UNCC was not primarily driven by concern for the interests of U.S. claimants. The damage to U.S. nationals and firms caused by the invasion and occupation of Kuwait, although hardly small, was modest in relation to that suffered by many other

---

[87] S/RES/778 (1992), Oct. 2, 1992. See Bettauer in Lillich, *The United Nations Compensation Commission, op. cit.*, 35. ("The United States then led an effort to develop another resolution under which frozen Iraqi assets and Iraqi-owned oil located outside Iraq could be used to fund humanitarian relief and UN activities under resolution 687, including the Compensation Fund.")

[88] Iraq began oil exports under Security Council Resolution 986 late in 1996, providing stable funding for the UNCC's later years.

[89] Transfer of Certain Iraqi Government Assets Held by Domestic Banks, Executive Order No. 12817, 3 C.F.R. 317 (1992).

[90] Veijo Heiskanen, *The United Nations Compensation Commission*, 296 Recueil des Cours 385 (2002). Under paragraph 17 of Security Council Resolution 1483 (2003), amounts of frozen assets advanced by the United States and other countries under Resolution 778 were repaid from funds held by the United Nations before the balance was transferred to Iraq.

countries. Overall, the UNCC received almost 2.7 million claims, seeking more than $350 billion in compensation (an asserted value that experience has shown to be much inflated[91]). According to the U.S. Department of State, the U.S. government "filed 3,254 claims valued at approximately $1.79 billion. As of December 5, 2001, 2,991 of these claims have been awarded a total of $665.3 million, which is being paid in installments as funds become available. The number of U.S.-filed claims still pending is 194, worth approximately $236.8 million."[92] Perhaps because of the comparatively limited U.S. commercial interests at stake, and because the organization was working well and to the general satisfaction of countries and claimants, the UNCC carried on for many years with little or no visibility in U.S. foreign policy circles or in Congress.[93]

The UNCC acquired visibility within senior levels of the U.S. government only following the March 2003 U.S.-led invasion of Iraq and subsequent U.S. efforts to develop political and financial support for a new Iraqi polity. Ironically, James Baker, who led in forging the Security Council consensus against Iraq as U.S. secretary of state in 1990–91, undertook the task of persuading Iraq's foreign creditors to defer or, better yet, forgive Iraq's external debts. During this period, some Iraqi political figures, international NGOs, and Washington think tanks came to focus on the UNCC process and on the significant amount of Iraqi oil revenues previously channeled to paying claims against Iraq.[94] Although some Iraqi and other critics denounced the UNCC process as a form of "odious debt" and called for its complete termination,[95] Kuwait and other countries or entities with claims still unprocessed or unpaid strongly opposed ending the process. (In my view, the "odious debt" argument rang hollow in respect of injuries addressed by the UNCC, which did not involve loans or commercial transactions voluntarily concluded by an outside party with the Iraqi regime.[96] There is no justice in denying UNCC claimants compensation because of the moral failings of the regime that injured them.)

---

[91] John R. Crook, *The UN Compensation Commission: What Now?* 5 Int'l L.- For. du Droit Int'l 279–80 (2003).

[92] See http://www.state.gov/s/l/3200.htm (visited May 4, 2007).

[93] I recall conversations in 1999 or 2000 with a well-informed assistant secretary of state, a former ambassador in an important Arab country and a "star" in the Foreign Service, who was largely unaware of the UNCC and its work.

[94] A January 2003 study by the Center for Strategic and International Studies called for the UNCC to stop all work on pending claims and to halt or reduce payments on claims already approved. Frederick D. Barton and Bathsheba N. Crocker, "A Wiser Peace: An Action Study for a Post-Conflict Iraq," at http://www.csis.org/media/csis/pubs/wiserpeace.pdf (visited May 8, 2007).

[95] See Crook, *UNCC – What Now? op cit.*, 281, n. 25.

[96] *Id.* at 281. The UNCC process did not address prewar or debt claims, which under paragraph 16 of Resolution 687 "will be addressed through the normal mechanisms."

In any event, the United States faced a dilemma regarding continuing withholdings from Iraq's oil exports to finance the UNCC claims program. The dilemma was resolved in May 2003, when the Security Council, with U.S. support, adopted a compromise maintaining funding for the UNCC from Iraqi oil exports but at a much reduced level. Security Council Resolution 1483 dealt broadly with international measures to support the reconstruction and rehabilitation of Iraq. Paragraph 20 provided that all proceeds of Iraqi export sales of petroleum, petroleum products, and natural gas "shall be deposited into the Development Fund for Iraq until such time as an internationally recognized, representative government of Iraq is properly constituted." Paragraph 21 provides that 5 percent of these proceeds then shall be deposited into the Compensation Fund. The paragraph continues that

> unless an internationally recognized, representative government of Iraq and the Governing Council of the United Nations Compensation Commission, *in the exercise of its authority over methods of ensuring that payments are made into the Compensation Fund*, decide otherwise, this requirement shall be binding on a properly constituted, internationally recognized, representative government of Iraq and any successor thereto.[97]

As of this writing (May 2007), no such agreement has been reached. In 2005, the UNCC Governing Council adopted procedures providing for significantly reduced payments of approved claims.[98]

D. CONCLUSION

Each of the three institutions discussed in this chapter has accomplished the task for which it was created.

The Iran–U.S. Claims Tribunal was the child of both necessity and invention. Despite its unhappy origins, it has largely accomplished what it was created to do. The claims of private U.S. claimants and of U.S. banks have long since been resolved, generally to claimants' satisfaction. In its later years, the Tribunal has survived, addressing (albeit at a slow pace) very large claims between the two governments, many involving pre-1979 military sales relationships. Notwithstanding the generally dismal state of U.S.–Iranian relations, it has continued to receive U.S. government support, and I know of no serious suggestions from the U.S. side that the Tribunal be terminated before its work is done.

---

[97] Italics added. The effect of the italicized language is to make any decisions to alter or rescind the 5 percent allocation subject to the veto by any permanent member of the Council.

[98] UNCC Press Release PR/2005/6 (April 7, 2005), at http://www2.unog.ch/uncc (visited May 4, 2007).

The Holocaust-related institutions created in the 1990s have likewise largely fulfilled their purposes. They gave effect to strong public and Congressional support for U.S. government action supporting victims of Nazi abuses and their heirs. The claimants embodied compelling human stories and often were represented by advocates able to present those stories in an aggressive, compelling way. The American Jewish community supported vigorous U.S. action. Arrayed on the other side were foreign corporate and financial interests whose wartime conduct left them properly subject to criticism, and for whom a positive image in U.S. markets was important. Support for the claimants was good politics at all levels of government.

These circumstances combined to create political space within which U.S. policy makers and officials worked to support the creation of new institutions. There was limited risk of domestic criticism, save perhaps from some claimants and class action lawyers arguing that more generous compensation eventually might be possible through litigation in U.S. courts. However, the unusual array of parties involved in the underlying disputes (private claimants and respondents, governments, groups representing claimants, aggressive trial lawyers, politicians) demanded an unusual measure of imagination, flexibility, and determination on the part of government officials and government lawyers involved.

The UNCC likewise has been a success. It has completed its enormous claims processing function, paid out more than $22 billion in compensation, and now has dramatically downsized. Only a few staff members remain to deal with future payments, archiving, and other remaining work. Given the small percentage of oil revenues allocated for paying claims under Security Council Resolution 1483, and the low volume of Iraq's oil exports given decrepit oil infrastructure and continuing terrorist attacks, it seems unlikely that UNCC funding will be available for most of the remaining awards approved by the Commission but not yet paid. In that case, the UNCC's claims assessments offer a reasoned basis for eventual lump-sum claims settlement agreements between a restored Iraq and its neighbors.[99]

All three of these institutions are examples of past U.S. ability to help create novel and effective international claims institutions to further U.S. policy goals. All three have in turn served as laboratories for creating new "mass claims technologies" – claims collection and processing techniques, software, powerful databases, and a generation of skilled people able to design and administer them. These skills and technologies exist and can be used again. (Unfortunately, some reinvention may be required, as successful programs such as the UNCC and the International Organization for Migration's

---

[99] See Crook, *UNCC – What Now? op. cit.*, 281–82.

Holocaust compensation programs close down and consign their records and software to archives.)

These institutions did not arise spontaneously. They all began with judgments by senior U.S. policy makers that law-based claims institutions had a role to play in addressing current foreign policy challenges. These judgments were backed up by serious commitments of skilled and dedicated people and other public resources. All three institutions then enjoyed political support inside the United States (or at least an absence of effective opposition), stood to benefit some U.S. claimants, and involved either negligible financial cost or risk to the United States or (in the case of the Iran Tribunal) risks seen as acceptable under the circumstances.

Such conditions have not existed in recent years. The years of the George W. Bush administration were dominated by the September 11 attacks on the United States and the administration's ensuing "global war on terrorism." These efforts preoccupied government policy makers and their lawyers and left little room for legal initiatives aimed at other kinds of problems. Moreover, some powerful administration officials saw little role for international law and institutions as elements of U.S. policy. With the advent of the new administration, circumstances will surely arise again in which the law-based, systematic resolution of large numbers of claims will support some U.S. foreign policy goal. When that occurs, the three mechanisms discussed here demonstrate that, with imagination, will, and resources, it can be done.

10

Does the United States Support International Tribunals? The Case of the Multilateral Trade System

JEFFREY L. DUNOFF[*]

The World Trade Organization's (WTO's) dispute settlement system represents an unprecedented grant of legal authority to international tribunals to enforce international legal norms, backed by the threat of economic sanctions. The United States was not only the principle *demandeur* of this system but also has been the most active participant. At first glance, the U.S. approach to dispute settlement in the trade area appears to contrast sharply with its approach to legalized dispute settlement in many other areas of international relations. Indeed, the United States' leading role in this area seems even more remarkable in light of the country's history of economic protectionism.

However, a closer look at the history of U.S. approaches to the resolution of trade disputes suggests that a more nuanced appraisal is in order. This history reveals that although the United States has generally supported rule-based approaches to settling trade disputes, at times it has evidenced ambivalence about the normative desirability and practical utility of a legalized dispute settlement process in the trade area. It also suggests that U.S. government support for judicialized dispute settlement in international trade is based less on an abstract commitment to the rule of law in international relations than on pragmatic, short-term, and highly contextual calculations that this mechanism serves U.S. interests better than alternative arrangements. Finally, this history suggests that the level of U.S. commitment to, and participation in, legalized

---

[*] Charles Klein Professor of Law and Government and Director, Institute for International Law and Public Policy, Temple University Beasley School of Law. Much of the research for this chapter was conducted when I was a visiting fellow at the Lauterpacht Centre for International Law at Cambridge University. Earlier versions were presented at a workshop, "U.S. Attitudes and Practices towards International Courts and Tribunals," at the Asser Institute at The Hague; a seminar at Georgetown University Law Center; and the conference "Next Steps in the U.S. Relationship with International Courts and Tribunals" at The George Washington University School of Law. I am grateful for helpful comments by participants at those events and for excellent research by Temple law student Ben Franks.

trade dispute resolution mechanisms reflects a two-level game in which U.S. officials mediate conflicting pressures generated by their foreign counterparts and domestic political actors. For these reasons, continued U.S. commitment to and support of judicialized dispute settlement in the trade area in general, and the WTO in particular, should not be assumed.

This chapter traces the history of U.S. attitudes toward judicialized resolution of international trade disputes. For ease of exposition, the analysis proceeds in chronological fashion; hence Part A provides a brief description of the United States' shift to a liberalized trade policy in the 1930s and its approach to resolution of trade disputes at that time. Part B reviews the birth of the multilateral trade system in the 1940s and, in particular, U.S. approaches to dispute resolution at the dawn of the international trade regime. Part C traces the twists and turns in U.S. attitudes to legalized dispute resolution during the General Agreement on Tariffs and Trade years and the U.S. role in creating the WTO's dispute settlement system. Part D briefly outlines the most salient features of the WTO dispute settlement system. Part E reviews the U.S. experience during the first decade of WTO dispute resolution. A brief conclusion speculates on what may lie ahead.

A. THE TURN TO LIBERAL TRADE POLICIES

The U.S. economy was largely agricultural from the nation's founding until the early nineteenth century. During these early years of the republic, there were few imports; however, with the growth in British manufacturing, imports of cotton and woolen goods, and later of iron manufactures, rose significantly. During the 1812 war with England, trade with the enemy was prohibited, and all import duties were doubled. These acts gave a tremendous stimulus to areas of economic activity previously served by imports. The consequent rise of a class of manufacturers, whose continued success depended largely on continued protection, formed an early political base for what would become a tradition of protectionist policies.[1]

The country's constitutional and political structure reinforced protectionist tendencies. The U.S. Constitution vests Congress with authority to "regulate Commerce with foreign Nations." As a historical matter, the legislature tended to enact protectionist trade policies. Congress's historical receptiveness to protectionist policy is often explained as a matter of interest-group politics.[2] The

---

[1] An early and still influential account of the nation's early trade politics is F. W. Taussig, *The Tariff History of the United States* (7th ed., 1922).
[2] To be sure, during the late nineteenth and early twentieth centuries, tariff policy was deeply associated with partisan politics. During these years, the Democrats pursued a largely rural

economic benefits of trade liberalization are widely diffused among numerous consumers who face large transaction costs in organizing to lobby for such measures. In contrast, the dislocations associated with trade liberalization will often fall on easily identifiable, concentrated, and well-organized groups. These groups have ample incentives to organize and lobby their representatives for protectionist legislation. As a result, these groups will tend to exercise disproportionate influence in the legislative process. As one Senator colorfully explained:

> [O]ur experience in writing tariff legislation . . . has been discouraging. Trading between groups and sections is inevitable. Log-rolling is inevitable, and in its most pernicious form. We do not write a national tariff law. We jam together, through various unholy alliances and combinations, a potpourri or hodgepodge of section and local tariff rates, which often add to our troubles and increase world misery.[3]

Congressional control over tariffs eventually led, in 1930, to passage of the Smoot-Hawley legislation, which raised U.S. import duties to their highest levels ever. In short order, Canada, Cuba, France, Mexico, Italy, Spain, Australia, and New Zealand all raised their tariffs; twenty-six states imposed quotas and exchange controls by 1931; and the United Kingdom abandoned liberalized trade the following year.

This experience helped trigger a sea change in U.S. policies. First, political elites could no longer ignore the reality that tariff policy was not simply a matter of domestic policy. As Congress came to appreciate the foreign implications of trade policy, the Roosevelt administration could persuasively argue that the president could only negotiate the opening of foreign markets if he had authority to open the U.S. market. This argument led Congress to pass the 1934 Reciprocal Trade Agreements Act (RTA), which authorized the president to negotiate executive agreements with other states for the purpose of expanding foreign trade; it also authorized the president to proclaim tariff rate reductions in the context of such agreements.[4]

---

electoral base in the South and West and were committed to lowering tariffs. Republicans generally championed protective tariffs that benefited manufacturing interests in the Northeast. Thus, Republican electoral triumphs in 1890, 1896, and 1920 produced sharp rises in tariffs; Democratic victories in 1892 and 1912 led to tariff reductions. However, the great realignment in domestic politics that occurred in the 1930s and the shift of tariff-making authority from the Congress to the president described in the text have greatly lessened the partisan nature of tariff policy. *See*, e.g., John J. Coleman, *Party Decline in America: Policy, Politics, and the Fiscal State* (Princeton University Press, 1996); James Sundquist, *Dynamics of the Party System: Alignment and Realignment of Political Parties in the United States* (Brookings Institution, 1983).

[3] 78 Cong. Rec. 10379 (1934) (remarks of Sen. Cooper), quoted in John H. Jackson et al., *Legal Problems of International Economic Relations* (4th ed., West, 2002).

[4] The Congressional dynamics behind the RTA are examined in Douglas A. Irwin, "From Smoot-Hawley to Reciprocal Trade Agreements: Changing Course of U.S. Trade Policy in

This historic legislation was designed, in part, to change the structural dynamics of U.S. trade policy. First, by placing tariff politics in the context of bilateral trade agreements, the RTA sought to create export-oriented constituencies who would benefit from trade agreements and who could countervail the protectionist voices of import-sensitive industries in the tariff context.[5] Second, shifting tariff authority to the president eliminated congressional logrolling and raised the political salience of the costs of protectionism to consumers that would otherwise have been neglected because they were widely dispersed across congressional districts.[6] Although the 1934 bill only granted the president tariff authority for three years and was introduced and supported as an emergency measure, advocates for liberalized trade within the administration never viewed the shift of tariff authority from Congress as a short-term policy.

The second critical event driving the change in approach to U.S. foreign economic policy was President Roosevelt's decision, early in World War II, to devote significant intellectual and political resources to planning the postwar international economy. Responsibility for generating economic policy fell within three main bodies: the State Department under Secretary of State Cordell Hull, Under-Secretary of State Sumner Welles, and Special Advisor Leo Pasvolsky; the Treasury Department under Treasury Secretary Henry Morgenthau, Jr., and his deputy in charge of international financial issues, Harry Dexter White; and the Board of Economic Warfare under Vice President Henry Wallace. These men believed that the United States' refusal to join the League of Nations had been a serious mistake with significant adverse consequences and were committed to basing future U.S. policy on participation in a world organization. They also believed that the breakdown of the last peace settlement lay largely in the mishandling of economic problems. Hull, in particular, was committed to the idea that "unhampered trade dovetailed with peace; high tariffs, trade barriers, and unfair economic competition, with war."[7]

---

the 1930s," in *The Defining Moment: The Great Depression and the American Economy in the Twentieth Century* (Michael D. Bordo et al. eds., University of Chicago Press, 1998), 337; William A. Diebold, Jr., *New Directions in Our Trade Policy* (Council on Foreign Relations, 1941).

[5] Michael Bailey, Judith Goldstein, and Barry R. Weingast, *The Institutional Roots of American Trade Policy*, 49 World Pol. 309 (1997).

[6] Robert Baldwin, "U.S. Trade Policies: The Role of the Executive Branch," in *Constituent Interests and U.S. Trade Policies* (Alan Deardorff and Robert M. Stern eds., University of Michigan Press, 1998), 65.

[7] Cordell Hull, *The Memoirs of Cordell Hull*, Vol. 1 (Hodder & Stoughton, 1948), 81. A large literature explores the connection between commerce and peace. For recent contributions, see Padideh Alai et al. eds., *Trade as the Guarantor of Peace, Liberty and Security? Critical, Historical, and Empirical Perspectives* (American Society of International Law, 2006). For a useful analysis of Hull's thinking on trade liberalization, see William R. Allen, *The International Trade Philosophy of Cordell Hull, 1907–1933*, 43 Am. Econ. Rev. 101 (1953).

Pursuant to the RTA, and under Hull's vigorous leadership, the United States entered into a number of bilateral agreements during the 1930s. In general, these agreements contained a series of bargained-for tariff reductions. The agreements also contained a number of provisions designed to ensure that the commercial value of tariff reductions would not be offset by alternative trade restrictions. Finally, because the negotiators knew that they could not anticipate all future contingencies that might diminish the value of tariff reductions, many of these agreements contained a clause calling for consultations in the event a party introduced "any measure ... even though it does not conflict with the terms of this agreement" that would "nullify or impair" the value of the treaty.[8]

These early treaties did not contemplate any form of legalized or judicial proceedings to resolve disputes, a pattern that mirrored a larger worldwide practice of providing for dispute settlement in commercial treaties by voluntary consultations, rather than through legalized dispute settlement.[9] The provisions for consultations and the lack of judicialized dispute resolution clauses suggest that states negotiating these agreements were much more concerned with maintaining a general sense of reciprocity and balance of trading

---

[8] See, e.g., U.S.-France Trade Agreement (opened for signature May 6, 1936) 199 LNTS 259 art XI (if either party adopts a measure that the other considers "to have the effect of nullifying or materially impairing any important object of the Agreement, such other Government shall be free to propose negotiations for the modification of this Agreement"); U.S.-Canada Trade Agreement (opened for signature November 17, 1938) 199 LNTS 91 art XV (if one party believes the other has adopted a measure "nullifying or impairing any of the objects of the Agreement, the Government which has adopted [the] measure shall consider any such representations and proposals as the other may make, with a view to effecting a mutually satisfactory adjustment of the matter").

The United States adapted this language from a recommendation by the 1933 London Economic and Monetary Conference that called for trade agreements to contain clauses calling for consultations in the event of a "new practice ... not covered by the treaties in operation ... considered by the other [party] to impair the value of the treaty." See League of Nations, Reports approved by the Conference on July 27, 1933, and Resolutions adopted by the Bureau (Official No. C.435.M.220.1933.II), at 30.

[9] For example, none of the seventy-three contemporaneous bilateral commercial treaties among European states provided for legalized, third-party dispute settlement. League of Nations, Memorandum Relating to the Pacific Settlement of International Disputes Concerning Economic Questions in General and Commercial and Customs Questions in Particular, Official No. E.666.1931.II.B.1. Perhaps as an alternative, these treaties typically permitted withdrawal in the event that one party was dissatisfied with another's performance. As a general matter, U.S. trade agreements were terminable on six months' notice.

One notable effort to provide for judicialized settlement of trade dispute failed. The International Convention for the Abolition of Import and Export Prohibitions and Restrictions (opened for signature November 8, 1927) 97 LNTS 391, provided for referral of "dispute[s] of a legal nature" to the PCIJ. This agreement did not attract a sufficient number of ratifications and was never implemented.

opportunities than with strict legal compliance.[10] The underlying premise – apparently widely accepted at the time – was that economic disputes could be better addressed through diplomatic rather than legalistic mechanisms.[11]

Against this backdrop – a shift in trade policy responsibility from the Congress to the Executive, a determination not to repeat the mistakes of the interwar years, a growing patchwork of bilateral treaties, and a tradition of thought that trade disputes are best resolved through diplomatic as opposed to legal means – the Roosevelt administration embarked on a plan to construct a multilateral, liberal postwar international economy.

B. THE BIRTH OF THE INTERNATIONAL TRADE SYSTEM: FROM THE INTERNATIONAL TRADE ORGANIZATION TO THE GENERAL AGREEMENT ON TARIFFS AND TRADE

The Roosevelt administration was acutely aware of the unsuccessful efforts to reach multilateral commercial agreements during the interwar years[12] and was committed to reaching a different outcome after World War II. Hence, during the latter stages of the war, the United States engaged the allies in a series of discussions concerning the shape of the postwar economic order.

As part of these efforts, the United States began developing plans for a new International Trade Organization (ITO) and in December 1945 circulated to other governments its "Proposals for Expansion of World Trade and Employment."[13] This document called for creation of an ITO within the United Nations (UN) system to oversee and govern compliance with rules concerning a wide range of economic issues including trade, restrictive business practices, commodity arrangements, and international labor issues. It provided that the ITO should include among its functions the duty "to interpret the provisions [of the treaty creating the ITO] . . . to consult with members regarding disputes growing out of [these] provisions . . . and to provide a mechanism for the settlement of such disputes." However, the Proposals did not set

---

[10] Robert E. Hudec, *The GATT Legal System: A Diplomat's Jurisprudence*, 4 J. World Trade L. 615 (1970) [hereinafter "Diplomat's Jurisprudence"].

[11] *See*, e.g., League of Nations, Procedure for the Friendly Settlement of Economic Disputes between States, Off. No. C.57.M.32.1932.II.B at 4.

[12] For example, the agreements reached at the 1927 Geneva Conference were not widely ratified, and the more ambitious 1933 London Monetary and Economic Conference could not even agree on proposals to be submitted for ratification. For an authoritative history, *see* League of Nations, *Commercial Policy in the Interwar Period: International Proposals and National Policies* (1942).

[13] The ideas contained in the Proposals had been discussed in the context of Anglo-American negotiations over U.S. loans to the United Kingdom. The United Kingdom expressed its "full agreement on all important points" in the U.S. Proposals when they were issued.

out in any detail how this proposed dispute settlement mechanism would be structured or operate.

Other states were receptive to the idea of an international body, and plans to commence formal negotiations ensued. In February 1946, the United States successfully introduced a resolution before the new UN Economic and Social Council creating a Preparatory Committee to draft an ITO Charter, which would then be adopted under the United Nations Conference on Trade and Employment.[14]

1. *The Original U.S. Draft*

Prior to the Preparatory Committee's first meeting, the United States circulated the "Suggested Charter for an International Trade Organization of the United Nations."[15] The Suggested Charter contained two dispute settlement mechanisms. The first, patterned on provisions in the U.S. bilateral trade agreements, was limited to the commercial provisions of the draft Charter and contemplated a three-step process. Article 30 provided that "if any Member should consider that any measure adopted by another Member, whether or not it conflicts with the terms of this Chapter, has the effect of nullifying or impairing any object of this Chapter" the parties shall enter into consultations "with a view to effecting a mutually satisfactory adjustment of the matter." If no agreement is reached, then "either Member shall refer the matter to the Organization, which shall investigate the matter and make appropriate recommendations to the Members concerned." Moreover, the Organization, "if it considers the case serious enough to justify such action," can authorize the complaining party to suspend the application to the non-complying Member of obligations or concessions.[16]

This language, with some modifications, would serve as the basis for nearly fifty years of dispute resolution under the General Agreement on Tariffs and Trade (GATT). For current purposes, two features of the U.S. proposal bear emphasis. First, the provision reflects a sense that disputes should be resolved on the basis of reciprocity and general balance of trading opportunities rather than through highly legalized processes; the U.S. administration emphasized

---

[14] For an excellent discussion, which informs the analysis that follows, *see* Clair Wilcox, *A Charter for World Trade* (Macmillan Co., 1949), 36–50. Wilcox served as chair or vice-chair of the U.S. delegation during much of the negotiations over the ITO Charter.

[15] The Suggested Charter is reproduced as Annexure 11 in the Report of the First Session of the Preparatory Committee of the United Nations Conference on Trade and Employment.

[16] In the event that obligations or concessions were suspended, the Suggested Charter also provided that the other member was then free to withdraw from the Organization upon sixty days' notice.

that the purpose of permitting sanctions is "merely to redress the balance between those members which are carrying out the provisions and purposes of the Charter and those which are not."[17] Second, the provision reflects the U.S. commitment to multilateralism in the trade realm. The U.S. perspective was that, independent of any Charter provisions, states possessed an inherent ability to retaliate against noncompliance. However, the nullification and impairment procedure

> introduces a new principle, the voluntary grant of authority to an international body to limit this power. The first objective is to tame retaliation, to keep it within bounds..., in sum to convert it from a weapon of economic warfare to an instrument of international order. The second objective is to preserve and adjust to changing circumstances by peaceful methods of consultation and adjustment the mutuality of benefits and obligations conferred by the Charter.... [T]he function of the Organization is to ensure that compensatory action [does] not tip the balance the other way. In the last analysis the procedure is not designed to invite retaliation or to invoke sanctions, but to maintain the net balance of interests provided for in the Charter as a whole.[18]

The Suggested Charter contained another dispute settlement provision, one that was highly legalized and applicable to all questions regarding the draft Charter (i.e., not simply the chapter on commercial policy). This provision outlined a three-step process for addressing "any question or difference concerning the interpretation of this Charter." First, the question would be referred to an Executive Board responsible for conducting the ITO's business "for a ruling thereon." These rulings could then be referred to the Conference, a plenary body of all ITO members. "Any justiciable issue" arising out of a Conference ruling could, with the Conference's consent, "be submitted by any party to the dispute to the International Court of Justice."[19] This article also provided that "[t]he [ITO] may, with the authorization of the [UN General Assembly] refer any question concerning the interpretation of the Charter to the International Court of Justice with a request for an Advisory Opinion thereon." This rather remarkable provision would have granted the

---

[17] U.S. Department of State, Nature of Enforcement in the New York Draft of the ITO Charter, reprinted in Hearings on Operation of the Trade Agreements Act and Proposed ITO before the Senate Finance Committee, 80th Cong., 1st Sess. (1947) 358 [hereinafter Senate Hearing].

[18] William A. Brown, *The United States and the Restoration of World Trade: An Analysis and Appraisal of the ITO Charter and the General Agreement on Tariffs and Trade* (1950), 92.

[19] Another clause provided that if the Conference ruling touched upon matters affecting national security (i.e., related to trade in fissionable materials, traffic in arms, etc.), it could be appealed to the International Court of Justice without the necessity of obtaining the consent of the Conference.

International Court of Justice (ICJ) jurisdiction[20] over not only trade disputes but also a host of other international economic issues addressed in the Suggested Charter, including employment issues, restrictive business practices, intergovernmental commodity arrangements, and other issues.[21]

This provision reflected a second strand of American thought. This strand, associated with Hull and others in the State Department, placed great weight on legal commitments, procedures, and enforcement mechanisms. Thus, many U.S. government officials contemplated that the role of the ITO "would be to interpret and, if need be, enforce the code; its role would thus be not unlike that of a court in determining whether crimes have occurred."[22] Hull's successor as secretary of state, Dean Acheson, summarized the rationale behind the push for legalized enforcement when he stated, "No code of laws is worth very much without an authoritative body to interpret it and administer it."[23]

2. The Drafting Process and Creation of the GATT

In all, four conferences to draft an ITO Charter were held. For current purposes, two developments during this process are of particular importance. First is the fate of the U.S. proposals regarding dispute resolution. Although the United States' proposed "nullification and impairment" clause was broadened in a few different ways through the course of negotiations,[24] it emerged

---

[20] The Suggested Charter provided that "the Members accept the jurisdiction of the Court in respect to any dispute submitted to the Court under this article."

[21] This second dispute settlement provision can be usefully contrasted with the International Monetary Fund Articles of Agreement, which provided that "any question of interpretation of the provisions of this Agreement arising between any member and the Fund or between any members of the Fund shall be submitted to the Executive Board for their decision." A member may require the Executive Board's decision to be referred to the Board of Governors, "whose decision shall be final." Articles of Agreement of the International Monetary Fund (opened for signature July 22, 1944) 2 UNTS 39 art XXIX. *See also* Articles of Agreement of the International Bank for Reconstruction and Development (opened for signature December 27, 1945) 2 UNTS 134 art 9 (setting out a similar procedure).

[22] Kenneth Dam, *The GATT: Law and International Economic Organization* (1970), 12–13.

[23] Dean Acheson, *Economic Policy and the ITO Charter*, 20 Dept. State Bull. 626 (1949). Acheson characterized the Havana Charter as "the first comprehensive code of international law to govern trade policies." *Ibid.*

[24] For example, one draft expanded the United States' proposed "nullification and impairment" clause by making it applicable to all of the Charter, not simply the Chapter on commercial policy. *See*, e.g., United Nations General Assembly, "Report of the Preparatory Committee of the United Nations Conference on Trade and Employment," 1st Session UN Doc A 6, A 17. The so-called Geneva draft slightly broadened the clause again to permit a complaint in cases where "the attainment of any objective in the Agreement is being impeded." John H. Jackson, *World Trade Law and the Law of GATT* (The Mitchie Company, 1969).

from the drafting process relatively unchanged. The clause contemplating ICJ review underwent more significant change.[25] Ultimately, the key debate was between delegations who argued that review by the Court would serve as a useful check on the Conference, which would inevitably be subject to political pressures, and other delegations who argued that the Court might be used to obstruct action by the ITO, and that on many issues the ITO, as an expert body, was a more appropriate decision maker than the Court.[26] This disagreement was never satisfactorily resolved and highlights the tension between seeking the security and predictability that a strongly legalistic process can bring and seeking the advantages that specialized expertise and flexibility can bring when dealing with complex economic and social questions.[27] More broadly, these debates are an early instantiation of a larger and recurrent debate between those who favor a legalized, "rule-oriented" approach to trade relations and those who advocate more diplomatic approaches.[28] At the time, the U.S. position was that referral of legal questions to the ICJ was desirable because, in the words of the vice-chair of the U.S. delegation, "a basis is thus provided for the development of a body of international law to govern trade relationships."[29]

The second relevant development is the creation of the GATT. To greatly simplify a complex process, in December 1945 the State Department announced that it had invited a number of states to negotiate a multilateral trade agreement. Negotiations over this agreement – which would eventually become the GATT – proceeded in parallel with negotiations over the ITO Charter, and many of the same individuals were engaged in both processes. For a variety of reasons, GATT negotiations over tariffs and commercial policy advanced more quickly than the ITO negotiations. By October 1947 – nearly a month before the final ITO Conference was to begin – negotiators had finalized the General Agreement on Tariffs and Trade. There was a general sense among the negotiators that it was necessary to implement this agreement

---

[25] An excellent overview of these changes can be found in Seymour J. Rubin, *The Judicial Review Problem in the International Trade Organization*, 63 Harv. L. Rev. 78 (1949), on which I draw heavily in this discussion.
[26] Ibid., 87.
[27] Ibid., 92–97.
[28] The literature here is vast. For a sampling, *see*, e.g., Dam, *op. cit.*; Oliver Long, *Law and Its Limitations in the GATT Multilateral Trade System* (1985); William J. Davey, *Dispute Settlement in GATT*, 11 Fordham Int'l L. J. 51 (1987); John H. Jackson, *Perspectives on the Jurisprudence of International Trade: Costs and Benefits of Legal Procedures in the United States*, 82 Mich. L. Rev. 1570 (1984). For a more recent discussion of this debate in light of contemporary challenges facing the trade system, *see* Jeffrey L. Dunoff, *Death of the Trade Regime*, 10 Eur. J. Int'l. L. 733 (1999).
[29] Wilcox, *op. cit.*, 160.

as quickly as possible; Assistant Secretary of State Will Clayton is reputed to have quipped that "we need to act before the vested interests get their vests on."[30]

Significantly, the negotiators intended for the GATT to be only a temporary arrangement; its commitments were to be effectively absorbed into the ITO when the ITO Charter came into force. This short-term perspective explains much of the GATT's language and structure. The GATT's substantive provisions closely track the ITO's commercial policy provisions as they then stood. However, given the expectation that the GATT would be temporary, its legal and organizational structure was rather less developed than the corresponding ITO provisions. Thus, for example, although the GATT included a "nullification and impairment" provision drawn from the Geneva draft of the ITO, it did not contain a provision to submit disputes to the ICJ.

Moreover, the GATT's underdeveloped institutional provisions also reflect concerns over U.S. ratification. The Truman administration was negotiating under the authority of the 1945 Trade Agreements Extension Act, which authorized the president to enter into "foreign trade agreements" but did not authorize entry into an international organization.[31]

A final complication was that legislative action was necessary before several GATT parties could accept many of the GATT's general clauses. Negotiators feared that this would unduly delay the implementation process, so a decision was taken not to apply the GATT directly. Rather, the Protocol of Provisional Application was signed in late 1947, which called on parties to effectuate the General Agreement to "the fullest extent not inconsistent with existing legislation."[32] The Protocol became effective on January 1, 1948; negotiations on the ITO ended in March 1948 with the signing of the ITO Charter in Havana, Cuba.[33]

---

[30] The quote, perhaps apocryphal, can be found in William Diebold, *Reflections on the International Trade Organization*, 14 N. Ill. U. L. Rev. 335, 336 (1993–94).

[31] Senate Hearing, *op. cit.*; Hearings on Operation of the Trade Agreements Act and Proposed ITO before the Senate Finance Committee, 80th Cong., 1st Sess. (1947).

[32] Protocol of Provisional Application (October 13, 1947) UN Doc E/PC/T/214 Add 2 Rev 1.

[33] Havana Charter for an International Trade Organization, in Final Act and Related Documents, United Nations Conference on Trade and Employment (November 21, 1947) UN Doc E/Conf 2/78. This document contained several articles titled "Settlement of Disputes" that provided for consultations, investigation, and ruling by the Executive Board; appeal to the ITO Conference; and referral of matters to the ICJ for an advisory opinion. For an analysis of the ITO Charter and negotiations from the perspective of various U.S. government officials involved in the process, *see* Wilcox, *op. cit.*; George Bronz, *The International Trade Organization Charter* 62 Harv. L. Rev. 1089 (1949); Percy W. Bidwell and William Diebold, Jr., *The United States and the International Trade Organization*, 27 Int'l Conciliation 185 (1949); Herbert Feis, *The Geneva Proposals for an International Trade Charter*, 2 Int'l Org. 39 (1948).

C. THE GATT EXPERIENCE

The idea that a trade body would be created after the war "was largely an American invention," and in both outline and detail, the Charter was very much "an expression of American policy."[34] However, for a complex variety of reasons, the United States did not ratify the ITO Charter, and it never entered into force.[35] As a result, the GATT and its skeletal institutional and dispute settlement provisions became, by default, the central international body addressing international trade.

The GATT was not well designed to play this role. First, because it was an agreement and not an organization, GATT itself could not act. GATT parties therefore engaged in little or no formal voting; instead, a practice developed in which the overwhelming majority of decisions were taken by joint action by all of the parties to the agreement, referred to as the CONTRACTING PARTIES. In practice, this meant that the GATT operated by consensus.

In addition, the GATT began operations with only the most rudimentary dispute settlement provisions in the form of the "nullification and impairment" language outlined earlier. In short, under GATT Article XXIII, if any party believed that a benefit accruing to it under the agreement was being nullified or impaired by another party, it could make written representations or proposals to that party. If this did not lead to a satisfactory adjustment, the complaining party could refer the matter to the CONTRACTING PARTIES, who were required to investigate and make recommendations. Article XXIII authorized the CONTRACTING PARTIES, in appropriate cases, to authorize the complainant to suspend the application of tariff concessions or other GATT obligations to the party found to be acting in a GATT-inconsistent manner. The GATT said nothing about the procedures that would govern this process.[36]

---

[34] Bidwell and Diebold, *op. cit.*, 190. *See also* Feis, *op. cit.*, 40 ("The Charter was from the beginning an American idea").

[35] In the face of opposition in the Republican-dominated Congress and, at best, half-hearted support from the business community, the Truman administration sensed defeat and did not seek ratification. For detailed examinations of the failure to win congressional approval of the ITO, *see* Richard Gardner, *Sterling Dollar Diplomacy* (Clarendon Press, 1956); William Diebold, *The End of the ITO* (Princeton Essays in International Finance, No. 16 (1952)). For more on President Truman's political calculations regarding the ITO, *see* John Odell and Barry Eichengreen, "The United States, the ITO and the WTO: Exit Options, Agent Slack, and Presidential Leadership," in *The WTO as an International Institution* (University of Chicago Press, Ann O. Kreuger ed. 1996).

[36] Dispute settlement provisions are contained in a number of specialized GATT provisions, such as article XVIII (12) (disputes over balance-of-payments restrictions) and article XXIV (7) (disputes over GATT consistency of interim agreements for customs union or FTA). Detailed discussion of these specialized provisions is omitted.

Two additional features of GATT dispute resolution deserve emphasis. Consistent with the notion that the GATT was an agreement and not an organization, Article XXIII required that all matters be decided and all actions approved by the CONTRACTING PARTIES. In practice, this meant that the dispute resolution system that evolved operated by consensus. Under this consensus requirement, a responding party in a dispute had a veto power over virtually every stage of the dispute resolution process. As we shall see, this consensus requirement would eventually become the fulcrum around which much of the debate over GATT dispute settlement would revolve.

Finally, Article XXIII empowered the CONTRACTING PARTIES to authorize a prevailing party to suspend concessions or other obligations to a noncomplying respondent; that is, retaliate by raising tariffs against imports from the offending party. However, like all other decisions, this, too, could only be decided by a consensus of the CONTRACTING PARTIES, and a losing party in a dispute could veto the authorization to retaliate. Thus, as a pragmatic matter, GATT parties could not utilize retaliation as a means to generate compliance with dispute settlement rulings.

1. *The Early Years*

At first, GATT Contracting Parties would refer disputes to GATT's biannual plenary session or ask the chairman to render a ruling or opinion as to the conformity of a measure. By 1949, matters were referred to ad hoc working parties, which were essentially negotiating bodies that included the interested states and the primary purpose of which was reaching an agreement acceptable to the parties with the most direct interests in the matter.[37] Over time, the GATT Secretariat urged working parties to act more like third-party adjudicators. In a very significant move toward increased legalization, the working party format evolved into a "panel" format by 1952. Panels did not include members from disputing states; rather, panelists were drawn from neutral countries. Panels received oral and written arguments from disputants and then met without the parties to draft, with Secretariat assistance, a "report" intended to resolve the dispute.[38]

The United States was a frequent participant in dispute resolution proceedings during these early years. Of the fifty-three disputes filed through

---

[37] *See*, e.g., Robert Hudec, *The GATT Legal System and World Trade Diplomacy* (Butterworth Legal Publishers, 1975), 78.

[38] *Ibid.*, 88–89. This third-party panel procedure was memorialized in Panel on Complaints (October 14, 1952) BISD Doc. W.7/20. For more on the panel procedure, *see* GATT (October 6, 1955) Doc. L/392/Rev.1 (Secretariat analysis of panel procedure).

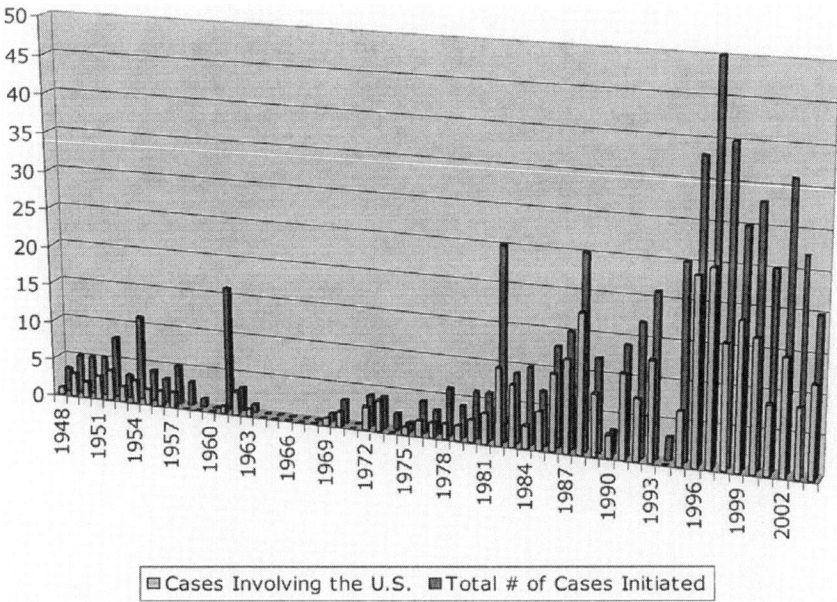

FIGURE 10.1. General Agreement on Tariffs and Trade/World Trade Organization Cases Involving the United States.

January 1, 1960, the United States initiated twelve cases, more than any other party. The United States was the defendant in nine of the fifty-three disputes, again more than any other party.[39]

Early panel reports were deliberately vague; they generally "said enough to indicate the proper legal conclusion, but... did not say it so clearly that it would embarrass the losing government."[40] The diplomatic vagueness of the reports afforded the parties some measure of flexibility in the event that compliance proved politically difficult. Relatedly, it protected the fledgling GATT from a perception that it was generating demands that states were unable or unwilling to meet.[41]

---

[39] See Figure 10.1. Although a number of disputes involved relatively technical matters, one bears mentioning. The Netherlands challenged limitations on its ability to sell dairy products in the United States by virtue of restrictions imposed under the federal Defense Production Act. A GATT panel found for the Netherlands and against the United States. The United States did not comply, and eventually the Netherlands sought, and received, authorization to limit by quota the amount of wheat flour imports from the United States. However, the Netherlands never exercised this authority, and the dispute marks the only time in GATT history that a party received authorization to suspend concessions pursuant to article XXIII.

[40] Hudec, *The GATT Legal System, op. cit.*

[41] Ibid.

During the 1950s and early 1960s, compliance with panel reports was relatively high.[42] Many attribute this success to the fact that the GATT largely consisted of a small number of like-minded states,[43] and many of the panelists had been involved in the drafting of the GATT and shared a common set of understandings and expectations. Panel proceedings were informal rather than adversarial, and panelists were typically diplomats rather than lawyers.

GATT's early years thus included an important move away from "diplomacy" and toward "law" in dispute settlement. The move to panels would be the first of many that inched the GATT away from negotiated settlement of differences by national representatives and toward independent third-party dispute resolution. However, this early move toward a form of third-party dispute resolution was embedded within a larger commitment to diplomatic traditions, which found expression in the form and content of panel reports, and the GATT's consensus decision-making processes. GATT's early forays into dispute settlement have aptly been characterized as "a diplomat's jurisprudence."[44]

2. The 1960s: The Fall of GATT Dispute Settlement and the Rise of Anti-Legalism

The 1960s were a period of transition for the GATT, its dispute resolution process, and U.S. attitudes toward the system. GATT's membership and policy agenda underwent significant change that represented a sharp departure from the "club" model that characterized the GATT's early years. As explained in this section, these changes produced higher levels of conflict, a sharp decline in the status of GATT law, a virtual halt to GATT dispute resolution, and an important shift in U.S. attitudes toward GATT dispute settlement.

First, GATT's membership changed dramatically. In particular, the European Community (EC) replaced its six original members as a GATT party. From the U.S. perspective, this change replaced six small and "generally law abiding [states] with one muscular superpower,"[45] which would become, along with the United States, a chief protagonist driving changes in the international trade domain over the next four decades. In addition, the number of developing

---

[42] For a detailed analysis of disputes during this period, see Hudec, *The GATT Legal System*, op. cit., 66–190. Hudec's analysis in this and other works constitutes seminal contributions to the empirical analysis of GATT and WTO dispute settlement. His work has strongly influenced much of the subsequent scholarship that empirically examines trade dispute resolution, including this chapter.

[43] By 1960, there were only thirty-six Contracting Parties.

[44] Robert E. Hudec, "Diplomat's Jurisprudence," op. cit., 615.

[45] Robert E. Hudec, *Enforcing International Trade Law: The Evolution of the Modern GATT Legal System* (1993), 12.

state members more than tripled; by the mid-1960s, developing states outnumbered developed states by more than two to one.[46] The simultaneous emergence of the EC and a coalition of developing states, along with the rise of Japan as a powerful economic force, combined to decrease the relative power of the United States within the GATT.

The new distribution of power was not as favorably inclined toward legalized forms of dispute resolution as the United States traditionally had been. In particular, at this time, the EC espoused a strongly anti-legalist approach to trade policy and dispute resolution. The EC approach reflected, in part, an effort to protect its Common Agricultural Policy and preferential trade arrangements with former colonies, which were in serious tension with GATT obligations. In addition, compliance with GATT norms began to decline noticeably at this time. In particular, conspicuous noncompliance in the areas of agriculture, safeguards, and the most favored nation obligation reflected a sense among many states that some GATT rules were outdated, unrealistic, or misguided as a matter of trade policy.

In light of these changes, the traditional U.S. commitment to the panel process was replaced with a more ambivalent approach. In part, this shift in U.S. attitudes reflected a strong determination to resist what was seen as overly aggressive demands by developing states – which had largely been excused from most meaningful GATT obligations – for heightened legal enforcement of developed state obligations. The United States believed that these demands ignored U.S. political realities. In addition, despite frequent tensions, the United States was committed to the success of the EC. To the extent that strict compliance with GATT norms threatened the delicate political balance that held the EC together, for geopolitical reasons the United States was prepared to choose accommodation over strict legal compliance.[47] The shifting U.S. position concerning dispute settlement during this decade suggests that the United States views dispute resolution mechanisms in instrumental terms. More specifically, when highly legalized processes are perceived to threaten U.S. economic or geostrategic interests, the United States will neither advocate for nor participate in such processes.

As a result of these various developments, GATT dispute settlement fell into virtual disuse during the 1960s.[48] We might best understand this decade

---

[46] Compare GATT, BISD 8th Supp. 99–100 (1960) (membership consisting of twenty-one developed states and sixteen developing states) with GATT, BISD 17th Sup. Vii (1970) (membership consisting of twenty-five developed states and fifty-two developing states).

[47] Hudec, *Enforcing International Trade Law, op. cit.*, 34.

[48] From early 1959 until late 1961, not a single complaint was filed. Six complaints were filed in 1962 and 1963; the system was then quiet until approximately 1967 and remained virtually unused for the rest of the decade. See Figure 10.1.

as a time when the United States and the GATT were adjusting to new GATT members, power dynamics, and agenda items. Many key GATT parties developed an understanding that formalized dispute settlement was unlikely to be an especially useful mechanism for advancing this adjustment process.

3. *The 1970s: Reconstruction and Revival*

The dynamics surrounding U.S. trade policy changed again in the 1970s, and the U.S. role in GATT dispute settlement evolved over the course of the decade. Two factors help explain U.S. actions during this period. First, congressional-executive relations began to shift. Despite occasional congressional grumbling, by and large the Congress had given the Executive wide latitude with respect to trade matters during the postwar era. However, political support for trade liberalization in the Congress, and in the country, was never particularly strong. As the relative economic power of the United States began to decline during the mid and late 1960s, this lukewarm political support began to evaporate.[49] Moreover, as import competition increased, trade policy assumed greater political significance, and Congress reinserted itself into the trade policy-making process.

The second key factor driving U.S. policy during the 1970s was heightened friction with the EC. A primary irritation was the EC's Common Agricultural Policy (CAP). U.S. efforts to liberalize trade during the 1960s met a stiff wall of EC resistance.[50] As the EC raised internal price supports to higher levels and as domestic calls for retaliatory action increased, the Nixon administration perceived CAP and other EC policies as growing economic – and political – problems.

I. Increasing Use of Dispute Settlement and Increasing Frustrations

To address these various pressures, the U.S. administration decided to pursue a two-track strategy. First, it called for a new round of GATT negotiations (the so-called Tokyo Round); its rationale was that creating economic gains

---

To the extent the United States used the system, it was largely in response to congressional pressure that the Executive Branch take action against foreign states that were violating GATT norms. The United States pursued disputes against French and Italian quantitative restrictions on agricultural products and Canadian duties on vegetables. These were resolved rather quickly. A fourth dispute, arising out of the "chicken war" with the EC, involved a high-profile conflict and symbolized larger frustrations with the GATT system, discussed in text.

[49] For example, in 1968 the AFL/CIO, a leading coalition of labor unions, abandoned its traditional support for trade liberalization and announced support for import restrictions.

[50] Hudec, *Enforcing International Trade Law, op. cit.*, 38.

through liberalization could help quiet domestic political complaints about rising import competition. At the same time, the administration decided to initiate a series of GATT claims and advocate the strengthening of GATT dispute settlement. Again, it is notable that this shift in U.S. policy regarding the utility of dispute settlement had little to do with an abstract commitment to the rule of law or the benefits of legalized dispute settlement but was instead a strategic policy designed to mollify congressional and private sector critics.

Important developments on the legislative front would soon follow. When Congress passed the 1974 Trade Act, strengthening GATT dispute settlement was not high on its agenda.[51] However, Congress wanted the administration to be much more aggressive vis-à-vis foreign states and enacted a new "Section 301" provision intended to spur Executive Branch action against laggard trading partners.[52] This section empowered private parties to initiate proceedings regarding unfair trading practices by other states before the United States Trade Representative (USTR). By providing a mechanism for private parties to bring foreign practices before USTR, Congress created a dynamic intended to generate strong political pressures in favor of pursuing complaints at the GATT. This strategy proved effective as, almost immediately, the United States initiated several GATT actions. Responding, in large part, to the United States' newfound enthusiasm for GATT dispute settlement, other states soon began to file complaints and GATT dispute settlement sprang back to life.

The new cases helped to highlight several problems with the dispute settlement process. First, under GATT's consensus rule, recalcitrant defendants could rely on GATT's consensus rule at various points in the process to delay greatly GATT dispute resolution. Thus, for example, in the response to one U.S. complaint over EC agricultural restrictions, the EC delayed creation of a panel, contested the panel's terms of reference, and then raised objections that delayed the naming of the members of the panel. As a result of these and other delays, the panel did not circulate its report until some two years and three months after the panel had been created. Similar delays occurred in other cases, both when the United States was a complainant and when it was a respondent.

Second, several of the new cases represented a dramatic escalation in the legal complexity of claims submitted and arguments presented to panelists.

---

[51] Near the bottom of a list of desired institutional reforms, Congress called for "any revisions necessary to establish procedures... to adjudicate commercial disputes among countries." Trade Act of 1974 s 121 (a) (9).

[52] The theory behind and practice under Section 301 have proven highly controversial. For a sampling of the debate, *see*, e.g., *Aggressive Unilateralism: America's 301 Trade Policy and the World Trading System* (Jagdish Bhagwati and Hugh Patrick, eds., University of Michigan Press, 1989).

In several of the cases, USTR lawyers submitted briefs of extraordinary complexity. The increased legal sophistication of the claims and arguments placed severe strains on the system, as many panelists were quite knowledgeable about GATT history but had no legal training.

Finally, perhaps reflecting the increasing number and complexity of the disputes and arguments presented, as well as the lack of legal expertise on the panels, several of the disputes generated "embarrassingly poor decisions."[53] Thus, these cases served to highlight the lack of any institutionalized source of high-quality legal analysis in the dispute settlement system. Moreover, GATT parties had no way to "correct" legal errors in the reports; hence, these disputes underscored the system's limited ability to address panel mistakes.

Nevertheless, for all these problems, the mid-1970s was a time of renewal for GATT dispute settlement. Between 1976 and 1978, fourteen separate complaints were filed – a dramatic upswing from the somnambulant sixties. The growing numbers of disputes is evidence that governments, including the U.S. government, once again viewed the GATT dispute system as a valuable tool in international economic relations. As a result, numerous governments were interested in strengthening the dispute settlement system in the ongoing Tokyo Round negotiations.[54]

II. The Tokyo Round Negotiations

In these negotiations, the United States emerged as a strong proponent of reforms designed to streamline the dispute settlement process and minimize respondents' ability to block the progress of an action. Not surprisingly, the EC opposed many U.S. proposals. In characteristic GATT fashion, both parties obtained some, but not all, of what they wanted. The Tokyo Round produced

---

[53] Robert E. Hudec, *The New WTO Dispute Settlement Procedure: An Overview of the First Three Years*, 8 Minn. J. Global Trade 1, 7 (1999). For example, in a 1981 case involving Spanish measures affecting the sale of soybean oil, the panel's reasoning was so troubling that the United States, which had brought the dispute, argued against adopting the panel report, not simply because it lost the case but on the systemic grounds of avoiding the incorporation of "bad" GATT law into the system. Andrew L. Stoler, *The WTO Dispute Settlement Process: Did the Negotiators Get What They Wanted?* 3 World Trade Rev. 99, 106, n. 12 (2004). Other cases that were heavily criticized include *United States: Income Tax Legislation* (November 12, 1976) GATT BISD 23S/98–114; *European Community: Program of Minimum Import Prices, Licenses, etc. for Certain Processed Fruits and Vegetables* (October 18, 1979) GATT BISD 25S/68–107; *United States: Imports of Certain Automotive Spring Assemblies* (May 26, 1983) GATT BISD 30S/107–28.

[54] For an overview of the Tokyo Round, not limited to debates over dispute settlement, *see* G. R. Windham, *International Trade and the Tokyo Round Negotiations* (Princeton University Press, 1986).

a number of "Codes" related to specific issue areas (i.e., the Tokyo Round Subsidies Code); these Codes had dispute resolution provisions that incorporated many U.S. ideas, including limits on a respondent's ability to use the GATT's consensus rules to frustrate the dispute settlement process.

The United States was less successful in reforming the Article XXIII nullification and impairment process. The Tokyo Round produced two relevant documents, the Agreed Description of Customary Practice and the Understanding on Dispute Settlement. On one hand, these documents advanced U.S. goals insofar as they described the adjudicatory nature of panel proceedings and committed GATT parties to work to make the process more effective. On the other hand, these documents did not remove a responding state's ability to block creation of a panel and emphasized the panel's conciliatory role: panels were to "consult regularly with the parties... and give them adequate opportunity to develop a mutually satisfactory solution."[55]

On balance, however, the Tokyo Round reforms on dispute settlement represented a significant strengthening of the system along the lines the United States sought. Particularly compared with the state of GATT dispute settlement at the start of the 1970s, the decade saw a dramatic revival of the process. Of course, not all problems were solved – there were still serious U.S.-EC frictions, and no effort was made to invest panels with greater legal expertise. However, at the time the moves to improve dispute settlement overshadowed the unresolved problems,[56] and Congress implemented the Tokyo Round Agreements by enacting the Trade Agreements Act of 1979.

4. *1980–1994: Aggressive Unilateralism and the Birth of the WTO*

The United States experienced a series of economic shocks during the 1980s, including an explosive growth in its trade deficit and a precipitous decline in the U.S. current account balance. As is often the case during difficult economic times, these developments led to increased political attention to trade issues, and in particular to increased congressional involvement. Following up on a 1979 statute that implemented the Tokyo Round agreements, Congress passed a major trade bill in 1984 over Executive Branch opposition and another major bill in 1988. In short, during the 1980s, Congress reasserted its historical primacy in trade politics.

---

[55] *Understanding Regarding Notification, Consultation, Dispute Settlement and Surveillance* (November 28, 1979) BISD 26S 210–19 (1980).
[56] *See, e.g.,* Robert E. Hudec, *GATT Dispute Settlement after the Tokyo Round: An Unfinished Business,* 13 Cornell Int'l L. J. 145 (1980).

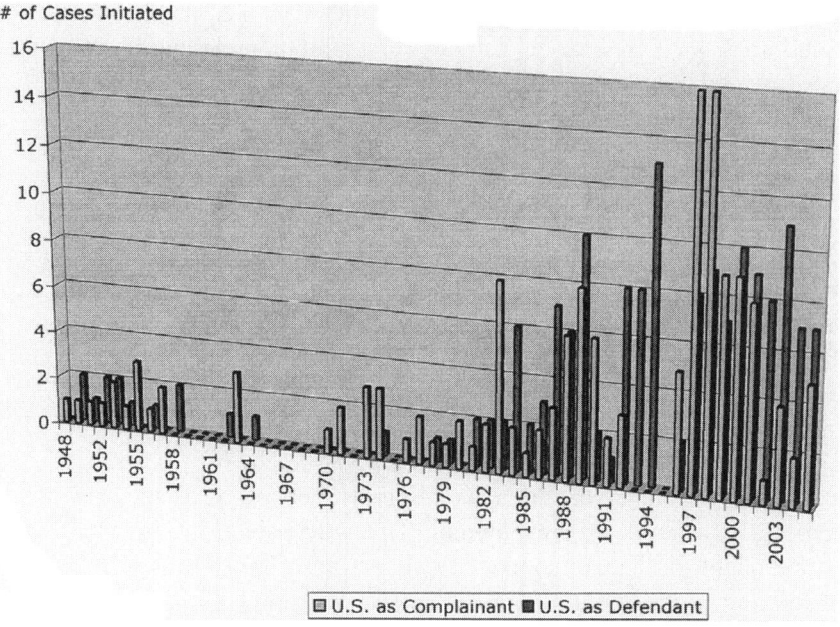

FIGURE 10.2. The United States as Complainant and Respondent in GATT Dispute Settlement.

I. Deflecting Protectionist Pressures

Congressional interest largely reflected growing protectionist pressures in the face of steadily increasing imports. By 1982, the Reagan administration was concerned about the rising tide of protectionist sentiment and responded, as the Nixon administration had done, with a two-track strategy.

First, it proposed expanding the GATT's substantive scope.[57] The rationale was that extending GATT benefits to other sectors of the U.S. economy could increase the domestic interests supporting liberalized trade. It took several years for this initiative to bear fruit, as described later.

The second strategy was to argue that growing trade deficits required lowering foreign trade barriers, as opposed to raising U.S. trade barriers. Hence, the United States once again took the offensive in GATT dispute settlement, filing eleven GATT complaints from 1980 to 1982.[58] Again, these U.S. actions

---

[57] Thus, in 1982 the U.S. proposed a new round of GATT negotiations that would include new codes in services, investment, and intellectual property. At the time, other states rejected this call; by 1986 they were prepared to launch the Uruguay Round.

[58] See Figure 10.2.

did not reflect an abstract commitment to the rule of law in international trade relations. Rather, many of these complaints were designed to demonstrate to Congress and others that the Tokyo Round agreements would deliver concrete results. In addition, the administration threatened several states with sanctions pursuant to section 301 in the event they did not remove specific trade barriers, particularly in the services and intellectual property sectors.

Nine of the GATT complaints were filed against the EC; as a general matter, the EC viewed these cases as attacking its CAP and seeking policy reforms through litigation that the United States had been unable to obtain through the Tokyo Round negotiations. In short, from the EC perspective, the U.S. litigation strategy bordered on an abuse of the system.[59] As a result, the EC employed all of the considerable procedural tools available to frustrate and stymie the dispute settlement process.

However, many of the threats of unilateral sanctions under section 301 produced results, at least when the target of the threat was a developing state. The threats made against the EC and Japan, in contrast, were properly understood by all parties as possessing a large element of political theater. However, U.S. trading partners strongly resented this form of U.S. unilateralism, and criticism of its unilateralist tendencies became a leitmotif of international trade relations throughout the decade.

II. The Spur of Unilateralism

Other states were not willing to agree to the U.S. call for a new round of negotiations in 1982. Hence, a November 1982 Ministerial Declaration said little regarding substantive trade issues. However, many states were troubled by procedural delays in several of the U.S.-EC disputes. The Ministerial Declaration recognized both EC concerns about abuse of the process and U.S. concerns about EC obstructionism; it then detailed ten specific recommendations for improving GATT dispute settlement.[60] In the aggregate, these recommendations sent a strong signal that the time for panels to adjust disputes through vague language and diplomatic nuance had passed and that it was time for GATT adjudication "to raise its ambitions and to become an objective legal arbiter capable of giving clear answers to all comers."[61] This document confirmed that the GATT had evolved into a rule-based entity that needed an effective dispute settlement procedure.

---

[59] Hudec, *Enforcing International Trade Law, op. cit.*, 146.
[60] Ministerial Declaration, L/5424 (November 19, 1982) BISD 29S/9, 10.
[61] Hudec, *Enforcing International Trade Law, op. cit.*, 166.

In 1986, with strong U.S. support, GATT parties launched a new negotiating round.[62] The United States brought an ambitious agenda to the new round, with dispute settlement reform a top U.S. priority. At this time, the United States was pursuing a relatively confrontational trade policy, including the filing of GATT complaints over politically contentious issues. The United States' aggressive posture, in turn, prompted the filing of a series of GATT complaints against it.

As is often the case, U.S. litigation activity in Geneva increased at a time when the administration was seeking negotiating authority from Congress in Washington. However, Congress was concerned by the country's large and persistent trade deficits. Echoing a pattern that past administrations had used, the Reagan administration made a series of demands on trading partners, backed by threats of unilateral, GATT-illegal retaliation. Against this backdrop, in 1988 Congress passed trade legislation that strengthened and expanded the use of "aggressive unilateralism" as a tool of trade diplomacy. At the same time, the 1988 legislation also identified the negotiation of a more effective and expeditious dispute settlement system as a principal U.S. negotiating objective for the Uruguay Round.[63]

The United States' increasing reliance on unilateralism during these years was widely, strongly, and repeatedly denounced by GATT parties. The EC and others became committed to seeking the elimination of unilateralism in the dispute settlement context. The United States argued that it acted unilaterally only because of weaknesses in the existing system and because existing GATT rules failed to address many trade issues. Implicit in this argument was the suggestion that, with stronger multilateral dispute resolution, the United States would not need to pursue unilateral policies.

As foreign concern over U.S. unilateralism increased, the outlines of a "grand bargain" began to emerge. By the time of the December 1990 Brussels ministerial meeting, trading nations made the dramatic decision to eliminate the veto power that parties had enjoyed under GATT's tradition of consensus decision making, a move the United States strongly urged.[64] As a result, respondents would no longer have the ability to block adoption of a panel report or authorization of retaliation. In exchange, trading nations obtained a U.S. commitment to pursue trade disputes through a greatly strengthened

---

[62] The willingness to launch a new round in 1986, as opposed to the unwillingness in 1982, reflects, in part, a defensive reaction to U.S. efforts to pursue bilateral trade agreements in the absence of multilateral negotiations.

[63] 19 U.S.C. section 2901.

[64] To be sure, important moves in this direction had occurred by the Montreal Midterm meeting in December 1988. However, that meeting clearly preserved consensus decision making over issues such as adoption of a ruling and authorization for retaliation.

multilateral system, rather than through unilateral measures. This bargain lies at the heart of the Uruguay Round's Understanding on Rules and Procedures Governing the Settlement of Disputes ("Dispute Settlement Understanding" or "DSU"), which is part of the Uruguay Round Agreements creating the WTO. Key aspects of the DSU are explained in the next section.

D. THE URUGUAY ROUND DISPUTE SETTLEMENT UNDERSTANDING

The Uruguay Round Agreements are the most important development in international economic relations since the Bretton Woods agreements. Creation of the WTO as a formal international organization – an idea first proposed by a prominent U.S. legal scholar and adopted by the Canadians – was meant to cure many of the GATT's "birth defects."[65] Thus, the WTO is formally endowed with existence, legal personality, and legal capacity as an international organization. In addition, the Agreements extend GATT rules into several new domains, including services, intellectual property, and investment. These agreements thus extend trade law disciplines into some of the most important and rapidly expanding areas of international economic activity. Finally, the Agreements include the DSU, which creates perhaps the most advanced and legalized form of dispute settlement found in international law.

1. Outline of the DSU

The DSU builds on and improves the procedures developed over time in the GATT. Most important, it replaces the traditional GATT consensus rule with a "reverse consensus" rule. That is, under the DSU, every stage of the dispute settlement process will move forward unless there is a consensus *against* doing so. Thus, a respondent state can no longer block the formation of a panel, refuse to select members of a panel, block the adoption of a panel report, or veto the authorization of sanctions in the event of noncompliance. The reverse consensus rule has transformed "WTO dispute settlement into what is, in all probability, the most effective area of adjudicative dispute settlement in the entire area of public international law."[66]

---

[65] John H. Jackson, *Restructuring the GATT System* (1990). For accounts of the influence of Jackson's proposals, *see* Jeffrey L. Dunoff, *Constitutional Conceits: The WTO's "Constitution" and the Discipline of International Law*, 17 Eur. J Int'l L. 647 (2006); *Tribute to John Jackson*, 20 Mich. J. Int'l L. 95 (1999).

[66] David Palmeter and Petros C. Mavoridis, *Dispute Settlement in the World Trade Organization* (2nd ed., 2004) 234.

Given the enhanced legal status of panel reports, the DSU also provides for a standing Appellate Body (AB). The AB has jurisdiction over issues of law covered in a panel report and legal interpretations developed by a panel.[67] It has authority to uphold, reverse, or modify a panel's legal findings and conclusions. As with panel reports, AB reports are automatically adopted unless there is a consensus not to adopt the report.

A party has thirty days from the adoption of an adverse report to announce its intentions with respect to the report. If it is not practicable to comply immediately with the report, the party shall have a "reasonable period of time" to do so. If it is not possible to agree on a "reasonable time" for compliance, the matter is referred to an arbitrator, who is authorized to issue a "binding" decision. Moreover, when there is a disagreement as to whether a party is complying with an adverse report, that issue may also be referred to WTO dispute settlement, whenever possible to the original panel. These panel reports may be appealed to the AB.

Finally, if a party fails to comply within a reasonable period of time, the prevailing party may request negotiations on appropriate "compensation," meaning additional trade concessions from the losing party. In practice this is rarely successful, so the prevailing party can then request WTO authorization to suspend concessions – that is, retaliate – against the noncomplying party. This request must identify the amount of retaliation, which should be at a level equivalent to the nullification and impairment caused by the WTO-inconsistent measure. As with other steps in dispute resolution, the request for authorization to retaliate will automatically be granted, unless there is a consensus to the contrary. However, if a losing party objects to the level of retaliation proposed, it may seek arbitration. This will be carried out by the original panel or an arbitrator chosen by the WTO director-general. If the arbitrators find that the retaliation requested is excessive, they calculate an appropriate figure. Thus, under this system, the WTO will both authorize and monitor retaliation; unilateral retaliation is prohibited.

2. U.S. Implementation and Debate over the DSU

Various aspects of the Uruguay Round agreements, including the DSU, proved controversial during congressional consideration of the agreements. In particular, many in Congress and elsewhere argued that the DSU would threaten U.S.

---

[67] The AB consists of seven members, three of whom comprise a "division" in any particular case. However, in response to U.S. (and EC) concerns, see Stoler, *op. cit.*, 99, the AB has adopted a collegial approach that provides in all cases for an "exchange of views" among all members. This procedure is widely credited with contributing to the "consistency and coherency" of AB decisions. See, e.g., Claus-Dieter Ehlermann, *Experiences from the WTO Appellate Body*, 38 Tex. Int'l L. J. 469, 478 (2003).

sovereignty[68] and undermine the effectiveness of section 301. To address these concerns, the Statement of Administrative Action submitted by the Clinton administration to Congress with the legislation implementing the Uruguay Round agreements emphasized that panel and AB reports "have no binding effect under the law of the United States"; that if a report recommends a change in U.S. law "it is for the Congress to decide whether any such change will be made"; that panel and AB reports "do not provide legal authority for federal agencies to change their regulations or procedures or refuse to enforce particular laws or regulations"; and that the DSU would "enhance the effectiveness" of section 301.[69] The implementing legislation contained several provisions designed to limit the domestic legal effect of adverse reports, including a provision explicitly precluding any private right of action or remedy against the United States on the grounds that a federal law is WTO-inconsistent.[70]

In addition, to help attract votes in a Republican-dominated Senate, President Clinton agreed to Senate Majority Leader Robert Dole's proposal to create a "Commission" of five federal judges who would evaluate WTO dispute reports adverse to the United States. If the Commission found that a panel or the AB either (1) exceeded its authority, (2) engaged in misconduct, (3) departed from panel procedures, or (4) deviated from the applicable standard of review, it would transmit a report to the Congress. Thereafter, any member of Congress would be entitled to introduce a resolution requiring renegotiation of WTO dispute settlement rules. If the resolution passed, the president would be required to initiate negotiations to reform the system. If the Commission found three instances of inappropriate panel behavior in a five-year period, then members of Congress could introduce a resolution, with privileged status, that the United States withdraw from the WTO. Either resolution would be subject to presidential veto. The Commission proposal enjoyed substantial support but was never enacted into law.[71] However, it does underline congressional anxiety about the greatly enhanced DSU.

---

[68] For a concise overview of the debates, see John H. Jackson, *The Great 1994 Sovereignty Debate: United States Acceptance and Implementation of the Uruguay Round Results*, 36 Colum. J. Trans. L. 157 (1997).

[69] Statement of Administrative Action for the Uruguay Round Agreements (September 24, 1994) H.R. Doc. 103-316.

[70] Relying on this statutory language, federal courts have not permitted private parties to rely on WTO law. See, e.g., *Corus Staal BV v. Dept of Commerce*, 395 F3d 1343 (C.A. Fed. 1005). For a discussion of these cases and arguments regarding the use by private parties of WTO law in domestic courts, see Jeffrey L. Dunoff, "Enforcing Trade Law: The DSU, Domestic Courts, and the Paradox of Embedded Legalism" (unpublished manuscript, on file with author).

[71] See A Bill to Establish a Commission to Review the Dispute Settlement Reports of the World Trade Organization and for Other Purposes, S. 16, 104th Cong. (1995). For more on the Dole Commission, see Gary N. Horlick, *WTO Dispute Settlement and the Dole Commission*, 29 J. World Trade 45 (1999); Rachel Brewster, *Rule-Based Dispute Resolution in International Law*, 72 Va. L. Rev. 251 (2006).

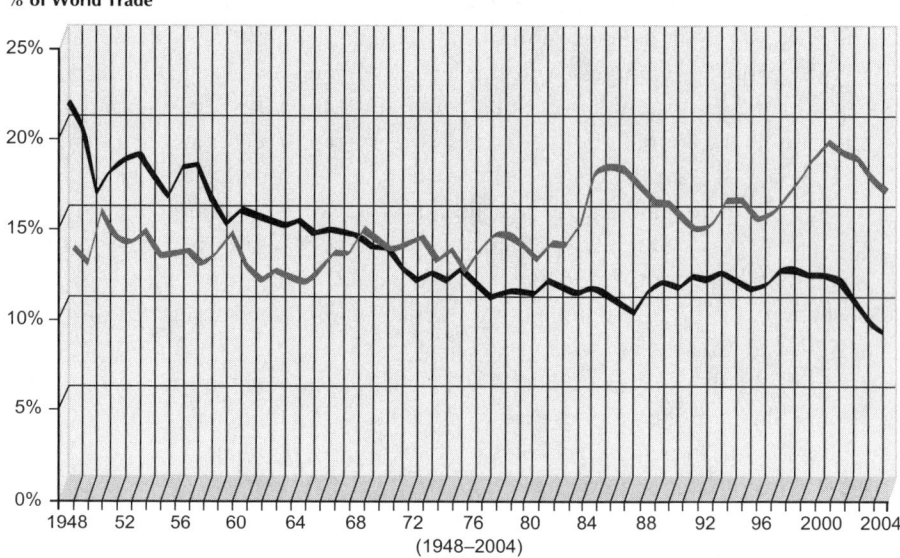

FIGURE 10.3. U.S. Proportion of Total World Merchandise Trade.

After extensive debate, the House of Representatives passed the implementing legislation on November 29, 1994, by a vote of 288 to 146, and the Senate passed the legislation on December 1, 1994, by a vote of 76 to 24. The WTO Agreements entered into force on January 1, 1995.

E. U.S. EXPERIENCE UNDER WTO DISPUTE SETTLEMENT

There is widespread agreement that, in its first decade, the WTO dispute settlement system has been a success.[72] The system has handled a large number of disputes expeditiously and professionally. Moreover, the United States has been a primary player in this system; it has initiated more complaints, been a respondent in more complaints, and participated as a third-party in more disputes than any other WTO member.[73]

---

[72] See, e.g., Report of the Chairman (June 6, 2003) TN/DS/9 (remarks by Chair of Doha dispute settlement negotiations that "the prevailing view of members is that the DSU has generally functioned well to date"); Procedures for the Review of the Dispute Settlement Understanding (February 26, 1998) WT/DSB/W/74 (remarks by Chair of DSB that, in context of discussions on reforming the DSU, members expressed general satisfaction with WTO dispute settlement).

[73] See Figures 10.1, 10.3, and 10.4.

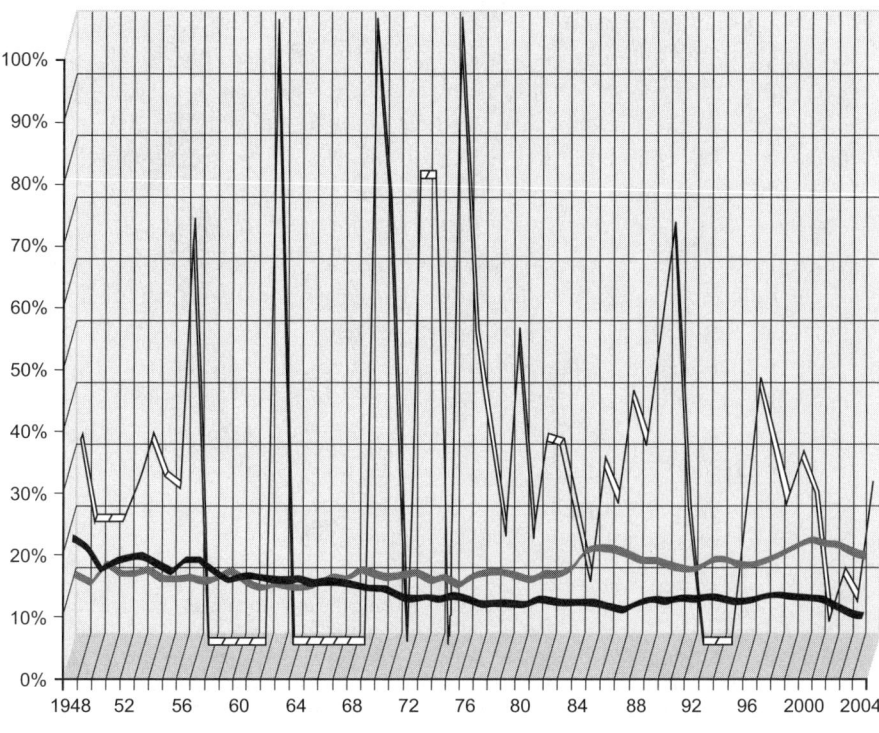

FIGURE 10.4. Proportion of U.S. Involvement in GATT Dispute Settlement and World Trade.

For current purposes, the first decade of WTO dispute settlement can be usefully divided into two parts.[74] During the first five years, the United States was an extremely active user of the system. During the first three years of the system, the United States initiated about 35 percent of the consultation requests made, and between 1995 and 1999, it initiated 60 of the 185 consultation requests made; the United States was an equally prominent respondent. Interestingly, both the total number of requests and the U.S. prominence as a user of the system have declined in recent years. During 2000–2004, the United States filed 18 consultation requests out of a total of 127 requests made.

As complainant, the United States has been successful in virtually all of the cases it has pursued seriously. In particular, it has initiated a number of

---

[74] See, e.g., William J. Davey, *The WTO Dispute Settlement System: The First Ten Years*, 8 J. Int'l Econ. L. 17 (2005). Professor Davey presents an excellent overview of dispute settlement activity, and I draw on his analysis in the paragraphs that follow.

consultation requests against the EC. These cases primarily involve intellectual property and agricultural issues, and the United States has, for the most part, prevailed in these actions.[75] However, implementation proved highly problematic in the *Bananas* and the *Beef Hormones* disputes, and a recent report on a U.S. complaint over European treatment of genetically modified organisms may do little to resolve the underlying dispute.

Apart from the EC, the United States has initiated multiple cases against only Canada, Japan, Korea, and Mexico. Against Canada, the United States successfully challenged rules for cultural industries that would be exempt under the North American Free Trade Agreement (NAFTA), reached mixed results in challenges to certain agricultural practices, and prevailed in a dispute involving an intellectual property issue. In addition, the United States and Canada engaged in several cases arising out of the long-running Softwood Lumber disputes;[76] notably, at the same time, the United States and Canada were litigating various aspects of the Softwood Lumber dispute before various NAFTA panels, domestic courts, and administrative agencies.[77]

---

[75] The cases involving intellectual property issues include the following: WTO *Portugal: Patent Protection under the Industrial Property Act – Notification of a Mutually-Agreed Solution* (October 8, 1996) WT/DS37/2; WTO *Ireland: Measures Affecting the Grant of Copyright and Neighbouring Rights – Request for Consultations by the United States* (May 22, 1997) WT/DS82/3; WTO *Denmark: Measures Affecting the Enforcement of Intellectual Property Rights – Notification of Mutually Agreed Solution* (June 13, 2001) WT/DS83/2; WTO *Korea: Taxes on Alcoholic Beverages* (January 18, 1999) WT/DS84/AB/R; WTO *European Communities: Enforcement of Intellectual Property Rights for Motion Pictures and Television Programs – Notification of Mutually Agreed Solution* (March 26, 2001) WT/DS124/2. The cases involving agriculture include WTO *European Communities: Duties on Imports of Grains – Communication from the United States* (May 2, 1997) WT/DS13/8 (settled); WTO *Belgium: Administration of Measures Establishing Customs Duties for Rice – Notification of Mutually Agreed Solution* (January 2, 2002) WT/DS210/6 (settled); WTO *European Communities: Measures Affecting the Exportation of Processed Cheese* (October 13, 1997) WT/DS104/1 (not pursued; EC compliance presumably demonstrated).

[76] WTO disputes related to the softwood lumber controversy include WTO *United States: Continued Dumping and Subsidy Offset Act of 2000* (January 16, 2003) WT/DS234/AB/R; WTO *United States: Preliminary Determinations with Respect to Certain Softwood Lumber from Canada – Notification of Mutually Agreed Solution* (November 16, 2006) WT/DS236/5; WTO *United States: Provisional Anti-Dumping Measure on Imports of Certain Softwood Lumber from Canada – Notification of Mutually Agreed Solution* (November 16, 2006) WT/DS247/2; WTO *United States: Final Countervailing Duty Determination with respect to Certain Softwood Lumber from Canada* (January 19, 2004) WT/DS257/AB/R; WTO *United States: Final Dumping Determination on Softwood Lumber from Canada* (August 11, 2004) WT/DS264AB/R; WTO *United States: Investigation of the International Trade Commission in Softwood Lumber from Canada* (March 22, 2004) WT/DS277/R; WTO *United States: Reviews of Countervailing Duty on Softwood Lumber from Canada – Notification of Mutually Agreed Solution* (November 16, 2006) WT/DS311/2.

[77] The U.S. experience with NAFTA dispute resolution is discussed in David Gantz, "The United States and Dispute Settlement under the North American Free Trade Agreement: Ambivalence, Frustration, and Occasional Defiance," and Susan Karamanian, "Dispute Resolution

Against Japan, the United States has won disputes involving the Sanitary and Phytosanitary agreement but lost a high-visibility case involving Japan's photographic film market. Against Korea, the United States enjoyed mixed success in cases seeking greater access for agricultural products. Against Mexico, the United States prevailed in disputes over telecommunications services, antidumping duties on high-fructose corn syrup, and settled a case involving countervailing duties on live swine.

U.S. cases are motivated by a variety of factors. Some cases seem to have little commercial value and appear to be pursued to generate "good law." But frequently disputes arise out of difficulties that powerful private interests confront in accessing foreign markets. A good example is the bananas dispute. No bananas are grown in the United States. However, the United States is home to the corporate headquarters of the world's largest banana producers. These firms helped persuade the USTR to, in effect, act on their behalf by challenging the EU's banana program at the WTO. The Kodak-Fuji case, involving a challenge to Japan's film market, is another example of the roles that private parties play in the government's decision to pursue GATT complaints.[78] Thus, many U.S. cases involve something of a "partnership" with interested private actors, who provide organizational, financial, political, and informational resources to the USTR.[79] In these cases, government and private actors reciprocally depend on each other to pursue their respective goals.

Not surprisingly, the United States has often been the target of WTO complaints. The EC is the key protagonist in this regard. The EC has successfully challenged a number of U.S. trade remedy rules and decisions, which have been followed by a decidedly mixed record of compliance. In addition, the EC has successfully used WTO dispute resolution to address its long-standing complaints about the U.S. tendency to act unilaterally and to impose measures with extraterritorial effects.[80] Canada has filed thirteen cases against

---

under NAFTA Chapter 11: A Response to the Critics in the United States," Chapters 11 and 12, respectively, in this volume. For a discussion of the multiple strands of the Softwood Lumber litigation and the implications of simultaneous litigation before WTO and NAFTA tribunals, see Jeffrey L. Dunoff, *The Many Dimensions of Softwood Lumber*, 45 Alberta L. Rev. 319 (2007).

[78] For a discussion of the ways that private parties influence WTO disputes, see Jeffrey L. Dunoff, *The Misguided Debate over NGO Participation at the WTO*, 1 J. Int'l Econ. L. 433 (1998).

[79] The term "partnership" comes from Gregory Shaffer, *Defending Interests: Public-Private Partnerships in WTO Litigation* (Brookings Institution Press, 2003).

[80] For example, the EC successfully established that section 301 must be used in a GATT-consistent manner, WTO *United States: Section 301–310 of the Trade Act of 1974* (December 22, 1999) WT/DS152/R; successfully settled a dispute over the Helms-Burton legislation, WTO *United States: The Cuban Liberty and Democratic Solidarity Act – Communication from the Chairman of the Panel* (April 25, 1997) WT/DS38/5; and deterred the United States from using a "carousel" approach to retaliation, WTO *United States: Section 306 of the Trade Act of 1974 and Amendments Thereto* (June 13, 2000) WT/DS200/1. See generally Davey, op. cit., 31.

the United States, focusing on the U.S. use of trade remedies. Japan, Korea, Mexico, Brazil, and India have also brought multiple complaints against U.S. use of trade remedies.

As a general matter, the United States as respondent has complied with many, but by no means all, adverse reports. Many of the cases the United States lost were of relatively minor economic or political importance.[81] However, compliance in a number of high-profile cases has been problematic. In cases such as Foreign Sales Corporation, the 1916 Anti-Dumping Act, and the Byrd Amendment dispute, U.S. noncompliance has created significant international tensions. In each of these cases, Congress resisted legislation designed to bring the United States into compliance. However, the United States has complied in some politically charged cases, notably that involving steel safeguards.[82]

Although a broad consensus holds that the WTO dispute settlement system has worked well overall, specific reports have triggered strong negative reactions in Congress and among private actors. In addition, the Executive Branch, the Congress, and private actors have identified several systemic concerns. In particular, in the Trade Act of 2002, Congress expressed its concern over a series of trade remedy cases that the United States lost.[83] The ultimate political and economic effects of these cases are unclear at this time, but "the major [U.S.] users of antidumping and countervail laws have argued vehemently that every U.S. loss in the trade remedy area is a huge disaster for U.S. interests and their influence in Congress has made these losses quite controversial, even if some of them are not that significant overall."[84] Members of Congress have also argued that some reports have created new obligations for members beyond those found in the WTO agreements. Congress has pressured the administration to address these and related issues.[85]

The United States has been active in the process of negotiating DSU reforms. In particular, it has repeatedly pressed for increased transparency in WTO dispute settlement, including open meetings, timely access to submissions and final reports, and guidelines for the participation of non-state actors

---

[81] See, e.g., General Accounting Office (GAO), World Trade Organization: U.S. Experience to Date in the Dispute Settlement System (June 2000) GAO/NSIAD/OGC-00-196BR.

[82] In terminating the steel safeguards, President Bush did not acknowledge the adverse panel and AB reports. Instead he argued that the restructuring of the steel industry constituted "changed economic circumstances" that justified termination of the steel tariffs. See Presidential Proclamation N. 7741, 68 Fed. Reg. 68483 (December 8, 2003).

[83] See 19 U.S.C. section 3801(b)(3)(A). Senator Max Baucus asked the U.S. GAO to prepare a report on this issue. See GAO, World Trade Organization, Standard of Review and Impact of Trade Remedy Rulings (July 2003) GAO-03-824.

[84] Davey, op. cit., 27.

[85] See, e.g., Trade Act sections 2101, 2105, 2106.

through *amicus curiae* submissions.[86] The United States has argued that these measures would increase the "accountability" of the dispute settlement system.

Another set of U.S. proposals seems designed to increase party control over the dispute settlement process.[87] At present, disputing parties have the right to review and provide comments on panel reports before they are circulated. The United States, acting jointly with Chile, has proposed to extend this right to the AB process. In addition, the United States proposed that disputing parties have the ability to agree to "delete findings in reports that hinder settlement or that are unnecessary or erroneous" and that the Dispute Settlement Body be able to decide, by consensus, not to adopt portions of a panel or AB report.[88] Finally, the United States, again acting with Chile, has referred to the desirability of providing "additional guidance to WTO adjudicative bodies," including with respect to the rules of interpretation of the WTO agreements, and ensuring that panel members have appropriate expertise.[89]

Whether any of these proposals are eventually adopted by WTO members, they reflect an important strand in current U.S. attitudes toward adjudication of trade disputes. The effort to impose political controls on the dispute settlement process following a string of defeats suggests that the United States views highly legalized dispute resolution in instrumental terms. To the extent adjudication of trade disputes is seen as advancing U.S. economic interests, it is likely that the United States will continue to support legalized dispute settlement. However, if a widespread perception takes root that, on balance, judicialized dispute settlement imposes politically difficult constraints on the United States and does not materially advance U.S. economic interests, then there is little reason to expect continued U.S. support. As other chapters in this volume illustrate, U.S. support for international tribunals in other issue areas has waxed and waned over time, and there is little reason to expect different behavior in the trade domain.

Two final recent developments deserve attention. The ongoing Doha Development Agenda negotiations are the first to take place against the backdrop of the WTO's enhanced dispute settlement system. A cluster of recent cases involve challenges that seemed aimed in part at influencing the ongoing negotiations. The United States has been both an initiator (the challenge to the EC's biotech approval scheme) and target (the Brazilian challenge to U.S. cotton

---

[86] Communication from the United States (February 11, 2003) TN/DS/W/46.
[87] Executive Branch Strategy Regarding WTO Dispute Settlement Panels and the Appellate Body: Report to the Congress Transmitted by the Secretary of Commerce (December 30, 2002).
[88] Textual Contribution by Chile and the United States (March 14, 2003) TN/DS/W/52. This proposal has not been fleshed out.
[89] *Ibid.*

subsidies) in these cases. Whether the United States and other WTO parties will accept a more frequent use of dispute resolution to improve positions in ongoing negotiations is an open question.

The other recent development is the April 2007 initiation of two cases against China at the WTO.[90] The timing of these complaints lends additional support to the thesis developed in this chapter regarding the contingent nature of U.S. commitments to legalized resolution of trade disputes. It also reflects the historic American pattern of initiating new disputes when the country is facing negative trade balances, rising protectionist voices at home, or when an administration is about to seek new trade negotiation authority from the Congress. Here, all of these factors are in play. The cases were filed shortly after Democratic Party leaders called on the president to generate a comprehensive plan to eliminate the rising deficit with China[91] and just as the administration was engaged in intensive negotiations with Congress regarding the approval of trade agreements signed with Columbia, Peru, and Panama and the extension of the administration's trade promotion authority.[92] Thus, notwithstanding USTR's statement that "[t]he timing [of these cases] relative to any other event is purely coincidental," these actions reinforce this chapter's claim that U.S. government use of highly legalized mechanisms to resolve trade disputes turns more on pragmatic and contextual calculations than on an abstract commitment to judicial dispute resolution.

F. CONCLUSION

The United States has been an essential driver in the movement to create a highly judicialized dispute settlement system in the international trade regime. However, a close examination of U.S. actions since the GATT's founding suggests that the U.S. commitment to highly legalized dispute settlement does not reflect an abstract commitment to the "international rule of law" in general or the use of tribunals in the trade domain in particular. Rather, U.S. pressure for increasing the legalization of dispute settlement for trade matters at various times in the past reflects pragmatic Executive Branch decisions designed to

---

[90] The disputes are WTO *China: Measures Affecting the Protection and Enforcement of Intellectual Property Rights* (April 16, 2007), WT/DS362 and WTO *China: Measures Affecting Trading Rights and Distribution Services for Certain Publications and Audiovisual Entertainment Products* (April 16, 2007) WT/DS363.

[91] See, e.g., G. Yerkey, "Democrats Call on Bush to Craft Plan to Eliminate Trade Deficits with 'Big 3,'" *WTO Reporter* (February 15, 2007).

[92] An alternative explanation, not inconsistent with that set out here, is that the timing of the United States' complaints sought to take advantage of China's relative vulnerability to international pressure in light of the Beijing Olympics. See, e.g., H. Cooper "Darfur Collides with Olympics, and China Yields," *New York Times* (April 13, 2007).

deflect protectionist pressures and silence Congressional critics. Similarly, the frequency with which the United States uses dispute settlement often reflects congressional-executive relations. For example, more aggressive use of dispute resolution by the United States in the early 1960s, the mid-1970s, and the fall of 1985 each occurred – not coincidentally – in anticipation of congressional consideration of trade legislation. Thus, the U.S. position at any point in time seems less a product of a long-term plan for the trade regime than a set of contextual decisions in light of then prevailing political and economic realities.

The WTO's dispute settlement system has just completed its first decade and is still very much a work in progress. The United States has been a frequent participant in panel and AB proceedings during this decade and has prevailed in almost all of the cases it has pursued. Although the U.S. government and key private actors view the system, in general, as a success, they have also expressed concern about a number of issues. Current U.S. proposals to modify the dispute settlement system seek to inject greater party control into the process, and hence appear to reflect something of a shift away from a desire for highly judicialized dispute settlement.

This discussion of changing U.S. attitudes about the use of tribunals to resolve trade disputes is, of course, only a partial and selective account of a process that continues to evolve. Had this chapter been written a decade or two ago, it would have told a very different story; we cannot know how U.S. attitudes will evolve in the next generation or how future historians will judge contemporary developments. Much will depend on the general state of the U.S. economy and corresponding pressures for protectionist policies. More specifically, much also turns on elite and business perceptions of whether extant dispute settlement machinery is performing satisfactorily. The history of ebbs and flows in U.S. enthusiasm for legalized dispute settlement suggests that in contexts where judicialized dispute settlement does not serve U.S. political or economic interests, continued U.S. support for the system will not be forthcoming.

11

The United States and Dispute Settlement under the North American Free Trade Agreement: Ambivalence, Frustration, and Occasional Defiance

DAVID A. GANTZ*

The North American Free Trade Agreement (NAFTA)[1] and its two parallel agreements on labor and on the environment[2] incorporate a broad and sometimes confusing variety of mechanisms for resolving the disputes that relate to the interpretation and application of certain NAFTA provisions in specific situations.

Essentially, there are six distinct dispute resolution procedures within the larger NAFTA framework:

- those relating to foreign investment and investor-state disputes (Chapter 11),
- financial services (Chapter 14, a variation on Chapter 20),
- appeals of antidumping and countervailing duty (unfair trade) actions by administrative agencies (Chapter 19),

---

* Samuel M. Fegtly Professor of Law and Director, International Trade and Business Law Program, University of Arizona, James E. Rogers College of Law; Associate Director, National Law Center for Inter-American Free Trade. Copyright © 2005–2009, David A. Gantz.
[1] North American Free Trade Agreement, December 17, 1992, 32 ILM 289 (1993) [hereinafter NAFTA], implemented by the North American Free Trade Agreement Implementation Act, 19 U.S.C. § 3312 et seq. [hereinafter NAFTA Implementation Act].
[2] North American Agreement on Environmental Cooperation, September 13, 1993, 32 ILM 1482 (1993) [hereinafter NAAEC]; North American Agreement on Labor Cooperation, September 13, 1993, 32 ILM 1502 (1993) [hereinafter NAALC]. Both agreements make it difficult for formal arbitration to take place. Under the NAAEC, arbitration is only available where there is "a persistent pattern of failure by that other Party to effectively enforce its environmental law" (art. 22). Under the NAALC, arbitration is mandated only where there is "a persistent pattern of failure by the other Party to effectively enforce such standards." ("Such" standards are limited to occupational safety and health, child labor or minimum wage technical labor standards) (art. 27:1). In each case, two of the three NAFTA parties must agree to move forward with arbitration. Thus, no arbitration is possible for violations that do not reach the "persistent pattern" stage.

- interpretation and application of the agreement generally (Chapter 20),
- failure to enforce environmental laws (North American Agreement on Environmental Cooperation, or NAAEC), and
- failure to enforce labor laws (North American Agreement on Labor Cooperation, or NAALC).

The latter two are not discussed herein because neither arbitral process has ever been seriously considered for utilization and it is thus impossible to measure U.S. attitudes toward them.[3] Likewise, financial services disputes, using a variation of the Chapter 20 mechanism, are discussed only briefly because no disagreement over financial services has yet been referred to arbitration.

It is evident that this impressive package was accepted with some ambivalence by the U.S. government; as we will see, each of these mechanisms was incorporated for a variety of mostly pragmatic and diplomatic, as well as legal, reasons. NAFTA, it should be recalled, was negotiated at a time when the General Agreement on Tariffs and Trade (GATT) Uruguay Round negotiations were largely stalled (1991–92), but after three years of more-or-less satisfactory operation of the United States–Canada Free Trade Agreement (CFTA).[4] As one of the authors in this book has opined,

> U.S. government support for judicialized dispute settlement in international trade is based less on an abstract commitment to the rule of law in international relations than on pragmatic, short-term, and highly contextual calculations that this mechanism serves U.S. interests better than alternative arrangements.[5]

Part A provides a short overview of the NAFTA dispute settlement process. Parts B through D treat, respectively, consider Chapters 11, 19, and 20 of NAFTA. A brief conclusion follows. In each instance, after a brief introduction to

---

[3] Although resolution of disputes that solely involve private parties is beyond the scope of this chapter, NAFTA incorporates a limited commitment by the governments to steps that may facilitate alternative resolution of commercial and agricultural disputes among private parties in the future. See NAFTA, *op. cit.*, arts. 707, 2022. Each party is required "to the maximum extent possible, [to] encourage and facilitate the use of arbitration and other means of alternative dispute resolution for the settlement of international commercial disputes between private parties in the free trade area."

[4] United States–Canada Free Trade Agreement, December 1987–January 1988 [U.S.–Can.], 27 ILM 281 [hereinafter CFTA].

[5] Jeffrey L. Dunoff, *Does the U.S. Support International Tribunals? The Case of the Multilateral Trade System*, Ch. 10, this volume.

the mechanism, I have tried, to the extent practicable, to discuss the threads common to this volume:

- Why did the United States favor (to the extent it did) each of these three NAFTA mechanisms?
- What branches of government and domestic constituencies have been supportive or opposed?
- How have the U.S. government and private interests participated?
- How have the U.S. government and the courts (where applicable) received the awards?
- How have attitudes of the government and private parties toward these mechanisms changed and evolved in the twelve years since NAFTA went into force?

In addition, I have provided, as Table 11.1, a chart illustrating the ambivalence created in the government by the pragmatic/contextual approach and the not-always-consistent views of various members of Congress, the business community, and nongovernmental organizations (NGOs).

Needless to say, there are some inherent risks in seeking answers to these questions. I have not served in the U.S. government since 1977 and played no role in the NAFTA negotiations, except as a generally supportive observer. Although I have served as a panelist or arbitrator in at least one proceeding each under Chapters 11, 19, and 20, I rely for government views primarily on the public statements and writings of active or former U.S. (or foreign) government officials, and on their official actions, particularly the changes to or omissions of NAFTA language that have been made as a result of the now-expired 2002 Trade Promotion Authority in subsequent agreements such as the free trade agreements (FTAs) with Singapore, Chile, and the nations of Central America.[6] This chapter was researched and written between 2005 and 2008, drawing on U.S. experience through 2008. It is much too soon to determine Obama administration views on NAFTA dispute settlement.

---

[6] United States-Chile Free Trade Agreement, June 6, 2003, U.S.-Chile, at http://www.ustr.gov/Trade_Agreements/Bilateral/Chile_FTA/Final_Texts/Section_Index.html (visited Apr. 15, 2007) [hereinafter Chile FTA]; United States-Singapore Free Trade Agreement, May 6, 2003, U.S.-Sing., at <http://www.ustr.gov/new/fta/Singapore/final/2004-01-15-final.pdf (visited Feb. 11, 2004) [hereinafter Singapore FTA]; United States-Central American-Dominican Republic Free Trade Agreement, May 28, 2004, U.S.-Guatemala, El Salvador, Honduras, Nicaragua, Costa Rica, Dominican Republic, at http://www.ustr.gov/Trade_Agreements/Regional/CAFTA/CAFTA-DR_Final_Texts/Section_Index.html (visited Feb. 27, 2009) [hereinafter CAFTA].

TABLE 11.1. *United States' attitudes toward dispute settlement under the North American Free Trade Agreement (NAFTA)*

Category	Chapter 11	Chapter 19	Chapter 20
Executive Branch – Pros	• Consistent with 60-year tradition of protecting U.S. investors abroad, mostly in developing nations • Minimizes diplomatic involvement in investment disputes • Encourages foreign investment in developing countries by promoting the rule of law	• For CFTA and NAFTA, was essential to conclude the agreements • Avoided any substantive changes in U.S. AD/CVD laws • Provided alternative for U.S. exporters who wish to avoid Mexican courts	• Largely ad hoc arbitral procedure is preferable to a NAFTA court • Even with WTO's Dispute Settlement Body, some NAFTA disputes not suitable for WTO resolution • Broader public U.S. commitment to international arbitration requires support for such provisions in NAFTA and more recent FTAs
Executive Branch – Cons	• Agencies do not like being sued, let alone losing • Skepticism that foreign investors in the United States need protection against alleged deficiencies in U.S. legal system • Concerns that creative lawyers are expanding scope of Chapter 11 beyond drafters' intent	• Duplicated review available in U.S. courts (CIT/CAFC) • Panelists less sympathetic to U.S. administrative agencies than courts • Scope of review of panel decisions by Extraordinary Challenge Committee is narrow • Panelists cannot properly apply applicable (national court) standard of review • Practical difficulties and costs of maintaining roster of objective panelists and a well-functioning secretariat • Conflicts between Chapter 19 and WTO decisions	• Suspicions that U.S. panelists are objective, whereas those from Canada and Mexico favor their governments • Some decisions are badly reasoned or wrong • Lack of appellate process creates risks that do not exist in WTO • Process is slow (often as result of U.S. actions/inactions in agreeing on panelists)

(continued)

TABLE 11.1 (continued)

Category	Chapter 11	Chapter 19	Chapter 20
Congress – Pros	• Business constituents continue to support strong investment protection • Belief that investment protection stimulates private foreign investment • U.S. has never lost a case under an FTA or BIT	• Did not weaken substantive U.S. AD/CVD laws • Administrative costs are not substantial	• No obvious objections to Chapter 20, distinct from opposition to NAFTA generally
Congress – Cons	• Business receives strong protection in Mexico, whereas labor and environmental interests do not • Foreign investors in the United States may receive greater protection under NAFTA than U.S. investors under Fifth Amendment • Applicability to regulatory takings requiring compensation could have a chilling effect on necessary government regulation • U.S. taxpayers will have to compensate foreign investors if NAFTA tribunal rules against the United States • Matters involving major public policy issues belong in U.S. courts rather than before unaccountable international arbitrators	• Substitutes ad hoc, largely unaccountable panelists for Article III federal judges whose appointment is subject to Senate advice and consent, raising political and constitutional doubts • Binational panel process is really another "international" tribunal	• Those who oppose WTO dispute settlement also oppose NAFTA Chapter 20

Category	Chapter 11	Chapter 19	Chapter 20
NGO/Civil Society – Pros	None	None	Same as Congress
NGO/Civil Society – Cons	• Same as Congress • Investor protection agreements encourage outsourcing of jobs	• Constitutionality of substituting panelists for federal judges questioned • "International" tribunals and arbitrations are a violation of U.S. sovereignty	Same as Congress
Business – Pros	• Investment protection necessary for foreign investment • Chapter 11 does not provide greater substantive rights than Fifth Amendment • Hysteria over indirect takings is unjustified given absence of any panel finding in 11 years of Chapter 11	• Provides some advantages over Mexican Tax Court, but some prefer *Amparo* courts • Importers feel panels are less likely to give undue deference to U.S. agencies • Panels may give more attention to administrative record than CIT	• Useful tool in some circumstances, e.g., border fishing dispute with Canada • General recognition that some issues better resolved within NAFTA than at WTO
Business – Cons	• Concerns generated by Chapter 11 have weakened investor protection in subsequent FTAs	• U.S. industry groups feel panels are too quick to challenge administrative agencies, and fail to follow U.S. AD/CVD law • Panel process, particularly in the United States, has become slow and costly, no longer saving time and money compared with court review • No effective appeal of panel decisions	None

(continued)

TABLE 11.1. (*continued*)

Category	Chapter 11	Chapter 19	Chapter 20
Summary	• Catch 22 for the United States; difficult to protect U.S. investors abroad when protection for foreign investors in the United States is weakened • General support in public matched by skepticism in private • Does a Calvo Clause mentality prevail? • Replicated in new FTA/BITs, but in somewhat weakened form	• Despite lukewarm support in public, U.S. government does not favor Chapter 19 • Not so benign neglect of processes, through underfunding of secretariat • "Never again" mentality with regard to subsequent FTAs	• Inability to appoint panelists reflects dissatisfaction with the mechanism • Replicated in new FTAs, but not likely to see much use there or in NAFTA in the future

AD = antidumping; BIT = bilateral investment treaties; CIT = Court of International Trade; CVD = countervailing duty; FTA = free trade agreement; WTO = World Trade Organization.

A. AN OVERVIEW OF DISPUTE RESOLUTION UNDER NAFTA

The wide and unique range of dispute settlement procedures reflects the apparent views of the three NAFTA governments that disputes regarding NAFTA implementation were inevitable and that third-party binding mechanisms for their prompt resolution were essential. National courts do not have or cannot exercise effective – and plausibly impartial – jurisdiction over most disputes between private individuals and foreign governments, or among governments, because of the sovereign immunity doctrine, act of state doctrine, concepts of comity, or other legal barriers,[7] with the possible exception of the unfair trade disputes area. In the foreign investment area in particular, resolution of investor-host government disputes through local courts has been highly unsatisfactory.

The Dispute Settlement Body (DSB) under the World Trade Organization (WTO) now provides a viable alternative to the NAFTA government-to-government dispute settlement process under Chapter 20 for most trade disputes among the three NAFTA governments; that alternative did not exist

---

[7] *See, e.g.,* Foreign Sovereign Immunities Act of 1976, 28 U.S.C. §§ 1330, 1332, 1391(f), 1441(d), 1602–11; *Banco Nacional de Cuba v. Sabbatino*, 376 U.S. 398 (1964) and subsequent cases relating to the act of state doctrine.

in its present form at the time the NAFTA negotiations were concluded. Yet the WTO and the DSB do not effectively extend to certain areas covered by NAFTA, such as foreign investment and land transportation services.[8]

The NAFTA mechanisms share common threads. First, the major three have largely been copied from previously existing dispute settlement procedures. Chapters 19 and 20 were cut and pasted, with minor modifications, from Chapters 19 and 18 of the CFTA, which preceded NAFTA by five years and the NAFTA negotiations by three years; likewise were the provisions guaranteeing certain rights to foreign investors, although the CFTA did not provide for mandatory investor-state arbitration.[9]

The Chapter 11 provisions at the time represented "the most recent stage in the evolutionary development of U.S. and international investment law." Logically enough they borrowed heavily from the several hundred bilateral investment treaties the United States and other Organisation for Economic Cooperation and Development (OECD) countries had concluded in the 1980s.[10]

Second, NAFTA did not create any permanent judicial dispute resolution body, akin to the European Court of Justice or the Court of Justice of the Andean Community. On this issue, Canada and the United States had been divided since the days of the negotiations of the CFTA. Canada had advocated a permanent tribunal, but the United States preferred the arbitration approach,[11] apparently because of a reluctance to create new international institutions and perhaps because of some unhappiness with Chapter 20's predecessor, Chapter 18 of the CFTA.[12] Eventually, during NAFTA negotiations a compromise was reached to create a mechanism that incorporates some elements of both courts and arbitral panels. In addition to U.S. resistance to a NAFTA "court," the complexity and breadth of the matters covered by NAFTA

---

[8] See NAFTA, op. cit., Chapters 11 (foreign investment) and 12 (cross-border trade in services), esp. Annex I (regarding transportation services); WTO, *Understanding on Rules and Procedures Governing the Settlement of Disputes*, Apr. 15, 1994, Annex 2 to the Agreement Establishing the World Trade Organization, at http://www.wto.org (visited Apr. 15, 2007) [hereinafter DSU].

[9] CFTA, op. cit., Chapter 16.

[10] Daniel M. Price and P. Bryan Christy, III, *Overview of the NAFTA Investment Chapter: Substantive Rules and Investor-State Dispute Settlement* in *The North American Free Trade Agreement: A New Frontier in International Trade and Investment in the Americas* (Judith H. Bello et al. eds., ABA, 1994), 165, 167; see also K. Scott Gudgeon, *United States Bilateral Investment Treaties: Comments on Their Origin, Purposes and General Treatment Standards*, 4 Int'l Tax & Bus. L. 105 (1986).

[11] Michael Hart, Bill Dymond, and Colin Robertson, *Decision at Midnight: Inside the Canada–U.S. Free-Trade Negotiations* (UBC Press, Vancouver, 1994), 302 [hereinafter Hart].

[12] A senior former United States Trade Representative official who was directly involved in the negotiations of Chapter 18 of the CFTA and Chapter 20 of NAFTA suggested both reasons. (Memorandum of Conversation, May 31, 2005, on file with author) [hereinafter Senior USTR Official].

have encouraged the use of highly specialized dispute resolution mechanisms and expert panelists. Although the Chapter 14, 19, and 20 mechanisms share a common secretariat – somewhat understaffed and underfunded (at least the U.S. Section) given the volume of Chapter 19 cases and the rare Chapter 20 case that it must administer – it is not, to the U.S. satisfaction, an international court of sorts, not even something akin to the Permanent Court of Arbitration (PCA).[13]

Third, none of the three mechanisms is equipped with effective appellate review. This is in stark contrast to the WTO's DSB and the Appellate Body functioning therein. As discussed later in this chapter, the lack of appellate jurisdiction has become a matter of concern to at least some U.S. government entities with regard to proceedings under both Chapter 11 and Chapter 19.

Fourth, the approach, like the GATT in its later years and the WTO, is clearly "rule-based" and more "juridical" with determinations that are effectively legally binding (although unlike the WTO no equivalent to the Dispute Settlement Body must approve the panel decisions).[14] Although all three mechanisms provide for some sort of soft diplomatic procedures (i.e., consultation and conciliation), by and large they are garden-variety international arbitral mechanisms designed to issue awards that technically do not require a Party to change its laws or regulation but are binding on the Parties in the sense that the Parties must either comply or face trade sanctions. They are not designed to be and in practice have not been simply a basis for a negotiated solution by governments.

Fifth, and finally, the U.S. government's perceptions of, and support for, all three mechanisms have waned significantly in the years since NAFTA entered into force.

B. INVESTMENT DISPUTES UNDER CHAPTER 11

There was nothing radical about Chapter 11 for the United States. The sources were the CFTA (i.e., for the obligations to investors language) and the various bilateral investment treaties (BITs) concluded by the United States with several dozen developing nations since 1980, particularly the 1992 "model" BIT.[15] Protection of U.S. foreign investment abroad has been a hallmark of U.S. international economic policy at least since the early 1960s, with various efforts to establish the international law principle of "prompt, adequate and effective

---

[13] On the PCA, see Mary Ellen O'Connell, *Arbitration and Avoidance of War: The Nineteenth-Century American Vision*, Chapter 3, this volume.
[14] See John H. Jackson, *The Jurisprudence of GATT and the WTO* (Cambridge, 2000) 165.
[15] Price and Christy, *op. cit.*, at 167, esp. n. 6.

compensation" following the Cuban and Brazilian expropriations.[16] For good reasons, the inclusion in NAFTA of a compulsory arbitration procedure to settle investment disputes must have been seen as a major achievement for State, Treasury, and the U.S. Trade Representative's Office (USTR), considering that it overturned many decades of Mexico's adherence to the Calvo Clause[17] and a long and troubled history of investment disputes with the United States.

The investment provisions of NAFTA were considered of major significance for U.S. and Canadian investors in Mexico, and for Mexico, which sought through NAFTA to encourage foreign investment, promote economic development, generate foreign exchange, and partially overcome the negative effects of a weak legal system. In this respect, Chapter 11 probably helped, generating an average of about US$9 billion annually in U.S. direct foreign investment in Mexico during the first ten years of NAFTA.[18] Although it is difficult to separate the influences of other NAFTA provisions, particularly the elimination of tariffs on most Mexican exports to Canada and the United States,[19] and the rules of origin that limit the NAFTA tariff benefits to goods that "originate" within North America,[20] the existence of "rules of the game" for foreign investment and the provisions applicable to investment disputes undoubtedly contributed to this strong growth.

As one senior U.S. State Department official, Mark Clodfelter, has commented, the United States, and, for that matter, Canada and Mexico

> took a very big step into the unknown when they signed onto Chapter 11. The NAFTA Parties have waived sovereign immunity from claims to an extent

---

[16] See Kenneth Vandevelde, *United States Investment Treaties: Policy and Practice* (Kluwer, 1992), 22–25.

[17] The Calvo Clause, named after the Argentine jurist Carlos Calvo, who first articulated the principle, posits that investors in the nation must agree to resolve disputes in the local courts and to forego seeking diplomatic protection by the home state in the event of difficulties. The Mexican version, Article 27 of the Constitution, reads "Only Mexicans by birth or naturalization and Mexican companies have the right to acquire ownership of lands, waters and their appurtenances, or to obtain concessions for the exploitation of mines, waters or mineral fuels, in the Mexican Republic. *The State may grant the same right to foreigners provided that they agree before the Ministry of [Foreign] Relations to consider themselves as nationals with respect to said properties and accordingly not to invoke the protection of their Governments in regard to them; under penalty, in case of breaches of the agreement, of losing to the benefit of the Nation the properties they may have acquired thereby*" (emphasis added).

[18] See [Mexican] Secretariat of the Economy, General Directorate of Foreign Investment, *Investment of the United States in Mexico*, September 2004, at 2 (estimating that since 1994, aggregate U.S. investment in Mexico was US$90.030 billion, about 62.6 percent of total foreign investment during the period), at http://www.economia.gob.mx/?P'1240.

[19] NAFTA, *op. cit.*, Chapter 3 and annexes 302.2 (tariff schedules of Mexico, the United States, and Canada).

[20] *Id.*, art. 401 and annex 401 (incorporating various rules of origin designed to ensure that goods enjoying NAFTA tariff benefits incorporate a high regional value).

far greater than they have consented to the jurisdiction, for example, of the International Court of Justice. They have agreed to be answerable to private claimants before arbitral tribunals that are subject to only very limited review. Even though the United States has been party to a fair number of BITs, which have arrangements resembling Chapter 11, we have never done so with states that have so much investment in our territory.[21]

This *was* radical, because the United States had never concluded a BIT in the past with another developed country, although that aspect of the coverage of Chapter 11 does not appear to have received much attention from U.S. government officials (or observers such as the author) until well after the fact, when thoughtful officials such as Mr. Clodfelter commented on it.[22]

Chapter 11 contemplates the possibility of disputes between a foreign investor or investing service provider and the host government or an agency thereof. Foreign investors may seek dispute settlement under Chapter 11 on the basis of any of the obligations guaranteed under Section A of Chapter 11, such as most favored nation treatment, freedom from export or local content performance requirements, and the right to make most financial transfers.[23] However, judging from the cases litigated through 2008, the most significant and controversial investors' protections in Chapter 11, Section A, are the rights to national treatment, to "fair and equitable treatment," and to fair compensation in the event of expropriation or nationalization, direct or indirect.[24] Tribunals established under Chapter 11 "decide the issues in accordance with this Agreement and applicable rules of international law."[25] National law is not relevant, except to

---

[21] Mark Clodfelter, *U.S. State Department Participation in International Economic Dispute Resolution*, 42 S. Tex. L. Rev. 1273, 1283 (2001). Mr. Clodfelter at the time the article was written was the assistant legal adviser, Office of International Claims and Investment Disputes.

[22] The State Department's guidance on the U.S. BIT program lists as one of the "basic aims" to "Protect investment abroad in those countries where investors' rights are not already protected through existing agreements." It says nothing about reciprocal actions by foreign investors against the United States. U.S. Dept. of State, Bureau of Economic and Business Affairs, *U.S. Bilateral Investment Treaty Program* (Mar. 15, 2005), at http://www.state.gov/e/eb/rls/fs/2006/22422.htm (visited Mar. 20, 2006) [hereinafter *U.S. BIT Program*]. Moreover, until 1998, the United States was actively engaged at the OECD in seeking to negotiate a multilateral agreement on investment (MAI), which if it had not failed would have extended Chapter 11-like provisions to the entire OECD membership. As the OECD Web site succinctly observes, "In 1995, OECD Ministers launched negotiations on a multilateral agreement on investment (MAI) with high standards of liberalisation and investment protection, with effective dispute settlement procedures, and open to non-Members. Negotiations were discontinued in April 1998 and will not be resumed." See http://www.oecd.org/document/35/0,2340,en_2649_201185_1894819_1_1_1_1,00.html (visited Apr. 15, 2007).

[23] NAFTA, *op. cit.*, arts. 1103, 1106, 1109, respectively.

[24] *Id.*, arts. 1102, 1105, 1110, respectively.

[25] *Id.*, art. 1131(1).

the extent tribunals must analyze the government measures (including national legislation) challenged, to determine whether they constitute violations of NAFTA or international law at large.

Chapter 11, Section B, provides a detailed mechanism designed to facilitate binding resolution of such disputes through compulsory arbitration,[26] normally through the World Bank's International Center for the Settlement of Investment Disputes (ICSID) "Additional Facility"[27] or under the arbitral rules of the United Nations Commission on International Trade Law (UNCITRAL). In theory, ICSID is available. However, in reality it is not. Neither Mexico nor Canada is a party to the Convention on the Settlement of Investment Disputes between States and Nationals of Other States, and arbitration under the ICSID Convention requires that both the host state and the investor's home state be parties. The ICSID Additional Facility, in contrast, is available if only one, the host state or the investor's home state, is party to the Convention.[28] In this respect, Chapter 11 differs significantly from Chapters 19 and 20 in that procedurally it takes advantage of existing arbitral mechanisms without creating any new ones. These mechanisms are not mandatory for the foreign investor who may elect to submit disputes to the local courts.[29]

NAFTA investment protection provisions have produced a significant volume of litigation in fifteen years. At least fifty notices of arbitration have been filed by foreign investors against NAFTA host governments, including those that are dormant or abandoned, and more than twenty Chapter 11 arbitral decisions on the merits, or other dispositive, or partially dispositive, opinions,[30] on

---

[26] *Id.*, arts. 1120, 1122.
[27] Convention on the Settlement of Investment Disputes Between States and Nationals of Other States, March 18, 1965, 17 U.S.T. 1270, T.I.A.S. 6090, 575 U.N.T.S. 159; ICSID Additional Facility Rules, art. 2(a).
[28] Disputes between Canadian investors and the Mexican government, or vice versa, could be submitted to binding arbitration only under the UNCITRAL rules. Canada signed the ICSID Convention Dec. 15, 2006, but approval at the federal and provincial levels was not complete as of March 2009.
[29] If the investor decides to bring a NAFTA claim for damages based on a NAFTA government's measure or measures, the investor must waive his or her right to initiate or continue a parallel action in a national administrative tribunal or court, except for certain injunctive relief. NAFTA, *op. cit.*, art. 1121(1)(b).
[30] *Metalclad Corporation v. United Mexican States*, Case no. ARB(AF)/97/1 (Aug. 26, 2000), 40 ILM 36 (2001) [hereinafter *Metalclad*]; *Pope & Talbot v. Canada*, Award on the Preliminary Motion of the Government of Canada to Dismiss (Jan. 26, 2000) [scope and coverage], hereinafter *Pope & Talbot I*; *Pope & Talbot v. Canada*, Interim Award (June 26, 2000), 40 ILM 258 (2001) [expropriation issues, merits], hereinafter *Pope & Talbot II*; *Pope & Talbot v. Canada*, Award on the Merits of Phase Two (Apr. 10, 2001) [national treatment and fair and equitable treatment, merits], hereinafter *Pope & Talbot III*; *Pope & Talbot v. Canada*, Award in Respect of Damages (May 31, 2002), 41 ILM 1347 (2002), hereinafter *Pope & Talbot IV*; and *Pope &*

occasion several in the same proceeding, have been issued. Another dozen or so are in various stages of proceedings.[31] A handful (*Metalclad, Loewen, Pope & Talbot, S.D. Myers, Methanex*) have generated considerable attention among the NAFTA member governments, the foreign investment bar, and NGOs that are concerned with environmental protection, alleged erosion of national sovereignty, or other problems, real or imagined. Six cases (*Metalclad, S.D. Myers, Pope & Talbot, Feldman, ADM*, and *Corn Products*) have resulted in monetary damages awards against Canada (two) or Mexico (four) as of early 2009; there have been no monetary damages awarded to date against the United States. Another group of cases (*Azinian, Waste Management, Gami, Mondev, ADF, Thunderbird, Loewen, Texas Water Claims*) resulted in a dismissal of all allegations against the respondent governments.

Each NAFTA Party has been a respondent in sixteen or more cases, still a virtually unique experience for the United States in investor-state claims

---

Talbot v. Canada, Award in Respect of Costs (Nov. 26, 2002) [procedural aspects of fair and equitable treatment, costs], hereinafter *Pope & Talbot V. Ethyl Corporation v. Government of Canada*, June 24, 1998, 38 ILM 708 (1999) [hereinafter *Ethyl*]; *Waste Management, Inc. v. United Mexican States*, Case No. ARB(AF)/98/2 (June 2, 2000) [hereinafter *Waste Management I*]; *Waste Management, Inc. v. Mexico* (Final Award) (Apr. 30, 2004) [hereinafter *Waste Management II*]; *Methanex v. United States* (Preliminary Award on Jurisdiction) (Aug. 7, 2002) [hereinafter *Methanex I*]; *Methanex v. United States* (Final Award on Jurisdiction and Merits) Aug. 3, 2005 [hereinafter *Methanex II*]; *S.D. Myers, Inc. v. Government of Canada* (Nov. 13, 2000) (Partial Award) [hereinafter *S.D. Myers*]; *Robert Azinian, Kenneth Davitian & Ellen Baca v. United Mexican States*, Case no. ARB(AF)/97/2 (Nov. 1, 1999), 39 ILM 537, 555 (2000) [hereinafter *Azinian*]; *Mondev v. United States*, Case no. ARB(AF)/99/2 (Oct. 11, 2002), 42 ILM 85 (2003) [hereinafter *Mondev*]; *ADF Group, Inc. v. United States*, Case no. ARB(AF)/00/1 (Jan. 9, 2003) [hereinafter *ADF*]; *UPS v. Canada* (Award on Jurisdiction) (Nov. 22, 2003) [hereinafter *UPS*]; *Marvin Feldman v. United Mexican States*, Case no. ARB(AF)/99/1 (Dec. 16, 2002), 42 ILM 625 (1993) [hereinafter *Feldman*]; *Loewen Group v. United States* (Award) (June 26, 2003), Decision on Request for Consideration (Sept. 13, 2004) [hereinafter *Loewen I* and *Loewen II*, respectively]; *Gami Investments v. United Mexican States* (Award) (Nov. 15, 2004) [hereinafter *Gami*]; *Int'l Thunderbird Gaming Corp. v. United Mexican States* (Award) (Jan. 26, 2006), 45 ILM 792 (2006); *Texas Water Claims v. United Mexican States* (Award) (Jun. 21, 2007); *Archer Daniels Midland v. United Mexican States* (Award) (Sep. 26, 2007); *Corn Products v. United Mexican States* (Partial Award on Liability) (Dec. 2007). See the Todd Weiler Web site, http://naftaclaims.com, the most comprehensive source for Chapter 11 decisions and other related documents discussed in this section.

[31] Although this was a more or less comprehensive list as of late 2008, based on the inclusive "NAFTA claims" Web site, the secrecy surrounding the Chapter 11 process does not ensure that disputes and the documents filed during the proceedings will be made public. NAFTA has no such requirements and one proceeding, *Cargill v. United Mexican States*, has been conducted in secrecy. However, an "Interpretation" issued by the Parties July 31, 2001, requires all documents relating to Chapter 11 provisions, excepting those containing confidential information, to be made "available to the public in a timely fashion." Compliance by the governments (and/or the claimants) appears to be good, except with regard to recent decisions affecting Mexico, *ADM*, and *Corn Products*, where release of the decisions was delayed by eight months or more in each instance.

practice, despite more than forty BITs in force.[32] As far as the author has been able to determine, no case has ever been brought by a foreign investor under any BIT against the United States. All of the NAFTA claimants against the United States have been Canadian individuals or investors; there have been no Mexican investor claims against the United States. This should be no surprise. Indeed, one result of the fact that the United States normally concludes BITs only with developing nations is a relatively small likelihood that any significant number of persons from those nations would have investments in the United States leading to investor-state disputes.

The cases against the United States have inevitably involved not only the State Department and USTR but also domestic agencies such as the Department of Justice and the Environmental Protection Agency (the latter particularly, for the *Methanex* claim that raised environmental issues arising out of California's banning of a gasoline additive for environmental – or maybe political – reasons). This obviously creates a potential for conflict between, on one hand, national agencies that are principally concerned with encouraging U.S. investment abroad and foreign trade (State and USTR) and, on the other hand, those that are more concerned with defending federal government and state actions[33] allegedly inconsistent with Chapter 11.

Most of the controversies that have led to at least some reevaluation of U.S. government support of investment disputes fall into one of several areas. First, there are disputes arising from conflicts between trade and "legitimate" government regulatory action, including but not limited to actions protecting the environment. This is particularly true with regard to the expropriation provisions, Article 1110 in NAFTA and the coverage of "indirect" expropriation and regulatory "takings." Second, there are concerns – primarily among NGOs and some members of Congress – regarding the appropriateness of having NAFTA tribunals effectively review decisions of U.S. courts. Third, there is an articulated concern –albeit probably unjustified – by the same NGOs and their supporters in Congress that foreign citizens may have greater rights regarding investment than do American citizens under the Takings Clause of the Fifth Amendment of the U.S. Constitution.[34] Finally, there appears to be a fear of a "rogue" tribunal establishing erroneous interpretations of international law that could not be overturned because of the lack of an appellate process.

---

[32] The United States has negotiated more than forty-five BITs of which about forty are in force. *U.S. BIT Program, op. cit.*, at 2–3.

[33] Under NAFTA Article 105, state and local governments are bound by NAFTA provisions unless otherwise provided.

[34] "[N]or shall private property be taken for pubic use, without just compensation."

The *Methanex* case[35] aptly illustrates the "regulatory takings" concern. The Canadian firm Methanex challenged the action of the State of California in banning the gasoline additive methyl tert-butyl ether (MTBE) because of the perceived risk that it might pollute the underground water supply.[36] Methanex manufactures methanol, which is the principal ingredient in MTBE, and argued that the measures taken by California constituted a "substantial interference and taking of Methanex US' business and Methanex's investment in Methanex U.S." These measures were characterized both directly and indirectly as "tantamount to expropriation." The arbitral tribunal did not reach the question of whether California's action constituted a compensable taking under Article 1110, because it initially dismissed the complaint on the procedural ground that the connection between the California MTBE ban and Methanex's operations was not "legally significant" so as to satisfy the "relating to" language in NAFTA, Article 1101.[37] Ultimately, the tribunal dismissed all claims by Methanex against the United States, both on jurisdictional grounds and on the merits.[38]

Anti-NAFTA groups in the United States had also seized on the *Loewen* case as "an all-out attack on democracy. If successful, it would undermine the jury system, which is fundamental to our system of justice."[39] In *Loewen*, a Mississippi state court trial, allegedly conducted in an intentionally prejudicial manner and stemming from a commercial transaction worth less than $5 million, resulted in a verdict against Loewen (a Canadian operator of funeral homes) of approximately $100 million in actual damages and $400 million in punitive damages.[40] Because the claimant allegedly could not meet bonding requirements for an appeal, set at $625 million, Loewen settled the case for $175 million "under conditions of extreme duress." Eventually it brought a Chapter 11 claim against the United States.[41] Among Loewen's contentions

---

[35] See discussion of *Methanex* and *Loewen* in Susan Karamanian, "Dispute Settlement under NAFTA Chapter 11: A Response to the Critics in the United States," Chapter 12, this volume.

[36] Executive Order D-5-99 of the State of California, Mar. 25, 1999, as modified by Executive Order D-52-02, Mar. 14, 2002, at http://www.governor.ca.gov (visited May 1, 2003).

[37] *Methanex I, op. cit.*, para. 172(2). Methanex's principal argument in the continuing proceeding is based on a denial of national treatment under Article 1102; that is, that California through its MTBE ban was seeking to favor domestic producers of the competing gasoline additive, ethanol. See Claimant Methanex Corporation's Second Amended Statement of Claim, at 58 et seq.

[38] *Methanex II, op. cit.*, Part V, Tribunal's Operative Order, at 300.

[39] *NAFTA: Consumer Group Brands Funeral Firm's NAFTA Suit an Assault on U.S. Protections*, Int'l Trade Daily (BNA) (Nov. 27, 1998) at D7 (quoting Joan Claybrook, president of Public Citizen).

[40] See *Loewen Group, Inc. v. United States, op. cit.*, Notice of Claim, October 30, 1998, paras. 3, 4, 6. Among other things, Loewen alleged that the court permitted "repeated appeals to the jury's anti-Canadian, racial and class biases."

[41] *Id.*, para. 6.

was that actions of the Mississippi trial court, the excessive judgment, and the bonding requirements amounted to a denial of justice and of fair and equitable treatment by the Mississippi courts in violation of NAFTA, Article 1105.[42] The arbitral proceedings were initially dismissed on procedural grounds, with the Tribunal holding that availability of the Chapter 11 mechanism had been lost when Loewen, in bankruptcy proceedings, transferred its interests to a U.S. firm. Although the Tribunal termed the process in the Mississippi state court a "disgrace," it concluded in what at the time was *dicta* that the decision was not cognizable under NAFTA and international law because Loewen had not exhausted legal remedies within the U.S. court system.[43] A subsequent ruling by the arbitral tribunal held that the action of the Mississippi court did not meet the high international law threshold for a denial of justice.[44]

Also, the NAFTA provision whereby "Each Party shall accord to investment of investors of another Party treatment in accordance with international law, including fair and equitable treatment and full protection and security"[45] has resulted in controversy. The scope of the concept "fair and equitable treatment" under international law has never been clear, and the water was muddied early on when the Tribunal in *Pope & Talbot* initially determined that this quoted language provided claimants with a right that was *in addition to*, rather than limited by, the phrase "treatment in accordance with international law."[46]

The concerns of the NAFTA Parties over this *Pope & Talbot* deviation prompted the first, and to date only, binding "Interpretation" of NAFTA Chapter 11,[47] which, inter alia, stated that "The concepts of 'fair and equitable treatment' and 'full protection and security' do not require treatment in addition to or beyond that which is required by the customary international law minimum standard of treatment of aliens."[48]

Of course, whether the regulatory actions such as those challenged in *Methanex* and challenges to state court decisions, as in *Loewen*, are "valid" is to be determined by the adjudicatory process. In both cases, the arbitral tribunal failed to reach a decision on the merits. However, the mere possibility that they might do so was enough to cause deep concerns within the NGO community and, in the United States, some U.S. government agencies. For

---

[42] *Id.*, paras. 7, 144–61.
[43] *Loewen, op. cit.*, paras. 119, 137, 217, 240.
[44] *Loewen, op. cit.*, Decision on Remand for Consideration (Sept. 13, 2004).
[45] NAFTA, *op. cit.*, art. 1105(1).
[46] *Pope & Talbot III, op. cit.*, at 48 (para. 110).
[47] NAFTA, art. 1131(2) provides that "An interpretation by the [Free Trade] Commission of a provision of this Agreement shall be binding on a Tribunal established under this Section."
[48] *See Notes of Interpretation of Certain Chapter 11 Provisions* (July 31, 2001), *at* http://www.international.gc.ca/trade-agreements-accords-commerciaux/disp-diff/NAFTA-Interpr.aspx?lang=en (visited Feb. 27, 2009).

example, environmental groups have been highly critical of the repeated use of investor protection provisions "to challenge the host country's environmental laws and administrative decisions," noting that "the provisions designed to ensure security and predictability for the investors have created uncertainty and unpredictability for environmental regulators."[49] Similarly, one American official suggested that "[the] promise [of NAFTA as a model for the FTAA and other agreements] . . . will only be fulfilled if Chapter 11 tribunals are successful in distinguishing valid claims under NAFTA and international law from claims beyond the bounds of what the Parties believed they were agreeing to when they entered into the NAFTA."[50]

Pressure on Congress to introduce changes to the president's "Trade Promotion Authority" led to new negotiating instructions in 2002:

> [T]he principal negotiating objectives of the United States regarding foreign investment are to reduce or eliminate artificial or trade-distorting barriers to foreign investment, while *ensuring that foreign investors in the United States are not accorded greater substantive rights with respect to investment protections than United States investors in the United States*, and to secure for investors important rights comparable to those that would be available under United States legal principles and practice, by:
>
> (A) reducing or eliminating exceptions to the principle of national treatment:
> . . .
>
> (D) seeking to establish standards for expropriation and compensation for expropriation, consistent with United States legal principles and practice;
>
> (E) seeking to establish standards for fair and equitable treatment consistent with United States legal principles and practice, including the principle of due process.[51]

These instructions to the president led to changes in subsequent FTAs and to a new 2004 "model" BIT. To illustrate, in the United States–Chile Free Trade Agreement, although the investment provisions are generally similar to those found in NAFTA, Chapter 11, Annex 10-D, is designed to restrict, perhaps significantly, the scope of the "indirect" expropriation provisions as they may apply to government regulatory activities:

---

[49] *See* Peter Menyasz, *NAFTA Chapter 11 Provisions Said to Threaten Environmental Protection Rights*, 16 Int'l Trade Rep. 1146 (1999) (quoting a report released on June 22, 1999, by the International Institute for Sustainable Development).

[50] Clodfelter, *op. cit.*, at 1283.

[51] 19 U.S.C. § 3802(b)(3) (2002) (emphasis added). Trade Promotion Authority also incorporates the substantive tests of *Penn Central Transportation Co. v. New York City*, 438 U.S. 104 (1978) for regulatory takings.

Except in rare circumstances, nondiscriminatory regulatory actions by a Party that are designed and applied to protect legitimate public welfare objectives, such as public health, safety, and the environment, do not constitute indirect expropriation.[52]

The United States–Chile FTA also attempts to resolve at least some of the doubts over the overly broad scope of "fair and equitable treatment" and review by investment tribunals of national court decisions. It does so by including the term "customary international law" in the fair and equitable treatment provision, defining that term in much greater detail, and limiting the scope of tribunal review of national court decisions to issues of due process:

1. Each Party shall accord to covered investments treatment in accordance with customary international law, including fair and equitable treatment and full protection and security.

2. For greater certainty, paragraph 1 prescribes the customary international law minimum standard of treatment of aliens as the minimum standard of treatment to be afforded to covered investments. The concepts of "fair and equitable treatment" and "full protection and security" do not require treatment in addition to or beyond that which is required by that standard, and do not create additional substantive rights. The obligation in paragraph [1] to provide:

(a) A fair and equitable treatment" includes the obligation not to deny justice in criminal, civil, or administrative adjudicatory proceedings in accordance with the principle of due process embodied in the principal legal systems of the world."[53]

The changes to the U.S. President's Trade Promotion Authority also generated interest, particularly among some in Congress, for some sort of an appellate body for investment disputes to replace the current system of review by courts of the state of the "situs" of the arbitration, but little progress toward such a mechanism has been made to date.[54]

---

[52] *Id.*, annex 10-C(4)(a).

[53] United States–Chile FTA, *op. cit.*, art. 10.4, annex 10.8; *see* David A. Gantz, *The Evolution of FTA Investment Provisions from NAFTA to the United States–Chile Free Trade Agreement*, 19 Am. Univ. Int'l L.R. 679, 724–28 (2004).

[54] *See* William H. Knull III and Noah D. Rubins, *Betting the Farm on International Arbitration: Is It Time to Offer an Appeal Option?* 11 Am. Rev. Int'l Arb. 531 (2000) (suggesting that internal appeals processes for investment disputes have a role for high-stakes and complex arbitrations); Susan D. Franck, *The Legitimacy Crisis in Investment Treaty Arbitration: Privatizing Public International Law through Inconsistent Decisions*, 73 Fordham L. R. 1521 (2005) (arguing that the expanding volume of investor-state arbitral decisions calls for, inter alia, an appellate court to discourage inconsistent decisions); David A. Gantz, *An Appellate Mechanism for*

Another concern raised by NGOs and U.S. government officials has been lack of transparency, which has likely contributed to broader skepticism of the process within the United States. Under the ICSID Additional Facility Rules – a popular mechanism for adjudicating Chapter 11 disputes – neither the written nor the oral proceedings are available to the public.[55] NAFTA itself provides that the final award may be made public if either the government or the private party wishes to do so (in the case of Canada or the United States) or in accordance with the applicable arbitration rules (Mexico).[56] Even the formal notice initiating arbitration may not be public if neither party decides to release it.[57] None of this is particularly surprising to those familiar with international commercial arbitration, because usually it is a confidential process. Yet when particular cases raise important public law and policy concerns, as with the potential impact of the Chapter 11 mechanism on the national or local government's ability to enact environmental or other regulations, then lack of publicity has become an issue.

In part because of public pressure, the degree of transparency of the process has increased significantly in recent years, at least for Canada and Mexico. In July 2001, the NAFTA Parties stated that "nothing in NAFTA imposes a general duty of confidentiality" and agreed that they would "make available to the public in a timely manner all documents submitted to, or issued by, Chapter 11 tribunals" subject to certain exceptions for confidential or privileged information.[58] In October 2003, Canada and the United States, but not Mexico, issued statements indicating that they would consent (and request disputing investors and tribunals to consent) to holding hearings open to the public, subject to measures to protect confidential business information.[59] At the same time, a statement was issued setting forth procedures for *amicus curiae* participation in Chapter 11 proceedings.[60]

Review of Arbitral Decisions in Investor-State Disputes: Prospects and Challenges, 39 Vanderbilt J. Transnat'l L. 1295 (2006) (discussing the complexities of creating such a mechanism in practice).

[55] ICSID Arbitration (Additional Facility) Rules, *op. cit.*, Article 39, gives the tribunal authority to decide, with the Parties' consent, what persons may be admitted to the hearing; publication of the minutes of the hearing requires the Parties' consent under Article 44.

[56] NAFTA, *op. cit.*, Annex 1137.4.

[57] See *California Democrats Press USTR to Clarify NAFTA Investor Provisions*, Americas Trade (Aug. 26, 1999), at 6.

[58] NAFTA Free Trade Commission, *Notes of Interpretation, op. cit.*, parts A(1), A(2).

[59] *Statement on Open Hearings in NAFTA Chapter Eleven Arbitrations* (Oct. 7, 2003), at http://www.ustr.gov; Statement of Canada on Open Hearings in NAFTA Chapter Eleven Arbitrations (Oct. 2003), at http://www.dfait-maeci.gc.ca.

[60] See *Statement of the Free Trade Commission on Non-disputing Party Participation* (Oct. 2003), at http://www.ustr.gov; *NAFTA Commission Meet, Announces New Transparency Measures*, USTR Press Release (Oct. 7, 2003), at 1.

To date, none of this subsequent reassessment of the various NAFTA Chapter 11 provisions and language in the 2002 Trade Promotion Authority Act (TPA) or FTAs has greatly affected the Chapter 11 language or the NAFTA arbitral process. However, it demonstrates the great extent to which the process is being second-guessed, reevaluated, and perhaps improved as a result of reactions of the American public, business community, and government.

C. REVIEW OF UNFAIR TRADE DISPUTES UNDER CHAPTER 19

The most innovative dispute settlement mechanism contained in NAFTA is Chapter 19, relating to antidumping and countervailing duty actions brought in one NAFTA member country against imports from another NAFTA country.[61] Antidumping (AD) and countervailing duty (CVD) cases are, of course, controversial.[62] Numerous such actions have been brought by national industries against the products of other NAFTA countries – in steel and steel products; beef, swine, and other agricultural products; high-fructose corn syrup; cement; and softwood lumber, among others.[63] Chapter 19 has been far and away the most frequently used NAFTA dispute settlement mechanism, with more than 120 actions filed by early 2009. This is not surprising considering the volume of unfair trade cases brought by domestic industries in the NAFTA nations against imports from NAFTA partners and the fact that "interested parties" in the various AD and CVD cases, as opposed to the governments, effectively determine whether actions are filed with "binational panels."

When Chapter 19 was drafted as part of the CFTA, Chapter 19 was only a procedural novelty. As one experienced trade attorney noted in 1994,

> At the time [1988], some regarded them [the Chapter 19 provisions] as insubstantial innovations: the Chapter 19 provisions creating panels neither adopted new substantive law nor established a right of review that would

---

[61] For a more extensive (but dated) discussion of the operation of Chapter 19 under NAFTA, see David A. Gantz, *Resolution of Trade Disputes under NAFTA's Chapter 19: The Lessons of Extending the Binational Panel Process to Mexico*, 29 Law & Policy in Int'l Business 297 (1998).

[62] Dumping generally occurs when goods produced in one country are sold in the territory of another country at below "normal value," usually where the adjusted price in the foreign market is less than the price in the producing country market, and the resulting sales cause injury to the domestic producers in the importing country. See [WTO] Agreement on Implementation of Art. VI of the GATT, Art. 2, Annex 1A, Agreement Establishing the World Trade Organization, April 15, 1994. Countervailing duties may be imposed to offset the effects of certain government subsidies to producers in one country that result in subsidized sales to another country when those sales cause injury to producers of like or similar goods in the importing country. See [WTO] Agreement on Subsidies and Countervailing Measures, Art. 1, both at http://www.wto.org (visited Apr. 12, 2007).

[63] See NAFTA Secretariat, Status Report of Dispute Settlement, at http://www.nafta-sec-alena.org/en/StatusReportResults.aspx (visited Feb. 27, 2009).

not otherwise exist. Rather, those provisions provided that Chapter 19 panels would serve simply as surrogates for reviewing courts and decide cases in accordance with the same legal standards that courts would apply.[64]

However, in many respects it *was* a more radical innovation than Chapter 11. The principal motivation for Chapter 19 was the adamant refusal of the United States to provide Canada with an exemption from the normal operation of U.S. AD and CVD laws, a position that threatened to prevent Canada and the United States from concluding the CFTA negotiations.[65] Chapter 19 was introduced in the CFTA at the behest of Canada. The United States agreed to the Chapter 19 process, and Canada temporarily abandoned demands for special trade remedy laws – distinct from those available in the WTO/GATT system – to be applicable in the United States and Canada.[66] It was initially suggested by Florida Congressman Sam Gibbons, the so-called decision at midnight that saved CFTA.[67]

The CFTA Chapter 19 mechanism also gave the Parties an opportunity to challenge each other's proposed changes in their unfair trade laws with regard to consistency with NAFTA and GATT/WTO principles[68] and incorporated a requirement for five more years of negotiations on Canada's proposal to eliminate AD and CVD actions relating to intra–Central

---

[64] Homer E. Moyer, Jr., *Chapter 19 of the NAFTA: Binational Panels as the Trade Courts of Last Resort*, in Judith H. Bello et al., *op. cit.*, at 291.

[65] One of the U.S. NAFTA negotiators, Jean Anderson, has suggested that there was some sympathy in the U.S. government for the argument that with the elimination of import duties and nontariff barriers for intraregional trade, the need for antidumping actions to control international price discrimination would be reduced or eliminated, although this was not the controlling view. There was little sympathy, however, on the U.S. side for eliminating CVD actions against existing and possible future federal and provincial subsidies in Canada. Conference remarks, "The Future of NAFTA Chapter 19 Dispute Settlement," D.C. Bar (May 11, 2005) [hereinafter "D.C. Bar Conference"] (notes on file with author).

[66] See U.S. General Accounting Office, *U.S.-Canada Free Trade Agreement, Factors Contributing to Controversy in Appeals of Trade Remedy Cases to Binational Panels*, June 1995; American Coalition for Competitive Trade v. United States, D.C. Cir. No. 97-1036, (brief for intervenor the Government of Canada at 4) (Sept. 5, 1997). Canada advocated, and later adopted in its 1996 FTA with Chile (but not in subsequent Canadian FTAs), a position that there was no need for AD actions within FTAs because there could be no international price discrimination where tariff and nontariff barriers had been abolished. Similar arguments were made for antisubsidy actions, with less economic justification in the absence of a centralized anticompetition authority, which NAFTA and most other FTAs lack.

[67] See Hart, *op. cit.*, at 321–34, for a detailed discussion of the development of the Gibbons proposal that became CFTA's Chapter 19. This Canadian perspective is confirmed by Anderson, *op. cit.*, noting that the Gibbons proposal, which in its original form was a somewhat vague suggestion of an international arbitral mechanism, was sufficient to restart the negotiations.

[68] CFTA, *op. cit.*, arts. 1902:2, 1903.

American Free Trade Agreement trade.[69] According to a Canadian official, the Chapter 19 compromise gave "Canada a voice both in determining whether legislative changes were consistent with the intent and purpose of the agreement, and... in determining whether the law had been properly applied."[70]

Other factors that prompted Canada to insist on the Chapter 19 mechanism included the costs and delays of the appellate process in AD and CVD appeals to the U.S. courts, and, ultimately, the belief that these courts had been overly deferential to the determinations of the Department of Commerce and the U.S. International Trade Commission. Chapter 19, significantly, removed AD/CVD appeals from the jurisdiction of the federal courts of the United States and Canada and ensured that at least two Canadians would sit on any binational panel reviewing a U.S. agency decision.

Because the United States was no more willing in NAFTA than it had been in the CFTA to adopt more favorable AD and CVD rules for the FTA, essentially the same mechanism was incorporated with relatively minor changes into the NAFTA. Canada insisted on carrying over the mechanism; it would have been politically impossible for Ottawa to give up the hard-won provisions that had secured the acceptance of CFTA only a few years earlier.[71] Mexico favored Chapter 11 for reasons basically similar to those articulated by Canada,[72] and it would have been impossible to provide the benefit to Canada without treating Mexico in the same manner. There was also some thought within the U.S. government that Chapter 19 would be perceived as a benefit by U.S. exporters to Mexico, who would be able to avoid litigating AD/CVD administrative appeals in the Mexican court system.[73] Mexico, as part of the package, agreed to make major procedural reforms in the administration of its AD and CVD laws and to create a general right of judicial review of AD and

---

[69] *Id.*, art. 1906: "The provisions of this Chapter shall be in effect for five years pending the development of a substitute system of rules in both countries for antidumping and countervailing duties as applied to their bilateral trade." The negotiations never progressed.

[70] Hart, *op. cit.*, at 334.

[71] Conference Remarks of Douglas Waddell, former assistant deputy minister of trade, International Trade Canada, D.C. Bar Conference, *op. cit.*

[72] Conference remarks of Beatriz Leycegui, former member of the Mexican Secretariat of Commerce and Industrial Development (SECOFI), D.C. Bar Conference, *op. cit.* Mexico was not seeking elimination of AD/CVD actions but saw Chapter 19 as a means of fairly and definitively resolving such actions at reduced time and cost compared to litigation before the U.S. Court of International Trade and the Court of Appeals of the Federal Circuit.

[73] E-mail exchange with a former U.S. government official involved in the negotiation and implementation of Chapter 19 (Apr. 30, 2005) (copy on file with author) [hereinafter Former Government Official].

CVD determinations.[74] In the author's personal experience, at least, these have been significant benefits for U.S., Canadian, and other exporters to Mexico, and were so perceived at the time.

Chapter 19 applies only to decisions of administrative agencies of the three countries in antidumping and countervailing duty cases. Cases relating, for example, to U.S., Canadian, or Mexican customs service rulings on classification, valuation, origin of merchandise, and so forth are not subject to panel review[75] but only to the usual review of the federal courts in the NAFTA nations.

Under Chapter 19, a binational panel replaces the federal courts of the Party imposing AD or CVD. Appeals from the administrative agencies are referred to five-person arbitral panels, comprised of trade experts who are nationals of the two countries whose citizens are involved in AD or CVD actions before the administrative agencies. However, it should be stressed that the binational panels are not international tribunals, although like international tribunals, they are made up of individuals coming from more than one country. The panelists are selected from standing rosters of at least twenty-five individuals designated by each of the NAFTA member states. "Candidates shall be of good character, high standing and repute, and shall be chosen strictly on the basis of objectivity, reliability, sound judgment and general familiarity with international trade law." They may not be "affiliated" with any of the Parties.[76]

Preference under NAFTA is to be given to judges and former judges, presumably because judges know how to apply a standard of review; however, no U.S. judge or former judge has yet served on a NAFTA Chapter 19 panel, although at least one Canadian judge has been designated.[77] Panelists are normally trade practitioners or law professors serving on an ad hoc, part-time basis and paid modest compensation.[78] Because many are simultaneously practicing before the national trade agencies at the same time they are serving as panelists, the risk of actual or apparent conflicts of interest is high, even though panelists are subject to a detailed code of conduct at the time of appointment and throughout their service as panelists.[79]

---

[74] NAFTA, *op. cit.*, Annex 1904.15 (Schedule of Mexico); the Former Government Official, *op. cit.* suggests that U.S. exporters subject to Mexican unfair trade proceedings have relied more on the Mexican writ of *amparo* than the binational panels for relief in difficult cases.

[75] NAFTA, *op. cit.*, art. 1904(1), limits Chapter 19 review to antidumping and countervailing duty determinations.

[76] *Id.*, Annex 1901.2(1).

[77] Telephone interview with Cathy Beehan, Esq., former secretary, Canadian Section, NAFTA Secretariat (Oct. 27, 1997).

[78] CDN$400 per day until 2002, when the amount was increased to CDN$800 per day (about US$832 at November 2007 exchange rates).

[79] Code of Conduct for Dispute Settlement Procedures under Chapters 19 and 20 of the North American Free Trade Agreement, 59 Fed. Reg. 8,720 (1994).

Crucially, unlike international tribunals, they do not apply international law (e.g., the provisions of the GATT and the WTO agreements governing AD or CVD actions) except to the extent international trading rules are incorporated directly into national law. Panels are governed by national substantive law, including court decisions in Canada and the United States. Procedurally, trinational rules and the Article 1904 Rules of Procedure as agreed by the three NAFTA parties apply but with reference to national law where the tri-national rules do not control.[80]

In contrast to the situation in Chapters 11 and 20, and reflecting the differing subject matter, Chapter 19 proceedings have been largely public and transparent from the outset. Although business proprietary information submitted by the interested parties or that is part of the agency's administrative record is kept confidential,[81] as, of course, are panel deliberations themselves, the briefs and hearings are normally public,[82] and the opinions are released to the public shortly after issuance to the interested parties.[83]

By almost any reasonable measure, the Chapter 19 panel process has been a success. As of February 2009, 124 Chapter 19 actions had been filed, 84 against U.S. authorities, 22 against Canadian authorities, and 18 against the Mexican authorities. Of these, more than a third were terminated by the request of the parties, and more than 50 decisions were rendered; a total of 14 remain pending.[84] Of the panel decisions rendered, a 2005 study determined that more than 80 percent resulted in unanimous rulings regardless of panel member nationality.[85]

Despite this notable success, political and financial support began to decline among the Parties around 1999, and controversy arose over several high-profile cases, such as softwood lumber and pork and live swine.[86] There is no general appeal of a panel decision. Challenges may be brought when there is an allegation of gross misconduct, bias, or serious conflict of interest; when the panel decision departs from a fundamental rule of procedure; or when the panel exceeds its power, authority, or jurisdiction (including, significantly, and in a change from the CFTA, fails to apply the proper standard of review) *and* such action materially affects the decision, *and* "threatens the integrity

---

[80] *See* 59 Fed. Reg. 8,686 (1994); NAFTA, *op. cit.*, arts 1904(2), 1904(10).

[81] NAFTA Article 1904 Panel Rules, at http://www.nafta-sec-alena.org/DefaultSite/index_e.aspx?DetailID=190 (visited Apr. 15, 2007).

[82] Proceedings are held in camera where proprietary or privileged information is presented: NAFTA Article 1904 Panel Rules, Rule 69.

[83] *Id.*, Rule 72.

[84] NAFTA Secretariat Reports, *op. cit.*

[85] Beatriz Leycegui, *op. cit.*

[86] GAO Report, *op. cit.*, at 68.

of the panel process."[87] In such instances alone, an "extraordinary challenge procedure," an appeal of the panel decision, is permitted to a special three-person review panel – the Extraordinary Challenge Committee (ECC) – for decision.[88]

The United States has been the only NAFTA Party to resort to this extraordinary challenge process, without success. In *Gray Portland Cement and Clinker from Mexico*, the panel unanimously determined that the United States and the U.S. industry petitioners failed to meet any of the three criteria.[89] In a U.S. challenge to a binational panel decision in *Pure Magnesium from Canada*, the ECC concluded that "(a) the Panel manifestly exceeded its powers by failing to apply the correct standard of review; and (b) such action materially affected the Panel's decision, *but* (c) ... the Panel's action did not threaten the integrity of the binational panel review process"[90] Accordingly, the "appeal" was dismissed, and the challenged panel decision stood.

Most significantly, a NAFTA binational panel effectively required the U.S. International Trade Commission (ITC) in 2004 to reverse its threat of material injury determination in the most recent U.S. AD and CVD cases against Canadian softwood lumber. In so doing, the ITC – clearly reflecting its frustration with the binational panel process – commented:

> The Panel's Decision and Order of August 31, 2004, can only be seen as a reversal of the Commission's affirmative determination of threat of material injury, despite the fact that neither the NAFTA nor U.S. law gives the Panel authority to reverse the Commission's determination in these circumstances. As such, the Panel's decision signals the end of this Panel proceeding. Because the Commission respects and is bound by the NAFTA dispute settlement process, we issue a determination, consistent with the Panel's decision, that the U.S. softwood lumber industry is not threatened with material injury by reason of subject imports from Canada. In so doing, we disagree with the Panel's view that there is no substantial evidence to support a finding of threat of material injury and we continue to view the Panel's decisions throughout this proceeding as overstepping its authority, violating the NAFTA, seriously departing from fundamental rules of procedure, and committing legal error.[91]

---

[87] NAFTA, *op. cit.*, art. 1904(13).

[88] NAFTA Annex 1904.13. This is in contrast to the WTO's dispute settlement procedures, which provides a standing Appellate Body that reviews panel decisions as a matter of course upon the request of any party, with the reviewing panel authorized to conduct a full appellate review of the initial panel decision. See DSU, *op. cit.*, art. 17.

[89] Case no. ECC-2000-1904-01 USA (Oct. 30, 2003), at 7, at http://www.nafta-sec-alena.org (visited Apr. 15, 2007).

[90] *In the Matter of Pure Magnesium from Canada*, ECC-2003-1904-01USA, Oct. 5, 2004, para. 42, at http://www.nafta-sec-alena.org/DefaultSite/index_e.aspx?DetailID'79 (visited Apr. 16, 2007).

[91] *Softwood Lumber from Canada*, Inv. Nos. 701-TA-414 and 731-TA-928, USITC Response to the Decision and Order of the Binational Panel, Sept. 10, 2004, *quoted in* USITC

The U.S. filed an extraordinary challenge in *Softwood Lumber*, which was also rejected.[92] The USTR's experience with ECCs makes it abundantly clear that the ECC is not an appellate process, as presumably was the original intent in the compromise language and coverage that were ultimately negotiated. Whether the ECC's statutory jurisdiction is so narrow as to make the process meaningless is another question.

The panel process has been criticized (mostly by U.S. NGOs and others who have opposed NAFTA generally) in several respects. First, it has been attacked for putting decision-making power in the hands of individuals, including foreign nationals, without judicial experience, who are not accountable for their performance, who have not been appointed in accordance with Article III of the U.S. Constitution, and who may disregard the requirement that they behave as would local courts and apply U.S. law.[93] The complexities and costs of a largely ad hoc system, which substitutes for what most believe is an acceptable national court system, have also been cited.

Constitutional challenges against the panel process have been raised in the United States, with plaintiffs arguing, inter alia, that the appointment of panelists without the advice and consent of the Senate is a violation of the "appointments" clause of the U.S. Constitution, Article II, sec. 2(2), and that the removal of jurisdiction of the federal courts in favor of panels violates Article III, sec. 1.[94] All constitutional challenges to the panel process to date have failed,[95] but efforts are likely to continue.[96] Counsel for U.S. industries that file AD/CVD cases tend to be much less favorably inclined toward the binational

---

Press Release 04-100 (Sept. 10, 2004), at 1, at http://www.usitc.gov/ext_relations/news_release/2004/er0910bb1.htm (visited Feb. 27, 2009); emphasis added; footnote omitted.

[92] *Softwood Lumber from Canada*, ECC-2004–1904-01USA, Extraordinary Challenge Committee (ECC) Proceeding relating to USA-CDA-2002–1904-07 Panel Review (Aug. 10, 2005), at http://www.nafta-sec-alena.org/DefaultSite/index_e.aspx?DetailID'796 (visited Mar. 20, 2006).

[93] *See* Written Statement in Opposition to Fast-Track Procedures for Trade Agreements Containing the NAFTA Chapter 19 Binational Panel Dispute System, submitted on behalf of AK Steel Company et al., to the Subcommittee on Trade of the Committee on Ways and Means (May 11, 1995), at 1–2.

[94] *See* Harry B. Endsley, *Dispute Settlement under the CFTA and NAFTA: From Eleventh-Hour Innovation to Accepted Institution*, 18 Hastings Int'l & Comp. L. Rev. 659, 671–72 (1995); *NAFTA: Group Files Constitutional Challenge to NAFTA, Binational Panel System*, Int'l Trade Daily (BNA) (Jan. 17, 1997) at D-5.

[95] *See, e.g., American Coalition for Competitive Trade v. United States*, 128 F.3d 761 (D.C. Cir. 1997) (dismissed for lack of standing); *Made in the USA Foundation v. United States*, 242 F.3d 1300, 1319–20 (11th Cir. 2001) (holding that plaintiffs had standing to bring the action but that the issue of whether NAFTA was a treaty requiring the advice and consent of the Senate, or had properly been concluded as an executive agreement, was a nonjusticiable political question).

[96] *See Coalition for Fair Lumber Imports Executive Committee v. United States*, D.C. Cir., Case No. 05-1366 (Sept. 13, 2005) [hereinafter *Coalition v. US*], apparently dismissed as part of the settlement that resulted in the 2006 Softwood Lumber Agreement (Sept. 12, 2006), at http://www.international.gc.ca/eicb/softwood/pdfs/SLA-en.pdf (visited Apr. 15, 2007).

panel process than those representing foreign producers, because the panels are thought to be less likely to affirm national administrative agencies than are the U.S. courts. In one of the constitutional challenges, several members of the Senate weighed in, arguing that the system

> supplants judicial review of antidumping and countervailing duty determinations involving Canadian and Mexican merchandise, removing affected appellate processes from the protected environment where political and financial pressures can influence outcomes. This system is both a policy debacle and, more importantly, an infringement of litigants' constitutional rights.
>
> The Chapter 19 system gives international panels a power for which they are ill-suited: the power to interpret and apply national law. It empowers foreigners and private U.S. citizens to decide, with no possibility of court review, whether U.S. law has been correctly applied at the agency level. The individuals replacing Article III judges under this system are seated inconsistently with the Appointments Clause, are subject to many of the kinds of entanglements and financial considerations that Article III guards against in the judicial review context, and routinely deny litigants a fair hearing and, thereby, of Due Process.[97]

In actuality, congressional unhappiness with Chapter 19 tends to focus on the handful of decisions involving the long-running softwood lumber dispute with Canada. Although that unhappiness is shared by the executive branch, USTR officials have indicated that they would "vigorously defend" the constitutionality of NAFTA, including Chapter 19.[98] U.S. government officials have also used considerable restraint in public criticism of various NAFTA Chapter 19 panel decisions involving softwood lumber that have effectively overruled determinations of the U.S. International Trade Commission.

Overall, the author's discussions over the years with various U.S. officials suggest some ambivalence on their part, but on balance there is at the very minimum a lack of enthusiasm for Chapter 19. Binational panels are generally perceived to be less likely to affirm U.S. Department of Commerce and U.S. International Trade Commission decisions than the U.S. Court of International Trade (CIT) and the U.S. Court of Appeals for the Federal

---

[97] Brief of *Amici Curiae* Senators Lindsey Graham, Susan Collins, Olympia Snow, Larry Craig, and Max Baucus Pursuant to F.R.A.P. Rule 29(a), Supporting Petitioner, in *Coalition v. US*, *op. cit.*, at 2.

[98] Rosella Brevetti, *Lumber Industry Files Federal Court Challenge to Constitutionality of Chapter 19*, 22 Int'l Trade Rep. (BNA) 1477 (Sept. 15, 2005), quoting USTR spokesperson Neena Moorjani.

Circuit (CAFC),[99] an obvious disadvantage for the government. However, for Commerce lawyers, the ability to present cases to the panels on their own, rather than under the direction of the Civil Division of the Department of Justice, which represents Commerce in the federal courts, makes the process attractive in that respect. At least one former U.S. official has indicated a belief that the trade attorneys and law professors who typically sit on binational panels undertake a more thorough examination of the administrative record than in most CIT proceedings but that these nonprofessional judges are much less skilled in applying the proper judicial standard of review.[100]

U.S. courts have had little direct contact with the panel process, largely because it substitutes for rather then supplements domestic court remedies. Binational panels sitting in review of U.S. AD/CVD determinations are bound by CAFC decisions, as is the CIT, but are not obligated to follow the court's decisions on the same or similar issues.

The frustration of the United States with the NAFTA binational panel process may be evidenced by the fact that the U.S. section of the NAFTA secretariat is understaffed, with only three employees from about 1999–2004 and four thereafter.[101] Also, proceedings have been periodically delayed, in part because of difficulties in finding and agreeing on panelists for the national rosters who possess the requisite international trade expertise (particularly in Mexico and Canada) or because of understandings between the governments to defer final action. However, most of the important and high-profile binational panel proceedings in *Softwood Lumber* resulted in initial decisions within about one year.[102] Overall, these staffing and funding problems appear to have reflected a lack of political will not only within the U.S. government but also in Canada and Mexico to make the process work more efficiently.[103]

A different kind of inaction is probably the best indicator of current U.S. government views of Chapter 19 procedures. Since NAFTA was negotiated in 1994, the United States has concluded FTAs, inter alia, with Jordan, Singapore,

---

[99] Under U.S. domestic law (28 U.S.C. § 1581, 1295), these two federal courts are responsible for review of Commerce and ITC decisions in dumping and CVD cases and have jurisdiction in other matters affecting customs and international trade.

[100] Former Government Official, *op. cit.*

[101] A fourth was added in December 2004, according to a telephone conversation with a staff member.

[102] *Status Report of Panel Proceedings, op. cit.*

[103] The chief counsel for Import Administration at the Department of Commerce, John McInerney, and the several former government officials at that conference who had participated in the negotiations of Chapter 19 have uniformly agreed that the major problem facing Chapter 19 today was not the legal structure or funding per se but a lack of political commitment on the part of the NAFTA governments to making the process work. D.C. Bar Conference, *op. cit.*

Chile, Australia, Morocco, the Central American nations and the Dominican Republic, Peru, Bahrain, Colombia, Panama, and South Korea.[104] None of these incorporates a Chapter 19 or similar mechanism. Thus, the suggestion that the United States "drew the line" at extending Chapter 19 beyond Mexico[105] seems accurate. Of course, this is not necessarily entirely a result of U.S. lack of enthusiasm for Chapter 19. All of these other FTA partners are members of the WTO, an organization endowed with a generally well-regarded DSB to which frequent actions have been brought over the past decade against U.S. AD and CVD determinations.[106] Probably the prevailing feeling in Washington, D.C., is that Chapter 19 is neither necessary nor desirable.

Even within NAFTA, the NAFTA Parties routinely bring AD and CVD challenges against each other in the WTO's DSB, including high-profile cases such as *Softwood Lumber* (four separate actions by Canada against the United States arising from the initial investigation alone),[107] *High Fructose Corn Syrup*, and *Wheat* (United States against Mexico, United States against Canada, respectively).[108] These are parallel cases; unlike Chapter 20, in which the complaining Party must choose between NAFTA and WTO remedies, there is nothing to prevent the "interested parties" in an AD/CVD case from seeking relief under Chapter 19 while the exporters' government is bringing a parallel action (under WTO law) before the DSB.

What, then, is the future for Chapter 19? It will not be replicated elsewhere, but is likely to be part of NAFTA for the foreseeable future. Amending Chapter 19, regardless of how attractive that might be to some U.S. government officials and to many NGO critics, would require (1) the agreement of Mexico and Canada and (2) a protocol to the agreement that would have to be submitted to the Canadian Parliament, the U.S. Congress, and the Mexican Senate.

---

[104] *See* USTR, Bilateral Trade Agreements, at http://www.ustr.gov/ (visited Apr. 15, 2007).

[105] Former Government Official, *op. cit.* Nor have Canada or Mexico incorporated a Chapter 19 into any of their subsequent FTAs.

[106] At least 16; *see* http://www.wto.org (visited Apr. 15, 2007).

[107] WTO, Report of the Appellate Body, *United States – Final Countervailing Duty Determination with Respect to Certain Softwood Lumber from Canada*, WTO Doc. WT/DS257/AB/R (Jan. 19, 2004), *adopted* Feb. 17, 2004; WTO, Report of the Appellate Body, *U.S. – Final Dumping Determination on Softwood Lumber from Canada*, WT/DS264/AB/R (Aug. 11, 2004), adopted Aug. 31, 2004; WTO, Report of the Panel, *United States – Investigation of the International Trade Commission in Softwood Lumber from Canada*, WTO Doc. WT/DS277/R (Mar. 22, 2004), adopted Apr. 26, 2004; WTO, Report of the Panel, *United States – Preliminary Determinations with Respect to Certain Softwood Lumber from Canada*, WT/DS236/R, (Sept. 27, 2002), adopted Nov. 1, 2002, all available at http://www.wto.org (visited Apr. 15, 2007).

[108] WTO, Report of the Appellate Body, *Canada – Measures Relating to Exports of Wheat and Treatment of Imported Grain*, WT/DS276/AB/R (Aug. 30, 2004), adopted Sept. 27, 2004; WTO, Report of the Appellate Body, *Mexico – Anti-Dumping Investigation of High Fructose Corn Syrup (HFCS) from the United States*, WT/DS132/AB/RW (Oct. 22, 2001), adopted Nov. 21, 2001.

The system would likely work far better, without amending the NAFTA, if the NAFTA governments, including but not limited to the United States, were to reaffirm at the highest levels their ongoing commitment to making the Chapter 19 process work, and would implement a few relatively minor changes to the Procedural Rules.[109] Whether or not this occurs, Chapter 19 is a process with which the United States and its traders will have to continue to live.

D. GOVERNMENT-TO-GOVERNMENT DISPUTES UNDER CHAPTER 20

State-to-state settlement of international trade disputes has a long history. Dispute settlement provisions were included in the 1947 GATT,[110] and nearly sixty years of third-party dispute resolution under the GATT and the WTO have proven their necessity. Thus, it should be no surprise that during NAFTA negotiations, the issue was not whether there should be such a mechanism but rather how it should be structured. There were several possible models. Chapter 18 of the U.S.–Canada Free Trade Agreement (CFTA) was the obvious one. Procedures under Article XXIII of the GATT, and the mechanism now provided by the WTO offered another.[111] In all such instances, panels of trade experts opine on disputes among member governments, based on the "law" of the international agreements (NAFTA or the GATT and the other WTO agreements), in a typical international arbitral procedure consisting of consultations, briefings, a hearing, and the issuance of an opinion or report. A draft of what is now the WTO's Dispute Settlement Understanding existed at the time of the NAFTA negotiations.[112] Although the NAFTA negotiators apparently reviewed the draft WTO Dispute Settlement Understanding (DSU) there appears to have been relatively little direct "borrowing" from the DSU in NAFTA Chapter 20, perhaps in part because of the desire of both Canada and the United States to avoid wholesale renegotiation of CFTA, Chapter 18.[113]

---

[109] John McInerney, *op. cit.*, thoughtfully suggested in 2005 that the Chapter 19 Procedural Rules be amended to increase the stipend paid to binational panelists, increase the number of staff members at the various sections of the NAFTA Secretariat, and impose strict page limits on party submissions to Chapter 19 proceedings. He also suggested clarifying the conflict rules in the Code of Conduct for Dispute Settlement Procedures under Chapters 19 and 20.

[110] GATT (1947), art. XXIII.

[111] GATT art. XXIII; *see* Cunningham and Smith, *Section 301 and Dispute Settlement in the World Trade Organization*, in the World Trade Organization (Terrence Stuart ed., ABA, 1996). *See also* DSU, *op. cit.*

[112] GATT Trade Negotiations Committee, "Draft Final Act Embodying the Results of the Uruguay Round of Multilateral Trade Negotiations," GATT Document MTN.TNC/W/FA, Dec. 20, 1991 [hereinafter, Dunkel Draft].

[113] Chapter 20 followed a similar approach to that of the DSU in seeking to put a limit on the level of retaliation by the prevailing Party in a dispute, through providing for additional panel review – never used to date – if the retaliation levels were "manifestly excessive" (art. 2019).

The CFTA general dispute settlement system was considered to offer "a significant improvement to the traditional, pre-WTO GATT proceedings" by making the formation of a panel mandatory on the request of either Party and by providing deadlines for each stage of the process. Yet the rulings there, as in GATT, technically were only recommendations, leaving the prevailing Party the option of retaliation.[114] The scope of Chapter 20 is broader than CFTA Chapter 18. This is largely because NAFTA itself is broader than the CFTA, covering, inter alia, financial services, intellectual property, standards, sanitary and phytosanitary measures, and, to some degree, the environment.[115] Chapter 20 of NAFTA applies

> with respect to the avoidance or settlement of all disputes between the Parties regarding the interpretation or application of this Agreement or wherever a Party considers that an actual or proposed measure of another Party is or would be inconsistent with the obligations of this Agreement or cause nullification or impairment.[116]

As in the case of Chapter 11 and 19 mechanisms, Chapter 20 of NAFTA raised concerns over loss of U.S. sovereignty among some in Congress and with NGO groups (particularly those concerned with environmental regulation). To some extent these concerns are dealt with in provisions permitting each NAFTA Party to maintain its own environmental, sanitary, and phytosanitary standards.[117]

Like the WTO's Dispute Settlement Understanding, Chapter 20 calls first for consultation between the Parties, followed by conciliation before the Free Trade Commission (the trade ministers of the three NAFTA countries), the convening of binational panels (arbitration), and, ultimately, implementation of the arbitral report.[118] The arbitral decision is not automatically applicable and in that sense is not "binding." Rather, after the decision is rendered, the Parties "shall agree on the resolution of the dispute, which *normally* shall conform with the determinations and recommendations of the panel."[119] However,

---

[114] Jeffrey P. Bialos and Deborah E. Siegel, *Dispute Resolution under NAFTA: The New and Improved Model*, in Judith H. Bello et al., at 315, 323; CFTA, *op. cit.*, art. 1807.

[115] *See, e.g.*, NAFTA, *op. cit.*, art. 104 (environmental agreements), Chapter 7B (sanitary and phytosanitary measures), Chapter 9 (standards), Chapter 14 (financial services), and Chapter 17 (intellectual property).

[116] NAFTA, art. 2004; matters covered by Chapter 19 (AD and CVD actions) are excluded. Private parties have no standing under Chapter 20, although those with political influence may be able to induce their respective governments to litigate on their behalf, as is evident from the cases.

[117] NAFTA, art. 1904; *see* Bialos and Siegel, *op. cit.*, at 327.

[118] NAFTA, *op. cit.*, arts. 2006–2017.

[119] *Id.*, art. 2018(1); emphasis added.

the prevailing Party may retaliate with trade sanctions thirty days after the issuance of the panel report, if the parties do not earlier reach an accord.[120]

The arbitral panel process contemplates the use of a standing roster of international legal experts, ten designated by each NAFTA party, although as of February 2009, the NAFTA Parties had not yet formally designated any of the roster members.[121] Because of the lack of a standing roster, the semi-automatic provisions in Article 2011 for choosing panelists by lot from rosters cannot be used, making each panel formation an ad hoc process subject to potentially long delays if either Party wishes to impede the process. For each proceeding, a group of five arbitrators is to be chosen, primarily from the rosters; the chairperson is to be chosen by the two governments by agreement, with the choice by lot if there is no agreement.[122] Interestingly, in a unique "reverse selection process,"[123] one Party chooses the two national arbitrators of the *other* Party (e.g., in the dairy products case, discussed later, the two Canadian panelists were selected by the United States from candidates offered by Canada).

In many instances – except for certain environmentally related matters including those arising under the standards provisions of NAFTA – the NAFTA parties have a choice between resorting to NAFTA, Chapter 20, or the WTO procedures. This is because the NAFTA Parties' existing rights and obligations under GATT and other agreements are explicitly reaffirmed or incorporated by reference in NAFTA.[124] Disputes relating to alleged conflicts between NAFTA and certain environmental agreements, and regarding the application of NAFTA provisions on the environment or human, animal, or plant life or health issues, must be resolved under Chapter 20.[125] However, certain disputes among the NAFTA Parties, such as disagreements over the consistency of national AD or CVD laws with the WTO agreements, must be resolved through the WTO's dispute settlement procedure.[126]

Procedurally, Chapter 20 offers both disadvantages and advantages in comparison to the WTO's procedures. The inclusion of nationals of the disputing

---

[120] *Ibid.*
[121] It appears that the Parties in the 1990s informally agreed on a roster of approximately five persons per Party, but it was never adopted formally.
[122] NAFTA, *op. cit.*, art. 2011. art. 2011(1)(c), provides that "[w]ithin 15 days of the selection of the chair, each disputing Party shall select two panelists who are citizens of the other disputing party."
[123] According to the Senior USTR Official, *op. cit.*, this approach was suggested by Guillermo Aguilar, one of the principal Mexican NAFTA negotiators, in the belief that it would encourage governments nominating members of the standing rosters to be careful about picking truly independent and objective individuals. Canada and the United States accepted the proposal.
[124] NAFTA, *op. cit.*, art. 103(1).
[125] *Id.*, art. 2005(3–4).
[126] There is no Chapter 20 jurisdiction over such matters under NAFTA art. 2004, and only new national AD or CVD laws may be challenged by the Parties under NAFTA art. 1903.

parties on NAFTA arbitral panels does not occur under GATT/WTO procedures; this may be an advantage, but it might also raise questions of favoritism. In addition, the NAFTA mechanism provides no process for appeals comparable to the WTO's Appellate Body, and the decision of the arbitrators may be more difficult to enforce given the lack of an independent international organization such as the WTO. Each government created a national section of the NAFTA Secretariat to provide assistance to the NAFTA Free Trade Commission and to panels established under Chapters 19 and 20.[127] However, there is no truly independent secretariat comparable to that of the WTO to ensure that panels are promptly appointed and that delays in the process are avoided,[128] nor is there legal staff to assist with the drafting of orders or decisions. This can help to explain why governments and NAFTA panelists regularly fail to comply with the relatively short deadlines provided in Chapter 20.[129]

During the first seven years of NAFTA, Chapter 20 was used periodically, but it has fallen into disuse since 2001. To date, there have been only three regular Chapter 20 panel decisions and one non-NAFTA proceeding using Chapter 20 rules.[130] In the first, the United States charged that NAFTA required Canada to eliminate duties on certain dairy products (*Dairy Products*). Under the WTO Agreement on Agriculture, Canada had agreed to "tarification" (conversion of quantitative restraints to tariffs) of dairy products, but there is no obligation under the WTO to eliminate tariffs, only to reduce them, if parties can agree. Under NAFTA, in contrast, all tariffs with a few exceptions must be eliminated within no more than fifteen years. Canada took the position that these items

---

[127] NAFTA, *op. cit.*, art. 2002(3).

[128] *See* David A. Gantz, *Dispute Settlement under the NAFTA and the WTO: Choice of Forum Opportunities and Risks for the NAFTA Parties*, 14 Am. U. Int'l L. R. 1025, 1083–95 (1999) [hereinafter Gantz, *Choice of Forum*].

[129] For example, art. 2011(1) provides that if the disputing Parties cannot agree on panelists with fifteen days, the panel members will be chosen by lot from the roster. This has never happened, because there is no formal roster. Art. 2016(2) also provides for the panel to render its initial report within ninety days after the selection of the last panelist. This also has never occurred; in some instances, the period required for briefings and a hearing have consumed almost the ninety days allotted for the entire process.

[130] The Softwood Lumber Agreement, May 29, 1996, 35 ILM 1195, that sought (unsuccessfully in retrospect) to resolve a long-running dispute between Canada and the United States over Canada lumber exports to the United States, contained an ad hoc dispute settlement mechanism that is based in part on NAFTA Chapter 20 (art. V). An arbitral panel was convened in November 1998 to address an alleged violation of the agreement as a result of British Columbia's reduction of certain charges for harvesting timber from government-owned lands, "In the Matter of British Columbia's June 1, 1998 Stumpage Reduction." The panel, operating generally under the NAFTA Chapter 20 Rules of Procedure and administered by the Canadian section of the NAFTA Secretariat, reviewed briefs submitted by the Parties, held a hearing and drafted a decision, but the case was settled by the Parties one day before the decision was due. *See* Exchange of Diplomatic Notes, dated Aug. 26, 1999.

are exempt from the NAFTA tariff reductions; the United States disagreed. Although NAFTA does not specify the use of a neutral country fifth arbitrator, a panel consisting of two Canadian and two U.S. law professors was chosen, with a British law professor as chairperson. The panel ultimately determined unanimously that Canada's actions were consistent with NAFTA.[131]

In a second action, Mexico challenged the United States' application of safeguards to corn brooms from Mexico (*Brooms*). Mexico argued that the application of the safeguards was inconsistent with NAFTA Chapter 8, and with the WTO Agreement on Safeguards. The panel, chaired by an Australian government official, found unanimously in favor of Mexico, holding that the U.S. ITC had failed to explain adequately its "domestic industry" determination in violation of NAFTA requirements.[132] Unfortunately, the United States declined to comply with the panel ruling immediately, maintaining the safeguards in place for nine months after the issuance of the panel decision.[133] The Presidential Proclamation lifting the safeguards cited only the failure of the U.S. industry to make a positive adjustment to import competition; the NAFTA decision was not mentioned.[134] Mexico continued to apply high tariffs to a series of U.S. products as retaliation permitted under NAFTA until the United States lifted the safeguards.[135]

The third proceeding involved the refusal of the United States to implement a NAFTA provision requiring the United States and Mexico, as of December 1995, to permit each other's trucking firms to carry international cargoes between the ten Mexican and four U.S. border states (*Cross-Border Trucking Services* or *Trucks*).[136] Investment by Mexican firms in U.S. trucking companies had also been precluded. Mexico had charged that the United States had violated the national treatment and most favored nation treatment provisions of Chapter 11 (investment) and Chapter 12 (cross-border services), as well as the specific provisions of Annex I imposing such obligations. The Panel ultimately agreed with Mexico, although in recognition of legitimate safety concerns in the United States, it held that "to the extent that the inspection and licensing requirements for Mexican truckers and drivers wishing to operate in the United States may not be 'like' those in place in the United States,

---

[131] Tariffs Applied by Canada to Certain U.S.-Origin Agricultural Products, Case no. CDA-95-2008-01 (Dec. 2, 1996), at http://www.nafta-sec-alena.org/DefaultSite/index_e.aspx?DetailID=76 (visited Apr. 15, 2007).
[132] U.S. Safeguard Action Taken on Broomcorn Brooms from Mexico, Case no. USA-97-2008-01 (Jan. 30, 1998), citing NAFTA Annex 803.3(12).
[133] *See Tariffs: Clinton Removes Safeguard Tariffs on Broom Corn Brooms*, Int'l Trade Daily (BNA) (Dec. 7, 1998) at D3.
[134] *See* Proclamation No. 7154, 61 Fed. Reg. 64,761, 64,762 (1998).
[135] *See* Americas Trade (Dec. 24, 1998) at 8.
[136] *In the Matter of Cross-Border Trucking Services*, op. cit.

different methods of ensuring compliance with the U.S. regulatory regime may be justifiable."¹³⁷

Insofar as the author has been able to determine, at least ten other matters have reached at least the consultation stage under Chapter 20, involving (1) Uranium Exports (U.S. v. Canada, 1994), (2) Import Restrictions on Sugar (Canada v. U.S., 1995), (3) Restrictions on Small Package Delivery (U.S. v. Mexico, 1995), (4) Restrictions on Tomato Imports (Mexico v. United States, 1996), (5) Helms-Burton Act (Mexico and Canada v. United States, 1996), (6) Restrictions on Sugar (Mexico v. U.S., 1998), (7) Farm Products Blockade (Canada v. United States, 1998), (8) Bus Service (Mexico v. United States, 1998), (9) Sportfishing Laws (United States v. Mexico, 1999), and (10) Restrictions on Potatoes (Canada v. United States, 2001).¹³⁸ Some, such as Uranium, Sportfishing, and Potatoes were resolved through consultations; others, such as Sugar (Canada and Mexico) and Tomatoes, were resolved among the governments in other contexts. Others, such as Restrictions on Small Package Delivery and Helms-Burton, appear to have been abandoned; there are no "active" Chapter 20 proceedings listed on the NAFTA Secretariat Web site.¹³⁹

There appear to be several reasons for the declining use of Chapter 20. The U.S. government had not been satisfied with the results under CFTA, Chapter 18; several of the five cases decided under those proceedings were thought to be poorly reasoned decisions, and there was no reason to believe that Chapter 20 would work better. Thus, even from the outset, there was healthy skepticism of the process.¹⁴⁰ Second, some of the major trade-related issues within the region – including post–September 11 security and immigration – are not easily addressed under NAFTA. NAFTA contains a "national security" exception in Article 2102 similar to Article XXI of GATT, which would make formal

---

¹³⁷ *Id.*, para. 301; *see also* paras. 295–300, 302. Although necessary implementing legislation was enacted by Congress in 2002, it was not until the court challenges were rejected that the United States was free to move forward with implementing NAFTA obligations. *See Department of Transportation et al. v. Public Citizen et al.*, 124 S. Ct. 2204, 541 U.S. 752 (2004). In April 2007, the Department of Transportation and Mexican authorities had agreed on a pilot program under which one hundred Mexican trucking firms, after verification of their operations for truck and driver safety, would be certified to operate in the United States. This approach was briefly implemented despite Congressional opposition. *See* Rossella Brevetti, *NAFTA: Reps. Hunter and Kaptur Introduce Bill Putting Limits on Mexican Trucking Plan*, 24 Int'l Trade Rep. (BNA) 522 (Apr. 12, 2007). By March 2009, it appeared highly likely that Congress would soon block even the pilot program. *See* Jane Winebrenner, *House Democrats' Omnibus Spending Bill Includes Mexican Truck Ban, Sales to Cuba*, 26 Int'l Trade Rep. (BNA) 284 (Feb. 26, 2009).
¹³⁸ For a discussion of these cases, *see* David A. Gantz, *Government-to-Government Dispute Resolution under NAFTA's Chapter 20: A Commentary on the Process*, 11 Am. Rev. Int'l Arb. 481, 456–549 (2002).
¹³⁹ *See Status Report of Panel Proceedings, Active NAFTA Panel Reviews, op. cit.*
¹⁴⁰ Discussion with Senior USTR Official, *op. cit.*

dispute settlement under Chapter 20 problematic. In fact, the NAFTA Parties appear to have been successful in addressing issues of border security through negotiations and joint planning without resorting to dispute settlement.[141]

Third, some issues, such as those involving dumping and subsidies, effectively require resolution by the WTO's DSB.[142] In addition, there appears to be a preference among all three NAFTA Parties for the WTO dispute settlement over Chapter 20 procedures. Undoubtedly, this is at least partially a result of the lengthy delays in several cases – notably *Trucks* – that indicate significant procedural imperfections in the system, particularly with regard to the apparent inability of the Parties to agree promptly on panelists.[143] Those who expect adjudicatory systems to come reasonably close to meeting set time limits and strict procedural rules, as at the WTO, are likely to find the NAFTA Chapter 20 system wanting. There is also a feeling among some U.S. government officials that it is better to exclude nationals of the Parties as arbitrators.[144] Canada and Mexico, on the other hand, may well believe that when they are seeking changes in U.S. trade law measures and policy it helps to have support from other Members of the WTO, who can participate in DSB actions as co-complainants or third parties.[145]

The U.S. reluctance to use Chapter 20 is probably best illustrated by the Mexican *Sugar* case – concerning U.S. market access to Mexican sugar – which Mexico considered directly related to a dispute over Mexican taxes on high-fructose corn syrup. The Chapter 20 case remained pending until 2008, while the U.S. authorities refused for more than four years to appoint panelists, a refusal with which a WTO panel and the Appellate Body refused to interfere.[146]

---

[141] *See* White House, *Fact Sheet: Security and Prosperity Partnership of North America* (Mar. 23, 2005), at http://www.whitehouse.gov/news/releases/2005/03/20050323-4.html (visited Mar. 21, 2006) (committing the NAFTA Parties, inter alia, to "develop a common security strategy to further secure North America").

[142] NAFTA, *op. cit.*, art. 1901(3) provides, "[N]o provision of any other Chapter of this Agreement shall be construed as imposing obligations on a Party with respect to the Party's antidumping law or countervailing duty law."

[143] *See* Gantz, *Choice of Forum, op. cit.*, at 1084. In *Trucks*, for example, there was a delay of approximately fifteen months between the formal request by Mexico for a panel and agreement by Mexico and the United States on the panelists.

[144] The author recalls a conversation with one of the U.S. NAFTA negotiators some years ago in which the view was expressed that the foreign (e.g., Canadian or Mexican) nationals on the panel would tend to favor their own governments, whereas the U.S. national panelists would make every effort to be absolutely objective without regard to nationality! This despite the fact that in all three cases to date, the panels were unanimous.

[145] DSU, *op. cit.*, art. 9.

[146] In *Mexico – Tax Measures on Soft Drinks and Other Beverages*, Appellate Body Report, WT/DS308/AB/R, adopted Mar. 24, 2006, the Appellate Body upheld a panel decision rejecting Mexico's request that the panel and appellate body decline to exercise WTO jurisdiction

Still, with the exception of *Cross-Border Trucking Services* – of which every aspect has been highly politicized in the United States – there has been relatively little criticism of Chapter 20 as distinct from criticism of NAFTA generally; even with *Trucks*, the criticism has been of safety issues and NAFTA, not the Chapter 20 process or the panel decision per se.[147] There are no apparent U.S. interest groups that oppose Chapter 20–type dispute settlement provisions in new trade agreements, except those that oppose any such agreements across the board. Only *Trucks* has been mentioned in a U.S. court proceeding; there Justice Thomas noted that "The Government of Mexico challenged the United States' implementation of NAFTA's motor carrier provisions under NAFTA's dispute-resolution process, and in February 2001, an international arbitration panel determined that the United States' 'blanket refusal' of the United States to consider *any* applications for operating authority by Mexican motor carriers breached the United States' obligations under NAFTA."[148] The relative lack of criticism may, of course, have resulted in part from the relative paucity of Chapter 20 panel proceedings.

Despite a strong preference among U.S. officials for the WTO's dispute settlement procedures, whenever available, the necessity for a dispute settlement procedure for matters that are unique to the NAFTA is generally recognized. Inevitably there will be disputes over NAFTA or other FTA provisions that have no direct parallel within the WTO system and cannot be litigated there, such as the disputes over cross-border trucking or sugar under specific NAFTA provisions or side letters. Thus, subsequent U.S. FTAs have invariably included Chapter 20–like language, usually with only minor modifications. For example, in Chapter 22 of the United States–Chile Free Trade Agreement, the basic Chapter 20 system consisting of consultations, mediation by the Commission, and arbitration is reproduced with only a few significant changes.[149] One change of note provides that six members of the twenty-person roster

---

because the matter was "inextricably linked to a broader dispute" that only a NAFTA [Chapter 20] panel could properly decide. The Appellate Body concluded that once it was established that a WTO panel had jurisdiction, it could not refuse to exercise it. *See* paras. 10, 40, 57.

[147] With the Teamsters Union and Ralph Nader's Public Citizen at the forefront. *See*, e.g., Public Citizen Press Release, *Serious Safety Concerns Must Be Resolved before Border Is Open to Long-Haul Mexico-Domiciled Trucks* (July 7, 2004): "A dozen key safety gaps remain," Smith told lawmakers, "What the federal government ignores will become a burden for Texans and others around the country."

[148] *DOT v. Public Citizen, op. cit.*, 124 S.C. 2211. The U.S. court challenge to allowing Mexican trucks to enter the United States concerned issues relating to agency authority, not to Chapter 20 or to the United States' NAFTA obligations.

[149] United States–Chile FTA, *op. cit.*, arts. 22.4–22.6. The principal additional changes relate to greater transparency and more detailed mechanisms for challenging the adequacy of post-arbitration compliance or sanctioning by the Parties.

"shall be selected from among individuals who are non-Party nationals.[150] One can hope that this innovation will facilitate panel selection if a dispute reaches arbitration, thereby avoiding the delays that have plagued the NAFTA Chapter 20 process. If the roster were appointed in a timely manner (which does not appear to have been the case as of early 2009), chairpersons from neutral countries would effectively have been preapproved, and, in appropriate circumstances, the entire (three-person)[151] panel could be chosen from non-American, non-Chilean nationals.

It is noted in passing that the financial services provisions of NAFTA (relating chiefly to banking, insurance, and brokerage) incorporate a variation of Chapter 20 for dispute resolution. Under the Chapter 20 procedures, only governments may bring actions. However, in financial services cases, the panelists are logically enough to be chosen from a special roster of financial services experts.[152] No cases have been brought to date under the financial services provisions, but it can be assumed that they would operate generally in the same manner as other Chapter 20 proceedings in the past.

E. CONCLUSION

The three major dispute settlement mechanisms in NAFTA have worked reasonably well in resolving the types of disputes for which they were designed. This has occurred, however, without generating much enthusiasm for any of them (and in some instances, such as softwood lumber, strong opposition) from the U.S. Congress, government officials, civil society, and the courts. All, for the reasons articulated earlier, are at least somewhat suspicious of third-party dispute resolution because of the loss of national control compared with national courts or diplomatic negotiations. There is, of course, a cadre of U.S. multinational corporations and their counsel who support strong investment protection in FTAs and BITs. The support of the business community for trade agreements remains important for U.S. national governments, whether Republican or Democratic, and thus can be influential. Besides, there is also a small group of law professors (the author and Dean Karamanian included) who enjoy writing about three very interesting processes in the history of international dispute resolution. Of course, these writings hardly shift equilibria in Washington.

Despite this general ambivalence, two of the three mechanisms, those relating to investment disputes and disputes over the application and interpretation

---

[150] *Id.*, art. 22.7(1).
[151] Instead of five, *id.*, art. 22.9(1)(a).
[152] NAFTA, *op. cit.*, art. 1414(3).

of NAFTA, have been replicated in almost all subsequent U.S. trade agreements,[153] albeit with significant changes in the case of investment disputes. Despite the entry into force of additional U.S. free trade agreements, given the volume of trade and investment with those nations (compared with that among NAFTA nations), it will probably be some time before there is a sufficient body of case law to permit comparisons with determinations under NAFTA Chapters 11 and 20.[154] Overall, in the case of dispute settlement under NAFTA, the U.S. government's attitudes are at best ambivalent. Be that as it may, in the final analysis attitudes are not as important as behavior, which in general reflect recognition that investor-state and government-to-government dispute resolution mechanisms are essential for new FTAs if U.S. government and private sector interests are to be adequately protected.

---

[153] The U.S.–Jordan and U.S.–Bahrain FTAs included no investment protection provisions because BITs with the United States had recently been concluded. The United States–Australia FTA contains an investment chapter but no mandatory arbitration of investor-state disputes (*see* Chapter 11). The Agreement between the United States and the Socialist Republic of Vietnam on Trade Relations, July 13, 2000 (not an FTA), provides for arbitration of investor-state disputes (Part IV) but no Chapter 20 equivalent.

[154] As indicated earlier, none of these subsequent agreements incorporate a Chapter 19 or equivalent. However, notices of intent to submit a claim for arbitration were filed in March 2007 against Guatemala and the Dominican Republic under the (Chapter 10) investment provisions of the DR-CAFTA FTA.

12

Dispute Settlement under NAFTA Chapter 11: A Response to the Critics in the United States

SUSAN L. KARAMANIAN*

The United States has authorized certain investor-state disputes arising under the North American Free Trade Agreement (NAFTA) to be resolved through arbitration.[1] The arbitral tribunals, which apply the NAFTA and applicable rules of international law to the disputes,[2] have come under substantial attack. Critics charge that the tribunals act as super-appellate courts and tower over domestic courts.[3] Others have pointed out the tribunals' alleged lack of "democratic legitimacy."[4] Tribunal procedures are believed to be shrouded in secrecy.[5] The legal soundness of tribunal awards has been questioned.[6]

---

* Associate Dean for International and Comparative Legal Studies, The George Washington University Law School. Thanks to Sri H. Peechara, a 2007 LLM graduate of GW Law School, for his help on this chapter. I also thank Professor David Gantz for his comments on an earlier version of this chapter.
[1] North American Free Trade Agreement, Dec. 17, 1992, Can.-Mex.-U.S., 107 Stat. 2057, 32 ILM 605, 639 [hereinafter NAFTA]. Articles 1115–1138 address dispute settlement.
[2] *Id.*, art. 1131(1).
[3] *See, e.g.,* Curtis A. Bradley, *International Delegations, the Structural Constitution, and Non-Self-Execution,* 55 Stan. L. Rev. 1557, 1576 (2003) (recognizing that "NAFTA is being used, at least indirectly, to conduct international review of the fairness and outcome of U.S. judicial decisions"); *id.* at 1577.
[4] Vicki Been and Joel C. Beauvais, *The Global Fifth Amendment? NAFTA's Investment Protections and the Misguided Quest for an International "Regulatory Takings" Doctrine,* 78 N.Y.U.L. Rev. 30, 137 (2003) (challenging the legitimacy of NAFTA Chapter 11 "because there was virtually no public awareness of or debate concerning the potential impact of NAFTA's investor protections"); Andrew J. Shapren, Note, *NAFTA Chapter 11: A Step Forward in International Trade Law or a Step Backward for Democracy?,* 17 Temp. Int'l & Comp. L. J. 323, 346–47 (2003) (noting, among other things, that Chapter 11 dispute settlement could allow "foreign corporations to radically change the way a domestic government may operate").
[5] *See, e.g.,* David Livshiz, Note, *Public Participation in Disputes under Regional Trade Agreements: How Much Is Too Much – The Case for a Limited Right of Intervention,* 61 N.Y.U. Ann. Surv. Am. L. 529, 548, 552, 554–55 (2005); David A. Gantz, *The Evolution of FTA Investment Provisions: From NAFTA to the United States-Chile Free Trade Agreement,* 19 Am. U. Int'l L. Rev. 679, 747 (2004) (mentioning concerns about transparency).
[6] Susan D. Franck, *The Legitimacy Crisis in Investment Treaty Arbitration: Privatizing Public International Law through Inconsistent Decisions,* 73 Fordham L. Rev. 1521, 1576–81 (2005)

These challenges should not be taken lightly. In addition to raising nagging issues that threaten dispute resolution, the assault reflects a concern from both within and outside of the United States about the loss of sovereign control over matters essential to governance. As more nations enter into bilateral investment treaties (BITs) or free trade agreements (FTAs), which may authorize arbitration of investor-state disputes, the criticism is likely to mount and come from a wider range of sources.

A measured and objective response to the criticism, which sorts the wheat from the chaff and constructively identifies areas of concern and means to address the concerns, is in order. This is the objective of this chapter. It also examines the response to the criticism to date, which has led to reforms of the arbitral process.

A. INVESTOR-STATE ARBITRATION UNDER NAFTA CHAPTER 11

1. *The Process*

An investor from one NAFTA Party that invests in another NAFTA Party may submit to arbitration a claim that the host Party has breached certain NAFTA obligations.[7,8] Arbitration of investment disputes "assures both equal treatment among investors of the Parties in accordance with the principle of international reciprocity and due process before an impartial tribunal."[9] The investor has access to an arbitral tribunal to settle certain of its differences with the host nation. The arbitration is conducted under established procedures. As a U.S. negotiator of NAFTA Chapter 11 has observed, the investor-state settlement process takes the dispute "out of a state-to-state forum and empower[s] investors to seek redress in their own right."[10] The investor, free from the unwieldy and

---

(showing inconsistency in Chapter 11 decisions); Been and Beauvais, *supra* n. 4 at 128 (observing "[e]arly interpretations by arbitral tribunals provide foreign investors with property protections that go beyond those afforded by the Fifth Amendment and the U.S. Supreme Court's 'regulatory takings' jurisprudence").

[7] NAFTA Chapter 11's dispute settlement process has been described and discussed in many books and articles. See, e.g., Todd Weiler (ed.), *NAFTA Investment Law and Arbitration: Past Issues, Current Practice, Future Prospects* (Transnational Publishers, Inc., 2004); Leon E. Trakman, *Dispute Settlement under the NAFTA: Manual and Source Book* (Transnational Publishers, Inc., 1997); Charles H. Brower, II, *Structure, Legitimacy, and NAFTA's Investment Chapter*, 36 Vanderbilt J. Transnt'l L. 37 (2003).

[8] NAFTA, *supra* n. 1, art. 1116(1). The obligations giving rise to claims that may be arbitrated are set forth in Section A of NAFTA Chapter 11, article 1503(2) (State Enterprises), and article 1502(3)(a) (Monopolies and State Enterprises). *Id.*

[9] *Id.*, art. 1115.

[10] Daniel M. Price, *Some Observations on Chapter Eleven of NAFTA*, 23 Hastings Int'l & Comp. L. Rev. 421, 427 (2000). Also, as the investor's home nation is removed from the dispute, the

uncertain process of relying on its home nation to espouse the claim, is given direct access to the allegedly offending Party in a designated forum under defined rules.

NAFTA Chapter 11, Section A, sets forth a Party's obligations that are subject to arbitration. Included among the obligations is the duty of a Party to provide to an investor of another Party, and investments of investors of another Party, the better of national treatment or most favored nation treatment, and under article 1105(1) to provide a minimum standard of treatment under international law to investments of investors of another Party.[11] Further, a Party cannot "directly or indirectly nationalize or expropriate an investment of an investor of another Party in its territory" or "take a measure tantamount to nationalization or expropriation of such an investment" unless certain conditions are satisfied, including specific compensation.[12] A Party must ensure that "all necessary measures are taken" to give effect to the NAFTA, which means it has the duty to assure that state and local governments comply with the NAFTA.[13]

An investor alleging that a NAFTA nation has breached the NAFTA investment obligations "may submit the claim to arbitration."[14] The word "may" means that the investor could elect not to arbitrate and rely on the remote chance that the home nation would espouse the investor's claim against the host nation. The investor can proceed to arbitration under the Convention on the Settlement of Investment Disputes between States and Nationals of Other States (ICSID Convention)[15] if both the disputing Party and the Party that is home to the investor are parties to the ICSID Convention.[16] If both Parties are not parties to the ICSID Convention, then arbitration could occur under ICSID's Additional Facility Rules (AFRs) if either the disputing party

---

claim "would be decided on the merits and would not be subsumed within a larger political or foreign relations dialogue between [the investor's] government and the host government." Id.

[11] NAFTA, supra n. 1, art. 1102 (national treatment); art. 1103 (most favored nation treatment); art. 1104 (investor and investments afforded the better of national treatment or most favored nation treatment); art. 1105(1) (requiring a Party to "accord to investments of investors of another Party treatment in accordance with international law, including fair and equitable treatment and full protection and security").

[12] Id., art. 1110. NAFTA Chapter 11, Section A, sets forth other obligations of a host nation.

[13] NAFTA, art. 105, 32 ILM 289, 298.

[14] Id., art. 1120. The parties should first try to settle the claim. Id., art. 1118. Further, at least ninety days before submitting the claim to arbitration, the investor must provide the host nation with written notice of its intent to submit a claim to arbitration. Id., art. 1119.

[15] Convention on the Settlement of Investment Disputes between States and Nationals of Other States, Mar. 18, 1965, Mar. 18, 1965, 17 UST 1270, 575 UNTS 159.

[16] NAFTA, supra n. 1, art. 1120(1)(a).

or the Party that is home to the investor is a party to ICSID.[17] A disputing investor may also elect to submit the claim to arbitration under the United Nations Commission on International Trade Law (UNCITRAL) Arbitration Rules.[18] NAFTA Chapter 11 includes provisions governing the arbitration process that supplement otherwise applicable rules.[19]

The International Centre for the Settlement of Investment Disputes (ICSID) is an "autonomous international organization" established under the ICSID Convention."[20] The ICSID Secretariat provides facilities for arbitration of investment disputes between State parties to the ICSID Convention and nationals of other State parties to the ICSID Convention.[21] ICSID's AFRs authorize the ICSID Secretariat to administer arbitrations between States and foreign nationals that the ICSID Convention does not cover.[22] NAFTA Chapter 11 arbitrations in ICSID involving the United States have been conducted under the AFRs because Mexico and Canada have not been parties to the ICSID Convention.[23] In 2006, however, Canada signed the ICSID Convention.[24]

ICSID has been described as a "self-contained" regime as it prescribes rules for arbitration and an annulment procedure for review of arbitral awards.[25] The UNCITRAL Arbitration Rules are not associated with any specific arbitral institution.

---

[17] *Id.*, art. 1120(1)(b).
[18] *Id.*, art. 1120(1) (c).
[19] *See, e.g., id.*, art. 1123 (requiring three arbitrators unless the parties otherwise agree; each party selects an arbitrator and the presiding arbitrator is appointed based on the parties' agreement); art. 1130 (requiring that the arbitration be held in the territory of a Party that is a Party to the New York Convention on the Recognition and Enforcement of Foreign Arbitral Awards, selected in accordance with applicable rules); art. 1133 (authorizing use of experts on certain factual issues); art. 1134 (allowing interim measures of protection in limited circumstances); arts. 1135–36 (setting forth standards for the final award and its enforcement).
[20] About ICSID, at http://icsid.worldbank.org/ICSID/ICSID/AboutICSID_Home.jsp.
[21] ICSID Dispute Settlement Facilities, at http://icsid.worldbank.org/ICSID/FrontServlet?requestType=CasesRH&actionVal=RightFrame&FromPage=Dispute%20Settlement%20Facilities&pageName=Disp_settl_facilities.
[22] *Id.*
[23] *Scorecard of Adherence to Transnational Arbitration Treaties*, News Notes Inst. for Transnt'l Arb. (Center Am. & Int'l Law) 12, 14, 15 (Winter 2006).
[24] *Scorecard of Adherence to Transnational Arbitration Treaties*, News Notes Inst. for Transnt'l Arb. (Center Am. & Int'l Law) 12 (Autumn 2006).
[25] *See, e.g.,* Andrea Giardina, "ICSID: A Self-Contained, Non-National Review System," in *International Arbitration in the 21st Century: Towards "Judicialization" and Uniformity?* 199 (Richard B. Lillich and Charles N. Brower, eds., Transnational Publishers, Inc., 1994); Charles N. Brower, *The Global Court: The Internationalization of Commercial Adjudication and Arbitration*, 26 U. Balt. L. Rev. 9, 11 (1997) (describing ICSID as a "completely self-contained regime for deciding investment disputes").

2. The Claims

Numerous claims have been filed under NAFTA Chapter 11's seemingly innocuous dispute settlement regime,[26] mirrored on the procedure the United States has routinely included in BITs and FTAs.[27] According to the U.S. Department of State, at least ten notices of arbitration have been filed against the United States.[28] Substantial amounts of alleged liability have been and remain at stake.[29] Although not yet resulting in an adverse award against the United States, the claims have presented and continue to present formidable challenges to U.S. regulations and governmental decisions and thus strike at the heart of U.S. sovereignty.

The trials and tribulations of NAFTA Chapter 11 investment cases have been documented at length and need not be repeated.[30] The cases have challenged domestic environmental or health regulations, including the executive order of the governor of California and California regulations restricting use of methyl tert-butyl ether (MTBE) in gasoline,[31] California regulations on open-pit metallic mining,[32] the laws of numerous states that require certain tobacco manufacturers (not named as defendants in the state cases against

---

[26] See http://www.state.gov/s/l/c3741.htm (identifying cases filed against the United States); http://www.state.gov/s/l/c3740.htm (identifying cases filed against Canada); and http://www.state.gov/s/l/c3742.htm (identifying cases filed against Mexico) (all last visited May 28, 2007).

[27] Renee Lettow Lerner, *International Pressure to Harmonize: The U.S. Civil Justice System in an Era of Global Trade*, 2001 B.Y.U.L. Rev. 229, 245 (2001) (noting that the "standard investor-state provision for arbitration in [the] U.S. BITs was the model for the investor-state provisions of NAFTA Chapter 11").

[28] See http://www.state.gov/s/l/3741.htm. As of May 28, 2007, the U.S. State Department Web site listed the following cases against the United States: *Cases Regarding the Border Closure due to BSE Concerns, Softwood Lumber Consolidated Proceeding, Domtar Inc., Grand River Enterprises Six Nations, Ltd., Glamis Gold Ltd., Kenex Ltd., ADF Group Inc., Methanex Corp., Mondev International, Ltd.,* and *Loewen Group, Inc.* Three cases, *Canfor Corp., Tembec Inc.,* and *Terminal Forest Products Ltd.*, were consolidated into the *Softwood Lumber Consolidated Proceeding. See In re* NAFTA and a Request for Consolidation by the United States (Order of the Consolidation Tribunal) Sept. 7, 2005, at http://www.state.gov/documents/organization/53113.pdf [hereinafter Consolidation Order]. Other investors have filed notices of arbitration against the United States but they appear not to have pursued the claims. This chapter does not address these claims. Since the writing of this article in 2007, Apotex, Inc. has filed a notice of arbitration against the United States arising out of judicial and other decisions relating to one of its pharmaceutical products. The Apotex case is not discussed in this chapter.

[29] See http://www.state.gov/s/l/c3741.htm (last visited May 28, 2007) (listing cases against the United States and including the Notice of Arbitration that specifies the alleged damages in each case). Claims as of May 28, 2007 collectively involved more than $1 billion. *Id.*

[30] *See, e.g.,* Gantz, *supra* n. 5, at 698–724; Brower, *supra* n. 7, at 86.

[31] *Methanex Corp. v. United States*, Second Amended Statement of Claim (Nov. 5, 2002), at http://www.state.gov/documents/organization/15035.pdf.

[32] *Glamis Gold Ltd. v. United States*, Notice of Arbitration (Dec. 9, 2003), at www.state.gov/documents/organization/27320.pdf.

the tobacco industry) to submit funds into state escrow accounts,[33] and federal regulations barring importation of cattle from Canada after discovery in Canada of a "downer" suffering from bovine spongiform encephalopathy (BSE).[34] One case tackled U.S. procurement laws, the Buy America Program, and regulations implementing the program.[35]

The cases have taken aim at U.S. and state agencies. For example, in *ADF*, the Canadian investor argued that the U.S. Federal Highway Administration (FHWA) misapplied case law, which ADF claimed gave it a legitimate expectation that it could fabricate steel outside of the United States. ADF also argued that the FHWA "acted *ultra vires* and in disregard" of applicable law.[36] Or, in *Glamis Gold*, the Canadian investor has challenged the refusal of the U.S. Department of Interior and the State of California to grant a permit for a gold mining project, the Imperial Project, in the California desert.[37] In *Softwood Lumber*, Canadian investors alleged Chapter 11 violations arising from the U.S. Department of Commerce's preliminary countervailing duty determination regarding softwood lumber imports from Canada and its preliminary antidumping determination.[38]

---

[33] *Grand River Enterprises Six Nations, Ltd. v. United States*, Notice of Arbitration (Mar. 10, 2004), at http://www.state.gov/documents/organization/30961.pdf.

[34] *Alexander v. United States*, Notice of Arbitration (May 19, 2005), *at* http://www.state.gov/documents/organization/52255.pdf. Other Canadian cattlemen filed similar NAFTA Chapter 11 claims, which the United States grouped and titled Cases Regarding the Border Closure due to BSE Concerns. Copies of the cattlemen's notices of arbitration can be found at http://www.state.gov/s/l/c14683.htm. The cases were consolidated and dismissed due to the lack of the Canadian cattlemen's investment in the United States. *See* Case Regarding the Border Closure due to BSE Concerns, Award on Jurisdiction (Jan. 28, 2008), http://www.state.gov/documents/organization/99954.pdf.

[35] *ADF Group, Inc. v. United States*, Notice of Arbitration (July 19, 2000), at http://www.state.gov/documents/organization/3351.pdf.

[36] *ADF Group, Inc. v. United States*, Award para. 190, ICSID Case No. ARB(AF)/00/1 (2003) at http://www.state.gov/documents/organization/16586.pdf [hereinafter ADF Award].

[37] Glamis Gold, *supra* n. 32.

[38] *See, e.g., Terminal Forest Products Ltd. v. United States*, Notice of Arbitration (Mar. 30, 2004) at http://www.state.gov/documents/organization/31360.pdf. Also at issue is the U.S. International Trade Commission's ruling that importation of Canadian softwood lumber threatened the U.S. softwood lumber industry with material injury. *Id.* The tribunal in the Consolidated Arbitration has issued a decision on a preliminary question and held that under NAFTA article 1901(3) it lacks jurisdiction over the claims of state conduct as to preliminary and final determinations on antidumping and countervailing duty law. The tribunal held, however, it has jurisdiction over claims of Canfor and Terminal to the extent they relate to the Byrd amendment, which distributed duties to affected domestic producers. *See* Softwood Lumber Consolidated Proceedings, Decision on Preliminary Question, June 6, 2006, at http://www.investmentclaims.com/decisions/NAFTA-Softwood_Consolidation-Preliminary_Decision-6_June_2006.pdf. Further, the consolidated tribunal did not issue rulings as to Tembec as it had dismissed its statement of claim and had filed suit in the U.S.

Two of the most controversial cases challenge State judicial decisions. *Loewen Group, Inc. v. United States*[39] is the most notable case given the conduct at issue. A Canadian funeral home company and its U.S. subsidiary faced a $500 million judgment from a Mississippi state court.[40] The Canadian claimants documented nationality-based comments (anti-Canadian) and race- and class-based distinctions during the trial, which the trial judge refused to defuse by issuing the appropriate jury instruction.[41] Matters became worse when the Mississippi courts refused to find "good cause" to reduce or dispense with the appeal bond for 125 percent of the judgment.[42] Ultimately, the Canadian company settled "under extreme duress."[43]

The NAFTA Chapter 11 claim was dismissed because of the Canadian corporation's failure to maintain itself as a Canadian investor.[44] Nevertheless, the tribunal took great liberty in reviewing the conduct of the Mississippi courts. The trial was "a disgrace" because "the trial judge failed to afford Loewen the process that was due."[45] After documenting instances of unfairness, the tribunal observed that "the whole trial and its resultant verdict were clearly improper and discreditable and cannot be squared with minimum standards of international law and fair and equitable treatment."[46]

The state court trial, however, was only one aspect of the judicial process in *Loewen*. For the United States to be responsible under international law for denial of justice, the claimants must have exhausted effective, adequate, and reasonably available remedies under municipal law.[47] Because the claimants had settled before all remedies had been exhausted, the municipal legal system was not shown to have denied them justice.[48] Jan Paulsson would later observe that "finality is thus a substantive element of the international delict."[49]

District Court for the District of Columbia to vacate the tribunal's consolidation order. *Id.*, para. 21–28.

[39] ICSID Case No. ARB(AF)/98/3, at http://www.state.gov/documents/organization/22094.pdf [hereinafter Loewen Award].

[40] *Id.*, para. 4. $75 million was awarded for emotional distress and $400 million was awarded in punitive damages. *Id.*

[41] *Id. See also id.*, paras. 45, 56–77, 84–85.

[42] *Id.*, paras. 5–6, 48–53.

[43] *Id.*, para. 7.

[44] *Id.*, paras. 223–25, 240. A Loewen family member later challenged the award because he is Canadian. The tribunal held its decision included a dismissal on the merits as to the family member and his claim. *See Loewen Group, Inc. v. United States*, ICSID Case No. ARB(AF)/98/3, Decision on Respondent's Request for a Supplementary Decision issued September 13, 2004, at http://www.state.gov/documents/organization/36260.pdf.

[45] Loewen Award, *supra* n. 39, para. 119.

[46] *Id.*, para. 137.

[47] *Id.*, paras. 168, 217.

[48] *Id.*, para. 217.

[49] Jan Paulsson, *Denial of Justice in International Law* (Cambridge University Press, 2005), 100.

In *Mondev International Ltd. v. United States*,⁵⁰ a Canadian investor charged that the United States violated NAFTA when Massachusetts courts essentially took away a jury verdict in its favor for breach of contract. The investor challenged the district court's granting a judgment notwithstanding the verdict (JNOV) on behalf of the Boston Redevelopment Authority due to immunity⁵¹ and the Massachusetts Supreme Court's reversal of a jury verdict against the City of Boston on the grounds that the investor had not taken the appropriate steps to hold the City in breach.⁵² One of the investor's arguments was that the conduct amounted to a breach of NAFTA article 1105(1), which sets forth the minimum standard for treatment of the investment.

Before analyzing denial of justice, the tribunal emphasized the minimum standard is as of no earlier than NAFTA's effective date, 1994, and the standard "has evolved and can evolve."⁵³ Further, the tribunal considered the interpretation of the minimum standard (Interpretation), which the NAFTA Free Trade Commission adopted in 2001,⁵⁴ and held that the minimum standard incorporated international law, "whose content is shaped by the conclusion of more than two thousand bilateral investment treaties and many treaties of friendship and commerce."⁵⁵ With these rulings, the tribunal cut off some of the NAFTA nations' argument that only the extreme standard of the *Neer* case, a 1920s decision of the United States–Mexico General Claims Commission, applied. *Neer* had held that actionable government conduct in the treatment of an alien "should amount to outrage, to bad faith, to willful neglect of duty, or to an insufficiency of governmental action so far short of international standards that every reasonable and impartial man would readily recognize its insufficiency."⁵⁶

The tribunal in *Mondev* was concerned about reviewing decisions of state courts.⁵⁷ After citing the International Court of Justice chamber decision in *ELSI*, which speaks of "willful disregard of due process of law, . . . which

---

⁵⁰ *Mondev Int'l Ltd. v. United States*, ICSID Case No. ARB(AF)/99/2, Award of Oct. 11, 2002 at http://www.state.gov/documents/organization/14442.pdf [hereinafter Mondev Award].

⁵¹ *Id.*, para. 1. The Massachusetts Supreme Court affirmed the granting of the JNOV.

⁵² *Id.*

⁵³ *Id.*, para. 124.

⁵⁴ *See infra* nn. 102–9 and accompanying text (discussing the Interpretation's clarification of NAFTA article 1105(1)).

⁵⁵ Mondev Award, *supra* n. 50, para. 125.

⁵⁶ *United States (L.F. Neer) v. Mexico* (U.S.-Mex. General Claims Comm'n Oct. 15, 1926), 4 R.I.A.A. 60, 3 ILR 213 (1927). *See also* Government of Canada Counter-Memorial (Phase 2), *Pope & Talbot, Inc. v. Canada* (Oct. 10, 2000) paras. 212, 238, 266, 309, at http://www.dfait-maeci.gc.ca/tna-nac/documents/B-2.pdf; Mondev Award, *supra* n. 50, para. 114.

⁵⁷ Mondev Award, *supra* n. 50, para. 126 (noting that "[i]t is one thing to deal with unremedied acts of the local constabulary and another to second-guess the reasoned decisions of the highest courts of a State").

shocks, or at least surprises a sense of judicial propriety,"[58] the tribunal in *Mondev* pronounced the test under article 1105(1):

> The test is not whether a particular result is surprising, but whether the shock or surprise occasioned to an impartial tribunal leads, on reflection, to justified concerns as to the judicial propriety of the outcome, bearing in mind on the one hand that international tribunals are not courts of appeal, and on the other hand that Chapter 11 of NAFTA (like other treaties for the protection of investment) is intended to provide a real measure of protection. In the end the question is whether, at an international level and having regard to generally accepted standards of the administration of justice, a tribunal can conclude in the light of all the available facts that the impugned decision was clearly improper and discreditable, with the result that the investment has been subject to unfair and inequitable treatment. This is admittedly a somewhat open-ended standard, but it may be that in practice no more precise formula can be offered to cover the range of possibilities.[59]

The tribunal in *Mondev* disposed of the claim of denial justice without any apparent shock or surprise. As to each principal complaint, the tribunal held the Massachusetts courts acted consistently with applicable legal principles. For example, the investor had argued that issues regarding contract performance should have been remanded under Massachusetts law and practice.[60] The tribunal refused to have "quintessentially matters of local procedural practice" become part of article 1105(1), and noted that if the investor's approach were adopted, "NAFTA tribunals would turn into courts of appeal, which is not their role."[61] The tribunal's analysis is consistent with Jan Paulsson's observation that a national court's application of national law, regardless of whether it is right or wrong, "does not give rise to an international delict unless there has been a violation of due process as defined by international standards."[62]

An issue in *Mondev* that caused the tribunal to draw on international jurisprudence involved the municipal court's holding that the Boston Redevelopment Authority, a public entity, was afforded statutory immunity for intentional torts under a Massachusetts statute. The investor argued that immunity, although appropriate under Massachusetts law, was "a failure to provide full protection and security to the investment" in violation of article 1105(1).[63] After discussing international decisions and comparative principles, the tribunal

---

[58] *Id.*, para. 127 (quoting Elettronica Sicula S.p.A. (ELSI) (United States v. Italy), ICJ REP. 1989, 15, 76).
[59] *Id.*
[60] *Id.*, para. 135.
[61] *Id.*, para. 136.
[62] Paulsson, *supra* n. 49, at 7.
[63] Mondev Award, *supra* note 50, para. 140.

easily dismissed the charge by noting that "within broad limits, the extent to which a State decides to immunize regulatory authorities from suit for interference with contractual relations is a matter for the competent organs of the State to decide."[64]

B. THE CRITICISM OF NAFTA CHAPTER 11

The attacks on the NAFTA Chapter 11 tribunals are wide ranging and come from both ends of the U.S. political spectrum. The most common ones can be grouped into two categories: (1) intrusions into U.S. sovereignty and (2) lack of due process. Although these categories have some overlap, they both reflect challenges to the legitimacy of the tribunals and thus help frame the analysis. Also, because the complaints are many, only two principal complaints in each category are examined.

1. *Intrusions into U.S. Sovereignty*

The U.S. Constitution establishes a federal system. Article III defines and sets forth the judicial power of the federal courts.[65] The Tenth Amendment acknowledges the role and authority of the states.[66] The system that has evolved over the years reflects a delicate and complex balance of power between the states and the federal government consistent with the Constitutional mandate.

The NAFTA Chapter 11 tribunals are allegedly at odds with the U.S. Constitutional regime. The tribunals in *Loewen* and *Mondev* examined decisions of state courts. Critics charge the tribunals afford a layer of review beyond the Constitutional structure. Ernest Young warns "[t]oo much supranational review of domestic court decisions on domestic law would threaten domestic courts' control over the content of their own law."[67] Curtis Bradley has noted that "[i]t is a new development to use non-U.S. adjudicators and international law to directly review the fairness of U.S. litigation."[68]

Renee Lettow Lerner goes beyond expressing concern that the NAFTA panels are super appellate courts. According to her, in resolving claims of denial of justice, the NAFTA panels could reach deeper into U.S. sovereignty and affect "federal-state relations and such tenacious institutions as civil jury trials and

---

[64] *Id.*, para. 154.
[65] U.S. CONST., art. III.
[66] *Id.*, amend. X.
[67] Ernest A. Young, *Institutional Settlement in a Globalizing Judicial System*, 54 Duke L. J. 1143, 1193–94 (2005).
[68] Bradley, *supra* n. 3, at 1577.

punitive damages."[69] As Professor Lettow Lerner has noted, *Loewen* threatened four elements of the U.S. justice system that are near and dear to various constituencies: "elected judges, jury awards, aggressive advocacy, and punitive damages."[70] Another commentator has proclaimed that NAFTA Chapter 11 panels are "the biggest threat to United States judicial independence that no one has heard of and even fewer people understand."[71]

American law professors are not alone in expressing concern about Chapter 11 and its potential for interfering with the established and respected U.S. judicial system. Chief Justice Margaret H. Marshall of the Massachusetts Supreme Court first learned about *Mondev* at a dinner party, and noted, "To say I was surprised to hear that a judgment of this court was being subjected to further review would be an understatement."[72] The chief justice of the California Supreme Court Ronald M. George stated, "It's rather shocking that the highest courts of the state and federal governments could have their judgments circumvented by these tribunals."[73]

In addition to raising concerns about the influence of the panels on decisions of domestic courts, critics claim NAFTA Chapter 11 tribunals undermine the ability of federal and state governments to govern in a democratic manner. They cite an early NAFTA Chapter 11 decision, *Metalclad Corp. v. Mexico*,[74] which awarded $16.85 million to a U.S. investor challenging a Mexican municipality's withdrawal of a permit to build a landfill.[75] The award found Mexico violated NAFTA article 1105(1) due to its lack of "a transparent and predictable framework" for obtaining the permit.[76] In addition, the tribunal found that Mexico had "taken a measure tantamount to expropriation"

---

[69] Lettow Lerner, *supra* n. 27, at 235.
[70] *Id.*, at 279.
[71] Adam Liptak, "Review of U.S. Rulings by NAFTA Tribunals Stirs Worries," *New York Times*, Apr. 18, 2004, 20 (quoting John D. Echeverria of Georgetown University Law Center's Environmental Law & Policy Institute).
[72] *Id.*
[73] *Id.*
[74] *Metalclad Corp. v. Mexico*, Award (Aug. 30, 2000), 40 ILM 36 [hereinafter Metalclad Award].
[75] *See, e.g.*, Been and Beauvais, *supra* n. 4, at 32–34, 72–74.
[76] Metalclad Award, *supra* n. 74, para. 99. The Mexican federal authorities, which had authority to issue the permit based on hazardous waste evaluations and assessments, had told the investor it was entitled to the permit yet local authorities ultimately denied the permit. *Id.*, para. 86. The municipality, however, only had authority over certain construction matters. *Id.* According to the tribunal, the "totality of these circumstances demonstrates a lack of orderly process and timely disposition in relation to an investor of a party acting in the expectation that it would be treated fairly and justly in accordance with the NAFTA." *Id.*, para. 99. The Supreme Court of British Columbia partially set aside the Metalclad Award as to this article 1105(1) finding. *See Mexico v. Metalclad*, 2001 B.C.S.C. 664 at http://www.investmentclaims.com/decisions/Metalclad-Mexico-BCSCReview-2May2001.pdf.

and thus violated article 1110(1).[77] According to Vicki Been and Joel Beauvais, *Metalclad* "opened the door for property owners to use NAFTA to assert what we in the United States think of as 'regulatory takings' challenges to land use and environmental regulations."[78] *Metalclad* was the precursor to *Methanex*, a high-profile NAFTA Chapter 11 case cited to support the charge that NAFTA is anti-environmental and gives multinational corporations more rights than U.S. nationals.[79]

Nongovernmental organizations (NGOs), citizens groups, and media commentators have joined the attack on the NAFTA Chapter 11 tribunals. An American Federation of Labor and Congress of Industrial Organizations (AFL-CIO) official has charged that "[c]ompanies have used NAFTA to challenge laws protecting the environment, public health, workers and consumers, arguing that these laws hurt their profits."[80] The journalist Bill Moyers, in defending his documentary *Trading Democracy*, claims NAFTA Chapter 11 has "created a private legal system for corporations that wish to challenge public laws, a system that operates outside the U.S. court system in a forum where U.S. citizens cannot even listen."[81] Describing the situation at issue in *Metalclad*, Mr. Moyers stated:

> In one case we investigated, the people of the Mexican state of San Luis Potosi were alarmed because an American company intended to reopen in their back yard a toxic waste facility that they believed was making their children ill. The community had blockaded the plant and brought an end to the dumping when it had had Mexican owners. These people and their elected representatives wanted the site cleaned up and demanded that the American company obtain the proper local permits. But under NAFTA, the foreign owners, who ignored the need for the local permit, had special rights to file a claim that was heard before a secret tribunal and win millions of dollars in compensation from the Mexican government.[82]

2. Due Process Concerns

The barrage does not stop with the concern that NAFTA Chapter 11 tribunals have usurped critical U.S. judicial and lawmaking processes. A

---

[77] Metalclad Award, *supra* n. 74, para. 104.
[78] Been and Beauvais, *supra* n. 4, at 33.
[79] *See, e.g.*, Lucien F. Dhooge, *The Revenge of the Trail Smelter: Environmental Regulation as Expropriation Pursuant to the North American Free Trade Agreement*, 38 Am. Bus. L. J. 475, 478–79 (2001) (describing the "firestorm of criticism" arising from the filing of *Methanex*).
[80] Statement of Thea M. Lee, Assistant Director for International Economic Policy, AFL-CIO, U.S. Senate Finance Committee, Subcommittee on International Trade, Federal Document Clearing House, May 13, 2003, *available at* LEXIS, News Library.
[81] Bill Moyers, "Talking Trade in Secret," *Washington Post*, Feb. 23, 2002, A19.
[82] *Id.*

common charge, which has taken on a life of its own, is that the NAFTA Chapter 11 tribunals are "secret tribunals." According to the accusers, no one knows the identity of panel members, the fact that a claim for arbitration has been submitted, by whom, and the results of the arbitration:

> Panel hearings are secret, panel members often unknown, and panel decisions not always published. These circumstances would not be troublesome if the panels dealt only with consenting private parties, but they deal with nonconsenting public parties, public treasuries and public laws, policies and regulations. None of the three member countries should be subject to NAFTA unless its serious substantive and procedural defects are corrected.[83]

As discussed later, the NAFTA nations have addressed concerns about the lack of transparency under Chapter 11. Yet within recent years at least one member of Congress and others have continued to claim that the tribunals are secret and act in secret.[84]

The second major charge about process concerns inconsistency in the arbitral awards. NAFTA acknowledges that a tribunal's award is only binding "between the disputing parties and in respect of the particular case."[85] A tribunal resolving a specific dispute is not bound to follow an earlier tribunal's decision or pronouncement of the relevant legal standard. Professor Susan Franck has documented how tribunals in *S.D. Myers, Inc. v. Canada*, *Metalclad*, and *Pope & Talbot, Inc. v. Canada* gave three different and arguably inconsistent meanings to the fair and equitable requirement under article

---

[83] "NAFTA Rules Supercede State and U.S. Regulations," *Asbury Park Press*, May 17, 2001, 17A, LEXIS, News Library.

[84] *See, e.g.*, "Hearing of the Subcommittee on Commerce, Trade, and Consumer Protection of the House Energy and Commerce Committee: Central American and Dominican Republic Free Trade Agreement," Apr. 28, 2005 available at LEXIS, News Library [hereinafter Hearing] (comments by Rep. Ted Strickland (D-Oh.)) (claiming that NAFTA Chapter 11 allows "foreign corporations to sue governments in *closed trade tribunals* over public health and safety laws that foreign countries claim cost them lost profits, and they demand our tax dollars in compensation" and further stating that "since NAFTA, $35 million has been ordered to be paid to foreign corporations by these *secret tribunals*") (emphasis added). *See also* Javier Sierra, "Congress Should Say No to a New Trade Pact," *Scripps Howard News Service*, May 20, 2005 available at LEXIS, News Library (claiming that the new dispute procedures under the Central American Free Trade Agreement (CAFTA) "would allow any corporation that feels its profits are threatened by local regulations to sue that country in a secret international tribunal for unlimited cash compensation" and then comparing these procedures to the NAFTA "experience").

[85] NAFTA, *supra* n. 1, art. 1136(1). *See also Grand River Enter. Six Nations, Ltd. v. United States*, Decision on Objections to Jurisdiction (July 20, 2006) para. 36, at http://www.investmentclaims.com/decisions/GRE-USA-Jurisdiction.pdf (stating that "NAFTA arbitral awards do not constitute binding precedent, and in any event are rooted in their specific facts").

1105(1).[86] After reading the awards it is difficult to say within any reasonable degree of certainty what obligations a NAFTA nation owes under article 1105(1).[87] According to Professor Franck, "conflicting awards based upon identical facts and/or identically worded investment treaty provisions will be a threat to the international legal order and the continued existence of investment treaties."[88] Predictability and stability, essential to attracting foreign investment, are undermined when a dispute settlement regime cannot develop a consistent meaning on investment standards. Concerned about inconsistency in the awards, the U.S. Congress passed the 2002 Trade Act and proclaimed that a principal negotiating objective for the United States in future free trade agreements would be to provide "for an appellate body or similar mechanism to provide coherence to the interpretations of investment provisions in trade agreements."[89]

C. A REALITY CHECK

A careful reading and analysis of the specific charges levied against NAFTA Chapter 11's dispute settlement regime establish that some of the concerns have been exaggerated to the point they are not credible. Some of the charges had, or have, merit, yet the consequences have been exaggerated.

1. Exaggerations

Leading the list of exaggerated complaints is the argument that NAFTA Chapter 11 panels are supranational courts that operate beyond the judicial regime established under the U.S. Constitution. The argument first suggests the United States had no involvement in creating the NAFTA. Instead, the United States championed the NAFTA Chapter 11 dispute settlement process as it sought to protect U.S. investors when they ventured into Mexico.[90] The U.S. president negotiated Chapter 11 along with other NAFTA chapters in

---

[86] Franck, *supra* n. 6, at 1576–81. *See also* Brower, *supra* n. 7, at 66 (observing that "incongruity has become the hallmark of decisions involving the minimum standard of treatment set forth in Article 1105(1)").

[87] *See also* Brower, *supra* n. 7, at 67–68 (establishing the "doctrinal incoherence" of the panels' decisions interpreting Article 1105(1)).

[88] Franck, *supra* n. 6, at 1583.

[89] 19 U.S.C. § 3802(b)(3)(G)(iv) (Supp. III 2003). *See* Dana Krueger, Note: *The Combat Zone: Mondev International, Ltd. v. United States and the Backlash against NAFTA Chapter 11*, 21 B.U. Int'l L. J. 399, 423 (2003).

[90] Jeffery Atik, *Repenser NAFTA Chapter 11: A Catalogue of Legitimacy Critiques*, 3 Asper Rev. Int'l Bus. & Trade L. 215, 220 (2003) (noting that "the Chapter 11 process was aimed at Mexico"). *See also* Sebastian Mallaby, "A Slanted Take on Trade," *Washington Post*, Feb. 18, 2002, A23

coordination with the U.S. Congress, which approved NAFTA and passed legislation implementing NAFTA.[91]

Second, the argument erroneously assumes that when a NAFTA Chapter 11 tribunal examines a decision of a national court to determine whether the United States has lived up to its promises under NAFTA Chapter 11 it somehow has the authority to reverse or vacate the judgment of the national court. An adverse arbitral award that is based on a domestic judgment imposes a liability on the United States. The argument erroneously assumes a "direct review" of the judicial decision. Mark Tushnet offers another approach to the issue by challenging Ernest Young's observation that the NAFTA panels are "making domestic law."[92] If *Loewen* had held that the conduct of the Mississippi courts violated NAFTA, then Congress, not the NAFTA tribunal, overrode Mississippi law.[93]

Third, the national court could have applied the wrong law or applied it incorrectly, or it could have been mistaken as to facts. These developments would be irrelevant, however, to the work of the NAFTA Chapter 11 tribunal unless the national court violated the NAFTA. One of the earlier Chapter 11 awards, *Azinian*, set out the rule clearly and succinctly:

> The possibility of holding a State internationally liable for judicial decisions does not, however, entitle a claimant to seek international review of the national court decisions as though the international jurisdiction seised has plenary appellate jurisdiction. This is not true generally, and it is not true for NAFTA.[94]

Fourth, the record to date as evidenced by *Mondev*, in particular, belies that any "supra" judicial review has disrupted or interfered with the U.S. legal

---

(Chapter 11 protections are "an effort to spread the American idea of legal rights to other countries").

[91] *See Made in the USA Found. v. United States*, 242 F.3d 1300, 1303 (11th Cir. 2001).

[92] Mark Tushnet, *Transnational/Domestic Constitutional Law*, 37 Loy. L.A. L. Rev. 239, 254 (2003).

[93] *Id.* (observing that "[i]t would be *Congress* that overrides Mississippi's laws after a NAFTA panel determination, not the NAFTA panel itself") (emphasis in original). As Professor Tushnet also observed, assuming the NAFTA is a treaty, which is the supreme law of the land, "[t]here could be no constitutional objection to a treaty that in its terms overrides Mississippi law on some ordinary commercial subject of the sort affected by NAFTA." *Id.* at 253.

[94] Azinian v. Mexico, Award, para. 99, ICSID Case No. ARB(AF)/97/2, 39 ILM 537 [Azinian Award]. *See id.*, para. 87 (holding that "NAFTA does not, however, allow investors to seek international arbitration for mere contractual breaches"); Mondev Award, *supra* n. 50, para. 136 (holding that "[e]xcept in extreme cases, the Tribunal does not understand how the application of local procedural rules about such matters as remand, or decisions as to the functions of juries vis-à-vis appellate courts, could violate the standards embodied in Article 1105(1)").

system. The United States has not been held liable under the NAFTA for any alleged denials of justice, let alone liable for breach of NAFTA Chapter 11. The tribunal in *Mondev* pronounced a relatively narrow test for denial of justice; for example, "shock or surprise" such that "an impartial tribunal" "on reflection" has "justified concerns as to the judicial propriety of the outcome."[95] The NAFTA tribunals, particularly after issuance of the Interpretation in 2001, are not basing their decisions on the perceived "unfairness" of local court proceedings. And the tribunal in *Mondev* cautioned it is not a court of appeal, which is similar to a pronouncement that an early NAFTA Chapter 11 tribunal, *Azinian*, made in 1999.[96]

Loewen found no breach of the NAFTA giving rise to liability, yet it persisted in examining and reexamining the conduct in the Mississippi court. The panel issued stern and harsh comments about what transpired in Mississippi but lacked power under the NAFTA to do anything about the travesty. Short of establishing liability, *Loewen* exposed a problem that has persisted in local courts in the United States, the "hometown" effect, and the effect is even more noticeable when the nonlocal party is from outside of the United States.[97] Having the "hometown" effect on the world stage could deter local lawyers and courts from relying on questionable antics when matters of justice are at stake. Far from being a threat to judicial independence, the NAFTA Chapter 11 tribunals could help promote a healthy and sound judicial system.

Equally suspicious and another example of a knee-jerk reaction is the sweeping charge that the NAFTA Chapter 11 tribunals are secret tribunals. From the outset, the fact of the dispute settlement process was public. The media reported the filing of some of the cases. Tribunal decisions have been published. The award in *Azinian*, issued on November 1, 1999, was published in 2000 in *International Legal Materials*.[98] Within two weeks of the issuance of the *Azinian* award, the Embassy of Mexico in Washington, D.C., issued a press release that quoted passages from the award.[99] The award in *Metalclad* was issued on August 22, 2000, and published in 2001.[100] The awards are

---

[95] See *supra* nn. 59–62 and accompanying text.

[96] Mondev Award, *supra* n. 50, para. 126 (holding that "it is not function of NAFTA tribunals to act as courts of appeal"); Azinian Award, *supra* n. 94, para. 99.

[97] I base this statement on having represented an agency of the People's Republic of China in a jury trial in Texas state court. During the voir dire and over objection, opposing counsel for a Texas company asked members of the venire panel if they were members of the Communist Party.

[98] Azinian Award, *supra* n. 94.

[99] "International Tribunal Resolves in Favor of Mexico on Waste Collection Concession," *U.S Newswire*, Nov. 9, 1999, LEXIS, News Library.

[100] Metalclad Award, *supra* n. 74.

rich with details. They identify the arbitrators, the parties, critical procedural and evidentiary issues, the investor's claims, the state's defenses, the evidence submitted, the conclusion, and the rationale for the conclusion based on the applicable legal authority.

At the outset, however, the NAFTA Chapter 11 tribunals conducted their business behind closed doors and the details became public only after the award was issued. The complaints about the secrecy did not fall on deaf ears. On July 31, 2001, the three NAFTA nations under the auspices of the NAFTA Free Trade Commission[101] issued an interpretation of Chapter 11 (Interpretation) to "clarify and reaffirm" the meaning of certain NAFTA provisions.[102] In the Interpretation, the Commission stated that NAFTA does not impose a duty of confidentiality on Parties to a Chapter 11 dispute and it does not preclude Parties from providing public access to documents submitted to or issued by tribunals.[103] The Interpretation included other statements about public access to the tribunals. A number of Web sites now have substantial information about the proceedings, including transcripts of hearings.[104] In *Methanex*, amici curiae were authorized to appear and submit memorials.[105] The hearings were open to the public, so anyone with government-issued identification could visit the World Bank in Washington, D.C., and watch the proceedings on a live video feed.[106]

Whereas before July 31, 2001, secrecy was a concern, it was never the case that the NAFTA Chapter 11 tribunals were "secret tribunals," and surely it is no longer correct to charge that the tribunals operate in secret. As a USTR official advised the Congress in correcting the statement of Representative Strickland, "And these international tribunals now are open to the public. The documents become public documents, except [when designated as] confidential; the practice that we have here in the United States."[107]

---

[101] The Commission, cabinet-level officials or their designees, "shall... (c) resolve disputes that may arise regarding [the NAFTA's] interpretation or application." NAFTA, *supra* note 1, art. 2001(2)(c). Under NAFTA, a Commission interpretation "shall be binding on a Tribunal." *Id.* art. 1131(2).

[102] *See* Interpretation at http://www.state.gov/documents/organization/38790.pdf.

[103] *Id.*

[104] *See, e.g.*, http://www.state.gov/s/l/c3439.htm; http://www.naftaclaims.com.

[105] *See, e.g., Methanex Corp. v. United States*, Decision of the Tribunal on Petitions from Third Persons to Intervene as "Amici Curiae," Jan. 15, 2001, at http://www.investmentclaims.com/decisions/Methanex_Final_Award.pdf.

[106] *See ICSID News Release* (June 8, 2004) at http://worldbank.com/icsid/highlights/methanex-form.htm. Although *Methanex* was filed under the UNCITRAL Arbitration Rules, the parties asked and ICSID agreed to administer the hearing. *Id.*

[107] Hearing, *supra* n. 84 (Statement of Regina K. Vargo, Office of U.S. Trade Representative and chief CAFTA negotiator).

2. Moderate Concerns

The attack on the jurisprudence of the NAFTA tribunals based on inconsistent awards or conflicting statements about the law in the awards has been mild yet accurate in many respects. Professor Charles Brower has documented how, aside from the confusion surrounding article 1105(1), the panels have been remarkably consistent and their awards "have reached a high level of coherence on many issues."[108]

In an effort to bring clarity to article 1105(1) and to avoid concerns that a tribunal would develop its own view of what is "fair" or "just" in evaluating State conduct, the NAFTA Free Trade Commission in the Interpretation also stated as follows:

> Minimum Standard of Treatment in Accordance with International Law
> 1. Article 1105(1) prescribes the customary international law minimum standard of treatment of aliens as the minimum standard of treatment to be afforded to investments of investors of another Party.
> 2. The concepts of "fair and equitable treatment" and "full protection and security" do not require treatment in addition to or beyond that which is required by the customary international law minimum standard of treatment of aliens.
> 3. A determination that there has been a breach of another provision of the NAFTA, or of a separate international agreement, does not establish that there has been a breach of Article 1105(1).[109]

The 2004 U.S. Model BIT likewise attempted to refine the minimum standard. It afforded covered investments "treatment in accordance with customary international law, including fair and equitable treatment and full protection and security."[110] For purposes of "greater certainty," the 2004 U.S. Model BIT clarified that the standard "prescribes the customary international law minimum standard of treatment of aliens as the minimum standard of treatment to be afforded to covered investments."[111] The U.S.–Uruguay BIT of 2004, modeled after the 2004 U.S. Model BIT, elaborated on "fair and equitable treatment" and denial of justice as follows:

---

[108] Brower, *supra* note 7, at 66. *See also id.* at 64 (noting most tribunals "have developed clear rules that strike a healthy balance between the interests of foreign investors with the regulatory obligations of host states").

[109] Interpretation, *supra* n. 102, § B.

[110] Treaty between the Government of the United States of America and the Government of [Country] Concerning the Encouragement and Reciprocal Protection of Investment art. 5(1), at http://www.state.gov/documents/organization/38710.pdf [hereinafter 2004 U.S. Model BIT].

[111] *Id.*, art. 5(2).

"fair and equitable treatment" includes the obligation not to deny justice in criminal, civil, or administrative adjudicatory proceedings in accordance with the principle of due process embodied in the principal legal systems of the world.[112]

By using "includes," the U.S.–Uruguay BIT and the 2004 U.S. Model BIT suggest that denial of justice is an element of the minimum standard of treatment owed to the foreign investor. In addition, "full protection and security" requires a party "to provide the level of police protection required under customary international law."[113]

Accordingly, the NAFTA States have established that the customary international law minimum standard is the applicable standard and the elements of "fair and equitable treatment" and "full protection and security" are subsumed within the standard. The United States, with the 2004 U.S. Model BIT, has also established that one of the subsuming elements, "fair and equitable treatment," includes the obligation not to deny justice in certain proceedings. Due process, as defined by the world's principal legal systems, is the governing standard.

Efforts to clarify article 1105(1) have not resolved all ambiguities[114] but they have resulted in relatively consistent decisions. NAFTA arbitral tribunals have rejected investors' misguided attempts to use the NAFTA tribunals as courts of appeal. Mere claims that the municipal court decisions violated municipal law are insufficient. Instead, the allegedly wrongful acts must give rise to violations of "due process" or "generally accepted standards of the administration of justice." Yet even these violations may not be enough. For example, the failure to give notice, even if harmful and in violation of principles of due process, may not violate the minimum standard. As the tribunal in *Mondev* observed, the result must engender "shock or surprise" that causes one to question the judicial propriety of the result. Also, the mere fact that one is caused to question the result is not enough. The outcome must be clearly improper and discreditable. In other words, the decision must be wrong, and one could argue clearly wrong. Further, the conduct arguably must be "arbitrary, grossly

---

[112] U.S.–Uruguay Treaty Concerning the Encouragement and Reciprocal Protection of Investments, art. 5.2(a), 44 ILM 268, 272 [hereinafter U.S.–Uruguay BIT]. *See also* 2004 U.S. Model BIT, *supra* n. 110, art. 5.2(a).

[113] U.S.–Uruguay BIT, *supra* n. 112, art. 5.2(b).

[114] As David Gantz has written, "[e]ven if everyone agrees that 'fair and equitable treatment' in Article 1105 means the standard required by '*customary* international law,' it still needs to be determined exactly what that means." David A. Gantz, *International Decision: Pope & Talbot, Inc. v. Canada*, 97 Am. J. Int'l L. 937, 949–50 (2003) (emphasis in original).

unfair, unjust, idiosyncratic" or be "discriminatory and exposes the claimant to sectional or racial prejudice."[115]

The NAFTA awards use broad phrases, such as due process, and unclear terms, such as "shock" and "surprise" in the case of *Mondev*, which likely means that more claims of denial of justice will be raised as enterprising lawyers attempt to deal with adverse decisions emanating from national courts that affect their investor clients. Although the bar for raising legitimate claims of denial of justice is indeed high, with the decisions of the NAFTA arbitral tribunals, we have the sense that neutrals are playing the important function of ensuring that nations are adhering to certain international law minimum standards.

In addition, the charge that the Chapter 11 process impairs the ability of local, state, and national governments to govern as they see fit and consistent with democratic principles is a serious one, yet one that to date has not materialized. The long-awaited decision in *Methanex*[116] should put fears to rest. The tribunal acknowledged the need for a nation to govern as follows:

> But as a matter of general international law, a non-discriminatory regulation for a public purpose, which is enacted in accordance with due process and, which affects, inter alios, a foreign investor or investment is not deemed expropriatory and compensable unless specific commitments had been given by the regulating government to the then putative foreign investor contemplating investment that the government would refrain from such regulation.[117]

In other words, the host nation that enacts nondiscriminatory laws and regulations in its usual course without having made promises to a foreign investor need not be too worried about a claim of expropriation.

And Methanex's venture into the Chapter 11 process was not without cost. The tribunal awarded to the United States more than $1 million in arbitration costs and nearly $3 million in legal costs.[118]

NAFTA recognizes that Chapter 11's dispute settlement procedure is designed to ensure "both equal treatment among investors of the Parties in accordance with the principle of international reciprocity and due process before an impartial tribunal."[119] Consistency in decisions is a value of the

---

[115] *Waste Mgmt., Inc. v. Mexico*, Award II para. 98, ICSID Case No. ARB(AF)/98/2, http://www.state.gov/documents/organization/34643.pdf [hereinafter Waste Management Award].
[116] *Methanex Corp. v. United States*, Award (Aug. 3, 2005), 44 ILM 1345.
[117] *Id.*, Pt. IV, Chap. D, para. 7.
[118] *Id.*, Pt. V, Chap. F, paras. 6, 12, 14.
[119] NAFTA, *supra* n. 1, art. 1115.

arbitration process.[120] The tribunal's obligation is to render decisions based "on the facts and by application of any governing treaty provisions."[121] As the Interpretation recognizes, most documents concerning the arbitrations are public, so it is possible to study the decisions of earlier tribunals and to examine the evidence and written submissions regarding the case.[122]

Further, NAFTA defines the law governing a tribunal, NAFTA, and applicable rules of international law. A tribunal is not at liberty to reach beyond the mandated sources of law. The article 1105(1) experience demonstrates that the NAFTA Free Trade Commission has the authority to interpret the NAFTA and its interpretation is binding on a tribunal. Thus, the NAFTA has built-in safeguards to keep tribunals in reasonable check. The tribunals have followed the Interpretation and rejected misguided attempts to ignore or undermine it.

Even in the context of article 1105(1), since the Interpretation, the arbitral awards have demonstrated relative consistency on the issue of denial of justice. The first major post-Interpretation award on the merits, *Mondev*, acknowledged that the tribunal "may not apply its own idiosyncratic standard in lieu of the standard laid down in Article 1105(1)."[123] Just before so ruling, the tribunal acknowledged the U.S. argument that the tribunal is "bound by the minimum standard as established in State practice and in the jurisprudence of arbitral tribunals."[124] *Mondev* acknowledged that NAFTA tribunals should consider decisions of arbitral tribunals in grappling with the minimum standard.

Relying on the first NAFTA arbitration award, *Azinian*, the tribunal in *Mondev* recognized it lacked free reign to exercise "plenary appellate jurisdiction" over decisions of national courts.[125] Citing *Mondev*, the tribunal in *ADF* later stated that "[w]e do not sit as a court with appellate jurisdiction with respect to the U.S. measures."[126] Consistent with this pronouncement, the tribunal in *Loewen* recognized the important principle that claims of denial of justice are subject to exhaustion requirements.

The substantive test *Mondev* pronounced as to article 1105(1) was followed by the tribunal in *ADF*, which acknowledged the standard is an evolving

---

[120] See, e.g., Consolidation Order, *supra* n. 28, para. 131.
[121] Mondev Award, *supra* n. 50, para. 118.
[122] See *supra* nn. 103 and 104 and accompanying text. See also Jack J. Coe, Jr., *The State of Investor-State Arbitration-Some Reflections on Professor Brower's Plea for Sensible Principles*, 20 Am. U. Int'l L. Rev. 929, 941 (2005) (noting that the fact "investment awards are more quickly becoming public may also play a moderating role" in the decisions of the tribunals).
[123] Mondev Award, *supra* n. 50, para. 120.
[124] *Id.*, para. 119.
[125] *Id.*, para. 126 (quoting Azinian Award, *supra* n. 94, para. 99).
[126] ADF Award, *supra* n. 36, para. 190.

standard not limited by *Neer* but one "disciplined by being based upon State practice and judicial or arbitral caselaw or other sources of customary or general international law."[127] The standard, although "constantly in the process of development," is a disciplined one.[128] In *Waste Management*, the tribunal cited *Mondev* and *ADF*, along with *S.D. Myers* and *Loewen*, in noting "a general standard for Article 1105 is emerging."[129] In *International Thunderbird Gaming Corp. v. Mexico*,[130] the tribunal acknowledged the minimum standard is evolving yet subject to a high threshold and relied on "recent international jurisprudence" to reach this conclusion.[131]

Even though NAFTA does not require a tribunal to follow the decision of another tribunal, at least as to article 1105(1) in the post-Interpretation environment, the tribunals have carefully examined and relied on earlier awards in shaping the jurisprudence. One commentator, a former lawyer for the United States in the Chapter 11 cases, has described prior awards as "persuasive authority."[132] Or, as another commentator has observed, reliance on prior awards "is not surprising – it is natural that lawyers and arbitrators trained in a common-law tradition would follow old habits in reasoning their way through these disputes."[133]

A strict system of hierarchy and deference is not in place. No specific rule mandates that the tribunal address and follow or distinguish prior NAFTA arbitral awards. In practice, however, the tribunals go beyond considering prior awards as simply "persuasive." With regard to article 1105(1), for example, the tribunals have relied on prior arbitral awards to shape the standard of denial of justice. At least one award, *ADF*, held that arbitral case law serves to discipline article 1105(1).[134]

Professor Raj Bhala, in his work on the role of *stare decisis* and precedent in dispute resolution in the World Trade Organization (WTO), effectively debunked the notion of varying standards of precedent.[135] Like the WTO

---

[127] *Id.*, para. 184.
[128] *Id.*, para. 179.
[129] Waste Management Award, *supra* n. 115, para. 98.
[130] *International Thunderbird Gaming Corp. v. Mexico*, Award (Jan. 26, 2006) at http://www.investmentclaims.com/decisions/Thunderbird-Mexico-Award.pdf.
[131] *Id.*, para. 194 (citing Mondev Award, ADF Award, and Waste Management Award).
[132] Andrea K. Bjorklund, *NAFTA Chapter 11: Contract without Privity: Sovereign Offer and Investor Acceptance*, 2 Chi. J. Int'l L. 183, 186 (2001).
[133] David MacArthur, Comment & Note: *NAFTA Chapter 11: On an Environmental Collision Course with the World Bank?*, 2003 Utah L. Rev. 913, 930 (2003). Questions remain whether this informal system is sufficient to establish predictability. *Id.*
[134] ADF Award, *supra* n. 36, para. 184. *See also* Mondev Award, *supra* n. 50, paras. 119–20.
[135] Professor Raj Bhala referred to *"de facto* precedent," *"de facto stare decisis,"* and *"de jure* doctrine of *stare decisis"* in his thorough analysis of dispute resolution in the World Trade Organization. *See* Raj Bhala, *The Myth about Stare Decisis and International Trade Law (Part*

bodies, the NAFTA tribunals do not operate in a vacuum. The lawyers appearing before the tribunals submit lengthy memorials in which they cite and argue prior decisions. The tribunals appropriately address the arguments and the prior awards. To not focus on this development is to neglect how an important body of law, the customary international law minimum standard of treatment of aliens, has been defined and refined in a fairly sophisticated and tempered manner.

The NAFTA Chapter 11 dispute resolution process is not airtight. Beyond article 1105(1), battles are fought over relatively open issues; for example, expropriation. Arbitral tribunals outside of the NAFTA process are frequently examining and defining the customary international law minimum standard or the principle of fair and equitable treatment. These developments, although challenging the system, offer opportunities for further refinement of relevant standards consistent with the principles and practices the tribunals have used in shaping the jurisprudence on denial of justice.

D. CONCLUSION

Contrary to the critics, the NAFTA Chapter 11 dispute settlement process has not turned the U.S. regulatory machine on its head or undermined the domestic judiciary. Unidentified tribunals are not operating in secret. The public treasuries are not being spent to reward foreign investors simply because their investments did not produce profits.

The sky has not fallen for various reasons. NAFTA Chapter 11 is rule based. The rules govern how tribunals operate. The tribunals have performed relatively well in various respects, particularly as to ensuring the appointment of qualified and diligent arbitrators. Because the Chapter 11 investment protections "were not written on a blank slate" and "have evolved over time,"[136] it has been critical that those charged with settling disputes understand these principles and appreciate their nuances. In fact, recent panels have consisted of serious international lawyers well versed in international investment law.

One of a Trilogy), 14 Am. U. Int'l L. Rev. 845, 847–48 (1999); Raj Bhala, *The Precedent Setters: De Facto Stare Decisis in WTO Adjudication (Part Two of a Trilogy)*, 9 J. Transnt'l L & Pol. 1, 3–4 (1999) (recognizing that "[a] *de facto* precedent is followed because of a variety of extra-legal and quasi-legal factors"); Raj Bhala, *The Power of the Past: Towards De Jure Stare Decisis in WTO Adjudication (Part Three of a Trilogy)*, 33 George Wash. Int'l L. Rev. 873 (2001). *See also* Susan D. Franck, *International Decision: Occidental Exploration & Prod. Co. v. Rep. of Ecuador*, 99 Am. J. Int'l L. 675, 678-79 (2005) (recognizing that "arbitration awards technically have no *de jure* precedential value, [however,] practitioners, investors, and states rely upon such decisions as *de facto* precedents and as indicators of their potential rights and liabilities").

[136] Price, *supra* n. 10, at 423.

Their comprehension of critical issues and sophistication in presenting and resolving the issues have alleviated concerns.[137]

NAFTA Chapter 11 has a built-in mechanism, Commission interpretations, that enable certain review and clarification of NAFTA provisions. When one considers NAFTA not as a static agreement but one that can adapt within reason, whether through the Commission or tempered arbitral decisions, it can hardly be seen as threatening as some have described.

Finally, like many non-U.S. tribunals, NAFTA's Chapter 11 tribunals have exposed and shed light on problems of domestic legal systems. The tribunals have taught the NAFTA nations more about their own systems of governance than what domestic introspection seemed capable of doing. The awards have caused scholars, policy makers, judges, and the like to analyze and confront aspects of domestic systems and perhaps cause them to see the systems in a different light. This studied reflection has the potential for substantial benefits, including improving the fairness of municipal courts, even U.S. ones, which ultimately benefits all investors.

---

[137] *See, e.g.*, Barton Legum, *Introductory Note to Methanex Corporation v. United States*, 44 ILM 1343, 1344 (observing that the *Methanex* decision is "a momentous award by an extraordinary tribunal in a great case").

13

The United States and International Courts: Getting the Cost-Benefit Analysis Right

CESARE P. R. ROMANO*

Our general approach to international courts and tribunals is pragmatic. In our view, such courts and tribunals should not be seen as an end in themselves but rather as potential tools to advance shared international interests in developing and promoting the rule of law, ensuring justice and accountability, and solving legal disputes. Consistent with this approach, we evaluate the contributions that proposed international courts and tribunals may make on a case-by-case basis, just as we consider the advantages and disadvantages of addressing particular matters through international judicial mechanisms rather than diplomatic or other means.[1]

Thus, John Bellinger, the legal adviser of the U.S. Secretary of State at the time he penned the opening chapter of this book, summarized the United States' approach to international courts. He could have said the same about any other nation in the world. It is difficult to disagree with such a commonsensical maxim. I am not aware of any government, democratic or dictatorial, that would create international courts and subject itself to them for the sake of it.[2]

---

* Professor of Law, Loyola Law School Los Angeles; Co-Director, Project on International Courts and Tribunals – PICT.
[1] John Bellinger, Chapter 1 of this volume, "International Courts and Tribunals and the Rule of Law."
[2] If, in general and on average, European nations seem to favor international courts more than the United States, any serious analysis of European practice and, in particular, of the major European nations would probably suggest a rather more nuanced picture once one looks beyond the federalist phenomenon of the European Communities/European Union, and its central judicial engine, the European Court of Justice (ECJ), and the system of human rights guarantees hinged on the European Court of Human Rights (ECHR). A book on European attitudes and behaviors toward international courts would need to ask whether it is correct to equate strong support for the judicialization of intra-European relations with support of international courts tout-court and whether motives for support or neglect, and patterns of use, by the United States are substantially different from those of Europe (as a whole or member by member). Since the Nicaragua case (1986), the United States has withdrawn its declaration of acceptance of the jurisdiction of the International Court of Justice (ICJ). Yet the only major European state having one standing (and full of reservations) is the United

Who would favor establishing an effective independent international authority, the sole purpose of which would be to constrain sovereignty, without significant benefits in return?[3] Pragmatic governments will base decisions to create or accept the jurisdiction of international courts on the basis of a cool-headed cost-benefit analysis.[4] Many factors are taken into account in that calculation,

> Kingdom. Since then, the United States alone has appeared before the ICJ about as often as the United Kingdom, France, Germany, and Italy combined. It is well documented that it was the United States that pushed for the judicialization of the dispute settlement system under the GATT/WTO regime, to the European objection. John Croome, *Reshaping the World Trading System* (World Trade Organization, 1995) 224–29, 277–81, 332; Robert E. Hudec, *The New WTO Dispute Settlement Procedure: An Overview of the First Three Years*, 8 Minn. J. Global Trade 1, 13–14 (1999). It is less well documented that, since the birth of the WTO, the European Community has made an instrumental use of the WTO dispute settlement system, often against the United States, to further its own goals. In sum, the danger is to exaggerate European idealism and American realism, as Robert Kagan did in his book *Of Paradise and Power: American and Europe in the New World Order* (Knopf, 2003), forgetting that Machiavelli and Hobbes are Europeans and that Americans have been idealists since the landing of the pilgrims from the Mayflower in Plymouth. As Margaret Thatcher once famously remarked, "European nations are not and never will be like [America]. They are the product of their history. While America is a product of philosophy." Cited in David Brinkley, *Everyone is Entitled to My Opinion* (Knopf, 1996), at 119.

[3] Andrew Moravcsik, *The Origins of Human Rights Regimes: Democratic Delegation in Postwar Europe*, 54 Int'l Org. 217, 219 (2000).

[4] The George W. Bush administration, and especially the first five years (2000–5), is probably not representative of long-term and general U.S. attitudes, nor could it be dubbed pragmatic. It is likely that those years will go down in history as the nadir of the relationship of the United States with international institutions, and in particular international courts. During that time, neoconservatives, deeply distrustful of any international institution, preferring nationalist and unilateralist options regardless of the cost to the United States, took the helm of American foreign policy. For a while, ideology displaced pragmatism and national interest. For instance, in March 2005, the National Defense Strategy of the United States of America, the document issued every few years by the secretary of defense to detail the official U.S. strategy and policy, bizarrely proclaimed that "our strength as a nation will continue to be challenged by those who employ a strategy of the weak using international fora, judicial processes, and terrorism." U.S. Department of Defense, *The National Defense Strategy of the United States of America* (March 2005) 5, at http://www.globalsecurity.org/military/library/policy/dod/nds-usa_mar2005.htm. However, during the second Bush administration, the most reactionary voices (e.g., John Bolton, Donald Rumsfeld, Douglas Feith, Paul Wolfowitz, and others) were removed from office because it had become clear that their positions had clearly ill served the U.S. national interest, and U.S. policy toward international institutions started the long return march toward its pragmatic tradition. Of course, populist politicians, who have found in international courts a new target to pander to the lowest instincts of certain parts of the national constituency, will keep on blaring against the existential threat posed by renegade international judges, but again, these are hardly representative of U.S. attitudes as a whole. For several examples of international courts bashing during the 2008 presidential campaign, see José E. Alvarez, *Judicialization and Its Discontents*, Am. Society of Int'l L. (Jan. 31, 2008) at http://www.asil.org/ilpost/president/preso80131.html. "Today, nary a thought is given when international organizations, like the UN, attempt to enforce their myopic vision of a one-world government upon America, while trumping our Constitution in the process. Moreover, many in our own government wilfully or ignorantly cede constitutionally guaranteed rights and

some of which can be empirically explained and pinpointed, whereas others are related to deep-seated cultural and historical forces. States create, utilize, and support international courts because international courts are instruments that render useful services to them.[5] However, if the "instrumental approach" is the necessary starting point of any analysis of how governments relate to international courts, then for the cost-benefit analysis to provide results that truly serve the national interest *all* factors need to be taken into account.[6]

I contend that the present U.S. attitude is exceedingly shortsighted and contextual, vitiated by a lack of sophisticated understanding of crucial differences between courts, or at least genera of courts, and of what international courts are for and about, what they can and cannot do for this country.

This chapter is more overtly normative than those that have preceded it. I put forward several arguments to explain how the United States frequently misses important benefits and exaggerates costs of participating in international courts. An attitude that focuses on praxis and rejects the ethos of international courts – that is to say, the ideals and principles they embody – unduly stresses the short-term benefits and grossly discounts medium and long-term ones. This in turn leads to a policy that is myopic and to decisions that ultimately ill serve U.S. interest. A sound policy is one that at the same time is based on both pragmatic and idealistic considerations because the former privilege the short-term benefits and the latter the long term. I surmise that the United States has more to gain, and less to lose, from more constructive engagement with international courts than superficial analysis might suggest.

I am fully aware that my considerations might not be something that other contributors to this volume would necessarily endorse and sound jarringly

---

freedoms to the international community." Rep. Bob Barr, *Protecting National Sovereignty in an Era of International Meddling: An Increasingly Difficult Task*, 39 Harv. J. Leg. 299, 323 (2002). Former U.S. Secretary of State Henry Kissinger warns that international adjudication "is being pushed to extremes which risk substituting the tyranny of judges for that of governments; historically the dictatorship of the virtuous has often led to inquisitions and even witch hunts." Henry Kissinger, "Does America Need a Foreign Policy?" in *Toward a Diplomacy for the 21st Century* (Simon & Schuster, 2001), 273.

[5] *See*, in general, Andrew Guzman, *International Tribunals: A Rational Choice Analysis*, 157 U. Pa. L. Rev. 171 (2008). *Cf.* Eric Posner and John Yoo, *Judicial Independence in International Tribunals*, 93 Cal. L. Rev. 1 (2005). For a rebuttal of Posner and Yoo's analysis, from a liberal theory perspective, *see* Laurence Helfer and Anne-Marie Slaughter, *Why States Create International Tribunals: A Response to Professors Posner and Yoo*, 93 Cal. L. Rev. 899 (2005).

[6] I prefer to use the expression "instrumental approach" rather than the less awkward "instrumentalism" because the latter has a specific meaning that is only partly fitting. "Instrumentalism" is used in philosophy of science to indicate the view that concepts and theories are merely useful instruments whose worth is measured not by whether the concepts and theories are true or false (or correctly depict reality) but by how effective they are in explaining and predicting phenomena. The American philosopher John Dewey (1859–1952) is considered to be the father of instrumentalism. Morton White, *The Origin of Dewey's Instrumentalism* (Columbia, 1943).

out of tune with contemporary national and international political reality. However, from time to time throughout history, there are transitional moments when old assumptions seem to be open for questioning and change seems to be looming on the horizon. As America experiences a change of leadership at the helm, after eight rocky years of administration by President George W. Bush, and much soul searching is done within both parties about what policies need to be changed given the alarming and increasing challenges the country faces, it seems the time is ripe to expand the horizon of U.S. foreign policy.

Before I move on to illustrate the limits of the narrow instrumental approach, there are two important problematic features that need to be highlighted. First, the thinking goes, international courts are just one of the many tools that the United States has at its disposal, along with classic diplomacy backed, to varying degrees, by its considerable economic and military muscle.[7] On any given issue, the United States should maintain the flexibility to be able to choose which option to resort to, including force (military, economic, or otherwise). Instrumentalists concede that there is a difference between a settlement reached by diplomatic means and one reached within legal parameters and according to legal procedure, "under the shadow of the law,"[8] so to speak. However, many are less ready to concede that there is a meaningful difference between legal settlement by way of a *permanent* international court and that by way of a *transient* arbitral tribunal, or between prosecution and trial by an ad hoc tribunal or a *permanent* international criminal court.

The whole point of international adjudication is to "settle disputes" by helping parties find a mutually acceptable settlement.[9] If they cannot do so by themselves, it is because either the facts or the law – or both – are not clear.[10] International courts are instruments that render useful services to states by "disseminating information"[11] between the parties, or, in other words, by providing "relatively neutral information about the facts and law relevant to a particular dispute."[12]

---

[7] "[I]nternational courts and tribunals are one tool among many to achieve these important ends." See Bellinger, *op. cit.*, *supra* n. 1.
[8] José E. Alvarez, *The New Dispute Settlers: (Half) Truths and Consequences*, 38 Tex. Int'l L.J. 405 (2003); José E. Alvarez, *International Organizations as Law-Makers* (Oxford, 2005).
[9] Posner and Yoo, *supra* n. 5, at 34–40.
[10] "... states do not need a tribunal if the law and the facts are clear. When the treaty or convention clearly governs the dispute and the states have the same information about the relevant facts, there is nothing a tribunal can contribute to the resolution of the dispute." Posner & Yoo, *supra* n. 5, at 22.
[11] Andrew Guzman, *International Tribunals: A Rational Choice Analysis*, U. Pa. L. Rev. 7–9 (2008).
[12] Posner and Yoo, *supra* n. 5, at 10.

Thus, a dispute can be settled by the International Court of Justice (ICJ), but it can be equally settled by an ad hoc arbitral tribunal. All that matters is that the settlement is implemented and complied with by the parties. Prosecution of those most responsible for serious international crimes can be done in various ways ranging from domestic courts to ad hoc international criminal tribunals, to full-fledged permanent courts, like the International Criminal Court (ICC). Ad hoc solutions, however, cost less (financially and politically) and probably have equal benefits.

Second, not only are international courts just one tool among many but they are also second best to most. They are unwieldy instruments, difficult to steer and control. If they rule in favor of the United States, their main problem is that they lack their own enforcement powers. If they do have bite, then they are dangerous because they might be used by another state against U.S. interests.[13] Hence, international courts should be created or resorted to only in very controlled circumstances. At all times, the United States should try to minimize its legal exposure, and when it cannot, it should strive to be the plaintiff or the judge, as opposed to the defendant or the indictee.

A. TOWARD A BALANCED INSTRUMENTAL APPROACH

There is a myopic instrumental approach, which privileges the "here" and "now," which is the currently prevailing approach. There is the hyperopic approach, which privileges the "there" and "then," which is the view of the starry-eyed internationalists. And then there is a balanced approach that takes into consideration all factors and reaches an optimal equilibrium between the need for short-term returns and long-term investments. I would like to suggest a few considerations that are usually overlooked when debating what the United States has to gain or lose from greater engagement with international courts.

1. *International Courts Are More than "Dispute Settlers" and "Problem Solvers," and, Surprise!, They Do What They Are Supposed to Do*

What are international courts for? If international courts are classified by *function*, that is to say by what they are supposed to do and how they do it, then it becomes immediately apparent that the first error is to posit that international courts are just dispute settlers, problem-solving devices that states can have

---

[13] According to Robert Bork, a former U.S. federal judge, states will cooperate with courts only when it suits their interests, so judges are reduced either to puppets (when the states approve) or to impotents (when the states choose not to cooperate). Robert H. Bork, *Coercing Virtue: The Worldwide Rule of Judges* (AEI, 2003).

recourse to at will or simply ignore.[14] Although historically that might have been correct, nowadays it is true only for certain kinds of courts and, for that matter, only a minority of them.[15] Indeed, it seems that, at this age in history, it is possible to identify four basic genera of international courts, each of which having four distinct functions. Let us consider them in the order in which they emerged.

The first genus is what we could call the *classical international courts*. The main purpose of these courts is to settle disputes between sovereign states, and *only* sovereign states, on matters of public international law (general or a special branch).[16] The quintessential specimen of this genus is the ICJ. The more recent International Tribunal for the Law of the Sea and the World Trade Organization (WTO) dispute settlement system, the judicial arm of which is the WTO Appellate Body, also belongs to this genus.

This "classical international courts" or the "state-only courts" genus was the first one to emerge in history (early twentieth century), and it is a direct offspring of the practice of international arbitration.[17] In these courts, diplomacy

---

[14] For some examples of limited appreciation of the scope and breadth of the functions carried out by contemporary international courts, see Robert H. Bork, *Coercing Virtue, op. cit.*; Jeremy A. Rabkin, *Law without Nations?: Why Constitutional Government Requires Sovereign States* (Princeton, 2005); Jack L. Goldsmith and Eric A. Posner, *The Limits of International Law* (Oxford, 2005); Posner and Yoo, *supra* n. 5.

[15] Several scholars recognize the complexity of the contemporary international judicial landscape. See, for instance, David Caron, *Framing Political Theory of International Courts and Tribunals: Reflections at the Centennial*, 100 Am. Soc. Int'l L. Proc. 55 (2006). José E. Alvarez, "The New Dispute Settlers," *supra* n. 8; José E. Alvarez, *International Organizations, supra* n. 8; Karen Alter, *Delegating to International Courts: Self-Binding vs. Other-Binding Delegation*, 71 Law and Contemporary Problems 36 (2008).

[16] The Seabed Disputes Chamber of the International Tribunal for the Law of the Sea is open, in some circumstances, to state enterprises and natural or juridical persons. United Nations Convention on the Law of the Sea, arts. 187, 189, Dec. 10, 1982, 1833 U.N.T.S. 397.

[17] Arbitration is the immediate previous historical precedent from which this genus of courts emerged and is still present in the structure of these courts. For instance, in the case of the ICJ, parties can decide to submit a case to a chamber of the court, instead of the full court, and influence its composition (ICJ Statute, art. 26). They can ask the court to decide the case *ex aequo et bono* instead of on the basis of international law (art. 38.2), a feature it shares with arbitral tribunals (e.g., Article 33 of the United Nations Commission on International Trade Law's Arbitration Rules (1976) provides that the arbitrators shall consider only the applicable law, unless the arbitral agreement allows the arbitrators to consider the case *ex aequo et bono*). The ICJ has been used in the past as a sort of appeal chamber of arbitral tribunals (e.g., *Arbitral Award of 31 July 1989* (Guinea-Bissau v. Senegal); *Arbitral Award Made by the King of Spain on 23 December 1906* (Honduras v. Nicaragua). See generally Michael Reisman, *Systems of Control in International Adjudication and Arbitration: Breakdown and Repair* (Duke, 1992). The WTO dispute settlement system consists of two levels: a first tier, in which disputes are decided by arbitral panels, and a second judicial tier, in which cases can be appealed before the Appellate Body. Finally, the International Tribunal for the Law of the Sea (ITLOS) is but one of the various dispute settlement procedures available under the Law of the Sea Convention,

and sovereignty play important roles, and dispute settlement is arguably the most important function they fulfill. Here, litigation is part of a longer diplomatic process of negotiation that usually both precedes litigation and follows it so as to make it possible for any eventual ruling to produce its effects.[18]

Because there are fewer than two hundred sovereign states in the world, these bodies serve a numerically small community, and accordingly, litigation is relatively sporadic. Their caseload tends to range from a few to several dozen per year. However, this kind of litigation tends to be high profile, involve high-level decision makers nationally, and attract considerable (albeit brief) public attention. This handful of courts also attracts a disproportionate level of attention by scholars, way beyond their actual significance in the day-to-day life of international relations. The real action, so to speak, is elsewhere. Indeed, international courts have evolved beyond the international, state-only, and "dispute-settler" model, giving way to a remarkable quantitative growth and qualitative differentiation.[19]

Thus, the second genus is that of *human rights courts*, such as the European Court of Human Rights (ECHR), the Inter-American Court of Human Rights (IACHR), and the nascent African Court of Human and Peoples' Rights. It emerged during the third quarter of the twentieth century. The purpose of human rights courts is to provide legal remedies (compensation, declaration, or specific performance) to individuals whose human rights have been violated. Individuals can submit to these courts – directly (in Europe) or indirectly through specific organs of international organizations called commissions (in the Americas and Africa)[20] – cases concerning the violation of their rights as provided for in the respective basic regional human rights agreements. Although states may raise violations of human rights by other states before

---

the others being various kinds of arbitral tribunals. *See generally* A. O. Adede, *The System for Settlement of Disputes under the United Nations Convention on the Law of the Sea* (Nijhoff, 1987); *see also* R. R. Churchill and A. V. Lowe, *The Law of the Sea* (3d ed., Juris, 1999). ITLOS can also issue provisional measures pending the constitution of an arbitral tribunal. United Nations Convention on the Law of the Sea, Annex VI, art. 25, *supra* n. 16.

[18] In other words, they are yet another forum for political maneuvering, or to paraphrase von Clausewitz, international adjudication is just the continuation of diplomacy by other means. Carl von Clausewitz, *On War* (Michael Howard and Peter Paret eds., Princeton, 1989). The original quote is "war is a continuation of politics by other means." *See* Cesare Romano, "Progress in International Adjudication: Revisiting Hudson's Assessment of the Future of International Courts," in *Progress in International Law* (Russell Miller & Rebecca Bratspeis eds., Nijhoff, 2008) 433, 444–48.

[19] Helfer and Slaughter call the new genera of courts "supranational courts." Laurence R. Helfer and Anne-Marie Slaughter, *Toward a Theory of Effective Supranational Adjudication*, 107 Yale L.J. 273 (1997).

[20] In the case of the ECHR, the filter of the Commission was removed with the entry into force, on November 1, 1998, of Protocol 11 to the European Convention for the Protection of Human Rights and Fundamental Freedoms, E.T.S. No. 155.

these courts, thus engaging in classical state-to-state litigation, it is an extremely rare event. Invariably, the defendant is a sovereign state and the plaintiff is a person, typically a citizen of the defendant. These courts tend to have large dockets – from dozens of cases per year, in the case of the IACHR, to tens of thousands in the case of the ECHR – as potential plaintiffs number in the hundreds of millions, and the range of issues they address is considerable and, in many regards, similar to those addressed by national supreme courts.

Although they do settle disputes between individuals and their own governments over whether a violation of human rights has occurred,[21] construing these courts as "problem solvers" or "dispute settlers" is reductive and beside the point. There are two public crucial functions that the "dispute settler" label misses. Over the years, human rights courts have justified their existence mostly by acting both as *custodians of the law*, sanctioning violations by abusive governments, and as *developers of the law*, fleshing out the bare-bones international human rights convention they have been asked to apply.[22] These are important *public* functions that transcend the narrow limits of the given case and the parties.

The third genus comprises *courts of regional economic and/or political integration agreements*. The European Court of Justice (ECJ), the Court of the European Free Trade Agreement, and the Caribbean Court of Justice (CCJ) are but just three examples among a dozen (all established from as early as the 1950s to the present day).[23] Indeed, numerically, this is the largest genus. The functions of these courts are many and diversified. One unique feature of courts of this genus is that they handle requests of interpretation of community law

---

[21] Besides the fact that the ruling is final and cannot be appealed at other courts or domestically, and thus is dispositive of the matter, human rights courts try to facilitate the settlement of the case *litis pendente*. Once an application has been declared admissible, the ECHR "place[s] itself at the disposal of the parties concerned with a view to securing a friendly settlement of the matter on the basis of respect for human rights as defined in the Convention and the protocols thereto." European Convention for the Protection of Human Rights and Fundamental Freedoms art. 38.1, Sept. 9, 1953, C.E.T.S. No. 005. The same happens in the Inter-American system. Organization of American States, American Convention on Human Rights arts. 48.1.f, 49, 50, 51, Nov. 22, 1969, O.A.S.T.S. No. 36, 1144 U.N.T.S. 123.

[22] See *A Europe of Rights: The Impact of the ECHR on National Legal Systems* (Helen Keller and Alec Stone-Sweet eds., Oxford, 2008); Michael Goldhaber, *A People's History of the European Court of Human Rights* (Rutgers, 2007).

[23] The Caribbean Court of Justice is unique because it has both original and appellate jurisdiction. In its original jurisdiction, like the ECJ, the CCJ is responsible for interpreting the *Revised Treaty of Chaguaramas*, which establishes the CARICOM Single Market and Economy. See Caribbean Court of Justice, "About the Court," http://www.caribbeancourtofjustice.org/about.htm (visited Nov. 26, 2008). Yet it also has appellate jurisdiction, as it acts as the common final court of appeal for those states that have accepted its jurisdiction (at the moment, Guyana and Barbados). This hybrid structure is unique among international courts.

from national courts (so-called preliminary rulings).²⁴ Acting as such, they are a continuum of the national legal systems, rather than a separate level of jurisdiction, as are most international courts. They also decide disputes between organs of the community and member states, and disputes between individuals or corporations and community organs or member states, on the content and implementation of community laws. Very rarely they decide disputes between member states, as classical, state-only courts do. In other words, courts of this genus are more akin to supreme courts of federal states, or supreme administrative courts, than classical international courts settling disputes between sovereign states.²⁵

Finally, the last genus of international courts to emerge in history – all since 1993 – is that of *international criminal courts*, such as the ICC, the International Criminal Tribunal for the former Yugoslavia (ICTY), and the International Criminal Tribunal for Rwanda (ICTR). A specific subgenus is that of the so-called hybrid or internationalized criminal courts, such as the Special Court for Sierra Leone, the Extraordinary Chambers in the Courts of Cambodia, the Special Panels for Serious Crimes in East Timor, or the Special Tribunal for Lebanon.²⁶

These courts do not really "resolve problems" by disclosing information on facts and law to the parties, or "settle disputes." Granted, one might say that the aim of a trial is to determine whether a crime has been committed and by whom, a problem between the indictee and the prosecutor that needs to be resolved by the judges, or a dispute of law and fact that needs to be settled, but, again, that misses the point. The function of international criminal courts is rather to rule on international crimes (war crimes, crimes against humanity, crime of genocide) through trials and, eventually and where appropriate, to

---

²⁴ In the case of the ECJ, most decisions of the court are, indeed, preliminary rulings. European Court of Justice, Annual Report (2007) 80. Available at http://curia.europa.eu/en/instit/presentationfr/index.htm.

²⁵ The ECJ has provided the archetypical model for several regional courts. It is also the most studied phenomenon. *See* Alec Stone-Sweet, *The Judicial Construction of Europe* (Oxford, 2004); Karen J. Alter, *Establishing the Supremacy of European Law: The Making of an International Rule of Law in Europe* (Oxford, 2001).

²⁶ The difference between hybrid courts and fully international criminal courts is that they are composed of a mix of international and local judges, and they decide cases by applying a mix of local and international procedural and substantive law. Some are more domestic courts with some international elements grafted on, like the internationalized panels in Kosovo; others approximate international courts but-for the presence of domestic elements, like the Special Court of Sierra Leone. On hybrid criminal tribunals, *see generally Internationalized Criminal Courts and Tribunals: Sierra Leone, East Timor, Kosovo, and Cambodia* (Cesare Romano, André Nollkaemper, and Jann Kleffner eds., Oxford, 2004); Cesare Romano, "Mixed Criminal Tribunals," *in Max Planck Encyclopedia of Public International Law* (3rd rev. ed., Oxford, forthcoming).

mete out criminal punishment, like loss of liberty or fines. Considering the ad hoc nature of most international criminal courts, bar the ICC, one could venture even to say that determining what happened, and if that amounts to a crime, is beyond the point because the very creation of the tribunal itself presupposes a sort of political "prejudgment" that some crime happened and that those highest in the chain of command are responsible for it.

From the foregoing, it should be apparent that the "problem-solving," "dispute-settlement" function is only one aspect of the work of modern international courts. When states create and subject themselves to the jurisdiction of international courts they seek more than just a clarification about the law or facts in dispute so that they can resolve disagreements. They ask international courts to review administrative decision making, to ensure international institutions do not exceed their powers, to enforce international agreements of all kinds so that states can capture the benefits they bargained for so hard to have included in them, and even to develop international law, just to name a few functions. The great news is that, in the vast majority of cases, international courts do exactly what states asked them to do.[27]

2. *International Courts Are Like Halloween Haunted Houses: They Spook Only the Naïve or Those Who Want to Be Spooked*

Judging from the fact that more, and not less, states are moving toward international courts – Russia and China the two latest most notable developments, countries that traditionally have shunned international adjudication – concerns about loss of sovereignty to unaccountable international adjudicators are grossly overstated.[28] The United States takes international courts and international adjudication very seriously, but perhaps, it can be said it takes them too seriously.

International dispute settlement and international criminal law are probably the activities of international courts with the greatest potential for touching raw nerves, but again, most international courts nowadays are not engaged in this kind of activity. Mostly, they hum in the background processing hundreds, if

---

[27] See generally Karen Alter, "Delegating to International Courts," *supra* n. 15.

[28] Russia joined the Council of Europe in 1996. The first ruling against Russia by the ECHR was in 2002 (*Case of Burodov v. Russia*). Russia has also appeared before the ITLOS in three "prompt release" proceedings – once as applicant in the *Volga* case (*Russian Federation v. Australia*) (2002); twice as respondent in the *Hoshinmaru* case and the *Tomimaru* case (*Japan v. Russian Federation*); and before the International Court of Justice in 2008, in the *Application of the International Convention on the Elimination of All Forms of Racial Discrimination* (*Georgia v. Russian Federation*). China has been a member of WTO since December 11, 2001. Since then it has been the complainant in three cases, respondent in eleven, and third party in sixty-two. To date, it has not yet appeared before the ICJ or the ITLOS.

not thousands, of cases involving the kinds of issues that, in the United States, are dealt with at the level of specialized courts, or low-level federal courts. Very rarely international court activity involves compromising national sovereignty in ways states did not intend and would not want.[29] Of course, critical issues might be at stake in those few instances, but a closer look, particularly at the aftermath of the decision, might indicate otherwise.

Currently, the only courts that are engaged in settlement of disputes between sovereign states in the light of international law – the classical and most ancient type of courts – are the ICJ, the International Tribunal for the Law of the Sea (ITLOS) arbitral tribunals, and the General Agreement on Tariffs and Trade (GATT)/WTO dispute settlement system.[30] The cases decided through these means are often, but not always, high profile, require attention directly from the highest national authority, and might affect or restrict sovereignty and national policy-making decisions. However, they are very few and far apart. The ICJ decides a few cases per year, the WTO Appellate Body a dozen, and there is, perhaps, one major international arbitration a year. ITLOS has decided only one case on the merits in more than ten years.

For all the hype and excitement that U.S. appearances before the ICJ cause, particularly in the United States, once the dust has settled, rulings have little or no practical effect on its foreign policy. The *Nicaragua* case did not jeopardize U.S. anticommunist activities in Central America. In June 1986, when the ICJ ruled on the case, finding that the United States had violated Nicaragua's sovereignty by carrying and aiding military and paramilitary activities on its territory, the Cold War in Latin American had already turned a corner.[31] Mikhail Gorbachev was announcing the perestroika, and Oscar Arias was bringing to a conclusion the negotiations of the Esquipulas Peace Agreements, which brought an end to the conflicts that had plagued Central America for many years. Libya's case against the United States for the sanctions imposed after the Lockerbie bombing did not go through.[32] Sanctions remained in place until those suspected for the bombing had been tried. It is Libya that changed its policy, not the United States. Again, Yugoslavia did not stop NATO bombs through the ICJ, and the case did not prevent the United States and its

---

[29] *See* Karen Alter, "Delegating to International Courts," *supra* n. 15.
[30] Although states can bring cases against other states in fora such as the IACHR, ECHR, and ECJ, it rarely, if ever, happens in practice.
[31] Military and Paramilitary Activities in and against Nicaragua (*Nicaragua v. United States of America*), Judgment (Merits), I.C.J. Reports 14 (1986).
[32] Questions of Interpretation and Application of the 1971 Montreal Convention Arising from the Aerial Incident at Lockerbie (*Libyan Arab Jamahiriya v. United States of America*). The case, together with the parallel one brought against the United Kingdom, was discontinued at the joint request of the Parties in 2003, after it had crept slowly forward for more than a decade.

allies from achieving their goals during the Kosovo campaign.³³ Likewise, Iran and the United States have wrestled before the ICJ three times in twenty-five years. There is no sign whatsoever that this has altered the diplomatic situation or the balance of power, or given Iran any edge over the United States.³⁴ Albeit the United States lost the case on the merits with Mexico and Germany over the question of the right of foreigners to consular notification, it is not yet clear whether and how this has prejudiced U.S. strategic interests or policy.³⁵ The United States had agreed, a long time before, to notify the consular authorities of those who were arrested, and it routinely did and still does so whenever those effectuating the arrest have a reason to believe they have arrested a foreigner. Probably, law enforcement agents are now more aware and, as a consequence, more willing to verify arrested people's nationality, but this is hardly an attack against U.S. security, sovereignty, interests, culture, lifestyle, or otherwise.³⁶

Arguably, international criminal courts might have greater impact. Although politicians might not lose sleep over decisions of international courts that have no independent enforcement powers but that rely for that on organs of the state they themselves govern, the parade of heads of state being prosecuted and incarcerated might send a chill down their spine. For example, Slobodan Milosevic, the powerful, former president of Yugoslavia who kept in check Western diplomacy for a decade, died in a prison in The Hague while on trial before the ICTY. The once-mighty Charles Taylor was forced to give up power in Liberia and is now awaiting trial before the Special Court for Sierra Leone. As a final example, take Sudan's President Umar Hassan Ahmad al-Bashir, the first ever head of state to be indicted for international crimes while still in power.

One might conclude that there is no longer a limit to the chutzpah of international prosecutors. In a world increasingly hostile to the United States, maybe one day, should the nation ever be so crazy as to accept the jurisdiction

---

33 Legality of Use of Force (*Yugoslavia v. Belgium; Canada; France; Germany; Italy; Netherlands; Portugal; United Kingdom; Spain; United States*), Provisional Measures, Order of 2 June 1999, I.C.J. Reports 124 (1999).
34 United States Diplomatic and Consular Staff in Tehran (*United States v. Iran*), Judgment (Merits), I.C.J. Reports 3 (1980); Aerial Incident of 3 July 1988 (*Islamic Republic of Iran v. United States of America*), Order of 22 February 1996 (discontinuance), I.C.J. Reports 9 (1996); Oil Platforms (*Islamic Republic of Iran v. United States of America*), Judgment (Merits), I. C. J. Reports 161 (2003).
35 *LaGrand (F.R.G. v. United States)*, 1999 I.C.J. 9 (Mar. 3); *Avena and Other Mexican Nationals (Mexico v. United States)*, 2004 I.C.J. 12 (Mar. 31).
36 Carsten Hoppe, *Implementation of LaGrand and Avena in Germany and the United States: Exploring a Transatlantic Divide in Search of a Uniform Interpretation of Consular Rights*, 18 Eur. J. Int'l L. 317 (2007).

of the ICC, a politically motivated prosecutor might investigate decisions of the U.S. political and military leadership. Although the United States could easily thwart prosecution by relying on the many guarantees included in the Rome Statute that would allow democracies and major powers to stop the ICC from proceeding, it could not prevent the prosecutor launching an investigation with the ensuing political fallout that such a step could have on the worldwide stage. As the movie industry – a field dominated by the United States – teaches, any scenario can be conjured.[37]

Yet reality suggests that international prosecutors are wiser – or timider – than that. Carla Del Ponte, the ICTY prosecutor, refused to investigate the U.S.–led NATO bombing campaign over Yugoslavia in 1999, although she had the power to do so.[38] Luis Moreno Ocampo, the ICC prosecutor, has not given any sign of inclination to investigate former Prime Minister Tony Blair, or anyone in the British military and civilian leadership, for the invasion of Iraq, Afghanistan, or anything that happened therein.[39] Prosecutorial action, at the international level, is discretionary but hardly harum-scarum.

In sum, anathemas of extreme opponents notwithstanding, it is hard to find a single ruling of an international court that has caused tangible and significant damage to any *major* power. International courts are not too powerful; if anything, they are not powerful enough.[40]

3. *You Cannot Have International Courts That Are Always on Your Side*

That the United States cannot have international courts that are always on its side should be a platitude. Alas, it is not. As suggested by Sean Murphy, when it comes to foreign affairs, the United States operates on the basis of a fundamental antinomy.[41] On one hand, it is animated by a desire for cooperation with

---

[37] "The Trial of Tony Blair" was being screened in the United Kingdom on January 15, 2007, by Channel Four. The same channel previously presented a drama on U.S. President George W. Bush being assassinated. See http://www2.irna.ir/en/news/view/menu-234/0701082293185740.htm.

[38] Final Report to the Prosecutor by the Committee Established to Review the NATO Bombing Campaign against the Federal Republic of Yugoslavia (June 13, 2000), at http://www.un.org/icty/.

[39] "Lawyers Sue Blair over War," *BBC News*, July 28, 2003, at http://news.bbc.co.uk/2/hi/europe/3101697.stm; "Blair 'War Crimes' Case Launched," *BBC News*, Mar. 2, 2004, at http://news.bbc.co.uk/2/hi/uk_news/politics/3524133.stm.

[40] On the limits of international courts, *see generally* Yuval Shany, "No Longer a Weak Department of Power? Reflections on the Emergence of a New International Judiciary," 20 Eur. J. of Int. L. (2009).

[41] *See supra* Murphy, Chapter 4 of this volume.

other states as equal sovereigns; indeed, the United States distinguishes itself by its strong predisposition for international law and its institutions and a certain legalistic approach to international relations. Yet at the same time, it has innate historical and cultural characteristics that push it toward "exceptionalism," claiming itself entitled, formally and informally, to be treated differently from other nations.[42]

It supports international criminal courts because they provide means that are relatively politically low cost to satisfy calls for accountability – from within the national electorate and the international community – for major international crimes. Yet it does so only when the U.S. government has, or is perceived by its officials to have, a significant degree of control over the court or where the possibility of prosecution of nationals is either expressly precluded or otherwise remote. International criminal courts are good only for everyone else, for the United States is hostile to the idea of having violations of the laws of war by its own military forces subject to third-party adjudication by any international or foreign court (arguably, during the G. W. Bush administration, by its own courts, as well).[43]

The United States believes itself to have one of the best, if not the best, constitutional systems for guaranteeing of human rights and fundamental freedoms; therefore, it sees little need for any external backup or second-guessing system, especially one that is not subject to the check of the American voters.[44] At the same time, it is acutely aware that democracy and human rights have not yet been firmly entrenched in most states of the world and believes it has a mission to spread them. Accordingly, it fosters and welcomes human rights courts and a large array of quasi-adjudicatory expert committees exercising supervisory jurisdiction, but it approaches them mostly as a one-way road, as tools to influence the conduct of other nations rather than instruments to affect internal change.

Finally, there seems to be also a sense – probably also shared by a vocal part of the population[45] – that any international court composed mostly of foreign judges, where the United States has no right of veto, could not possibly correctly apply the law and decide a case involving the United States fairly.[46] At the same time, the United States prides itself for providing the world with first-class judges who will invariably apply the law correctly and decide a case involving other nations fairly.

---

[42] See supra Preface to this volume, n. 7.
[43] See supra Cerone, Chapter 6 of this volume.
[44] See supra Abi-Mershed, Chapter 7 of this volume, and Melish, Chapter 8 of this volume.
[45] Yet Kull and Ramsey (see Chapter 2 in this book) suggest this might not be the attitude of the majority of the U.S. population.
[46] See, e.g., José E. Alvarez, "Judicialization and Its Discontents," supra n. 4.

Justice Robert H. Jackson of the U.S Supreme Court, in his first address to the American Society of International Law, in 1945, provided the best reply to this nonsensical attitude:

> It is futile to think, as extreme nationalists do, that we can have an international law that is always working on our side. And it is futile to think that we can have international courts that will always render the decisions we want to promote our interests. We cannot successfully cooperate with the rest of the world in establishing a reign of law unless we are prepared to have that law sometimes operate against what would be our national advantage. In our internal affairs we have come to rely upon the judicial process to settle individual controversies and grievances and even those between states of the Union, not because courts always render right judgments, but because the consequences of wrong or unwise decisions are not nearly so evil as the anarchy which results from having no way to obtain any decision of such questions; in which case each will take the law into his own hands. And in a somewhat similar sporting spirit we must look upon any international tribunal, not as one whose decision always will be welcome or always right or wise. But the worst settlement of international disputes by adjudication or arbitration is likely to be less disastrous to the loser and certainly less destructive to the world than no way of settlement except war.[47]

Granted, Jackson was a unique Supreme Court Justice, the only one ever to have acquired an insider's knowledge of an international court, having served as chief U.S. prosecutor at the Nuremberg trials.[48] Considering the diffidence a majority of judges of the U.S. Supreme Court seems to have toward international courts nowadays, it is hard to believe any could utter something like this.[49]

4. International Courts, and the Services They Render, Are Global Public Goods

Justice Jackson reminds us that the wise policy is the one that reconciles the short-term need to avoid tactical legal defeat in court on any given case, with the

---

[47] *"A Decent Respect to the Opinions of Mankind...": Selected Speeches by Justices of the U.S. Supreme Court on Foreign International Law* (Christopher Borgen ed., ASIL, 2007), 40.
[48] See Robert H. Jackson, The Nürnberg Case as presented by Robert H. Jackson, chief of counsel for the United States, together with other documents. (Cooper Square, 1947).
[49] More troubling still, José Alvarez recently dismally concluded that "any U.S. judge today who would dare to suggest that she (much less her fellow U.S. citizens) should be bound by 'supra-national' law as found by an international court, especially when these decisions are not in accord with the immediate 'national interest,' would likely find herself target of an impeachment campaign – or at least the subject of a Congressional inquiry and a media circus." See Alvarez, *Judicialization and Its Discontents*, supra n. 4.

long-term benefits of having a respected and effective system of international adjudication in place. In a way, Jackson reminds us that the services that international courts produce – that is, the settlement of a dispute, but also the judgment itself, which adds to the body of international law – are public goods.[50] In particular they are "global public goods," goods whose benefits reach across borders, generations, and population groups, like the ozone layer, the earth climate, or global financial stability.[51]

Narrow instrumental approaches to international courts pay way too little attention to the important positive externalities of international courts and their activity. For instance, in 1995, Venezuela (later joined by Brazil) complained to the WTO Dispute Settlement Body that the United States applied stricter rules on the chemical characteristics of imported gasoline than it did for domestically refined gasoline. By 1997, the dispute had been resolved.[52] A purely instrumental approach would carefully measure how many millions of dollars it cost the United States to implement the report of the dispute settlement body and how much, if anything, because it lost the case, it gained. However, one could also consider that by settling the dispute, the WTO dispute settlement machinery might have defused escalation, averting a larger and more expensive retaliatory spiral that would have, directly or indirectly, harmed the United States and several other nations. Or one could also consider the precedential value of the report issued by the WTO Appellate Body in that case, which set new standards for interpretation of WTO law, thereby affecting all present and future WTO members.[53]

---

[50] "Public goods" are those for which the use by one person does not reduce availability for others (nonrivalrous), and, once created, it is impossible (or too costly) to exclude third parties from their benefits (nonexcludable). A textbook example of a public good is a street sign. It will not wear out, even if large numbers of people are looking at it; and it would be extremely difficult, costly, and highly inefficient to limit its use to only one or a few persons and try to prevent others from looking at it, too. Conversely, *private* goods are both excludable and rivalrous. I can buy a cake and have exclusive property rights over it (excludable). Once I have eaten it, no one else can enjoy that same cake (rivalrous). Paul A. Samuelson, *The Pure Theory of Public Expenditure*, 36 R. of Econ. Statistics 387 (Nov. 1954); Paul A. Samuelson, *A Diagrammatic Exposition of a Theory of Public Expenditure*, 37 R. Econ. Statistics 350 (Nov. 1955). International courts and their jurisprudence are highly nonrivalrous goods because their use does not decrease – and perhaps even increases – their availability. They are also highly nonexcludable.

[51] *See* Inge Kaul, Isabelle Grunberg, and Marc A. Stern, "Defining Global Public Goods," in *Global Public Goods: International Cooperation in the 21st Century* (Oxford, 1999), 2–19; William Nordhaus, *Managing the Global Commons: The Economics of Change* (MIT, 1994). An excellent early study surveying the area is Todd Sandler, *Global Challenges: An Approach to Environmental, Political, and Economic Problems* (Cambridge, 1997). *See also Global Public Goods: International Cooperation in the 21st Century* (Inge Kaul, Isabelle Grunberg, and Marc A. Stern eds., Oxford, 1999).

[52] *U.S. – Gasoline* (WT/DS2/AB/R).

[53] "The general rule of interpretation [as set out in Article 31(1) of the Vienna Convention on the Law of Treaties] has attained the status of a rule of customary or general international

There are even greater imponderable, but momentous, benefits. International courts "socialize" states to the idea of international adjudication.[54] The multiplication of international tribunals with specialized and regional competence experienced since the end of the Cold War has gradually enabled governments – many of which are of developing countries, some of which are not quite democratic – to experiment with and observe the effects of international adjudication. Processes of persuasion and acculturation, and learning by doing, might explain why there are certain countries that resort to some judicial bodies more often than others, but it is clear that the more states – at all latitudes and of all kinds – resort to international adjudication, the less reluctant they seem to become to the idea – the United States being an egregious exception.[55]

The United States stands to benefit from the judicialization of international relations even when it opts out of it or when it takes place elsewhere. For example, the Court of Arbitration of the Organization for the Harmonization of Business Law in Africa (OHADA), an African regional court, helps ensure that domestic courts of several African countries will enforce multilaterally negotiated rules regarding foreign direct investment, including those of American companies.[56] Again, U.S. corporations are understandably concerned about reaping the benefits of their research and development and want international intellectual property rules respected. That is what they get from some regional courts. The overwhelming majority of cases decided by the Andean Court of Justice are about ensuring that Andean countries (Ecuador, Bolivia,

---

law. As such, it forms part of the 'customary rules of interpretation of public international law,' which the Appellate Body has been directed, by Article 3(2) of the [Dispute Settlement Understanding], to apply in seeking to clarify the provisions of the *General Agreement* and the other 'covered agreements' of the *Marrakesh Agreement Establishing the World Trade Organization* (the '*WTO Agreement*'). That direction reflects a measure of recognition that the *General Agreement* is not to be read in clinical isolation from public international law." *U.S. – Gasoline*, p. 17, DSR 1996:I, p. 3 at 16. (WT/DS2/AB/R). *See generally* Joost Pauwelyn, *Conflict of Norms in Public International Law: How WTO Law Relates to Other Rules of International Law* (Cambridge, 2003).

[54] On the "socializing effects" of international litigation, *see generally* Thomas Buergenthal, *Proliferation of International Courts and Tribunals: Is It Good or Bad?* 14 Leiden J. Int'l L. 267 (2001).

[55] On the role of persuasion and acculturation (as opposed to coercion) in socializing states, *see generally* Rayan Goodman and Derek Jinks, *Socializing States: Promoting Human Rights through International Law* (Oxford, 2009). On trends in international dispute settlement and patterns of utilization, particular by developing countries, *see* Cesare Romano, *International Justice and Developing Countries: A Quantitative Analysis*, 1 Law and Practice of International Courts and Tribunals 367 (2002). On the effect of "learning-by-doing," *see* Cesare Romano, *International Justice and Developing Countries (cont.): A Qualitative Analysis*, 1 Law and Practice of International Courts and Tribunals (2002), 575–576, at 539.

[56] Boris Martor, *Business Law in Africa: OHADA and the Harmonization Process* (2nd ed., GMB, 2007).

Colombia, and Peru) respect international intellectual property rules.[57] Likewise, U.S. corporations do not want to be discriminated against by foreign regulatory decisions (e.g., antidumping, countervailing duties, antitrust). The ECJ provides checks that American individuals or companies can activate to challenge the legality of decisions both of the European Community organs and its several member States that could, and sometimes, do jeopardize American interests. When human rights of American citizens are violated by foreign governments, international courts might be able to provide a form of redress that would be otherwise unavailable or that would require the U.S. government to spend considerable political capital to exercise diplomatic protection. Indeed, the United States' refusal to accept the jurisdiction of the IACHR notwithstanding, Americans brought cases before that court to challenge actions by Latin American governments that have jeopardized their human rights.[58] Less known and publicized is the fact that Americans could, and actually have, brought cases before the ECHR.[59]

5. *Easy-Riding Will Cost You*

Yet one might object that, if the United States stands to benefit from the judicialization of international relations even when it opts out of it or it takes place elsewhere, then why should it have greater and deeper engagement with international courts?[60]

---

[57] *See* Laurence Helfer, Karen Alter, and Florencia Guerzovich, *Islands of Effective International Adjudication: Constructing an Intellectual Property Rule of Law in the Andean Community*, 109 Am. J. Int'l L. (2009).

[58] E.g., *Case of Lori Berenson Mejía vs. Perú*, Judgment of November 25, 2004, I/A Court H. R. (Ser. C), No. 119 (2004).

[59] E.g., *Case of Quinn v. France*, Judgment (Merits and Just Satisfaction) 22/03/1995; *Case of Custers Deveaux and Turk v. Denmark*, Judgment (Merits) 03/05/2007; *Case of Medenica v. Switzerland*, Judgment (Merits) 14/06/2001; *Case of Hartman v. Czech Republic*, Judgment (Merits and Just Satisfaction) 10/07/2003.

[60] The free-rider problem (or easy-rider problem, if the consumer's contribution is small but nonzero) is the crux of the public good theory. Public goods cannot be created by market forces alone. Because public goods are nonexcludable, they provide benefits equally to those who bear the costs of producing the good and those who do not. The most rational strategy for a utility-maximizing individual (the free-rider or the easy-rider) is to let others go first and seek to enjoy the good without contributing to its production. Utility-maximizing individuals would not serve in a jury. The cost in terms of time can be high and the duty can be taxing. The direct benefits of participating and making juries possible are low because they would be distributed among all of the millions of other people in the country. Knowing that an individual cannot be excluded from the benefits of trial by jury, regardless of whether he or she ever sat or will ever sit in a jury, the free rider would not serve. However, if everyone free rides, public goods are never produced or are not produced in the necessary quantity. The free-rider problem can be resolved only through some sort of collective-action mechanisms (e.g., the government

There is a price to be paid for easy-riding on these international public goods. The more that international courts shape and make international law, the less the United States is going to be able to influence it and steer the direction of development of this new "international common law."[61] By being indifferent, if not hostile, to the rise of international courts on the international scene, the United States is giving up the driving role it has played since World War II in international institutions that shape international law. To put it simply, easy riders sit in the backseat; they do not steer.

During the past decade, the ECHR has become the driving engine of human rights law on a global scale. Relying on a massive jurisprudence of several hundreds of cases per year, many of which tackle unprecedented issues, the Strasburg court is de facto writing much of international human rights law of the twenty-first century. Its precedents are cited not only by all other international courts and human rights bodies but also by national courts outside Europe. As a matter of fact, it can be argued that the ECHR's influence is on the way to replace the U.S. Supreme Court as the democratic world's legal beacon on civil rights issues.[62] Had the United States a long-term strategy on international courts, it would try to foster the growth of the IACHR into an equally authoritative voice to balance the European choir across the Atlantic.

It is not far-fetched to imagine that, should the ICC establish itself as an effective and authoritative court, its jurisprudence might become the central voice on international criminal law – an area of international law where the United States has strategic stakes. Strengthened by its permanent nature and by acceptance by a majority of the countries of the world, including a majority of countries in each continent but Asia, it will stand in the field taller than any other international criminal body. It does not have any credible rival. It will stand taller than any hybrid court, the impact of which on international law is diminished by the fact that each speaks a vernacular made of a mix

---

adopting and enforcing laws that make jury duty compulsory), forcing free-riders to bear their fair share of the cost of producing the good.

The crucial difference between public goods at the national level and at the international level is that nationally there are governments that can authoritatively intervene to ensure the production of the good. They control all factors that determine availability and quality of the public goods. However, at the international level, largely lacking an authoritative supra-national authority, public goods can only be produced (or protected from destruction, if they are naturally occurring) by way of international cooperation and, crucially, only if all major actors are better off as a result.

[61] Andrew Guzman and Timothy Meyer, "International Common Law: The Soft-Law of International Tribunals," U.C. Berkeley Public Law Research Paper No. 1267446 (2008). Brown used this same expression, but more narrowly, referring to common procedures between various international courts and tribunals. Chester Brown, *A Common Law of International Adjudication* (Oxford University Press, 2007).

[62] Adam Liptak, "U.S. Court Is Now Guiding Fewer Nations," *New York Times*, Sept. 18, 2008.

of international and local laws; taller than the ICTR and ICTY, which are in the process of being discontinued; taller than any other ad hoc court the United Nations might establish, should the UN ever find again the concord necessary to do so; and definitively taller than the U.S. Supreme Court, the influence of which on courts around the world is steadily declining. It is exactly the realization that this might happen that led George W. Bush's administration to oppose aggressively the creation of the ICC, but it is also the realization that the Court is here to stay and the United States cannot single-handedly stop it that led, eventually, to milder tactics. Still, it is not yet enough. The United States needs to get on the bus, preferably in a front seat.

By shunning international courts, the United States is renouncing its authority to shape the international courts of the twenty-first century, and American legal discourse and structures are giving way to European archetypes. In particular, the success of European economic and political integration has provided a model for most regional integration schemes around the world. Additionally, as the ECJ is celebrated for having been able to keep European integration on track, sometimes in the teeth of political opposition, it should be no wonder that nowadays most regional economic and political integration endeavors feature at their core a judicial institution that, to varying degrees, mimics the ECJ. The list is remarkable, including the periphery of Europe (e.g., Economic Court of the Commonwealth of Independent States and the European Free Trade Area Court of Justice); Latin America and the Caribbean (Court of Justice of the Andean Community, and, to a certain extent, the Caribbean Court of Justice); and Africa (Court of Justice of the Common Market for Eastern and Southern Africa, Court of Justice of the Economic Community of West African States, Court of Justice of the Economic and Monetary Community of Central Africa, Arab Maghreb Union Judicial Authority, and, last but not the least considering it is probably the closest to the ECJ template, the African Court of Justice). Only in South America, in the Mercosur, is the dispute settlement template favored by the United States that stresses arbitration in favor of permanent judicial institutions resisting. Yet the creation of the Permanent Review Tribunal of the Mercosur in 2002 signals that states of the southern cone are veering toward the permanent and fully judicialized model preferred by the Europeans and away from the à la carte model preferred by the United States.[63]

Missing out on the opportunity to mold international courts on familiar American templates is not the only price that United States pays for riding in the

---

[63] The Olivos Protocol for the Settlement of Disputes in Mercosur, art. 33, Feb. 18, 2002, 42 ILM 2 (2003). *See generally* Raúl Emilio Vinuesa, *The MERCOSUR Settlement of Disputes System*, 5 Law and Practice of International Courts and Tribunals 77 (2006).

backseat. There are more tangible costs. For instance, by its foreswearing of the ICC, the United States opened the way for the court to be eventually located at The Hague, reinforcing the quasi-monopoly that that European town has on major international judicial institutions. Nowadays, The Hague boasts that it is the "Legal Capital of the World."[64] Hosting major international institutions on one's own territory provides considerable diplomatic and economic advantages and a few minor drawbacks. As a matter of fact, toward the end of World War II, the United States insisted on, and obtained, headquartering the new, major international organizations emerging from the conflict, including the United Nations, the World Bank, the International Monetary Fund, and the Organization of American States.[65] Think what New York or Washington, D.C., would be without those institutions and the business they bring with them.

However, that is not the only thing that the United States lost when it turned its back on the ICC and the new court was pushed out of the United Nations, to be created as a self-standing international organization. The ICC became the first international organization operating on a global scale to have a budget in euros and not in U.S. dollars, a harbinger of the beginning of the end of predominance of the U.S. dollar as the only truly world currency.[66]

6. *If You Do Not Understand Your Instruments, You Risk Blunting Them Unnecessarily*

If international courts are instruments to serve its national interest, then U.S. decision makers need to conceptualize them correctly to avoid blunting them unnecessarily. International courts are peculiar instruments. Trying to explain why any government would favor establishing an effective independent international court, social scientists have argued that Principals (i.e., "States") delegate decision making to Agents (i.e., "international courts") because they know that their recontracting powers will keep the agent within their comfort zone of acceptable jurisprudential outcomes.[67] Yet, as Karen

---

[64] See, e.g., *The Hague: Legal Capital of the World* (Peter J. van Krieken ed., T.M.C. Asser, 2005); David Vriesendorp, *The Hague Legal Capital?: Liber In Honorem W.J. Deetman* (Hauge, 2008). See also "The Hague Justice Portal" http://www.haguejusticeportal.net/.

[65] *See generally* Robert Hilderbrand, *Dumbarton Oaks: The Origins of the United Nations and the Search for Postwar Security* (University of North Carolina, 1990).

[66] International Criminal Court, *Financial Regulations and Rules*, adopted by the Assembly of States Parties, First session, New York, September 3–10, 2002 (ICC-ASP/1/3), Regulation 3.2.

[67] Under the Principal-Agent theory, one party (the Principal) delegates to another (the Agent) performance of a task that the Principal cannot do by itself, or can do only at too high a cost. The fundamental problem any Principal faces is how to ensure that the Agent, whose desires or wishes might differ, remains faithful to the mandate and does not deviate. Principals will

Alter convincingly argued, courts of law, including international courts, are better understood as "Trustees" rather than "Agents."[68] Agents are chosen because they are expected to be faithful to the Principal; they have *delegated authority* based on the Principal having authorized the Agent to act within a certain domain. Trustees are instead chosen because either they personally or their profession in general brings their own source of legitimacy and authority.[69] Indeed, in addition to delegated authority, trustees have *moral authority* that comes from embodying or serving some shared higher ideals; their moral status as a defender of these ideals provides the basis for their authority. Trustees have *rational-legal authority* to the extent they apply pre-existing rules impartially in a like fashion across a body of cases, thereby imparting a perception of procedural justice and neutral fairness in their decisions.[70] Trustees are chosen by Principals exactly because either their persona or their profession in general provides a source of legitimacy and authority. Yet, arguably, the legitimacy and authority of international courts are not a given and a constant. They can increase over time, usually at a slow pace. The more a court is resorted to, and the higher the degree of compliance with its rulings, the greater the perceived legitimacy and its authority. However, legitimacy and authority can be equally reduced when states neglect courts by refusing to submit to, or withdrawing from, their jurisdiction or when they attack, on political and legal grounds, the decision once it has been rendered.

One would expect the Principal to have an interest in seeing the legitimacy and authority of Trustees increase. If courts are instruments of the Principal, then the Principal might want to keep them sharp for when they are needed. This should hold true even if the Principal contracts Trustees only occasionally or even just wants to keep the option open. Only those who rule out ever resorting to an international court would deliberately try to undermine their legitimacy and authority. Yet when in the United States the decisions of the ICJ are rejected by prominent public voices as politically motivated, illegitimate, morally dubious, or plainly, legally wrong, the authority of the court is reduced. When Congress considers legislation to create an ad hoc body to track rulings of the WTO Appellate Body and, should the United States lose too many

---

nonetheless contract Agents, because they have the power to sanction the Agent by changing the terms of the contract (e.g., firing or not reappointing the Agent, rewriting contractual terms to undercut the Agent's realm of authority, or cutting the Agent's budget). For a primer on the Principal-Agent theory, *see* Norman E. Bowie and R. Edward Freeman, *Ethics and Agency Theory: An Introduction* (Oxford, 1992); Joseph E. Stiglitz, "Principal and Agent," in 3 *The New Palgrave: A Dictionary of Economics* (Palgrave Macmillan, 1987), 966.

[68] Karen Alter, *Agents or Trustees? International Courts in their Political Context*, 14 Euro. J. Int'l Rel. 33 (2008).
[69] *Ibid.*, at 39–40.
[70] *Ibid.*

cases, be able to withdraw the United States from the WTO, legitimacy of the dispute settlement system is reduced. When the United States argues that it will not accept the jurisdiction of the ICC because, despite the fact that it can effectively block any prosecution against its own citizens, it is concerned by politically motivated investigations that an anti-American prosecutor might initiate, it puts in doubt both the moral and the rational-legal authority of the court.

States have available a fairly large range of tools to regulate ("recontract," in principal/agent theory parlance) overreaching in international courts.[71] Some operate *ex ante*, before any given case is decided, such as precisely defining interpretive methodologies or standards of review in the court's constitutive treaties. Others can be deployed *ex post*, such as renegotiation of a court's jurisdiction or procedural rules, or forum shopping to tribunals with competing jurisdictions. Some are formal and structural; others are political. The matrix is complex, but the trustee/principal theory seems to suggest that modes of contestation that are rhetorical, persuasive, and jurisprudentially based, as opposed to delegitimizing, material, or threatening (the modes of choice of the United States during much of the past decade) are less likely to produce long-term deleterious effects on the targeted international court and the international judicial system as a whole, making it possible for the United States to rely on strong and legitimate international courts if and when needed.

There are also some powerful internal constraints that limit the possibility of international judges going rogue. Indeed, international judges are typically more concerned about their reputation and maintaining their authority – personal and of their profession – than they are about displeasing governments, however powerful and influential they might be. Granted, international courts and their judges are not apolitical or immune from pressure. They are susceptible to all sorts of legitimacy and rhetorical prods. Logically, relying on sovereign states and their organs to execute their decisions, they necessarily worry about maintaining their support.[72] However, international judges understand that Principals (states) contracted them as Trustees exactly because they have moral authority that comes from embodying or serving some shared higher ideals, and rational-legal authority that comes from their impartiality and loyalty to the law. If they neglect those ideals and start applying law in a way that might be perceived as biased, or as a cave-in to states' pressure, they undermine their own rationale. Some judges might be inclined to use the

---

[71] *See* Laurence R. Helfer, "Why States Create International Tribunals: A Theory of Constrained Independence," 23 *Conferences on New Political Economy* (Mohr Siebeck, 2006), 265–72.
[72] *See generally* Daniel Terris, Cesare Romano, and Leigh Swigart, *The International Judge: An Introduction to the Men and Women Who Decide the World's Cases* (Oxford, 2007), 147–79.

bench to do politics and not serve the law, but systemic bias of a whole court, or group of courts, as some critics of international courts in the United States seem to suggest, smacks of paranoia and is hardly believable.

7. *The United States Needs International Courts, and International Courts Need the United States*

What is more likely to happen is that the generally antipathetic U.S. attitude toward international courts might induce international judges to have less reason to tread with care when it comes to American interests. When given the chance, international judges might be tempted to use the bench to lecture the United States. Truth be told, international courts have their own level of responsibility for the current troubled relationship with the United States. Not all criticism leveled against them by the United States is unfounded. The process of selection/election/nomination of international judges is opaque – perhaps too much to stomach for the United States, a country that is accustomed to electing some of its judges, and to having those who are appointed undergo fierce public scrutiny. International judges often act as if their independence and impartiality are a dogma rather than something that can, and should be, legitimately questioned. The United States has been seeking greater transparency of international judicial proceedings and public participation (at the WTO, in the North American Free Trade Agreement, at the ICJ) and has often been baffled by finding resistance both from other states and the courts themselves.

It is also difficult to deny that certain countries have tactically used international courts to harass, embarrass, and influence the United States. The use of courts by adversaries of the United States is understandable; use by allies, however, is more questionable. In recent years, Mexico has used the ICJ and the IACHR to chastise the United States' treatment of Mexican nationals – with little practical effect but with the result of further alienating the United States from international courts.[73] The EC has similarly used international tribunals on occasion to score easy political points against the United States. For example, in response to the United States' successful challenges at the WTO of the EC's bananas regime, the EC started a case at the WTO against the United States that it was virtually certain to win (and where it would be

---

[73] *Avena and Other Mexican Nationals (Mexico v. United States of America)*, *supra* n. 38; Request for Interpretation of the Judgment of March 31, 2004 in the Case Concerning Avena and Other Mexican Nationals (*Mexico v. United States*); The Right to Information on Consular Assistance in the Framework of the Guarantees of the Due Process of Law, Advisory Opinion, Inter-Am Ct. H.R. (Ser. A) No. 16 (Oct. 1, 1999); Juridical Condition and Rights of the Undocumented Migrants, Advisory Opinion, Inter-Am Ct. H.R. (Ser. A) No. 18 (Sept. 17, 2003).

politically difficult for the United States to comply with an adverse ruling), largely in an effort to bolster domestic support for the WTO dispute system and to gain easy bargaining chips to be used in other WTO disputes where its hand was not that strong.[74]

It is a vicious circle. Negative U.S. attitudes lower the incentives that international courts have to tread carefully when U.S. interests are at stake. This, in turn, gives more voice to opponents and further alienates the United States from the process, leading to harsher criticism down the line. Its military and economic preponderance and unilateralist stance force other nations to try to find alternative ways to challenge it, but the United States, having little confidence in these mechanisms and in its own capacity to control them, resents it.

The circle must be broken. It is in everyone's interest. The United States needs international courts; and even if this notion is rejected, the truth is that, for all the unilateralist rhetoric, it cannot completely disengage from the system, remaining exposed to litigation it cannot effectively control. In turn, international courts suffer from U.S. lack of interest or even hostility because they cannot rely on the legitimization and borrowed clout they could have with the largest and most powerful democracy of the world accepting their jurisdiction. Nor can they count on the material and diplomatic assets that the United States can make available to them to carry out their respective missions.

International courts need more support and engagement than the United States is currently willing to provide.[75] To illustrate, the hostility of the United States toward the ICC affects its capacity in multiple ways. It denies it the possibility to count on American financial support, which limits its resources.

---

[74] In 1999, the European Union challenged the Foreign Sales Corporation provisions of U.S. tax law as a violation of the Uruguay Round Code on Subsidies & Countervailing Measures (*United States – Tax Treatment for "Foreign Sales Corporations,"* DS108). This was a surprise to the United States because the tax treatment for foreign sales corporations had not been challenged during the course of the Uruguay Round negotiations.

[75] In March 2009, an Independent Task Force convened by the American Society of International Law to assess attitudes and behaviors of the United States toward the ICC recommended that "the President take prompt steps to announce a policy of continued positive engagement with the Court, including: a stated policy of the U.S. Government's intention, notwithstanding its letter of May 6, 2002 to the U.N. Secretary General [i.e., the un-signing of the Rome Statute], to support the object and purpose of the Rome Statute of the Court; examination of methods by which the United States can support important criminal investigations of the Court, including cooperation on the arrest of fugitive defendants, the provision of diplomatic support, and the sharing of information, as well as ways in which it can cooperate with the Court in the prevention and deterrence of genocide, war crimes, and crimes against humanity." Independent Task Force, *U.S. Policy toward the International Criminal Court: Furthering Positive Engagement* (ASIL, 2009), available at http://www.asil.org.

That, in turn, makes the ICC overwhelmingly dependent on financial support from EU member states, thwarting its universal aspirations. It undermines efforts to expand ICC jurisdiction to countries that the United States might arguably have an interest in having subject to a permanent mechanism of accountability for war crimes and crimes against humanity (e.g., Indonesia, Syria, Iran, Sudan, Eritrea, Zimbabwe, but also geostrategic rivals such as Russia and China). It denies the ICC and its investigators the diplomatic power that they need to investigate crimes in countries whose governments are unwilling to cooperate. It denies the transport, intelligence gathering, and protection capacities of its military and governmental agencies. It is simple. One just needs to look at what difference active U.S. support of the ICTY, ICTR, and Special Court for Sierra Leone has made to start appreciating how much difference U.S. endorsement of the ICC could make.

Between the historical lows that the U.S. attitude toward international courts has reached since the end of the Cold War, and in particular since September 11, and the attitude the United States could have, given its power, role, history, culture, and constitutional structure, there is much room for maneuver. America needs change the world can believe in, to paraphrase President Obama's campaign slogan, on many issues, including international courts. It is becoming increasingly apparent that what Americans call a realist attitude is perceived around the world as a cynical one; what Americans call pragmatism is perceived as callousness and egotism; that à la carte commitment betrays insecurity; and that American exceptionalism and sense of mission come across as odious arrogance. Benignant support of international courts – and the ideals of peace, justice, and equality they stand for – is a practical, effective, low-cost, and low-risk way to reassure the world that the United States still stands by those ideals and is ready to lead the way as it did for the second half of the twentieth century.

Index

Abolitionism, 33–34
Abortion
  American Convention on Human Rights
    and, 200, 271–272
  human rights courts and treaties and,
    271–272
  insulationism and, 262
Abu Ghraib scandal, 27–28, 157–158
Accountability in international criminal
  tribunals, 180
Acheson, Dean, 330
Adams, Charles Francis, 35
Addams, Jane, 30–31, 41–43, 44
Ad hoc tribunals *versus* permanent courts,
  422–423
Advisory opinions
  IACHR (*See* Inter-American Court of
    Human Rights (IACHR))
  ICJ, 4, 74, 79, 80, 83–85
African Court of Human and People's Rights,
  160–161, 425–426
African Court of Justice, 438
African Union, 160–161
Agent and Principal analogy, 439–442
Alabama Claims Arbitration, 34–37
Albright, Madeleine, 144
Alfaro, Richard, 136
Algiers Accords, 302–303, 304–306
Alter, Karen, 439–440
Ambivalence of US toward international
  courts
  generally, 431–433
  human rights courts and treaties, 210–212,
    222–223, 235
  NAFTA, dispute resolution under, 357
American Bar Association (ABA), 189–190
American Convention on Human Rights

abortion and, 200, 271–272
Article 4, 200–201
Article 28, 201–202
Article 64, 196–198
Article 74, 198
Article 75, 198
death penalty and, 200–201
drafting of, 187–188
enforceability, 206
federalism and, 201–202
future trends, 283–284
IACHR advisory opinions regarding,
  191–192, 193, 198–199
obstacles to US ratification, 200–202
prospects for US ratification, 189–191
signing by US, 226–227
American Declaration of the Rights and
  Duties of Man
adoption of, 187
commitments of US under, 268
complaints under, 243
death penalty and, 206–207
enforceability, 206
IACHR advisory opinions regarding,
  191–193, 196–198
OAS Charter and, 223–224
participation of US under, 245
American Federation of Labor and Congress
  of Industrial Organizations
  (AFL-CIO), 406
American Fellowship of Reconciliation, 41–42
American Peace Society (APS), 33–34
American Servicemembers' Protection Act
  (ASPA), 154–155, 163, 164–165, 166–167
Americans Talk Issues Foundation (ATIF), 16
Americans Talk Security (ATS), 14, 15
American Union Against Militarism, 43

Andean Community, 363–364
Andean Court of Justice, 435–436, 438
Annan, Kofi, 171
Anti-Dumping Act of 1916, 352
Antidumping cases. *See* North American Free Trade Agreement (NAFTA)
Anti-Imperialist League, 38–39
Anti-legalism, 336–337
Arab Maghreb Union Judicial Authority, 438
Arbitration, 30–45. *See also* Dispute resolution tribunals
  Alabama Claims Arbitration, 34–37
  bilateral agreements, 40–41
  decline of, 44–45
  generally, 30–31
  NAFTA, under
    government-to-government disputes under, 387
    investment disputes under, 367, 396–398
  pragmatism and, 41
  St. Croix River Arbitration, 31–32, 297
Argentina
  realism *versus* institutionalism in, 52
Autonomous national law, 48–49, 55–57
Avena case
  death penalty in, 3
  generally, 48
  horizontal dialogue and, 119–120
  IACHR and, 195, 196
  ICJ and, 85–96, 127–129
  procedural default rule and, 116, 122–123, 124–125
  "respectful consideration" and, 122
  vertical dialogue and, 125–128, 129

Baker, James, 315–316, 318
Bámaca, Efraín, 205
Bani-Sadr, Abolhassan, 300
Bashir, Umar Hassan al-, 430
Bayer, 311
Beauvais, Joel, 405–406
Been, Vicki, 405–406
Bellinger, John, 161–162, 163, 182–183, 419–421
Berenson, Lori, 205
Bettauer, Ron, 316–317
Bhala, Raj, 416–417
Biddle, Francis, 138
bin Laden, Osama, 18
Blair, Tony, 431
Blake, Nicholas Chapman, 205
BMW, 311

Board of Economic Warfare, 325
Bolton, John, 149, 150–151, 152, 156, 166
Bosnia and Herzegovina
  Bosnian War Crimes Chambers, 178
Boston Redevelopment Authority, 402, 403–404
Bradley, Curtis, 404
Brazil
  WTO and, 351–352, 434
Breard, Angel, 114–115
Breard case
  death penalty in, 3, 114–115
  generally, 48
  horizontal dialogue and, 122
  IACHR and, 195
  ICJ and, 85–96
  procedural default rule and, 126–128
  vertical dialogue and, 125, 129
Breyer, Stephen, 88–89, 113
Bricker Amendment, 256–257
Brooks, Preston, 33–34
Brower, Charles, 412
Brown, John, 33–34
Buergenthal, Thomas, 2–3, 201, 204
Bulgaria
  ICJ cases involving, 66
Bulloch, James, 34–35
Burritt, Elihu, 34
Bush, George H. W.
  human rights courts and treaties and, 223–224, 226–227
  ICC and, 437–438
  UNCC and, 315–316
Bush, George W.
  American Servicemembers' Protection Act and, 154–155
  change of leadership from, 421–422
  hostility toward international courts, 432
  human rights courts and treaties and, 223–224, 226–227, 231, 291
  ICC and, 156–157, 158–159, 166
  ICJ and, 6, 93–94, 196
  realism of, 50–51
  Rome Statute and, 150–151, 152
  SCSL and, 168, 173–174
  War on Terror, preoccupation with, 321
Bustillo, Mario, 117
Byrd Amendment, 352

California Holocaust Victim Insurance Relief Act, 314
Calvo Clause, 364–365
Cambodia

Extraordinary Chambers in the Courts of
    Cambodia, 132, 174–178, 427
Khmer Rouge, 175
Canada
    consent to ICJ jurisdiction, 61–62
    Gulf of Maine case, 3, 70–71
    ICJ cases involving, 3, 70–71
    International Joint Commission and, 40
    NAFTA and, 350
    non-self-execution clauses in, 287–288
    U.S.-Canada Free Trade Agreement
        (CFTA), 357, 363–364, 375–377,
        385–386
    WTO and, 350
Capital punishment
    American Convention on Human Rights
        and, 200–201
    IACHR and, 194
    ICJ and, 3, 85–96
    juveniles and, 206–207
Caribbean Court of Justice, 426–427, 438
Carnegie, Andrew, 43
Carter, Jimmy
    human rights courts and treaties and,
        226–227
    IACHR and, 189
    institutionalism of, 50–51
    Iran hostage crisis and, 299–300
    Iran-U.S. Claims Tribunal and, 304
Cassel, Douglass, 208
Catholics for Christian Political Action,
    271–272
Catt, Carrie Chapman, 41–42
Cauthern v. Tennessee, 91–92
CEDAW. *See* Convention on the Elimination
    of All Forms of Discrimination Against
    Women (CEDAW)
Central African Republic
    ICC and, 165–166
Central American Court of Justice, 40
Central American Free Trade Agreement,
    376–377
CERD. *See* Convention on the Elimination
    of All Forms of Racial Discrimination
    (CERD)
"Chauvinist" vision of courts, 51
Cheney, Dick, 150–151
Chicago Convention, 63–64
Chicago Council on Foreign Relations
    (CCFR), 16–17, 18–19, 26–27
Chile
    U.S.-Chile Free Trade Agreement,
        372–373, 392–393

WTO and, 353
China
    compulsory ICJ jurisdiction and, 68
    international courts and, 428
    realism *versus* institutionalism in, 51–52
    WTO and, 354
Christopher, Warren, 189–190, 295–296, 301
Churchill, Winston, 137
Civil rights movement, 256–257
Civil War, 33–34
Claims and compensation tribunals
    generally, 297–298, 319–321
    Holocaust victim claims (*See* Holocaust
        victim claims)
    Iran-U.S. Claims Tribunal (*See* Iran-U.S.
        Claims Tribunal)
    UNCC (*See* Compensation Commission
        (UNCC))
Claims Resolution Tribunal for Dormant
    Bank Accounts in Switzerland,
    307–311
Clarendon, Earl of, 35–36
Clayton, Will, 331–332
Clinton, Bill
    human rights courts and treaties and,
        189–190, 223–224, 226–227, 230, 291
    ICC and, 147, 150, 156, 157
    ICTR/ICTY and, 143, 144–145
    Uruguay Round and, 346–347
Clodfelter, Mark, 365–366
Cold War, 256–257
Commerce Department, 382–383, 400
Commission on Responsibility of Authors of
    the War, 134, 136
Common law, 204–205
Compensation Commission (UNCC),
    314–319
    generally, 79, 314, 320–321
    Iraqi oil revenues supporting, 317, 318–319
    role of US, 315–318
Conference on Jewish Material Claims
    against Germany, 311
Congo. *See* Democratic Republic of Congo
    (DRC)
Congressional Research Service, 149, 166
Congress of Christian Nations, 33
Connally Reservation, 65–68
Constitution
    Fifth Amendment, 369–370
    foreign commerce, regulation of, 323–324
    NAFTA, challenges to, 381–382
    Supremacy Clause, 55–56, 126–127
    Takings Clause, 369–370

Constitution (cont.)
  Tenth Amendment, 404
  treaties under, 55–56
Consular notification
  Avena case (See Avena case)
  Breard case (See Breard case)
  Cauthern v. Tennessee, 91–92
  IACHR advisory opinions regarding, 193–196
  LaGrand case, 3, 48, 85–96, 115–116, 127
  Medellín, Ex parte, 129–130
  Medellín v. Dretke, 91–94, 116–117
  procedural default rule and, 90–92, 117, 124–127
  Sanchez-Llamas v. Oregon case (See Sanchez-Llamas v. Oregon case)
  stare decisis and, 127
  Torres v. Oklahoma, 91–92
Convention of 1907 Respecting the Limitation of the Employment of Force for the Recovery of Contract Debts, 40
Convention on the Elimination of All Forms of Discrimination Against Women (CEDAW)
  failure of US to ratify, 224–226, 261–262
  future trends, 283–284
  incorporationism and, 264–265
  signing by US, 226–227
  support by US for, 189–190
Convention on the Elimination of All Forms of Racial Discrimination (CERD)
  insulationism and, 267–268
  periodic reporting under, 235–236
  ratification by US, 223–224, 261–263
  signing by US, 226–227
  support by US for, 189–190
Convention on the Law of the Sea, 64–65
Convention on the Rights of Persons with Disabilities, 226–227, 268–271, 283–284
Convention on the Rights of the Child (CRC)
  failure of US to ratify, 224–226, 267–268
  future trends, 283–284
  Optional Protocols, 223–224, 261–262
  periodic reporting under, 235–236
  signing by US, 226–227
Council of Europe, 52
Countervailing duty cases. See North American Free Trade Agreement (NAFTA)
Court of International Trade (CIT), 382–383
Court of Justice of the Common Market for Eastern and Southern Africa, 438
Court of Justice of the Economic and Monetary Community of Central Africa, 438
Court of Justice of the Economic Community of West African States, 438
Cramer, Myron C., 137–138
Crane, David, 168–169, 171–172
Customary international law, 412, 417

Daimler-Chrysler, 311
D'Amato, Alphonse, 307–309
Darfur
  ICC and, 9, 159–163, 165–167
Dayton Accords, 146
Death penalty
  American Convention on Human Rights and, 200–201
  IACHR and, 194
  ICJ and, 3, 85–96
  juveniles and, 206–207
Defense Department
  human rights courts and treaties and, 231–232
  ICC and, 150
  SCSL and, 168–169, 171
DeLay, Tom, 151, 157, 166
Del Ponte, Carla, 431
Democratic Republic of Congo (DRC)
  ICC and, 165–166
  realism versus institutionalism in, 52
Dewey, John, 42–43
Dispute resolution tribunals
  arbitration (See Arbitration)
  GATT (See General Agreement on Tariffs and Trade (GATT))
  generally, 2
  ICJ (See International Court of Justice (ICJ))
  NAFTA (See North American Free Trade Agreement (NAFTA))
  public opinion regarding (See Public opinion regarding international courts and tribunals)
  Uruguay Round (See Uruguay Round)
  US support for, 1–2, 10–11
  WTO (See World Trade Organization (WTO))
Djibouti
  realism versus institutionalism in, 52
Dodge, David Low, 32
Dogger Bank Inquiry, 39–40
Doha Development Agenda, 353–354
Dole, Robert, 347

Domestic resolution
  ICC compared, 158–159
  international criminal tribunals, preference for, 180–181
Due process concerns regarding NAFTA, 406–408

Eagleburger, Lawrence, 313–314
East Timor
  international criminal tribunals and, 178
  Special Panels for Serious Crimes in East Timor, 178–179, 427
Economic Court of the Commonwealth of Independent States, 438
Effectiveness of international courts, 428–431
Eizenstat, Stuart E., 306, 309–312
ELSI case, 3, 63, 70–71
Embedded international law, 48–49, 55–57
England. *See* United Kingdom
Environmental Protection Agency, 369
European Community
  GATT and, 336–337, 338, 340–341, 343, 344
  WTO and, 349–350, 351–352
European Court of Human Rights (ECHR), 52, 61, 96, 425–426, 435–436, 437
European Court of Justice (ECJ), 52, 96, 363–364, 426–427, 435–436, 438
European Free Trade Area Court of Justice, 426–427, 438
European Union (EU)
  realism *versus* institutionalism in, 52
  subsidiarity principle, 217–218
Exceptionalism
  generally, 431–432
  ICJ and, 48–49, 53–55
  public opinion regarding, 20–24
  sovereign equality *versus*, 48–49, 53–55
Ex post facto nature of international criminal tribunals, 135
Extraordinary Chambers in the Courts of Cambodia, 132, 174–178, 427

Falk, Richard, 98
Federal Highway Administration, 400
Federalism, 201–202
Feldman, Mark, 301–302
Field, David Dudley, 34
Fifth Amendment, 369–370
Fish, Hamilton, 35–36
Flemming, Ken, 171
Forced labor claims by Holocaust victims, 311–313
Foreign Assistance Act, 229–230

Foreign trade. *See* Multilateral trade system
France
  compulsory ICJ jurisdiction and, 68
  Holocaust victim claims and, 313
Franck, Susan, 407–408
Franck, Thomas, 51
Frankfurter, Felix, 73
Franklin, Benjamin, 31–32
Frazer, Jendayi, 162–163, 164
Functions of international courts, 423–424, 428

Gallup Poll, 14, 19
Garrison, William Lloyd, 33–34
GATT. *See* General Agreement on Tariffs and Trade (GATT)
General Agreement on Tariffs and Trade (GATT)
  anti-legalism, move toward, 336–337
  creation of, 330–332
  dispute resolution under
    complexity of cases, 339–340
    consensus rule, 339
    decline during 1960s, 336–338
    move from diplomacy to law, 336
    NAFTA compared, 385, 387–388
    panel process, 334, 335–336
    poor quality of decisions, 340
    revival during 1970s, 338–340
    shortcomings of, 333–334
    US participation in, 334–335
  European Community and, 336–337, 338, 340–341, 343, 344
  expansion proposed, 342
  Japan and, 343
  protectionism and, 342–343
  Tokyo Round, 340–341, 342–343
  unilateralism of US in, 343–345
  Uruguay Round (*See* Uruguay Round)
  US role in, 333
Geneva Committee of the UN General Assembly, 141–142
Geneva Conventions, 24
Genocide Convention, 3, 62–63, 140–141, 223–224, 226–227
George, Ronald M., 405
Germany
  Hague Peace Conference of 1907 and, 40, 41
  Holocaust victims, forced and slave labor claims, 311–313
  LaGrand case and, 85, 88–89, 90–91, 115–116
  procedural default rule in, 124–125, 128

Gibbons, Sam, 375–376
Government-to-government disputes. *See* North American Free Trade Agreement (NAFTA)
Great Britain. *See* United Kingdom
Grossman, Marc, 152–153
Grotius, Hugo, 31
Guantanamo Bay, 12–13, 24, 25, 243–244
Gulf of Maine case, 3, 70–71
Gulf War, 316

Hague Peace Conference of 1907, 39, 40, 41, 58–59, 133
Haig, Al, 303
Harbury, Jennifer, 205
Hariri, Rafiq, 8, 179
Health and Human Services Department, 231–232
Helms, Jesse, 151, 155, 166
Higgins, Rosalyn, 6
High Court of International Justice, 136
Hobbes, Thomas, 49–50
Holbrooke, Richard, 169
Holocaust victim claims, 306–314
   California Holocaust Victim Insurance Relief Act, 314
   Claims Resolution Tribunal for Dormant Bank Accounts in Switzerland, 307–311
   forced and slave labor claims, 311–313
   France and, 313
   generally, 306–307, 319–320
   insurance claims, 313–314
   International Commission for Holocaust Era Insurance Claims (ICHEIC), 313–314
   Swiss bank claims, 307–311
Homeland Security Department, 231–232
Hudson, Manley, 137
Hull, Cordell, 325–326, 330
Hull House, 42
Human rights courts and treaties
   ambivalence of US toward, 210–212, 222–223, 235
   categorization of, 425–426
   complaints against US, 242–248
   conservative opposition to, 227–229
   domestic policy interests of US and, 256–259
      abortion, 271–272
      incorporationism, 256, 258–259, 263–268, 286
      insulationism, 256, 257–263
      local laws, 264–265
      social issues, 262
   foreign policy interests of US and, 250–255
      institutionalist position, 251–254
      realist position, 254–255
   future trends, 283–284
   implementation and monitoring in US
      coordination mechanisms, 291
      generally, 289–291, 296
      government focal points, 291–292
      independent bodies, 292
   inter-branch responses to, 232–233
   jurisdictional position of US toward, 273–276
   legitimization, effect of US participation on, 253
   mediating techniques to promote US engagement with
      domestic interest groups, role of, 222
      generally, 272–276
      limited acceptance of jurisdiction, 281
      "no-go" zones, 276–279
      non-self-execution clauses, 280–281
      preference for political over judicial control, 279–282
      procedural requirements, 281–282
      prospects for greater engagement, 213–215
      retention of discretion, 282–283
   motives of US regarding, 295
   need for US engagement with, 295–296
   negative effects of US nonparticipation, 252–253
   non-self-execution clauses, 262, 265–266, 280–281
   overview, 215–217
   periodic reporting by US, 235–241
      appreciation of usefulness, 240
      extensiveness of response, 237–238
      high-level delegations, 238–239
      lex specialis and, 240–241
      recognition of imperfections, 239–240
   precautionary measures, 246–247
   public opinion regarding (*See* Public opinion regarding international courts and tribunals)
   "push-pull" factor of US interests and, 249–250
   quasi-judicial functions of, 234–235
   ratification of treaties by US, 223–226

rule-based position of US toward, 273–276
signature of treaties by US, 226–227
sovereignty concerns, 273, 282
subsidiarity principle (*See* Subsidiarity principle)
supervisory mechanisms, 233–235
UN, within, 212–234
Hussein, Saddam, 19

IACHR. *See* Inter-American Court of Human Rights (IACHR)
ICC. *See* International Criminal Court (ICC)
ICCPR. *See* International Covenant on Civil and Political Rights (ICCPR)
ICESCR. *See* International Covenant on Economic, Social and Cultural Rights (ICESCR)
ICJ. *See* International Court of Justice (ICJ)
ICTR. *See* International Criminal Tribunal for Rwanda (ICTR)
ICTY. *See* International Criminal Tribunal for the Former Yugoslavia (ICTY)
ILO. *See* International Labor Organization (ILO)
Immigration and Naturalization Service, 243–244
Incorporationism, 256, 258–259, 263–268, 286
Independent Committee of Eminent Persons (ICEP), 308–309
Institutionalism, 49–53, 251–254
Instrumental approach, 419–423
Insulationism, 256, 257–263
Interagency Working Group on Human Rights, 230–231
Inter-American Commission on Human Rights
 abortion and, 271–272
 complaints against US, 242–248, 268, 283–284
 creation of, 187
 engagement with US, 202, 248
 generally, 185–186, 208–209
 influence on US law and policy, 206–208
 jurisdiction of, 212–234
 jurists from US, role of, 204, 205
 procedural requirements, 281–282
 support of US for, 203–204
Inter-American Court of Human Rights (IACHR)
 advisory opinions
  American Convention on Human Rights, regarding, 191–192, 193, 198–199
  American Declaration of the Rights and Duties of Man, regarding, 191–192, 196–198
  consular notification, regarding, 193–196
  generally, 191–193
 attempts to embarrass US in, 442–443
 Avena case and, 195, 196
 Breard case and, 195
 cases brought by US citizens, 435–436
 categorization of, 425–426
 common law, role of, 204–205
 creation of, 187–189
 death penalty and, 194
 effect of US indifference toward, 437
 engagement with US, 191–200, 202–203
 generally, 185–186, 208–209
 influence on US law and policy, 206–208
 initial US support for, 187–189
 judges, 204
 jurists from US, role of, 204–205
 LaGrand case and, 195
 non-acceptance of jurisdiction by US, 96, 241–242, 283–284
 obstacles to US acceptance, 200–202
 prospects for US acceptance, 189–191
 protection of US citizens, 205
 references in US to, 199–200
 Vienna Convention on Consular Relations and, 192–195
Inquiry, *Dogger Bank*, 39–40
Interior Department, 231–232, 400
International adjudication, public opinion regarding, 20–24
International Bar Association, 10
International Centre for the Settlement of Investment Disputes (ICSID), 64–65, 367, 373–374
International Civil Aviation Organization Council case, 63–64
International Commission for Holocaust Era Insurance Claims (ICHEIC), 313–314
International Court of Justice (ICJ)
 advisory opinions, 4, 74, 79, 80, 83–85
 Article 26, 70–71
 attempts to embarrass US in, 442–443
 autonomous national law *versus* embedded international law in, 47–49, 55–57
 Avena case and, 3, 85–96
 Breard case and, 3, 85–96
 Bulgaria, cases involving, 66
 Canada, cases involving, 3, 70–71
 "chauvinist" vision of, 51
 circumscribed jurisdiction, 61–68

International Court of Justice (cont.)
compulsory jurisdiction, 69
China and, 68
France and, 68
Russia and, 68
Soviet Union and, 61
UK and, 68
withdrawal of US from, 5–6, 46, 196
Connally Reservation, 65–68
consent to jurisdiction, 61–62
death penalty and, 3, 85–96
direct enforcement, lack of, 71–72
ELSI case, 3, 63, 70–71
exceptionalism *versus* sovereign equality in, 47, 48–49, 53–55
foreign policy matters and, 98
future trends, 98
growing assertiveness of, 97–98
Gulf of Maine case, 3, 70–71
ICC debate in US, effect on, 151
individuals, no jurisdiction over, 61
International Civil Aviation Organization Council case, 63–64
Iran, cases involving (*See Oil Platforms* case)
Israel, cases involving (*See Legal Consequences of the Construction of a Wall in the Occupied Palestinian Territory* advisory opinion)
Italy, cases involving, 3, 63, 70–71
ITO, jurisdiction over, 329–331
Kosovo, cases involving, 3, 62–63, 429–430
LaGrand case and, 3, 85–96
Legal Consequences of the Construction of a Wall in the Occupied Palestinian Territory advisory opinion, 3, 4, 48, 79, 83–85
Libya, cases involving, 3, 429–430
mediation of antinomies
circumscribed jurisdiction, 61–68
direct enforcement, lack of, 71–72
generally, 48, 57–61
individuals, no jurisdiction over, 61
political constraints, 72–74
state influence on selection of judges, 69–71
"messianic" vision of, 51
Nicaragua, cases involving, 63, 66–68, 429–430
"no-go" zones and, 276–277
Nuclear Weapons advisory opinion, 74, 79
Oil Platforms case, 3, 4–5, 48, 79–83
"optional clause," 65–68
Palestinians, cases involving (*See Legal Consequences of the Construction of a Wall in the Occupied Palestinian Territory* advisory opinion)
political constraints, 72–74
politicization of cases, 3–4, 5
public opinion regarding, 14–15, 17
realism *versus* institutionalism in, 46–47, 48–53
relationship of US with
antagonism between, 48
cases involving, 74–75, 79
generally, 46
support for, 2–3, 5–6, 44
reservations to jurisdiction, 62–63, 65–68
"respectful consideration" of rulings (*See* "Respectful consideration" of ICJ)
Serbia, cases involving, 3, 62–63
state influence on selection of judges, 69–71
transparency, need for, 442
treaties conferring jurisdiction on, 62–65, 99
volume of litigation, 429
International courts. *See specific court*
International Covenant on Civil and Political Rights (ICCPR)
commitments of US under, 268
complaints under, 241–242
federalism and, 201
ICJ cases involving, 4
"no-go" zones and, 277–278
periodic reporting under, 235–236
ratification by US, 202, 223–224, 261–263
signing by US, 226–227
International Covenant on Economic, Social and Cultural Rights (ICESCR)
failure of US to ratify, 224–226, 261–262, 268
future trends, 283–284
signing by US, 226–227
support by US for, 189–190
International Criminal Court (ICC)
categorization of, 132
Central African Republic and, 165–166
charging of individuals, public support for, 25–27
Darfur and, 9, 159–163, 165–167
domestic resolution compared, 158–159
DRC and, 165–166
effect of US indifference toward, 437–439, 443–444
exceptionalism and, 54
historical background, 140–143

Index

hostility of US toward, 156–157
military members, attempts to exempt, 153–155
moderation of US position on, 164–167
"no-go" zones and, 276–277
notification of US intent not to become party to, 150–153
objections of US to, 8–9, 148–149, 151
peacekeeper exemption, 154
public opinion regarding, 16–17, 25–27
Rome Statute (*See* Rome Statute)
SCSL and, 9
Sudan (Darfur) and, 9, 159–163, 165–167
support by US for, 44, 147
Taylor, Charles and, 9, 163–164, 165–167
Uganda and, 164, 165–166
International Criminal Tribunal for Rwanda (ICTR)
categorization of, 132
decline in US support for, 145–146
emergence of, 427
jurisdiction, 143–144
role of US in creation of, 143
support by US for, 6–7, 143–144, 145–146, 443–444
International Criminal Tribunal for the Former Yugoslavia (ICTY)
categorization of, 132
decline in US support for, 145–146
emergence of, 427
jurisdiction, 143–144
role of US in creation of, 143
support by US for, 6–7, 143–144, 145–146, 443–444
International criminal tribunals
accountability in, 180
attitude of US toward, 131–132
Bosnian War Crimes Chambers, 178
categorization of, 427–428
defined, 131–132
domestic resolution preference, 180–181
effectiveness of, 430
exceptionalism and, 54
ex post facto nature of, 135
Extraordinary Chambers in the Courts of Cambodia, 132, 174–178, 427
historical analysis of policy formation, 182
ICC (*See* International Criminal Court (ICC))
ICTR (*See* International Criminal Tribunal for Rwanda (ICTR))

ICTY (*See* International Criminal Tribunal for the Former Yugoslavia (ICTY))
Iraqi High Tribunal, 10, 132, 179
Kosovo and, 178
position of US toward, 180, 181–182
pragmatism, limits of, 182–183
public opinion regarding (*See* Public opinion regarding international courts and tribunals)
SCSL (*See* Special Court for Sierra Leone (SCSL))
Security Council authority and, 181
Special Panels for Serious Crimes in East Timor, 178–179, 427
Special Tribunal for Lebanon, 8, 179, 427
support by US for, 1–2, 6–8, 10–11
International Joint Commission, 40
International Labor Organization (ILO)
Committee on Freedom of Association, 242
complaints before, 247–248
Convention 182, 226–227, 261–262
engagement with US, 248
human rights court, as, 212–234
ratification of conventions by US, 235–236, 268
International Law Commission (ILC), 140–141, 142–143
International Legal Assistance Consortium, 10
International Monetary Fund, 54, 438–439
International Organization for Migration, 310, 320–321
International Trade Commission (ITC), 380–381, 382–383
International Trade Organization (ITO)
drafting of Charter, 330–332
historical background, 327–328
ICJ jurisdiction over, 329–331
US draft of Charter, 328–330
International Tribunal for the Law of the Sea, 424, 429
Investment disputes. *See* North American Free Trade Agreement (NAFTA)
Iran
assets frozen by US, 300–301
hostage crisis, 299–300
ICJ cases involving, 3, 4–5, 48, 79–83
invasion by Iraq, 301
nationalization of commercial enterprises, 299
Oil Platforms case, 3, 4–5, 48, 79–83
Revolution in, 298–299
seizure of US embassy, 3, 298–300
U.S.-Iran Treaty of Amity, 4–5, 79, 82–83

Iran-U.S. Claims Tribunal, 298–306
  Algiers Accords, 302–303, 304–306
  Claims Settlement Declaration, 302, 304
  generally, 319
  negotiations behind, 301–302
  proceedings of, 304–306
Iraq
  Abu Ghraib scandal, 27–28, 157–158
  Gulf War, 316
  invasion of Iran, 301
  invasion of Kuwait, 315–316
  Iraqi High Tribunal, 10, 132, 179
  Regime Crimes Liaison Office, 10
  UNCC and, 314–319
    generally, 79, 314, 320–321
    Iraqi oil revenues supporting, 317, 318–319
    role of US, 315–318
Israel
  Holocaust victim claims and, 311
  ICJ cases involving (See *Legal Consequences of the Construction of a Wall in the Occupied Palestinian Territory* advisory opinion)
  Legal Consequences of the Construction of a Wall in the Occupied Palestinian Territory advisory opinion, 3, 4, 48, 79, 83–85
Italy
  ELSI case, 3, 63, 70–71
  ICJ cases involving, 3, 63, 70–71
  U.S.-Italy Friendship Commerce and Navigation Treaty, 3
ITO. *See* International Trade Organization (ITO)

Jackson, Robert H., 432–434
Japan
  GATT and, 343
  Treaty of Peace with, 307
  WTO and, 350–352
Jay Treaty, 31–32, 297
Johnson-Sirleaf, Ellen, 173
Jurisdiction. *See specific court*
Justice Department
  Holocaust victim claims and, 307, 309–311
  IACHR and, 194, 202
  NAFTA and, 369, 382–383

Kant, Immanuel, 50–51
Karadzic, Radovan, 146
Kerry, John, 156–157
Khmer Rouge, 175

Khomeini, Ruhollah, 298–299
Knowledge Networks, 12–13
Kony, Joseph, 164
Korea
  WTO and, 350–352
Kosovo
  ICJ cases involving, 3, 62–63, 429–430
  international criminal tribunals and, 178
  war in, 146, 429–430, 431
Kroman, Edward R., 309–310
Krupp, 311
Kuwait
  claims against Iraq, 317–318
  invasion by Iraq, 315–316

Labor Department, 231–232
Ladd, William, 33
LaGrand, Walter, 115–116
LaGrand case, 3, 48, 85–96, 115–116, 127, 195
Lawyers for Life, 271–272
League of Nations, 43, 44, 59, 136–137
Lebanon
  Hariri assassination, 8, 179
  Special Tribunal for Lebanon, 8, 179, 427
Lettow Lerner, Renee, 404–405
Lex specialis, 240–241
Liberia
  Taylor and, 7–8, 163–164, 430
Libya
  ICJ cases involving, 3, 429–430
Lieber, Francis, 34
Lieber Code, 133
Limitations of international courts, 423
Lincoln, Abraham, 35
Locke, John, 49–50
Lockerbie bombing, 3, 429–430
Loewen Group, Inc. v. United States, 370–371, 400–401, 410
Lomé Accords, 168
London Charter, 138–139

MacArthur, Douglas, 138–139
Madrid Peace Conference, 83
Maine, sinking of, 38–39
Marshall, George C., 137–138
Marshall, Margaret H., 405
McKinley, William, 38–39, 41
Medellín, Ex parte, 129–130
Medellín v. Dretke, 91–94, 116–117
Mercosur, 438
"Messianic" vision of courts, 51
Metalclad case, 405–406
Methanex case, 369–370, 414

Mexico
  Avena case and, 85, 116
  WTO and, 350–352
Milosevic, Slobodan, 430
Mladic, Ratko, 146
Model BIT, 412–413
Mondev International, Ltd. v. United States, 402–404, 409–410, 415–416
Moravcsik, Andrew, 54–55, 228, 257
Moreno Ocampo, Luis, 431
Morgenthau, Hans, 49–50
Morgenthau, Henry, 325
Morris, George, 141–142
Multilateral trade system
  anti-legalism and, 336–337
  GATT (*See* General Agreement on Tariffs and Trade (GATT))
  generally, 354–355
  historical background, 323–327
  ITO (*See* International Trade Organization (ITO))
  NAFTA (*See* North American Free Trade Agreement (NAFTA))
  protectionism and, 342–343
  Tokyo Round, 340–341, 342–343
  Uruguay Round (*See* Uruguay Round)
  US support of dispute resolution, 322–323
  WTO (*See* World Trade Organization (WTO))
Murphy, Sean, 431–432

NAFTA. *See* North American Free Trade Agreement (NAFTA)
National Security Council, 172, 189–190, 231–232
Need for international courts, 442–444
Nethercutt Amendment, 154–155, 164–165
New York Convention, 305–306
New York Peace Society, 32, 33
Nicaragua
  ICJ cases involving, 63, 66–68, 429–430
  realism *versus* institutionalism in, 52
Nigeria
  Taylor and, 7–8
9/11 attacks, 151–152, 166
Nixon, Richard, 338
"No-go" zones, 276–279
Non-self-execution clauses, 262, 265–266, 280–281, 287–288
North American Free Trade Agreement (NAFTA)
  Canada and, 350

  criticism of
    due process concerns, 406–408
    generally, 395–396, 404
    sovereignty concerns, 386, 404–406, 414
  dispute resolution under
    advantage over national courts, 362
    ambivalence of US toward, 357
    attitude of US toward, 359–362
    CFTA compared, 363–364
    decline in US support for, 364
    generally, 356–358, 393–394
    lack of appellate review, 364
    lack of permanent body, 363–364
    rule-based approach, 364
    WTO compared, 362–363, 364
  due process concerns, 406–408
  financial services provisions, 393
  government-to-government disputes
    arbitration, 387
    CFTA compared, 385–386
    claims involving, 388–390
    criticism of, 391–392
    decline in use, 390–391
    GATT compared, 385, 387–388
    necessity of, 392–393
    sovereignty concerns, 386
    WTO compared, 385, 386–388, 391
  investment disputes under
    agencies involved in claims, 400
    arbitration, 367, 396–398
    claims against US, 368–369, 399
    environmental issues, 371–372
    fair and equitable treatment requirement, 371
    generally, 64–65
    lack of transparency, 373–374
    Loewen Group, Inc. v. United States, 370–371, 400–401, 410
    Metalclad case, 405–406
    Methanex case, 369–370, 414
    Mondev International, Ltd. v. United States, 402–404, 409–410, 415–416
    Pope & Talbot, Inc. v. Canada, 371
    regulatory takings concerns, 369–370
    significance of, 365
    sources of provisions, 364–365
    subject matter of claims, 399–400
    types of disputes, 366–367
    volume of litigation, 367–368
  response to criticism of
    consistency of decisions and, 412–414
    customary international law, reliance on, 412, 417

North American Free Trade (*cont.*)
  denial of justice standard, limited use of, 409–410, 414, 415
  generally, 417–418
  lack of direct review and, 409
  lack of plenary appellate jurisdiction and, 409, 415
  precedential value of cases and, 416–417
  procedural safeguards, 414–415
  role of US in creating NAFTA and, 408–409
  transparency of proceedings and, 410–411
Rules of Procedure, 379
sovereignty concerns, 386, 404–406, 414
transparency, need for, 442
unfair trade disputes under
  applicability, 378
  CFTA compared, 375–377
  Constitutional challenges, 381–382
  debate regarding, 377–378
  Extraordinary Challenge Committee (ECC), 379–381
  future trends, 384–385
  innovativeness of, 375–376
  other free trade agreements, effect of, 383–384
  panel process, 378–379, 380–383
  success of, 379
  transparency of, 379
  volume of litigation, 375
  WTO compared, 384
Nuclear Weapons advisory opinion, 74, 79
Nulla poena sine lege, 136
Nuremberg Tribunal, 137–140

OAS. *See* Organization of American States (OAS)
Obasanjo, Olusegun, 173–174
Oil Platforms case, 3, 4–5, 48, 79–83
Organisation for Economic Co-operation and Development (OECD), 363
Organization for the Harmonization of Business Law in Africa (OHADA), 435–436
Organization of American States (OAS)
  Charter, 223–224
  effect of US indifference toward, 438–439
  engagement with US, 248
  generally, 185–186
  human rights and, 203–204
  IACHR and, 187–189

Inter-American Commission on Human Rights and, 206, 212–234
U.S. Mission to, 202–203
Overview, xiii–xxiii
Owen, Roberts B., 300–301

Pacifism
  abolitionism and, 33–34
  Civil War and, 33–34
  generally, 30–31
  slavery and, 33–34
  Spanish-American War and, 38–39
  War of 1812 and, 32–33
  World War I and, 43–44
Palestinians
  ICJ cases involving (*See Legal Consequences of the Construction of a Wall in the Occupied Palestinian Territory* advisory opinion)
Paris Peace Conference, 134, 139
Paris Peace Treaty, 38–39
Paris Principles, 293
Paslovsky, Leo, 325
Paulsson, Jan, 401
Peace of Westphalia, 31
Permanent Court of Arbitration, 39, 133, 363–364
Permanent Court of International Justice, 13–14, 41, 43–45, 58–59
Permanent courts *versus* ad hoc tribunals, 422–423
Pew Poll, 25
Policy Coordination Committee on Democracy, Human Rights, and International Operations (PCC), 231, 291
Pope & Talbot, Inc. v. Canada, 371
Powell, Colin, 159
Pragmatism
  arbitration and, 41
  international criminal tribunals, limits in, 182–183
Principal and agent analogy, 439–442
Procedural default rule, 90–92, 117, 124–127, 128
Program on International Policy Attitudes (PIPA), 12–13, 16–17, 20, 24–25, 27–28
Prosper, Pierre, 145, 153, 158–159, 171, 175
Protectionism, 342–343
Public opinion regarding international courts and tribunals, 12–29
  American exceptionalism and, 20–24
  Bush administration, during, 20

Cold War, during decline of, 14–15
generally, 12–13
Guantanamo Bay and, 24–25
historical background, 13, 19–20
ICC and, 16–17, 25–27
ICJ and, 14–15, 17
international adjudication and, 20–24
Iraq War, during, 18–19
9/11 attacks and, 17–18
post-Cold War period, during, 15–17
torture and, 27–28
UN and, 14, 28–29
Vietnam War, during, 14
World War II, during, 13–14
WTO and, 19

Reagan, Ronald
human rights courts and treaties and, 226–227
Iran-U.S. Claims Tribunal and, 302–303, 304
Latin American policy of, 67–68
protectionism and, 342
Realism, 49–53, 254–255
Reciprocal Trade Agreements Act of 1934, 324–326
Regional economic and political integration agreement courts, 426–427
Rehnquist, William, 304
"Respectful consideration" of ICJ
conservative view, 120, 122–125, 128–129
different conceptions of, 117–118
generally, 112–114
greater deference to ICJ, 120–121
horizontal dialogue, 120, 122–125, 128–129
international court *versus* court of foreign nation, 119–120
liberal view, 120–121, 125–128, 129
Scalia on, 118–119, 120
stare decisis and, 127
vertical dialogue, 120–121, 125–128, 129
Rewards for Justice Program, 145–146
Rice, Condoleezza, 6–7, 163
Roberts, John, 113
Rome Conference, 148–149, 151
Rome Statute. *See also* International Criminal Court (ICC)
Article 98, 153–155
notification of US intent not to become party to, 150–153
politicized prosecutions under, 8–9
public opinion regarding, 16–17
signing by US, 150
support by US for, 9
Roosevelt, Franklin D.
foreign trade and, 324, 325, 327
international criminal tribunals and, 137
UN and, 59–60
Yalta Conference, at, 138
Roosevelt, Theodore, 41
Root, Elihu, 30–31, 40–41, 44, 58–59
Roper Poll, 14–15
Rosberg, Gerald, 301
Rousseau, Jean-Jacques, 49–50
Rumsfeld, Donald, 150–151, 166
Russia
compulsory ICJ jurisdiction and, 61, 68
Dogger Bank Inquiry, 39–40
Hague Peace Conference of 1907 and, 39
international courts and, 428
realism *versus* institutionalism in, 51–52
Rwanda
ICTR (*See* International Criminal Tribunal for Rwanda (ICTR))

St. Croix River Arbitration, 31–32, 297
Sanchez-Llamas v. Oregon
dissenting opinion, 125–128, 129
generally, 112–114, 117
majority opinion, 122–125, 128–129
"respectful consideration" of ICJ (*See* "Respectful consideration" of ICJ)
Scalia, Antonin, 118–119, 120
Scheffer, David, 145, 148–149, 169, 175
Schelling, Thomas, 49–50
Schiavo, Terri, 269–270
SCSL. *See* Special Court for Sierra Leone (SCSL)
Security Council
exceptionalism and, 54
ICJ judges, selection of, 69–70
international criminal tribunals and, 181
noncompliance with ICJ rulings and, 72
Resolution 242, 83
Resolution 338, 83
Resolution 674, 315–316
Resolution 687, 316–317
Resolution 692, 316–317
Resolution 706, 317
Resolution 778, 317
Resolution 1422, 154
Resolution 1483, 318–319, 320
Resolution 1593, 159–160, 161
Resolution 1654, 159
Semmes, Raphael, 35

Serbia
  ICJ cases involving, 3, 62–63
Seward, William, 35
Shelton, Dinah, 191–192
Shortsighted attitude of US toward international courts, 421
Siemens, 311
Sierra Leone
  SCSL (*See* Special Court for Sierra Leone (SCSL))
Slave labor claims by Holocaust victims, 311–313
Slavery, 33–34
Smoot-Hawley Act, 324
Social contract, 49–50
Solana, Javier, 9
Sovereignty
  human rights courts and treaties, concerns regarding, 273, 282
  insulationism and, 256, 257–263
  NAFTA, concerns regarding, 386, 414
Sovereign equality, 48–49
Soviet Union
  compulsory ICJ jurisdiction and, 61
Spanish-American War, 38–39
Special Court for Sierra Leone (SCSL)
  categorization of, 132
  emergence of, 427
  hybrid court, as, 167
  internationalization of, 174
  Management Committee, 167
  peacekeeper exemption, 170–171
  role of US in creating, 167–168
  support by US for, 7–8, 9, 169–170, 443–444
  Taylor and, 172–174
Special Panels for Serious Crimes in East Timor, 178–179, 427
Special Tribunal for Lebanon, 8, 179, 427
Stare decisis, 127
State Department
  GATT and, 331–332
  Holocaust victim claims and, 307–308
  human rights courts and treaties and, 229–230, 231–232, 246–247, 269–270, 295
  IACHR and, 189–190, 194, 195–196, 202–203
  ICC and, 147, 153–154
  Iran-U.S. Claims Tribunal and, 305
  ITO and, 330
  multilateral trade and, 325
  NAFTA and, 364–365, 369
  Office of the Legal Advisor, 202, 305
  SCSL and, 171–172

UNCC and, 314–315
States-only international courts, 424–425
Status of Force Agreements, 153
Stettinius, Edward, 59–60, 138
Stevens, John Paul, 88–89
Stimson, Henry L., 137–138
Subsidiarity principle
  assistance principle, lack of attention in US, 286–287
  bifurcation of, 287
  challenges for US regarding, 288–289
  EU, in, 217–218
  generally, 217–222
  implementation and monitoring of human rights treaties in US based on, 294
  non-interference principle, 287
  non-self-execution clauses and, 287–288
  paradox regarding, 285–286
Sudan
  ICC and (Darfur), 9, 159–163, 165–167
  international criminal courts and, 430
  Sudan Tribunal, proposal of, 160, 161
Sumner, Charles, 33–34
Supremacy Clause, 55–56, 126–127
Switzerland
  Holocaust victim claims against Swiss banks, 307–311

Taft, William Howard, 41
Takings Clause, 369–370
Tariffs, 324
Taylor, Charles
  ICC and, 164, 166–167
  indictment of, 172–174
  relocation of prosecution to Hague, 9, 163–164, 165–166
  SCSL and, 7–8, 174, 430
Taylor, Telford, 134, 137–138
Tenth Amendment, 404
Thucydides, 31
Timor-Leste. *See* East Timor
Tokyo Round, 340–341, 342–343
Tokyo Tribunal, 137–140
Torres v. Oklahoma, 91–92
Torture, public opinion regarding, 27–28
Torture Convention, 223–224, 235–236, 241–242, 261–263, 267–268
Trade. *See* Multilateral trade system
Trade Act of 1974, 339
Trade Act of 2002, 352, 407–408
Trade Agreements Act of 1979, 341
Trade Agreements Extension Act of 1945, 332
Trade Promotion Authority, 372–373, 374–375

Treasury Department
  multilateral trade and, 325
  NAFTA and, 364–365
Treaties. *See also specific treaty*
  Constitution, under, 55–56
  ICJ, treaties conferring jurisdiction on, 62–65, 99
  UNCC and, 317
Truman, Harry, 138, 332
Tushnet, Mark, 409

Uganda
  ICC and, 164, 165–166
UN. *See* United Nations (UN)
UNCC. *See* Compensation Commission (UNCC)
Unfair trade disputes. *See* North American Free Trade Agreement (NAFTA)
United Kingdom
  Alabama Claims Arbitration, 34–37
  compulsory ICJ jurisdiction and, 68
  Dogger Bank Inquiry, 39–40
  Foreign Enlistment Act, 34–35
  Hague Peace Conference of 1907 and, 39
  Proclamation of Neutrality, 34–35
  proposed arbitration treaty with, 37
United Nations (UN)
  Charter, 59–60, 72
  Commission on Human Rights, 12–13, 24
  Commission on International Trade Law (UNCITRAL), 64–65, 302, 367
  Committee against Torture, 212–234
  Committee on the Elimination of All Forms of Racial Discrimination, 212–234
  Committee on the Rights of the Child, 212–234
  Compensation Commission (*See* Compensation Commission (UNCC))
  Conference on Trade and Employment, 328
  Conventions (*See specific Convention; specific Conventions*)
  Declaration on Principles of International Law, 53
  Economic and Social Council, 328
  engagement with US, 248
  General Assembly, 53, 69–70
  Human Rights Committee, 212–234, 267–268
  human rights courts within, 212–234
  Office of Legal Affairs, 168, 171
  Office of the Controller, 169–170
  public opinion regarding, 14, 28–29
  Security Council (*See* Security Council)
  Special Rapporteur on the Human Rights of Migrants, 248–249
  Special Rapporteur on the Promotion and Protection of Human Rights and Fundamental Freedoms while Countering Terrorism, 248–249
  US in, 59–60
United States. *See specific topic*
United States Trade Representative (USTR)
  GATT and, 339–340
  NAFTA and, 364–365, 369, 380–381, 411
  WTO and, 351, 354
Universal Peace Conference, 37
University of Maryland, 12–13
Uruguay Round
  Dispute Settlement Understanding (DSU), 345–346
    Appellate Body, 345–346
    debate in US over, 346–348
    generally, 344–345
    implementation by US, 346–348
  generally, 345
  WTO (*See* World Trade Organization (WTO))
U.S.-Canada Free Trade Agreement (CFTA), 357, 363–364, 375–377, 385–386
U.S.-Chile Free Trade Agreement, 372–373, 392–393
U.S. Human Rights Network, 228–229
U.S.-Iran Treaty of Amity, 4–5, 79, 82–83
U.S.-Italy Friendship Commerce and Navigation Treaty, 3
USTR. *See* United States Trade Representative (USTR)

Vattel, Emerich de, 31–32
Venezuela
  WTO and, 434
Versailles Treaty, 133–136
Victoria (UK), 34–35
Vienna Convention on Consular Relations
  Additional Protocol, 5–6
  Article 36, 122, 124–125, 126–127
  Avena case and, 85–96, 122–123, 124–125, 127–129
  Breard case and, 85–96, 114–115, 126–128
  consular notification cases and, 3, 112–113, 114, 120, 122–123, 124–127
  enforceability in US courts, 196
  IACHR and, 192–195

Vienna Convention (*cont.*)
  ICJ jurisdiction over, 46
  Iran hostage crisis and, 3
  LaGrand case and, 85–96, 115–116
  Optional Protocol, 206–207
  Sanchez-Llamas v. Oregon and, 112–114
Vienna Convention on the Law of Treaties, 198, 202, 276
Volcker, Paul, 308–309

Wallace, Henry, 325
Waltz, Kenneth, 49–50
War of 1812, 32–33, 323
War on Terror, 151–152
Warsaw Convention, 118
Washington, George, 31–32
Washington, Treaty of, 35–36
Weld, Abelina Grimke, 33–34
Welles, Sumner, 325
Whelpley, Samuel, 32
White, Harry Dexter, 325
Wilhelm II (Germany), 133–134
Wilson, Woodrow, 43, 50–51
Woman's Peace Party (WPP), 41–42
World Bank, 54, 367, 438–439
World Conference on Human Rights, 189–190
World Court. *See* International Court of Justice (ICJ)
World Trade Organization (WTO)
  attempts to embarrass US in, 442–443
  Brazil and, 351–352
  Canada and, 350
  Chile and, 353
  China and, 354
  creation of, 345
  criticisms of, 352
  debate in US over, 346–347
  dispute resolution in, 348–354
    Appellate Body, 345–346, 364, 424
    cases filed against US, 351–352
    cases filed by US, 348–351
    Dispute Settlement Body, 362–363
    generally, 355
    NAFTA compared, 362–363, 364, 384, 385, 386–388, 391
    success of, 348
    Uruguay Round and, 345–346
    volume of litigation, 429
  Doha Development Agenda, 353–354
  European Community and, 349–350, 351–352
  future trends, 353
  Japan and, 350–352
  Korea and, 350–352
  Mexico and, 350–352
  public opinion regarding, 19
  reform proposals, 352–353
  submission of US to jurisdiction of, 96
  support by US for, 44
  trade disputes before, 64–65
  transparency, need for, 442
  Venezuela and, 434
World War I, 41, 43–44, 297–298
World War II, 13–14
WTO. *See* World Trade Organization (WTO)

Yalta Conference, 138
Young, Ernest, 404, 409
Yugoslavia
  ICTY (*See* International Criminal Tribunal for the Former Yugoslavia (ICTY))